Calculating the Value of the Union

CIVIL WAR AMERICA

Gary W. Gallagher, *editor*

CALCULATING THE VALUE *of* THE UNION

SLAVERY, PROPERTY RIGHTS, AND THE ECONOMIC ORIGINS OF THE CIVIL WAR

James L. Huston

THE UNIVERSITY OF NORTH CAROLINA PRESS

Chapel Hill and London

Designed by Gary Gore
Set in Haarlemmer MT
by Keystone Typesetting, Inc.
Manufactured in the United States of America

The paper in this book meets the guidelines for permanence and durability of the Committee on Production Guidelines for Book Longevity of the Council on Library Resources.

Library of Congress Cataloging-in-Publication Data
Huston, James L., 1947–
Calculating the value of the Union : slavery, property rights, and the economic origins of the Civil War / by James L. Huston.
p. cm. — (Civil War America)
Includes bibliographical references and index.
ISBN 0-8078-2804-1 (alk. paper)
1. Slavery—Economic aspects—United States—History. 2. Right of property—United States—History. 3. United States—History—Civil War, 1861–1865—Causes. 4. United States—History—Civil War, 1861–1865—Economic aspects. I. Title. II. Series.
E441.H895 2004
973.7′1—dc21
2003008363

Portions of this work have appeared earlier, in somewhat different form, as "Abolitionists, Political Economists, and Capitalism," *Journal of the Early Republic* 20 (Fall 2000): 487–521, reprinted with permission of the journal; "Property Rights in Slavery and the Coming of the Civil War," *Journal of Southern History* 65 (May 1999): 249–86, reprinted with permission of the journal; and "Southerners against Secession: The Arguments of the Constitutional Unionists in 1850–51," *Civil War History* 46 (December 2000): 281–99, reprinted with permission of Kent State University Press.

07 06 05 04 03 5 4 3 2 1

To my wondrous wife, Kathy Jane Simmons Huston,
and to her feline companions

Contents

Tables

Figures

Preface

Many reasons impel people to study the United States before and during the Civil War, for there are many worthwhile stories to explore, lessons to learn, and conundrums to ponder. But for myself, a central story has been to explain precisely the forces that led to separation and then to armed conflict. After all, the experiment in self-government in a sense had failed; democracy was no cure for whatever insoluble problem was tearing at the innards of the nation; reasonable compromises no longer seemed possible. Obviously slavery was at the center of the sectional quarrel—efforts to downplay the institution or replace it are will-of-the-wisps—and those seriously engaged in understanding the origins of the war have ever grappled with one line of Abraham Lincoln in his Second Inaugural: "All knew that this interest was, somehow, the cause of the war." The polar star for historians of the period has always been removing the "somehow" in Lincoln's phrase and rewording it to say, "All knew that this interest was the cause of the war for the following reasons. . . ."

My initial starting point several decades ago was that the source of the conflict had to be economic, for the basic function of slavery was to provide cheap labor. Tying all the pieces together, however, took quite some time. By the early 1990s I believed I had assembled a reasonable, logical, and historically verifiable explanation. Aiding me in my thoughts were two theories from political science and economics: realignment theory for American electoral politics and the property rights paradigm. I thought a small book would suffice to put forth the essential propositions and yet provide enough primary research to give the thesis credibility.

The conventions of the profession unexpectedly intruded on my plans. In the 1970s and into the 1980s, historians seemed to prefer smallness in research monographs and in theoretical works, in which evidence was implied rather than presented. Sometime in the late 1980s and especially in the 1990s came the return of the fat narrative. Why large books on restricted topics have again become so popular is something of a mystery to me; it certainly does not derive from historians having an abundance of spare time or from a paucity of historical writing—historians are now so overwhelmed with monographic production that a fair prediction would have been that the monograph would have disappeared in favor of journal articles. A skeptic might try to locate the origins of the big book in the designs of publishers who sought to mimic the automobile makers of Detroit—small books, like small cars, yield small profits; what the book publishing companies require for large profits are books that are the equivalent of SUVs—big, fat, environmentally unfriendly but blessed with huge profit margins. Unfortunately, historians only have themselves to blame. Among social historians the adoption of the technique of "thick description" ruled out thin volumes. From another quarter, the complaint of many that the discipline had too much (pretentious) theory and too little research led to a demand for more proof, which of course meant more pages.

Although many of the conceptual structures of this book were complete by 1995, I found it necessary to engage in a broader, richer research effort to sustain my propositions. Probably the point of diminishing returns was reached early, but the additional years of effort proved invaluable. Those years of extra investigation reinforced the basic premises of this book and removed any lingering doubt of their validity; moreover, they also extended the ideas into subsidiary areas so that a number of unconnected ends could be nicely tied together.

The thesis of this book is that property rights in slaves generated the sectional conflict, that the concentration of valuable property in one region thwarted any attempt at compromise and undermined the genius of the democratic process. Southern slaveholders searched for a sanctuary founded on the absolute guarantee that all members of the Union would view slaves as property and agree that no law at any level of government anywhere within the Union could directly or indirectly harm the value or ownership of that property—the absolute sanctity of property rights in slaves. Northern resistance to southern demands about property rights in African Americans stemmed from a number of sources, but the crucial one was economic. Property rights in slaves created an unfair labor market that ruined the opportunities for free northern village labor. Northerners saw the growing slavery system as a ruinous competitor to their system of free village labor.

For the South, the dilemma was clear. Property rights were granted by government; if control of government fell into the wrong hands, then the definition of property rights became a potential casualty of the new regime. Southerners would not risk the "potential" of the situation—slavery was worth too much for such tinkering. Northerners could not afford to let the South win control over defining property rights in slaves because it meant the possible extension of slavery into the North and the ruination of their society.

This book is organized into two parts and two important appendixes. The first part, consisting of five chapters, relates the theme of property rights to the sectional conflict. One chapter deals with the birth of the problem at the formation of the United States. Another examines the South, its wealth, and the nature of slavery; it explains how property rights in slaves was so essential to the region's political leaders. Next I examine the northern economy and its basis vis-à-vis the slaveholding states. A separate chapter is given to the question of politicians, abolitionists, and the sanctity of property rights, a subject that has gone virtually unnoticed and unrecorded but one that throws a revealing light on the way contemporaries understood the collision between the free and slave states.

Part II, consisting of three chapters, turns to the politics of the sectional struggle between 1846 and 1860. The purpose for these chapters is to put the property rights perspective into the narrative of Civil War history. Twenty-first-century Americans have no dearth of Civil War textbooks to choose from, and I did not want to write another. However, it did seem reasonable to show how the property rights perspective worked its way through the events of the era and how well it fit the arguments and concerns of the historical actors in their chronological setting. An analytical purpose guided research of antebellum politics as well, but has been relegated to Appendix B so as not to disturb the narrative flow. It was determined to present present election data in a useful way—in this case, figures—showing how well the realignment synthesis works for antebellum politics, and revealing when and where realignment occurred. The figures argue strongly that the collapse of the Second Party System was due to the slavery issue. However, quantitative and qualitative literature has been inspected by at least two generations of historians, and their reactions have revealed only two obvious truths: no proposition ever laid down by a historian will ever be acceptable to all the specialists in a field or probably even half of them; and, second, no argument in history will ever be solved by a pure numerical approach. Quantitative history can inform, educate, refine, and assist historical inquiry, but will never yield conclusive answers (well, for a majority of historians quantitative history may not, but such is not the case for me). Appendix A offers a theory that proposes that struggles over property rights have been the engine producing the phenomenon of political realignment over the course of American national development.

Producing this volume has led to a number of strange observations. One has to do with sources. Eventually I looked at several hundred newspapers and manuscripts. The reader should understand, however, that this was not a full search; rather, I looked only through certain time periods because I expected that then I would most likely find relevant material. In terms of understanding how contemporaries understood and argued positions, newspapers and printed sources were easily the most informative. Indeed, I came away amazed at the power of congressional debates and was almost convinced that many historians had not read them but had only turned to the speeches of their favorite orators. A wealth of information lies therein that is still amazingly untouched.

Manuscripts were more of a disappointment. While personal correspondence revealed much about political movements, alliances, designs of opponents, and such, they were not particularly educational about issues. My own belief is that letters took too much time to write, so people virtually used code words (like slave power) to sum up large and intricate arguments. Moreover, my sense is that individuals put most of their thinking into formal speeches and public statements—they had no grand need to reiterate them to friends, relatives, and constituents. If it might be argued that letter writers were more truthful in letters than in public speeches because they knew the public had to be appeased or assuaged, I would counter that the same is true with authorial intent in letters. The speaker or writer is always aware of his or her audience and thereby either alters arguments or phrases them with different nuances and emphases.

About this point in a preface, the historian then thanks all those who have assisted him or her. The present convention is to list half the practicing members of the profession and lavish praise upon them all. Such will not be the case here. To Gary W. Gallagher and Shearer Bowman Davis, the reviewers of this manuscript for the University of North Carolina University Press, I wish to offer my sincere gratitude for their encouraging and positive comments as well as their helpful suggestions. After nearly two decades of publishing articles and books, it has been a singular pleasure to receive reviews in which the compliments outweighed the criticisms. I also want to acknowledge the interest, courtesy, and kindness shown to me by the staff of the University of North Carolina Press, especially its chief editor, David Perry, and those who worked on this manuscript, Ron Maner, managing editor, and Brian MacDonald, copyeditor.

Of all those who aided me, librarians were clearly the most important. Historical societies and centers throughout the nation are wondrous places indeed, and the people who staff them are uniformly diligent, courteous, and supportive. However, I will note that unlike my experiences in researching two previous books, the interlibrary system was much more creaky and resistant; some material that I should have been able to obtain I never did. I ascribe this phenomenon to a new financial situation that for some institutions makes many transactions either difficult or impossible.

Those who have aided and assisted me most in developing my particular ideas about the genesis of sectional discord are the authors of the books and articles I have read. From their ideas and theories I have pieced together my explanation, along with some reshaping once the evidence became more voluminous. These individuals are pointed out in the endnotes, and it should be obvious whom I have paid attention to and learned the most from. Not that these authors will appreciate wholly or even partly what I have written. Indeed, I make considerable use of the "property rights paradigm" in numerous places in this book—but one should not assume I ascribe to the theory as presented by others. Indeed, most people working in the area of property rights draw the conclusion that the best society is a libertarian one; I think a logical inference from their theory, given an additional assumption or two, is that the best society is one powered by advanced New Deal intervention in the economy.

Many friends have encouraged me in my efforts, although they generally do not know the contents of these pages, and to them I owe far more gratitude for their kind words than they would ever expect or understand. As always, my mentor, Robert W. Johannsen, has been interested and supportive. On my ideas concerning realignment over time, I want to thank Robin Baker, Scott Barton, Mark Stegmeier, Randy Roth, Paula Baker, Lex Renda, and Morgan Kousser. Many friends have urged me to flesh out my ideas fully, even though they frequently challenged my views concerning the nature of the sectional conflict: Dan Feller, Heather Cox Richardson, Phil Paludan, Vernon Volpe, Stan Harrold, Louis Gerteis, and the late Bill Cecil-Fronsman. I was given helpful criticism at a Library of Congress Civil War Symposium by Michael F. Holt, Ira Berlin, and Rob Forbes. None of them has seen this manuscript, and a few have seen only slices of it; but their charitable words were received with great appreciation.

PART ONE

THE THEMES OF SLAVERY AND PROPERTY RIGHTS, 1776–1860

With them [abolitionists] the right of property is nothing; the deficiency of the powers of the general government is nothing; the acknowledged and incontestible powers of the States are nothing; a civil war, a dissolution of the Union, and the overthrow of a government in which are concentrated the fondest hopes of the civilized world, are nothing. A single idea has taken possession of their minds, and onward they pursue it, overlooking all barriers, and regardless of all consequences. . . .

A third impediment to immediate abolition is to be found in the immense amount of capital which is invested in slave property. The total number of slaves in the United States, according to the last enumeration of the population, was a little upwards of two millions. Assuming their increase at a ratio, which it probably is, of five per cent. per annum, their present number would be three millions. The average value of slaves at this time is stated by persons well informed to be as high as five hundred dollars each. To be certainly within the mark, let us suppose that it is only four hundred dollars. The total value, then, by that estimate, of the slave property in the United States, is twelve hundred millions of dollars. This property is diffused throughout all classes and conditions of society. It is owned by widows and orphans, by the aged and infirm, as well as the sound and vigorous. It is the subject of mortgages, deeds of trust, and family settlements. It has been made the basis of numerous debts contracted upon its faith, and is the sole reliance, in many instances, of creditors within and without the slave States, for the payment of debts due to them. And now it is rashly proposed, by a single fiat of legislation, to annihilate this immense amount of property! To annihilate it without indemnity and without compensation to its owners! Does any considerate man believe it to be possible to effect such an object without convulsion, revolution, and bloodshed?

I know that there is a visionary dogma, which holds that negro slaves cannot be the subject of property. I shall not dwell long on this speculative abstraction. *That is property which the law declares to be property.*

—Speech of Henry Clay on abolitionist petitions in the Senate, February 7, 1839, in Swain, *The Life and Speeches of Henry Clay*, 2:398, 410 (emphasis added)

1

Slavery, Property Rights, and the American Revolution

When the English settled at Jamestown, they began creating a European civilization in North America, and thus they imprinted upon the early English outposts all the elements of their culture, bad as well as good. From the unhealthy side came the planting of slavery in the English colonies. Slavery grew in the American colonies because it was profitable, and by the time of the Revolution it was a massive institution representing one and one-half centuries of investment. That investment required state protection. As the newly formed United States found out, a central government with some power was necessary if the nation were to survive. At the formation of the Constitution came then the marriage of politics and economics that haunted six decades of the nineteenth century. To create a nation, the Constitution makers pulled together different and antagonistic strands of English political and cultural ideals as well as American colonial practices: the necessity of protecting private property from majoritarian assault, the requirements of individual liberty, the enshrinement of local authority, and an acknowledgment that African slaves in North America were in some manner property. The well-understood antagonism lodged within the nation was that the nation was founded upon the principle of individual liberty while it sanctioned chattel slavery. At the same time, however, leaders broadcasted all the deficiencies of slavery, a list to which the later decades would add virtually nothing. But the afterglow of the Revolution bathed many difficult problems in a warm, optimistic light. Slavery would disappear, and property rights, instead of being used as a device to make aristocracy impregnable, would instead be instrumental in protecting the rights of common folk, thus helping to preserve popular government and the principle of majority rule.

Several conditions led to the establishment of slavery in North America. Upper-class Englishmen had low opinions of those who did manual labor, and the elite used various forms of servitude to obtain cheap labor. The English were also interested in amassing wealth. North America was strangely unpopulated compared with the other continents of the Earth, and at the time of the arrival of the English, diseases had decimated the resident Indian tribes. There was thus a vast amount of land but little population—a unique condition in the world of 1600. When the English found a commercial crop in tobacco, they were able to supply their needs through servants brought over from England by the system of indentured servitude. In Maryland, Virginia, and South Carolina (where rice became the important commercial staple), the rise of large farms using some form of controlled labor had fully blossomed by the last half of the seventeenth century. Slavery had been dead in England for about 400 years or so, its demise slowly being recognized in statutes and judicial proceedings, but servitude continued to possess certain aspects of slavery. The master had some conditional property rights in the labor of the servant and control over the servant's mobility; he had the capacity to sell the property rights in labor to other parties. The conditional aspects of those property rights were limitations on punishments, a limit to term of service, the nonhereditary quality of servitude, and the fact that servants could sue masters for breach of contract. The essential difference was that the law recognized servants as human beings (usually English human beings) possessing nonbarterable rights. That is, servitude did not reduce a person to the level of an animal, to personal property.

Dutch traders brought the first Africans to Jamestown in 1619 for sale as servants, although the normal tendency in today's scholarship is to stress the early emergence of chattel slavery. Slavery for Africans may have developed rapidly, but it is clear that the numbers of slaves did not. Planters until the 1660s depended on English labor in the form of indentured servants to take care of their labor requirements for tobacco cultivation. Between 1660 and 1700, however, the supply of English labor dwindled because wages in England improved, and the planters suddenly lacked an adequate servile labor force—which simply meant they lacked cheap, manageable labor. Moreover, English servants in the colonies became unruly. For these reasons, the colonial planters, through their legislators, turned to Africans for a labor supply. They wrote the laws of slavery that defined slaves by race, made the condition hereditary, and denied that emancipation could be achieved by conversion to Christianity. In these laws the slave also became a chattel—a piece of property over whom, except for certain public safety reasons, the slave master had total dominance, as much as a property holder had over land, animals, or other articles of personal possessions.[1] As of 1660, there were probably barely 3,000 Africans on the North American mainland. The engine of the slave trade then roared; by 1680, there were 7,000, by 1700, 28,000, by 1720, 69,000, by 1740, 150,000, and in 1770, 460,000. Imports from Africa would reach their height after the Revolution, between 1800 and 1820.[2]

Why slavery manifested itself in North (and South) America just when its death was being recorded in Europe has two reasons. The first was economic. Europeans in either of the Americas were few, but the land mass was great. To obtain labor, the Europeans turned to forced labor, either of Indians or of some imported race. Second, the Europeans carried with them an ethnocentrism that easily rationalized the enslavement of people different from themselves. The skin color difference between Indians, Africans, and Europeans led to an obvious rationale for enslavement of people of different color: they were easily identified and controlled. But the ethnocentrism element among Europeans operated in a particular way to promote slavery. European society had been built on communities of quite homogeneous population types; they noted the differences among themselves, let alone between them and the rest of the world's population. Within their group they incorporated individuals into the existing community; that is, they bestowed upon individuals the community notion of rights, privileges, and activity. Those outside of the community did not receive the same treatment; they were the "others." In North America in 1610 or 1660 or 1700, English men and women were not made slaves—they were members of the English community and had the "rights and privileges" of English people. The crown and Parliament would never have allowed English colonials to have enslaved other English colonials.[3] Nor could the English have easily enslaved other Europeans without risk of retaliation from their mother countries. The Spanish were in Florida and parts of Georgia, the French in Canada, and other Europeans could rely upon their descent to ward off the labor-hunger of the English. But none of these rules applied to Indians or to Africans. They were not members of the community, and they, except for the Indians, lacked a national power base to threaten the English. In short, Indians and Africans were vulnerable and so became the obvious sources for some sort of servile labor pool for the English.

To this must be added the inchoate stage of economic development of Europe. Economic rules, except for vague ones supplied by church and government, did not exist in terms of how individual and national wealth could be best accumulated. Theorists were only beginning to promote the ideas that became mercantilism; physiocracy awaited the opening of the eighteenth century; and Adam Smith would not begin the codification of the rules of a market economy until 1776. Shortly after 1650 or so, the Atlantic economic community assumed a distinct shape, and the benefits of extended trade would teach people how individuals and nations acquired wealth by exchange of goods. Prior to 1600, however, the way to wealth was fairly simple and had been simple for 2,000 years. Wealth was obtained, it was somewhat true, by trade, but mostly from the employment of servile labor—a cheap labor made to work to benefit a social superior—and more generally by conquest. The earth yielded its fruits, grains, and minerals, and individuals by their own labor could obtain a modestly healthy living; but to live in grandeur one had to conquer others and force them into a cheap labor pool, into some form of servility.

When the English (or the French or the Spanish) came to the Americas, they brought this older notion of wealth accumulation with them. Some trade or barter with the indigenous people might occur, but the invaders knew that the wealth they wanted could only be obtained via conquest and servile labor. And so we come to one of the major original sins of the English founding of North America. They condoned and legitimized violence in the pursuit of wealth—violence against the "others" not wrapped in the protective folds of European community. In modern economic terms, a market economy is ethical and legitimate (among these type of economists) only so long as all actors make *uncoerced* choices, and the existing alternatives represent *real choices* (not alternatives that deny a choice, such as life or death). Servitude could be an uncoerced choice; but slavery was the offspring of unrelenting violence.[4]

Given the conditions of early America, the English should not have established slavery. Had the rules of a market economy been formulated and enforced, coercion of either labor, yeoman farmer, or aristocrat would have been forbidden. The result would have been small farms producing subsistence crops and a vastly reduced tobacco and rice yield. Such a result was foretold by the conditions of North America in the seventeenth century: extensive land that could be obtained at a low price, few settlers, and the observance of the rule of noncoercion. Remove the rule of no violence to obtain material goals, that all economic activity had to be done by mutual consent, and the result was slavery.[5]

Even then, Virginians and South Carolinians might have established slavery without the chattel principle. Other means existed to deal with the labor shortage than by legally transforming people into property. In particular, the colonial governments or even Parliament or the king could have maintained ownership of all slaves and merely have leased them out to planters. Through some arrangement, planters could have been allowed to obtain the labor of slaves without acquiring property rights in the bodies of slaves and their progeny. Under that circumstance, emancipation might in the future have been more easily accomplished. But domination of others via the right of an individual to an absolute control of his or her property was to be the guiding principle of American slavery. That principle created the snowball effect. The slave became an asset, a thing representing invested wealth; as the use of slaves became economically effective in certain types of agricultural activity, the wealth grew in a compound fashion. As the slaveholders recognized that their wealth in slaves was compounding, they became more and more resistant to any infringement upon their rights of ownership. So it came to pass that a system of human relations founded in violence, nurtured by violence, and maintained by violence, while constantly augmenting wealth, could only be removed by violence.[6]

While Virginians and South Carolinians fashioned the legal bulwarks of American slavery, other aspects of the colonies evolved along different lines. The customs, values, institutions, and practices of England came over to the American mainland but began mutating. Those changes were in general toward a leaner, less intrusive government, a more open economy, a society marked by the emergence of the yeoman farmer, the rise of a ruling business class rather than a true aristocracy, and a diversity of Western European ethnic and religious groups.[7] Because England failed to govern the American colonies directly, with a firm hand strengthened by an active on-site bureaucracy, American and British customs started diverging. That separation of customs and ideals grew large enough so that when Parliament tried to extend its governing power over the colonies after 1763, the colonists resisted. Indeed, the colonists began to understand that their differences with England socially, politically, and economically were irreconcilable, and that separation from the empire was the only alternative the American colonists had to preserve their own traditions and ideals. So when the British Parliament attempted to tax and regulate trade in the American colonies in 1763, it sparked off a process that led to the American Revolution, a period that may be considered as extending from 1763 to 1790. Out of the Revolution came a host of ideas about personal freedom, relations between church and state, monopolies and special privileges, republican forms of government, social values, and the nature of aristocracies. As well, the Revolution broadcast the central message that the rights of property were to be observed and made sacrosanct.

The heart of the American Revolution politically, economically, socially, and ideologically was a strident defense of the individual's right to property, in particular the right of individuals to earn, keep, and dispose of their property without the interference of any other power, especially the power of government. The rebel insistence on property rights—at times appearing to be a monomania—has unsettled historians. Property with its earthy, material connotations evokes emotions that at best seem primitive and uncivilized—undiluted greed, selfishness, and mean-spiritedness. Scholars wish to see in revolutions more exalted sentiments and arguments for the future welfare of society. Thus, rather than dwell on the colonials' obsession with private property, they have (rightfully) emphasized the revolutionaries' advocacy of representative government, antiaristocratic laws, local control of domestic affairs, freedom of expression, and citizen participation in politics. Yet all these concerns have strong connections to the revolutionaries' understanding of property rights. When historians have dealt with the topic, the discussion tends to become dichotomous—sheer good or sheer evil—and the generalizations usually have not located some of the ambiguities, problems, and promises that the American doctrine of property rights evoked. One observation has not been sufficiently stressed: the doctrine of property rights can at certain times have distinct egalitarian purposes.

The American struggle over property rights during the Revolution set the stage for the Civil War and, indeed, for the tumults of American elections for the next two centuries. Property rights were central in both the ideological defense and attack on slavery. The economic consequences of private property doctrines made secession inevitable. And it was the political consequences of property rights, and particularly the strains they necessarily imposed on popular government, that led to the realignment of the 1850s. Most of these results flowed from the property rights decisions made by the revolutionary generation.

American colonial rebels meant physical property when they spoke of property rights, and only infrequently offered a broadened sense of property. At times, leaders used property to include personal rights to religious opinion, speech, assembly, and use of talents and faculties. Yet the common written or verbal expression about property rights was unmistakably precise: the revolutionaries meant the right of individuals to possess material property.[8]

Parliament's attempt to tax the colonists directly or indirectly drew a shriek from the colonials that they were being taxed without their consent and thus being deprived of their property. And there was no mistaking that the colonists meant physical property. Wrote Virginian Richard Bland in 1766 against the Stamp Act, "If a Man invades my Property, he becomes an Aggressor, and puts himself into a State of War with me; I have a right to oppose this Invader." Two years earlier, Massachusetts lawyer James Otis argued against taxation without representation, "For what one civil right is worth a rush after a man's property is subject to be taken from him at pleasure without his consent? If a man is not his *own assessor* in person or by deputy, his liberty is gone or lays entirely at the mercy of others." The Continental Congress did not leave much to the imagination about the meaning of property when it issued addresses, petitions, and appeals to various groups and governing bodies. "*Know then,*" the Congress declared in a 1774 address to the people of Great Britain, ". . . that no power on earth has a right to take our property from us without our consent." In another address in 1775, the congressional members narrowed down the constitutional dispute with England to one sentence: "We contend for the Disposal of our Property." Explaining the position of the Americans to the British inhabitants of Quebec, the Continental Congress made clear why representation was so vital a principle: the first right the Americans wanted was the right of representation as "This is a bulwark surrounding and defending their [the people's] property, which by their earnest cares and labours they have acquired, so that no portions of it can be legally taken from them, but with their own full and free consent[.]"[9]

Fewer ideas had a more secure place in the minds of the Americans than the belief that civilization rested on property rights. As John Adams wrote in 1778, "Property is surely a right of mankind as really as liberty." James Madison made it apparent in *Federalist* 10 that the reason for the adoption of the Constitution was to secure more strongly for Americans their property even if that meant protecting the unequal distribution that property ownership naturally took. In fact for many of the late eighteenth century, the equation linking civilization and property rights was perfect: to have civilization, one had to have property rights of individuals protected. If property rights were not protected, then civilization could not exist.[10]

Many sources fed the American belief of the centrality of property rights in the mid to late eighteenth century. Some proclaimed that property rights elicited the good character traits of sobriety and industry in the general population and thus benefited all of society.[11] Others stressed that unless persons were allowed to accumulate property by hard work, they would not exert themselves and the result would be economic stagnation.[12] Many insisted that property was basic for a republican polity as it gave citizens independence and acted as a bulwark against tyrannical government; of recent years, historians have incorporated this view of property under the synthesis termed "republicanism."[13] Most commonly, Americans upheld the idea of private property by referring to it as a natural right, and justified it by using the natural right argument of the late seventeenth-century philosopher John Locke.[14] Just as important as the heritage of European ideas was the physical circumstance of the colonies: for white men, the expanse of land far exceeded the numbers of people inhabiting it, thus ownership of property in the form of land was common. Therefore, popular allegiance to doctrines calling for individual property rights was not irrational for this type of society. Whatever its source, early American society was almost maniacally devoted to maintaining the rights of individuals to property.

The commonplace method of handling property rights in the American past is for historians to divide the society politically into conservatives, those who elevated property rights above all other rights, and democrats (or reformers or radicals) who placed property rights below social and human welfare. In the early history of the United States, the struggle over control of state governments, paper money laws, Shays's Rebellion, the framing of the Constitution, its ratification, and the emergence of political parties in the 1790s have frequently been described as fights over property rights between conservatives and democrats. Usually, the conservative pro-property rights side has been identified with privilege and high status. Indeed, the interpretive brunt of such studies is simple enough: property rights doctrines when they appear invariably are used by individuals seeking to protect the wealth, status, and power of the existing elite at the expense of those unfortunately situated. American politics has been frequently reduced to a fight between democracy and the rights of property.[15] This interpretation, it might be noted, is generally true.

However, there is a hidden egalitarianism operating in the eighteenth-century American doctrine of property rights. That egalitarianism arises from the contemporary description of how property was to be obtained and who were the enemies of the legitimate means of acquisition. The answers were that only industry and labor legitimized personal property, actions that all humans could partake in. The enemies of property were aristocrats who used government to usurp for themselves the small holdings of the multitude. The doctrine of property rights among aristocrats was indeed conservative, status quo dogma; but property rights when used to protect those who labored and added value to the world had something of a democratic character.[16]

When Americans complained in the 1760s and 1770s that British policies deprived Americans of their property, they continuously and overwhelmingly identified property as the "fruits of labor." American colonials had adopted a labor theory of property and justified property in possession because the property was the result of labor. John Locke had used the labor theory of value or property to explain the origin and legitimacy of property rights by asserting that as every person "owned" himself, he also owned his own labor; when a person bestowed labor upon some object, only that person was entitled to ownership of the value produced. Locke had used the labor theory of value ultimately to defend inheritances and the property distribution obtaining in late seventeenth-century England—the property holdings (primarily land) of aristocrats were to be sancrosanct because aristocrats had possession of them.[17] This was not the case with the Americans. Property rights were to be observed because individuals labored assiduously to obtain property and therefore deserved to possess it. For the Americans the key was activity in the form of labor.

Nearly all the leaders in the revolutionary period justified private property with a fruits-of-labor argument. The Philadelphia legalist, political moderate, and Constitutional Convention delegate James Wilson wrote approvingly of property rights in the early 1790s. "Man is intended for action," he asserted. "Useful and skilful industry is the soul of an active life. But industry should have her just reward. That reward is property; for of useful and active industry, property is the natural result." More emphatic was the agrarian radical George Logan: "Our rights over the other species of property arise from the labor we have bestowed in acquiring them, or from the bounty of others." During the Revolution, the Massachusetts radical Joseph Warren claimed that Parliament's taxation policies assumed the right of taking "*that property* which the Americans have earned by their labor."[18]

American revolutionaries and continental radicals identified an enemy to the just and ethical distribution of property implied by the fruits-of-labor argument. Aristocrats, the ruling elite of Europe, amassed their excessive landed and personal fortunes by leeching away the fruits of labor of commoners. They accomplished this feat by monopolizing the powers of government. By unfair taxation, creation of government bureaucracy, instigation of wars, manipulation of religious establishments, creation of monopolies, and general economic legislation, aristocrats forced the rest of society to pay them tribute. The injustice of property accumulations in aristocratic societies was that aristocrats obtained their wealth without labor; they were a leisure class that received wealth not by laboring but by the effect of unjust laws that favored them—what the rebels called "partial legislation."[19]

Property rights doctrines thus could contain an egalitarian edge. Property rights in an aristocratic system certainly were unjust because the means of wealth acquisition were unjust. But in a republic, property rights doctrines protected all people in the enjoyment of the fruits of their labors. In particular, property rights protected the masses from the designs of actual or would-be aristocrats. James Wilson wrote that property rights gave to each person a security of possession: "This security is afforded by the moral sense, which dictates to all men, that goods collected by the labour and industry of individuals are their property; and that property ought to be inviolable." Admitting that different talents would produce potentially great differences in wealth accumulations, Wilson nonetheless saw property rights as a defense for lesser folk as well as the talented elite: "If much labour employed entitles the active to great possessions, the indolent have a right, equally sacred, to the little possessions, which they occupy and improve."[20]

Throughout most of the nineteenth century, the revolutionaries' ideas about property rights prevailed. The institutions of the United States forbade aristocratic distortions in property acquisition, although ramifications of federal policy were hotly debated. Orator, statesman, and Whig luminary Edward Everett made precisely this point in 1838. European property was unjust as it was founded originally on "military violence" and conquest. But in the United States wealth was earned by "industry and frugality." Agreeing with Everett was the Whig warhorse and textile magnate Nathan Appleton. He remarked in 1844 upon the differences between Europe: "Nothing is more striking that the distinction made, more especially in Europe, between labor in possession, and labor in action: in other words, between capital and labor." European aristocrats had always relied upon force to amass their personal empires, and so brought property rights into disrepute. That means of acquisition was denied in republican America: "[I]t is not surprising that the acquisition of property, by one's own labor and skill, should be held in equal, or even higher estimation, than the inheritance by the accident of birth."[21]

Jacksonian Democrats substantially agreed with their Whig counterparts on the general importance of property, if nonetheless disagreeing on much else. William Leggett, perhaps the most famous Jacksonian antimonopolist, left no doubt that the main duty of government was to protect property rights, but he placed it in an egalitarian context: "The fundamental principle of all governments is the protection of person and property from domestic and foreign enemies; in other words, to defend the weak against the strong." Property rights only injured the multitude when government engaged in favoritism to the elite. The New York Democrat Samuel J. Tilden in 1840 argued for equality through the security of property—"to the laborer in the immediate results of his toil. The motive to labor is the enjoyment of its fruits." Governmental activity, Tilden argued, upset that enjoyment. Using the example of England, Tilden postulated that the government's security of property for the

the capitalist was secured "but the earnings of the laborer are largely consumed by taxation, or transferred to the privileged classes."[22]

Thus the American Revolution had created these three principles that would direct the controversy over slavery: the sanctity of property rights, the justification of personal property by individual labor, and the repudiation of aristocratic mechanisms. These set the parameters of the legal and ideological conflict over slavery. But the Revolution also produced a fourth contribution to the slavery discussion that was indispensable. It was also unclear and imprecise. The Revolution sanctified property rights but could not define the term "property."

Several revolutionary leaders struggled with the origin, justification, and social tendencies of the doctrine of property rights. Property rights were supposed to be a bulwark against the designs of aristocrats and thus bestow upon a nation a measure of social equality. Yet John Adams knew, at least by the early nineteenth century, that property rights might produce a new elite: "I repeat it, so sure as the idea and existence of *property* is admitted and established in society, accumulations of it will be made; the snowball will grow as it rolls." Others railed at the idea that property rights reduced popular government to impotency and that protection of property was the sole purpose of government.[23]

Samuel Adams, the Boston radical who trumpeted Lockean doctrines about the sanctity of private property as much as anyone, showed that the central ambiguity about property rights was that they were the creation of society. "Men therefore *in society having property*," he explained, "they have such a right to the goods, which by the law of the community are theirs, that no body hath the right to take *any part* of their subsistence from them without their consent." Property depended upon legal definition, but nature did not do the defining; society through government determined what was or was not property. The moderate James Wilson accepted the fact that even if one argued in favor of property being a natural right, it was a natural right that could be modified by positive institutions—that is, by government.

The radicals of the Revolution, at times upset by the uncooperative attitude of those who found the sanctity of property rights a ready defense for their political positions, went much further than Wilson. Benjamin Franklin in 1783 stated that all property "seems to me to be the creature of public convention" and that the public therefore had the right of "regulating descents, and all other conveyances of property, and even of limiting the quantity and the uses of it." Thomas Jefferson dismissed the idea of a natural right to property, while the radical Tom Paine in *Agrarian Justice* proclaimed, "Personal property is the *effect of society*; and it is impossible for an individual to acquire personal property without the aid of society, as it is for him to make land originally."[24] The centrality of property rights could not be denied, but there arose the very real problem of what agency actually determined what was property.

For all the verbiage surrounding the word property during and after the Revolution, no one offered a definition as to what items were to be considered property and what items were not. What functioned as a definition of property was entirely circular. Property was an object of personal possession that the law protected; yet possession was secured by the right to property. Neither possession nor property was defined separately. Unlike other substances in life—trees, animals, humans, houses, streets—property did not have any specific definition for it had no "natural" form or content. People could (and do) invest enormous amounts of labor into activity that society declares illegal, but their labor is declared criminal, not productive. In short, the labor theory of value only operates when society in a collective capacity allows it to operate, just as Samuel Adams stated. No legislation in the colonial or revolutionary period listed the material objects that constituted property. Rather, society in the form of judicial decisions, English common law, or explicit legislation determined over time what was and what was not property.

Because property is so crucial to any society that has anything like a market system for exchange of commodities—and early American society was at least a potential market society—the forces determining the social definition of property require some comment and observation. The determination of what constitutes property is distinctly a nonmarket operation. Governments, for whatever reasons, declare what shall and shall not be considered property. The decision probably reflects values of the society, the state of its technology, and the control various groups may exercise over legislation. But ultimately government—through its use of its coercive powers—delineates the rules of the economic game; government makes the initial step in declaring how economics in a society operates.[25] Indeed, government makes the initial determination about what objects a market economics will and will not operate on. All societies decide that some items will not be designated as property and are beyond the pale of barterable items—in present-day America, narcotics would serve as an obvious example (or prostitution or aborted fetuses or, as this book is about, human beings).

This discussion points to one obvious conclusion. Because no prior definition of property exists—no "eternal" definition—then societies continuously decide what objects are property and what ones are not. Periodically societies revise the list of items they have designated as property. And this function of government—this unavoidable function of all governments—means that at times what was once considered property may in the future be considered as nonproperty and inappropriate for private possession; the power of the state will not condone and enforce private possession. When such alterations in the list of the things considered as property occurs, major ramifications can reverberate through society and shake it to its core, depending on the size of investment that had been made in the form of property and the stream of income flowing from it. The application of this condition—that property receives validation only through political legitimation—to southern slavery is obvious. Slavery only existed because governmental authority declared slaves as property. Let the authority be removed, and slavery would cease to exist.

"They who have no property can have no freedom," declared Rhode Island's Stephen Hopkins in 1765, "but are indeed reduced to the most abject slavery." The association the revolutionaries made between their property and the social state of slavery was omnipresent during the years of controversy with England over imperial policy. Although their discourse was aimed at securing a civil liberty, and not necessarily connected with the economic form of plantation slavery because it was beyond the realm of the rights and duties of citizens and so could be ignored, the dialogue nonetheless indicated a precise definition of freedom and slavery regardless of civil condition. Contemporary Americans knew as well the inconsistency of their demands for their individual freedom while at the same time practicing slavery for others.[26] It was at this juncture that the Revolution began the process of generating the confrontations that eventually would produce southern secession. The major economic doctrines of the Revolution—the labor theory of property or value and the inequitable results of aristocracy—were invoked to denounce American slavery.

Attackers of slavery readily put slavery into the framework of individuals being unnaturally deprived of the fruits of their labor. David Rice, an early abolitionist, mocked slaveholders and their attitude toward emancipation; emancipation would mean "that black men in the next generation shall enjoy the fruit of their own labour, as well as white men." Philadelphia physician and early antislavery agitator Benjamin Rush exclaimed, "How great then must be the amount of injustice which deprives so many of our fellow creatures of the *just* reward of their labor!" Tom Paine also placed the question of slavery in the fruits-of-labor context; he advocated gradual emancipation so that former slaves might have "the fruits of their labors at their own disposal, and be encouraged to industry."[27]

Slavery was also rearing up an aristocracy in the youthful United States. An aristocracy did not labor but took the fruits of labor of others, and, as Quaker abolitionist John Woolman noted, the labor of slaves was used to "support us [slaveholders] in those Customs which have not their Foundation in right Reason," or, in other words, in dissipation and luxury. A free black at the time of the Revolution complained that slaveholders engaged in aristocratic leisure that "can only be supported by the sweat of another person's brow." By the middle of the eighteenth century, Ben Franklin had noted that slavery inculcated habits in the masters leading them and their progeny to "become proud, disgusted with Labour." Slaves were also handed down from generation to generation and thereby mimicked aristocracy's mechanism of maintaining wealth by inheritance. And the connection between slavery and aristocracy—and the overthrow of aristocracy—was made explicit by an Englishman who had written to Washington arguing for an end to slavery: "France has already burst her shackles, neighboring nations will in time prepare, and another half century may behold the present bespotted Europe, without a Peer, without a Hierarchy, and without a Despot"—and without a slave.[28]

Because slavery denied the worker the fruits of his or her toil, and because an aristocracy stole the fruits of others' labors and did not labor for itself, the economic result was an impoverished region that contained a few extremely rich individuals and a mass of poor people. This was the reasoning that the rebels had used against British policy in the 1760s. Now it was used against southern slave masters to explain southern economic problems. Well before the year 1800, northerners blamed the South's economic woes on its peculiar institution.[29]

Slavery had failed to develop significantly in the North, although in New York, New Jersey, and Pennsylvania it was developing some strong roots, and so northerners could end the institution within their borders without great upheaval. Prodded on by revolutionary ideology and abetted by the slim economic strength of slavery there, northerners removed the institution either abruptly or gradually. The point that was not lost upon southerners, however, was that the North no longer had a material interest in the maintenance of slavery. The slave South and the nonslave North, soon to be known as the free labor North, had come into existence.

The northern attack upon the peculiar institution drew upon many sources. Natural-rights ideas informed the question of the legitimacy of slavery. So did religious doctrines and sensitivity to the sufferings of the slave population.[30] However, prominent among the arguments composing the attack that overthrew northern slavery and denounced southern slavery were two vital principles of the revolution: that the individual deserved the fruits of his labor and that aristocrats sought to impoverish and dominate commoners.

In response to this attack, and while admitting at times that slavery did violate certain natural rights and posed unusual problems for republican government, southerners immediately grabbed another vital principle of the Revolution: no individual could be deprived of his or her property without his or her consent. Government was not to abridge property rights. The major lines for the defense of slavery evidently had not yet formed except the crucial one of the sanctity of property rights[31] (although, without too much effort, it could be inferred that the racial argument for slavery must have already been in operation). Perhaps the most emphatic declaration of the rights of property in slaves occurred in July 1776 in the Continental Congress. In a discussion about an appropriate frame of government, Samuel Chase of Maryland wanted the word "white" to be inserted concerning citizenship: "Negroes are a species of property, personal estate." James Wilson then attacked slavery and its effects upon prosperity; "It [slavery] is attended with many inconveniences." Judge Thomas Lynch then laid down the law of any union between the slave states and nonslave states: "If it is debated, whether their slaves are their property, there is an end of the confederation."[32] From the beginning of the Union, southerners demanded a basic contract that at all times had to be observed: slaves were property and property rights were inviolable. This was the foundation of all political defenses of slavery.

People committed to the extirpation of the institution of slavery in the aftermath of the Revolution had to combat property doctrines because property rights constituted the frontline defense of the peculiar institution. Much of the attack, perhaps the bulk of it, stressed living up to Christian doctrines, following the Golden Rule (do unto others as you would have others do unto you), protecting the institution of the family, and eliminating the excessive cruelty so visible in slavery.[33] One line of attack was that no one could claim the sanctity of property rights if the property was obtained by theft; because slaves had been kidnapped from Africa, no social or governmental power could be invoked on behalf of property rights in slaves because they were stolen property.[34]

A frequent way that antislavery proponents dismissed property rights as a legitimate defense of slavery involved the Enlightenment's exaltation of natural rights. Freedom was the natural right of each human being, curtailed only slightly due to need of humans to aggregate into society. One form of the natural-rights argument was quite specific and easily blended into the newly established discipline of political economy. David Cooper, an early antislavery advocate, approvingly quoted John Locke for saying that the natural right of each person was the ownership of his or her body, and thus the person owned the results of the labor of his or her body. John Wesley celebrated the dictum of the eminent English jurist William Blackstone, who declared in the *Somerset* case (1772) that slavery could not exist in England; though a person might sell his labor to another, no Englishman could ever alienate his body to another. Adam Smith then put these sentiments into an economic doctrine, rather widely quoted in the infant United States: "The property which every man has in his own labour, as it is the original foundation of all other property, so it is the most sacred and inviolable." The concept of property rights in humans was thus invalidated by a natural-rights theory that postulated original ownership began with the person and the person's labor.[35]

How powerful the property-in-oneself approach was in rejecting property rights in slaves is unclear. For some it was simply a convenient argument that made sense. More generally, the natural-rights argument of the Enlightenment simply led to the idea, however expressed in specific terms, that individuals should suffer as few artificial social and political restraints as possible, and slavery was an artificial social restraint on individuals. The thrust of the Enlightenment and specifically of the American Revolution was antiaristocratic and antihierarchical. Slavery, an example of unnatural hierarchy, was therefore illegitimate.

Whatever the exact source of why antislavery individuals rejected the doctrine of property rights in slaves, the result was undeniably finely chiseled. Property rights as previously defined were incorrect; a new definition of property rights was necessary. And here the antislavery element drew upon the fourth lesson—but not principle—of the Revolution; property rights might indeed be natural but the definition of property was in fact derived from popularly elected legislatures. The challenge was made explicit by Tom Paine in *The Rights of Man*, his response to the pronouncements of Edmund Burke on the French Revolution: "Man has no property in man."[36]

The Constitutional Convention in Philadelphia in the spring and summer of 1787 revealed the currents of American thought about minority rights, property rights, democracy, slavery, and slavery's social effects. Many forebodings brought the leaders of the states to this meeting; the national finances were disastrous, the country appeared to be breaking apart into smaller confederations, few believed the nation had the power to repel a foreign attack, problems of trade both internal and external plagued the states, and the people had undergone the stress of an economic downturn. What had struck fear into the minds of numerous leaders, however, were the attempts to remedy some of these problems by the state legislatures. States had passed tariff acts against other states and foreign nations, and they had emitted paper money to overcome the depressed economy, raising fears that obligations between debtors and creditors would be governed by popular vote instead of by moral principle. And Massachusetts endured an uprising of western farmers against the state's taxation policies in 1786 in Shays's Rebellion.

Conventioneers immediately pointed to the essential framework in which all the problems of the country would be addressed. "Life & liberty were generally said to be of more value, than property," explained Gouverneur Morris of Pennsylvania. "An accurate view of the matter would nevertheless prove that property was the main object of society," a sentiment to which John Rutledge of South Carolina, James Madison of Virginia, and Pierce Butler of South Carolina, at one point or another, agreed.[37] The danger to property rights, and hence to civilization, was that the states during the Revolution had become too democratic and so had passed laws undermining the rights of property holders to their property; or, in the words of Connecticut's Elbridge Gerry, the "evils we experience flow from the excess of democracy."[38] Although the sense was nearly unanimous that only a republican form of government was suitable for the United States, and that republics required the principle of majority rule, the delegates nevertheless felt that minority rights had become endangered. Minority rights almost invariably meant the rights of the propertied to be left alone with their property. Madison thus made speeches crying for a diversity of interests to dilute a majority that might appear on any particular interest, and that condition, he felt, best suited a republic that extended over a great amount of land; he asserted that the enemies to property rights were small republics in which dominating majorities could easily form.

Madison did believe in majority rule and a republican form of government, but the basic argument he propounded in the convention was a fear of majority rule on property rights. No "agrarian attempts" at property redistribution had yet been made in the United States, he said, but who could doubt that over time the condition will arrive when "the proportion of those who will labour under all the hardships of life . . . secretly sigh for a more equal distribution of its blessings." The Constitution should be formed so that future agrarian attempts would fail.[39]

As the members contemplated a stronger Union, they had to address the role of slavery under a new frame of government. These concerns most naturally arose during discussions of representation and taxation. Outside of the obvious clash of self-interest between the slaveholding representatives and the nonslaveholding ones (that is, free states members wanted to count slaves for taxation purposes but not representation, the opposite being the desire of southerners), members made tangential comments that showed how deeply rooted had become prejudices about slavery. The definition of slaves elicited a troubled interchange. Elbridge Gerry of Massachusetts used the beast analogy: why should slaves be counted in representation when in the South they were accounted property, and if they be counted as property then why not representation for "the Cattle & horses of the North." Gouverneur Morris wanted slaves to be counted as either property or as people but not both; he was concerned about Pennsylvanian sentiments about slavery in general. In discussion over tariff policy and the international slave trade, Roger Sherman of Connecticut wanted to avoid labeling slaves as "*property*," while James Madison later agreed that he "thought it wrong to admit in the Constitution the idea that there could be property in men."[40]

Northern politicians at the time caved into the demand of southerners that slaves be considered property and that slaves were included in the doctrine of the sanctity of property rights. At the ratification convention of New York state, Alexander Hamilton justified the three-fifths compromise and noted that northerners had acceded to the southern insistence that slaves be considered property. He inserted, however, that slaves were "men, though degraded to the condition of slavery." In the monthly magazine the *American Museum*, a contributor addressed the possibility of emancipation. The difficulty confronting the country was the inviolability of property rights; government could never simply effect emancipation by legal declaration "since, to deprive a man, at once, of all his right in the property of his negroes, would be the height of injustice" and would "never be submitted to."[41]

The southern response to northern quibbles about slaves as men and not property was forthright. South Carolina's Charles Cotesworth Pinckney "desired that the rule of wealth should be ascertained, and not left to the pleasure of the legislature; and that property in slaves should not be exposed to danger under a government instituted for the protection of property." The Virginians

George Mason and John Randolph apologized for the institution's existence, but nonetheless argued that as it did exist, in Randolph's words, "the holders of it would require this security." When the exchange became more heated over slavery's representation, Pierce Butler laid down the rule of Union under the Constitution: "The security the Southn. States want is, that their negroes may not be taken from them, which some gentlemen within or without doors have a very good mind to do."[42]

The framers acknowledged that by 1788 a moral argument against slavery existed and that it was based on the Protestant version of the Bible. This is a logical inference to be made from Edmund Randolph's argument against continuance of the Atlantic slave trade for an extra twenty years because "it would revolt the Quakers, the Methodists, and many others in the States having no slaves." The answer to moral charges against slavery was revealing. South Carolina's John Rutledge dismissed such emotions for "Religion & humanity had nothing to do with this question." Rather, slavery within the states of North America should be treated like an issue between nations: "Interest alone is the governing principle with nations." And so interest alone governed the entire subject of slavery, the interest of property rights. To this position Oliver Ellsworth of Connecticut agreed, giving an early example of the use of the doctrine of states' rights: "The morality or wisdom of slavery are considerations belonging to the States themselves. What enriches a part enriches the whole, and the States are the best judges of their particular interest." At least one delegate, South Carolina's Charles Pinckney, justified slavery on the grounds of past civilizations and insisted that the history of the human race had been the history of slavery.[43]

Discussion of slavery went well beyond questions of morality and humanity, however, and easily permeated questions of national strength and economic vigor. A few comments were made about the fact that the new powerful government would find that its new duty would be the suppression of slave insurrections, but such internal strife would weaken the nation in foreign affairs.[44] More to the point was the declaration by some delegates that slavery retarded economic growth. Chief among these was Gouverneur Morris, who, in an irate speech about the prosouthern tendencies of the Constitution, demeaned the institution as a curse: "Compare the free regions of the Middle States, where a rich & noble cultivation marks the prosperity & happiness of the people, with the misery & poverty which overspread the barren wastes of Va. Maryd. & the other States having slaves." To this assessment George Mason later added, "Slavery discourages arts & manufactures. The poor despise labor when performed by slaves."[45] Gouverneur Morris inferred the source of the dislike between free and slave labor: free labor wanted, it would be assumed, a competence and a decent standard of living, but the "miserable slave" had no more "than his physical subsistence and the rag that covers his nakedness." Thus began the continual comparison of free states versus slave states that would be so prominent between 1846 and 1860; thus commenced the charge that slavery produced economic backwardness; but thus also began a rebuttal of these comments by southerners.[46]

And so also commenced the free labor diatribe against slavery. The Constitution makers merely reiterated an argument in the Continental Congress in August 1776 over how to assess taxes to finance the war, the requisitions required from the states. In this debate, the main question was whether a slave contributed as much to national wealth as a freeman. John Adams of Massachusetts, wanting the southern states to pay as much as possible, said there was no difference between kinds of laborers save the name: "that in some countries the labouring poor were called freemen, in others they were called slaves: but that the difference as to the state was imaginary only."[47] James Wilson added that freemen did work harder (but they consumed more, so the surplus available for taxation was the same as for slaves), but current ideas now stipulated that slave labor was the "dearest" of all labor.[48] North Carolina's delegate, William Hooper, recognized the operation of the incentive theme and how whites feared competing with slave labor: "Whites and negroes cannot work together. Negroes are goods and chattels, are property. A negro works under the impulse of fear, has no care of his master's interest." Benjamin Harrison agreed that slaves did not work as assiduously as did freemen; he determined that the ratio of output between them was two slaves to one free person. Indeed, this idea of comparing the labor output of slaves and freemen was the basis for the three-fifths ratio for taxation and representation in the Constitution.[49] In any event, many citizens had the notion that slave labor and free labor were antagonistic labor systems.

Also born at the Constitutional Convention was a fear of the political power of the slaveholding states. In the debates over representation and taxation, both Madison and Gouverneur Morris stated that the real dividing line between the states was not big versus little, but slave versus nonslave.[50] During the debate on representation, southerners got political representation for their property; they were taxed less for their property; they obtained a prohibition against taxes on exports, and nearly obtained a rule that taxation of imports required a two-thirds majority. Morris charged that the "Southn. Gentlemen will not be satisfied unless they see the way open to their gaining a majority in the public Councils." By August, not only did Morris declare slavery immoral and economically injurious, but now slavery "is the most prominent feature in the aristocratic countenance of the proposed Constitution." Slaveholders, in short, wielded too much power in the national government. Madison later supported that observation by pinpointing slavery as the wellspring of aristocracy. "In proportion as slavery prevails in a State, the Government, however democratic in name, must be aristocratic in fact. The power lies in a part instead of the whole; in the hands of property, not of numbers." The southern states were, in short, aristocracies due to the existence of slavery.[51] In forty years, Morris's complaint would be termed the "slave power" by the abolitionists who labeled the slaveholders an aristocracy.

In the ratification conventions that followed, northerners, to the extent that such a generalization can be made, acceded to the southern demand that they recognize property rights in slaves, while southerners hotly debated whether to join the new government.[52] At least one major question emerging in the discussions was whether slavery got sufficient protection under the new system. In these exchanges there was no doubt that southerners were thinking in terms of their investment.

In the Virginia debates over ratification, Patrick Henry moaned about the three-fifths ratio compromise for counting slaves for the purposes of representation and taxation; it was oppressive to the South "who alone have slaves!" By the taxation power slavery could be doomed; and, in one of the first planter outcries against democracy at the federal level, he warned that "The efforts of our ten men will avail very little when opposed by the northern majority." He exclaimed, "This government subjects every thing to the northern majority. . . . We thus put unbounded power over our property in hands not having a common interest with us."[53]

South Carolinians also worried about the fate of slavery under a new national government. Charles C. Pinckney, who favored the Constitution and had been a delegate to the convention, tried to tame heated imaginations by pointing out that the three-fifths compromise worked to the advantage of the South because "we thus obtained a representation for our property." It was certainly true that in the Philadelphia Convention southern delegates "had to contend with the religious and political prejudices of the Eastern and Middle States," but over all, and "considering all circumstances, we have made the best terms for the security of this species of property it was in our power to make."[54]

Even George Mason fretted that the new Constitution would not make slavery safe from northern designs. While lambasting the Philadelphia Convention for not outlawing immediately American participation in the international slave trade, he, in a bizarre twist of logic, found the Constitution inadequate for the security of property in slaves already in the country: "This government does not intend our domestic safety. It authorizes the importation of slaves for twenty-odd years, and thus continues upon us that nefarious trade. Instead of securing and protecting us, the continuation of this detestable trade adds daily to our weakness. *Though this evil is increasing, there is no clause in the Constitution that will prevent the Northern and Eastern States from meddling with our whole property of that kind. There is a clause to prohibit the importation of slaves after twenty years; but there is no provision made for securing to the Southern States those they now possess.*"[55]

When Quakers petitioned the early Congresses of the United States to abolish slavery, southern statesmen quickly reminded northerners what they had agreed to in the constitutional compact. Representative William Smith of South Carolina launched probably the first explicit proslavery speech in American history, dragging in white supremacy, the indolence of Africans, the greatness of Rome and Greece, and fears of racial amalgamation. He also made it clear that slaves were property and northerners had agreed to that definition: "There was then an implied contract between the Northern and Southern people, that no step should be taken to injure the property of the latter, or to disturb their tranquility."[56] Somewhat later, John Taylor of Caroline, the strange plantation owner who became among antebellum southerners the master source for slavery-based agrarianism and hostility to northern capitalism, aired the heartfelt fear of southerners about their new national government: "Unhappily for the southern states, they possess a species of property, which is peculiarly exposed, and upon which, if this law stands [the carriage tax], the whole burden of government may be exclusively laid."[57] Representative John Rutledge Jr. of South Carolina in 1800 in another debate over an abolitionist petition charged flatly that "so improper was it to consider this subject that some of the States would never have adopted the federal form of Government if it had not been secured to them that Congress would never legislate on the subject of slavery."[58]

The impact of slaves as property upon the formation of the Constitution deserves a brief comment. From the proceedings of the convention it appears that slavery did not directly dominate the discussion. In some ways, though, its surrogates did. Slavery was intimately bound up with concern over the basic issues that created the most consternation at the convention: representation, taxation, trade policy, majority rule, and power of the states to regulate their internal affairs—that is, a consolidated government or a federation. Although the term slavery did not emerge prominently in most of these debates, its presence was unmistakable. Slaves represented too much a property interest for it not to have been a factor in these kinds of discussions.

The end result, however, was a little strange. Supposedly the Constitutional Convention originated in the fear of northerners that majority rule had run amok, that agrarian rebellions were soon to overtake the nation, that a more powerful government was necessary to handle trade and defense. But what actually came out of the convention? The new government barely touched the northern states in the ways that the framers intended: the Dorr rebellion, the New York rent riots, and labor unrest in the 1820s and 1830s proceeded without any intervention by the federal government, and the Constitution was nearly incapable of stopping states from doing what they wanted in foreign affairs and in halting settlers from taking public lands in the West. And in trade policy, northerners obtained little more than the proposed impost that the Confederation stupidly refused to pass. In short, the North obtained virtually nothing that the preamble of the Constitution had promised. State governments ruled. Rather, the Constitution ended up protecting exactly what slaveholders wanted it to protect: property rights in slaves. The federal government marshaled an impressive record between 1790 and 1845 in making sure that the private property of slaveholders was immune to attack. It is an ironic twist that in the process of making the Constitution, the wishes of northerners were lost while the desires of slaveholders were built into the structure.[59]

Virtually all the arguments against slavery were present at the time of the writing of the Constitution. In embryonic form the free labor critique of slavery had taken shape, and individuals had announced as well the political fear that slaveholders were aristocrats who sought their elevation above freemen in the counsels of government. Southerners had made it clear that their peculiar institution had a defense. A racial argument existed, as did one based on the history of humankind. Moreover, no one doubted that slaves represented property, and southerners expected their property rights to be observed. People understood the antagonisms between North and South and had already determined that the difference was between slaveholding and nonslaveholding states. All that was necessary was for some train of events to heighten the antagonisms and allow them to erupt in anger and violence.

The Origins of Slaveholder Aggressiveness

The rotund but famed Alabama fire-eater William Lowndes Yancey told a Louisville audience in late October 1860 that the election of Lincoln would be the clap of doom for southern society. Extension of slavery, he insisted, was not the issue, but the existence of slavery itself. And he urged the crowd to consider how intertwined slavery was in the fabric of the South. In particular: "Again: Look at the value of that property.—These slaves are worth, according to Virginia prices $2800,000,000—an amount easy to pronounce, but how difficult to conceive of to one who knows anything about the power of multiplication of numbers. . . . Twenty-eight hundred millions of dollars are to be affected by the decision of this question. Four millions of people are to be affected by it—four millions of slaves. Not only that, but the social and domestic relations of the eight millions of whites of the South are of necessity more or less affected by the decision of this question." Here in one paragraph Yancey pointed to all the variables necessary to explain southern secession and the coming of the Civil War.[1]

Yancey's stress on the amount of property invested in slaves was not unique but was indeed a major theme in the southern defense of slavery. In numerous speeches, southern writers and orators revealed that they knew quite well the dollar amounts connected to slavery. And they also knew that the legal protector of those dollar amounts was the doctrine of property rights.

Thomas R. Dew in his famous review of the debate over emancipation in the Virginia legislative assembly of 1831–32 figured that Virginia slaves were worth $94 million while the value of all the houses and land in the state was $206 million—slaves represented about one-third the value of Virginia.[2] John C. Calhoun, when defending his resolutions in the Senate calling for a denunciation of abolitionists, stated that antislavery radicals were waging war upon "institutions that involve not less than $900,000,000 of property, and the prosperity and safety of an entire section of this Union." During the heated struggle over the provisions of the Compromise of 1850, James D. B. De Bow wrote in his influential monthly periodical that "$2,000,000,000" of southern property was in peril. Governor James J. Pettus of Mississippi, in the wake of John Brown's failed raid on Harpers Ferry Armory, exclaimed that southerners could not permit northerners to abuse $2.6 billion of property. In his reminiscences, Mississippian J. L. M. Curry wrote that after the election of Lincoln the southern states "in unequivocal language" told northerners that they would not permit violations of the Constitution, discriminations against their property, or making "insecure a property valued at $3,000,000,000."[3]

Understanding the relations between wealth, slavery, and property rights in the South provides a powerful means of understanding southern political behavior leading to disunion. First, the size dimensions of slavery are important to comprehend, for slavery was a colossal institution. Second, the property rights argument was the ultimate defense of slavery, and white southerners and the proslavery radicals knew it. Third, the weak point in the protection of slavery by property rights was the federal government. Because nonslaveholders participated in the federal Congress, they lacked the perspective, the cultural awareness, and the financial commitment to preserving the peculiar institution. They could foster laws that injured the economic viability of slavery or weaken property rights in people. In short, the federal government endangered the basic means of maintaining slavery: the legal definition of property. Fourth, the intense need to preserve the sanctity of property rights in Africans led southern political leaders to demand the nationalization of slavery—the condition under which slaveholders would always be protected in their property holdings.

The basic statistics of the divisions within the nation are given in Table 2.1. A few elements of that table require elaboration as they play a role in one way or another in several parts of this book. The first aspect of the table is the superficial realization of the overwhelming population advantage of the nonslaveholding states. In fact, three Garantuas ruled antebellum America: New York, Pennsylvania, and Ohio alone accounted for nearly one-third of the nation's population. And in the category of white males, one can read the potential political supremacy of the North, for until the 1870s white males mostly accounted for political representation. However, of importance for the Civil War and for much population theory floating about antebellum America is the amount of square mileage per section. The entire South had twice the area but only one-third the population.[4] The clear dividing line was between the immigration states and the slaves states; indeed, one is almost tempted to say, looking at the table, that the real division between the states was the locus of cheap labor: in the North it was the immigrant, in the South it was the African slave. A feature of this table that will play an absent role in national politics is the potential of the Border South. The states of the Border South have tended to be pushed out of the picture in antebellum politics so as to get to the mentalities of New Englanders, Yorkers, and Carolinians. Yet Table 2.1 reveals

TABLE 2.1. *General Population, Wealth, and Areal Characteristics of the States and Regions of the United States, 1860*

State and Region	*Total Population*	*White Males Age 15–69*	*Total Wealth ($ Million)*	*Total Aliens*	*Total Slaves*	*Square Miles*
New England						
Connecticut	460,147	94,831	444	80,696	0	4,750
New Hampshire	326,073	69,018	156	20,938	0	9,280
Massachusetts	1,231,066	251,287	815	260,114	0	7,800
Maine	628,279	120,863	190	37,453	0	35,000
Rhode Island	174,620	35,209	135	37,394	0	1,306
Vermont	315,098	63,781	122	32,743	0	10,212
Total	3,135,283	634,989	1,862	469,338	0	68,348
Middle Atlantic						
New York	3,831,590	1,179,374	1,843	998,640	0	47,008
New Jersey	672,035	194,852	468	122,790	18	8,320
Pennsylvania	2,906,215	826,654	1,417	430,505	0	46,008
Total	7,209,840	2,200,880	3,728	1,551,935	18	101,336
Great Lakes						
Illinois	1,711,951	524,061	716	324,643	0	55,410
Indiana	1,350,428	386,905	529	118,184	0	33,809
Iowa	674,913	197,086	247	106,081	0	55,045
Michigan	749,113	236,674	257	149,092	0	56,451
Ohio	2,339,511	672,166	1,193	328,254	0	39,964
Wisconsin	775,881	231,658	274	276,927	0	53,924
Minnesota	172,023	54,111	52	58,728	0	83,531
Total	7,773,820	2,302,661	3,268	1,361,909	0	378,134
Deep South						
Alabama	964,201	146,664	495	12,352	435,080	50,722
Florida	140,424	22,460	73	3,309	61,745	59,268
Georgia	1,057,286	162,203	646	11,671	462,198	58,000
Louisiana	708,002	113,341	602	81,029	331,726	41,346
Mississippi	791,305	101,138	607	8,558	436,631	47,156
South Carolina	703,708	81,863	548	9,986	402,406	34,000
Texas	604,215	126,520	365	43,422	182,566	[274,356]
Total	4,969,141	754,189	3,336	170,327	2,312,352	564,848
Border South						
Arkansas	435,450	103,134	219	3,741	111,115	52,198
Delaware	112,216	27,071	46	9,165	1,798	2,120
Kentucky	1,155,684	262,320	666	59,799	225,483	37,680
Maryland	687,049	151,748	377	77,536	87,189	11,124
Missouri	1,182,012	321,275	501	160,541	114,931	65,350
North Carolina	992,622	171,059	358	3,299	331,059	50,704
Tennessee	1,109,801	230,214	494	21,226	275,719	45,600
Virginia	1,596,318	293,833	793	35,058	490,865	61,352
Total	7,271,152	1,560,654	3,454	370,365	1,638,159	326,128

Sources: Total population and white males 15–69 figured from U.S. Department of the Interior, *Eighth Census*, vol. 1: *Population*, 339; wealth from ibid., vol. 4: *Statistics*, 295; immigration from ibid., vol. 1: *Population*, xxix; area from ibid., vol. 4: *Statistics*, 339.

that the Border South housed a large population capable of throwing much weight around politically and was a region that possessed impressive wealth. But the main purpose of this table is to yield the census calculations for wealth (personal and real estate) in the United States. On the surface, it appears to be lodged in the North, especially in the Middle Atlantic and Great Lakes states. Therein lies a strange tale.[5] However, the impressive features of slavery can be demonstrated by a few additional but simple tables and a little narrative.

Slavery was a huge institution. Its size may not have been in some ways comparable with its counterpart in the Caribbean and Latin America where slaves far outnumbered free people, but in the context of southern daily life slavery was omnipresent and unavoidable. Table 2.2 provides the population statistics of the Old South. The slaveholding states in 1859 had a total of 12,240,300 people; 65.7 percent of these were white, 2.0 percent were free blacks, and 32.3 percent—some 3,950,511 or about 4 million—were slaves. As one went into the cotton South, the number of slaves relative to free people changed dramatically. Indeed, the eleven states of the Confederacy had 5,449,463 whites and 3,529,110 slaves; the border states of Delaware, Kentucky, Maryland, and Missouri probably did tilt the outcome of the Civil War in favor of the Union because those states housed 2,589,533 whites and only 429,401 slaves. However, the key is first to recognize the size of the institution: nearly 4 million out of a population of 12 million is large in both relative and absolute terms.[6]

The second paramount feature of slavery is the unbelievable amount of wealth it comprised compared with other sectors of the United States economy in 1860. Table 2.3 offers the dollar values of the basic categories of wealth that may be derived from the census of 1860 (in terms of 1860 dollars). The category of unaccounted-for wealth probably reflects urban residences, investments in canals, river and oceanic transportation devices and supply facilities, and various sundry items of personal wealth. The $3 billion figure for slaves is a compromise over economists' varying estimations.[7] Outside of the somewhat obvious fact that in terms of wealth the United States was overwhelmingly an agrarian nation, it has to be underlined that slaves accounted for approximately 18.75 percent of the national wealth ($3 billion divided by $16 billion), or less precisely between 15 and 20 percent of the total store of national wealth.

What is shocking is the comparison of wealth in slaves to wealth (or investment dollars) in other areas of the economy. Table 2.3 shows that slaveholding comprised far more national wealth than railroads and manufacturing enterprise *combined*; the $3 billion in slaves was almost 50 percent more than the $2.2 billion invested in railroads and manufacturing. For decades now, political and business historians have almost been obsessed—at the least transfixed—by the dynamics of northern industrial and transportation development. Yet in terms of wealth holding, railroads and manufacturing pale when compared with slaveholding.

TABLE 2.2. *Percentage of Slave Population in the Southern States in 1859 (1860)*

State	*% White*	*% Slave*	*% Free Black*	*Total*
Border States				
Arkansas	74.4	25.5	01.1	435,450
Delaware	80.7	01.6	17.7	112,216
Kentucky	79.6	19.5	00.9	1,155,684
Maryland	75.1	12.7	12.2	687,049
Missouri	90.0	09.7	00.3	1,182,012
North Carolina	63.6	33.4	03.0	992,622
Tennessee	74.5	24.8	00.7	1,109,801
Virginia	65.6	30.7	03.7	1,596,318
Old South				
South Carolina	41.4	57.2	01.4	703,708
Georgia	56.0	43.7	00.3	1,057,286
Alabama	54.6	45.1	00.3	964,201
Florida	55.4	43.9	00.7	140,425
Mississippi	44.7	55.2	00.1	791,305
Louisiana	50.5	46.9	02.6	708,002
Texas	69.7	30.2	00.1	604,215

Source: Kennedy, *Preliminary Report on the Eighth Census*, 131.

Another way to buttress this point is to look more closely at the wealth of the planters, those who possessed twenty or more slaves. This group amounted to 46,274 individuals by the census of 1860, representing 00.58 percent of the southern population or perhaps 3 percent of southern families. But the planters owned more than one-half of all the slaves. This means this small segment of southern society probably owned at least $1.5 billion in slaves.[8] On the other hand, according to the census enumerators, the value of southern railroads and

TABLE 2.3. *Value of Wealth of the United States per Economic Sector, 1860*

Category (All U.S.)	*Estimated $ Value*
Slaves	$3,000,000,000
Value of farms	6,638,414,221
Value of farm implements	246,125,064
Investment in manufacturing	1,050,000,000
Investment in railroads	1,166,422,729
Bank capital	227,469,077
Home productions	27,484,144
Value of livestock	1,098,862,355
Total	13,452,000,000
Total assessed real estate and personal property	16,159,616,068
Value unaccounted for	2,707,616,000

Source: Kennedy, *Preliminary Report on the Eighth Census*, 190, 192, 193, 195, 196, 209, 230–31.

industry, in terms of value of investment, was $522,850,000. Subtracting the value of southern investment in railroads and industry from the national total of $2,216,422,729 leaves an amount invested in northern railroads and industry of $1.69 billion. In other words, *the worth of the slaves owned by the planters alone was almost equal to all northern investment in railroads and manufacturing combined.* And this does not even include the value of land that southern planters possessed. If we assume the simple equation that wealth is power, or even the more circumspect and more accurate equation that power is partially a function of wealth, then no one should have any question where power lay in the antebellum period. It lay with the slaveholders. With only a modest effort one can easily imagine the massive wealth imbalance that must have existed prior to 1840, before railroads and industrial development gave the free states a wealth position that could even modestly compare with that of the planters.

How dramatic the wealth in slaves was compared with that in other endeavors can be illustrated another way. The wealth of the states can be ranked from first to last, and when that is done, northern states look impressive. But when the states are ranked according to wealth per capita, suddenly the slave states all leap forward in the rankings (columns one and two of Table 2.4). But in the South, slaves were not exactly population, especially in connection with the subject of wealth. If the total amount of wealth (real estate and personal) is divided by the white population, the totals for the free states remain essentially the same (the figures in Table 2.4 are not adjusted for the free black population in the North because the numbers are so small) but the wealth per white capita in the South leaps far beyond the free states. Indeed, as column 3 of Table 2.4 shows, the highest ranking states in wealth per white capita are exactly the seven states, with the exception of Connecticut, that seceded the Union in the winter of 1860–61. After those states comes the parade of the border slave states. At the bottom of the list, interestingly, are the agricultural states of the Great Lakes and New England. In terms of wealth, the mighty economies of Pennsylvania, Ohio, and New York, from Table 2.4, column 3, look like the sick and underdeveloped economies that Republicans called the slave states. One could almost say that the war between the states was not between the slave and free states, but between the rich and poor states.

Gavin Wright explained that the antebellum difference between the sections could be summed up as the difference between laborlords and landlords: northerners invested in land, whereas southerners invested in slaves. The truth of that powerful interpretation can be seen in Table 2.5, which presents the simple ratio of real estate (per white population) wealth divided by personal estate (per white population) wealth. Southern wealth was lodged in slaveholdings, which the census enumerators listed under personal estate. This difference in the way northerners and southerners invested made a huge difference in the way the sections sized up each other. Northerners had trouble "seeing" southern wealth because it was in slaves, although they knew slaves repre-

TABLE 2.4. *Ranking of States by Wealth Adjusted for Population, 1860*

Ranking of State by Wealth, Total Wealth (Millions $)	*Ranking of State by Wealth per Capita (Total Population) (Thousands $)*	*Ranking of State by Wealth per White Population Only (Thousands $)*
New York, 1,843	Connecticut, 965	South Carolina, 1,883 (12/20/1860)
Pennsylvania, 1,416	Louisiana, 850	Mississippi, 1,715 (1/9/1861)
Ohio, 1,194	South Carolina, 778	Louisiana, 1,686 (1/26/1861)
Illinois, 872	Rhode Island, 771	Georgia, 1,091 (1/19/1861)
Massachusetts, 815	Mississippi, 767	Connecticut, 965
Virginia, 793	New Jersey, 696	Alabama, 941 (1/11/1861)
Kentucky, 666	Massachusetts, 662	Florida, 936 (1/10/1861)
Georgia, 646	Georgia, 611	Texas, 867 (2/1/1861)
Mississippi, 607	Texas, 604	Rhode Island, 771
Louisiana, 602	Kentucky, 576	Virginia, 757 (4/17/1861)
South Carolina, 548	Oregon, 558	Maryland, 731
Indiana, 529	Maryland, 549	Kentucky, 725
Missouri, 501	California, 547	New Jersey, 696
Alabama, 495	Florida, 521	Arkansas, 676 (5/6/1861)
Tennessee, 494	Alabama, 513	Massachusetts, 662
New Jersey, 468	Ohio, 510	Tennessee, 597 (6/8/1861)
Connecticut, 444	Illinois, 510	North Carolina, 570 (5/20/1861)
Maryland, 377	Arkansas, 503	Oregon, 558
Texas, 365	Virginia, 497	California, 547
North Carolina, 359	Pennsylvania, 487	Ohio, 510
Wisconsin, 274	New Hampshire, 479	Illinois, 510
Michigan, 257	New York, 475	Delaware, 505
Iowa, 247	Tennessee, 445	Pennsylvania, 487
Arkansas, 219	Missouri, 424	New Hampshire, 479
California, 208	Delaware, 410	New York, 475
Maine, 190	Indiana, 392	Missouri, 471
New Hampshire, 156	Vermont, 387	Indiana, 392
Rhode Island, 135	Iowa, 366	Vermont, 387
Vermont, 122	North Carolina, 362	Iowa, 366
Florida, 73	Wisconsin, 353	Wisconsin, 353
Minnesota, 52	Michigan, 343	Michigan, 343
Delaware, 46	Maine, 303	Maine, 303
Kansas, 31	Minnesota, 303	Minnesota, 303
Oregon, 29	Kansas, 290	Kansas, 290

Sources: Total population computed from U.S. Department of the Interior, *Eighth Census*, vol. 1: *Population*, 339; white population from ibid.: vol. 1: *Population*, 593; wealth from ibid.: vol. 4: *Statistics*, 295. Date in parenthesis in column 3 is date of passage of secession ordinance.

sented wealth. For them the outward sign of wealth was land and buildings. Thus northerners would have a dim picture of southern development even though, simply put, they were peons compared with southerners.[9]

Given these tables, the question naturally arises about the economic debate between northerners and southerners for the two decades prior to the Civil War. The tables given here are not the usual ones depicting North-South differences; indeed, they are radically different. Usually the North is character-

TABLE 2.5. *Ranking of States by Ratio of Real Estate per White Population Divided by Personal Wealth per White Population, 1860*

State	*Ratio*
Wisconsin	3.85
Pennsylvania	3.57
Minnesota	3.57
Vermont	3.45
New York	3.33
Michigan	3.13
Illinois	2.78
Iowa	2.63
Kansas	2.63
Ohio	2.56
Indiana	2.44
Rhode Island	2.04
Delaware	2.00
Louisiana	1.82
Virginia	1.75
Massachusetts	1.59
Tennessee	1.35
Missouri	1.35
Maine	1.28
Connecticut	1.27
Kentucky	1.11
New Jersey	1.01
New Hampshire	0.93
California	0.92
Texas	0.72
North Carolina	0.66
Alabama	0.56
Arkansas	0.54
Florida	0.47
Oregon	0.46
Mississippi	0.45
Georgia	0.41
South Carolina	0.36
Maryland	0.28

Source: Computed from U.S. Department of the Interior, *Eighth Census*, vol. 1, *Population*, 593; wealth from ibid., vol. 4: *Statistics*, 295.

ized as the dynamic, growing economy while the South is described as sinking into backwardness and poverty—usually by some comparison of New York to Virginia or Ohio to Kentucky. Part of the answer lies in the use of income statistics versus wealth statistics: the productions of the farm, miles of railroad, extent of manufactures. Seldom did these debates turn on wealth figures. Moreover, it does not appear—as fantastic as this claim seems to be—that contemporaries used the census statistics on wealth. James D. B. De Bow superintended the *Seventh Census* and provided a table of the real and personal wealth of the states but added no narrative to it. A brief table gave an accounting of all persons who owned over $100,000 in various counties in the states of Kentucky, Michigan, Pennsylvania, Rhode Island, South Carolina, Louisiana, and Ohio; they were southerners. De Bow's counting, however, was not comprehensive and few if any made any debating points from this knowledge.[10]

The census of 1860 was a little different. In the final publication, the narrator fixed upon western growth in the Great Lakes region, particularly Iowa. He provided an example of wealth per capita for Iowa and Pennsylvania. But he did not do so for all the states and for none of the southern states. One would have thought he might have noticed the peculiarity of wealth in the nation when he listed the top ten wealthiest states: New York, Pennsylvania, Ohio, Virginia, Illinois, Tennessee, Alabama, Massachusetts, Kentucky, and Mississippi: five of these wealthiest states had been slave states, yet the narrator provided no comment. Perhaps the reason for the lack of analysis and summation came from the date of publication—1866. By the time the statistics came out, the value of slaves made no difference, for the Civil War had settled the matter of slavery.[11] Nonetheless, in the sectional debates over the economics of slavery, there was a real blind spot in regard to wealth. In an 1855 speech Charles Sumner threw out the line that he would not take the time to disprove the notion that slavery assisted economic growth, for the idea that slave labor was more advantageous than free labor was "all exploded by the official tables of the census."[12] His position was absolutely simply incorrect.

Wealth in slaves, however, carried an important meaning for all white southerners. Wealth in slaves economically stitched together the region. It did more than that. Because Africans were legally permitted to be counted as wealth, the institution of slavery defined progress, social mobility, and economic growth for white southerners. The peculiar institution simply grafted itself onto every economic and ideological feature of southern antebellum life.

Wealth invested in slaves was productive wealth that produced a stream of income, making the white South generally prosperous. Whether due to economies of scale or to a nearly insatiable world demand for cotton, slavery produced for southerners a per capita income comparable to the national average and a growth rate that augured a sanguine future (the average national per capita income for whites in 1860 was about $144; for white southerners, it was $150.)[13] It is likely that the wealth was distributed more unevenly in the South than in the North, especially when rural areas are compared, but most concede that the white South contained a type of broad rural middle class—small property holders who were not plunged into poverty.[14] Moreover, the South did have an industrial beachhead and possessed considerable railroad development.[15] The slaveholding states may not have had the dynamism of the northern free labor economy, but they were not particularly laggards either.[16]

It was this stream of income coming from the wealth of slavery that stitched southern white society together. Wealth that is essentially unproductive—

hoards of gold, diamonds, or other kinds of non-income-producing assets—would have evoked far more turbulence in the white South and ultimately have resulted in class collisions. Because slavery produced income, however, it generated secondary and tertiary effects, which provided employment opportunities for nonslaveholders and created a generally prosperous economic climate. Income from slavery was financing industry, transportation, government, and various urban and legal services.[17]

Antislavery northerners insisted that the South was poor, but southerners never agreed to those claims. Thomas Prentice Kettell wrote a pamphlet in 1860 detailing the wealth of the South, and at the beginning of the 1850s David Christy of Cincinnati coined the phrase, "Cotton is King." The "South has not been lacking in skill and enterprise," contended Georgia's A. H. Colquitt in 1854, and in 1850 Mississippi governor John A. Quitman warned the legislature that antislavery northerners might attack slavery, "this great social interest upon which are founded the prosperity, the happiness, and the very existence of the people of fourteen States of this Union." Toward the end of the 1850s, a contributor to a Georgia newspaper testified that, "Talk of robbery, if you will; rail against tariffs, and merchants, and manufacturers, dependent or not dependent, the most highly prosperous people now on earth, are to be found in these very [slave] States."[18]

Although the slaveholding states differed among themselves in important ways, they nonetheless exhibited certain basic similarities. The southern states were simply agricultural (see Table 2.6), as farming remained their central occupation.[19] Factory labor did not penetrate the slaveholding South, so it seems (Table 2.7); the Border South had more occupational diversity than the Deep South, and the smaller states of Maryland and Delaware had to turn to activity other than agriculture. Elsewhere in the Border South some significant manufacturing and artisanal activity appeared.[20] Yet, if one assumed that the total number of families in a state stood for a better measure of household production than the number of white males aged fifteen to sixty-nine, and the number of farms an accurate measure of the number of proprietor farmers, then the ratio of those who owned farms was about .46 for the Border South and .44 for the Deep South. What is not factored into Tables 2.6 and 2.7, however, are the occupations of slaves. The impact is significant, because slaves would show up in the various categories of labor and agricultural labor.

In whatever state slavery became entrenched, however, it had one immediate visible feature: it fostered the large farm. Farms containing more than 1,000 acres were almost exclusively limited to the slaveholding states, and even in the category of farm size 500–999 acres, the slaveholding states far outstripped northerners (see Table 2.8). These large farms were the plantations, and slavery thus gave birth to the plantation elite, the planter class. Whether these large agricultural units were as productive as some historians assert need not detain us; their existence would certainly play an important role in heightening sectional tensions.[21]

TABLE 2.6. *Southern Occupational Categories and Ratios of Category to Total White Males, 1850 and 1860*

State	*Total White Males 15–69*	*Farms*	*Farmers*	*Commerce*	*Skilled Labor*	*Factory/ Manual Labor*	*Common Labor*	*Professions*
Border South, 1850								
Arkansas	44,525	.399	.656	.025	.057	.001	.126	.035
Delaware	17,367	.349	.454	.066	.205	.045	.374	.114
Kentucky	211,617	.353	.545	.036	.109	.005	.128	.031
Maryland	125,216	.175	.233	.080	.223	.010	.301	.030
Missouri	172,728	.315	.379	.056	.104	.009	.109	.029
North Carolina	146,104	.390	.568	.028	.082	.006	.198	.028
Tennessee	197,283	.369	.606	.025	.077	.002	.085	.028
Virginia	235,320	.327	.476	.045	.135	.005	.047	.035
Total	1,150,160	.332	.488	.043	.117	.006	.165	.032
Border South, 1860								
Arkansas	103,134	.322	.562	.029	.057	.000	.068	.034
Delaware	27,071	.243	.426	.060	.200	.020	.267	.035
Kentucky	262,320	.236	.569	.050	.105	.006	.102	.034
Maryland	151,748	.166	.278	.093	.201	.010	.219	.035
Missouri	321,275	.276	.515	.052	.154	.001	.096	.038
North Carolina	171,059	.392	.621	.029	.087	.010	.115	.032
Tennessee	230,214	.338	.572	.050	.088	.005	.106	.035
Virginia	293,833	.294	.495	.052	.099	.016	.099	.030
Total	1,560,654	.286	.491	.073	.094	.009	.114	.034
Deep South, 1850								
Alabama	116,132	.361	.607	.048	.065	.002	.066	.035
Florida	14,563	.296	.419	.048	.092	.001	.212	.074
Georgia	137,355	.377	.623	.040	.075	.009	.080	.033
Louisiana	90,323	.149	.226	.146	.153	.002	.169	.036
Mississippi	82,964	.409	.634	.038	.065	.005	.067	.043
South Carolina	74,867	.400	.576	.058	.076	.002	.107	.039
Texas	48,060	.254	.530	.024	.080	.001	.111	.063
Total	564,264	.332	.538	.060	.085	.004	.099	.040
Deep South, 1860								
Alabama	146,664	.341	.567	.059	.075	.008	.070	.044
Florida	22,460	.285	.417	.063	.088	.009	.134	.052
Georgia	162,203	.332	.562	.061	.085	.020	.072	.046
Louisiana	113,341	.135	.213	.122	.151	.006	.151	.047
Mississippi	101,138	.366	.578	.050	.077	.002	.071	.053
South Carolina	81,863	.348	.540	.067	.104	.015	.073	.058
Texas	126,520	.295	.470	.041	.084	.000	.080	.041
Total	754,189	.303	.491	.073	.094	.009	.114	.034

Note on method: The categories to the right of the number of white males aged 15–69 were divided by the number of white males aged 15–69. Because the numbers in the censuses of 1850 and 1860 included women and free blacks, and because not all census categories were used, the "percentages" do not add up to 100 across each row. The number of families in the census of 1860 was also tried as a denominator, but the results so far exceeded 100 when added that that procedure was dropped. The table provides a rough comparison of how occupations were divided for household heads and voters, which is all that is intended. The census offered breakdowns for the states, but only manufacturing totals for counties.

For the 1850 categories, the information was taken from the U.S. Department of the Census, *The Seventh Census*, vol. 1: *Population*, lxvii–lxxx. *Farmer*: farmers, gardeners, overseers, planters; *commerce*: agents, bankers, bank officers, barkeepers, boardinghouse operators, boatmen, brokers, clerks, dealers, grocers, apothecaries, innkeepers, market men, merchants, peddlers, produce and provision men, railroad men, storekeepers, and traders; *skilled labor*: apprentices, blacksmiths, brewers, brickmakers, butchers, cabinetmakers, carpenters, coopers, cordwainers, drivers, drovers, joiners, machinists, masons, mechanics, millers, painters, printers, saddlers, sawyers, ship carpenters, stonecutters, tailors, teamsters, tinsmiths, weavers, wheelwrights, and jewelers; *factory/manual labor*: factory hands, fishermen, iron founders, iron mongers, iron workers, lumbermen, unspecified manufacturers, molders, and miners; *common labor*: laborers, mariners; *professions*: city and town officers, clergymen, dentists, lawyers, physicians, soldiers, teachers, U.S. and state officers.

For the 1860 categories, the information was taken from the U.S. Department of the Interior, *Eighth Census*, vol. 1: *Population*, 656–79. *Farmer*: farmers, gardeners, overseers, farm laborers; *commerce*: bankers, bank officers, boardinghouse keepers, clerks, commission merchants, dealers, druggists, grocers, innkeepers, merchants, railroad men, saloonkeepers, storekeepers, traders, boatmen; *skilled labor*: apprentices, blacksmiths, brewers, bricklayers, butchers, cabinetmakers, carpenters, coopers, harness makers, machinists, masons, mechanics, millers, painters, plasterers, printers, saddlers, sawyers, ship carpenters, shoemakers, stonecutters, tailors, teamsters, tinsmiths, weavers, wheelwrights, jewelers, joiners; *factory/manual labor*: factory hands, fishermen, lumbermen, miners, molders, iron founders, iron mongers, iron rollers, ironworkers; *common labor*: laborers, mariners; *professions*: civil and mechanical engineers, clergy, lawyers, manufacturers, officers (public), physicians, teachers, U.S. officers, dentists.

Number of farms in 1850 from De Bow, *Statistical View of the United States* (1854), 169; total farms in 1860 from U.S. Department of the Interior, *Eighth Census*, vol. 2: *Agriculture*, 221. Population of white males taken from earlier tables.

TABLE 2.7. *Workers in Factories, Border South and Deep South, 1850 and 1860*

State	*Number of Factory Workers Divided by Number of White Males, 15–69, in*	
	1850	*1860*
Border South		
Arkansas	.000	.001
Delaware	.042	.043
Kentucky	.024	.017
Maryland	.033	.052
Missouri	.005	.008
North Carolina	.014	.008
Tennessee	.015	.013
Virginia	.043	.024
Deep South		
Alabama	.005	.009
Florida	.002	.002
Georgia	.013	.019
Louisiana	.004	.018
Mississippi	.001	.006
South Carolina	.010	.010
Texas	.001	.003

Note on method and source: The census takers took the job description of individuals at their residences but as well asked factory owners who made more than $500 worth of product annually to provide the number of workers employed. Not all categories were used as many did not seem pertinent to the idea of "factory" work. For 1850, the categories used were cottons, woolens, iron, carpets, steam engines, calico, locomotives, coal mining, carding mills, smelting lead, coal, tobacco, shingles, coach making, lead furnaces. In the 1860 census, the numbers came from the introductory remarks and the particular tables given on manufacturing; the categories used were cotton men hands, woolens men, worsted, hosiery, wool carding, carpets, men's clothing, boots and shoes, iron bar sheet and railroad, railroad engines, hardware, nails, iron workers, paper, printing, hats, coal mining, iron mines, iron booms, and pig iron.

Sources: U.S. Department of the Census, *Seventh Census*, vol. 1: *Population*; U.S. Department of the Interior, *Eighth Census*, vol. 3: *Manufactures*, xxi–clxxx.

TABLE 2.8. *Farm Size, Southern States and Northern Regions, 1860*

State	*Total Number of Farms*	*Farms 1,000+ Acres*	*Farms 500–999 Acres*	*Farms 100–499 Acres*	*Farms 50–99 Acres*
Deep South					
Alabama	50,064	696	2,016	13,455	12,060
Florida	6,396	77	211	1,432	1,162
Georgia	53,829	902	2,622	18,821	14,129
Louisiana	15,281	371	1,161	4,955	3,064
Mississippi	37,007	481	1,868	11,408	9,204
South Carolina	28,456	482	1,359	11,369	6,980
Texas	37,363	87	408	6,831	7,857
Total	228,396	3,096	9,645	68,271	54,456
Border South					
Arkansas	33,190	69	307	4,231	6,937
Delaware	6,588	0	14	2,862	2,208
Kentucky	61,969	166	1,078	24,095	24,163
Maryland	25,244	35	303	12,068	6,825
Missouri	88,552	95	466	18,497	24,336
North Carolina	67,022	311	1,184	19,220	18,496
Tennessee	77,741	158	921	21,903	22,829
Virginia	86,477	641	2,882	34,300	21,145
Total	444,783	1,475	7,155	137,176	126,939
Northern Regions					
Middle Atlantic	378,940	42	303	93,253	140,313
New England	183,016	21	225	43,750	63,706
Great Lakes	651,418	404	1,944	138,356	209,898
Total South	673,179	4,571	16,800	205,446	181,395
Total North	1,213,374	467	2,472	275,359	413,917

Source: U.S. Department of the Interior, *Eighth Census*, vol. 2: *Agriculture*, 221.

The question of classes in the antebellum South has remained among historians a bone of contention. Certainly the planters had the wealth, amassed vast estates of the best land, had the greatest incomes, and commanded people (slaves) more directly than any other group in the United States; they composed 70 percent of the richest persons in the United States in 1860. Slaveholders were an exclusive group as only 25 percent of southern white families owned slaves, although by slave hiring a much larger proportion could experience being a slavemaster. Planters, however, were much more exclusive than mere slaveholders. The majority of slaveholders only held one to five slaves, representing almost 55 percent of all slaveholders. Those holding twenty slaves, the planter class, were only 12 percent of slaveholders. The 46,274 individuals in the planter class, assuming they were heads of families, constituted a mere 3.03 percent of southern society.[22]

Planters probably did set the tone for society—its interests, fashions, and customs. In terms of politics, they dominated state senates and controlled virtually all southern United States senators as well as a majority of the region's governors. But their position was not necessarily stable, and entry into and exit out of the planter class was extensive. Planters were an economic class but not an aristocracy in a formal sense: they could not perpetuate their families the way European aristocrats could.[23]

Slavery of course pitted the slave owner against the slave: it was the economic interest of the slaveholder to make the slave labor for the master's benefit, whereas the slave desired to labor only for himself or herself. As the potential ruling class of the South, however, the planters had to consider the desires of the majority of white southerners, the nonslaveholders, who composed 75 percent of the population. The great body of nonslaveholders were small farmers—that is, property holders—who, evidently, practiced family-first agriculture but who raised enough commercial crops to earn cash. However, their connections with the larger commercial economy—totally unlike the planters—was tenuous. Evidently the yeomen farmers of the Border and Deep South had the character traits of the northern middle-class commercial farmer —hard work, industry, frugality—but not the connections to markets that drove those traits into a frenzied drive for accumulation. Eventually, the railroad, already penetrating yeomen strongholds in the mid-1850s, would transform the South by eliminating these pockets of isolated economic activity. Prior to the generation of a market environment, however, the yeomen, nonslaveholding farmers of the South continued to practice a customary agriculture and semitraditional social relations.[24]

Planters had tremendous wealth, whereas nonslaveholders had small plots of land, and the tendency is to think of the two as natural enemies—a form of the rich against the poor. Potentially the nonslaveholder could be envious of the slaveholders' ownership of slaves and angry that the cotton planters monopolized the best land. But up to 1860, specific class conflicts were rare between slaveholders and nonslaveholders. There were some; in North Carolina in 1860 slaveholders were aghast that nonslaveholders demanded an ad valorem tax on slaves (instead of a low per capita tax), urban artisans petitioned against slave artisans, the settled plantation areas did not want to pay the taxes to extend transportation improvements to the (usually) nonslaveholding western parts of the states, and frequently nonslaveholders and slaveholders divided between Whigs and Democrats. But beyond these rumblings, and perhaps some resentments at planter presumptions, few fights broke out that pitted the two sides against each other. On state and federal policy, both sides seemed politically united in desiring low taxes and noninterventionist government.[25]

Southerners knew that the general economic well-being of their region came from slavery, and this knowledge produced something of a common economic bond. Slaveholders and nonslaveholders wanted to maintain a remunerative economy, and their experience had shown that slavery was capable of producing such an economy. Other means of wealth creation were theoretically possible; but practice and custom led southerners to prize slaveholding as the best means to prosperity.

The economy of slavery gave birth to the social economy of slavery, which may be defined as the set of ideas and social practices that southerners used to justify their economic arrangements. At this point, difficulties of interpretation arise, for antebellum southerners gave two different and, in a sense, antagonistic descriptions of the peculiar institution. One was a justification of one group's mastery over another group. This was the proslavery argument that in its extreme form sanctified aristocracy, feudalistic relationships, patriarchy, and anticapitalist values; its hallmark, as exemplified by its most renowned practitioner George Fitzhugh, was to show how slavery shielded the worker from material deprivation while free labor (or, more accurately, free market) systems left the worker unprotected from the capitalists' avarice.[26] Historians have at times also assumed, as some southerners stated and abolitionists continuously charged, that because slave labor was coerced, unwilling, and poorly paid, slavery cast into disrepute all labor and crippled the white southern work ethic, a proposition still echoed in historical writings.[27]

On the other hand, southerners expressed attitudes that had much in common with the "free labor ideology" of the modernizing North. The free labor ideology emphasized hard work, independent production, intelligent labor, and social mobility via property acquisition. Southerners seemed to seize economic opportunities when available, especially railroads in which southerners invested with an ardor equal to northern speculators.[28] One of the key phrases in the northern free labor economy was the "fruits of labor"; the fruits of labor were the rewards for arduous economic activity, and they belonged solely to the person who did the actual work. Southerners used the phrase as frequently as northerners in spite of the fact that their prosperity came from the sweat not of their labor but of their slaves. So Virginia representative Philip P. Barbour could exclaim in 1820—evidently with no sense of hypocrisy—that "What villein will labor like a freeman? None; until human nature is so formed as that we will labor with as much ardor for the benefit of others as we do when we ourselves are to reap its fruits." Thirty-four years later William S. Barry of Mississippi said in the U.S. House of Representatives that "The laboring men of the South, sir, will compare with those of any section of the Union, in intelligence, in self-respect, and in the qualities of head and heart which command the respect of others . . . there are no barriers which prevent the free and cordial intercourse of men in all conditions of life."[29]

Numerous southern leaders demanded that northerners and others recognize the progressive, democratic, hardworking, and meritocratic qualities of their society. Thus Samuel Wolfe responded to Hinton Rowan Helper's denunciation of the southern economy by asserting, "There is no place on earth where the industrious, enterprising, and upright poor man—no matter what his calling—is more cordially aided and abetted in all his honorable undertakings than in the South, or slave-holding states."[30] In terms of economic thought, southern editors and politicians embraced extreme laissez-faire views and openly advocated economic competition and antimonopoly. The editor of the *Charleston Mercury*, the fire-eating newspaper of the South, defined southern radicalism in Adam Smithian terms: "*Laissez nous faire*, is the doctrine of free trade men. It is the doctrine of states rights men in this country."[31] And many southern publicists argued that social mobility was a fact of life, that the "elites" of the South had earned their positions "by the sweat of their brow[s]."[32]

Southern understanding of democracy seemed to be thoroughly individualistic, as the editor of the *Mississippian* explained: "The Democratic theory has been to rely less upon the government and more upon the unfettered energies of a free people in shaping and determining their own good." One contributor to the *United States [and Democratic] Review* argued strongly for "THE VOLUNTARY PRINCIPLE" in the organization of American life, for it was the basis of antimonopoly, antichurch and antistate, antibank, and favorable to laissez-faire. Then the writer insisted that fanatics on slavery violated the "let alone" principle because they were denying the voluntary principle of letting slaveholders do whatever they wanted. Parties in much of the South by 1845 were fiercely competitive, and through a series of constitutional conventions between 1845 and 1860 most of the property qualifications for voting and holding office were eliminated, as they had been in the North. Indeed, on the economic issues of the tariff, banks, western lands, internal improvements, and states' rights, Democrats North and South used pretty much the same language to include hosannas to the common man. Whigs perhaps were more divided, but by 1845 even southern Whigs agreed to a more active federal government than did their Democratic opponents. The Prospectus of the Democrat sheet the *Mississippi Free Trader* in 1858 could have been used by any Democratic paper in the North: "Equal and exact justice to all men, of whatever State or persuasion, religious or political. Peace, commerce, and honest friendship with all nations; entangling alliances with none. The right of States and territories to administer their own domestic affairs. Freedom and equality; the sovereignty of the people, and the rights of the majority to rule, when their will is constitutionally expressed. Economy in the public expenditures and a sacred preservation of public faith. Freedom of religion, freedom of the press, and general diffusion of information. . . . No bigotry or pride of caste, or distinction of birth among American citizens. . . . Opposition to all chartered monopolies."[33]

The South had a ubiquitous and strident free labor ideology that has been overlooked due to the proslavery argument.[34] Southern intellectuals who wrote extensive treatises on southern slavery tended to focus on the question of labor in general and to argue about which system, slave or free, acted to secure the laborer a better existence. Even still, except with George Fitzhugh and perhaps one or two others, every proslavery tract invariably justified southern slavery because the enslaved were Africans, an "inferior variety of the human race."[35] The quest for social mobility, equality, and democracy concerned only whites; the South was a "herrenvolk democracy" that rested on a large base of African slaves. Southern politicians made it explicit that African slavery produced white equality: wrote Georgia senator Alfred Iverson, a white man "walks erect in the dignity of his color and race, and feels that he is a superior being, with the more exalted powers and privileges than others." Mississippi governor John Pettus said the true issue between parties was the "Superiority and Supremacy of the White Race." Even the aspiring proslavery intellectual James H. Hammond of South Carolina rebuked an English editor who denounced slavery: "You speak of African slavery as if it were the slavery of . . . [the Anglo-Saxon or Celt.] But it is not & you are wholly wrong."[36]

Southerners used race to divide their society in terms not only of labor but also of spheres of life. The slave sphere was the one of domination, but was also, according to them, the slaves' natural fate. White males enjoyed the complete flowering of democracy and all its economic, social, and spiritual promises. By this bifurcation—this radical division of their social, political, and economic world by race—southerners insisted that they completely marched in step with the advancing democracy of their age. Some prior to 1860 understood the contradictions, but the contradictions had not yet swept away the optimism of participating in the advance tide of modernity. How long the South could have maintained this bifurcation if the Civil War had not intervened is, of course, a completely conjectural question; it can only be stated that until 1860 the South was capable of maintaining a free market, democratic, socially mobile society for whites while vigilantly imposing an ancient Roman world for Africans.

But slavery did figure in the free labor ideology world of southerners in a way that northerners could not or would not understand. Social mobility, or earning a competence, was made possible by hard work, saving, and then purchasing property so as to obtain independence either in owning one's own farm, shop, or store. In the South, acquiring property to climb the social ladder meant acquiring slaves, for slaves were defined as property. The free labor ideology in the North did not recognize slaves as property. For northerners, property was either inert matter, some form of currency, animals, or land—but it was not people. Northerners could not easily think of slaves as a mere investment; they had trouble with statements like the one Richard Lathers, a transplanted South Carolinian living in New York, made: a rice plantation having 200 slaves supported a family of five to ten in luxury, and "the natural increase of the negroes in twenty or thirty years was sufficient to educate the children in high-grade seminaries."[37] Thus one obtained a difference that the perceptive cliometrician Gavin Wright pinpointed: mobility and industry in the South created laborlords, whereas in the North it generated holders of largely inanimate forms of property—buildings, stocks and bonds, houses, and merchandise.[38] Both societies were at heart free labor societies for whites, but the difference boiled down to one simple legal doctrine: southerners sanctioned private property in Africans, whereas northerners did not. Northerners simply could not or would not recognize social mobility via slaveholding. Rather, northerners would see control of slaves not as control of property but as control of people; they would see the slaveholder as a medieval lord commanding the people, his serfs; they saw an aristocracy on North American soil.

All types of issues and conditions divided the antebellum slaveholding states. The tidewater areas along the Atlantic tended to be heavily slave populated and politically conservative, whereas the western reaches tended to be nonslave and receptive to enlarged state activity. Slavery in some states, especially Delaware, was barely alive in 1860, while in Mississippi and Texas it was thriving. Border states had strong economic ties with the old Northwest, while the Cotton states had almost closer ties with England. Eastern slave states tended to be parochial, whereas the western slave states exhibited nationalistic fervor. Within the states, Whigs battled Democrats over internal improvements and banking facilities, and in the Border South the Whigs were close to having the upper hand. An antislavery South continued to exist, although as the sectional crisis mounted in the 1850s those voices became fewer and fewer.[39]

Diversity did not extend to all things, however, and on at least three matters southerners were united. First, slaves were property. Second, the sanctity of southerners' property rights in slaves was beyond the questioning of anyone inside or outside of the South. Third, slavery was the only means of adjusting social relations properly between Europeans and Africans. These tendrils of slavery wrapped around the slaveholding states and gave them a unity that no other section of the country possessed or ever would possess, from Delaware with its 1.6 percent of the population held in slavery to South Carolina with its 57.2 percent. Indeed, slavery—not agriculture, ethnic grouping, states rights' beliefs, or warm climate—defined the South. As the Mississippi Democrat Felix Huston explained, "with us the institution of slavery existing in the Southern States and not in the Northern, [has made] a broader line of demarkation than has existed in any other country" and had made two separate peoples.[40] When the issue of the territorial expansion of slavery arrived in 1846, it is revealing that southern statesmen talked about the rights of the South when restriction of slavery's expansion could at best be said to limit the movement of one-quarter of the South's white population, not the dominant three-quarters white majority.

Property rights in Africans—the bulwark of all southern white society—established the ways southerners accumulated wealth, earned income, enjoyed prosperity, enunciated egalitarian doctrines among themselves, boasted of the ideals of free labor advancement, and thrived under free institutions and representative government. Without property rights in black people, all these social pathways crashed to the ground. It was through this door that the economy of slavery and the social economy of slavery produced the political economy of slavery: a set of political principles and policies that were the result of the economic ownership of slaves. The political economy of slavery centered about a hysterical defense of property rights and gave birth to the collateral doctrines of preservation of minority rights, the dangers of majority rule, abhorrence of agrarianism, reliance on states' rights, and absolute equality of treatment under the Constitution.[41]

For centuries in Europe, property rights had been considered the foundation of all civilization, and holders of property—usually a minority—had lived in fear of efforts of the masses, the poor, the government, or of any agency that might seek to divest them of their possessions. The North's wealthy class had similarly expressed its apprehensions about democratic politics—giving the vote to propertyless people—that could lead to an attack on the property of the rich; this unease was especially visible during the revolutionary and the Jacksonian eras. Property holders' fears of the lower class were put into precise form by the English historian Thomas Babington Macaulay, a famous contemporary historian. Macaulay in 1859 wrote a letter to American historian Henry S. Randall, who had sought the renowned author's view of the democratic politics of Thomas Jefferson; Macaulay belittled them. The extensive quote is given here because it explains the anxiety that existed throughout Europe about democracy and extending the suffrage to the unpropertied:

> I have long been convinced that institutions purely democratic must, sooner or later, destroy liberty, or civilization, or both.
>
> In Europe, where the population is dense, the effect of such institutions would be almost instantaneous. . . . Either the poor would plunder the rich, and civilization would perish; or order and property would be saved by a strong military government, and liberty would perish.
>
> You may think that your country enjoys an exemption from these evils. I will frankly own to you that I am of a different opinion. Your fate I believe to be certain, though it is deferred by a physical cause. As long as you have a boundless extent of fertile and unoccupied land, your laboring population will be far more at ease than the laboring population of the Old World; and, while that is the case, the Jeffersonian polity may continue to exist without causing any fatal calamity. But the time will come when New England will be as thickly peopled as Old England. Wages will be as low; and will fluctuate as much with you as with us. You will have your Manchesters and Birminghams; and in those Manchesters and Birminghams, hundreds of thousands of artisans will assuredly be sometimes out of work. Then your institutions will be fairly brought to the test. Distress everywhere makes the laborer mutinous and discontented, and inclines him to listen with eagerness to agitators, who tell him that it is a monstrous iniquity that one man should have a million while another cannot get a full meal. In bad years, there is plenty of grumbling here and sometimes a little rioting. But it matters little. For here the sufferers are not the rulers. The supreme power is in the hands of a class, numerous

> indeed, but select, of an educated class, of a class which is, and knows itself to be, deeply interested in the security of property and the maintenance of order. Accordingly, the malcontents are firmly yet gently restrained. The bad time is got over without robbing the wealthy to relieve the indigent. . . . I have seen England pass three or four times through such critical seasons as I have described. Through such seasons the United States will have to pass, in the course of the next century, if not of this. How will you pass through them? I heartily wish you a good deliverance. But my reason and my wishes are at war; and I cannot help foreboding the worst. It is quite plain that your government will never be able to restrain a distressed and discontented majority. For with you the majority is the government, and has the rich, who are always a minority, absolutely at its mercy. The day will come when, in the State of New York, a multitude of people, none of whom has had more than half a breakfast, or expects to have more than half a dinner, will choose a Legislature. Is it possible to doubt what sort of Legislature will be chosen? On one side is a statesman preaching patience, respect for vested rights, strict observance of public faith. On the other is a demagogue ranting about the tyranny of capitalists and usurers, and asking why anybody should be permitted to drink champagne and to ride in a carriage, while thousands of honest folks are in want of necessaries. Which of the two candidates is likely to be preferred by a working man who hears his children cry for more bread?

For most of the nineteenth century, the reigning view in Europe was that property rights and democracy were incompatible systems.[42] Macaulay's entire analysis of American politics suffuses the southern defense of slavery and states' rights.

However, the southern defense of property rights went beyond the normal trepidations of the wealthy at sharing political power with the middling and lower elements of society. Slavery had economically ensnared slaveholders. Over time, because useful occupations for slaves were found, the value of slavery mounted and mounted through a process of compound interest. By the middle of the nineteenth century, the investment was enormous. All that wealth hinged on the definition of slaves as personal property, and in truth the discussion over slavery throughout the South was a discussion of property rights. Although historians have not stressed the fact as much as they should have, the word "property" was almost a synonym for slavery during the sectional debate, and it was omnipresent.

Defining slaves as property had a myriad of difficulties, not the least of which was convincing northerners that such a definition was just. Why could not northerners look upon slaves as simple property, asked Jefferson Davis in the United States Senate in 1850; "What is there in the character of that property which excludes it from the general benefit of the principles applied to all other property?"[43] The reason was, as the abolitionists screamed, that human beings could not be property. Proslavery writers offered other definitions, such as "*a right to the services* of a man" rather than property, or "any system of involuntary servitude, by which the time, service, and toil of one person becomes the property of another by compulsion."[44] Yet the enduring aspect most southerners insisted upon was that slaves were property, and slaveholders had property rights in slaves that others must observe. And the effect of property rights was straightforward: it "consists in the free use, enjoyment, and disposal of our acquisitions, without any control or diminution save only by the laws of the land."[45]

The reason for southern hypersensitivity was the nature of the property itself. Property was usually in the form of inert matter or domestic animals. To whom the matter or animals belonged could be determined by social consensus or political rules; disputes over ownership of property might lead to the creation of courts and a police force of some kind. But in disputes over ownership, the property itself, except for certain kinds of domestic animals, was not a combatant. Coal, iron, oil, glass, gold, lumber, land, pigs, and chickens did not contest ownership—a statement that is so obvious it is almost vacuous. This is the quality, however, that made slaves a different sort of property requiring extra vigilance.[46] People, who could reason and act—who had the quality of volition—were transformed into inert property, but the legal transformation could never eliminate the volition of human beings. Thus the property itself, the slaves, could contest the rule of the property holder (the slave master), a condition unlike any other property-holding arrangement. Fear of slave revolts was merely the extension of the fact of slave rationality and volition.

Slavery as an institution of property holding could only operate if force were applied. Slaves were sentient beings with volition; but as a form of property their function was to earn income for their owners. Because they did not share equally or share by mutual agreement in the rewards of economic activity, slaves had no motivation to remain slaves. Hence, they had a desire to escape their condition. Slaveholders had to apply physical violence to stop slaves from acting on their desires; this is why the synonym for slavery was involuntary servitude. As the son of one slaveholder in Virginia told Mary Livermore, employed as a teacher on a plantation, "You haf t' lick niggers, or they'd run over you. You don't know the South yit." His father reiterated the fact of slaveholding: "If you have slaves, you must first, last, and always keep them in their place."[47]

How law and physical force were so vital to slavery requires further examination. The central problem was that slaves had volition. Eventually a slave would quarrel with his or her master, become dissatisfied, or simply want to depart. A slave master confronted with this situation had no alternative if the slave master wanted to keep possession of the slave: physical violence had to be applied. If physical violence were not applied, the slave, and eventually those around that slave, learned that he or she could escape with impunity. Then slavery died. However, it might have been possible that the master could have individually applied physical violence to his or her slaves but that the larger community of free people refused to respect the slave master's claims of ownership. By himself, the slave master might be able to terrorize the slave for a while, but eventually the slave would find means to escape. When the slave did, the slave master could not turn to police authorities or to members of the community to force the return of the slave. Eventually, escape opportunities would arise for the bulk of the slave population, and the slave masters would be unable to reclaim them. Then slavery died. This is why physical violence was a practical necessity in maintaining the system of slavery, and why property rights in slaves had to be recognized and enforced. Without them, slavery perishes because of the human quality of the slaves themselves, their capacity of volition.

Southerners knew these connections between slave volition, property rights, and violence. During the first year of the Civil War, Joshua F. Speed of Louisville wrote Secretary of the Treasury Salmon P. Chase to demand the suppression of emancipation pronouncements from federal officials. The reason was the impact of such statements on border state unionists who were slaveholders: "Slave property is unlike any other—It is the only property in the world that has locomotion with mind to controll it—All men know this—and hince the jealousy of any people where it exists with any outside interference with it." In Georgia a discussion erupted over the use of slave mechanics, and a Georgia editor wrote about the controversy that "Slaves are human beings, and as such, are endowed with volition and reason—This fact makes the tenure of property in slaves more delicate and precarious than that of any other species of property." Even northerners recognized this aspect of slavery. Julius Rockwell of Massachusetts once wrote that laws had to be obeyed, and that admonition included the one in the Constitution "in relation to locomotive property—property which has legs." During the fight over the Compromise of 1850 in South Carolina, the politician Armistead Burt wrote in a public letter that not only was the settlement of the territorial question risking the fate of "fifteen hundred million dollars," but "the great function of government, in modern times, is the protection of property. Property in slaves, of all other property, can least endure aggression, and most needs the arm of government."[48]

Without property rights in people, masters lost their capacity to direct and discipline labor. Society could restrict former slaves and reduce them to a low-wage earning class, they could limit their mobility, they could deny to ex-slaves judicial proceedings and political processes, but they simply could not directly manage people in the same manner that they previously had. Voluntary labor could not be directed, redirected, and commanded as when involuntary. Without the law defining Africans as property, involuntary labor was impossible to obtain. As South Carolina's Christopher Memminger explained to an audience at Pendleton, "In other words, here would be a property without protection of a law, which is only another name for that which is no property at all."[49] And property rights in slavery produced the involuntary labor that made slaveholders and the whole of the white South rich.

Southern law made slaves property but never resolved the incongruities arising from defining humans as property. Because slaves were property, masters supposedly had all the rights over their slaves that any property holder had over his or her property. Yet because slaves were humans, both slaves and masters were held to standards of conduct that neither property nor property holders in other situations were held to. Pieces of property could not engage in crime, murder, or self-defense, but slaves could. Masters of other types of property could destroy ("murder") their property but not if the property were slaves.[50]

However inconsistent the law may have been, it possessed a singular virtue from the slaveholder's position: the law of slavery was written by a slaveholding society. Thus a society with an interest in the preservation of the institution manipulated the laws and tried to write them coherently so that the laws recognized slaves as both human and property. That at times laws were confused and inconsistent was inconsequential. What mattered was that because individuals interested in slaveholding wrote the laws, the essential qualities of property in humans were maintained; the slaveholder's wealth and income from slaveholding were not jeopardized.

It was probably this legal aspect of slavery that made southerners so hypersensitive to criticisms about slavery and movements to terminate the practice. Slavery's existence, unlike most other forms of property, depended on the positive sanction of the law; physical force had to be applied to make operable the "involuntary" part of "involuntary servitude." This was what made slavery stand out from other forms of property and in fact made the "peculiar institution" peculiar—it was a peculiar form of property. No other form of property in the United States required so much legal care to make it function properly. Southern slaveholders knew how singular slavery was from a legal standpoint and how valueless slavery could become if the laws were tampered with. Thus when the abolitionist movement in the North commenced with vigor after 1830, southern slaveholders reacted immediately with denunciations and concerted political actions. Besides their obvious fear of slave revolt, slaveholders responded almost hysterically to the abolitionists because of the singular importance of maintaining inviolable the legal definition of slavery.[51]

Property rights concerns thus produced an anxiety over the role of government and its actions vis-à-vis slavery and thus generated the political economy of slavery. Slaveholders had two entities to guard over: state and national governments. For a variety of reasons, state government did not present a great problem. Such was not the case for the federal government.

Within the southern states, the planters left a visible trail of concern for their property rights. Taxation was kept minimal out of fear of injuring the profitability of slavery.[52] Public education was not funded for fear of rising tax rates. Despite the advent of democracy to southern states by the 1850s, planters had fought to insure an overrepresentation of property (that is, slave) interests in the selection of state senators and governors and also sought to insure more electoral districts in planting areas than in nonslaveholding areas—which usually pitted easterners against westerners. The most famous clash of this kind was the Virginia legislative assembly of 1831–32, in which one Virginian believed the members from West Virginia sought to emancipate the slaves in the eastern part of the state: "Their course has too fully verified the suspicions of the opposition, who said when they got due weight in the Legislature, they would as they intended, attack the property of our slaves."[53]

Planters learned, as most propertied elites now have, that democratic forms do not endanger property so long as the entire society operates under the same definitions of property. If property produces income, it stitches societies together in a pragmatic manner such that people are more concerned about maintaining the flow of income than in rearranging the distribution of property. It is unlikely that legislators will attack the property basis of society because acquisition of property is perhaps the most obvious way that individuals have to show their leadership abilities. Most people, it seems, defer politically to those who exhibit talent. In a society that allows (at least some) mobility based on talent, the end result will be that the talented will obtain position by earning property. In a slave society, the talented earned slave property. When it came time to choose individuals to operate the government, the voters chose from the people who had demonstrated talent—and in the South's case that meant they almost invariably chose people who had accumulated slave property. Hence, slaveholders, but not necessarily planters, ruled the statehouses of the South. Planters could generally rest secure in the notion that, although state politicians could enact laws that might momentarily injure the profitability of slavery, slaveholding legislators would never undermine the legal basis of slaveholding itself.[54]

The South, however, belonged to a country in which the legal dictum of slaveholding did not extend to the entire society. Northerners lived beyond the web of loyalties to slavery that the institution spun. The only real danger to southern slavery came from the North. Southern statesmen, politicians, intellectuals, and orators pointed precisely to the weak area: a national government not under the cultural spell of slavery that could tamper with property rights in slaves. That recognition immediately elicited from southerners a clamor for states' rights, minority rights, a dread of centralization, and hostility to majority rule. The solitary source for all these doctrines was the need to protect the legal definition that turned people into property.

Southerners feared the federal government because nonslaveholders not only had a majority in Congress but hailed from nonslaveholding societies. Northern congressmen had no umbilical cord from a slaveholding society that would sustain a conviction to nurture and protect the peculiar institution. Thus under the direction of nonslaveholders, Congress could directly affect the profitability of slavery by federal policy and even alter the sanctity of property rights in slaves.[55]

Southern statesmen had a long history of beating back federal initiatives to stimulate the economy. They had most often been free traders and opposed to high tariffs; they denounced internal improvements as sectional favoritism; they saw in national banking statutes a sinister design to bleed the agrarian regions in order to fatten the urban ones; they only saw northern avarice in plans to carve up the western territories. Of course, party allegiances destroyed unanimity on these questions, as the Whig Party especially in the Border South frequently desired an interventionist national government. It had long been one of the several political staples of southern radicals that the North only grew wealthy at the expense of southerners. One D. H. London raised the question in 1860 as to the origin of New York's material advantage over Virginia: "To these questions there is but one, and only one answer, and that is this: IT IS THE PERNICIOUS HAND OF GOVERNMENT which has degraded us and benefited others." Another late antebellum writer complained that the "legislature of the Union has been shaped to favour and foster their navigation interest, fisheries and manufactures. The South has wrought out her fortunes by her own unassisted efforts." Robert Barwell Rhett warned northerners in Congress against propagating the idea that the North "can only prosper by destroying the South."[56]

Most realized that federal legislation had an influence upon the economic health of slavery. By interfering with international trade and overseas markets, tariffs could destroy southern markets and hence southern prosperity. That slavery might be crushed by federal taxes had always occurred to some southern politicians. And by internal improvements and an active government, the federal government could damage the profitability of slavery in two distinct ways. To build improvements, the government needed taxes, and so slavery could be taxed to build up other pursuits. Moreover, by bolstering other pursuits, the federal government was fostering activities that might not be adaptable to slave labor. In any case, southerners were well aware that federal policy could abolish slavery simply by making the institution unprofitable. John Claiborne, a Mississippi secessionist, declared the tariff a deceitful abolitionist measure: "The Abolitionist would rob us of our slaves; the government will let us retain them, but contrives to diminish the profits of their labor, well knowing that thus the institution itself is sapped. So they accomplish, by different means, the same end—the ruin of the slaveholder." And few tied the potential effects of federal economic policy to the fate of slavery as concisely as did John C. Calhoun in 1830: "[The tariff is the] occasion, rather than the real cause of the present unhappy state of things. . . . It is the system of slavery, which has given direction. . . . [Slavery] has placed them in regard to taxation and appropriations in opposite relation to the majority of the Union, against the danger of which, if there be no protective power in the reserved rights of the States, they must be forced to rebel, or submit it to have their paramount interests sacraficed [*sic*], their domestick institutions subordinated by colonization and other schemes, and themselves & children reduced [to] wretchedness." One cannot find a more simple statement bringing together federal economic policy, slavery, and states' rights.[57]

The second means by which the federal government could impinge upon the economic health of slavery was by tinkering with the doctrine of property rights in slaves. For southerners, this power was far more deadly to slavery than economic legislation, which is why the territorial issue evoked a visceral response. With federal economic policy, southern slaveholders could hope to obtain northern allies and defeat federal legislation that required higher taxes, redistribution of rewards, and subsidization of various enterprises; this was the basis for the oft-expressed hope for a western-southern alliance against the Northeast. Ultimately southerners could count on some sort of reaction among northerners if federal legislation ever became too oppressive for the consuming or tax-paying public. But on the legal definition of slavery, southern slaveholders had no natural allies. No northerner had a direct social or economic interest in preserving property rights in slaves. On questions about legal definitions of slavery, southerners had to fend for themselves.

Southerners testified frequently to this chasm of experience between themselves and northerners. As William H. Trescot wrote to James H. Hammond, "It [slavery] is an institution that can only be understood by experience, and its enemies can never be made to see the *unreality* of their convictions."[58] The difference was enunciated precisely by the fire-eater William Lowndes Yancey at the 1848 Democratic National Convention: "It is idle to call the question an abstract one. . . . They [northerners] own not a dollar of property to be affected by the ascendency of the principle at issue. They have not a single political right to be curtailed by it. With them opposition to the South on this point, is purely a question of moral and political ethics. Far different is it with the South. They own the property which the success of this principle will prevent them from carrying with them to the Territories."[59]

Through a variety of actions the federal government could invade and alter the doctrine of property rights in slaves. By diplomacy, the federal government determined whether the United States would define Africans as property on the oceans. The federal courts ruled on property rights between citizens of different states, and thus could have some say on the property rights of slaveholders. As well, the federal government was given power over interstate commerce; theoretically, it could deny legal sanction to slaves as property in interstate slave trading or even to interstate migration with slaves. Finally, the federal government could determine whether Africans in the western territories would be treated as property, via instructions to territorial marshals, courts, and governors.[60]

In all these cases, the federal government determined whether property in slaves would be a legal doctrine or not. If the federal authorities determined not to treat Africans as property, then the federal government was weakening the property rights of slaveholders. Once the process began of whittling away the absolute right of slaveholders to treat slaves as property, then the value of slaves falls and the income stream from slavery begins to diminish; the courts become an uncertainty (and the more the uncertainty, the less the value), and investors will be less attracted to further investment in slavery. The federal government's treatment of the doctrine of property rights in slaves was a Pandora's box for southerners, and they wanted to keep the lid as tightly shut as possible to stop any federal incursions into the law of property rights in slaves.

In formulating their political ideals to handle the challenge of participation in the federal Union, southerners drew together a number of separate economic and political ideas that served as the background to their famous theories about states' rights. First, the purpose of society was to protect property rights, a theme that had emerged out of the British heritage, had been reaffirmed in the American Revolution, and had become dominant in American political thought.[61] As slaves were property, government had to defend the slaveholders' rights to his property. Because property holders in all past ages were a minority of the population, the need to guarantee property holders their possessions became translated in American idiom in the nineteenth century as "minority rights." Obviously, the twentieth century has a different notion of minority rights, based on the need to treat equally people from different races and ethnicities, as well as equal treatment for men and women. But in the nineteenth century, the political concern for the "minority" was a concern for the property of the wealthy.

Concern for property rights in slaves thereby led southerners to cast highly suspicious eyes on democracy. "The lesser, numerically, and richer interests," complained South Carolina governor Whitemarsh Seabrook to the state legislature, "[have] always been the subject of plunder by the greater and poorer interest." Popular governments under no restraint of power endangered property rights, and for southerners such a circumstance was intolerable. The Virginia radical Beverly Tucker wrote to James Hammond explaining why the Democratic Party was of no value to the South: "The cardinal principle of the sect is that the majority should do its pleasure in all things, and I can only wonder how it comes to recognize any limitation on the powers of the federal government, through which alone the majority can act." This was, of course, the radical position. One contributor to *De Bow's Review*, while explaining the growth of the North, warned that southerners had to defend themselves from the "unspeakable tyranny of majority rule." Many more southern voices, from all over the South, wanted popular government, but they usually also wanted a limitation on the power of government as well.[62]

Apprehensions about democracy filled the works of proslavery writers but in a particular way. While proslavery arguments have now become largely known for their biting criticism of factory labor under capitalism, three other separate concepts filled their works—and indeed, much of all southern thought.[63] The first, and somewhat unexplored area, was population theory. Southerners gulped down Malthusianism and, in a fit of ideological inebriation, applied it everywhere. They found it eminently suited to their sectional arguments, for they contended that slavery slowed down population growth, kept wages high, let the majority of whites remain yeomen farmers, and kept the propertyless (the common laborers, who in the antebellum South were slaves) out of politics. This was not the case with the North where immigration and the small amount of available of land were producing a growing propertyless class that had the vote.[64]

From proslavery writers and a host of southern politicians then came the cry that "agrarianism" threatened the land. Antislavery agitators were indoctrinating northern society with the idea of majority rule without boundaries, and the result would be a war on the wealthy. The term agrarian meant a political redistribution of wealth and originated in the experience of Rome when the two Gracchi proposed to give farms to landless army veterans out of the public domain; that proposal drove the Roman senators, the great property holders of their time, to murder both Tiberius and Gaius Gracchus. In the United States by 1840, proslavery warnings about the agrarian spirit filled the air and increased right up to the day of secession. John Claiborne wrote that northern capitalists used antislavery to "divert the socialists and infidels from their own palaces . . . forgetting that, when the knife of fanaticism leaves its sheath, it soon ceases to discriminate between its victims. What cares the political or religious monomaniac for constitutional restraints or the rights of property?" E. N. Elliot also warned the North: "Ye Capitalists, ye merchant princes, ye master manufacturers, you may excite to frenzy your Jacobin clubs, you may demoralize their minds of all ideas of right and wrong, but remember! the gullotine [*sic*] is suspended over your own necks!! The agrarian doctrines will ere long be applied to yourselves." Fitzhugh warned that abolitionism was begetting socialism which was begetting revolution, and the "revolution, directed at first against negro slavery, now proposes to destroy all religion, all government, and all private property."[65]

A third doctrine prevalent among southerners justifying slavery used natural law. Among proslavery extremists, natural "rights" were pretty much discarded as useless concepts. For them, rights only came from society and the definitions of rights that compacts among people delineated; this was one of the ways they rejected abolitionist and antislavery claims that Africans were denied their natural rights.[66] This was not popular among southern politicians, editors, and others because it was also a means to disparage poor and middling whites. Much easier was a resort to natural law that was coincidental with Darwin's thinking on species survival and was an early example of social Darwinism. Congress, said one report of the Southern State Convention in Mississippi in 1849, had no power over slavery: "[T]he right of property preceded the constitution—it is coeval with the history of man; it exists by a paramount law of nature; it is the subject of control by State sovereignty only." Africans were slaves by nature; and the state of their servitude came from the fact of the commingling of superior and inferior races in the same locality. "It is asked upon what principle slavery can be justified," wrote George Sawyer in a book published in 1859, and he answered, "upon the principle of the superiority of mind over matter, of intellect and intelligence over instinct and brute force." When the state of Kentucky in 1849 reaffirmed its statutes maintaining the peculiar institution, the legislature passed a law declaring the "right of property is before and higher than any constitutional sanction," and the reference to property was specifically to property in slaves.[67] Southerners thus claimed sanctity for slavery because it was the social setting by which the strong ruled the weak.

The essence of the southern position on slavery had much in common with the aristocrat Thomas Babington Macaulay. Macaulay rejected democracy because it enabled the propertyless to redistribute the wealth of the rich by political means, thereby undermining the sanctity of property rights and destroying civilization. Southern writers on slavery and politics virtually said the same thing, and one only needs to substitute the phrase "property rights in slaves" for "property rights" in Macaulay's analysis to obtain the essential proslavery position.

But the southern literary production that northerners had to deal with and which has continued to be the subject of scholarly and popular debate was the doctrine of states' rights. Yet the doctrine of states' rights actually mimicked the aristocratic position of Macaulay and was barely, if at all, a concept that supported popular government and majority rule. A close look at the debate over slavery finds that states' rights was largely a constitutional means to protect property rights in slaves and had virtually no other function in the antebellum period. And southerners were explicit about this before the Civil War: the purpose of states was to protect property rights in slaves, and the purpose of the Constitution was to stop all others from meddling with those rights.[68]

States' rights mixed together a batch of concerns about who ruled over what geographical area. The reigning view was that local government permitted the "people," however defined, to have more control over their legislative representatives and the laws legislators promulgated than when the seat of government was at a great remove. Thus citizens could guard their individual liberties from attack by political demagogues, rogue bureaucrats, and corrupt ministerial sycophants. When government became removed, it had the possibility of becoming centralized and consolidated—as Parliament had done in England. Once removed from the immediate oversight of the people, government could foster laws that leached away the rights of persons and property. Within the American context, a diversity principle was added. Because the American republic was spread over such a vast landmass, variations in geography, climate, and productions arose so that local government allowed for rational adaptation; a centralized government trying to legislate for the whole landmass would only promulgate laws that would be irrational in some places.

Beyond the philosophical defense of local rights and local control was the set of constitutional ideas that buttressed states' rights formulations. The first was a strict reading of the Constitution in which the powers and duties of the federal government were specifically listed. All powers not so listed were to be denied to the central government, and all rights and powers not enumerated belonged to the states or the people via the Tenth Amendment to the Constitution, the "reserved" powers clause. A strict-construction view denied the ability of certain phrases to enlarge the powers of Congress, such as the wording of the preamble ("general welfare") or Article 1, section 8 (the "necessary and proper" clause). On these grounds, states' rights advocates had the text of the Constitution and an argument to support their views.

But then states' rights supporters supplied theories that were actually hypotheses about the way the Constitution was constructed, the meaning of its architecture, and the intent of its founders. These were extrapolations, or inferences, made from existing information, but the theories themselves had no textual basis in the Constitution itself. The first, devised by Jefferson in the Kentucky Resolutions of 1798, was the "compact theory" of the origin of the Constitution. Not the people but the states had created the Constitution and the federal government; therefore, the states had original sovereignty and the federal government was to act merely as the agent of the states under specified circumstances. States had the power to deny the legality of congressional laws under certain conditions (nullification). During the battle over the tariff of abominations and its brood of lesser tariffs between 1828 and 1833, two additional claims were added. The first held that as the states created the Constitution, then all its laws must operate equally on all the states, for no state would have agreed to have joined the Union with the knowledge that laws of the central government might result in poverty for some and prosperity for others. This became known as "equality of the States under the Constitution" or "equality of benefits and burthens." Added to this was a distinct minority rights argument: the Constitution should observe the rights of the minorities and not deprive citizens who lived in small states of life, liberty, and property.[69]

Behind these ideas, however, was the fervent desire to maintain the property rights in slaves. John C. Calhoun of South Carolina, the extreme states' rights proponent of the South, exhibited this trait. From the beginning of the abolitionist agitation, he thundered against such northern movements that disparaged southern institutions "that involve not less than $900,000,000 of property." He feared any extension of federal power would eventually lead to an attack on slavery, and he saw the essential division in the country as between the nonslaveholding majoritarian North and the minority slaveholding South.[70]

Calhoun's concern over property rights in slaves in the Union is most easily seen in his treatise on the appropriate form of government, *A Disquisition on Government*, and his pet theory of the "concurrent majority." Calhoun wanted to protect individual liberty, particularly the freedom of an individual to possess and dispose of private property. In a republic where the dictum of majority rule operated, property was in danger of being legislated away. Popular voting rights were only workable where the "whole community had the same interests so that the interests of each and every portion would be so affected by the action of government that the laws which oppressed or impoverished one portion would necessarily oppress and impoverish all others." That is, if all had the same type of property, then the property would not be endangered by popular voting or democratic rules, as long as it was distributed widely. But in the case where different societies were joined whose "interests" —that is, forms of property—were not the same, then the majority had no stake in preserving the rights of property they did not possess. To avoid this nonchalance about the property of the minority, or worse, the evil intentions of the majority, Calhoun offered the "concurrent majority." Such a divided society required voting by "interests" rather than by numbers, and each interest should possess an absolute veto over all legislation to make sure no law enriched the majority while impoverishing the minority. In the American context, this became a plea for a dual presidency, one from the South and one from the North, each with an absolute veto over all legislation.[71]

Calhoun's defense of minority rights was a defense of propertied interests, and as such it breathed hostility toward democratic forms of government, for it was majority rule that endangered the property holdings of the minority. Thus Calhoun showed the path by which individualism without limitations paved the way for despotism. Calhoun's theory led to the establishment of a society upon grounds that several groups, or interests, agreed. After that, however, an individual could thwart the actions of the group by insisting that any proposed action not injure his or her interest. This resulted in policies being passed that were only favorable to the individual's interests; it was in effect minority rule. It translates into the worst form of individualism: allegiance to the group is based entirely and exclusively on whether one's self-interest is being promoted and satisfied, and if it is not, then a veto of the allegiance results. The standard brooks no compromise, concession, or willingness to retreat on any subject whatsoever. Calhoun demonstrated this numerous times. He had followers in New England, Pennsylvania, and New York, where some thought the southern proslavery clique had sympathies for northern white workers. In reply to an inquiry by Robert L. Dorr about the Wilmot Proviso, Calhoun took the occasion to denounce majority rights. Dorr later responded in the press—the correspondence was published—"I cannot see with the limited information I possess into the correctness of any other theory of republican government but in the admitted right of the majority to rule." Anything else, said Dorr, was a form of "Divine right."[72]

Few people agreed with Calhoun's political arguments, but almost all did see states' rights as a protection of property. Indeed, as the furor over the Wilmot Proviso crescendoed after August 1846, southern spokesmen virtually defined states' rights as the right to hold property beyond the touch of the federal government. They insisted that not only could the federal government not intervene in matters of property in the states, but that the federal government even lacked the power to declare what was or was not property, that power belonging exclusively to the states.[73] On the hustings and in the newspapers, however, states' rights meant nothing more than state control over property rights in slaves. "The Constitution is a compact between the slave and non-slave States. Slavery is recognized in it, throughout, in some form or other." The editor of the *Mississippi Free Trader* listed the agreements the northern states made about slavery in 1787–89; they were required to "securc the rights and property of the People of the South," and these provisions "may be said to contain the essence of the Union." Moreover, the editorial continued, "It is from these considerations that the People of the South have been, from the commencement of our national existence, so earnest and perservering in their demands for a strict construction of the Constitution." A southern convention held in Jackson, Mississippi, agreed: "This Union never would have been formed, without the full and entire recognition of slavery, and property in slaves, and the guaranty to the owner which is contained in the Constitution." Southerner after southerner, in Congress and out, maintained that "the property in slaves is specifically secured—the only instance of the kind in the whole instrument [the Constitution]"—and "it would be the height of madness to contend that the states in which slavery existed, would have ever consented to become members of the union, unless the institution was recognised and guaranteed." In the speakership fight of 1859–60, Jabez L. M. Curry of Alabama put the matter succinctly. After charging the Republicans with the crime of having the "conviction that property in man is a sin and a crime," he connected his fears about slavery with states' rights: "[F]ree governments, so far as their protecting power is concerned, are made for minorities, and the Jeffersonian, State-rights theory protects minorities"; the South was a minority and looked at states' rights as its "sheet-anchor."[74]

Orators and writers also let it be known what this attack on property rights in the territories portended. "No," declared a call for a southern congress, "the Southerners feel the necessity of being, themselves their watchmen, and of keeping their own property in safe custody." The northern verbal attack on slavery and expansion "will depreciate property," said an editor; "many will wish to sell; few will buy; credit will be destroyed; no one can raise money on negro property."[75] From the concern that debate over slavery's extension by itself would depreciate property came a parade of statements escalating the situation to the final abolition of slavery itself and the loss of the property invested.[76]

Many southerners from the cotton states insisted that the Constitution be considered an immutable agreement between the sections, one incapable of changing at the whim of public opinion. On property rights in slaves, the South indeed demanded permanence and immobility of the rules of the nation, and because of that stand southerners insisted that the Constitution could never be altered. Thus states' rights became a truly conservative doctrine, and one that southerners would press incessantly any time some federal policy had the potential even in the slightest to touch the profitability of slavery. Therein lay a host of problems.

James Seward of Georgia once said in the House of Representatives that the South must stand by the Constitution: "We are bound by the Constitution, and if it operates injuriously to us we must submit to it." But the reality was that southerners always found a way to declare unconstitutional federal policies they disliked. States' rights was not a stagnant doctrine but one that reshaped itself to meet any development in the national Congress that could be construed as hostile to southern propertied interests. Northerners were quite aware of this tendency. As the Whig editor of the *Toledo Blade* said, slaveholders always "exercise the right of construing the constitutional powers of congress to suit their own interests." Even the editor of the *New Orleans Picayune* shook his head at the obvious tendency of Calhoun's theories: "He requires that the slave element in the United States shall have a distinct representation, directly," and Calhoun's demands were "inadmissable." The Democrat Lewis Cass as well found the states' rights doctrines of Calhoun and other extremists an impractical annoyance. "Sir, the objection of the Senator from South Carolina," he said in 1850 in the Senate, "is repeated here to-day by his colleague, and it amounts to this: that if you give power to a government, it may be abused. So it may; and I should like to see the Government where power cannot be abused. It would be another new thing under the sun."[77]

States' rights was anything but a precise doctrine. It shifted and reshaped itself to meet every contingency, and usually did so under the cover of theory, implied conclusions, and "correct" inferences. In some instances the idea of states' rights might actually have had some merit and have been a practical guide, but its use indicates that it served another function. For most political southerners, states' rights was their "higher law," their moral code that dictated their response to criticism about slavery. It was virtually the southern twin of the northern abolitionists' abstract morality. By appealing to abstract morality, the abolitionists felt no compulsion to obey laws not to their liking—their moral code was higher than human institutions. States' rights operated much the same way for southerners. They really did not have to obey the Constitution because they could always reshape the Constitution via states' rights to meet their needs. In the battle over the extension of slavery, states' rights ended up being the higher moral principle of the South, and its application meant the local relationships existing in the South would brook no outside intrusion, constitutional or not.

When Congress debated raising the tariff to unprecedented heights in 1827, South Carolinians reacted in horror, and one of them, the political economist and president of South Carolina College, Thomas Cooper, uttered a line that has reverberated in historical treatments of the South ever since. "Wealth will be transferred to the North, and wealth is power. Every year of submission rivets the chains upon us, . . . we shall, before long, be compelled to calculate the value of our union."[78] This phrase—"to calculate the value of our union"—is most telling indeed, because it reflects precisely the property basis of southern society. Planters always knew the value of their slaves; southern politicians and publicists dropped value amounts frequently enough in their writings and speeches. The calculation of the value of the Union was rather simple and ruthlessly logical: whenever the Union promoted and preserved the value of property in slaves, then the South found the Union acceptable. But if ever events occurred that damaged or augured future damage to the value of property in slaves, then disunion was the cure. The Union was not a mystical entity at all; it was a simple cost-benefit calculation. And when the worth of slavery as property was involved, the calculation was exceedingly simple to make.

Interpretations of why the South seceded have varied considerably over the years, and most have not stressed property rights in slaves in the fashion of this chapter. It is worth some effort to explore other explanations of southern secession and demonstrate why the issue of property rights in slaves offers a more reasonable assessment of the force motivating slave states to separate from the Union. My approach is the topical, not chronological, development of interpretations.

The trunk of the tree of explanation for southern secession has always been that the South was agrarian and the North was industrial. Virtually all perspectives on antebellum American life revert to that circumstance—a circumstance, incidentally, that is not undisputed. From the main body have come three major branches: political, cultural, and economic. Although each branch in fact intertwines with the others, and all employ the agrarian-industrial dichotomy, each generally is responsible for a particular kind of interpretation of southern actions. Political explanations for southern departure have usually been variants on states' rights. Cultural interpretations have found the roots of secession in a separate culture within the South. And the economic explanations usually blame northern industrial capitalism. Except for the cultural interpretation that southerners left because they wanted to preserve white supremacy and keep a racially based caste system intact, all the interpretations of southern secession have had flaws and have ultimately been unconvincing. The root problem is that except for a small coterie of economic historians, no one wishes to believe slavery represented a mountain of wealth.

Outside of the northern explanation that the slave power took the slave states out of the Union to maintain its sovereignty, the most persistent political explanation of secession has been states' rights. In its earliest manifestations, as with Frank Owsley or D. L. Osborne, it was an idealistic formulation: the South left to preserve local autonomy.[79] Yet one can substitute the phrase "sanctity of property rights in slaves" for the phrases of community control, states' rights, or minority rights virtually every time they appear. All those constitutional doctrines were explicitly linked to property rights in slaves. Nor does the nonsense of the South being a minority in the nation struggling for minority rights merit any lengthy contemplation.[80] All regions of the country were by definition minorities: so was New England; so were the Yorkers, so were the midwesterners, so were the far westerners. They had grievances and they were minorities; yet none of them grasped secession as a solution for their complaints. And the reason is plain. The laws of property were the same in all those states, and the rights of property were not only secure in law but also in public opinion (generally). The South talked about itself as an aggrieved minority because it had a form of property unique to itself and, though the law supported its property rights, the national consensus was falling apart over property rights in people.

Another political interpretation of secession was revisionism, a school of thought that postulated that sectional agitators heated up the political atmosphere so much that rational thought was vaporized. Thus secession became an act of passion.[81] This passion is not especially difficult to understand, at least for southerners. Their property, and lots of it, was at stake. Why modern historians are so reluctant to understand that persons of great property get agitated over having their property *taxed*, let alone devalued, is a far greater mystery to me than why southerners screamed secession when they saw their 20 percent of the national wealth being undermined.

Some current historians are bringing southern secession within the explanatory grip of republicanism, a massive interpretation of American history that focuses on the revolutionary generation's beliefs in individual liberty, fear of centralized power, and abhorrence of corruption and tyranny. This interpretation has been applied by Lacy Ford and Kenneth Greenberg to explain the emotionalism of southerners and their fear of a modernizing North.[82] This interpretation has distinct limits. It is somewhat amusing to think of a mortal combat over interpretation of southern secession that pits the puny ideals of republicanism against the brute fact that slaves were worth $3 billion as property. Someone expects readers to believe that southerners would destroy the Union of the states to avoid a spoils system, high tariffs, and the danger of a potent government; they, of course, would never have been swayed by anything so crude as money. The language of republicanism certainly existed in the South; it certainly existed everywhere in nineteenth-century America in one form or another. But so did the discourse over property rights in slaves, and in extensive amounts. Moreover, property rights not only had a rhetorical dimension; it had as well a very vivid statistical dimension, which I believe makes it a more prominent explanation. It has for many centuries been known, and has become something of a social law, that money talks; nonetheless, to hear the speech one still has to listen.

Many historians have always insisted that slavery was the heart of the problem between North and South. The ways of explaining how it was so much a problem that it created secession has been the interpretive barrier. Some have argued that southerners feared eventual abolition; others have posited that secession was an act to preserve slavery from attack from inside as well as from outside southern borders.[83] The mechanism driving this desperate gambit, however, was the wealth that had been invested in the peculiar institution.

The second major branch of the tree that explains southern secession uses cultural explanations, normally pivoting around the idea that the South was a different society from the North. Actually, commentary on the differences between North and South are nearly as old as the Constitution. In recent times, topics such as soil composition, climate, and ethnic type (Celtic fringe theory) have been used to mark the differences between North and South.[84] Many of the explanations of North-South contrasts have been based on the existence of slavery and the determination to maintain white supremacy, the agricultural nature of the southern economy and the romantic view of nature it inspired, and the lack of development in the southern economy.[85] These generalizations have not gone unchallenged. Any number of authors point out that southerners adhered to many of the same economic and political values as did the North. The regional peculiarities of the South were no more than any region's peculiarities—with the exception of slavery.[86]

Out of the belief that North and South represented different civilizations have come three basic interpretations to explain southern secession. The first is "modernization." The term was coined in the 1950s and 1960s by sociologists and others to explain the difference between developed European nations and undeveloped Third World nations. The process of going from a traditional society to an European late twentieth-century economy was the process of "modernization," and, among other socioeconomic phenomena, it entailed a market economy, industrialization, urbanization, powerful government, suppression of localism, and growth in bureaucratic structures. Modernization was then applied to the United States in 1860; the South was a traditional (undeveloped) society, whereas the North was a modern (developed) society. *Somehow* this difference generated friction. The most obvious form of the friction was political: control of the economic policy of the federal government. Not infrequently in modernization scenarios—especially, for example, in its "prebourgeois" manifestation—the North becomes the aggressor section seeking to extend its suzerainty over the localist-minded arcadian dwellers of the southern hinterland.[87]

Modernization, as far as explanations go, is a gun without a trigger. As applied to the United States in 1860—and its application to the North is debatable indeed—the interpretation is little more than the old agrarian South versus the evil industrial North. If one really pushed the economics of modernization theory, then one would have the South and the West against Massachusetts, Rhode Island, New York City, Philadelphia, Pittsburgh, and about ten northern counties. Most of the North was rural and centered in villages. Furthermore, nothing is precisely posited as to why differences in economics or speeds of development should result in war. No economic policy of the federal government was going to damage slavery much, regardless of the exaggerated fears expressed by some southerners. Beyond the general policy impotence of the federal government is the obvious condition that the history of the United States has been a history of regions that have experienced different rates of growth. War has not resulted between sections except once; and modernization cannot map out an explicit mechanism for secession without resorting to vague, metaphysical concepts that have never produced such massive conflict in any other period of American history. Simply remove slavery from the South, and modernization explains nothing.

In the 1980s the efforts of Bertram Wyatt-Brown led historians to appreciate the concept of "honor" in the antebellum culture of the South, distinguishing it from the Puritan, pietistic, modern culture that arose in the North. Honor cultures cannot accept challenges or insults without striking back; thus southern secession was the result of a society that could no longer bear the moralistic assaults of the North.[88] It may very well be true that southerners held values reflective of an honor culture, and perhaps any number of southerners responded to insults with immediate physical violence. Yet it is not at all clear why it took southerners so long to find their honor that they only seceded in 1860–61 rather than earlier, nor is it obvious why a society should respond to national issues in the same way individuals do. The real test for the interpretation of southern honor is whether honor operated over society at large when money was not concerned. As a rule of thumb, when any great property holder is threatened with changes in the laws describing property or with confiscation of his or her wealth, one can expect an avalanche of verbiage about honor, hard work, and honest effort. Individuals of wealth normally act with rage when the origin and morality of their wealth is questioned. Would honor have been so important in promoting southern secession if slaves had not been worth so much money? On a theoretical level, I would argue the answer would be no.

The third interpretation derived from cultural history is that the South left the Union to preserve white supremacy. This interpretation is on much more solid ground than any other in the cultural school. Virtually no defense of slavery was ever enunciated or written that did not at some point use racial inequality as a justification for enslaving African Americans. Several distinct arguments composed the rationale. First, proslavery orators and writers insisted that Africans and Europeans were different and unequal types of "races"; that inequality meant one "race" had to dominate the other because the two could not live in a social and political framework of equality—the lesser race would always seek to obtain the privileges and rewards of the superior race and therefore had to be restrained. Otherwise, the result could only be race war. Second, southerners insisted, and many northerners agreed, that Africans were naturally lazy. In Congress, Georgia's Lucius Gartrell said Africans were "idle, dissolute, improvident, lazy, unthrifty. . . . [These are the] inherent laws of their nature." Because whites could not work in semitropical climates and blacks could, southerners insisted that only by the directing mind of white southerners were Africans made productive; only enslavement let Africans participate in the grand progress of European civilization in the nineteenth century.[89]

However, the most potent racial argument that southern politicians made was that black slavery permitted white equality. Regardless of the economic origins and function of slavery, slaveholders tried to convince nonslaveholders that African slavery made all whites equal, and that if slavery were ended, then white inequality would ensue. An economic logic lay behind this claim. By having African slavery, southern politicians and proslavery advocates claimed that all the rude manual work of their society was done by slaves; no white person, therefore, needed to be a servant or perform menial tasks. Instead, whites became the propertied members of society—farmers large or small. Thus slavery preserved the hallowed idea of citizen independence by making all citizens property holders, but the institution denied dependents—slaves—civic participation. They thereby kept political power in the hands of the propertied and did not let the unpropertied have a chance to redistribute wealth. Societies without a racial divide ran the problem of creating such a chasm of inequality among members of the same race that they invited revolution.[90] The South avoided that problem by letting only whites become citizens while restricting the status of dependency to Africans. Southern politicians verbally pounded their audiences with statements about the necessity of white liberty upon black slavery, predicting catastrophe if emancipation ever came about.[91]

Few should doubt that maintenance of white supremacy was so culturally important to white southern society that they would indeed have left the Union for that reason alone had they reason to believe northerners sought to terminate the peculiar institution. Indeed, most current assessments of Reconstruction promote the interpretation that while white southerners could accept the loss of independence in a civil war, they could not accept political and economic equality with blacks; therefore, they fought and won a guerrilla war to ensure white supremacy.[92] Regardless of whether "race" has any scientific legitimacy or any stable definition, white southerners had used a racial argument so frequently and so often that racial differences had become an accepted truth of nineteenth-century American life and had become an independent factor in social and political life.[93]

In the case of Civil War causation, however, race may not have played the most prominent role in promoting southern separation. First, the entire country was bitterly racist, North as well as South. On the question of the racial inferiority of Africans, there was no debate but nearly consensus (save the abolitionists). Time after time northerners insisted that, as David Wilmot said, they had "no morbid sympathy for the slave," for they pled "the cause and the rights of white freemen." Time after time northern politicians claimed that they cared not about Africans, whom they thought inferior, but about the fate of white farmers and workers. Northern politicians often said that they disliked slavery and hoped that someday it would die out, but that they would take no action against it in the states; and most of the time they indicated that its death should be "natural," leaving to everyone's imagination just what the natural death process of the institution was.[94]

The debate over slavery in the antebellum years was about the effects of slavery on the white population nationally, not about the injustice done to Africans. If slavery had been only a racial institution without economic overtones, then the North would never have challenged it. No scholar argues that the antebellum North was bereft of racism. In fact, it was probably precisely because slaves were of African descent that northerners did not seriously attack slavery earlier than the 1850s. What created consternation in the North was not the racial aspects of slavery, which many northerners could agree with, but with the economic ramifications of the doctrine of property in people. If slavery had had no economic reverberations for the North, it is more than likely that northerners would have permitted white southerners to arrange racial relations any way they wanted without northern interference; that, in a sense, is about what happened anyway in the postwar years.

Evidence exists indicating that the southern elite in regard to slavery wanted economic rather than racial questions answered first. Slaves represented too much money to permit wild talk of emancipation. The pertinent example of this concern with wealth was the Virginia Assembly's debate over emancipation in 1831–32. Thomas R. Dew, one of the first proslavery writers, analyzed the possibilities of emancipation and found them nonexistent. Although he underscored the importance of race in emancipation, the insuperable roadblock was money. He estimated that Virginians had about $206 million in houses and land and $100 million in slaves. How could Virginia emancipate its slaves and recompense their owners when the value of slaves was one-third the value of the entire state? The taxation level for such a scheme would have bankrupted the people. And the state had to recompense the owners because that was the rule of civilization. Partial compensation would have been unjust and "subversive of the rights of property and the order and tranquillity of society." Over time, the amount of wealth slavery represented simply grew and compounded; what was unthinkable in 1832 was more unthinkable in 1850 or in 1860. The property aspect of slavery was more important for slaveholders than anything else, including race relations and morality. Dew presented a powerful and nearly irrefragable argument.[95]

Economic explanations for southern secession, the third major branch of interpretive schemes about the South, have had some variation but usually have revolved around the rather simple idea that the South was agrarian and the North was industrial. The progressive historians Charles A. Beard and Louis Hacker were perhaps the most famous promoters of this viewpoint. Such historians held, except for Beard, a sort of sympathy with the South because it was agrarian and therefore not really capitalist; slavery simply did not matter. What did matter was the advent of industry in the northeastern states. Here rose the demon, the industrialist, who ran a feudalistic hierarchy, who exploited thousands of workers, who amassed undreamt of riches (until the late twentieth century, that is), and who controlled local and state politics. Progressives fought the industrialist in their era; certainly the beast was no better in an earlier time period. The mechanism for Civil War was political in the progressive interpretation of southern secession. A class war broke out between northern capitalists and southern slaveholders over control of the federal government and its economic policies. When southerners saw that they had lost in the election of 1860, they expected the new industrialists to leech the wealth of the South away by federal legislation. Unwilling to become a colonial dependency of the North, southerners decided to leave the Union.[96]

This depiction of southern secession leaves no doubt that northern capitalists were the aggressors. According to Eugene Genovese, southerners could not coexist with northerners due to the "increasingly hostile, powerful, and aggressive Northern capitalism" transforming the North; the southern economic agenda "clashed more and more dangerously with the North's economic needs." The most current restatement of the progressive viewpoint comes from Richard F. Bensel, who argues that southern leaders feared "the increasing penetration of the South by institutions and processes associated with the northern political economy" and which, when implemented after Reconstruction (homestead, tariff, subsidies), permitted the South to be "systematically impoverished."[97]

The progressive interpretation, very similar to some analyses made by antebellum slave masters, suffers from two disastrous assumptions.[98] The first was that the South was not rich and the North was. Progressives and those following in their footsteps never sat down and looked at the wealth-holding patterns; their assessments of northern wealth versus southern wealth were empirically wrong.[99] The second was the failure to understand the dilemma over property rights and its implications in the long run. Southerners were striving to control property rights in people and were fearful of letting representatives from a nonslaveholding society control federal definitions of property, a control that could seriously damage the monstrous investment in slaves that southerners had made.[100] On this basis, however, it was not a battle between northern capitalists and southern planters because the property rights of each were not in conflict.

The reason the progressive interpretation drags in federal policy is because that is the only place they can find such combat. Progressive historians assumed that control of the federal government outweighed any other economic influence in the country. Yet the northern economy—to include industry and railroad construction—had soared when a laissez-faire shroud covered federal government policy between 1832 and 1860. The low tariffs of 1846 and 1857, the attack on transportation subsidies, and the lack of a national banking system caused no wave of poverty among northern elites. They prospered. Any gains northerners might expect from a federal program had to be marginal, especially when compared to the income generated by King Cotton. To insist that the northern upper class was desperate for political control indicates that that group was filled with irrational, non-calculating fools who felt a small tariff increase would outweigh southern credit demands, southern shipping needs, and southern industrial consumption purchases.

More to the point, it has to be asked: why would the northern economic elite fear the planter class at all? How were planters going to injure the northern wealthy? When the question is considered, the inescapable answer becomes that the southern planters offered no danger to northern industrialists. Slavery was not going to reduce their profits or wages; slavery might reduce their workers' wages, however, but in theory that should make industrialists rejoice, not strike out in anger. So slavery moved into the territories and inhibited free-labor migration. That merely meant that slavery's expansion would keep the eastern labor markets clogged and labor cheap—again, not exactly a phenomenon that induces upper-class tears. Slavery was in many ways the ultimate control of labor. Why that should arouse the industrial upper class's concern is unclear. To argue that industrialists wanted laborers to internalize controls so they would not have to be externally applied (that is, rule by pain inflicted by conscience instead of the whip) misses the essential point: what was desired was control of labor, and any way it could be obtained was acceptable. And if slavery became nationalized, the rich of the North would hardly be victimized. They had the money; they could have bought slaves for any chores they so desired, industrial, commercial, or agricultural. And up to 1860, industrialists and planters produced different commodities; they were not in direct competition with one another.

Simply put, northern capitalists had little to fear from the nationalization of slavery. Their position was secure because they already had the wealth to take care of themselves. The damage nationalization of slavery might inflict upon the North was really limited to the middle and lower classes, where an actual conflict of economic interest might occur. This is the reason that most empirical voting studies now reveal two aspects of the antebellum Republican Party: the party represented the middle in American society in 1860, and antebellum upper-class northerners were far less radical than even the moderates of the Republican Party.[101]

An accurate depiction of the class conflict over slavery was made in 1896 by a pioneer in discovering the nation's distribution of wealth. Charles B. Spahr went over the history of the United States in terms of wealth distribution and easily summarized slavery's role: "The influence of slavery in creating property for the whites out of the robbery of the blacks was hardly more marked than its influence in concentrating the property of the whites in the hands of a comparatively few of their number." Why disunion occurred was also easily summarized: "The rebellion of 1861 was a rebellion of the richer classes in America against the rule of the middle classes." Interpretation of the origins of the Civil War has experienced a devolution over time; Spahr had it right, and historians have been going in the wrong direction ever since.[102]

Cliometricians have come closer than political and cultural historians to ferreting out the real economic forces producing Civil War. Gavin Wright, Gerald Gunderson, Richard Sutch, and Roger Ransom have mapped out the mountainous investment made in slavery and its potential influence in the sectional animosity.[103] However, some of their work has not been amenable to historians' understanding (and some of it has not been amenable to anyone's understanding), while at other times the basic points have been buried in a host of (highly legitimate) economic questions relating to the economic health of slavery. What has been missing in this fruitful and promising analysis has been an awareness of the role of property rights. In particular, the paranoia exhibited by southerners was a simple one. They were living in one of those frightful times when the rules of the game were being rewritten, when the basic principles of market activity were being redesigned. And southerners realized that they were to be the losers in the revision.

Historians and economists have exercised as much ingenuity in figuring out the reason for southern secession and the American Civil War as on any topic in American history. In all this amazing display of creativity in analyzing what people will fight for—honor, white supremacy, local autonomy, states' rights, economic freedom from northerners—they have oddly and stubbornly refused to recognize the oldest social law that virtually all political philosophers have underlined: many men will kill other men to keep their property or to extend it. Great property holders usually do not lie down to let the forces of history roll over them and seize their possessions, regardless of how those possessions were obtained. There are two ways to demonstrate the importance of wealth in the coming of the Civil War.

One is to conduct a simple thought experiment. If slaves had only been worth \$300 million instead of \$3 billion—that is, a reduction of slavery's economic power by a factor of ten—would there have been a Civil War? Would northerners have attacked an institution that only represented 2 percent of total wealth? Would southerners have been so hypersensitive to attacks when so little money was involved? My answer would be: absolutely not.

The second way to understand southern motivations in secession is to look at how they expected slavery to end. They did not imagine slavery's demise by talking about the death of states' rights, the conversion to northern moral standards, an uprising of the slaves, the mutation of everyone's skin color to one shade, or the replacement of republicanism with an Enlightenment egalitarianism. *Slavery was to end when the slaves became worthless.* Here population theory permitted southerners to foresee the end of the peculiar institution. Population growth would occur and eventually produce a dense population. Yeomen farmers would lose their land, and the South would experience the creation of "free" laborers. The wage rate of these free workers would decline over time, as it had in England and as it was doing in the 1850s North. Eventually, the pauperized free laborer would emerge who earned only subsistence wages. At that point slavery would disappear—because free labor would then be cheaper than slave labor. So said South Carolinian Preston Brooks in 1854: "As population increases, poor laborers will be so plenty as to render slaves useless." And slaveholders would not hold onto an asset that had become a constant debit.[104] Thus would endeth the patriarchal institution, the best socialism for the worker—and its demise would take with it all that talk about honor, racial kindness, family, and republicanism. Slavery and all the ideals surrounding it were sustained by one thing: profitability. And when profitability vanished, so did slavery and its long train of justifying rhetoric.

At the root of the controversy over slavery was the wealth invested in slavery. Remove the wealth, and the controversy, like a Cheshire cat, fades away with a knowing grin.

3

Free Labor and the Competition of Slaves

At nearly the same time William L. Yancey was explaining to a Louisville audience why southerners could not live in a Union where their immense investment in slaves was threatened, two Illinois Republicans, Richard Oglesby and Richard Yates, both destined to be governors of the state, made clear the apprehension that northerners had about an expanding slave-based economy. In June 1860 Yates made a long free labor speech at Springfield, and he explained the struggle between the northern and southern labor systems in this manner:

> Now the question comes, how shall we advance this labor. As presented in our politics, the question is, whether unpaid, unwilling slave labor is better than voluntary, intelligent, free paid labor? I was not so young when I left Kentucky, but that I recollect the time when a poor man toiled all day, with a hod upon his shoulder, up the scaffold of a rich man's edifice for three shillings a day, because a slave could be hired for seventy-five dollars a year. Do you recollect what Senator Hammond said of the free white population of South Carolina? That a majority of that unhappy class subsisted by hunting and fishing, and trading with the negroes for what they were stealing from their masters and they cannot live and prosper in competition with unpaid slave labor.

Two months later, Richard Oglesby offered a similar tale to listeners at a meeting in Clinton:

> I came myself from a slave State. Poor white girls washed there all day over a hot and steaming tub, and under a blazing sun, for ten cents a day. [Cries of "That's a fact; I saw such things."] And why was this? Simply because a negro wench, equally strong, could be hired for that price. In Kentucky I was a laboring man. I hired out for six dollars a month. Why couldn't I get more? Because a negro man, of of [*sic*] equal physical strength, could be hired for $75 per year. He could be fed on coarser food than I, and would be submissive. . . . Do you want such an institution in your territories?[1]

The brunt of these speeches is plain: a competition between free and slave labor leads to the ruin of free labor.

In understanding the forces that led to secession, the North has been something of an enigma. Explaining why southerners seceded from the Union in 1860–61 is in fact not that difficult, once one recognizes the amount of property at stake in the sectional controversy. Coming to terms with the North's paranoias about slavery, however, is more complex. To comprehend the sudden northern dread of southern institutions in the 1850s, various authors have emphasized northern moral abhorrence of slavery, the demand of northern elites for control of the federal government, a northern arrogance that originated in their region having surging industrial growth while the southern region seemingly stagnated in agrarian backwardness, emotional unease that turned to aggression because of the instability in economic and social life produced by the rise of a market economy, and politicians who rode their "hobby"—their means to attract voters—to power by denouncing southern society.[2] Two explanations currently reign. One, northerners feared slaveholders constituted the "slave power," an aristocracy that wanted to seize control of the federal government, destroy the northern economy, end civil liberties, and eventually expand slavery into the North. Second, northern society was ideologically committed to an ideal of free labor, the "free labor ideology," that praised the American capacity for work, its economic reward, and social mobility; slavery was the hostile and aggressive antithesis of free labor.[3]

Northern fears about slavery and why northerners felt the South was aggressive can be fruitfully explained by looking at the northern economy and drawing out the implications of the doctrine that slavery was defined as property rights in people. Both sections had founded their civilizations on property rights, but in the South property rights encompassed people of African descent whereas in the North such rights either were not permitted to operate on people at all or were very limited (apprenticeships, indentures). The sectional controversy over slavery was in truth a struggle over property rights and their implications for both societies. For the South, the role of property rights in the fight over the expansion of slavery is easy to observe and therefore to understand: slaves represented property and southerners gathered round to protect the property they had built up over centuries, not to mention all the social and political mores they had grafted onto the ownership of that property.

How property rights operated in the North to push that section into an adamant stand on slavery's expansion was not quite so visible but was no less potent. Northern society grew and developed according to the rules of property rights that did not allow one person to enslave another. That meant that wealth and earning a livelihood followed different rules in the free states than in the slave states. The fight between the sections occurred when the possibility arose that the two systems of property rights might merge and no longer be kept separate. The economic implication of these two sets of property rights was that one set was privileged over the other and could inflict grievous, irrevocable damage on the other. Ultimately, property rights in slaves was the aggressor. Property rights in slaves threatened to transform northern society—and northerners, or many of them, ferociously resisted adaptations to property rights in slaves.

This chapter elucidates the way that property rights in slaves threatened the North's social and economic foundations. First, northerners had a clear and well-founded fear of the potential results of free labor competing against slave labor—a competition that could not occur without property rights in people being sanctioned. Second, the issue of competition between free and slave labor arose largely due to the transportation revolution. The transportation revolution created a national market and suddenly enabled the economic effects of slavery to escape its geographical confinement to the southern states. Third, the economic situation made slavery the aggressor; instead of northern economic practices invading the South, the reality was that southern economic practices were invading, or suddenly had the capacity to invade, the North. Fourth, the northern middle and lower classes were the ones the antislavery leaders directed their appeals to because they were the portion of northern society that most obviously might experience competition with slave labor.

By 1850 the northern states had grown into an economy that gave substance to the ideology of free labor and that provided a basis for a rational northern fear of southern aristocracy. The northern economy was one of small shops and small farms in a commercial setting, buttressed by a few large industrial firms. In this economy, the appeal that a person by hard work, diligence, and a modicum of intelligence could expect to become a property holder and independent made some sense. The social mobility creed of the mid-nineteenth century was not a creed of unimaginable wealth but of independent citizenship. Indeed, labor, in its general sense, may have been at the core of the northern experience. Because this was an economy based on smallness, on individual effort, the economic enemy was bigness in enterprise, a bigness that could throttle individual activity, individual reward, and individual social mobility. The northern economy of proprietorships and partnerships was in a social sense, to extend Philip S. Paludan's apt description, the economy of the commercial northern village.[4]

At the time of the Revolution, the northern colonies were primarily agricultural communities with an important appendage of transatlantic commerce from the major cities of Boston, New York, and Philadelphia. Certainly a portion of the population dwelled in seaport areas and earned a living by fishing, artisanal work, and manual labor. But the agrarian tenor of the economy was overwhelming. Probably 80 percent of northerners were farmers, and only 10 percent or so lived in communities over 2,500 souls. In some places farming was extensively commercial, such as along the Hudson and Connecticut Rivers, but elsewhere a form of subsistence agriculture was the standard. The lack of transportation facilities dictated a local economy that only occasionally managed trade with the wider state and country. A true subsistence economy probably never existed in North America, but certainly great portions lived in areas of highly restricted commercial access. Farmers probably consumed three-quarters of what they raised.[5]

Change came in the early nineteenth century in two forms. The War of 1812 disrupted New England's trade patterns and led investors into building textile factories. Thereafter textile factories boomed in those states until the late 1840s. A more powerful effect on the economy came from new means of transportation. The steamboat opened up the inland rivers to commercial intercourse on a vast scale, while the building of canals stitched isolated areas into a market. Railroads soon pushed canals aside as the primary way Americans conquered space and time, and by 1860 some 20,000 miles of track were in operation in the North.

The new transportation facilities made important changes in northern society. A national market was beginning to take shape, and the creation of a national market meant that the final price of a product had fewer deviations from one locale to another. Thus transportation reshuffled the internal activities of the nation as each region sought its "comparative advantage" within the broad market area. Eastern states turned more to manufacturing, marginal farmers moved to the West, and areas with reserves of coal and iron flourished, commerce swelled, and employments multiplied.

However, the transition from a semisubsistence to a commercial economy took more time and had more stages than many historians have recognized. The major impact of commercialization on the northern states was to augment the proprietorship quality of economic endeavor, not to aggregate businesses together. And much of the activity was not industrial, but rather artisanal or skilled work. It would appear, a proposition offered with some hesitation, that the impact of transportation improvement elevated the demand for skilled workers—blacksmiths, carpenters, coopers, bricklayers, shoemakers, cabinetmakers, millers, painters, machinists, tailors, and wheelwrights. Evidently, the village economy of the North was not simply agrarian but had a considerable skilled-labor base.[6]

Table 3.1 attempts to place census tabulations for occupations into categories that might have some interpretive merit. The table, however, requires some explanation. For purposes of determining the status of the economy, the household seemed the most important economic unit. Unfortunately, using the number of families for a denominator to determine percentages of what portion the category was of the whole yielded poor results—totals far exceeding 100 percent. The reason was that wives, sons, and daughters were included in the occupational listings; indeed, the youth of American society probably skewed the results when households were used as a denominator. Thus for a

TABLE 3.1. *Northern Occupational Categories and Ratios of Category to White Males, 1850 and 1860*

State	*Total White Males, 15–69*	*Farms*	*Farmers*	*Commerce*	*Skilled Labor*	*Factory/ Manual Labor*	*Common Labor*	*Professions*
New England, 1850								
Connecticut	121,085	.185	.264	.043	.181	.022	.165	.019
New Hampshire	104,469	.280	.465	.027	.201	.001	.136	.020
Massachusetts	326,700	.104	.172	.075	.288	.015	.212	.021
Maine	184,072	.254	.419	.040	.153	.013	.185	.017
Rhode Island	38,795	.139	.250	.051	.319	.066	.266	.024
Vermont	102,754	.290	.471	.035	.118	.004	.215	.020
Total	877,875	.191	.310	.052	.216	.016	.194	.020
New England, 1860								
Connecticut	143,431	.175	.298	.065	.215	.080	.134	.048
New Hampshire	102,692	.296	.446	.049	.240	.070	.094	.051
Massachusetts	382,761	.093	.170	.085	.310	.102	.153	.036
Maine	194,265	.287	.418	.048	.155	.071	.155	.048
Rhode Island	52,938	.101	.206	.082	.216	.110	.160	.041
Vermont	99,167	.312	.535	.038	.158	.017	.088	.037
Total	975,254	.188	.306	.066	.237	.081	.138	.042
Middle Atlantic, 1850								
New York	960,342	.178	.327	.078	.186	.010	.194	.024
New Jersey	137,605	.174	.239	.064	.205	.017	.274	.023
Pennsylvania	658,254	.194	.316	.055	.234	.033	.230	.026
Total	1,756,201	.183	.316	.068	.206	.019	.214	.025
Middle Atlantic, 1860								
New York	1,179,374	.166	.319	.092	.195	.016	.145	.040
New Jersey	194,852	.141	.256	.075	.221	.025	.177	.032
Pennsylvania	826,654	.189	.306	.063	.221	.025	.171	.036
Total	2,200,910	.172	.306	.079	.198	.027	.158	.038
Great Lakes, 1850								
Illinois	248,621	.307	.567	.030	.101	.006	.114	.019
Indiana	269,194	.349	.606	.033	.123	.002	.105	.023
Iowa	53,856	.275	.608	.031	.124	.009	.093	.029
Michigan	122,100	.279	.539	.033	.134	.012	.118	.022
Ohio	560,396	.257	.482	.042	.153	.009	.157	.023
Wisconsin	98,885	.204	.414	.035	.118	.001	.144	.026
Minnesota	2,557	.061	.133	.088	.150	.050	.234	.117
Total	1,355,609	.283	.527	.037	.132	.007	.132	.023
Great Lakes, 1860								
Illinois	524,061	.272	.385	.037	.098	.004	.102	.028
Indiana	386,905	.328	.512	.036	.112	.003	.088	.029
Iowa	197,086	.300	.521	.040	.117	.005	.080	.043
Michigan	236,674	.264	.529	.042	.129	.012	.115	.038
Ohio	672,166	.258	.450	.050	.143	.008	.119	.037
Wisconsin	231,658	.297	.544	.042	.125	.020	.125	.039
Minnesota	54,111	.322	.518	.042	.099	.086	.099	.038
Total	2,302,661	.283	.478	.042	.121	.010	.106	.034

Note on method: The categories to the right of the number of white males aged 15–69 were divided by the number of white males aged 15–69. Because the numbers in the censuses of 1850 and 1860 included women and free blacks, and because not all census categories were used, the "percentages" do not add up to 100 across each row. The number of families in the census of 1860 was also tried as a denominator, but the results so far exceeded 100 when added that that procedure was eliminated. The table provides a rough comparison of how occupations were divided for household heads and voters, which is all that is intended. The census offered breakdowns for the states, but only manufacturing totals for counties.

For the 1850 categories, the information was taken from the U.S. Department of the Census, *Seventh Census*, vol. 1: *Population*, lxvii–lxxx. *Farmer*: farmers, gardeners, overseers, planters; *commerce*: agents, bankers, bank officers, barkeepers, boardinghouse operators, boatmen, brokers, clerks, dealers, grocers, apothecaries, innkeepers, market men, merchants, peddlers, produce and provision men, railroad men, storekeepers, and traders; *skilled labor*: apprentices, blacksmiths, brewers, brickmakers, butchers, cabinetmakers, carpenters, coopers, cordwainers, drivers, drovers, joiners, machinists, masons, mechanics, millers, painters, printers, saddlers, sawyers, ship carpenters, stonecutters, tailors, teamsters, tinsmiths, weavers, wheelwrights, and jewelers; *factory/manual labor*: factory hands, fishermen, iron founders, iron mongers, ironworkers, lumbermen, unspecified manufacturers, molders, and miners; *common labor*: laborers, mariners; *professions*: city and town officers, clergymen, dentists, lawyers, physicians, soldiers, teachers, U.S. and state officers.

For the 1860 categories, the information was taken from the U.S. Department of the Interior, *Eighth Census*, vol. 1: *Population*, 656–79. *Farmer*: farmers, gardeners, overseers, farm laborers; *commerce*: bankers, bank officers, boardinghouse keepers, clerks, commission merchants, dealers, druggists, grocers, innkeepers, merchants, railroad men, saloonkeepers, storekeepers, traders, boatmen; *skilled labor*: apprentices, blacksmiths, brewers, bricklayers, butchers, cabinetmakers, carpenters, coopers, harness makers, machinists, masons, mechanics, millers, painters, plasterers, printers, saddlers, sawyers, ship carpenters, shoemakers, stonecutters, tailors, teamsters, tinsmiths, weavers, wheelwrights, jewelers, joiners; *factory/manual labor*: factory hands, fishermen, lumbermen, miners, molders, iron founders, iron mongers, iron rollers, ironworkers; *common labor*: laborers, mariners; *professions*: civil and mechanical engineers, clergy, lawyers, manufacturers, officers (public), physicians, teachers, U.S. officers, dentists.

Number of farms in 1850 from De Bow, *Statistical View of the United States*, 169; total farms in 1860 from U.S. Department of the Interior, *Eighth Census*, vol. 2: *Agriculture*, 221. Population of white males taken from earlier tables.

denominator I used white males fifteen years or older as a proxy for the basic economic unit of northern society. Moreover, where to place various occupations in which category has obvious subjective problems. In the table, I made the following choices. Agriculture includes both farmers and farm laborers, and it seems likely that most of the reported farm laborers were kinfolk of proprietors. Skilled labor presented a problem not only because of where to place occupations but also because in some locales the occupation might be highly skilled but in another place be a "hand" in a factory. The greatest example of this problem is shoemaking. In Massachusetts in the 1850s shoemaking was the largest category of employment and a factory setting (though without machinery) had arrived, but elsewhere in the country shoemaking was a skilled craft. The divisions in labor were made because the census takers included the category "factory hands," which indicated the presence of industrialization in the manner most think and write of—large numbers of unskilled workers housed in central locations responding to bureaucratic management. The category of "common labor" was created because the census takers made such a category, and it is difficult to determine what the term meant. It might possibly mean unskilled and lowly labor in cities; it could mean agricultural laborers (by individuals who did not call themselves farm laborers); it might indicate youth just finding employment; it might also be a reflection of the massive immigration wave that came to the United States between 1845 and 1860. Let it also be noted that not all the occupations given in the census reports were used in the table; some occupations were not classified under male labor, some were too small to be important, and some I had no idea to which category it belonged. The occupations chosen were those that had the most substantial numbers. Thus these tables have their warts and should not at all be taken to be definitive.[7] The numbers are *ratios* of the occupational category to the estimate of males aged fifteen to sixty-nine; they are not proportions or percentages because they do not add up to unity. Despite the various imperfections, they shed some light on the northern mid-nineteenth-century economy and yield useful generalizations.

Table 3.1 reveals that for all the writing on the *industrial* North by scholars and others, the main fact was that the region was primarily agricultural. Even New Jersey, Pennsylvania, and New York had one-third of their populations in agriculture, while the Great Lakes states were close to half. New England was a split region. Massachusetts, Connecticut, and Rhode Island housed a non-agrarian economy, but the states of Vermont, New Hampshire, and Maine had numbers more in common with the Great Lakes states than with their Puritan brethren. In terms of "factory hands," industrialization could hardly be said to have existed save in certain select counties of the country. Indeed, northern contemporaries knew that the question of labor encompassed far more than factory hands. During the debate over the tariff of 1846, the editor of the *Buffalo Courier and Pilot*, a Democratic paper, argued that 75 percent of American labor was agricultural; of the remainder most were "mechanics such as shoemakers, tailors, carpenters, tanners and others, resident among the farmers and directly dependent on them." This antiprotectionist argument was basically claiming that factory labor in the North was a rarity while village skilled labor was the norm.[8]

Three general categories of occupations stand out for the North in 1850 and 1860. First was agriculture and next came the two divisions of labor, skilled and common. In the New England and Middle Atlantic states, skilled labor—at least skilled labor as defined in Table 3.1—was a sizable portion of the working community and of the head of households. Many of these individuals must have done work that fitted both urban and rural environments (like carpentry, blacksmithing, and milling) because even in the frontier states of Iowa, Minnesota, and Wisconsin a relatively large ratio (.12 or so) of the male work force could be labeled skilled. Of nearly equal size both in urban and rural communities was common labor, a category whose meaning, as mentioned earlier, is unclear. But the three categories of skilled labor, common labor, and agriculture represent in one sense an emphasis on manual labor; the categories in which manual labor is suspect, commerce and the professions, are minute by comparison. By stretching out the meaning behind the numbers in Table 3.1, I would assert that the free labor ideology of the mid-nineteenth century was originating in the northern experience of agriculture and skilled labor.

Much of the literature on the North has now veered to redefining free labor as wage labor, in anticipation of the rise of industrialization in the form of factories manned by unskilled labor. Although it is not always said, there is an additional important translation of terms. Wage labor means not merely work for hire but work that yielded subsistence wages. Thus the free laborer of the 1850s is transformed into a subsistence factory worker, a definition that partly derives from the British experience and English writing on political economy.[9] In the United States during the 1850s evidence of miserably paid factory workers in the North abounded, and in general the decade was a difficult one for wage earners because of inflation and labor supply pressures.[10] But those individuals were not the referents for the free labor ideology.

Because in one way or another the question of industrialization in its modern factory, machine-driven form haunts discussions of the Civil War era, some additional information may bring a sense of proportion to the topic. Table 3.2 provides the extent of factory work, defined by census takers as the number of people working in shops that made more than $500 worth of product per year (in 1850 and 1860) and puts those ratios next to manufacturing in 1900. The comparison between the decadal points is imprecise, however, because in 1900 the census takers did not attempt to include in the manufacturing population only those working in factories. Nonetheless, the basic numbers and the ratios tell the vital story. Industrialization and manufacturing had begun early in the nineteenth century true enough, but that process did not dominate American life until late in the nineteenth century. The numbers are presented as well as the ratios so that the leap can be appreciated. Massachusetts, Pennsylvania, and New York in 1860 had, respectively, totals of factory workers equaling 76,100, 90,432, and 48,985; by 1900 those numbers had ballooned to 341,783, 574,606, and 605,686. This transition came more dramatically in the last two decades of the century. According to the twelfth census, in 1870 some 1,615,000 males above age sixteen worked in manufacturing; by 1900 that number was 4,114,000. Almost 84 percent of that increase came between 1880 and 1900.[11]

Another way to demonstrate the economic evolution that the United States experienced is to show the occupational division of the nation in 1900 and compare it with the situation in 1850 and 1860 (Table 3.3). Once again, the comparison is beset with difficulties. While a division between skilled, factory, and common labor may be possible in the earlier decades, it is not by 1900. The census takers in 1900 did not even try, and categories no longer provide clues because almost all work became "wage work" and factory work could include both skilled and unskilled labor.[12] What is clear in Table 3.3 is the reduction of agriculture in the North; its virtual collapse in Massachusetts, Rhode Island, and Connecticut, along with the Middle Atlantic states of New York, Pennsyl-

TABLE 3.2. *Workers in Factories, Total Number, and Ratio to White Males Fifteen Years of Age or Older*

Region/State	*Workers 1850*	*Ratio 1850*	*Workers 1860*	*Ratio 1860*	*Workers 1900*	*Ratio 1900*
New England						
Connecticut	5,905	.049	18,073	.126	130,610	.401
New Hampshire	4,060	.039	9,813	.096	46,847	.309
Massachusetts	20,600	.063	76,100	.199	341,783	.348
Maine	1,875	.010	5,528	.028	53,701	.212
Rhode Island	6,290	.162	10,839	.205	64,508	.433
Vermont	1,509	.015	1,977	.020	24,714	.197
Central Atlantic						
New York	18,515	.019	48,985	.042	605,686	.237
New Jersey	5,213	.038	15,201	.078	181,879	.279
Pennsylvania	39,579	.060	90,432	.109	574,606	.264
Great Lakes						
Illinois	578	.002	4,113	.008	325,713	.195
Indiana	676	.003	3,063	.008	133,009	.152
Iowa	101	.002	577	.003	48,417	.063
Michigan	433	.004	1,416	.006	136,627	.160
Ohio	8,360	.015	20,714	.031	287,789	.198
Wisconsin	350	.004	1,192	.005	120,131	.173
Minnesota	0	.000	45	.001	66,889	.110
Deep South						
Alabama	634	.005	1,346	.009	45,530	.086
Florida	28	.002	44	.002	32,188	.186
Georgia	1,758	.013	3,099	.019	66,540	.105
Louisiana	383	.004	2,006	.018	35,531	.088
Mississippi	70	.001	615	.006	23,643	.053
South Carolina	759	.010	811	.010	29,823	.080
Texas	52	.001	363	.003	44,199	.047
Border South						
Arkansas	21	.000	152	.001	25,158	.063
Delaware	722	.042	1,153	.043	17,765	.277
Kentucky	5,056	.024	4,347	.017	51,101	.075
Maryland	4,180	.033	7,911	.052	72,824	.186
Missouri	875	.005	2,684	.008	106,782	.102
North Carolina	2,015	.014	1,355	.008	44,549	.083
Tennessee	3,024	.015	3,000	.013	42,492	.068
Virginia	10,020	.043	7,174	.024	86,424	.098

Note on method and source: The census takers took the job description of individuals at their residences but as well asked factory owners who made more than $500 worth of product annually to provide the number of workers employed. Not all categories were used as many did not seem pertinent to the idea of "factory" work. For 1850, the categories used were cottons, woolens, iron, carpets, steam engines, calico, locomotives, coal mining, carding mills, smelting lead, coal, tobacco, shingles, coach making, lead furnaces. In the 1860 census, the numbers came from the introductory remarks and the particular tables given on manufacturing; the categories used were cotton men hands, woolens men, worsted, hosiery, wool carding, carpets, men's clothing, boots and shoes, iron bar sheet and railroad, railroad engines, hardware, nails, ironworkers, paper, printing, hats, coal mining, iron mines, iron booms, and pig iron. Material from 1900, the twelfth census, includes male wage earners 16 years and older employed in manufacturing; the ratio is division of the number of wage earners by the total males 15 years and older. The comparison is loose because the 1850 and 1860 censuses was explicit about workers in factories, while the 1900 census was simply wage earners in manufacturing. However, a rough but not precise understanding of the transition is fairly obvious.

Sources: U.S. Department of the Census, *Seventh Census*, vol. 1: *Population* U.S. Department of the Interior, *Eighth Census*, vol. 3: *Manufactures*, xxi–clxxx; U.S. Census Office, *Twelfth Census*, vol. 2: *Population*, part 2, p. lxxxii; ibid., vol. 7: *Manufactures*, part 1, pp. cxxix–cxxxii.

vania, and New Jersey. There the occupations of commerce and manufacturing obtained a ratio to workers between .65 and .80. In the Great Lakes states, agriculture remained vital to the society but at a much reduced level, a ratio of .50 to .35. As in the East, manufacturing and commerce in the Great Lakes became prominent. Somewhat interesting, the South appears not to have changed much at all, except to have become more agricultural than it was in 1860. However, the earlier censuses reported the occupations of whites while the 1900 census gave the occupations of blacks and whites, and that probably accounts for the much greater percentage of people in agriculture. In any event, the sectional difference in economic evolution is striking: the Deep South and most of the Border South remained agricultural, while the northern states blossomed into manufacturing and mercantile states with an agricultural appendage.

Table 3.4 makes a regional comparison of occupations. Clearly New England and the Middle Atlantic states had less agriculture than the other regions but still a substantial amount. What is more intriguing is the area of difference between the northern and southern regions. That difference is labor, in the amount of skilled and common labor per white adult males above age fifteen. All the northern areas are well above the Deep South and moderately above the Border South. Table 3.5 makes the same point in a slightly different way. Taking the categories of skilled labor, factory labor, and common labor by states from the earlier results and then ranking the states from highest to lowest produces lists that show for skilled labor and common labor the slave states dominate the lower end while the free states monopolize the upper end. Factory labor was not all that revealing because the spread among the states was not that extensive and because the Lake States had almost as little factory manufacturing as the South. The chasm between North and South was defined by skilled labor and common labor. (It should be noted here, as given in Chapter 7, that the rise of the Republican Party was first strongest in the *West*, not the East.)

What accounts for this division among the regions is slavery. The occupation categories were for whites in the South because slaves were treated separately; the North did not have this division. Because all communities needed certain amounts of manual labor, the only conclusion is that the South supplied these needs with slave labor, an inference that agrees with much secondary literature on the use of slaves. Thus an analysis of occupations in the United

TABLE 3.3. *Male Occupational Categories and Ratio of Category to White Males in 1900, All Regions*

Region/State	*Males Age 15+*	*Number of Farms*	*Agri-culture*	*Profes-sional*	*Domestic Service*	*Trade and Transportation*	*Manufacturing and Mechanic*
New England							
Maine	255,332	.233	.290	.027	.145	.153	.271
New Hampshire	152,133	.193	.243	.026	.118	.151	.355
Vermont	127,197	.261	.378	.031	.102	.134	.236
Massachusetts	983,459	.038	.066	.038	.127	.243	.421
Rhode Island	150,492	.037	.073	.033	.140	.213	.473
Connecticut	326,809	.083	.131	.031	.138	.190	.419
Middle Atlantic							
New York	2,555,281	.089	.141	.042	.160	.257	.308
New Jersey	652,435	.053	.103	.037	.164	.245	.374
Pennsylvania	2,176,041	.103	.152	.033	.180	.185	.378
Great Lakes							
Ohio	1,454,446	.190	.275	.036	.142	.172	.269
Indiana	873,115	.254	.381	.033	.135	.143	.203
Illinois	1,674,164	.158	.269	.038	.146	.207	.242
Michigan	858,170	.237	.354	.028	.146	.147	.225
Wisconsin	694,160	.245	.376	.026	.140	.134	.210
Minnesota	609,196	.254	.414	.028	.126	.167	.164
Iowa	772,250	.296	.470	.031	.102	.153	.135
Border South							
Delaware	64,857	.151	.277	.031	.169	.154	.292
Maryland	391,759	.117	.235	.033	.176	.209	.265
Virginia[a]	879,188	.297	.482	.025	.140	.121	.177
North Carolina	542,295	.414	.618	.018	.098	.076	.124
Missouri	1,047,568	.272	.427	.034	.115	.172	.175
Kentucky	679,499	.345	.574	.028	.109	.113	.128
Tennessee	622,301	.361	.609	.026	.116	.119	.113
Arkansas	400,267	.446	.745	.025	.083	.085	.083
Deep South							
South Carolina	376,325	.413	.742	.019	.090	.074	.114
Georgia	641,427	.350	.650	.023	.115	.105	.105
Florida	172,191	.237	.442	.029	.186	.128	.169
Alabama	535,287	.417	.723	.021	.090	.092	.129
Mississippi	451,706	.489	.803	.018	.080	.075	.058
Louisiana	411,306	.282	.552	.022	.168	.131	.109
Texas	935,416	.376	.626	.031	.109	.113	.075

Sources: Number of those aged 15 and older from U.S. Census Office, *Twelfth Census*, vol. 2: *Population*, part 2, table XLV, p. lxxxii; number of farms from ibid., vol. 13: *Special Reports*, table XII, p. lxxiii; number of persons in gainful occupations from ibid., table XXIII, pp. xc–xci.

a. Includes West Virginia.

TABLE 3.4. *Regional Summaries of Ratios of Occupational Category to White Males, 1850 and 1860*

Region	*Total White Males, 15–69*	*Farms*	*Farmers*	*Commerce*	*Skilled Labor*	*Factory/ Manual Labor*	*Common Labor*	*Professions*
1850								
Deep South	564,264	.332	.538	.060	.085	.004	.099	.040
Border South	1,150,160	.332	.488	.043	.117	.006	.165	.032
Great Lakes	1,355,609	.283	.527	.037	.132	.007	.132	.023
Middle Atlantic	1,756,201	.183	.316	.068	.206	.019	.214	.025
New England	877,875	.191	.310	.052	.216	.016	.194	.020
1860								
Deep South	754,189	.303	.491	.073	.094	.009	.087	.048
Border South	1,560,654	.285	.518	.051	.130	.009	.114	.034
Great Lakes	2,302,661	.283	.478	.042	.121	.010	.106	.034
Middle Atlantic	2,200,910	.172	.308	.079	.198	.027	.158	.038
New England	975,254	.188	.306	.066	.237	.081	.138	.042

Sources: Compiled from previous tables.

States in 1850 and 1860 leads inevitably to the conclusion that the economic area that southern slaves and northern workers shared was common labor and skilled labor, the economic meeting point of free labor and slave labor. To anticipate, this explains some of the North's fears about residing with the South in a national market and why the free labor ideology took the form it did.

Moreover, the statistics of the census also reveal the foundation of northern yeoman farmer apprehensions about slavery. In Table 3.6, panel A, the distribution of farms according to numbers in size of acreage category are given. It is clear that the modest farmer dominated throughout the nation, as every region had the majority of farms within a range of 50 to 500 acres, and if the acreage boundaries are pushed to 20 to 500 acres, then 70 percent of all farms in the nation fell into this category. What is obvious is that the North did not have farms above the 500-acre boundary; those farms were in the South. In panel B of Table 3.6, an attempt is made to determine the percentage of total acreage each size category contained. An estimate was made by multiplying the number of farms in each category times the midpoint of acres the category represented. The inevitable problem occurred: the last category, farms above 1,000 acres, had no upper boundary. To make the calculation, the last category was found by multiplying the number of farms times 1,500 acres; thus the results in Table 3.6 are erroneous but are nonetheless sufficient for broad generalization. Northern farms overwhelmingly remained in the intermediate-size category, but in the Deep South, the large farms—assumed to be the plantations—may have accounted for 30 percent of the acreage, and a modest 13 percent in the Border South.

Northern travelers to the South had to be impressed with plantations.

TABLE 3.5. *Ranking of States by Labor Categories, 1860*

Skilled	*Factory*	*Common*
Massachusetts, 31.0	Rhode Island, 11.0	Delaware, 26.7
New Hampshire, 24.0	Massachusetts, 10.2	Maryland, 21.9
New Jersey, 22.1	Minnesota, 8.6 (?)	New Jersey, 17.7
Rhode Island, 21.6	Connecticut, 8.0	Pennsylvania, 17.1
Connecticut, 21.5	Maine, 7.1	Rhode Island, 16.0
Maryland, 20.1	New Hampshire, 7.0	Maine, 15.5
Delaware, 20.0	Pennsylvania, 4.4	Massachusetts, 15.3
Pennsylvania, 19.9	New Jersey, 2.5	Louisiana, 15.1
New Jersey, 19.5	Delaware, 2.0	New York, 14.5
Vermont, 15.8	Wisconsin, 2.0	Connecticut, 13.4
Maine, 15.5	Georgia, 2.0	Florida, 13.4
Missouri, 15.4	Vermont, 1.7	Wisconsin, 12.5
Louisiana, 15.1	New York, 1.6	Ohio, 11.9
Ohio, 14.3	Virginia, 1.6	Michigan, 11.5
Michigan, 12.9	South Carolina, 1.5	North Carolina, 11.5
Wisconsin, 12.5	Michigan, 1.2	Tennessee, 10.6
Iowa, 11.7	Maryland, 1.0	Illinois, 10.2
Indiana, 11.2	North Carolina, 1.0	Kentucky, 10.2
Kentucky, 10.5	Florida, 0.9	Virginia, 9.9
South Carolina, 10.4	Ohio, 0.8	Minnesota, 9.9
Minnesota, 9.9	Alabama, 0.8	Missouri, 9.6
Virginia, 9.9	Kentucky, 0.6	New Hampshire, 9.4
Illinois, 9.8	Louisiana, 0.6	Indiana, 8.8
Florida, 8.8	Iowa, 0.5	Vermont, 8.8
Tennessee, 8.8	Tennessee, 0.5	Texas, 8.0
North Carolina, 8.7	Illinois, 0.4	Iowa, 8.0
Georgia, 8.5	Indiana, 0.3	South Carolina, 7.3
Texas, 8.4	Mississippi, 0.2	Georgia, 7.2
Mississippi, 7.7	Missouri, 0.1	Mississippi, 7.1
Alabama, 7.5	Arkansas, 0.0	Alabama, 7.0
Arkansas, 5.7	Texas, 0.0	Arkansas, 6.8

Sources: Compiled from previous tables.

They were situated on the best land and visible along the routes of transportation.[13] Yeoman farms, populous though they were, may have been overshadowed by the plantations because many of them were in mountain regions or on poorer soil. Thus what northerners saw was plantation domination of the agricultural South, the victory of the large landowner over the small farmer—in a European sense, the triumph of the aristocracy over the yeomanry. This is the material base that gave rise to observations about the dangers of monopolization of the soil by slaveholding aristocrats: "White men will not see individuals holding five or ten thousand acres of land, with one hundred or two hundred slaves, and go hungry for themselves for want of bread with the ballot in their hands," spoke Representative Bishop Perkins of New York in 1854. After the Civil War, the Democrat John A. McClernand lauded the yeoman farmer as

TABLE 3.6. *Northern and Southern Farm Size Comparison*

Panel A. Distribution of Number of Farms in Each Farm Size Category by Region (in Percent)

Region	*% Farms 3–19 Acres*	*% Farms 20–49 Acres*	*% Farms 50–99 Acres*	*% Farms 100–499 Acres*	*% Farms 500–999 Acres*	*% Farms 1,000+ Acres*
Deep South	11.5	29.7	23.6	29.7	04.2	01.3
Border South	09.5	31.0	27.7	29.9	01.6	00.3
Great Lakes	10.0	35.1	33.3	21.2	00.3	00.1
Middle Atlantic	10.1	28.2	37.0	24.6	00.1	00.0
New England	11.7	31.7	34.8	21.7	00.1	00.0

Panel B. Distribution of Number of Acres Farmed in Each Farm Size Category by Region (in Percent)

Region	*% Acres in Category 3–19 Acres*	*% Acres in Category 20–49 Acres*	*% Acres in Category 50–99 Acres*	*% Acres in Category 100–499 Acres*	*% Acres in Category 500–999 Acres*	*% Acres in Category 1,000+ Acres*
Deep South	00.8	06.1	10.4	52.3	18.6	11.9
Border South	00.8	07.8	14.9	64.6	08.9	03.5
Great Lakes	01.1	11.7	23.7	60.5	02.1	00.9
Middle Atlantic	01.1	08.7	24.5	65.1	00.5	00.1
New England	01.3	10.6	24.9	62.2	00.5	00.1

Source: Computations made from U.S. Department of the Interior, *Eighth Census*, vol. 2: *Agriculture*, 221.

Note on method: For panel B, the amount of acres was calculated by using the total farms in the category times the midpoint of the interval of category size (that is, 11.5, 35, 75, 300, and 750). Because no interval existed for the 1,000+ category, I arbitrarily chose 1,500 to multiply times the number of farms in the category. The states in each category are those used in previous tables.

the foundation of the republic and found the cause of the conflict in slaveholding land monopoly: "And, even, in our own times and country, the engrossment of the best portion of the cotton and sugar growing lands in the South by the local class of Slave-holders, gave a character to human bondage in that section which, at the same time feeding the pride and arrogance of that class and offending the dignity of the free laborers of the North, at length, forced the train of civil war between those sections."[14]

Northern observations of the southern economy easily became imbedded in the sectional controversy. When northerners traveled South, especially the Deep South, they saw the extensive landholdings of the planters and equated that with wealth. They may have had more problem in understanding slaves themselves as a facet of wealth, for they had no valid point of comparison at the North. For northerners, wealth meant land, buildings, carriages, and tangible objects, not people; for southerners, accustomed to thinking of slaves as property, ownership of slaves revealed success at worldly endeavors. What northerners probably saw in slaves if not wealth exactly was something very alien: an overwhelming mastery over other men and women. Slaveholders saw wealth when they looked at slaves; northerners saw an ancient mastery reminiscent of civilizations built on force and conquest. Finally, northerners also observed who labored. It could hardly have escaped notice that manual labor was done by slaves.[15]

For northerners looking at the material base of the South, the lessons seemed unmistakable. In the North, labor was the means of advancement; in the South, it was the mark of servility. In the North, independent small agents conducted farming; in the South, a monopolizing planter class controlled the soil. In the North, individuals commanded themselves; in the South, planters commanded others. This was not an accurate picture. But given the way the South presented itself and the statistics of ownership, wealth, and labor, there was enough of a basis to substantiate northern fears. And those fears were that an aristocracy had grown up in the South that monopolized the soil and deprived labor of its reward.

An aristocrat was one who possessed great wealth, controlled other men and women, and escaped a life of labor. Aristocrats obtained their wealth by using their dominant political position to leech away the fruits of labors of commoners, thus reducing commoners to penury and producing a society composed of the few rich and the many poor. This conceptual apparatus about aristocracy and labor was the inheritance of the American Revolution, and over time northerners came to articulate fully its meaning. The Revolution and the society thereafter established was antiaristocratic; all would labor and each would retain the fruits of labor for the family household. The result would be a society of the middle, of independent producers, of near equals in income and wealth.[16]

In the decades after the Revolution, the view that the laborer deserved the fruits of his or her labor became the free labor ideology. The free labor ideology was in the mid-nineteenth-century North a joyous noise praising the capacity of all people to work assiduously when assured of the fruits of their labor, thus generating a society of equals and an economy that grew rapidly and incorporated new ideas and techniques. Because the free worker was guided by incentive—the rewards of labor—he or she applied intelligence and ingenuity to industriousness and thrift. While most started out poor in life, the genius of free labor institutions and the absence of enervating (that is, fruits of labor-stealing) aristocracy allowed people to work for wages initially, save and accumulate property, eventually become an independent producer, and finally an employer of youths starting on their road to maturity. This was the vision of Daniel Webster, Abraham Lincoln, Theodore Parker, and countless other northern spokespeople.[17]

In 1819 the political writer Hezekiah Niles wrote, "Emancipation from political tyranny, without the means of preserving personal liberty, is a nullity.

The gift of life without the means of living, is destitute of value." Northerners increasingly came to realize that their vision of a middling society rested on two assumptions: a vast extent of uninhabited land and high wages. The existence of unoccupied land negated the Malthusian dilemma of an increasing population that pushed down wages. For others, high wages should be the natural result of a free economy. If economic activity was uncoerced and voluntary, labor should be adequately remunerated; wrote the political economist Alonzo Potter, "labour cannot, under a system of freedom be a source of suffering."[18] Yet the United States experienced great labor unrest in the cities between 1830 and 1860; strikes were prominent and alternative schemes of organizing society were promoted. From proslavery writers came a cascade of denunciations of wage labor, declaring it far worse than slave labor, the latter system insuring the worker shelter, food, and raiment. Moreover, throughout Europe the condition of free laborers was disgraceful, and American editors knew it. For this reason, the protectionist evangelical Stephen Colwell proclaimed that the "great social problem is not merely the largest production, nor the freedom of the distribution, but that the laborers shall be enabled to enjoy adequately the fruits of their own industry."[19] Although the path had pitfalls, by 1860 many northerners continued to believe in an equation that stated that a free economy, without distortion from aristocratic devices, naturally produced high wages and ensured the worker of all the fruits of his or her wages.

The free labor analysis of a properly functioning economy set the standards by which many northerners judged the slave economy of the South. First, the slave master was in all respects an aristocrat. Northerners mentioned the dollar amounts involved in slaveholding as frequently as did southerners. "To argue down American slavery," said Abraham Prynne, an abolitionist who debated Tennessee's Parson Brownlow, "I must meet 1200,000,000 of dollars with logic and ethics." In 1856 on the stump, Abraham Lincoln told his audience that slavery was worth $1 billion and "is looked upon by men in the light of dollars and cents." Henry Bennett of New York in the debate over the Nebraska Bill in 1854 declared that the 300,000 slaveholders of the South have more governmental influence "*than any aristocracy of Europe have in theirs,*" and the reason for its power was its being "a great property interest—more than three millions of slaves, covering fifteen States, and worth over $2,000,000,000."[20] A Democratic representative from New Hampshire, Mason W. Tappan, made explicit his belief in a southern aristocracy by another route. "Mr. Chairman, the power wielded by large combinations of capital is well known," he said, and for an example he pointed to the "aristocratic" Second Bank of the United States. But that institution only had a few million dollars; how small its power was when compared to the $2 billion of slave property.[21]

Northerners charged that slaveholders exhibited the single trait of aristocracy: they grew wealthy not by laboring themselves but by usurping the fruits of others' labors. James Wilson of New Hampshire lauded the ability of northern labor to bargain with their employers, but the slaveholder "has no bargains to make, no disagreeable chaffering with a laboring man about prices of labor per day, or week, . . . [and no] consent of the laborer" was asked. John Calhoun once told John Quincy Adams that servitude was not intended for intelligent work, "It was only manual labor—the proper work of slaves." Abolitionists took the meaning of slavery from a quotation of North Carolina Judge Ruffin who said the purpose of slavery was profit for the master: "The [slave] is doomed, in his own person and his posterity, to live without knowledge, and without capacity to make anything his own, and *to toil that others may reap the fruits*." The abolitionist Wendell Phillips responded to the southern cry that northerners attempted to take from them the fruits of their labor: "Calhoun said, when talking on another subject, that nothing was clearer than that what a man dug out of the earth is his. But he had, at the same time, sixty human beings, to whom he denied that right."[22]

Property and power over the labor of other men and women made southern slaveholders an aristocracy, and of course that condition translated into excessive political power. Due to the three-fifths compromise in the Constitution, slaveholders obtained extra representation for themselves, so numerous northerners thought, in Congress. Because of the way the founders constructed the Constitution, the interest of slavery dominated federal legislation. Thus, antislavery northerners loathed the control the "slave power" exerted over the federal government. This belief that slaveholders ran the government solely for the benefit of slavery, thereby leaving the free labor North to get whatever scraps came its way, was of ancient vintage. The idea commenced during Jefferson's administration, swirled around during the Missouri Compromise, was prominent in the Nullification controversy of 1832–33, and became a leading proposition of abolitionists.[23] After the Mexican War, northern use of the phrase "slave power" flooded correspondence and speeches. A correspondent of Senator Benjamin F. Wade wrote that people needed to know that "the degraded negro is not the only class of *slaves* among us; but that the arrogance of the '*Slave power*' tramples ruthlessly upon *all* who presume to fix limits to its dominion." Gideon Welles had grown tired of southern demands by 1846 and argued to Martin Van Buren that northern Democrats had to take a stand as "[e]very thing has taken a southern shape and been controlled by Southern caprice for years." Charles Ray of Chicago was not certain in 1854 that he wanted to back Abraham Lincoln's claims to become a U.S. senator, "But I *do* desire to lend a helping hand to checkmate the rascals who are making our government the convenient tool of the slave power." Moses M. Davis of Wisconsin worried that "The tyrannical Slave power has got possession of the people, and will crush out their liberties before many more years pass by."[24] In 1848 the *National Anti-Slavery Standard* took eight columns of small print to show how southerners had dominated the offices of government: presidents, vice-presidents, cabinet ministers, senators, representatives, speakers of the house, Supreme Court judges, ambassadors, and government clerks.[25] Northerners wanted the government to revert back to the founding principle of promoting freedom, not the interests of slavery. Massachusetts politician Nathaniel P. Banks in 1857 complained that "in our Government, no Legislative enactment—no appropriation of money—no executive vigor is given to any measure until its effect upon the institution [of slavery] has been carefully considered." Throughout the North rang the cry that some 350,000 slaveholders ruled 25 million freemen the way aristocrats ruled peasants.[26]

Analysis of the economic effects of slavery was as prominent as the depiction of slaveholders as aristocratic monopolizers of politics. Indeed, the economics and the politics of slaveholding melded together, for aristocracy implied the robbery of the fruits of labor of commoners. Although northerners knew southerners were rich, they looked upon the southern economy with contempt. Output was small, buildings appeared dilapidated, common people seemed unintelligent and poor, fields required clearing, and everything looked disorganized and slovenly.[27] Northerners blamed the low state of the southern economy on slavery and offered three basic explanations for its miserable performance. First, slavery robbed the worker of incentive. Vermont senator William Upham explained that, unlike the free laborer who obtained all the fruits of his labor, "the slave has no stimulus to industry because he has no hope of bettering his condition. . . . The slave labors from compulsion, and to enrich his master; the freeman voluntarily, and to enrich himself."[28] Incentive spurred the free laborer to devise ways to increase the fruits of his labor; thus he (and she) applied intelligence to production. As the abolitionist C. C. Burleigh explained, "As much as brain and muscle are worth more than muscle only, as much as moral jointed to mental power is a better wealth than mere brute force," then so was free labor better than slavery. Or, as William Kellogg explained in the House of Representatives, "Free labor *thinks, acts, progresses* and *improves.* Slave labor is denied *thought*; it is driven; corrupts and retrogrades."[29] From these two conditions came low productivity for slave labor but high productivity for free labor. Free labor earned high wages because of productivity, but slave labor dragged down a region's, or a nation's, total output. Adam Smith pointed out this productivity gap in 1776 between slave labor and free labor, and in the United States a pamphleteer gave it full numerical expression by 1824. John G. Palfrey, a Massachusetts Free-Soiler, phrased it this way: "It is ruinous economy to give small pay for the grudged and clumsy labor of a slave, instead of giving larger for the cheerful and intelligent labor of a freeman," and "Good labor costs more money; but to pay it, we find to be the only good thrift."[30]

"On a field of open competition, if free labor does not demonstrate its superiority, and win the reluctant and in time the hearty suffrage of its opponents, we are content to take issue on the side of slavery; for we do not believe that economical and moral laws can work otherwise than harmoniously."[31] So wrote James Russell Lowell of the *North American Review*, and so agreed virtually all writers and speakers on the subject: free labor was in all ways a superior economic system to slavery. Yet northerners endlessly repeated that slavery and free soil were "antagonistic systems" that could not live side by side. In the early stages of the debate over slavery's extension into the newly acquired territories, Representative Preston King of New York said that either slave labor could go into the new land, or free labor, but "One or the other it must be; it cannot be both . . . free white labor will not be degraded by such association."[32] As some southerners pointed out, there was a weakness in the northern argument: if free labor was so superior, then why were antislavery people so upset? Would not the superior system win regardless of political activity?

For antislavery groups in the North, free labor was not going to defeat slave labor but was indeed destined to lose. The reason for this unexpected result was not to be found in performance but in the nature of economic competition and the rules that undergirded competition. In a market system, the low-priced commodity won; and in the labor market, slave wages were below free wages.

Northerners had two prominent arguments about the collision of slave labor and free labor in the same market area. The first was that slavery degraded free labor, or, as the *Appeal of the Independent Democrats* said in reaction to Stephen Douglas's Kansas-Nebraska Act of 1854, "Freemen, unless pressed by a hard and cruel necessity, will not, and should not, work besides slaves. Labor cannot be respected where any class of laborers is held in abject bondage." The free laborer was stripped of his "dignity" or was "degraded" when placed beside a slave.[33] The notion of degraded labor seemed at times to indicate that the free laborer lost vital personality traits when placed next to slave laborers—what contemporaries probably called moral abilities. Because certain types of labor was done by slaves, that type of labor became disgraceful, suited only to slaves, and freemen would not do it because it then became a sign of servility instead of independence. In such a view, wages were not necessarily uppermost in the analysis. Indeed, a laborer could be poor, receive little for work done, but still retain independence because of frugality, honesty, and industry. Slavery dragged an economy down because slave labor brought industriousness and perseverance into disrepute; people no longer labored with intensity and intelligence because they refused to be identified with slaves. All manual labor was thus divested of the honors that made people work diligently. With all work in disgrace, people exerted themselves but slightly and thus output faltered; the slave region or nation fell into backwardness and poverty.

George W. Julian, an Indiana Free-Soiler, received a letter from a person who removed to Missouri who exhibited this view of slavery. On the one hand, abolitionists were crazy, for slaves were seldom whipped and "They appear to be the happiest of mortals." But poor white men have no standing; they were "despised by the most pious slaveholder." "I have often thought," he continued, "that the working men, the mechanics and laboring men of the free states, act like fools in their opposition to abolition lecturers, when if these same white working men were in the slave states, they would be despised (unless they owned niggers). Many of them would be placed along side of a big odoriferous buck negro and would receive about as much respect." About the South's economic values, he added: "I never knew a slaveholder permit his son to learn a trade," because they think it disgraceful "to work at mechanical vocations."[34]

But the second interpretation of the incompatibility of slave labor and free labor is more substantial and economically potent. Slave labor was ill-paid labor because the slave master monopolized the rewards of the slave. The wages of the slave were pushed to the lowest level possible to maximize the profits of the slaveholder. In a competitive situation, then, the low wages of the slave become the standard, driving down the high wages of the free worker to that of the slave. Once wages hit the subsistence level, all the attributes of free labor disappeared. At subsistence wages, there was no incentive to work harder, no capacity for savings, no desire to use intelligence to increase output, no productivity—and no social mobility and no society of the middle. For northerners, a direct competition between slave labor and free labor meant the end of northern society and its replacement by the form of southern society: a few aristocratic lords ruling over the poverty-stricken multitude of manual and skilled workers.

Northern antislavery leaders had no illusion about the purpose of slavery: it was to obtain cheap labor. Representative Sidney Dean of Connecticut showed his understanding of the remuneration of slavery in 1858: "No hired pauper of Europe, even though his scanty pittance, can compete with the owners of the human-labor machines in the South. You can restrict his daily allowance to the stand-point of actual necessity. You can compel him under the lash to labor for a number of hours per day, which, if forced upon the paupers of Europe, would revolutionize every nation." An African American minister denounced slavery economically for withholding "from him all the proceeds of his labor, except a scanty subsistence." All the slave obtained for his labor, said William Lloyd Garrison, was "a little meal and a few herrings." More commonly, antislavery advocates said slaveholders did not remunerate labor: they compel "them to labor without compensation," said the *Prairieview (Wisconsin) American Freeman*, or, as Charles Sumner emphasized, slavery sought "*to compel labor without wages.*" George M. Weston, a Democratic Maine editor, made his position known in the title to a pamphlet he published: *Southern Slavery Reduces Northern Wages.*[35]

Frequently northerners made transparent their fears about placing slave labor and free labor in one market. When the two types of labor competed for jobs, the low wage laborer would win, and inevitably that would be the slave laborer. Frederick Law Olmsted produced a trenchant economic analysis of the situation in his famous work, *The Cotton Kingdom.* Free whites could not live in competition with slave labor because "the holder of slave-labour controls the local market for labour [hence, the slaveholder is a monopolist], and the cost of slave-labour fixes the cost of everything which is produced by slave-labour." Historians of the South have time after time depicted a growing hostility among southern white artisans toward the introduction of slave labor into their trades. In fact, artisanal complaints about competition with slave labor started in the seventeenth century.[36] Frederick Douglass, the ex-slave abolitionist orator and editor, showed in his autobiography how the rules of competition subjected the free worker to misery when brought into contact with slave labor. After dwelling on how slavery was a robbery of his earnings, Douglass remarked that "the white laboring man was robbed by the slave system of the just results of his labor, because he was flung into competition with a class of laborers who worked without wages." That fear of competition between free and slave labor suffuses the literature of antislavery northern politicians about slavery's expansion into the territories. Cassius M. Clay, Kentucky's courageous abolitionist, put the matter squarely at the feet of the competitive system as early as 1843: "It is an evil to the free laborer, by forcing him by the laws of competition, supply and demand, to work for the wages of the slave—food and shelter."[37] When the Kansas-Nebraska Act was under debate in Congress, the editor of the *Lebanon (Pennsylvania) Courier* objected to the legislation because "Slavery brings slave labor into competition with free labor, most evidently; and free whites cannot exist, side by side, with the labor of slaves. One or the other must give up."[38]

Nor were Republicans or other antislavery northern groups willing to confine the analysis strictly to the territories, which were simply the first obvious manifestation of a dreaded collision between the slave laborer and the free laborer. The proprietor of the *Springfield Daily Illinois State Journal*, battling Stephen A. Douglas's doctrine of popular sovereignty, said that the Republican policy "is emphatically opposed to southern slaves being brought in competition with free white laborers every where." No chance for slavery's extension was to be allowed; "the Republican party seeks to dignify and exalt the honest laborer for his daily bread[;] the entire struggle of the Democracy now is to put a curse upon free labor, by placing it alongside of the labor of slaves, and reduce it at last to a species of serfdom."[39] John Wentworth of the *Chicago Daily Democrat* generalized the battle between free and slave labor in 1848. Slave labor limited the field and lessened the demand for free labor and reduced "its wages." Like many others, Wentworth said the question "is between Free Labor and the Slaveholding Capitalist; and he who mystifies this question, so as to represent that the issue is between the white and black races, instead of Free Labor and the Slaveholding Oligarchy, has too little information . . . to attempt its discussion."[40]

Some of this appeal to people engaged in manual labor to fear the economic consequences of an expanding slave system came out in numerous newspaper articles about slave mechanics, strikes of white laborers against slave operatives in the South, or inflammatory pronouncements by southern leaders. "Negroes as Master Mechanics" was the column of one issue the *National Anti-Slavery Standard*, while the *Rochester Advertiser* in 1848 had a blurb, "MECHANICS FOR SALE." During the election of 1860, editors and spokesmen used an 1856 speech of Herschel V. Johnson of Georgia, who was Douglas's running mate, in which Johnson declared under certain conditions that "Capital should own Labor." And Republicans obtained much support for their insistence that they sought the welfare of manual laborers when South Carolina senator James H. Hammond in 1858 declared that labor was nothing but a "mudsill," leading Republican papers to write columns about "Labouring Men but Mud Sills" and "White Workingmen no better than Slaves."[41]

The northern dread of having free labor compete with slave labor in the same vicinity was not a phantom conjured up by unusually active northern imaginations. Dislike of competition with slave labor had been recorded since colonial days and had been responsible for keeping immigrants from streaming into the South. Moreover, the Great Lakes states housed many people who came from the slave states fleeing the peculiar institution—and specifically for economic, not moral, reasons.[42] But the dread of the consequences of competition came from no less a source than the great proslavery spokesman and states' rights fanatic, John C. Calhoun. Calhoun had commenced his congressional career as a national statesman during the War of 1812 but by the mid-1820s retreated to states' rights due to fears that slavery's viability could be threatened by a powerful central government. As the push for protection mounted between 1824 and 1828, Calhoun's restless mind focused on the heart of the dilemma. Writing in August 1828 to John McLean, he stated, while all the time denouncing an ongoing protectionist agitation, that slaves were made for raising tropical staples and should not be allowed to be used in manufacturing. The reason was simple. "Can we conceive a more dangerous political condition, than for free and slave labour to come into competition[?] . . . Do you think, that the free laborers, the voters of the North, would permit bread to be taken out the mouths of their wives and children, by the slaves of the South?" Calhoun then repeated this fear in his famous South Carolina "Exposition and Protest" against the tariff of abominations. But the point was clear: pitting free labor and slave labor against one another was asking for social and political upheaval. And Calhoun was not here disturbed by the possible reaction of the northern wealthy and capitalists; he was fearing the potential reaction of the common man in the North who earned wages.[43]

The antislavery argument that a reduction in American wages by unfair competition—here, by slaves—had a pedigree. Indeed, the basic structure of the argument had existed for years in debates over tariff legislation. A pauper labor theory emerged in the 1820s that pitted the free American worker against the aristocratically controlled European worker. European aristocrats by taxes on labor, laws favoring themselves, and monopolization of political power artificially reduced wages. That was a basic unfairness. Trade between equals, who lived under laws giving to the laborer the fruits of labor, was fine; but trade between peoples who had different competitive rules meant disaster for one side. These ideas formed an argument for protection, for prohibiting trade with nations that artificially depressed wages out of the fear that such trade would lower wages in North America, and thereby bring about disastrous social and political tumult.[44]

Since the 1820s protectionists had based their advocacy of high tariffs on the necessity of maintaining sufficiently high wages to enable the bulk of the American population to save and then to obtain property and thereby to become, over time, independent producers. Low wages destroyed northern social mobility. In countless speeches protectionists hammered away at the need of a republic with high wages; the threat they conjured up to the American public was the free American worker competing against the degraded pauper laborer of Europe, degraded because aristocrats had ground those workers down to subsistence—an unfair competition because of the monopoly power of the aristocrat. The economic disparagement of free trade because of its effects on American free workers was structurally identical to the antislavery analysis of free laborers competing against slave laborers. In a protectionist speech in 1824, well before the developed abolitionist movement beginning in the 1830s, New York's Henry C. Martindale gave this depiction of the battle between American workers and European workers: "The foreign tyrant, who compels his slaves to work for nothing, and to go naked and hungry, could not wish more subtle and sophisticated advocates than those who urge this [free trade] doctrine here. . . . The price of living is the price of labor; and, inasmuch as freemen will live better than slaves, and therefore consume more than slaves, in just so much will their labor cost more than slaves, as between them and their employments; in just so much will their condition approach the condition of their employers, and in just so much will they divide the profits of the business with the employer." He then launched into a fear of American free labor competing against European pauper labor. Simply remove the word "foreign tyrant" and replace it with "slave master" and the antislavery analysis of bondage emerges. By the 1840s and 1850s, northerners had been inundated with the question of high wages and unfair labor competition. All that was required was to make the obvious leap of imagination: slaves were like pauper laborers because slave masters were like aristocrats who drove down the wages of labor. Protectionists, who usually shied away from radical antislavery, had prepared the public for the economic argument of the antislavery coalition.[45]

Northern fears and southern attitudes about free and slave labor can be displayed in three simple graphs. Figure 3.1, panel A, offers the standard economic

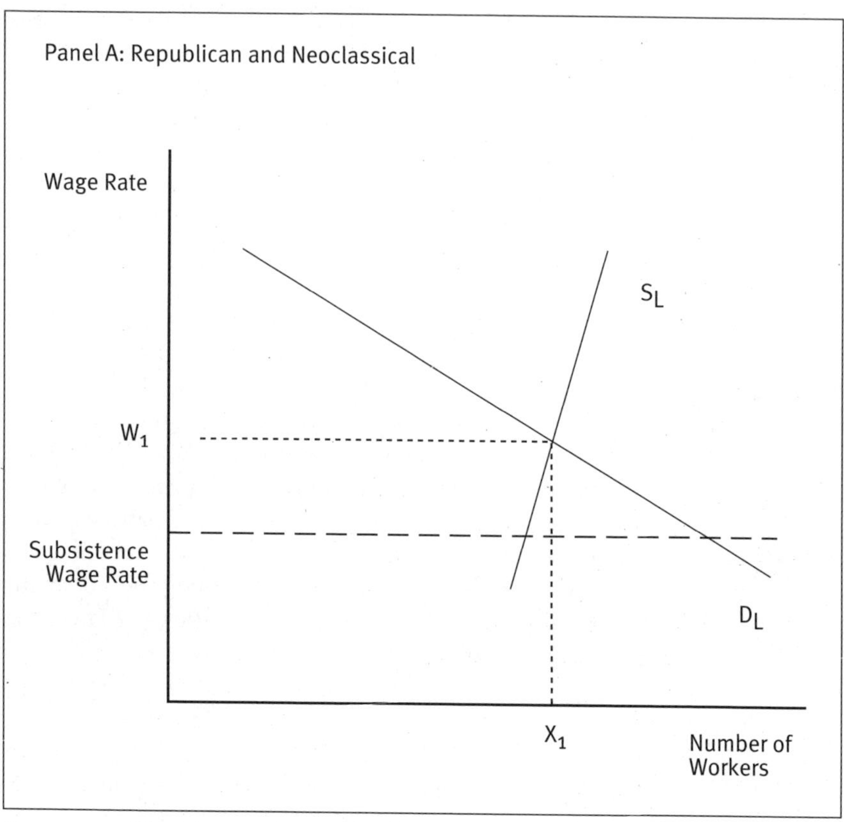

FIGURE 3.1. *Wage Determination by Proslavery, Free Labor, and Subsistence Labor Theories*

explanation of the determination of wages. The demand curve D_L stands for demand for labor by employers and curves down and to the right. When the price of labor (its wage) is high (the ordinate or y axis), few workers will be hired (the abscissa or x axis, indicating the number of workers). The supply of workers, S_L, which is a schedule according to microeconomic theory of individuals who are willing to work, indicates that when wages are low, few individuals will work at that wage. As the wage increases, more individuals offer their labor services. Thus we have the operation of supply and demand. Equilibrium is achieved at the intersection of D_L and S_L, where the demand for labor equals the supply of labor, and X_1 number of workers will be employed at a wage rate of W_1. This is the free market, competitive depiction of wage rate determination. Under certain conditions, namely a restricted number of workers relative to a growing demand for workers, wages will rise—basically the Republican position of the 1850s—to which must be added their belief that education and

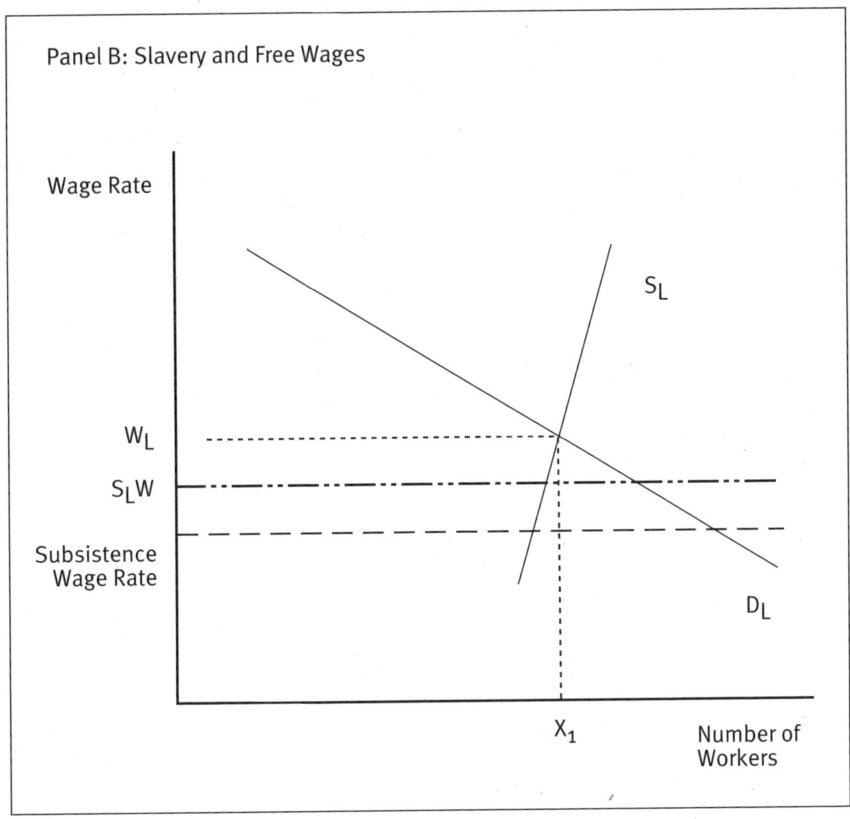

productivity will in fact constantly augment the demand for labor (or, in graphical terms, D_L shifts to the right faster than S_L shifts to the right).

Slavery's main economic function is to depress the wage for labor. In a free market, planters (or slave masters generally) could not obtain a labor force by consent or voluntary agreement. That is to say, given the opportunities that the economy afforded, workers had the option of doing other things or working at different pursuits than those offered by planters. To attract workers, planters would have had to bid up the price of labor so high as to make cotton planting, for example, unprofitable. The only way around the planter's dilemma of an inadequate labor supply by free consent—if the planter was bent on continuing production of the staple—was to enslave workers. Thus the reason for slavery was simply to depress wages: to force individuals to work at a wage rate (in this case, the amount for food, shelter, clothing, and any other amenities that planters provided) that would make planting profitable, regardless of the other opportunities workers had in the economy. In panel B, the slave wage rate, S_LW, is given as a horizontal line at the planter's chosen wage rate, the one the

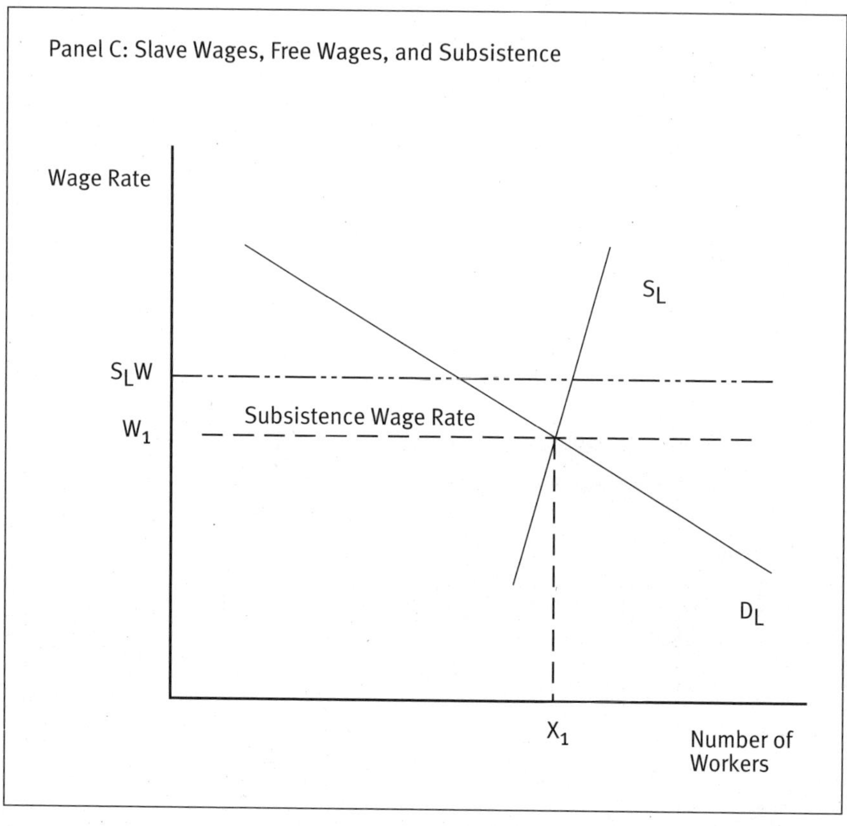

planter sets. Supply and demand are not the determinants of wages; only the master's discretion is.

The point of antislavery leaders was that S_LW is, of course, below the equilibrium point of S_L and D_L in panel B of Figure 3.1. The market wage rate should be W_1 but is suppressed to S_LW, because that is the only way planters can secure a labor force to make planting profitable. The masters obtained the power to suppress wages by the establishment of laws that permitted property rights in Africans. It was property rights in Africans that made the master a monopolist over labor and gave him the capacity to appropriate the earnings of his slaves. Panel B in Figure 3.1 thus also depicts the economic oppression of slavery, for the antislavery or Republican charge was that slavery's economic oppression for the slave was the difference between the wage levels S_LW and W_1; that difference went to the slave master instead of the slave (in nineteenth-century terms, "the fruits of labor" taken by the master instead of being awarded to the worker).

Any other reading of the situation made no sense. For the slave master to have offered higher wages to slaves than could be obtained by the free market wage was a bizarre proposition. Why would one pay more for labor than one had to? If the wage of slaves equaled the wage of a free worker or were higher, there was no economic justification for slavery. It indeed became an irrational institution. In discussions about free and slave labor that occurred in the antebellum period, panel B of Figure 3.1 has to be kept in mind. For the Republican or general antislavery perspective was that, *of course*, free labor wages were higher than slave wages; by economic logic they had to be. And when northerners talked of emancipation, they ultimately were saying that blacks would improve economically because they would be recovering the part of their wages lost due to the oppression of slavery.

When free labor and slave labor were brought together to compete for the same occupations, then what happened to the wage rate? Because the slave master set the wage rate, and until the number of slaves was exhausted, the actual rate of wages was the slave's wage. To obtain employment in a competitive economy that included slave labor, free labor would have to accept the effective wage rate of slaves. If the wages of free people came down to those of slaves, then social mobility, property ownership, middling economic activity, and intelligent labor would all disappear.

In this presentation, however, there is one qualification. It has been noted by several economic historians that southern wages for free workers were actually high instead of low.[46] The reason for this aberration is that slave masters in the practice of "hiring out" slaves to employers acted as agents for their slave labor, seeking for their labor the highest possible wage. On all occasions, the slaveholder set the wage of the slave. But the effect of slavery upon the labor market depended on who owned the slave. If the employer-entrepreneur did not own the slaves, then essentially a free market for labor existed. But if the employer-entrepreneur did own the slaves, he or she controlled the labor market and depressed wages.

This analysis can additionally explain the position of southern proslavery writers. Proslavery advocates were the greatest exponents of classical economy in the nation. And classical economics meant specifically the analysis and predictions of David Ricardo and Thomas Malthus concerning population and rent. Due to population pressure and the finite amount of arable land, wages would drift to brute subsistence—enough to sustain physical existence and the propagation of the species and nothing else. Demand for labor reached a limit due to the doctrine of rent; but population kept advancing due to the lusts of the lower class, and so while the demand for labor remained constant, the supply of labor kept increasing and pushing down wages. Eventually one obtained a wage rate of W_1 in panel C of Figure 3.1—the wage rate of subsistence. For proslavery writers, this was the wage rate to which free competitive economics inexorably moved. One may call it the Fitzhughian wage rate. And the opinion of Fitzhugh was that slavery was inefficient compared with free labor because slavery offered workers a wage above subsistence and insured a level of comfort for workers that free markets could not.

Panel C also explains a host of writing on the fate of slavery. Despite the proslavery argument of Fitzhugh, countless southerners announced that slavery would end when population pressures mounted sufficiently so that the wage of free labor was less than the effective wage rate of slaves. For most southerners, panel C illustrated the conditions that would lead to emancipation in the South.[47]

These three panels in essence map out the positions of the major participants in the sectional controversy. Panel A, the optimistic view of labor relations, saw wages rising over time due to increased demand for labor from productivity, intelligence, and growth of capital stock. Panel B represents the fear of northern statesmen that the wage rate of slavery would dominate the wage rate of free labor. Panel C exhibits the thinking of the proslavery school: slaves were treated better in the long run than workers under free markets.

Thus the economic fears of northern antislavery groups centered about a dread of the consequences of a competition between free and slave laborers. Yet for decades northerners understood the mechanics of that competition, had been opposed to it, but had not pressed for a political or economic resolution. Suddenly in the 1840s and 1850s, though, the topic acquired an urgency that it had not before possessed. Two conditions generated the sense of foreboding that pushed the North into political activity. The first condition resulted from Manifest Destiny, the acquisition of new territories due to the Mexican War. Out of that war came a number of northern frustrations that resulted in a demand that the new territories be preserved for free labor by placing a ban on slave labor. But the deeper condition arose from the economic process of market integration across the nation that commenced in the 1830s and accelerated in the late 1840s. The market revolution was responsible for this suddenly heightened awareness and dread of bringing slave and free labor into direct competition. The continuous antislavery cry that the United States had to become either a free labor nation or a slave labor nation only makes sense in the setting of a national market.

Until the 1830s the United States was largely divided into local trading areas with a few transatlantic markets. Areas along the Atlantic coast and locations on or next to navigable rivers were able to create market economies—that is, an aggregation of suppliers and consumers who experienced roughly similar prices. The obvious areas of commercial activity—a synonym for market activity—were New York City, Philadelphia, and Boston; various communities along the Hudson, Delaware, and Connecticut Rivers; and the plantation, tidewater South, which by virtue of its many navigable rivers started off North American life as transatlantic commercial entities. But for the rest of the nation, economic life was circumscribed by geography. The only mode of transportation for most inland communities was overland wagon travel, and overland wagon travel added so much cost to a product that it was nearly impossible to conduct trade.

Prior to 1830 the labor market effects of slavery were limited geographically.[48] Within a local slave area, the hiring-out of slaves to employments besides those of raising staple crops should have depressed wages, so long as within these communities there were free laborers seeking a livelihood in the same occupations. Avoiding the competition of slave labor in this situation was relatively easy: migrate out of the community. Because the effect of slavery on the labor market was local, one could with some ease escape the effects of slavery. The transportation revolution changed this equation dramatically.

Between 1830 and 1850, state governments and entrepreneurs added 10,000 miles of railroad track and 4,500 miles of canals. At the same time, the steamboat by midcentury made the Mississippi River the major artery of internal commerce for the nation.[49] Then in the late 1840s, almost coincident with the end of the Mexican War, a boom in railroad construction resounded across the United States, North and South. By 1860 the nation had 30,000 miles of track in operation, and though there were significant gaps and problems in connecting all points frictionlessly to one another, the backbone of a national transportation system was in place.[50] These developments created the skeleton of a national market and modified significantly the local nature of American society and its economy (incidentally, a far more "centralizing" force than any proposal by any political party in the nineteenth century). How the transportation revolution remolded the economy of the United States needs a precise understanding: it broke down the price barriers that separated local economies. By lowering the price of transportation so enormously, individuals from a locality at a huge distance from another locality could nonetheless *compete* in the *distant* locality's *market.*

The application of this economic change to the sectional controversy over slavery is obvious. The effects of slavery on the labor market could no longer be confined to small geographical areas in the South. It had the potential of affecting the national labor market. The means of affecting the national labor market was by employing southern slaves in the same occupations as northern workers. Products made by slave labor then competed against products made by free labor—and the cost advantage would be to the southern producer on the basis of the wages paid to slaves. Free labor wages would be forced by competition to the level of slave wages, because ultimately in a competitive system the low-price producer wins.

Northerners were reacting to the new market realities. The first place the competition between free labor and slave labor would take place would be in the territories. So the advocates of free labor felt the pressure to stop slavery's expansion. But in a real sense, northerners were also arguing for the welfare of their existing free states, not simply the territories. The transportation revolution had produced a new danger to the stability and longevity of northern society. Regardless of the fate of the territories, northerners had to fear the economic effects of slavery in the states where the institution did not exist. The national market insured that economic effects of slavery could no longer be isolated to the South.

Contemporaries did not expect the improvements in transportation to work this way. Wrote a thoughtful contributor to the *Southern Literary Messenger*, "The confident hopes entertained by many, that the agencies of steam and the railway would so knit together the Union in commercial interest, as to render all chance of separation an impossibility, appears to be doomed to disappointment. . . . Indeed, the railway, and its winged sister, the telegraphy *politically* considered, seem to have been instrumental only in bringing the opposing views of the sections into more concentrated action."[51]

The transportation revolution heightened sectional tensions in two specific ways. First, it let more northerners than ever witness slavery in operation; the experience of seeing such a blatantly coercive society did nothing to enhance the reputation of southerners as part of an empire of freedom. In addition, thoughtful northerners, as they witnessed the reshuffling of northern society due to increased competition stemming from the market revolution, could only project what would ultimately happen when southern slavery was brought within the embrace of a national market. No one captured the role the transportation revolution played in bringing about sectional hostility more than William Henry Seward, antislavery senator from New York and until 1860 the most prominent Republican in the nation. In 1858, Seward announced his famous "irrepressible conflict" thesis that an inevitable conflict existed between northern and southern labor. Generations of historians have interpreted Seward's pronouncement as an incitement to armed conflict that heightened the boiling sectionalism in the country and magnified southern fears of a Republican Party capture of the federal government. Seward's reasoning has not been as exactingly dissected. In the paragraph before he uttered the fateful phrase of "irrepressible conflict," he pointed to transportation improvement as the agent that brought the clash to a political precipice:

> Hitherto, the two systems have existed in different states, but side by side within the American Union. This has happened because the Union is a confederation of states. But in another aspect the United States constitute only one nation. Increase of population, which is filling the states out to their very borders, together with a new and extended net-work of railroads and other avenues, and an internal commerce which daily becomes more intimate, is rapidly bringing the states into a higher and more perfect social unity or consolidation. Thus, these antagonistic systems are continually coming into closer contact, and collision results.
>
> Shall I tell you what this collision means? It is an irrepressible conflict between opposing and enduring forces, and it means that the United States must and will,

sooner or later, become either entirely a slaveholding nation, or entirely a free-labor nation.[52]

A second observation on the effects of the transportation revolution in connection with the slavery controversy needs to be made. Northern fears about competing against slave labor meant that northerners felt that their society was under attack from southern slaveholders. And, indeed, the mechanics of competition work in that direction. The market revolution in its national effects was not going to change one feature of southern economic, social, or political life. Southerners were facing no invasion of northern practices or customs via market economics; all the economic practices and customs of the North were already present in the South—property rights, legal procedures, free white labor, a general laissez-faire creed, small government, and so on. The market revolution did not threaten the South with alien northern business practices.

The reverse was not true: the market revolution was allowing slavery to affect northern economic practices and customs. Southerners had an institution that northerners did not, slavery, and its effects were no longer circumscribed by the high cost of inland transportation. Northerners were faced in a real sense with adaptation to slavery. Slavery might not have actually gone northward—that is, northerners actually owning slaves—but its economic effects in a national market economy could not be stopped at the Mason-Dixon line. A continued Union between North and South in a national market system meant the North was going to have to adapt to the influence of slave labor in the labor markets. In a sense, this was the invasion of the North by the slave power that politically rocked the North.[53] And the source of aggression that made northerners dread a competition between free and slave labor was the southern doctrine of property rights in Africans.

Northerners like William H. Seward had no difficulty in declaring that slavery and freedom were radically antagonistic, that either slavery or free labor was destined to triumph.[54] Northern antislavery advocates also claimed that free labor produced a healthier society, an intelligent and well-rewarded work force, an equitable distribution of wealth, an egalitarian society lacking an elite, and a participatory form of government. But in the competition between free labor and slave labor systems, which system would actually prevail? Just because free labor produced healthier social and political results and, in the long run, better economic results was not reason to believe that in the short run free labor would triumph. In point of fact, most Republicans believed that slave labor would win the contest. George Weston realized this. He admitted that "It is certainly true that wealth is more rapidly augmented under free, than under slave systems, and that, in a large sense, free labor is cheaper [due to productivity] than slave labor." Yet in direct competition, the better system would not win. "But although exhausting and impoverishing in all its results and all its influences, it [slavery] is irresistibly and unmistakably cheaper, when applied to the ruder processes of agriculture, than free labor, which it overpowers and reduces to its own level."[55] Slave labor was cheap labor; and the rule of competition was that the inexpensive won over the expensive. Slave labor was going to win the contest unless some provision was made to restrict its influence. In the new national market, restricting the economic effects of slaveholding would require not only ingenuity but considerable institutional reshuffling.

The source of the trouble was clear: it lay entirely with the laws in the South that allowed whites to have property rights in Africans, for it was that foundation that gave rise to inequalities in labor market competition. Slavery was a monopoly over a person's labor. That monopoly condition arose because slave masters had property rights in slaves. Thus the wage of labor was suppressed below its natural level (or market determination) because of the legality of defining some people as property. A competition between free labor and slave labor was unfair and unjust because one side had been unnaturally repressed. And this was a necessary economic by-product of the different regimes of property rights; it created unfair advantages that the marketplace inevitably magnified. At times, this struggle between southern capital and northern labor was captured in words. Wrote the conservative editor of the *Ohio State Journal* in 1854, "The issue is now fairly joined between the North and South, between SLAVERY and FREEDOM, between *Representation based on property in Slaves* and the *Free Voters and Free Laborers of the Land!*"[56]

Southerners and northern Democrats were miffed by these long-winded jeremiads concerning the competition of free and slave labor. Slave labor, according to southerners, was the fate of Africans, not whites. The necessity of enslaving Africans arose from their biological ability to work in a tropical climate, which, according to southern proslavery writers, Caucasians could not. As one correspondent to Indiana Democrat William H. English argued, in Kansas whites could outwork slaves "and hence the public can dispense with Slave labor there without detriment." But in the tropics, whites die and cannot work, "where the Negro *can* work, and *revel in health* and joyousness, *but he won't*, unless he has a *master*." The climatic explanation of slavery satisfied many northerners.[57]

Proslavery southerners also quickly pointed out that a dual system of labor operated in the South, one that kept free labor and slave labor separate. Slaves worked at tropical agricultural staples; whites did other work. Thus the occupations of free and slave labor were separate and so there were two distinct markets for labor. As Georgia Representative Alfred H. Colquitt explained in 1854, "where labor is exercised in small combinations, and where greater economy and skill are required than is usually attained by slaves, there free labor, as it is termed, may be found most profitable. The line of separation is natural and well-marked." By 1847 Calhoun convinced himself that no invidious competition plagued free and slave labor. After suffering a bout of Wilmot Provisoism in the Senate, he asked a Charleston meeting why the North acts against the extension of slavery, for there was no antagonism: "The labor of our slaves does not conflict with the profit of their capitalists, or the wages of their operatives, or in any way injuriously affect the prosperity of those States." Although the southern response to the northern charge of unfair labor competition was surprisingly tepid and uninspired, southerners, when they replied to such charges, denied that slave labor degraded free labor.[58]

Were the fears of northerners rational or not? As long as slaves continued to work in the staple fields of the South, the collision between free and slave labor was not likely to occur directly. By the 1850s, however, agriculture was not the only pursuit of the slave population. Slave masters had hired out slaves in a variety of occupations, including manufacturing and transportation. Some 200,000 slaves found employment in nonagricultural activities. A scenario was developing that probably would have pitted slave labor directly against free labor.[59]

Slavery's source of strength lay in the production of cotton, by which the institution became profitable for slaveholders. Gavin Wright argues, probably correctly, that the height of world cotton demand came in the mid-1860s. After that, world demand for cotton rose at a much less spectacular rate.[60] Given that the rate of demand for cotton began to lessen, it is reasonable to assume that the profitability of slavery would decline—perhaps not enough to kill the institution but sufficient to make it less attractive. As the profits generated by the institution began to fall, the net value of slaves—that is, the wealth of slaveholders—would also begin to drop. In short, southern planters faced the prospect, if the Civil War had not intervened, of lessened profitability from slavery and a drop of some magnitude in their wealth holdings.

Under those conditions, it would seem likely that planters would scramble either to unload their failing assets or shift them into alternative employments. Southern planters could afford to be anti-industrial when their annual rate of return from slaveholding during the glory days of King Cotton ranged between 8 and 12 percent. But a significant drop in that return would have led a substantial number to seek alternatives for their slaves. Planters may have been wedded to the land, to a prebourgeois viewpoint, to a paternalism, and to anti-industrialism in the 1850s. They could afford to be all those things in the 1850s. But most of all they were married to their wealth. And when that wealth began to deteriorate, they would undoubtedly have taken steps to preserve it. Those steps would have been selling slaves or renting them to industrial enterprises.

An extensive literature claims that industrialists could not have employed slave labor profitably in industrial enterprises, that free labor was both cheaper and more productive. Slaves were too expensive a capital investment for manufacturing, slaves had no incentive to be industrious as did free labor, slaves were incapable of learning the necessary skills for tending machines, and slaves aggregated into factories would represent a frightening revolutionary class.[61] Some of these claims may have validity in the early stages of industrialization, but they have less potency in a matured industrial economy. These analyses do not look carefully at the economic trends that unfolded in the United States after 1880. The obvious trends were mass production in large hierarchical business units; machinery to replace skilled labor; unskilled, virtually brute, labor to tend the machines; a bureaucracy to oversee the system; and an internal police to keep laborers from organizing.[62] What in this scenario offers an argument against the use of slave labor? Does not it instead look like the manufacturing processes in the United States moved exactly in the direction in which slave labor could be employed in manufacturing?[63] Had it not been for emancipation, the use of slave labor in southern manufacturing would have become a very real possibility after the 1870s and 1880s. If such had actually happened, then free labor and slave labor would have directly competed by producing the same product in a *national* market. If such a course of events had ever come to pass, it is not inconceivable to think that around 1890 or 1900 the North would have seceded from the Union to protect its economy from slave labor domination.

This was not exactly the circumstance that northern workers feared or the analysis they used. Egged on by Democratic orators, workers expressed more often a fear that emancipation would release hordes of ex-slaves out of the South to clog up northern labor markets and drive down wages.[64] The analytical apparatus of abolitionists and antiextensionists was also not exactly to working-class liking. Competition had reduced free wages in the North badly in the 1840s and 1850s, and most workingmen expressed disgust at the treatment of labor as a commodity in a marketplace. For this reason, workers at times found the antimarket statements of various proslavery writers to their liking because proslavery advocates tended to upbraid northern factory owners for their dismal treatment of operatives.[65]

Northern workers, regardless of their animus to the antislavery movement and misgivings about the Republican-Whig wing of northern politics, could not ignore the potential effects slavery could have on their material well-being.[66] Fears of a freed black population moving to the North was an argument that perhaps had some political strength with workers. But the national market could accomplish the same effect by letting slaves remain in the South. For workers, there was no escape from the dilemma. The national market made inevitable a competition between free and slave labor.

In the ad infinitum exhortations about the glory of labor and laborers from antislavery northerners, a vital matter of interpretation has emerged. What did the antislavery contingent mean by the phrase "free labor"? What workers were they pointing to, and, perhaps more significantly, what system of work were they lauding? These questions have become a bone of contention because it is involved with the passage of the United States from a precapitalist economy to a capitalist one. Defining capitalism has always been a terror among scholars, but the current approach centers on the emergence of "wage labor" as the key.[67] Currently, wage labor in capitalism is taken to mean the propertyless worker who is "free" to make contracts with the employer of his or her choice, free of coercion by person, company, or government. The wage worker is thus a "free worker" or an example of a "free laborer." However, the implication is that this freedom is materially worthless, for without property the free worker has only the choice of employment at subsistence wages or starvation. Thus the slave, who is guaranteed income in the form of housing, clothes, and food, is actually better off than the free worker who is guaranteed nothing and who can only obtain enough money to hold together life and limb. Normally, the abolitionists bear the brunt of being the torchbearers for wage labor (that is, subsistence wage labor), but the Republicans are usually included by a form of guilt by association—antislavery people who were not at the same time willing to end the market system in labor were all guilty of justifying the human misery of industrial capitalism.[68]

Nothing is easy in history when it comes to cosmic interpretations, and this case is no different, but parts of it may be resolved. Although the concept of subsistence wages, in the classical sense meaning the absolute lowest that wages can sink before life is lost, is no longer seen as necessary to the analysis of capitalism by neoclassical economists or Marxist theorists, it still has surprising power in the historical literature that describes nineteenth-century American economic conditions. To sidestep various intellectual land mines on this matter, wage labor may be taken to mean a low recompense for workers, if not actual starvation wages.[69] It is demonstrable that neither abolitionists nor antislavery politicians ever argued for such wages; they always insisted that the United States be a high-wage economy so that social mobility and property ownership be the hallmark of the vast majority of its citizens.[70] Besides subsistence wages and high wages as categories of free labor, we also have to deal with the proposition, crucial it appears, in deciding whether labor was precapitalist or capitalist—whether the "laborer" owned property, for it is the lack of property that defines the subsistence-wage laborer.

The assertion that the rise of the free labor ideology was an attempt to justify industrialism's desire for propertyless, and thereby powerless, workers ("free laborers") builds on the viewpoint that the ideal of freedom arose from the analysis of slavery and the coercion involved. To remove that coercion was tantamount to creating a free laborer. However, slavery was not the foundation for northern understanding of "freedom" either in the antebellum era or any earlier period. The basic referent for American freedom was European history, in particular its past and present practices of aristocracy and serfdom as well as Europe's record with slavery in ancient Rome and Greece. Freedom for the Americans in its broadest form meant individualism without restraint from outside sources except for community laws—the latter being a concession to the need for civilization. Northerners constantly referred to serfdom as a form of slavery; they expressed opinions about the hierarchy of Europe and how it impinged on natural liberties. In short, Americans did not need southern slavery to teach them the meaning of freedom, of external restraint imposed by force on the individual: all they had to do was look at monarchical and aristocratic Europe—England, France, Prussia, Italy, and Russia. And they did.[71]

In the case of the 1840s and 1850s, antislavery advocates indicated with little obfuscation that their "free labor" was people who worked with their hands and who accumulated property. The "wage" was simply a generic term meaning reward, the fruits of labor. Cydnor B. Tompkins of Ohio said in Congress in 1858 that slavery deprived white labor of its reward: "It builds up no middle class of intelligent farmers, artisans, and mechanics, who constitute the real wealth [of the free states.]" In this particular session of Congress, northerners flailed away at the "mudsill" speech of James H. Hammond, and Daniel Clark of New Hampshire, besides denying Hammond's depictions of the desperation of factory workers, defined free laborers as "the men who cultivate their farms; they are the men who work in mechanic shops; they are the men who are at the various trades; they are the men and women in the mills who are called operatives." In 1854 E. W. Farley of Maine defined the "great working classes of the North" as "the men who cultivate our lands, build our ships, construct our railroads," and work in industry. John Wentworth started a Free-Soil speech by defining the "free labor democracy" as farmers, mechanics, and operatives.[72]

Of key importance is the emphasis that antislavery leaders, especially Republicans, placed on landownership and the existence of small, independent farms. This should come as no surprise given the statistics of farming for the North; northerners virtually had no large farms, and the debate from 1846 to 1860 was over slavery in the territories. To say that northerners argued that the territories had to be preserved for subsistence wage factory workers is ludicrous. If slaveholders went West, said Bishop Perkins of New York in 1854, they would monopolize the land "so that a man cannot work his own little farm for himself." In 1847 a New York Barnburner meeting passed a resolution stating "That we respect the dignity of labor and in the name of the farmer, mechanic, and laborer, we protest against its degradation." In Wisconsin, a movement against land monopoly was thriving, and a resolution of the Free-Soil Democracy in 1850 claimed that "every man should inherit a portion of the earth," that it was an inalienable right of "man," and that "as a party, we believe it to be the duty of every man to labor for the independence of himself and his race." One could hardly have a more emphatic belief in the benefit of a yeoman farming republic that the Free-Soil declaration in Chester County, Wisconsin, that slavery was to be forbidden entry into the west as that "almost boundless region shall become the happy home of millions of independent and intelligent free laborers." Many others were explicit: free laborers were yeomen farmers. After the Civil War, Henry Wilson, senator from Massachusetts and somewhat a Radical Republican, gave a speech at Bangor, Maine, where he made the equation between free laborers and yeoman farmers absolutely unmistakable: "This demand of land for the landless, of small farms tilled by men standing on their own acres, was made in the interests of freedom, culture, development, and Christian civilization. It was the idea of the farm against the plantation—of free labor against slave labor—of the perennial verdure of liberty against the blight and mildew of slavery."[73]

The Democrat political economist Theodore Sedgwick analyzed slavery in the 1830s and decided that in the abstract "Slavery is the natural enemy of every man who performs manual labour, of every working-man in the United States, whether he lives in a slave, or a free state." That sentiment should not be terribly difficult to understand. Its applicability to the free labor argument of the antislavery politicians in the 1840s and 1850s resides in the crude state of the American economy, not its sophistication; hard manual labor was the lot of the vast majority of people, property-holding or not. Most northerners could identify with the act of labor and have an unease about a potential competition with slave labor. James Garfield may have been closer to the truth than many historians like to think, although one can never discount useful exaggeration for politicians seeking election. In a speech dedicating a monument to Joshua Giddings in 1870, Garfield rhetorically asked, where antislavery came from? "It did not [come from] the high places of political or ecclesiastical power. It sprang up among the common people who lived remote from the centres of power and influence,—people who ate their bread in the sweat of their faces."[74]

The free labor argument was not about subsistence wages or emerging industrialism; it was about maintaining the social middle of northern American village life.

4

The Antislavery Debate over Property Rights

Slavery elicited arguments that touched a host of exciting and stimulating topics. Involved in the attack and defense of the institution were the subjects of Christianity, humanitarianism, natural rights, race, the fate of labor, control of politics, and the nature of democratic government. Missing from the scholarly treatment of either the proslavery defense or the antislavery attack on slavery, however, is the subject of property rights. Usually, researchers have mentioned property rights among abolitionists and politicians only in passing, but the institution of slavery unavoidably evoked a consideration of the meaning of property rights, and the ensuing discussion has gone largely unrecorded. This neglect has produced a misunderstanding about the antislavery hosts and their connection with events in the latter part of the nineteenth century.

Antislavery groups were ultimately of two minds on the question of property rights. Some found slavery a violation of "true" property rights because property in slaves was false to begin with and a violation of natural law; this position, of course, maintained the ideas of the Enlightenment about natural laws governing the human social world and the duty of all institutions to bow to those decrees. Others held that property rights were at all times the creation of law and were determined by the exercise of governmental power—a view existing somewhat coincidentally and paradoxically with the natural-law position. Not nature but society acting through government decided what was and what was not going to be property. This perspective on property rights made them not only conditional and conventional but subject to change whenever the needs of a society so dictated. Property rights were not sacrosanct; they were simply useful conventions to help society function better—and in the nineteenth century, that usually meant to help the economy grow more rapidly. The economic justification of property rights, however, did not exclude the need of rearranging property rights so as to secure "justice." Whichever strand emerged dominant among antislavery people at whatever time, a basic proposition came flowing out: property rights were second to human rights, to humanitarian sensibilities. This idea about the superiority of human rights became a cornerstone of the antebellum Republican Party.

As abolitionists, Free-Soilers, Liberty Party followers, and Republicans talked about the ephemeral nature of property rights, southern slaveholders turned red in fury. The security of their wealth—their ownership of slaves—depended on a doctrine of property rights in Africans, and they could not allow those rights to be tinkered with in any manner, especially by those who had no interest in that form of property. True "conservatism" meant absolute sanctity of property rights. Southerners defined radicalism as those people for whom property rights were not sacred and who might alter or abolish them. By this line of reasoning proslavery advocates called abolitionists—and later Republicans—socialists.

Abolitionists and Republicans were not socialists. The antislavery groups did not repudiate property rights, although they questioned their sanctity and usefulness. The reason was the labor theory of property or value. What made property rights just was not mere possession of property but the act of labor. Individual labor that created values useful to other members of society deserved a reward, and that reward was the right of the individual to dispose, keep, transfer, or even to destroy the values he or she created, and those values were termed property. The labor theory of value in its broad form is, after all, a justification of property ownership, and in the United States of the mid-nineteenth century the celebration of the act of individual labor reached a zenith. Labor without a reward made no sense. For this reason, antislavery groups did not reject individual rights to property.

This antebellum debate over property rights has relevance for postbellum developments. Instead of focusing on how antislavery people developed doctrines that proved of some use to industrial organization later on, it should first be noted that antislavery proponents were criticizing existing doctrines of property rights. That criticism moved planters to strengthen property rights in new ways, two of which became obvious: the nationalization of property rights in people instead of reliance upon municipal or state regulation, and the establishment of the legal doctrine of substantive due process instead of procedural due process (substantive due process meant that laws that devalued property were unconstitutional even if the the appropriate procedures were followed; procedural due process ruled that laws that devalued property were not a deprivation of property so long as the appropriate procedures were followed). Chief Justice Roger B. Taney's decision in *Dred Scott v. Sanford* (1857) was the first Supreme Court ruling in favor of a doctrine of substantive due process. The force motivating those changes in property law concerning slaves was obvious: slavery had become consolidated among a few southerners who felt very much like a minority under siege from a hostile majority. After the Civil War, the changes in property laws—the law of contract, the fellow-worker rule, and substantive due process—arose because owners of a new form of concentrated property, large-scale corporations, feared that their right to property might be imperiled by the unpropertied majority. So the new corporate business form took existing doctrines and warped them to frame a new security for their property—just as the slaveholders had tried to do in antebellum times. Thus changes in postbellum property laws came not from abolitionist and antislavery doctrines but from the need of those holding concentrated property to protect themselves from the potentially hostile intrusions of popular government. In this sense, the slaveholders of the Old South and the industrial elite of the late nineteenth-century had a commonality: a quest for the sanctity of *their* property rights from majority rule.

The American Revolutionaries produced four doctrines that became central themes in the question of property rights in slaves. First, individual labor justified the existence of property rights. Second, the unnatural accumulation of property in a few hands originated in an impure political organization in which a few people used the coercive powers of the state to enrich themselves —the economic incubus that came from the system of aristocracy.[1] Third, civilization required the existence of property rights, a position that had been seen as a truism since the Roman Republic. Fourth, republics were political systems of representative government in which laws were enacted by majority rule.

These four doctrines produced a Janus-faced outlook on the future. The optimistic side held that by keeping aristocratic practices out of the American Republic and by insisting that all property be earned as the "fruits of labor," all the citizenry would enjoy property ownership and thus majority rule would never produce agrarian laws that upset the right to property; hence, the American Republic successfully brought together majority rule and respect for property rights, thereby saving civilization. The Revolution's other visage was pessimistic. Because property distribution depended on civic virtue, talent differences, or population pressure (depending on the orator speaking), a maldistribution of wealth would occur. Then the unpropertied citizens would exercise their franchises to take the property of the wealthy class and bestow it upon themselves. Such were the apprehensions of several at the Constitutional Convention. It was the fear of the populace passing agrarian laws to rob the rich of their possessions that led Madison to say, "An increase of population will of necessity increase the proportion of those who will labour under all the hardships of life, & secretly sigh for a more equal distribution of its blessings."[2]

After the Revolution, politically minded Americans continued to carry this trepidation of the antagonism between property rights and majority rule. No literate American, save labor leaders after 1820, questioned property rights.[3] But as the nation altered suffrage requirements and moved to white adult male suffrage by dropping property qualifications for the vote, numerous people warned that including the unpropertied among the voters set the stage for an attack on the wealthy. Noah Webster in 1837 wrote to Daniel Webster about the fallacy of permitting universal manhood suffrage, predicting that the adoption of the principle would end up destroying property rights. He decided that the revolutionaries had been overly optimistic: "They seem to have supposed that, to obtain liberty and establish a free government, nothing was necessary but to get rid of kings, nobles, and priests."[4] In his memoirs, Thurlow Weed remembered the fear many had about the poor uniting to defraud the rich, although he dismissed the notion in his old age. But during the outbreak of reform activity during the 1840s and under the experience of the French Revolution of 1848 many expressed doubts about the future of democracy. Wrote one Massachusetts citizen to Artemas Hale: "We shall suffer much in Massachusetts from the spirit of Modern Reform. It is of the same character that now shakes Europe to its centre. The only thing that saves us is that we have made the most of [the] concessions already. There is much of the spirit of agrarianism abroad even among us. If a division is not demanded, the spirit aims in that direction. An inalienable home stead, a participation in the profits of manufactures by the operatives—that the government must employ the poor. These are but intimations of the same spirit. A reorganisation of Society what is it? We hardly know as yet the import of the term."[5]

Frequently combatants characterized the fights between Whigs and Democrats in the Second American Party System of 1828–54 as one that pitted the property-conscious Whigs against the populace-worshiping Democrats. Early Democrats insisted that men were above property, while Whigs feared that the masses would trample property rights. As one Whig wrote, a radical Democrat was opposed to all established practices and advocated that "instead of giving each man his own, he divides and distributes in equal shares."[6] Early political economists of course stressed the sanctity of property rights and usually added that governments must be careful never to transgress upon them. Across the Atlantic came the warning of Thomas Babington Macaulay that the American experiment in self-government was doomed to a total implosion because eventually the impoverished masses would use the ballot to seize by law the riches of the wealthy, a proposition rebutted by many editors.[7]

In the midst of these dark forebodings about the potential antagonisms of majority rule and property rights came the subject of slavery. The revolutionary generation (say roughly 1765 to 1800) analyzed slavery thoroughly and produced every critique of it that would prevail during the abolitionist agitation between 1830 and 1860. Antislavery revolutionaries attacked slavery by using biblical injunctions, denouncing the institution's cruelty, declaiming against its economic results, insisting it violated the natural law of individual liberty, and denying its justification because of alleged racial differences between Europeans and Africans.[8] Two important strands of this discussion led to the free labor ideology and the slave power conspiracy theory of the mid-nineteenth-century North. First, slavery violated the labor theory of value: only the individual who labored created value, but in slavery those values were stolen by slave masters, or as Benjamin Rush wrote, "How great then must be the amount of injustice which deprives so many of our fellow creatures of the *just* reward of their labor!"[9] Likewise, many tract writers believed slavery built up a type of aristocracy, people who lived in splendor by usurping the fruits of others' labors.[10]

Writers on slavery did not ignore the question of property rights. By the end of the Revolution, any number of Americans claimed that English law as described by Blackstone and by Lord Mansfield in the *Somerset* decision (1770) had established that slavery was incompatible with common law. Men had a natural right to liberty that could not be alienated except in the instance of positive municipal law. The operative phrase became man cannot have property in man, that each person had a right to own himself—that is, to self-ownership.[11] For the politicians, property rights in people, regardless of qualifications and reservations, had to be recognized at the state level if the union under the Constitution were ever to take form. This was not the case for antislavery writers. They found the defense of property rights in slaves totally deficient.

Antislavery proponents insisted that slavery violated property rights, thereby voiding any argument that slavery had to be accepted because of respect for property rights. The path most often taken by these individuals was a natural-rights formulation. Each individual by nature had a right to himself or herself and a natural liberty to his or her labor and its fruits. Timothy Dwight of Connecticut, a staunch Federalist minister, claimed that the natural right to liberty preceded any right to property at all, and therefore the defense of slavery by using property rights was entirely bogus. Some years earlier, another Massachusetts resident, Nathan Appleton, argued against slavery because "A Briton has the free disposal of his time, to employ it in that way he likes best; all he gains by his industry, he hath sole right to." Another early antislavery writer, David Cooper, quoted "that celebrated master of reason" John Locke on the principle of self-ownership.[12]

Thus the revolutionary generation of antislavery people insisted that they did not injure the vitality of property rights but only wanted a proper rendition of those rights. Slavery was a system of "robbery." The robbery was manifold. First, people became slaves when others robbed them of their natural rights by force of arms; thus the origin of the institution was one of "theft." Then the masters stole the fruits of the slave's labor. As David Rice, a Kentucky abolitionist, wrote, if a person has "a right to enjoy that property he acquires by an honest industry, so has another."[13] Finally, slavery was a robbery of the progeny of the family. Even if slavery could be justified by conquest or a penalty imposed by crime, antislavery writers did not see how such a condition could then be passed on to children. John Woolman, for example, struck at the hereditary nature of the institution when he asked how it could be just to hand slaves down "from Age to Age in the Line of natural Generation, without Regard to the Virtues and Vices of their Successors."[14]

In 1791 Tom Paine wrote *The Rights of Man* and declared in it that "Man has no property in man; neither has any generation a property in the generations which are to follow." Already the definition of slavery had advanced to the point that slaves were persons reduced to the status of property. And, as David Rice noted, this reduction to property permitted "an absolute, unconditional subjection" of the slave to the slaveholder that violated the natural right of humans to liberty. Rice even offered the observation that property rights in people debased the idea of property in general and would eventually lead to the destruction of property rights; people would associate the transparent injustice of property rights in people with all property rights.[15]

Thus at the beginning of the nineteenth century, early antislavery writers had already staked out a rejection of the doctrine of property rights in slaves. They, however, did not usually (if ever) question the validity of property rights themselves. What was wrong with property rights in slaves was the misapplication of the doctrine by a willful violation of its internal standards. Nineteenth-century abolitionists and antislavery politicians delved deeper into the subject of property rights in general.

When William Lloyd Garrison published his first issue of the *Liberator* in Boston on January 1, 1831, he commenced what has been termed the "modern" abolitionist movement. Modern abolitionism differed from the crusaders against slavery during the revolutionary era by being more demanding, vituperative, and righteous in its pronouncements and tracts; Enlightenment ideals had suffused the first attack on slavery; evangelical emotionalism filled the second. Moreover, abolitionism after 1830 lacked a central organization, and instead abolitionists acted either in small groups or individually. Some abolitionists, like the Garrisonians, were "universal reformers" and perfectionists; others retained religious affiliations; after 1840 a number became politically active and formed the Liberty Party and then the Free-Soil Party; others were moral reformers like Arthur and Lewis Tappan of New York City; and then some were religious anarchists. However, abolitionists had an ideological core argument against slavery—it was morally wrong and had to be ended immediately—and most of their preachments contained common themes. Property rights were at the center of abolitionist analysis of slavery.[16]

Abolitionists assaulted the property rights basis of slavery in two distinct ways. The first was a free labor argument. Each person had the right to the fruits of his or her own labor, and to take the fruits of labor (property) of the laborer was theft. The black abolitionist Nathaniel Paul reminded audiences that the Bible proclaimed that man "should obtain his bread by the sweat of his brow," while the Kentucky advocate of emancipation, John G. Fee, wrote, "Every man has by nature a right to the products of his own labor. Whatever value I create by my labor, or by the innocent use of the other means which God has given me, is mine," adding that the "defense of this right, was the ground of the American Revolution." Frederick Douglass claimed that the property relation in slavery violated the right of the laborer to his fruits: "He toils that another may reap the fruit; he is industrious that another may live in idleness."[17]

This abolitionist argument against slavery based on the fruits of labor, also common among antislavery politicians, was totally sufficient by itself to condemn slavery in the American cultural context. No other argument was needed; dissection of slavery by a fruits-of-labor approach was wholly complete and unanswerable, even from proslavery defenders. Indeed, advocates of the peculiar institution even admitted the substance of the charge. Often quoted was the famous definition of slavery by North Carolina judge Thomas Ruffin: the slave had no right to private property, for "The subject is doomed in his own person and his posterity, to live without knowledge, and without capacity to make any thing his own, and *to toil that others may reap the fruits.*"[18] Once the admission was made that slaves were deprived of the fruits of their labor by force, no justification of slavery by reference to the American Revolution existed. The ideas coming out of the Revolution could only result in condemnation of the peculiar institution.[19]

The second abolitionist assault based on property rights was more complex. Abolitionists constructed a property rights analysis and then applied biblical strictures to reveal the institution's immorality. What was slavery? "By slavery, I understand the property principle," said George M. Bassett in 1858. Theodore Weld wrote that the crucial element of the institution was "ENSLAVING MEN IS REDUCING THEM TO ARTICLES OF PROPERTY." In 1834 James M. Dickinson defined slavery as "the claiming and exercising of the right of property in man." Abolitionists commonly began their treatises with understanding how the principle of property rights operated in slavery.[20]

Abolitionists understood slavery as the reduction of a human to the status of property, and from there a specific moral argument against slavery emerged.[21] The first sin was changing people into parcels of property, for, "MAN CANNOT BE PROPERTY."[22] Behind this common assertion lay two specific strands of biblical reasoning. God made man in His image, and therefore to reduce humankind to a lesser being was sin. One correspondent of James G. Birney charged that slaveholders made "merchandise of the image of God," whereas the editor of the *Augusta (Maine) Kennebec Journal* held that slavery "transformed [men], made in the image of their God, to brutes and chattels, to be owned, bought and sold like cattle in the market." At one religious conference in New England in 1846, the attendees resolved that "holding and using human beings as property, and degrading those whom God made but 'a little lower than the angels,' to the condition of brutes and things, is sin—complicated sin."[23] From this line of reasoning came the "beast analogy," by which abolitionists denounced slaveholding because human beings were turned into animals. The beast analogy suffuses abolitionist writing.

This biblical condemnation of slavery led to one conclusion: humans could not be transformed into property. From this injunction that no person could have property rights in another person, antislavery advocates made a leap to the principle of self-ownership. Said Abraham Prynne in a debate with "Parson" William G. Brownlow, "God inscribed upon man's forefront the law of self-ownership as clearly and distinctly as he revealed the fact that twice two makes four." Because people owned themselves, they also owned the labor of their hands, and thus the antislavery exhorters married their entire biblical attack on slavery to a very explicit economic doctrine. A good example of this was Joshua Giddings in the U.S. House of Representatives. According to Giddings, God gave man dominion over fish, fowl, and all earthly creatures: "This is the title by which we claim property in the brute creation; but man can claim no such title to his fellow man." And with the abolitionists and other antislavery groups, the doctrine of self-ownership was indeed omnipresent.[24]

Antislavery extremists constantly explained that slavery built up an aristocracy that endangered democratic practices in the United States. In this they followed the trail of the revolutionaries who insisted that aristocracy was the prime enemy of republics. However, the way abolitionists defined aristocracy and democracy was interesting. Slave masters became aristocrats not only because of their command over people, their slaves, but also because they were the owners of vast amounts of property. "What is the Slave Power?" asked Wendell Phillips in 1860; and he answered his rhetorical question with "it is two thousand millions of dollars invested in one kind of property. You know the power of money." During the Civil War, one abolitionist, after calling slaveholders a "haughty and intolerant aristocracy," reminded readers that the "disposition on the part of the rich [is] to trample upon the poor, and of the strong to crush the weak."[25] At the same time, abolitionists claimed they represented the forces of democracy—and that force economically was manual labor. Wrote Gamaliel Bailey in the *National Era*, the "Mission of Democracy" was Jefferson's goal of "self-ownership," and while southerners had one vision of the third president, "great numbers of the free laborers of the Northern States—the mechanics and small farmers"—had another. The *New York Independent*, perhaps more antislavery than abolitionist, said the South became addicted to "compulsory" labor, while in the North "Labor and Laborers are the foundations of a community. . . . a community must be measured by the condition of its laborers, and not by the polish [of] its surface."[26]

One very good reason for abolitionists to look askance at property accumulations was that they frequently met the propertied as political and ideological enemies, not as allies. Charles Francis Adams took over editorship of the *Boston Whig* in 1846, and he addressed the problem of property rights between abolitionists and Whig politicos. For some people, Adams explained, Whig principles were narrowed to "very small limits. They are conservatives, only in reference to the preservation of the right of property and care little to go any further." Adams did not want to attack property, but insisted that "the only real safeguards to a happy community [were] the maintainece of justice and of right." A Maine antislavery editor wondered why the Liberty Party was so hated; nothing on the same scale had happened to other reform movements such as temperance. The truth was antislavery received the "wrath of men of property and standing" in and out of churches. In his memoirs, James Freeman Clarke remembered that the commercial interests opposed abolitionists for fear of injuries to trade.[27]

Abolitionists did not mount an attack on property rights, but they did reveal a somewhat ambivalent attitude to them. Usually they said the right of property was a natural right, and slavery was incorrect because other natural rights had been violated to make certain kinds of people slaves; this was the position antislavery writers of the eighteenth century staked out. And some abolitionists, such as Richard Hildreth, James Russell Lowell, and Henry B. Stanton, proposed that slavery defiled property rights and brought them into disrepute. Property distributed justly caused no social upheaval; but when unjustly distributed, then cataclysm was an inevitability.[28] However, it was unlikely that abolitionists would ever totally repudiate property rights because they so rigorously argued the labor theory of value.

Some abolitionists forthrightly declared that property rights were conditional in any event. When Henry Stanton argued in the Massachusetts legislature in 1837 against slavery extension and for the abolition of slavery in Washington, D.C., he insisted that slavery violated property rights and made them unstable, that it was only just to give the slave back his or her property right. And he then, somewhat remarkably, responded to those who cried that such legislation would be tinkering with existing property rights. In effect, Stanton said, "So what?" He pointed out that laws constantly regulate property and transactions between people, but "This has never been considered as any violation of private property." In other words, the law shaped property rights and that function of the law was entirely appropriate. Richard Hildreth had an even more pragmatic approach: property was entirely the result of convention. "Property, it is to be recollected, is a thing established among men by mutual consent, and for mutual convenience."[29]

And some abolitionists questioned the beneficence of property rights altogether. Theodore Parker had many doubts about property rights, at one point writing in his journal that "seventeen-twentieths of crimes are against property, which shows that something is wrong in the state of property." Nathaniel P. Rogers embraced communalism of some sort, arguing that all people deserved competence and that pauperism was unnatural; property rights created injustice, the most galling example being slavery itself. The Free-Soiler William Elder of Pennsylvania took the abolitionist concern about labor to its obvious conclusion. Abolitionists did not do well with wage earners because they had their own "privations" and desired a better distribution of income: the great problem was the "*system of property*, that occupies these people." He wanted to create a "new Democratic party" based on laborers, free and slave. The conservative abolitionist Charles Francis Adams began one of his speeches in 1860 by noting how property rights dominated discussion of slavery, and while he did not wish to demean property rights, he nonetheless insisted there were other rights of humans more important than property rights: "It is not a good sign when the tendency of public men is to set up property—the most palpable of appeals to self-interest—above the higher sentiments of humanity."[30]

When John Greenleaf Whittier, the poet abolitionist, lambasted Massachusetts senators in 1847 in the columns of the *National Era*, he wrote a line that probably all abolitionists could agree to: "Here as elsewhere, the greed of Gain, the intense selfishness of Traffick, have a natural aversion to the doctrine that the Rights of Persons are more sacred than those of Property." Abolitionists were aware that their crusade was, after all, an attack on property rights and a demand that they be redefined. Their entire movement swirled around individual rights, and it was clear from their commentary that they saw property rights as a hostile force that belittled their arguments, strengthened their opponents, and justified the institution they detested. Hence, protection of property rights was not central to their antebellum work; rather, the corpus of the literature they left tends more to the conclusion that property rights had to be judged by their usefulness and their contribution to the general welfare; they were only absolute in the sense of reward to individual laborers but were otherwise to be shaped and reshaped by circumstances. For the abolitionists, property rights represented as much a danger to human rights as they did a benefit. As James Russell Lowell explained, antislavery ideals were promoted "not by any unthinking hostility to the *rights* of property, but by a well-founded jealousy of its usurpations." He was one of those northerners "who believe that, besides meum and tuum, there is also such a thing as suum—who are old-fashioned enough, or weak enough, to have their feelings touched by these things, to think that human nature is older and more sacred than any claim of property whatever, and that it has rights at least as much to be respected as any hypothetical one of our Southern brethren."[31]

In the political realm, the formulations of the abolitionists found constant reiteration by antislavery northerners. Indeed, the property rights analysis of slavery was fundamentally the same across the political spectrum of the North—to include the Whigs and Democrats. The differences among the political groupings lay beyond property rights. Democrats and Whigs largely agreed to abide by southern property rights in the states but not necessarily in the territories. Their sense of the sanctity of the Union, their understanding of the evolution of the institution, and their belief in the superiority of Europeans outweighed any moral concerns about enslaving Africans. Republicans went quite a distance with the abolitionist analysis, but they did not break away from constitutional obligations nor did they call for immediate emancipation. Abolitionists were radical in the sense that their willingness to override all other obligations in order to obtain emancipation was nowhere duplicated in the political parties. Nor were any of the parties close to the one doctrine held dear by abolitionists: all people of all races were equal.

When the Republican Party formed, it drew disproportionately in its first several years of existence from the former Whig Party, and it may be conjectured that Whigs largely held the same ideas about property rights and slavery that Republicans espoused between 1854 and 1860. At least some segment of the Democrat leadership held the same views and became a prominent element in the early Republican Party. Hence Republicans were often speaking for the members of the Second Party System, only under new conditions and with a new urgency.

Property rights could hardly be avoided as a topic when the issue of slavery's expansion arose in 1846–47 because southerners defended slavery in Congress on the basis of property rights. In the early stage of the territorial debate, the Whig warhorse Nathan Appleton wrote that "it is the question of property, after all, that is the insurmountable difficulty."[32] Republicans of course grounded their belief in property rights in the free labor ideology. At an 1851 mass meeting in Wisconsin about homestead proposals, one resolution read "that in our political system all property . . . is a right which society creates for the recompense of Labor; that with us all property is simply industry rewarded with its just fruits."[33]

Republicans attacked the property basis of slavery with the same doctrines the abolitionists had used. Slavery was not an institution formed from natural right; it only existed "by the might of [the slaveholder's] power."[34] Slavery denied the divine creation of humanity and thus there could be no property in man.[35] Edward Wade insisted that "a man's *right to himself* is, of course, the highest and most sacred of all his rights."[36] Republicans objected to the reduction of blacks to the level of brutes—the beast analogy abounded in their comments—and they also said only local law created slavery and that even in those localities slavery was unlike other property. Asked one correspondent of Senator James Doolittle, "What other property but the negro is subject to penal law?"[37]

Republicans also recognized that property rights were not sacrosanct but subject to change and to legislative burdens. When the Wilmot Proviso first emerged in Congress to stop slavery's expansion into any newly acquired territories, Horace Greeley's *New York Tribune* insisted that southerners had to abide by the fact that laws by legislatures determined property; northerners generally agreed with a statement made by Henry Clay in 1839 about property in slaves: "[W]hat the law declares to be property is property."[38] Republicans reminded audiences that property "has its duties, as well as its rights." During the Lecompton Constitution battle in Congress, Republicans made a tempest over the part of the constitution that read "The right of property is before and higher than any constitutional sanction; and the right of the owner of a slave to such and its increase is the same, and as inviolable, as the right of the owner of any property whatever." To this Representative Henry Waldron declared, "a constitution indorsing and avowing such a principle is not a republican constitution." In short, republics had control over property rights, and property rights were not beyond political processes.[39]

Two Republicans made extended comments about property rights and pushed the Republican analysis in interesting directions. William H. Seward of New York, that state's former Whig governor, a U.S. senator throughout the 1850s, and leading contender for the Republican presidential nomination in 1860, was given to making interesting comparisons between European society, ancient republics, and the United States. He used such comparisons to show how slavery weakened ancient societies, especially Rome, and promoted an unequal distribution of wealth. Seward held most of the standard antislavery notions of self-ownership, reduction of humans to animals, and enervation of labor.[40] But on one occasion he dipped into the troubled waters of property rights. True, he said, property "is an essential element of civil society," but then he added so "is liberty." He divided the two, which often had been joined: private property had been for many philosophers the guarantor of individual liberty. Seward described a more complex relationship. They could act together and produce harmony and progress; but they could become unbalanced and war on each other. "How to adjust the balance between property and liberty in States, is the great problem of government." Property was "jealous of liberty" and always had "a bias toward oppression"; property accomplished the oppression of liberty by gathering all property holders together for a common attack on the rights of others. True liberty only existed when "the rights and duties of the property classes are defined and regulated" while at the same time liberty was "so bounded as to secure property against social or individual aggression." It can only be conjectured, but Seward's analysis of the dangers of property—rare among popular politicians—probably came from his experience of constantly battling slaveholders who insisted their slaves be looked upon as property.[41]

The other Republican who dissected the question of property rights was the Illinois lawyer, Whig politician, and staunch opponent of popular sovereignty, Abraham Lincoln. Although Lincoln has become most known for his insistence upon treating slavery as a moral issue, he had one of the more sophisticated views of the influence of property rights upon the southern mind. In 1856 Lincoln recorded his belief that the value of slave property determined the southern position, and in 1859 he responded to a comment by Douglas that all that the slaveholders wanted was their property rights: Of course, they did; "If they want anything else, I do not comprehend it."[42] When he spoke in Connecticut in the spring of 1860 during an eastern visit, Lincoln carefully laid out the property basis for the sectional conflict. In the South, he said in a speech at Hartford, slaves were looked upon as property, and this was the obstacle to a political settlement because the property in question was worth $2 billion. That amount of property would have the same effect upon the northern mind if a similar amount were endangered. Moreover, "Public opinion is formed relative to a property basis. Therefore, the slaveholders battle any policy which depreciates their slaves as property, what increases the value of this property, they favor." When northerners tell southerners that slavery is immoral, "they rebel, because they do not like to be told they they are interested in an institution which is not a moral one." And so the South was thoroughly comprehensible because of the nature of southern property. The reason slavery was immoral, said Lincoln, was that "God gave man a mouth to receive bread, hands to feed it, and his hand has a right to carry bread to his mouth without controversy"—in other words, the right of self-ownership.[43]

Lincoln also enunciated another viewpoint, one that appeared in Republican newspapers. In an 1859 letter that celebrated Jefferson's birthday, Lincoln noted that in Jefferson's day human rights were held higher than property rights. The Republican Party had indeed now become the true heir of Jefferson, for the "democracy of to-day hold the *liberty* of one man to be absolutely nothing, when in conflict with another man's right of *property*. Republicans, on the contrary, are for both the *man* and the *dollar*; but in cases of conflict, the Man *before* the dollar." In this Lincoln was not alone.[44]

During the debate over the Lecompton Constitution, fought in the growing shadow of the *Dred Scott* decision of 1857, Republicans made some remarkable speeches about property rights. None was more impressive than that of Senator James Harlan of Iowa. After detailing various legal aspects of *Dred Scott*, Harlan said that the idea of property rights in slaves destroyed the northern Democracy's hope for popular sovereignty as a solution to the problem of slavery's extension into the territory. Moreover, the basic division between parties was whether property rights in man could exist; the concept could be maintained only by "the law of force, by the law of physical power, and can be maintained in no other way." Summarizing numerous strands of antislavery thought on property rights, Harlan then declared: "A man's right to the use of himself, to the use of his own will and his own body and his own intellect and his own conscience and his own moral emotions, is as old as the right to property; and by the common consent of mankind even more sacred, because wherever these two come in necessary conflict, the right to property must give way before the right of person."[45]

As Republicans and abolitionists debated the meaning and limits of property rights, southerners could only look on in horror. The property being debated was theirs. Northerners had fallen into the tyranny of majority rule, and agrarianism was sweeping their region. The war of numbers upon property had commenced. The editor of the *Charleston Mercury* asked, "When the majority of the people in the North who go to the polls shall be non-property holders, will they respect the rights of property?" Would they not rather legislate a general confiscation? "But we must pause on this fruitful subject, although not half exhausted. Red Republicanism will never arise in the South."[46] The debate over slavery was a debate over property rights, and as that controversy mounted in the North from the South came the cutting shriek of agrarianism.

It is befuddling that some scholars believe that the legal doctrines that ruled relations between government and the economy came from the antislavery vanguard. Sanctity of contract, substantive due process, and the fellow servant doctrine may have had some intellectual roots in the ideas of self-ownership, voluntary association, individual moral responsibility, and natural-rights doctrines.[47] Whether other groups simultaneously touted the same values has not yet been explored, but a reasonable guess is that politicians of all stripes plus the nonabolitionist (and maybe even proslavery) Protestant denominations trumpeted the same views. But even that misses the point. The application of the antislavery position to late nineteenth-century economic development is contextually wrong.

Antislavery in both its abolitionist and political forms was an outright attack on the property rights that had been previously established. Slavery represented, at least for nineteenth-century northerners, a fearful concentration of property and power—indeed, *the* fearful concentration of property and power of their time period. Industrialization and commercialization might have revealed disturbing tendencies, but those tendencies had not yet manifested themselves so blatantly as had concentration of ownership of slaves. When the antislavery groups battled with slaveholders, they knew precisely what was going on: they were telling the great property holders of the nation that their possessions were immoral, irresponsible, and dangerous. They took the position that though property rights *might* be beneficial to a society, there was no guarantee that they would be. And when property ownership matured or evolved in such a manner as to create dangers to the ideals of the body politic and to "first" principles, then it was indeed the duty of statesmen to rewrite the laws of property. Property rights were utilitarian and subject to legislative change—not on whims, of course, but property rights were not more valuable than the society itself. Thus, the antislavery groups in toto could legitimately claim that they represented the force in American history that called for the primacy of human rights over property rights.

What happened in the late nineteenth century was not dissimilar to what happened in the early nineteenth century in terms of property. When property ownership in slaves became more concentrated, especially along geographical lines, the slave masters grew more and more fearful of popular majorities and more demanding about the application of the rules of property rights. Slaveholders in fact extended the Constitution in their search for security for their human wealth; after all, it was the proslavery decision in *Dred Scott* that produced the first example of substantive due process. In the late nineteenth century, industry concentrated into large business units that, except for the railroads and a few textile mills, had not been seen in North America before and was alien to its economic experience of proprietorships and partnerships. That realization of being remarkable and different, with all the property involved in these new organizations, led the innovators to demand new forms of protection of property from legislative majorities. They then turned to various ideas in existence and warped them to their needs—sanctity of contract, fellow servant doctrine, and substantive due process. What was propelling history was not the ideological position of reform groups but the changing nature of property ownership and its tendency to concentration.

The analogy has not been yet made, but the outlines are clear. Between 1890 and 1920 a resurrection of the battle between antislavery and proslavery arose. This time, antislavery became known as progressivism and socialism, while proslavery was conservatism, standpatism, or laissez-faire social Darwinism. Even the use of the word "slavery" in that period was reminiscent of antebellum America. But the true comparison was always present. One side stood for human rights as the primary quality of a civilized community, while the other side demanded a privileged and unassailable place for property rights.

5

The Constitutionality of Slavery Prohibition in the Territories

Wending its way through a tumultuous Congress in late summer 1846 was a bill providing President Polk $2 million to negotiate an end to the Mexican War. On the last day of the Congress, August 8, David Wilmot of Pennsylvania rose and offered a provision to the bill that forbade slavery in any territory acquired from Mexico. He thereby initiated the fourteen-year struggle between the North and the South over the expansion of slavery and its future in the republic. That controversy took many twists and included an enormous range of topics, but certainly one of the major ones, especially for congressional representatives, was the constitutionality of the policy of congressional restriction of slavery's expansion. Out of the rhetorical battle arose the southern cry that the issue was states' rights versus centralization, local control versus federal control, multitudes of communities versus consolidation into a national entity. Ever since the introduction of Wilmot's Proviso the legend has continued that the controversy between the sections was not over slavery but over the rights of the states to control their internal affairs.

States' rights had virtually no meaning in the question of the constitutionality of prohibiting slavery's expansion, and it was entirely a bogus application of the doctrine. Indeed, the question of slavery's expansion into the West invoked states' rights only as a by-product of property rights. From the beginning of their defense of slavery's ability to expand into the West, southerners used a property rights argument, and that defense continued unabatedly until the moment of secession. Southern angst about the prohibition of slavery expansion arose from a number of specific concerns about the future viability of slavery, but the key component was the viability of the right to property in slaves. Southerners in both the Deep South and the Border South agreed about the sanctity of property in slaves, and their concern was one that has always mobilized great property holders to a truculent demand for an absolute and eternal status quo: if one gives an inch, then someone will take a mile. Once they yielded property rights in slaves in the territories, their enemies would next move on the sanctity of property rights in slaves in the states—by some mechanism not well explained, true, but the fear constantly filled southern speeches.[1]

However, constitutionality and constitutional doctrines are not about the just, the fair, and the wise: they are about the power to be able to do certain acts and the inability to do certain other acts. Congress alone posses the war-making power. That power is lodged in a specific governmental body and no other. The Constitution cannot detail the circumstances by which Congress may declare war, or whether any specific declaration of war is just, fair, or wise. All it does is allocate the power. This is the heart of the territorial issue after 1846. The Constitution put the power to govern the territories in Congress and nowhere else. Numerous southerners understood that in this instance they were on the losing end of the constitutional stick. Their cry was really that congressional prohibition was unfair and unjust to southern slaveholders. That complaint, when considered wholly among the ruling groups in the nation, was true; congressional restriction of slavery expansion was unfair to southern slaveholders and did bias the end result toward the creation of nonslaveholding societies in the West. But the policy was not unconstitutional.

The Indiana Whig Richard W. Thompson in 1847 found himself asked to answer a list of questions about his views on the Mexican War, territorial acquisitions, and slavery's potential expansion. He responded that he thoroughly rejected acquisition "by *conquest*" as "a war of conquest is opposed to the first principles of our government, and is, in every way unsuited to the genius of our people." As to slavery's expansion, it was an "*original* question" that could only be vexing to national politics, but he did not doubt Congress's authority to prohibit the peculiar institution in the territories, although he feared the consequences of enacting such a policy. By 1851 Daniel Webster of Massachusetts, leading Whig, member of President Fillmore's cabinet, and famed orator, told a crowd at Buffalo, that slavery in the states was "beyond the reach of Congress. It is the concern of the States themselves." However, "when we come to speak of admitting new States, the subject assumes a new and entirely different aspect."[2]

Northerners insisted that they had the power and the right to block slavery from entering the territories. Their argument had a constancy that lasted from the introduction of the Wilmot Proviso until the firing on Fort Sumter. It was based on a number of specific doctrines, constitutional phrases, and property rights considerations. Almost all of them emerged in a few months after August 1846, for when Wilmot offered his proviso there was virtually no debate. Before Calhoun submitted his famous resolutions on the constitutionality of restricting slavery's expansion on February 19, 1847, the northern position was complete, requiring for closure only a few legal references and some additional refinements to rebut novel southern assertions. Indeed, the northern position among Whigs, Democrats, and others took shape almost instantaneously.

More than anyone else, Supreme Court justice and rabid presidential aspirant John McLean of Ohio provided the framework for the restrictionists. Taking the opinion formally from Justice Storey in the Supreme Court case of *Prigg v. Pennsylvania*, McLean said slavery was wholly a domestic institution, regulated by municipal law. Its reach could not extend beyond the jurisdiction —the sovereignty—that sustained the institution. Without laws to make slavery operative, slavery did not exist. According to McLean, Congress had not the power to establish slavery in any territory. If slavery did not exist in a territory when acquired, it effectively became a free territory because neither the territorial government—a creature of Congress—nor Congress itself could establish slavery. Thus if territories when acquired prohibited slavery, then slavery was prohibited until the time of a statehood convention when delegates constructed a state constitution; only at that moment could slavery be established, not before. And Mexico had abolished slavery in 1822, thus making any territory acquired from Mexico free territory. McLean's argument served many northern political parties well, and Democrats, future Free-Soilers, and Whigs could use his formulations to justify their positions.[3]

Restrictionists relied upon these pivotal doctrines. Northerners believed that, of course, property was crucial to civilization and that the role of government was, at a minimum, to protect property of those people who acquired their property according to the laws in the jurisdiction over which the law-making power held sway. In the American experiment, the Constitution, said Samuel Lahm of Ohio, did not list property "and it only requires legislation to make that property which is not universally conceded to be property." That meant that the states created for their jurisdictions certain types of property that might not exist elsewhere in the country. This made slavery a "local institution, depending for its existence solely and exclusively upon the laws and constitutions of the States on which it is sanctioned." Later on, as the *National Era* explained, "Slavery is a *State* institution, not a *Federal* one," and therefore slavery "is *sectional*, not *national*."[4]

Of all the phrases that antiextensionists used to buttress their position, the most repeated was, as the editor of the *Ohio State Journal* printed in September 1846, "The free States will not consent to establish slavery in countries where it does not exist." One of the resolutions at a Buffalo Democratic meeting was "we are decidedly opposed to the extension of slavery over any territory that may be hereafter acquired where slavery does not now exist." This phrasing, no slavery in territories "now free," was continuous throughout the 1850s. The doctrine northerners rallied behind in the extension controversy was that slavery could not be permitted to expand into territories that had abolished the peculiar institution or had never allowed it to take root. Democrats, Whigs, and others responded to the call, and those who tarried were warned of the consequences. So wrote a friend to Charles Lanphier, editor of Springfield's *Illinois State Register*, Stephen A. Douglas's organ in the state: "But Charly, my old friend, it will not do for the State Register to denounce every man as a demagogue, who advocates the policy of keeping all territory now free, *forever free*. And if I am not greatly mistaken, you will find many of your best friends, at Springfield, this minute, urging with all their power, the passage of resolutions, instructing our Senators to use their best efforts to prevent the introduction of Slavery into all territory where it does not already exist. And for them, to oppose with all their might every attempt to extend the *Missouri Compromise* to the Pacific." A few argued against any new slave states whatsoever, but the precise position taken throughout the controversy was to deny slavery's establishment in territories that at the moment of acquisition did not permit slavery.[5]

Mexican law was crucial to the antiexpansionist position. Mexico had abolished slavery in its domain in 1822. When (and, prior to 1848, if) the United States obtained territory in recompense for hostilities, any land acquired by treaty from that nation had an express prohibition against slavery—that is, if by municipal regulation these lands had outlawed slavery—then such land was free and could not have slavery introduced. According to Robert Dale Owen, "the law of nations will exclude slavery thence, unless, by some positive act of legislation, we establish it there." Owen said that international law declared that a conquering nation left alone the property of a conquered people until changed by special enactment of the conquerors. The state of freedom in Mexican land—that is, no property in people—could only be altered by positive law from the new possessor, the Congress of the United States. In short, the land acquired from Mexico was "free." For some northerners, this analysis produced the argument that the Wilmot Proviso was an unnecessary redundancy, because, if correct, slavery was already effectively prohibited from the land ceded by Mexico.[6]

So far as the ability of Congress to restrict slavery in the territories, northern antiextensionists had two lines of attack. The first and most obvious one was precedent. By the Northwest Ordinance of 1787, then readopted by the Constitution after 1789, and the Compromise of 1820, Congress had already demonstrated the constitutionality of prohibiting slavery from the territories. The power had been claimed and then used. Indeed, John A. Dix wrote to Charles Francis Adams to see if the elder Adams had recorded in his notes the meeting of Monroe's cabinet when Congress first formulated the Missouri restriction. Adams wrote later to John Palfrey that Dix had guided him correctly: "*All the Cabinet officers* of that day, including Crawford, Wirt and *Calhoun* gave written opinions affirming the constitutionality of interdicting slavery in the territories of the Union."[7]

The second text of the restrictionists was Article IV, section 3, paragraph 2, of the U.S. Constitution. It read: "The Congress shall have power to dispose of and make all needful rules and regulations respecting the territory or other property belonging to the United States; and nothing in this Constitution shall be so construed as to prejudice any claims of the United States, or of any particular State." Any number of northerners emphasized this text in the Constitution. In 1854 George W. Morrison of New Hampshire told Congress that in the territories there was "no divided sovereignty"; the sovereignty specifically belonged to the federal Congress. Territories could not elect governors, judges, or even set up a legislature at first; those offices belonged to the national government, and even afterward the territories could not execute their own laws without the consent of Congress. According to Joseph R. Chandler of Pennsylvania, the Constitution permitted sovereignty in states, but not in territories.[8] Moreover, under any circumstance there was no provision in the Constitution that permitted Congress to extend slavery. Slavery only existed by local law, and the Constitution, spoke Massachusetts representative Tappan Wentworth, "carries slavery nowhere, and protects it nowhere." When a territory was free at the time of acquisition, slavery could only be instituted by positive law (that is, a legislative enactment). As the governing power of a territory was the Congress of the United States, the only body that could allow slavery was Congress—but that power was forbidden it, at least according to Barnburning Democrats.[9] Indeed, New York senator John A. Dix, a Free-Soiler in the campaign of 1848, stated that when a territory already had slavery established, then Congress could not prohibit it; but when a territory was free, Congress should prohibit slavery until the time of its statehood.[10]

Restrictionists coupled with every assertion that slavery should not be allowed into the territories the affirmation that they would not touch slavery in the states and that they would live in full compliance with every constitutional compromise concerning slavery. Northerners did not accept the charge that somehow they were betraying the Constitution and meddling with a state institution. Asked the *Cincinnati Daily Enquirer*, "Do we interfere with slavery in South Carolina, when we say it shall not exist in Oregon or California?" Richard W. Thompson of Indiana called the "*conservative* position" in 1847 the one "denouncing Slavery as an evil, on the one hand, and admitting all the constitutional rights of the Slave States on the other." In the Senate, Maine's Hannibal Hamlin in 1858 uttered a phrase that northern restrictionists had uttered thousands of times after the introduction of the Wilmot Proviso: southerners "denied that the Government of the United States had any right to interfere with slavery in the States: so say we all." The antiextensionist position was that the Constitution said nothing about expansion of slavery, and on that question the Constitution gave powers to Congress to determine the fate of slavery in the territories. There was no constitutional provision detailing how territories were to be treated in regard to slavery.[11]

Any number of individuals enunciated the complete constitutional argument justifying restricting slavery's admission into territories already free. A mass meeting of antislavery Democrats of New York City produced such a document in a letter to Martin Van Buren, and Van Buren repeated the arguments in his response to them. Their opinions rested on the idea that slavery was a local institution supported by local laws, that those laws did not migrate naturally into a territory acquired by the United States, and that Congress had the power to regulate conditions in the territories. Most of the restrictionists claimed the prohibition stemmed from the unnatural quality of property, or, as the governor of Maine, John W. Dana, wrote in 1847, the right of an individual to a slave (that is, property right in slaves) "is an unnatural, an artificial, a statute right." If a person took a slave to a territory where no statutes concerning slavery existed, "then, at once, the right ceases to exist. The slave becomes a free man." Everyone had accepted that slavery was a local institution. Edward Bates complained that "Even the hottest politicians of the South understood it so, for they had habitually denounced the 'northern fanatics' for presuming to intermeddle with their 'domestic institution.'" Property was defined by state law; where state law did not hold sway, only common understandings of what constituted property could operate. If no common ground on a form of property existed outside of a state's jurisdiction, then that form could not be construed as property. Slavery in the territories only existed if prior law recognized it. For northerners, this was the acknowledged truth of the case and had been since the establishment of the Constitution.[12]

Of course, the reason for restriction of slavery was different from its Constitutional justification. The antiextensionists used a legal argument to demonstrate that the power existed for Congress to prohibit slavery in the territories, and they considered their argument flawless and irrefutable. The reason why they wanted to halt slavery's territorial advance was different and offensive to southerners. All the ideological reasons for antislavery emerged. First, northerners wanted to stop the "slave power" from growing in strength—that is, no more slave states to add representatives and senators who only thought of legislation in terms of how it affected the peculiar institution.[13] Second, slavery produced a sluggard economy and deprived free laborers of their just reward; slave labor ruined free labor because of its unfair cheapness, and thus destroyed a healthy society of the middle. The proof of this was in the comparison of the Old Northwest to any part of the slaveholding South.[14] Third, antiextensionists insisted that the intention of the Founders was to found a nation based on individual freedom, not slavery, and it was thus their hope to see freedom, not slavery, expand.[15] Fourth, as the Democrat newspaper and supporter of the regular part of the party, the *Hartford Times* printed in the early phase of the Wilmot Proviso debate, "There is no diversity of opinion at the North. [Slavery] is looked upon as wrong." Hence, it made no sense to northerners to allow the expansion of an institution thought to be morally wrong and at odds with the national principle of freedom, especially when they had the constitutional power to prohibit it.[16]

Northern constitutional scrupulousness totally unimpressed southerners. Rather, "we hold the Wilmot Proviso, then, to be unjust, unconstitutional, and not to be tolerated." The Wilmot Proviso was an "outrage upon their [southerners'] rights and institutions," wrote one correspondent to the *Charleston Mercury*. South Carolina's James H. Hammond, former governor and later to be senator, wrote others that "The north has offered as deep insults and consummated as great outrages upon the south as ever one nation did upon another. . . . [The North] deliberately and openly aims to revolutionize our whole social system—to destroy all our property and effect our ruin." Thus the words constantly poured forth from southern lips and pens: northern aggression, a trespass against states' rights, violation of constitutional guarantees, equality of the states in the Union. The debate was joined.[17]

Special circumstances surrounded the Wilmot Proviso that made the initial rebuttal of its proposal for slavery restriction interesting. Wilmot announced the policy on the last day of the session of Congress, and no debate attended it. When Congress reconvened in December, no prominent statesman had staked out a constitutional position on the idea. When the proviso reentered debate again in early January, under the motion of Preston King of New York, serious debate commenced. Yet it would not be until late February 1847 that the southern analysis of the Wilmot Proviso took shape under the guidance of John C. Calhoun.

Before Calhoun made known his views, southerners immediately took shelter from the deluge of Free-Soil sentiments under the canopy of property rights. Henry Hillard warned that the subject would lead to dissolution and that the South wanted its political rights observed; Edward Dargan, preferring to leave the fate of slavery to God rather than to Congress, said that a compromise based on the 36 degree 30 minute line was possible. But Virginia's James A. Seddon demanded observance of equality of states and that protection of slave property was an inherent part of the bargain between the North and the South in 1787–89. The Constitution, he said, "never would have been endured if it had been believed that the rights or property of one section were of less worth and less to be protected than those of another." Shelton F. Leake, also from Virginia, argued that "the property in slaves is specifically secured—the only instance of the kind in the whole instrument." Because of the recognition of the rights of property in slaves, said James Dobbin of North Carolina, a prohibition against slaveholders from entering the territories "*violates most palpably the faith and compromises of the Constitution.*" In South Carolina, the editor of the radical states' rights paper, the *Charleston Mercury*, quoted approvingly a piece by a Georgia writer stating that the territories were "common property both of the free and of the slave States."[18] Two individuals, however, fleshed out as much as possible the constitutionality of the southern demand for slavery's expansion—or at least detailed the unconstitutionality of the restrictionist position: John C. Calhoun and Jefferson Davis. Both of their analyses were based on the southern right to property in slaves.

Calhoun and other southerners probably expected some political compromise over slavery's expansion, particularly the extension of the Missouri Compromise line, but the almost unanimous and constant support by northern Whigs and Democrats for the Wilmot Proviso demanded a response based on the Constitution. In Calhoun's first move, on February 19, 1847, he proposed four resolutions concerning slavery and the territories. First, the territories were common territory owned by all the states for which the federal government was only the trustee; second, each member of the Union had the right, due to the equality of states, to migrate to the territories with their property, including slave property; third, if localities lost the right to determine their own institutions and have Congress dictate those institutions, self-government was at an end, and in this case the federal government was imposing institutions upon localities; and fourth, the debate over slavery's extension was ruining the Union. In his comments on both February 19 and 20, Calhoun insisted that the Constitution was based on fairness and equity among the states, whereas the Wilmot Proviso obviously placed a discrimination against some of the states and treated them unequally. His understanding of the Constitution was that it was a compact among states, not people, and that it portended a union of states and not a consolidated nation in which the central government could determine local rights and institutions. At this point, he also added nonconstitutional reasons for opposing the Wilmot Proviso: it sought to ruin the South by dramatically increasing the free states, and it would promote white emigration from the slave states leaving only a vast black population in the older states, thereby inviting slave insurrection.[19]

In June 1848 Calhoun gave a much more extensive scrutiny of constitutional powers in regard to congressional authority over the territories. Again, all who joined the Constitution expected to be treated equally, and all knew that southerners in 1787 demanded protection for slave property as they were "very jealous" about that property. Calhoun then asked whether the Constitution had any provision that gave "the North the power to exclude the South from a free admission into the Territories of the United States with its peculiar property and to monopolize them for its own exclusive use?" The answer was both no and obviously not—no to an exact provision and obviously not to any wording anywhere about one section having a monopoly to the detriment of another section; this last was pure rhetorical flourish, and rather nonsensical at that. He then focused on Article 4, section 3, paragraph 2, which gave Congress the right to govern the territories until they entered as states. Calhoun read this passage as proving that Congress was not given absolute power but only power to dispose of real estate—the territorial land—but not power over persons.

Without a power over persons, Congress could not restrict a person's property, and thus could not prohibit someone from taking slave property into the territories. That part of the Constitution restricts Congress "beyond the possibility of doubt, to territory regarded as property."[20] He then tackled the precedent of the Northwest Ordinance of 1787; he called it a compromise between the North and South in 1787, not a constitutional principle, and claimed that there was no surrender of southern rights in the territories. While it was true that Congress had some power over the territories, those powers were limited to titles of nobility, ex post facto laws, bills of attainder, writs of habeas corpus, and the like.[21]

But the heart of his claims, it seems, was that the spirit giving the Constitution life and meaning dictated against any policy that discriminated against any state for any reason. He compared the Constitution with the legal form of a trust; congressional representatives were "agents, or, more properly, trustees," who were restricted in their activities by "the nature and the objects of the trust." As the nature of the Union was a compact between the states, power could only be used that inured to the "common and joint benefit" of the states. Thus, neither Congress nor territorial governments could stop slaveholders from taking their property into the territories—indeed, Congress and territorial authorities had to protect the property of the slaveholder in the territories because the nature of the trust was equality between the states and prohibition of discriminatory legislation against any state or group of states. Hence the application of the cry of "the equality of states" or "equality of rights within the Union."[22]

Mexican laws, Calhoun continued, did not matter because Mexico had lost its sovereignty over the land when it lost the war. Then U.S. laws took effect, and that meant the trustee condition applied. Municipal government, in this case territorial government, certainly could make needful laws to regulate the land, but only laws "not inconsistent with the condition and the nature of our political system." Calhoun lapsed then into a discussion of free labor versus slave labor, and declared that the comparison misrepresented the relationship between them because the two systems were complementary and not antagonistic (largely because he defined them as mechanical and agricultural systems). He dismissed the Declaration of Independence as it applied to slaves and emphasized the difference between races that was the bedrock justification of southern slavery. As well, Calhoun denied Locke and Sidney on natural rights and rejected all legitimations of social structures by reference to a state of nature.[23]

Jefferson Davis offered much the same argument, although with some additional and interesting observations. In a long and important speech made on the admittance of Oregon in 1848, Davis recited much of Calhoun's position: the states retained full sovereignty and only delegated a small portion of it to the federal government; the federal government acted as agent for the states and had to insure its policies benefited all; Mexican laws in western territories were superseded by American conquest; the territories were the common property of the states, and territorial governments had no ability to prohibit slavery; democratic government could not overrule fundamental rights; the Northwest Ordinance was a compromise not a principle; slavery was justified by race, which would only end when population pressure reduced wages below the cost of maintaining slaves; and the alleged antagonism between free and slave labor did not exist because of climate. Davis found the North guilty of a more profound racism than the South's. "The only conclusion is, that you are prompted by the lust of power, and an irrational hostility to your brethren of the South."[24]

The subject of property rights, however, ran throughout Davis's peroration. He raised some ideas that must have scared northern hairs straight. Local laws, he claimed, sustained slavery but did not create the institution. When the Constitution was framed, property in humans was recognized and "made coextensive with the supremacy of the Federal laws, its existence subject only to the legislation of the sovereign States possessing powers not drawn from, but above, the Constitution." The meaning of this line became clear: in all its dealings until 1815, the federal government acted under the premise that property rights in people was the same as all other property rights, and so the federal government must recognize property in slaves in all its functions. That is, the Constitution recognized property rights in slaves beyond municipal jurisdiction, and only state sovereignty could override such property rights. As many other southerners said, the Constitution recognized slave property and was the only type of property named. Thus, "The Constitution recognizes the institution of slavery, which thence acquired a general, instead of its previous merely local character." For northerners, this was the nationalization of slavery; the Constitution really meant, if Davis were right, that slavery was national and freedom was sectional, that freedom was a municipal regulation. This was certainly a stunner.[25] At one point Davis declared, "I deny, then, that the Federal Government may say to any class of citizens, you shall not emigrate to territory which belongs in common to the people of the United States; equally deny that it can say what property shall be taken into such territory."[26]

Davis and Calhoun represented the extreme proslavery interpretation of the Constitution regarding the territorial question, yet southern politicians reiterated their basic premises time and time again. At the bottom of the argument was the sanctity of property rights and the need for the federal government to recognize those rights in all its actions. The cadence of the southern argument about territories proceeded in this fashion. First, southerners insisted the purpose of all government was to protect property rights.[27] Slaves were property. The Constitution came into existence because of a basic compromise between northerners and southerners that northerners would not assail property rights in slaves—indeed, among some southerners, the institution of slavery was responsible for "our peculiar form of Government and Constitution," and that the security of "the rights and property of the People of the South" was "the essence of the Union."[28] Besides expecting northerners to live up to the compromises on slavery spelled out in the Constitution, they usually insisted that the federal government could not define property, only the states could. As William O. Goode of Virginia phrased it in 1854, the federal government was "bound to treat as property, and protect as property, whatever has been decided to be property by the supreme sovereign authority of an independent State."[29]

Whether anti-proviso southerners used the compact theory of the origin of the Constitution—that is, the Constitution was formed by the states, not the citizenry, and thus the states reserved sovereignty and only delegated a few specific powers to the central government—almost all insisted that territory was "common territory" for North and South and thus the property rights of all sections had to be observed. This insistence upon property rights in slaves in the territories drew forth the states' rights argument. The states were equal members of the Union and had equal rights; they then drew the inference of equal treatment in the territories. The federal government acted illegally when it used its power to allow members of some states access to the territories but not other members from other states.[30] Sometimes anti-proviso southerners argued that the federal government had to protect slave property throughout the territorial stage, sometimes they opted for the solution of Lewis Cass and then Stephen A. Douglas to allow citizens migrating to the territories to determine immediately the fate of slavery for themselves.[31] The base point of the whole argument, however, was not states' rights or consolidation but property rights. In the Democratic Convention of 1848 in Baltimore, the resolution the radical William Lowndes Yancey of Alabama failed to have adopted was a declaration of adherence to the doctrine of noninterference "with the rights of property . . . be it in the State or in the Territories, by any other than the parties interested in them."[32]

In a speech on the Nebraska bill in Congress, Alabama representative Philip Phillips stated that the "great test" of all congressional legislation was, "is it constitutional?" Certainly southerners thought that the arguments of Calhoun and other states' rights southerners were irrefutable. According to the editor of the *Georgia Weekly Constitutionalist*, Calhoun's Oregon speech was "unanswerable"; another editor, on considering Calhoun's February 1847 resolutions, declared them and constitutional rights "the high and holy ground." When Calhoun returned to South Carolina after the short session of Congress, 1846–47, he said to a public gathering in Charleston that the South would defeat the Wilmot Proviso: "We have, in the first place, the advantage of having the Constitution on our side, clearly and unquestionably, and in its entire fabric; so much so, that the whole body of the instrument stands opposed to their scheme of appropriating the Territories to themselves."[33] But the truth was the states' rights argument of southerners about congressional prohibition of slavery in the territories was a very poor argument. On this issue, the northern position was an unassailable fortress.

Northerners had explicit constitutional provisions and precedents on their side. In the Northwest Ordinance of 1787, a number of other congressional laws in the early nineteenth century ensuring slavery did not enter the Northwest, and the Missouri Compromise, the precedent of Congress prohibiting slavery in certain territories had been established. Second, they pointed to Article 4, section 3, which even in a strict-construction sense gave the ruling power of the territories to Congress. Sovereignty is neither mentioned nor explained in the Constitution, but the power to appoint marshals, governors, and judges to the territories, the capacity of Congress to review and to veto territorial legislation when a territorial legislature commenced operation, and the ownership of land that the federal government possessed were certainly all that was necessary to establish sovereignty. Indeed, the federal government had far more potential power over the territories—just the establishment of a police function alone—than it did over the states.

Finally, the law of property was on the side of the North. All the states varied in their property laws, perhaps the most obvious being in banking laws and rights of incorporation. By the 1840s it was well established that the laws of property of one state only operated within that state's confines and could not extend to another state or jurisdiction. The federal government did not, at that time, intervene in such matters. The provision in the Constitution (Article 4, section 2) that stipulates that citizens of each state "shall be entitled to all the privileges and immunities of citizens in the several States" did not permit the laws of persons and property to go from one state to another. Rather, it stated that a citizen of the United States could not be discriminated against in another state, that each state's rules and regulations applied equally to all U.S. citizens residing in that state; a state government could not discriminate against its citizens and citizens from other states in its laws. Thus when a South Carolinian removed to New York, the South Carolinian faced the same New York laws that a New Yorker lived under and not under a different set of rules for non–New Yorkers.

The southern argument was shot full of holes. Southerners referred to the compact theory of the Constitution, to the doctrine of states' rights, perhaps to the "principles of [17]98," to the sanctity of property rights. What they did not point to were explicit provisions of the Constitution that allowed slavery as property to be protected outside of state jurisdictions. They had nearly no precedents to back their case. In short, their position depended on a favorable reception of their theories about the Constitution. It was not based on a strict construction of the document that referred to explicit powers. Indeed, the only explicit citation made was Article 4, section 3, and then the effort was made to deny the obvious—to deny the federal government had power over the evolution of the territories. Calhoun's distinction that the power granted was only over landed property and not over people might have been excellent lawyer case argument—making the best case possible given the existing evidence and statutes—but it was largely ludicrous. The federal government from the beginning had exercised every known element of sovereignty when ruling the territories, including the power to tax—and without the consent of the inhabitants to boot.

Moreover, most of the component parts of the southern defense of slavery's right to expand into the territories were dubious. Southerners tried to extend states' rights into the controversy, but the issue was about territories, not about states. In the states' rights formulation, the states had sovereignty and tried to stop the central government's growth of power by a rigid construction of the specific areas given to the federal authority. Territories have nothing to do with that concern. In the Constitution the fate of the territories vis-à-vis the federal government and the states was specific: the states gave up all claim to the territories, giving up all possibilities of expanding their borders, and yielded total sway over the territories to the federal government. In the Constitution the states had not one attribute of sovereignty in regard to the territories; the Constitution vested all those powers in the federal government. States' rights was simply inapplicable to the condition of the territories to begin with.

In the debates over the Compromise of 1850, Robert Toombs of Georgia said that "I stand upon the great principle that the South has the right to an equal participation in the territories of the United States. I claim the right for her to enter them all with her property and securely to enjoy it."[34] Such statements could probably be multiplied a thousand times, and they all exhibit serious defects. First, note that Toombs defined the South as those states that permitted slavery. What else could the meaning be, for the issue was the prohibition of *slavery* into the territories and nothing else. The whole debate ends up proving that southerners defined their section by no other standard than the existence of slavery—no other condition mattered. States' rights as a theory does not recognize congregation of states into sections; the plea that the "South" was being injured had no bearing because states' rights only works for states, not sections. Second, Toombs confused the rights of citizens with the rights of property. No citizen of the South, or of the North, was denied access to any of the territories. The Wilmot Proviso did accord equal treatment of citizens—all lived under the same set of rules that Congress formulated. But the Wilmot Proviso did not treat property equally. Congress did not deny citizens access but denied slave property governmental protection.

The question of citizenship brings up another fallacy in the southern argument. The group most decidedly discriminated against was the slaveholders. Slaveholders only accounted for 30 percent of the southern population in 1850 and 25 percent in 1860. By a numerical standard, then, the prohibition against slavery in the territories did not discriminate against *southerners* because most southerners were nonslaveholders. Rather, the discrimination fell upon a minority group in the South. One then comes around again to the willingness of southern politicians to equate the South with slaveholding. If that equation were untrue, then southern states had no basis for complaint against the proviso because for the bulk of the citizens it was a meaningless restriction.

Thus we come to the sticking point of state property laws moving beyond their jurisdictions.[35] When it came to the laws of property, the Southern anti-provisoists fostered a grand contradiction. Congress could not establish rules of property for the states, and many northerners and southerners also stipulated that Congress could not define property in the territories either. The agency that did define property was state government. So in the "Address of the Southern Delegates in Congress to Their Constituents" in early February 1849, Calhoun quoted Judge Storey that "slavery is a domestic institution. It belongs to the States, each for itself to decide, whether it shall be established or not." All sorts of southerners insisted that slavery was entirely a municipal institution over which Congress and other states had no authority; Armistead Burt even claimed authority for local control of slavery from Justice John McLean, who had used the municipal argument to justify prohibition of slavery in the territories! The radical South Carolinian Robert Barnwell Rhett in 1850 spelled out what the South required of northerners: "[W]hy, they simply ordain that the Northern people shall let us alone (as the Constitution designed) with respect to our property and our institutions."[36]

How then does one move from an explicit embrace of the doctrine that a local authority defines property only for its own jurisdiction and denies any other authority to intrude on its decisions to the position that such a local authority can define property beyond its jurisdiction? The laws of property in the United States of the nineteenth century, and even in the twentieth century, are local laws of municipalities and states. Southerners had no right under any circumstance to define property anywhere other than in their own states. The price of exclusive control of slavery from outsiders was that southerners could not define slavery outside their borders. Southerners in the territorial issue were seeking the power to project the laws of property (slavery) beyond state borders, a power that under the Constitution no state had.

Nevertheless, the territories had to have rules about property or else all would have been chaos. In the territories, people might claim different things property, and part of the duty of the law—that is, government—is to produce uniform and understandable rules about property. The only agencies left there for determining the rules of property were either the territorial government or the Congress of the United States. Calhoun's argument that the federal government was only a trustee of the states and could not pass legislation that undermined the activities of any of its members totally missed the point. The

Constitution gave the central government control over the territories and denied the states participation in that control. The "trusteeship" that Calhoun mentioned was provided for in the machinery of law making. Congress made laws by majority voting in the Senate and the House of Representatives, then finally approved by the president. That was the arena for states to work out their trusteeship. But that principle of majority rule was precisely the principle Calhoun found abhorrent because the laws might not be to his liking. Majority rule on matters relating to slavery by nonslaveholders in any governmental body was not to be tolerated.

Northerners also quickly found the practical weakness of the southern argument. Slavery was a form of property established by state law, yet southerners claimed that this one type of property required recognition by other migrants to the West. Northern states had different types of laws about property, too, governing such matters as banking, corporations, patrimonies to sons, the wages and possessions of wives, and inheritances. These laws differed from state to state. Did settlers from different states carry their state's property laws with them? "But the southern man complains that he cannot carry his local laws with him," argued Israel Washburn in 1854. "The northern man cannot carry his, and yet he does not complain." If all state laws concerning property were observed in the territories, "what a jumble and confusion of rights would ensue."[37] Given the multiplicity of property laws in the states, some agency had to determine which specific laws actually operated in the territories, and that agency could either be the Congress or the territorial legislature, but it simply could not be a state.

Northerners believed southerners were seeking a privileged status for slavery as property, and indeed this was the only way that southerners could enable the law of slave property to escape its state boundaries. They argued that the Constitution recognized property rights in slaves, thus giving to that property a national presence. This claim had its strengths and weaknesses. Although northerners denied that the Constitution directly recognized slaves as property, southerners on this point had the better argument. Southerners would never have consummated a union if the rights to slave property and control of its definition by the states had not been guaranteed at the time of the framing. But the reverse of the situation also had to be recognized. Northerners never would have agreed to union if southerners had pressed upon them the idea that slavery had a national standing—that in all things the new government would recognize property rights in slaves. Upon this point, northerners came to see southerners as changing the rules of game and creating innovations to which their northern ancestors had never assented.

Moreover, northerners had a sufficient counterattack on claims that slavery as property had a special legal status under the Constitution. The Constitution did not mention slavery as an institution, and when it referred to bondage it referred to human beings, not property. The various clauses that dealt with people bonded to others were specific in their application (the three-fifths compromise, the fugitive slave law) rather than being general. The Fifth Amendment declared that no person should be deprived by the federal government of "life, liberty, or property, without due process of law." In the states, this provision operated to protect property in slaves from the federal government because the state had defined property in slaves. That was not the condition of territories where the agency to define property was not a state government. Because the federal government or a territorial legislature may assume the right—or even duty—to define property, there was no violation of the Fifth Amendment because the act of definition by the appropriate authority was a formulation of property rights, not a violation of them.[38]

Many southern politicians claimed that their ancestors would never have joined the Union if they had known that Congress in the future would have forbidden them to take their property into the territories. Perhaps that was so, but the Constitution was strangely mute on the question of territories and slavery. No real discussion of the matter emerged in the Constitutional Convention, and all one can offer is speculation. Perhaps northerners and southerners in that era realized that such a question was too explosive to bring up and yet hope to cement a new national government, that the best policy was to remand the question to their distant progeny. Perhaps they thought time would effect a solution before slavery expansion became a political issue. After all, in 1790 the United States was still largely an Atlantic seaboard nation with tremendous landholdings to the Mississippi River that American settlers had barely touched. When Jefferson consummated the Louisiana Purchase in 1803, he hoped that the nation had sufficient land to maintain its yeoman farmer status for the next millennium. Perhaps the founders believed that the nation had enough land so that by the time settlement spilled beyond the Mississippi River either slavery had commenced its death spiral or northerners would have fully accepted it. Whatever their intentions, they were not written into the Constitution. No provision of the document spelled out specifically how the question of slavery in the territories was to be handled. All that was certain was that the territories were given to the new Congress and taken entirely away from the influence of the states.

Northerners of all political opinions found the Calhoun school and most of the anti-provisoist camp to be incomprehensible and wrong. The *New York Globe* called southern rights doctrines a "ridiculous unconstitutional platform," while another antislavery editor summed up the southern position as slaveholders exercising "the right of construing the constitutional powers of Congress to suit their own interests." Lewis Cass in 1854 complained that southerners sought too expansive a power for slavery and that such activity was destroying states' rights. At the Buffalo Free-Soil convention in 1848, one speaker complained that "A Virginian thinks the Constitution is a great jug with the handles all on the Southern side." A Democratic Pittsburgh editor declared

Calhoun "a perfect enigma" who "thinks South Carolina is the whole Union, and most faithfully does he represent his constituents."[39] Of Calhoun's speech in the Senate on Henry Clay's compromise measures (March 4, 1850), John A. Dix remarked, "I certainly never read a speech so replete with false premises and illogical deductions from them; and it will detract much in the public estimation from Mr. Calhoun's high reputation as a Statesman and a logician."[40]

Moreover, northerners specifically and instantly went to the weaknesses in the anti-provisoist interpretation. One was the status of the law; southerners simply had no right to extend slave law beyond their borders. After reading of the *Charleston Mercury*'s attempt to argue for the sanctity of slave law everywhere, the editors of the antislavery paper the *National Era* responded by saying, "So utterly extravagant and groundless is this doctrine, that we can hardly frame a serious answer to it. If it be true, the slaveholders . . . can migrate with their slaves to Ohio, settle there, . . . and perpetuate slavery there, despite all the laws of the State."[41]

Others said the obvious: where were the texts that defined slaves as inviolable property in the territories? In the Address of the Democratic Members of the New York Legislature, they inserted a line about southern constitutional doctrine concerning the territories, "we are called upon to interpolate this new theory upon the constitution as a sort of mystical common-law, not expressed, not implied, in any particular part, but to be inferred from the general nature of that instrument." A correspondent of Joshua Giddings, Arnold Buffum, complained that "Slaveholders would take their stand upon the utterance 'The *Compromises* and *Guaranties* of the *Constitution*.' But I never knew an instance in which, they quoted, or gave a reference to those 'Compromises and guaranties' and the reason was that there are no compromises and guaranties which authorize the enslavement of human beings." In 1858 Vermont representative Eliakim P. Walton complained that Calhoun based his position "upon no express provision of the Constitution, and no previous interpretation of it."[42] The conclusion of northerners generally was that the states' rights doctrine of the sanctity of property in slaves in the territories was founded only in some nebulous theory that really was a guise for naked self-interest.

Southerners had their share of trouble in adjusting to some of the claims of the Calhoun school. For almost all southerners, the concept of property rights in slavery was sacrosanct, and no one questioned that fairness dictated that slavery should be permitted to expand into the territories when profitable to do so. Beyond that, however, the question of slavery in the territories rankled as both an abstract and practical problem. "So great is the diversity of opinion which unfortunately prevails among Southern men as to the mode of settlement of the disturbing subject of slavery," wrote Alabama senator William R. King to James Buchanan, "that I am unable to say what they will insist on, or what they will yield." As to Calhoun, he was "not merely impracticable as usual," wrote James H. Hammond of South Carolina, "but absurd." Calhoun's opinion that the property aspect of slavery obliged the federal government to carry slavery into the territories stumped Henry Clay. The doctrine was "so irreconcilable with any comprehension or reason, which I possess, that I hardly know how to meet it."[43]

Within the South a dissenting view about the advanced anti-provisoist interpretation appeared, and not merely on practicalities but on constitutional grounds. Alexander H. Stephens and Robert Toombs, possibly for internal Georgia political reasons, warned that Mexican law was a real obstacle to slavery expansion, and that if the Supreme Court handled such a case, the judges might well indeed decide that Mexican law prohibited slavery in the western territories.[44] They demanded Congress pass a law repealing the Mexican prohibition and specifically allow slavery to enter the lands acquired from Mexico. But most southerners shied away from giving Congress any power over slavery, be it in the territories or the states. Many voiced their favor of "nonintervention," which ultimately gave Lewis Cass's popular sovereignty a plausibility of southern support.[45] One writer said that he preferred the ideas of Daniel Webster because "he repudiates what is *not* in the Constitution & with us, he insists upon whatever *is* in that paper." Others noted that the precedent of the Missouri Compromise acted against southern hopes for slavery's expansion into the territories.[46]

Calhoun's pronouncements on the inability of Congress to rule the territories found southern challengers. North Carolina representative Thomas Clingman called Calhoun's doctrines "shallow and superficial" and ended up, in a not particularly masterful oration, agreeing with northerners that Congress had the right to determine what was property in the territories. More shattering was the view of John A. Campbell of Alabama, soon to be a Supreme Court justice and participant in the *Dred Scott* case. In an 1848 letter to Calhoun, Campbell got right to the point.

> I think congress has the power to organise the inhabitants of a territory of the U.S. into a body politic, and to determine in what manner they shall be governed. As incident to this power I think that congress may decide what shall be held and enjoyed as property in that territory, and that persons should not be held as property. I think farther that when a territory is acquired by conquest or by treaty and the laws in force in the territory are not changed by the treaty of cession or by an act of congress that they remain in force. . . . I think further that slavery is purely a municipal institution and falls under this principle. . . . [The Constitution] does not sanction the tittle [*sic*] of a master in his slaves except in certain specified cases . . . it no where provides that the rights of the slave owner shall be protected in all the territories of the U.S. or that the master shall be free to carry them as slaves to those territories.

And so Campbell undercut every one of Calhoun's propositions.[47]

And many understood not only the benefits but the limitations of the municipal law defense of property rights in slavery. One contributor to the *Charleston Mercury* pointed out that until the present all that the South demanded was to "be let alone" and for Congress to be kept from interfering in the territories. Behind this was the fact that "Slavery exists nowhere in the Union but by legislative or positive enactments. It is a municipal regulation." But this particular writer drew out an obvious problem. What entitled slavery to the privileges of property sanctification in the territories but not other forms of property? When people from different states entered the territories, they could not all bring the property laws of their states with them. "Does the slave-owner carry with him the laws of South Carolina in favor of slavery? Then the free laborer of the West carries with him also the laws of his State against slavery. Which law shall prevail and be paramount?" The privileging of slavery as property over northern forms of property had no justification.[48]

The editor of the Whig journal, the *Raleigh Weekly Register*, fought the tendency to demand federal promotion of slavery into the territories. The only safe position was nonintervention by Congress in the territories, for if one admitted Congress had the power to protect slavery there, then it also had the power to deny slavery's expansion. Rather, said the editor, "The *Constitution* guarantees ample protection, in its provisions, for our slave property." Let it stay that way. "Under the local municipal law, the Constitution found slavery, there left it, and there, and there alone, every true friend of the South ought to wish it to remain."[49]

In Georgia, the Whig and later Know-Nothing Judge Garnett Andrews contributed some interesting letters on the territorial issue and brought forth the real dilemma. He ascribed to the belief that property rights in slaves depended on positive municipal law, and he advocated nonintervention by Congress in the territories on the slavery question. He hoped that New Mexico would become a slave state as "it would strengthen the slave power" but doubted it would happen. However, it might come to pass that the North would overrule the southern demand for nonintervention. If it did, the North would be guilty of prejudice and unfair actions toward the South—but not of acting unconstitutionally. For the majority had the right to rule. And if nonintervention came to be the rule and no new slave states emerged from the territories, then the South had to accept the result. The true safety for the South, he claimed, lay in recognizing that the North possessed the majority: "Southern Rights can be maintained only by combining Southern power with the Northern politicians who abide the constitution . . . [to maintain] our rights and security."[50] In short, southerners would find no assurances for slavery in fantastic constitutional theories; rather, they would have to do the hard work of forming and maintaining political coalitions. The majority resided in the North, and southerners had to accommodate themselves to the reality that on some issues they might lose—that was the inevitable fate of political life in a republican government that operated by majority rule. Judge Andrews could accept the possibility of losing some political battles in order to preserve republican government; John C. Calhoun and the radicals could not.

Both northerners and southerners probed further into the nature of property rights in slaves rather than limiting themselves to the question of the constitutionality of prohibiting slavery in the territories. Some of the expressions were purely concerns about sectional advantages, while others were contemplations of a more practical bent—how to get beyond the problem. Yet out of this particular nature of property rights in slaves came an extended look into natural rights, the common law, and the meaning of the constitution. Moreover, their analyses help to clarify the "aggression" that each side saw in the other's actions, and especially the charge of northerners that the territorial issue had elicited new doctrines out of the South that were fundamentally altering the nation.

Almost all southern defenders of the right to extend slavery in the territories insisted that the act of prohibiting slaves was an act of aggression. Northerners responded by labeling the South the aggressor. George W. Julian said that there could be no aggression when northerners agreed that slavery in the states "is beyond our control." The problem was southern control of the government, the "slave power," requiring northerners to participate in maintaining the peculiar institution. In 1858 Benjamin Wade responded to the famous "mudsill" oration of James Henry Hammond by querying how could southerners howl about "aggressions at the North" when "the slaveholders of the South have ruled this Government for sixty long years."[51] Beyond this, northerners generally claimed that they sought nothing new in the political arena: territory once free remained free, they claimed, and the policy of restricting slavery in the territories was as old or older than the Constitution itself.

But another southern argument elicited a sense of aggression, especially from those knowledgeable about law. Southerners claimed that slaves were property, property rights were recognized in the Constitution, and the Constitution was in fact a machine designed to protect slave property. Northerners immediately repudiated these southern positions.

Northerners dived into an analysis of property rights in man. They insisted that slavery existed only by municipal law and was therefore localized.[52] The Constitution promoted freedom, not slavery, for the intention of the founders was a republic of freeholders, not of slaveholders. Rather, the founders, said the antiextensionists, wanted slavery to die out over time, but territorial expansion had permitted the institution to thrive.[53] Such claims, regardless of the quantity of ancestor quotations, were inconclusive, and the proposition that the Constitution was an antislavery document was merely a convenient interpretation, as much as was the extreme proslavery claim that it was a proslavery document.

Northern provisoists were most upset with the southern claim of property rights in man. They could agree that law could make men or women property, but not that it was a general principle. In 1847, Samuel Gordon of New York declared that "Man cannot hold property in man; slaves are not property except in the slaveholding States," and, moreover, they were slaves "only upon the principle that might makes right." Indiana's Caleb Smith remarked that even as property slavery had a different quality than other property: it was permissible to shoot a horse in the head, but not a slave. "Why? Because he was not property." A host of northerners testified that property rights in humans was a false idea but one that could only be brought into being by positive legislative enactment. The Cass supporter, Massachusetts representative Benjamin Hallett, while supporting nonintervention in the territories, added some informative views about the southern argument. Noting that the South wanted more than the Constitution yielded, Hallett explained that "Property does not exist by nature. It is the creature of legislation." Therefore, property rights in people—to include apprentices or others—requires "a law of that place." Hence, all property was local and limited to a local jurisdiction; southern claims for extension of slavery into the territories via property rights could not stand.[54]

Most northern antiextensionists, while admitting slavery was protected by local law, bitterly denounced the idea that the Constitution protected property rights in slaves. The radical interpretation was that the Constitution was fundamentally antislavery and gave power to emancipate those in bondage, a position favored by almost no congressman. But most provisoists pointed out that not only did the word "slave" not appear in the Constitution, but that whenever the phrasing intimated slaves—persons owing labor to others—the Constitution treated them as persons, not property. Early in the fight over extension, a few extreme northerners pushed this idea in the Antonio Pacheco case, a situation in the Flordia Indian wars in which a slaveholder sued the federal government for compensation for the loss of his slave who had been pressed into service. In 1848 James Wilson of New Hampshire argued against compensation because slaves by the Constitution were not property, and compensation in this case would be a bad precedent. In a superior speech showing the conflict of state laws of slavery with the Constitution, Martin Grover of New York said he permitted and obeyed local laws on slavery but not national ones—"Why? Because slaves are not the kind of 'property' that is within the meaning of the Constitution." By 1858 the Republican Nehemiah Abbott simply said, "The doctrine that slaves are property by the Constitution of the United States, I hold to be utterly false. . . . If established, it will nationalize slavery, and denationalize freedom."[55]

As northerners talked about the legal aspects of property rights in slavery, they made two additional claims. The first was that slavery violated natural rights. Salmon P. Chase, the radical antislavery leader from Ohio, boasted in 1854, "I could quote the opinions of southern judges *ad infinitum*, in support of the doctrine that slavery is against natural right" and dependent solely on local law. Although not fully developed among northern congressional figures, they seemed to intimate that natural rights meant a right to act in the absence of outside force. Cyrus Dunham of Indiana stated that the title to slave property "is no natural right" but existed only "by the might of [the slaveholder's] power, and no longer." Ben Wade declared that the use of force in slavery was akin to the justification of the divine right of kings and all privileged orders. Northerners made such declarations to divorce the Constitution and any theory of natural right from any justification of slavery except that of municipal law.[56]

Another northern assertion, which greatly agitated southerners, was the claim that the common law did not support slavery. In the case of the territories, the importance of the common law was that many figured that in the absence of any real authority—that is, a formal government in operation with police powers—one could claim that the law in operation was the common law borrowed from England at the time of the Revolution. Was the common law friendly or hostile to slavery? According to the proviso supporters, English common law—surprise of surprises—was always inimical to slavery. For their proof, the restrictionists pointed to Blackstone's *Commentaries* on the English law and to the decision of Lord Mansfield in the 1772 *Somerset* case that declared that people in England could not have property in other men. In reaction to Roger B. Taney's decision in the *Dred Scott* case, Republicans dredged up cases to show that well before the Revolution Africans were considered people and not property.[57] Again, the brunt of the restrictionist argument was to drive slavery's legality back to municipal authority solely and thus close off any legal route to extend slavery beyond a local jurisdiction.

Southern extensionists did not let these arguments pass without comment. As to the idea that the Constitution did not observe property rights in slaves, southerners, though shocked by the assertion, dismissed the idea. Supreme Court cases time and again had shown that the court recognized property rights in slaves, and southerners time and again said that had not property rights in slaves been guaranteed in 1787, no Constitution would have ever been constructed or ratified. On this question, southerners undoubtedly were correct. Although northern antiextensionists could try to finesse the situation by various arguments about the federal government observing property rights in slaves only in slaveholding jurisdictions, the Constitution obviously recognized those types of property rights. Whether the recognition of those rights extended into matters of federal policy was another question.

Antirestriction arguments based on the common law and natural rights evoked a more powerful counterattack. Southerners fought the notion that slavery only existed where positive law permitted it and that common law was naturally antislavery. Early in the debates over extension, some southerners stated that slavery preceded law: "Slavery existed as a form of property without being instituted," said South Carolina representative Joseph A. Woodward. In 1854 Virginia's William Smith told Congress that slaves arrived in Virginia in 1619 and the practice of slaveholding developed before slave laws were promulgated, circa 1660. In fact, most of the colonies in the seventeenth century had African slaves without slave laws. By 1858 Virginian Muscoe R. H. Garnett said in a stunning oration, "Yes, sir, property is not the creature of legislation; but it is coeval with government, with society, with man himself." Property arose, said Garnett, out of the desire of humans to master their environment, government or no, and property sprung "from the capacity and instinct of the superior races to command, and of the inferior to obey, and thus mutually to aid each other in fulfilling the work of God in the universe." South Carolina's Lawrence Keitt argued that England had slavery at the time of the Revolution, and thus the common law supported the institution of slavery.[58]

This particular phase of the southern argument denied the claim of northerners that slavery required "positive law" for the institution to take root. By invalidating the proposition that slavery required law and was not contrary to common law, southerners asserted that slavery was a natural phenomenon that occurred rather spontaneously and only positive law prohibited it. As a consequence, slavery went into the territories because slavery could only be stopped by legislation; in the absence of legislation prohibiting it, slavery existed. This argument of southern politicians was historically correct, save for the common law, and theoretically interesting. On the history of slaveholding in colonial America, they were absolutely correct: slavery was practiced long before laws were passed making Africans chattel property. The theoretically interesting aspect of the argument is how it redounds on economic theories regarding choice and the absence of the state. Slavery, an obvious deprivation of a person's ability to choose, evolved as an economic custom without legal sanction and without enforcement largely due to a consensus, it appears, on the part of the white majority in early America (or, rather, Virginia). In short, given the chance to bargain freely, actors choose against bargaining with Africans and instead determined to exercise nongovernmental power to deprive people of their economic "rights" to choose economic activities freely. This example hardly accords with Pareto optimality or with the "win-win" scenario so often given by libertarians as an argument against government.[59]

Interestingly, one prominent Republican agreed with part of the southern claim that slavery had access to the territories because of the lack of a prohibitive law—Abraham Lincoln. Lincoln in most matters tended to repeat the arguments made throughout the North, albeit in far more memorable language, and was characteristic, not unique, in most of his thinking on sectional matters. But on this one instance he was unique among Republicans. He did not believe, as virtually all other Republicans did, that land without slavery meant slavery was prohibited, that without positive law slavery could not exist. "That *is* good book-law," he said in Peoria in 1854, "but is not the rule of actual practice." He agreed with southerners that the law did not create slavery in the colonies but was created to regulate what had already been established. Without a prohibitory law, slaveholders might try to get into a territory because they well might know "the negative principle that *no* law is free law." In short, in a fluid situation where the law was not specific, one might take chances that what is not prohibited is then allowed. Lincoln's scenario then was once property holders got into the territories with slaves, they became the wealthiest and most influential people, well able to guard against political intrusions on their property. Thus once established, slavery could grow from a small beginning, partly from the reluctance of people to dispossess people of their property.[60]

Unlike virtually every other aspect of sectional debate between 1846 and 1861, the question of the relationship between common law and slavery had a final closure. Louisiana senator Judah P. Benjamin delivered in 1858 an erudite and informative speech on the common law and how in 1776 the common law supported slaveholding. He noted, or argued, that slavery persisted in England into the eighteenth century via villeins regardant and villeins ingross, both of whom he called slaves and chattels. Benjamin made this distinction: people might have property, but law only covered the right of recovery of property when lost. He thereby proposed that property in people could exist and be recognized, but the right of recovery might not. Thus at the time of the Revolution, the common law recognized slavery, and the founders, as people of that time, also saw slaves as property.[61] Both senators John P. Hale and Daniel Clark of New Hampshire responded to Benjamin and gave a final answer to common law's position on slavery. In particular, Clark cited 2 Lord Raymond Reports, *Smith v. Gould*, 1703, in which the judge, Lord Holt, decided the case by applying the doctrine of "trover" that "for the common law takes no notice of negroes being different from other men," and that "By the common law no man can have a property in another . . . but in special cases." The court then declared, "There is no such thing as a slave by the law of England." And with that pronouncement, battles of the meaning of common law in regard to slavery ceased in Congress.[62]

On natural rights, however, defenders of property rights in slaves never capitulated. It was a defense greatly at odds with much of American enlightenment thinking at the time and had much in common with extreme proslavery assertions that natural rights did not exist. A number of southerners concluded that their right to slave property was the result of the natural law of force and not due to legislation at all. When Alexander H. Stephens in the summer of 1848 argued against a proposed compromise on slavery in the lands ceded by Mexico (the Clayton Compromise), he based his views on the need for Congress to pass a positive law establishing slavery there and repealing Mexican law. His stance produced a violent reaction from a Mississippi editor. If Stephens's position were correct, then "slavery is a mere civil right depending on the municipal law of a locality," that there is no "natural right to hold slaves, as there is to our horses or cattle." Stephens's ideas reduced "the tenure by which we hold our slaves [to] no greater strength than a mere statute of limitations." The editor concluded that slavery was a natural right.[63] Jefferson Davis put the matter bluntly. Property in slavery did not owe its existence to local law but "resulted from the dominion of mind over matter." In short, the legal argument of southerners stretched to the point of their stating that slavery reflected the property rights of the superior to dominate the inferior—Social Darwinism before its time.[64]

Out of the continuous battle with northern restrictionists, many southerners came to several unsettling conclusions. The conviction grew widespread, and was as well matched with the actual condition of the North American continent, that northerners would not permit any new slave states, and many southerners for reasons of political power in the U.S. Senate demanded that more slave states be admitted.[65] If restricted, then the operation of majority rule in the Congress could only injure the South and destroy southern political equality in Congress (basically, the Senate). Thus, as some said, the South needed more constitutional guarantees if it was to stay within the Union, for as the Philadelphia conservative Sidney Fisher noted, "The South is afraid to *trust* the protection of slavery to the Constitution."[66] One way already mentioned was to alter the Constitution in its interpretation of the Fifth Amendment and the protection of property—to create substantive due process. In an address in 1849, Georgia senator John M. Berrien said the South should not allow any attempt of the federal government to interfere or "to diminish the value" by "direct or indirect means" the value of slave property. Indeed, the final demand of the South was in some sense the "nationalization of slavery" in that property rights in slaves came before any other consideration. The federal government should be dedicated to the propagation and preservation of slavery. Said Georgia's Robert Toombs in 1854, "Therefore, so far from its being true that the Constitution localized slavery, it nationalized it; and it is the only property which it does nationalize except the works of genius and art."[67]

Driving southern behavior and projections was a fear that northerners would jeopardize property rights in slaves. The property rights nature of the debate over slavery started from the introduction of the Wilmot Proviso and lasted to the end of the Thirty-sixth Congress in June 1860. Certainly southerners had to withstand a lot of aggravating self-righteous northern posturing on moral laws, God's laws, and the design of Nature's god over these years, and political considerations certainly were not far from their calculations. But arguments over property rights in a property worth nearly 20 percent of the nation's wealth was not a quarrel over abstract principles. Southern slaveholders, or at least a goodly number of them, had reason to suspect that their wealth was about to be diminished by a hostile northern majority. They wanted new guarantees that it would not. The abstract nature of the debate was the way some southerners projected the battle over property rights in the territories into property rights in the states. Extremists constantly saw Republicans increasing their demands. Complained James F. Dowdell of Alabama, "Once concede the power to Congress to legislate slavery out of a common territory, and what barrier can be set up against its unlimited sway?"[68] Many southerners lived under this fear that the attack on property rights in slaves would not stop with the territories. Perhaps that fear was induced by the size of the property at stake.

Between 1846 and 1848, virtually all northerners believed Congress had the constitutional right to restrict slavery's expansion into the territory, and the doctrines of southerners that such restriction was unconstitutional was something of both a shock and insult to them. Initially northerners did not declare that they would no longer tolerate the admission of more slave states, although given the geography of the country by 1848 and the dictum that once free always free, the only conclusion to be made was that the filling out of the continental borders would result only in free states and no slave states. Moreover, northerners believed the South had all the guarantees necessary to protect slavery in the states and required no more. As the secession crisis deepened in February 1861, some northern congressmen were questioned as to compromise possibilities with the South and particularly about new constitutional safeguards for the slaveholding states. Replied Godlove Orth, "While I shall always feel ready to yield to the Institution of Slavery all the protection granted by the Constitution, I will never consent to confer upon it any additional guarantees."[69]

Many northerners found the debate over slavery in the territories unsettling because they saw the South evolving in a way that portended ill for the future, and the reason was the maniacal attachment of slaveholders to their property. Property holdings in slavery were, to some northerners, endangering republican liberty and the process of self-government. The tendency of the southern argument was to elevate property rights above all other rights, and in particular the right of the majority to pass laws. Stephen A. Douglas tried to overcome that tendency by ignoring it, offering the possibility of popular governance in the territories by the settlers themselves; he believed climate would ultimately dictate the establishment of slavery or not. The persistence of the South on the supremacy of property rights in slaves over all other considerations finally drove Douglas to an explicit rejection of southern claims in the Lecompton Constitution episode in 1858. Tension between the rights of property in slaves and majority voting had been obvious to other Democrats as well.[70]

In the same years, many northerners also came to the conclusion that under the guise of property rights the South was changing the nation and forcing it into a new direction. Certainly the provisoists and the antislavery advocates charged aggression against slaveholders often enough, and just as frequently they tied that aggression to the use of the government to expand slavery into new territory.[71] But their fears were deeper than that—southerners in their quest for security of slave property were altering the entire country. This was the northern antislavery charge that the North remained true to the old Constitution, but that southerners were foisting upon them a new framework.[72] The results of demanding that slaves, as property, had rights beyond state jurisdiction led inevitably to the conclusion that slavery could not even be prohibited in the North. Upon this basis the abolitionist William Goodell sent out letters to Republicans warning them of the consequences of property rights doctrines connected with slaves: "If slavery be legal & Constitutional in *some* of the States why not in *all* the States? If human beings are property *any* where, are they not property *every* where?" The nationalization of the law of slavery as property meant that the Constitution, as the "supreme law of the land," recognized the sanctity of property rights in slaves everywhere, making them "paramount to all State laws and constitutions. . . . The effect would be to carry slavery into every State in the Union, and the Union from that day would stand dissolved."[73] In the *Dred Scott* decision, Republicans believed their worst fears had come to pass.

Seward had warned that an antagonism dwelled between property and liberty, and that concentrations of property could become so dangerous as to overwhelm other freedoms and liberties. The concentration of property in slaves between 1840 and 1860 did represent a danger, an imbalance, that led to a growing southern animus toward democracy and majority rule. By 1860, most white southerners were well within the folds of northern beliefs in natural rights, democratic government, and majority rule, but slavery was an exception. Yet the tendency existed and was apparent in a few figures like Calhoun. By late 1847 northern passage of personal liberty laws exasperated him as much as the Wilmot Proviso. He already believed a majority should never be allowed to dictate his rights, and of his rights one of the most precious was his property in slaves. He showed how the belief in slaveholders' right to slave property escalated to the point of overriding the liberties of others: "I go farther, and hold that if we have a right to hold our slaves, we have the right to hold them in peace and quiet, and that the toleration in the non-slaveholding States of the establishment of societies and presses, and the delivery of lectures, with the express intention of calling in question our right to our slaves [and enticing runaways and abolition, is] not only a violation of international laws, but also the Federal compact."[74] By this route, concentrated property became a danger to the right to press, religion, speech, and assembly.

Northerners by any objective standard held all the aces in the constitutional battle over slavery in the territories. The South made as good a defense as possible, but it was entirely inferior, based on nonconsensual theory instead of constitutional referents and precedents. The power to prohibit slavery belonged constitutionally to Congress. But constitutionality only indicates the ability to do; it has nothing to do with fairness. And the southern complaint was really not about the constitutionality of prohibiting slavery in the territories, but about the justice of doing so. The "outrage" expressed by so many southerners was that their institution was being discriminated against, that their property was being demeaned and possibly devalued, and that their society was being castigated. In that sense, southerners were right. The northern position was that slavery produced a morally, socially, and economically defective society that then became an obstacle to good government by giving representation to a faulty economic system; that was why northerners did not wish it to spread. Southerners had the right to declaim against this depiction and demand some kind of compromise about slavery in the territories, but they had no constitutional defense against the imposition of a nonextension statute.[75]

This type of unfairness is almost inescapable in a scheme of representative government. Any law will produce winners and losers because by making specific some rule, some individuals will have more of an ability to take advantage of the opportunities afforded than others. For representative government to work, society has to accept the fact that someone will lose when rules are made by the legislative authority. Usually, people who endure these setbacks have little difficulty in incorporating the defeat because so many avenues are open to advancement that the losses incurred are irritating, not monumental. Moreover, fairness in society comes not only or even primarily from the intellectual constructions inferred from a set of rules, but from argumentation, trial and error, and retrospective judgments. Some rules simply have to be tried before their results, good or bad, can be evaluated. Representative government allows this type of trial and error or learning by doing, permitting the majority then to change as its understanding of fairness evolves.

What is interesting about the history of constitutional dispute in the United States between the founding and southern secession in 1860–61 is that by constitutionalism southerners hoped to control the actions of the federal government and never lose. Constitutional doctrine in the hands of radical southerners always changed to satisfy the interests of the peculiar institution. By constitutional arguments, a number of southerners hoped they could negate any policy they deemed antagonistic to the peculiar institution regardless of what the Constitution actually permitted—for example, on issues of the tariff, internal improvements, and interstate commerce. Over the years, constitutional arguments came not to act as protectors of minority rights, but rather as a means for the minority to dominate federal policy. It was by this route that northern and southern constitutional doctrines, and the insistence of radical southerners that they never lose, came to produce a battle over the right of the majority to govern.

Certainly the constitutional question of the right of Congress to prohibit slavery in the territories has an abstract quality to it. But in a more theoretical sense about whether states would be free or slave, it made little difference. The territories in question might have sustained slavery, but in 1860 that was not clear, given the fact that most viewed slavery's profitability as being determined by the ability to raise the staples of cotton, sugar, tobacco, or rice. The key element in the whole debate was profitability, and in a sense it overrode the constitutional question of Congress's control over the territorial stage. A number of non-provisoist Democrats and newspapers saw part of the reality. If the economics were right, constitutionality did not matter. The territorial stage lasted only so many years. Once the territory became a state, it could do whatever it wanted.[76] It is at this point that profitability ruled the question of the establishment of slavery. Take two hypothetical examples.

Imagine that, in a fit of rage, southerners teamed with northern agrarian Democrats and laissez-faire Free-Soilers to pass a law prohibiting the corporate form of property in Colorado. Only agricultural property would be recognized. Congress, as ruler of the territory, had the right to impose such legislation under the guise that the "general welfare" of the nation would be better served by having yeomen farmers there rather than servile manufacturing wage earners. So it might have been imposed and even enforced. But by 1859 Coloradoans knew that precious minerals lay in their mountains, and within ten years they found out that placer mines and individuals could no longer retrieve gold and silver from the earth. Rather, they needed advanced hydraulic systems, deep mining, and huge ore crushers to get just ounces of mineral from tons of rock. And only corporations could raise the capital for these kinds of operations. Would the early prohibition against corporations stand? Not on your life. Where there's a buck, there's a will and a constitutional way. If Colorado tried to enter the Union as a state allowing corporations, maybe Congress would have said no. So what. Coloradoans could change their state constitution to forbid corporations; Congress then lets them into the Union; and then within months after admission Colorado amends its constitution and permits corporations, which Congress now has to allow because of state sovereignty over property rights. What is economically feasible—even disgustingly feasible—may triumph in the long run.

The same was true for areas in which slavery would have been immediately profitable by raising the types of staples white southerners were used to cultivating. Suppose a part of Mexico, or Cuba, or a Central American state had been annexed to the United States, and Congress slapped on a prohibition against slavery. But the white Americans going to those lands would have immediately recognized the economic profitability of raising sugar or cotton by slavery, be those white Americans northerners or southerners. So the prohibition would have been overturned as soon as these lands became states—either opting for slavery at the time of statehood or waiting for statehood and then amending their state constitutions. Economics drove the choice between slavery and nonslavery, and morality was hardly going to prevent an American from taking full advantage of the situation regardless of who got run over. The Constitution was no roadblock to action when money was involved.

It turned out, however, that expansion in the 1840s economically favored the northern labor system to a large extent rather than the southern, except for southern California and New Mexico, and even there it was unclear how profitable slavery might be. Southerners could have easily shrugged their shoulders in Congress and let the Wilmot Proviso pass. It would have made very little difference. One way to explain the hostility, then, to the proviso is to refer to southern honor and the unwillingness of southerners to being stigmatized as having an inferior civilization.[77] But the source of the fear appears to be the sanctity of property rights in slaves. The escalation of northern sentiment that southerners dreaded was clear: if property rights in slaves could be endangered in any form by the federal power, property rights in slaves in the states would be next on the agenda. Such fears made sense in consideration of the size of the institution, how concentrated it was in the hands of the politically active, and how it was so geographically isolated. The South would not allow itself to lose on the issue of slavery in the territories, and that is why they developed such strange constitutional theories in spite of the obvious powers the Constitution gave to Congress.

P A R T

TWO

THE POLITICAL REALIGNMENT OF THE 1850S

The entire value of the slave population of the United States, is, at a moderate estimate, not less than $2,000,000,000. This amount of *property* has a vast influence upon the minds of those who own it. The same amount of property owned by Northern men has the same influence upon *their* minds. . . . Public opinion is formed relative to a property basis. Therefore, the slaveholders battle any policy which depreciates their slaves as property. What increases the value of this property, they favor.

—Abraham Lincoln, speech at Hartford, Connecticut, March 5, 1860, in Basler, Pratt, and Dunlap, *Collected Works of Lincoln*, 4:3

The immediate question before the country is, Shall slavery be extended into free territory? In the settlement of this, it needs no elaborate arguments to show that the interests of the nonslaveholding white people and those of all the "blacks" are identified. The extension of slavery into free territory tends to prolong the existence of the system, to perpetuate the bondage and augment the sufferings of its victims, and, at the same time, to injure the working classes of the whites, by excluding them from such free territory, and by reducing their wages. . . .

The real question, is between Free Labor and the Slaveholding

Capitalist; and he who mystifies this question, so as to represent that the issue is between the white and black races, instead of Free Labor and the Slaveholding Oligarchy, has too little information (whatever his intelligence in other respects) to attempt its discussion.

—*Chicago Weekly Democrat*, March 12 [21?], 1848

We have time and again attempted to impress upon our readers the idea that this matter of slavery involve[s] something more than a mere servitude of the blacks. It is a question of *labor* in which every laboring man, and every man who believes it essential that labor be free has an interest. The fact is plain and patent that the south enslaves not the *black* but the *labor*. The South cares not a copper what the *color* of its slaves are, so [long as] their title is good. [The ascendancy of the Slave Power is] the ascendancy of a power which seeks to enslave, crush, and degrade *labor*, without a particle of reference to *color*.

—*Milwaukee Daily Free Democrat*, November 14, 1857

All property is best managed where Governments least interfere, and the practice of our Government has been generally founded on that principle. . . . What is there in the character of that property [slaves] which excludes it from the general benefit of the principles applied to all other property?

—Jefferson Davis, Speech in Senate, February 13, 14, 1850, in Rowland, *Jefferson Davis: Constitutionalist*, 1:279, 283

The whole theory of property will be questioned, and it will be found inconsistent with the higher law. The moment this theory becomes popular among the laboring classes of the North, the titles to estates will begin to be very precarious. It is surprising that the property-holders of the North do not see the dangerous consequences in the higher law principle of the slavery agitation.

—Representative William W. Boyce of South Carolina, May 20, 1854, *Cong. Globe*, 33d Cong., 1st sess., *Appendix*, 725

[Many in a] light and almost flippant manner . . . have spoken of changing and annulling constitutions, at any time and upon the least provocation, by a popular vote. . . . What safeguard have the rights of property, always in the hands of a minority, if this doctrine be true?

—Representative William Porcher Miles of South Carolina, March 31, 1858, *Cong. Globe*, 35th Cong., 1st sess., *Appendix*, 287

Mr. Clerk, free governments, so far as their protecting power is concerned, are made for minorities, and the Jeffersonian, State-rights theory protects minorities.

—Representative J. L. M. Curry of Alabama, December 10, 1859, *Cong. Globe*, 36th Cong., 1st sess., 96

The Politics of Southern Upheaval, 1846–1853

It was near the end of the day in Congress on August 8, 1846, at the close of the First Session of the Twenty-ninth Congress, that David Wilmot of Pennsylvania, the youngest Democratic member of the House of Representatives at age thirty-four and one of the most radical of Jacksonian Democrats, obtained the floor. He moved that a paragraph—a provision—be added to the legislation under consideration, legislation that authorized the president to use $2 million to negotiate an end to the Mexican War. That paragraph read: "That, as an express and fundamental condition to the acquisition of any territory from the Republic of Mexico . . . neither slavery nor involuntary servitude shall ever exist in any part of said territory, except for crime, whereof the party shall first be duly convicted."[1] For the next fourteen years northerners and southerners wrangled over the Wilmot Proviso but to no common understanding. Here was the issue that would finally evoke secession and afterward armed conflict.

The first years of debate over the Wilmot Proviso were crucial. Most of the important stands on the question of slavery's expansion into the territories were then fleshed out and fears for the future given voice. From the very start, however, southerners saw the conflict over the status of slavery in the territories as an attack on their property rights and wealth. Indeed, property rights was the crux of the debate, for it centered on the question of what governmental entity had sovereignty over the definition and enforcement of property rights. While numerous politicians believed the issue of slavery in the territories was exaggerated, the polar positions increasingly viewed the battle as one that would decide the future of their societies, free labor or slave labor. For many southerners, the issue became so important that in 1850 and 1851 it disrupted party lines and commenced the collapse of the Democrat-Whig party system. The realignment of the 1850s had a distinct sectional cadence to it, and its origins began in 1851.

This chapter does not provide a comprehensive narrative of the events and political issues between 1846 and 1853. Rather, it focuses on crucial features of the Wilmot Proviso, the congressional debate, the election of 1848, the southern response to the Compromise of 1850, and the aftermath of sectional discord in 1852 and 1853.

Turmoil characterized Congress in the waning two months of 1846. The Polk administration had either fallen into or connived its way into war with Mexico in May 1846; by June 1846 the administration had arranged a treaty to settle the Oregon question and the United States–Canadian boundary at the 49th parallel (instead of at the 54 degrees 40 minutes which ardent northern Democratic expansionists wanted). Then in July and early August came important measures through Congress—a new tariff and warehousing system, river and harbor appropriations, an independent treasury to hold government monies, and U.S. governmental recompense to victims of French depredations in the 1790s, otherwise known as French Spoilations. Within two weeks these mighty bills rolled to their conclusions. Of the issues, observers most ardently followed the new tariff proposal of Secretary of the Treasury Robert J. Walker and its accompanying measure, a warehousing act that permitted storage of foreign goods until ad valorem duties could be assessed. The vote was close; one North Carolina Whig senator, William H. Haywood Jr., refused to obey instructions from his state legislature and resigned his post. Eyes focused on William Jarnigan of Tennessee, as all knew he was the "swing" vote. Jarnigan voted for the tariff and produced a tie in the Senate, thus enabling Vice-President George M. Dallas, from the obsessively high-tariff state of Pennsylvania, to cast his vote for it and send the bill to the president. By August 2, the new tariff and warehousing bills became law. At the same time the Congress passed a subtreasury plan into law, the new Independent Treasury. Then came President Polk's veto of the river and harbor improvement bill on August 4, the announcement of ratification of the Oregon Treaty the next day, and a few days later his veto of the French Spoilation bill. All this activity was crammed into just a few weeks.[2] Whigs felt crushed by the press of administration activity. Out in Illinois, the editor of the *Alton Telegraph and Democrat*, a Whig paper, wrote of the tariff bill that it was a "bill to protect and encourage the foreign at the expense of the American manufacturer." The next week, the paper cried, "ANOTHER VETO!" referring to the fate of the harbor bill, and then the week after that, "ANOTHER VETO!" responding to the Polk's disposition of the French Spoilation bill.[3]

In the midst of this volcanic uproar by politicians over issues that were the core of national debate, Polk pressed Congress to appropriate $2 million for the administration to use to negotiate a peace treaty with Mexico, leaving the ways to which the money might be applied unstated. On August 8 when the House considered the legislation, Wilmot obtained the recognition of the Speaker and read his proviso prohibiting slavery in any territory acquired from Mexico. Virtually no debate occurred and almost on the spot congressmen had to decide how to vote—without time to consult party chieftains, to figure out constitutional positions, or to seek guidance from counselors or opinion makers. The vote was 83 to 64 in favor of the proviso, and, unlike all the other measures flowing through the last two months of this Congress, the vote was almost totally sectional. All southerners, Whig and Democrat, voted against the Wilmot Proviso; all but six northerners voted for it. The six northerners not favoring the Proviso were William W. Wick and John Petit of Indiana, Joseph P. Hoge, Orlando B. Ficklin, and John A. McClernand of Illinois, and John S. Chipman of Michigan. The tariff, the warehouse bill, the Oregon treaty, rivers and harbor improvements, and the Independent Treasury had been party measures, not sectional ones; but the Wilmot Proviso crushed party affiliation and left a sectionalism naked of party trappings for all to see. In the Senate a small filibuster by Massachusetts senator John Davis killed the chance of the Senate voting on the measure, and the $2 million bill with the Wilmot Proviso was lost for that congressional session.[4]

Wilmot's bold action created a significant stir in the country but no firestorm. Antislavery people read into the measure more than was actually there. A *New York Tribune* editor said southern Democrats were "pale with excitement, anger, and consternation," a sentiment repeated by William Lloyd Garrison's *Liberator*. A correspondent of antislavery Ohio representative Joshua Giddings commenced a letter on the proviso with "Fire! Fire!! Fire!!!" and wrote "You never saw a madder set of men [southerners] in your life." Salmon P. Chase prophesied on September 1 that "Wilmot's Proviso will exert a tremendous influence. Let the people stick to that and we will be soon ready for an aggressive movement en mass."[5] But these were people interested in the antislavery cause, and the second they saw anything favorable to their movement they immediately magnified its significance.

Southern congressmen may well have been vexed and angry at Wilmot's resolution, but it is not certain what particularly angered or vexed them. Few seemed to have mentioned the proviso in their letters. Calhoun saw it as a potential "apple of discord" among the parties, but otherwise he did not dwell on it. The editors of the radical *Charleston Mercury*, usually most vigilant on any northern aspersion toward slavery, were silent even though their Washington correspondents related the incident. Throughout the South the proceedings of Congress had been reported, yet editors and correspondents wrote little or nothing about Wilmot's Proviso. In the immediate aftermath of this session of Congress, everyone had plenty to mull over, and the Wilmot Proviso had not yet achieved any stature. Most likely politically minded southerners saw the action as the North presenting a bargaining chip to obtain future concessions of some sort or other from the Democratic Party. Southerners probably considered the Proviso irritating and obstructionist but no more consequential than abolitionist petitions or northern antislavery meetings.[6]

Northern editors did respond to the Wilmot Proviso—the press was not entirely silent.[7] For the Whigs, prohibition of slavery was mixed with other issues dear to the hearts of members of the party, such as the national bank, the Independent Treasury, and internal improvements. In the precious few days after August 8, the *Philadelphia North American* explained that expansion would make slavery eternal and the North could never condone it, while the editor of Columbus's *Ohio State Journal* took from the *Ohio Statesman* the phrase the "free States will not consent to establish slavery in countries where it does not exist." An Alton, Illinois, editor praised at least the majority given to Wilmot's Proviso, indicating that no expansion of slavery would be permitted, while the *Pottsville (Pennsylvania) Miner's Journal* offered a withering assessment of southern power—even before debate in Congress became strident: "The disposition of the South to rule the nation has become too strong to be born even by Brinkerhoff and the other 'whipped in' who on this question would not vote with their party."[8] Democrats may have been more reluctant to discuss Wilmot's motion, but a few papers did bring the matter up. Perhaps the strongest statement came from the *Cleveland Daily Plain Dealer*: "We will forgive and forget all past sins of the South if they will now come in, although at too late a day, and join the Democracy of the North in their efforts to constitutionally limit, curtail, and finally abolish slavery in this country. The Fathers of the Revolution . . . intended that we should thus finish the work they so patriotically began."[9]

In the fall of 1846, however, comments on slavery in the territories ran a poor second to other issues. Polk's veto of legislation providing for river and harbor improvements drew forth a mighty response from the Great Lake states, although Democrats often did agree that Polk's veto message contained much Democratic constitutional wisdom.[10] The issue that seemed to drive politics in the fall was the tariff. Northern Whigs denounced the Walker tariff and the accompanying warehouse bill, labeling it the "British Tariff Bill," warning that American wages would shortly fall to the European standard and that American manufacturing would become extinct. Interestingly, southern Whigs backed northern Whig complaints about the new tariff, perhaps indicating that the sectional wings of the party were finally about to coalesce around a moderate activist government. While southern Whigs did not screech the protectionism of the state of Pennsylvania, they nonetheless indicated the necessity of a moderate protection that preserved manufacturing and stimulated a home market.[11] Except for Pennsylvanians, Democrats North and South supported the new tariff, the only dissidence perhaps being that some in the Deep South believed the new tariff too protectionist and only a partial step to treating southern interests fairly.[12] From the space editors and politicians gave to the tariff, that issue looked as if it would be the center of the political storm for the next presidential election.

Congressional elections came in September, October, and November of

1846—evidently quite unexciting—and they proved inhospitable to the Democrats. The Whigs scored heavily in Pennsylvania, Ohio, and New York. In 1844, Pennsylvania had elected thirteen Democrats and ten Whigs; in 1846 the results were seven Democrats and sixteen Whigs; Ohio in 1844 produced thirteen Democrats and eight Whigs; in 1846 those numbers were eight Democrats and thirteen Whigs; and New York gave the Democrats twenty-five representatives in 1844 and only nine Whigs; but in 1846 the numbers were eleven Democrats and twenty-three Whigs. Elsewhere (Maine, Vermont, Georgia, South Carolina, Florida, Missouri, Illinois, Arkansas, and New Jersey) the results showed little change between 1844 and 1846.[13] No one ascribed these alterations to the Wilmot Proviso, if that measure were even mentioned at all. Few ascribed the results to the Mexican War. For most observers and for political strategists, the tariff seemed to dominate the results. Thus the comment of Virginia Democratic editor Thomas Ritchie made sense: "The tariff is likely to be the great question of the Day. It will enter vitally in the next Presidential Election."[14]

The next session of Congress (the second session of the Twenty-ninth Congress) began deliberations in mid-December and initially members brought up the Mexican War and whether or not the United States would seek territorial concessions, the Whigs arguing for no war of territorial conquest. At first northern Whigs confined their remarks to the iniquity of the war and only obliquely referred to the Wilmot Proviso, warning that the North would not sanction a war of conquest to expand the boundaries of slavery. Massachusetts representative Charles Hudson lectured that the expansion of slavery was a subject "on which there can be no compromise," and as proof he referred to the division of northern and southern Democrats on the proviso during the last session. During December congressmen debated the legitimacy of the Mexican War, not the question of the future status of slavery in any possible acquisitions.[15]

Preston King, Democrat from New York, then set off the powder keg. President Polk again requested Congress that it appropriate monies for the administration to use to negotiate an end to the war, raising the sum to $3 million. On January 5, King slapped the proviso on the president's request and made the first important Wilmot Proviso speech in this session of Congress. The moment had arrived, he said, when the nation had to decide the question of expansion of slavery; northerners believed the final outward thrust of slavery was Texas and there was to be no more territory given to the peculiar institution. King then provided the reason for the North's hostility to slavery: northern labor—free labor—could not operate fruitfully when in competition with slaves. "[Shall the territories be open to the] laboring man of the free States, or shall it be slave territory given up to slave labor? One or the other it must be; it cannot be both. The labor of the free white men and women, and of their children, cannot and will not eat and drink, and lie down, and rise up with the black labor of slaves; free white labor will not be degraded by such association.... [The pioneers of Illinois, Indiana, and other states] would never have consented, in the workshops or in the field, to be coupled with negro slaves."[16]

Almost immediately, after the shock of King's remarks subsided, the southern defense of slavery expansion began, and it instantly turned to property rights. Two days after King's oration, James A. Seddon of Virginia insisted that equality of the states was a paramount condition of the Union, without which the Constitution "never would have been endured." After all, Seddon claimed, the Constitution was written to protect slavery. The Wilmot Proviso was an attack on southern property rights and the federal government's equal protection of those rights. Martin Grover of New York picked up the gauntlet thrown down by Seddon. First, no constitutional rights were being violated because no northerner was suggesting any interference with slavery in a state. Second, slaves were not property in a national sense but only under a state jurisdiction. Even within the southern states, Grover claimed, the definition of slaves as property varied. "Why? Because slaves are not the kind of 'property' that is within the meaning of the Constitution." The constitutional doctrines began to spill forth, and the debate then raged over all sorts of matters connected with the slavery question. At its core, nonetheless, was the status of property rights in slaves.[17]

After King's speech, the press throughout the Union picked up the battle over the extension question in Congress. Southerners immediately found the Wilmot Proviso offensive, unfair, and, therefore, unconstitutional. Party divisions mattered. Southern Whigs bemoaned the Mexican War and saw the divisive slavery issue as the bastard offspring of Polk's policy of aggressive expansionism. William C. Rives in Virginia wanted installation of the 36 degree 30 minute line as the only way to avoid "the terrible agitation of the antislavery question," and he blamed the condition of politics on "this most deplorable & shameful war" brought on by "wicked acts & folly of the little men" who had come to power.[18] Southern Democrats justified the war and insisted on having the right to migrate to the territories with their slaves; one letter writer had elevated the struggle to the last stand for the final rights of southern freemen—"the last and most ignoble of all the rights of a freeman: that of his property—his dollars and cents—his slaves and his cotton fields."[19]

Certainly southerners made calculations as to the impact of the prohibition of slavery's expansion into the western territories. Most of them voiced a brooding suspicion that the North's movement to stigmatize the South's primary economic institution foreshadowed future and stronger penalties. Calhoun reached an early conclusion. If the South were not allowed to expand the peculiar institution, the final result would be an overwhelming majority of free states—Calhoun simply rejected the possibility of reliance upon political parties for protection—and eventually that majority would find other means to attack slavery, constitutional or not.[20]

On February 19, 1847, Calhoun answered the northern demand for the Wilmot Proviso with a set of resolutions for the Senate to approve. In those resolutions he argued that the United States was a confederation of states, that the federal government acted as the agent of the states and in their actions had to treat states as equal members of the confederation, that the Constitution protected the rights of property, and that as citizens of the United States southerners had a constitutional guarantee that they could take their property —namely slaves—into the territories, that Congress had no power or right to exclude slavery from the territories. While not all southerners agreed with the various parts of Calhoun's constitutional theories, his resolutions elicited considerable comment from southern editors. Most of them approved. One Georgia editor remarked that, although he did not like Calhoun as a politician, he liked Calhoun as a defender of southern rights.[21]

What immediately struck southerners, however, was that the issue was not driven by partisanship. Rather, the instigators of the agitation against slavery's expansion into new territories came from northern Democrats. As the Whig North Carolina congressman James Graham wrote to his brother, "you see the Locos have introduced the Slavery or Abolition Question, and I believe they intend to press it." Southern Democrats had come to expect abolition explosions from certain Whigs, but to find northern Democrats leading the antiextensionist charge was a shock. Indeed, southern editors watched northern state legislatures nearly unanimously pass resolutions instructing their representatives to obtain a prohibition against slavery extension. The northern Democratic defection to an antislavery position was the immediate impetus that drove Calhoun to proclaim that party loyalty now meant nothing, and the only way to protect southern institutions was a "united & determined resistance of the South."[22]

Northern Whigs had little reservation about their constitutional power to curb the spread of slavery into the territories, and their representatives in this session of Congress remained loyal to the Wilmot Proviso through two more votes. More intriguing to them was the dilemma of the Democratic Party. Joshua Giddings excitedly wrote to Charles Francis Adams that the only "fear now entertained by a portion of our party, [is] that the northern democrats will steal the 'abolition Thunder.'" Whigs still distrusted the northern Democrats, however, and expected them to crawl back to the party once the chieftains began cracking the patronage whip.[23]

Much of the national crisis over the Wilmot Proviso between 1846 and 1850 was in reality the crisis of the Democratic Party. A certain group of northern Democrats initiated the proposal and then sustained it until the beginning of 1848 when the breach between antislavery Democrats and party Democrats became obvious. Explaining the reasons for the defection of these Democrats has lain at the heart of the controversies about the coming of the Civil War. Exactly why the proviso made its appearance when it did, what the motivations were for the band who promoted it, and why the northern Democrats instantly supported it have become questions lacking compelling answers.[24]

The northern Democracy's problems with the Polk administration and with southerners generally began with the clique of New York politicians who looked to Martin Van Buren as their pole star. Van Buren had been cheated, in their view, out of the Democratic nomination in 1844 by southerners who had imposed a two-thirds rule for any individual to receive the party's nomination, thus making the majority bow to the deliberations of a minority. Moreover, northern Democrats faced an active political abolitionist movement in the Liberty Party that was slowly attracting a small percentage of the total votes cast at elections. Normally 3 or 4 percent of the total vote cast meant little, but in very tight races such small numbers meant the difference between victory or defeat. Added to those matters was a belief that southerners had engineered the annexation of Texas and had ignored the concerns of northern Democrats that the policy of the country not seem proslavery. Polk's patronage appointments did not satisfy the desires of Van Buren's New York supporters, and then came the Mexican war and a streaming number of policy changes in the months of July and August. As the editor of the *Cincinnati Daily Enquirer* stated, "it may be unfortunate that we are to have the Tariff clamor, the Banking clamor, and Harbor clamor, at one and the same moment."[25]

Before the Wilmot Proviso had been introduced, northern Democratic rumblings about their southern brethren had become audible. In a long letter to Van Buren, Connecticut senator Gideon Welles castigated southern—and he specifically meant Calhounite—control of the party and government. The treasury report of Walker was "insane" and should have been called "a bill of confiscation, which will desolate the East & North." The reduction of rates was "an act to bring down the free labor of the North, and to try to bring up the Slave labor of the cotton planters & tobacco growers of the South." All this meant the "time has come, I think, when the Northern democracy should make a stand. Every thing has taken a southern shape and been controlled by Southern Caprice for years. The Northern States are treated as provinces to the South." In the aftermath of the veto of the rivers and harbors bill, the *Cleveland Daily Plain Dealer* cried, "Combination is the word. Let the boundaries of Slavery, as contemplated by the framers of the Constitution, be set!" From the *Buffalo Courier and Pilot* came an attack on southern constitutionalism: the editor claimed that when policies served the interests of northerners, southerners immediately find "the Constitution stands in the way—they are north of Mason & Dixon's line!" In Indiana, one editor in the middle of July editorialized, "We have no sympathy for the southern members: their course does not entitle them to much from the north, & should have no objection to northern democrats opposing any measure that was purely for the interest of the south." The Whig paper, the *Toledo Blade*, was more blatant: the tariff of 1842 had been replaced by the "Slavo-Polko-democrats" and the country was now in the hands of "The Slave Power."[26] Indeed, even before the Wilmot Proviso was introduced, northern Whigs and Democrats in regard to sectional affairs were referring to "free labor" and "the slave power."

Yet the policies of the Polk administration should not have upset most Democrats, particularly those who first promoted the idea of restricting slavery's advance into the territories. The clique that developed the prohibition were Barnburners, radical New York Democrats who insisted upon laissez-faire government policy, hard money, and strict economy in government. They had been the moving force in crafting the New York State Constitution of 1846, a constitution noted for limiting the power of state government. In the meeting in which the proviso was drawn up, the individuals supporting the move were Barnburners and their allies in neighboring states. The reason they choose Wilmot to move the restriction passage may have been that Wilmot was most likely to attract the Speaker's notice and thereby gain the floor, but it was also because if ever a person had shining Locofoco, Barnburning, Jacksonian credentials, that individual was David Wilmot. Alone of the representatives from the state of Pennsylvania, he voted for the Walker tariff and defied the rampant protectionism of his own state. Indeed, southerners lionized him before the proviso proved so contentious an issue in January 1847.[27]

When Barnburning Democrats talked about southern control of the federal government and its policies, exactly what control they objected to requires some additional exploration. Certainly New York Democrats felt the political side of the question, for the patronage policies of the Polk administration greatly upset them, and the faction harbored deep resentments over the treatment of Van Buren in the convention of 1844. But when it came to policy, Polk's actions, and indeed the program of the South Carolinians, was indistinguishable from that of the Barnburners. Polk after all obtained the passage of Van Buren's pet creation, the Independent Treasury, and the lower tariff Polk signed into law was part of the Locofoco free trade program. Vetoing appropriations for river and harbor improvements might involve some constitutional finessing, and surely the veto tried the patience of some Great Lakes Democrats, but curbing government expenditures and refraining from intervention in the economy harmonized perfectly with Barnburner strictures.

Southern domination of federal policy manifested itself in one instance: expansion of the domain of the United States by war, and because of southern mastery of the federal government, that expansion meant the expansion of slavery. Northerners might take exception to any number of policies about the domestic economy that southerners favored, but they had no unity on questions of tariffs, internal improvements, and banking. On those questions northerners divided, and over time northern divisions tilted in favor of the South Carolinian advocacy of laissez-faire. But to use the power of the central government—to involve all citizens, not just southerners; to use all tax monies, not just southern tax money; to ask young men, not just southerners, to go to war—was another matter entirely. And to do so for the seeming purpose of extending the realm of slavery was unthinkable; that purpose immediately brought forth northern objections to the peculiar institution. The war policy of the government, moreover, was emphatically not a state matter but a national issue, thereby justifying northern commentary and agitation. Slavery might be unquestionably a state institution, but the war powers of the federal government were national in scope, not local; and thus the possibility of slavery meriting expansion under the aegis of the war power of the federal government gave northerners every right to debate the subject and vote on it as they saw fit. The Texas annexation had been troublesome enough; with a war added to it almost immediately, the anger over the use of government power to expand slavery exploded, and the politicians triggering the detonation, the ones who had most battled southerners internally over Texas and Democratic politics, were the Barnburners.

"The truth is," wrote John Law to Martin Van Buren, "the Mexican War is not popular with the thinking and reflecting majority of our party." Of the many reasons for objecting to the war was the issue of slavery: "And though we are [a] very conservative [sort] of people, we want no addition of Slave States." Democrats feared the damage at the polls that an accusation of initiating an "unjust and cruel war with a sister Republic" might do. In Jacob Brinkerhoff's letter about the meeting leading to the proviso, he wrote that northerners wanted an honorable peace but not one that extended slavery and thereby "lay still wider and deeper the foundation of another sectional power—a power all grasping in its disposition—which has for years manipulated nearly all that is valuable in official station and quite all in territorial acquisition." Brinkerhoff specifically mentioned the Texas experience as the point of revelation for the Locofoco Democrats.[28]

Much more so did Whigs register their wrath at the idea of war power being used to expand slavery—to "see the power and influence of the federal government prostituted to the propagation and perpetuation of that institution." One Maine meeting of Whigs declared in a resolution that slavery was a great evil, and although no interference with it could be allowed as it was a state institution, "yet the National Government ought not, nor have they the constitutional power, in any way to be involved in the sin of aiding to extend or sustain it, by war, legislative action, or in any other manner." This attitude suffused the Whig Party between July 1846 and April 1847.[29] Northern Whigs as well as southern Whigs reached beyond the slavery issue, however, and simply feared the matter of expansion altogether. Part of their reaction reflected apprehensions about the stability of their party, but the Mexican War also mightily disturbed their notion of the proper behavior for a republic. Republics should be pacific and not be engaged in military conquest and domination of others. A constituent of Massachusetts representative Artemas Hale wrote that the United States entered upon a new epoch with the Mexican War, because "when we were young . . . we had territory enough, had better be satisfied, and cultivate peace with all nations." In 1850 Millard Fillmore confided that the framers had never contemplated "that our army is ever to go beyond the boundaries of the United States or conquer a foreign territory.—and I wish with all my heart that it might never do either." John C. Calhoun was realizing that territorial expansion through the war was producing domestically a political disaster, and the Whigs in general sought to avoid sectional disputes by decrying any acquisition of Mexican land at all.[30]

Democrats found themselves in a very trying position. Except for the Barnburning fragment, most party members supported the war with Mexico as a just war and believed indemnification via land cession was appropriate. Slavery threw a sectional wrench into the war machinery of the party. By the end of the second session of the Twenty-ninth Congress, the painful divisions of the party due to the Wilmot Proviso were obvious. Wrote the Maine partisan Edmund Burke to Franklin Pierce, "I think we are to have a *sectional division* of parties; or a coalition of the South and West against the North," all of which was due to the "foolish" actions of "our democratic friends in the Northern States on the Wilmot Proviso." Joshua Giddings agreed, believing that there was by January "a perfect breach between the northern and southern wings of the democratic party."[31]

Unlike the Barnburners, most northern Democrats approached the Wilmot Proviso issue with circumspection. A few simply said the whole issue was a "federalist" trick designed to weaken the national Democratic Party, and some said southerners had an equal right to expand into the territories with their slaves as did northerners without slaves. The common stance was to avoid mentioning the Wilmot Proviso as long as possible and, when it became no longer feasible to do so, to exhort people to be patriotic and win the war first and argue about slavery second.[32] Some of this insistence upon postponing the subject of slavery's expansion may have been a simple bid for time. Even by March 1847 it was clear that the Wilmot Proviso was tearing the party to pieces. A few openly acknowledged that, due to the wealth slavery represented, any congressional debate touching the institution elicited a visceral response from southerners. As one editor explained, arguing for readers to refrain from joining the Liberty Party in New York, "And we cannot ask, or expect, that they [southerners] will voluntarily—except in isolated individual instances—dispossess themselves of so large an amount of personal property, from mere abstract notions of human rights." Charles Lanphier of the *Daily Illinois State Register* was more explicit: Southerners could not be expected to end slavery and give up all at once "seven hundred millions of dollars worth of property."[33]

Democrats wrestled with the Wilmot Proviso because it exposed the huge sectional division of opinion on the institution. Southerners justified slavery, but northern Democrats frankly admitted that "We are no advocates of slavery," and even the most conservative Democratic editors wrote "there is no diversity of opinion at the North. It [slavery] is looked upon as wrong."[34] Nevertheless, in virtually every commentary by Democrats between August 1846 and June 1847 appeared the statement that slavery, no matter how one felt about it, was a state institution over which northerners had no right to meddle. But throughout the North, save for a few individuals who immediately placed the Union above all else, Democrats insisted that the issue of slavery's expansion into the territories went beyond the confines of states' rights and involved national deliberation. Democrats agreed, perhaps not quite so emphatically, with the conclusion of the editor of the *Portland (Maine) Daily Argus*: "*But we say, with frankness, with firmness, and with a full consideration of all the responsibility of the avowal,* THE DEMOCRACY OF MAINE OUGHT NOT AND WILL NOT SANCTION ANY VOTE, WHICH WILL LEAD TO THE INTRODUCTION INTO THE UNION OF ANOTHER INCH OF SLAVE TERRITORY, WHICH IS NOW FREE."[35] When southerners denounced congressional attempts to block the expansion of slavery into new territories by arguing that such legislation represented a violation of states' rights, northern Democrats reacted with amazement and skepticism. States' rights had no role to play in the controversy, and Democrats usually insisted that Congress certainly had the power to act.[36]

Within this growing commentary on the Wilmot Proviso during 1847 flowed a host of Democratic statements about why northerners disliked slavery. Such expressions anticipated the three major criticisms against slavery to appear in the Republican Party of the 1850s: slavery was morally wrong, it raised a power hostile to freedom, and it ruined the prospects of free workers. In 1847 the whole of the northern Democratic Party voiced the concerns that would later power the Republican party to political supremacy.

Democrats in 1846–47 frequently denounced slavery on the basis of the Declaration of Independence and the ideals of Thomas Jefferson. As Jacob Brinkerhoff said in Congress, slavery was an evil. In New York, a General Clark in the New York Senate denounced slavery for being inconsistent with republicanism, an incubator for oppression, and a device that lessened people's attachment to equal rights; slavery "violated the first great principles on which the revolution was based."[37] In all this debate, the Democrats made few racial remarks about African Americans. At one point in 1848, John Van Buren, not known for his friendliness to northern free blacks, told a crowd that slavery "is most unjust to the black population, whom it degrades into chattels." In Congress, both David Wilmot and John Pettit announced that whites were the center of their attention, not blacks. Nonetheless the defense of slavery on the basis of race came from southern congressmen; race had not entered northern political debate to any appreciable extent.[38]

In their support of the proviso, Democrats in 1846–47 relied most heavily upon a glorification of the free worker and the economic ruin that forms of servitude wrought. They considered slavery a "curse" and most often used an agricultural metaphor by calling it an economic "mildew"—such as Governor John W. Dana of Maine who wrote that "the influence of slavery upon productive energy is like the blight of mildew."[39] Northern Democrats insisted that a competition between free labor and slave labor was unthinkable, because the slave would always pull down the free laborer into economic degradation. Some of their analysis was explicitly Jacksonian in emphasis. One resolution of a February 1847 Locofoco meeting in New York read:

> Resolution 2: That we respect the dignity of labor and in the name of the farmer, mechanic, and laborer, we protest against its degradation. We will never give our consent that a barrier shall be drawn around any new territory to be added to our Union, impassable by us, except upon the condition that we, and our children, shall be forced to hold slaves or stand on the same level with them. [Wilmot's Proviso] is the "white man's Proviso."

In the Senate, Barnburner John A. Dix explained his economic hostility to slavery by pitting the property rights of the slaveholder against the property rights of the freeman. The free laborer would not emigrate to territory open to slavery: "The property of the free laborer is in himself—in his powers of exertion, his capacity for endurance in the labor of his hands. To him these are of as much value as the property which the master has in his slaves." Such attitudes had been widespread among Democrats for a long time. The New York popular economist and Jacksonian supporter, Theodore Sedgewick, had denounced slavery a decade earlier. In his explanation of why the American economy was better than those of aristocratic nations, he insisted that it was due to the fact that all Americans were hearty, willing laborers; but "it [was] *free* labour"—they labored for themselves and for their own family but not for a master.[40]

At the same time northern Democrats gave voice to the free labor ideology, they denounced the "slave power." Free labor advocacy and dread of the slave power marched together in 1846–47 and were nearly always present in any northern speech on the Wilmot Proviso; one almost never obtained a speech, editorial, or tract that centered on only one of these ideas. In many respects, the slave power thesis and the free labor ideology were ideological twins; free labor could not exist unless the power of the master class was overthrown. Northern Democrats used the phrase "the slave power" during the proviso controversy without any sense of impertinence. Indeed, it appeared as if Democrats assumed that slavery represented an interest like agriculture, industry, or commerce, but unlike the other interests slavery united its political representatives into a formidable bloc and nearly always obtained its way.[41] Some felt southerners snubbed the requests of the North and that the entire electoral process had been tilted to meet southern demands. One Indiana Democrat retold a conversation with a follower of New York senator Silas Wright: " 'I'll be damned if I ever vote for a man *South* of Mason & Dixon's line till the North gets a President—nor will I ever vote for one not against the extension of Slavery!' "[42] Some openly said slavery reared up an oligarchy hostile to American liberty. Northern Democrats thus ended with a flat statement that they would abide by all rights granted to the South in the Constitution but that the interest of slavery, and the oligarchy reared up by stealing the fruits of others' labors, should be curtailed; northerners could stop the power of slavery by stopping its expansion, and let freedom, in the form of the accession of new nonslave states, tip the balance of the Union in favor of nonslaveholding states.[43]

By 1846 northerners had become accustomed to hearing or reading that a slave power controlled national legislation. Northern Whigs exhibited a pronounced belief that southerners dominated national politics. And the Liberty Party, the organization of political abolitionists, propagandized its existence. Charles Sumner in his speeches referred continuously to the slave power, John Palfrey of Massachusetts wrote editorials on the slave power and then in 1846 collected them into a book, and in 1844 Salmon P. Chase wrote an appeal to Pennsylvanians that included a section entitled "The Slave Power Controls the Great Interests of Our Country." One correspondent to Congressman Artemas Hale complained, "Have not the South wisdom enough to know that their present assumption of power [is] as great as can be endured? Will they presume further?" In case any one missed the point, the *National Anti-Slavery Standard* in a November 1848 issue printed seven entire columns that showed how the slave power ran the government by listing the sectional character of the selections of president, cabinet officers, senators, representatives, Supreme Court justices, and ministers to foreign countries. Before Wilmot stood up on August 8, 1846, to offer his proviso, the slave power was already a pervasive northern view of southern political leaders.[44]

Congressmen recorded two more votes on the Wilmot Proviso in the second session of the Twenty-ninth Congress. Both times in the House, the proviso passed by a northern sectional coalition of Whigs and Democrats against the opposition of southern Whigs and Democrats. Offered as amendments to a Three Million bill, that is, an appropriation to the Polk Administration of $3 million to expedite an end to the Mexican War, the proviso passed 115-105 on February 15. However, near the end of the session in the beginning of March, the Senate managed to eliminate the proviso from the Three Million bill, sent it to the House where House members first reinserted the measure but then narrowly removed the proviso (102-96) and then passed the entire bill. Even at the last, the restriction was not truly defeated because a number of northerners simply decided to wait until some new territory had actually come into the possession of the nation.[45]

Newspapers quickly picked up on the northerners that joined the anti-proviso southerners: Stephen Strong from New York; Richard Brodhead, James Black, and Jacob Erdman of Pennsylvania; Francis Cunningham, Joseph

Morris, Isaac Parish, William Sawyer, and Henry St. John of Ohio; William Wick and Robert Dale Owen of Indiana; John Chipman of Michigan; and Orlando Ficklin, John A. McClernand, and Stephen Douglas of Illinois. Northern solidarity against the "slavocracy" impressed Joshua Giddings and Edwin Stanton. However, the original proviso in August 1846 registered only six defections; by February 1847 the number had grown to sixteen, and at the end totaled twenty-three. Clearly second thoughts were invading the minds of some of the northern Democracy.[46]

Efforts to avoid confrontation over slavery prohibition in the territories focused on two measures after March 1847. One was to extend the Missouri Compromise line across the Rocky Mountains to the Pacific Ocean. That solution was offered in an Oregon territorial bill in February 1847, but northerners voted it down, and it was defeated in the Senate as well in March. Many southerners, including Calhoun, Polk, and Jefferson Davis, initially favored the compromise line as an acceptable and practical way to break the deadlock, even if theoretically they found the Missouri Compromise distasteful. In August 1848 Stephen A. Douglas moved the application of the Missouri Compromise to another Oregon territorial bill but it was soundly defeated in the House of Representatives.[47]

Among northerners a small element favored extending the Missouri Compromise line and jettisoning the Wilmot Proviso. Some conservatives fretted that the agitation would lead to southern separation. A few, like James Buchanan, believed it unfair to deprive slaveholders entrance into all the public domain.[48] But most northerners who favored extending the compromise line did so because they did not believe the climate in the supposed territorial acquisitions would support slavery. They held that slavery's economic past was its economic future, and only land that could produce cotton, rice, sugar, or tobacco could ever support slavery. In short, nature stopped the spread of slavery, and there was no need of congressional intervention: free labor, not slave labor, would populate the West. As Buchanan wrote, the difference between the Wilmot Proviso and congressional nonintervention on the question was the difference between "tweedledum & tweedledee. Non-Intervention however saves the feelings of the South & enables them to triumph over the free soilers."[49]

From the beginning active northern Whigs and Democrats rejected the Missouri Compromise. No constitutional argument of southerners made any sense to them; the sovereignty of the Congress over the territories was for northerners indisputable and the cry of states' rights misplaced. Certainly the fear of the consequence of adding many more slave states was there, but the essential reason northerners refused the Missouri Compromise line was its inapplicability: by Mexican law in 1846, 1847, and 1848, the lands the United States wanted and obtained from Mexico had no slavery—it was already free territory. Thus, slavery could only be introduced from the outside, and northerners refused to allow free territory to become slave territory—territories in which slavery came to be sanctioned had the institution prior to acquisition. Moreover, the Missouri Compromise only covered the Louisiana Purchase area, not land acquired from Mexico. Northerners believed that they had completely won on this question, and the only reason to legislate the Wilmot Proviso was to seal the victory and stop southerners from overturning it by migrating to the new territories with their slaves.[50]

A Senate committee fashioned out another compromise attempt in mid-1848 to steer the country out of its deadlock on the Wilmot Proviso. Senator John M. Clayton of Delaware headed the committee and, with Calhoun on the committee, proposed that Congress not legislate on slavery in the territories but let the matter be decided by the Supreme Court if and when in the territories a slaveholder should demand observance of property rights in slaves (this became known as the Clayton Compromise). People quickly tried to figure out whether the justices would be proslavery or antislavery. However, the bill never passed the House. Alexander H. Stephens led seven southern Whigs to oppose the bill on the basis that the Supreme Court might agree that Mexican law held sway in the new territories, and the only means to enable southern rights to prevail was to have Congress pass a law establishing slavery in the territories. Meanwhile, most northerners still persisted in declaring that free territory was antislavery and slavery could not exist except by a law-making power. One correspondent from Rochester, New York, wrote to Clayton that he found the debate upsetting because in it was the admission that slavery probably would gain a foothold in some of the territories: "That Slavery not only *may* be, but that it inevitably *will* be extended into parts of the new territory (now free) is so opposed to all my opinions of right & justice." He refused to believe that Clayton could be sponsoring it.[51]

Propelling the sectional hostility to a crisis point was the end of the Mexican War. By February 1848 Mexico had ceded the lands of New Mexico, California, and the disputed lands involved in the Texas Boundary question. Gold was discovered in California in early 1848, and within one year had sufficient population to become a state. Likewise, New Mexico had the population needed for statehood. Yet Congress had not yet organized these lands into territories and offered them civil government.

Continued northern hostility to the expansion of slavery hardened the southern heart. Although a majority of southerners probably would have accepted an extension of the Missouri Compromise line to the Pacific, more than a few insisted that the line discriminated unfairly against southern property and was unjust—and therefore unconstitutional.[52] More important, southerners increasingly saw the whole debate in terms of property rights. For southerners it was not merely that they wished to take slaves into the territories, it was that, in Florida Senator Yulee's phrase, "*we have the full and indisputable right to emigrate with our property into any territory belonging to the whole*

Union, and that the Federal Government is bound to protect us in the possession of such property." The lengthy speeches of Calhoun and Jefferson Davis were largely about the right of property in slaves, not defenses of slavery generally.[53]

Although the debate was about slavery in the territories, the escalation in the southern mind was that the concept of property rights in slaves was under attack. Given the insecurity of property rights in sentient human beings who could contest the will of the property holder, slaveholders could not let pass a questioning of their rights to human chattels. To exist, slavery required much law and a social consensus among nonslaveholders; it needed the exercise of the police power of the state or its equivalent, a social conformity among members of the society to maintain the institution. If those broke down, then the slave master's ability to control and reclaim slaves became tenuous. Property rights in slavery needed to be enforced. Thus one obtained affirmations from southerners that slavery was not merely a local institution. The radicals at the *Charleston Mercury* explained that slavery had rights beyond state borders: "Now the law of property, whether in slaves or any thing else, is local. But although local, the Constitution in this case, and *only in this case,* has provided for its recognition throughout the United States." The editor of the *Mississippi Free Trader* even flatly stated that the purpose of the Constitution and states' rights was to protect property rights in slaves from majoritarian tinkering. And Jefferson Davis reasoned that if Congress be allowed to legislate on slavery in the territories, then it "will be exercised in others."[54]

By 1848 the danger that the territorial issue raised was clear to southerners —their property rights in slaves could be made insubstantial by the northern insistence that the Constitution was not beholden to observe state legislation beyond state boundaries. The same was true for northerners but in a different direction. If the Constitution recognized slavery in its framework, then slavery was effectively nationalized and could legally move into northern free states. Joshua Giddings remarked on the Pacheo case that, although Congress had no right to "legislate upon the relation of master and slave" in the states, there was a danger in the southern claim for slavery as a form of property recognized by the Constitution: "If the doctrine intended for by southern men be correct, no State can exclude slave markets from its territory, or consecrate its soil to freedom"; eventually, "if slaves be property, slave markets may be opened in Boston."[55]

Anger over the territorial issue in late 1847 and early 1848 was ripping the Whigs and Democrats into warring sectional fragments. Northern Whigs were largely staunchly opposed to slavery's expansion, and certain clumps of Whigs—the followers of William H. Seward in New York and "conscience Whigs" in Massachusetts—were nearly abolitionist in their outlook. Southern Whigs knew this but hoped to evade the question by demanding that the United States not take any territory from Mexico. The Treaty of Guadalupe Hidalgo, February 2, 1848, ended that prospect, and the Whigs were going to have to find some common ground on the territories.[56]

Democrats, however, found an odd solution—actually, a brilliant solution, albeit not recognized at the time. Senator Lewis Cass of Michigan was a functionary of the party, a former cabinet minister under Andrew Jackson and U.S. ambassador to England, who was most noted for his indecipherable handwriting, long-winded speeches, and devotion to the Democratic Party. He had voted for the Wilmot Proviso in early 1847, but then he witnessed the mounting southern reaction. Alarmed, he sought shelter for the Democratic Party in some device that would allow the northern and southern wings to override the slavery issue. Never known especially for his originality, Lewis Cass hit upon the themes of nonintervention by Congress in the internal regulation of territorial life, and territorial life to be guided by popular sovereignty or the will of people in the territory. He expressed these ideas in a long letter to Tennessee senator A. O. P. Nicholson in December 1847, and the letter then quickly made the rounds among northern and southern Democrats and was known forever after as the "Nicholson Letter."

Cass made a number of interesting points. In a concession to the Calhounites, he agreed that the Constitution gave authority over property in the territories to Congress but not authority over domestic relations. To soothe northerners, he admitted the Northwest Ordinance did establish a precedent, but there might have been extenuating circumstances and unless Congress faced some unusual situation, such Congressional power could be avoided. This was another way for stating that the North might have the constitutional argument on its side, but practicality would be the better guide. Moreover, he agreed with both James Buchanan and Secretary of the Treasury Robert J. Walker that climatic conditions in the Far West determined that slavery would not root there and that soil and weather conditions had already determined the triumph of free labor, making the entire argument over forms of labor pointless. Given these facts, he advised northerners to prize the Union rather than their constitutional rights in the territories. As to the exercise of sovereign power in the territories over matters of domestic relations, Cass wrote: "But certain it is, that the principle of interference should not be carried beyond the necessary implication, which produces it. It should be limited to the creation of proper governments for new countries; acquired, or settled, and to the necessary provision for their eventual admission into the Union; leaving, in the meantime, to the people inhabiting them, to regulate their internal concerns in their own way. They are just as capable of doing so, as the people of the states [*sic*]; and they can do so, at any rate, as soon as their political independence is recognized by admission into the union." A few paragraphs later, he summed up the position: "I am opposed to the exercise of any jurisdiction by Congress over this matter; and I am in favor of leaving to the people of any territory, which may be hereafter acquired, the right to regulate it for themselves, under the general principles of the constitution."[57] Thus the doctrines of congressional nonintervention in the territories and popular sovereignty commenced their mighty and torturous course through American politics for the next thirteen years.

Few recognized Cass's achievement immediately. In truth, the idea of popular sovereignty had already been broached and probably someone else would have picked it up before the Democratic Party convention in May 1848. Ellwood Fisher, a Cincinnati conservative, had virtually outlined Cass's idea in a letter to Calhoun on August 22, 1847; a New York correspondent of Illinois senator Sidney Breese claimed to have popularized the idea first; and the doctrine was foreshadowed in an editorial of the *Springfield Daily Illinois State Register* in October 1847.[58] But few, including Cass, understood its power. They thought only in terms of stopping the sectional rift between North and South and finding a way out of the interminable and dangerous debate over constitutional principles. What they did not see was how mighty the doctrine of popular sovereignty was in combating the antislavery cry of freedom. In ideological terms, the power of antislavery to attract public sympathy lay in claiming that the legacy of the Revolution was human freedom, individual freedom, and that slavery clearly violated the intent and momentum of the founding period. What Cass had done was to give the Democrats a counterclaim equally as appealing: the legacy of the Revolution was also the right of the people to frame their own laws, that ultimate sovereignty lay with the people. Instead of being apologetic about slavery and being on the defensive, Democrats by exhorting "popular sovereignty" could claim the mantle of the Revolution and, without flinching, contest the claims of antislavery speakers to the heritage of the founders. It would take several years before Stephen A. Douglas came to this realization.[59]

Popular sovereignty in 1848 was not sufficiently developed to save the Democratic Party from debacle. Cass's affirmation placed him as a frontrunner for the nomination. Polk had declared he would not run again, James Buchanan had a circle of followers in Pennsylvania and few elsewhere, and no generals from the Mexican War were forthcoming to take the nomination. Indeed, the only general interested in politics went over to the Whigs. As the Democrats moved to their convention in Baltimore, divisions over popular sovereignty emerged. The Barnburning element in New York saw Cass as a "doughface," a northerner bowing to southern interests. Calhounites as well declaimed against popular sovereignty. They saw the right to take slaves into the territories as a constitutional right, and no power—exercised either by the Congress or by a territorial government—could take that right away. In the Alabama Democratic Party convention in early 1848, the position of the Calhounites took exacting form. The second resolution of the Alabama platform read, "That it is the duty of Congress to protect and secure to the slaveholder in case of such [territorial] cession, by adequate laws, the full, free, and uninterrupted privilege of moving into and living with his slaves upon such territory, and the enjoyment of his property in such slaves, as long as the ceded territory remains under the jurisdiction of the federal government."[60]

The Democratic Party's problems in 1848 rested more with New York than the Deep South, however. New York's Democrats had divided into Barnburners—the antislavery faction—and Hunkers, those who towed the administration line.[61] The split became apparent in the state Democratic convention at Syracuse in September–October 1847; there, the convention refused to accept the Wilmot Proviso formally. The Barnburners then met shortly thereafter at Herkimer to adopt an antislavery platform. In late January 1848 the Hunkers convened at Albany to send a slate of delegates to the national convention, while the Barnburners did likewise at a congregation at Utica in mid-February. Both New York delegations converged on Baltimore to demand recognition of their legitimacy, but the party officials determined to let in both sets of New York delegates on the condition that they would have to split their voting privileges between themselves. The Barnburners refused. They then held a convention at Utica on June 22 and announced the formation of a new political organization and tossed out the name of Martin Van Buren as the presidential nominee. In August another gathering was held at Buffalo to unite Barnburners with Conscience Whigs, and a potential ticket of Martin Van Buren and Charles F. Adams, a Massachusetts Conscience Whig, was concocted. Finally, a national convention of the antislavery politicians met in Utica on September 14 to announce formally the Free-Soil Party and its nominees.[62]

The Free-Soilers left little doubt that they wanted to keep slavery out of the territories and that their great fear was the competition between slave and free labor. In several letters in response to the nomination, Martin Van Buren adhered fairly closely to constitutional arguments as to the legality of congressional restriction, denied the property argument of southerners by saying that without congressional guidance one would have thirty sets of property laws trying to coexist in one place, referred to the vision of liberty of the founders, and only obliquely mentioned free labor. His followers did not so hesitate. Slave labor and free labor were antagonistic, and slave labor drove free labor from the field of enterprise due to unfair competition. The address of the Barnburners of the legislature of New York laid the matter quite bare: "The wealthy capitalists who own slaves, disdain labor, and the whites who are compelled to submit to it, are regarded as having fallen below their natural condition in society. They cannot act in terms of equality with the masters for those social objects which, in a community of equals, educate, improve, and refine all its members. In a word, society, as it is known in communities of freemen—with its schools and its various forms of voluntary association for common benefit and mutual improvement can be scarcely said to exist for them or their families."[63] An Oneida Free-Soil editor added that he wanted always to keep slavery out of land that had been free because "we never should allow . . . one generation of selfish men, who can make money out of Slavery, while the soil is rich and the wages of labor high, to curse their children and children's children with a system that in the end destroys the man, the master and the land, and blackens the fairest heritage of God."[64]

So the national Democratic Party lost the formal allegiance of an important faction of Democrats in the most populous state of the Union, but the organization did not lose the South. This circumstance was not due to a failure of effort on the part of William Lowndes Yancey. Yancey, along with John C. McGehee of Florida and J. M. Commander of South Carolina, wrote a minority report objecting to the Platform Committee's embrace of federal nonintervention in the territories and popular sovereignty as a cure for the slavery question. The difference in the reports was a single sentence; Yancey wanted the convention to approve the resolution "That the doctrine of non-interference with the rights of property of any portion of the people of this Confederation, be it in the States or in the Territories, by any other than the parties interested in them, is the true republican doctrine recognized by this body." He gave a speech in support of his resolution. "It is idle to call the question an abstract one," he insisted, for it was only abstract to northerners:

> They [northerners] own not a dollar of property to be affected by the ascendency of the principle at issue. They have not a single political right to be curtailed by it. With them opposition to the South on this point, is purely a question of moral and political ethics. Far different is it with the South. They own the property which the success of this principle will prevent them from carrying with them to the Territories. They have a common right in the Territories, from which they are to be excluded, unless they choose to go there without this property. . . . [The Democratic party must] give assurance to the public mind of our entire country that the democracy of the Union will preserve the compromises of the constitution . . . that it recognizes entire political equality to exist among the people, and their right to people unmolested in the rights of property, the vast territories.[65]

Yancey was answered by McDowell of Virginia. "The gentleman mistakes a personal right to hold property, under general laws, for a governmental right to make laws." At this stage, it seems, southerners were not ready to bolt the Democratic Party and were willing to give alternative solutions a chance for success. Even the effort of Freman of Georgia to have the Wilmot Proviso officially repudiated by the party was voided; intense pressure (so it was reported) made Freman withdraw his motion. The delegates rejected Yancey's resolution by a vote of 36 yeas to 216 nays.[66]

The convention went on to nominate Lewis Cass for the presidency and William Butler for the vice-presidency. The platform reflected the movement of the party to popular sovereignty but in a vague manner. During the election, however, many northern Democratic papers began to feel quite comfortable with the idea and explicitly rejected federal restriction, most of the editors freely admitting that they wanted no extension of slavery.[67] Southern Democrats somewhat reluctantly campaigned for Cass, but they were aware that within popular sovereignty lay a major problem. When did the populace get to vote on the institution of slavery? The northern reading of popular sovereignty was that the territorial settlers determined the question throughout the territorial stage; the southern position generally was that sovereignty only occurred when the territory became a state and wrote its constitution, and until that time neither the territorial legislature nor the federal government could ban or establish slavery.[68] One suspects, however, that in 1848 most southerners were willing to let climate make the determination on where slavery might be established, and therefore let this basic question slumber undisturbedly.[69]

In early June the Whigs held their convention in Philadelphia. Southern Whigs took advantage of the occasion to press remorselessly the need for the nominee to be a southerner, and in particularly they urged the claims of General Zachary Taylor, a Louisiana slaveholder and the hero of the battle of Buena Vista. As a running mate southern Whigs accepted the nominally antislavery northerner Millard Fillmore, who had a record of antislavery statements and pro–Wilmot Proviso voting, but southerners would not accept nominees from the avowed antislavery wings in New England, Ohio (Giddings), or New York (Seward). The Whigs could not agree on a platform and so did not produce one. The party had suffered severe sectional splits, southerners demanding a candidate safe on the slavery issue so that they could match the southern Democracy's proslavery pronouncements, northerners insisting on a pro–Wilmot Proviso candidate so that they could capture northern antislavery sentiment.[70]

The election of 1848 exhibited an oddity that has ever since been remarked upon by historians. In the South, Whigs painted Cass as an abolitionist and Democrats denounced Taylor for having the antislavery Fillmore for a running mate. In the North, the Democrats denounced Taylor for being a slaveholder while the Whigs painted Cass as a proslavery doughface. Party electoral appeals were Janus-faced; in truth, there was no national party appeal by either Whigs or Democrats, only sectional ones that transformed into polar opposites as one moved from North to South or South to North. However, party unity generally withstood this test, Whigs continuing to maintain party loyalty and Democrats holding on to theirs. Taylor won the election, however, because his popularity in the South overcame his liabilities in the North. Cass suffered a northern split in the party plus being treated coolly by southerners.[71]

In the unpalatable political stew of 1848 bobbed the undigested lump of the Free-Soil Party. The party lasted only one year and then disappeared, but there were many portents connected to it because it was the first major party to be explicitly antislavery. The Free-Soil episode was a revelation about coalition-forming among antislavery northerners, particularly when the Free-Soil experience is compared with the Republican Party of the 1850s. And at the center of the storm was the person of Martin Van Buren. Although no writer in the antebellum decade exactly pointed it out, Van Buren was a major warning sign of impending sectional collision. The United States had had only three northern presidents since the adoption of the Constitution: John Adams, John Quincy Adams, and Martin Van Buren—because William Henry Harrison died one month after taking his oath of office, he may be omitted from the list. They had all gone antislavery in their postpresidential lives; John Adams somewhat mildly, John Quincy Adams as a leader of the opposition to the "gag" resolution on abolitionist petitions to Congress and as counsel to the mutinous slaves on *La Amistad*, and then Martin Van Buren as presidential candidate for the Free-Soil Party. All three presidents had only served one term, usually at southern insistence. Party affiliation had made no difference. Southerners should have wondered about the mysterious process that manufactured antislavery standard-bearers out of former leaders of northern parties.

Indeed, the impact of the Van Buren nomination yields much valuable information about third-party politics. The leaders of the movement were the Barnburners, and because they had been the ones who had broken with the administration party and had been willing to risk all to secure adoption of the Wilmot Proviso, sympathetic antislavery politicians deferred to their wishes. Barnburners made no secret that their inspiration was Van Buren, and they pressed others interested in a third party into accepting him. Antislavery Whigs and political abolitionists accepted the mandate.[72] All this made sense given that the New Yorkers had long harbored a grudge over southern treatment of Van Buren in the Democratic convention of 1844 and over the patronage policies of the Polk administration as well as their hostility to slavery expansion. But it was a political blunder. Antislavery sentiment in the North was rising and the Free-Soil Party failed to capture it.

The central difficulty was overcoming past party affiliations to forge a new political identity—to fuse existing political fragments into a new entity. Those fragments in 1848 were Democrats, Whigs, Liberty Party members, and probably many young voters just entering political consciousness and activity. Martin Van Buren may have been a giant to the Barnburners, but he was a loathsome insect to others. Instead of his presence on the Free-Soil ticket assisting the fusion, his nomination practically dissolved it.

Whigs, conscience Whigs, and Liberty Party men found Van Buren as the leader of an antislavery party a difficult potion to swallow. William Sprague told Charles Francis Adams that "Almost any other Free Soil man (especially John McLean) would suit them. With Van Buren it will be utterly impossible." Henry Stanton recognized the power of Van Buren's name in New York, but where else? For a vice-presidential choice, the party required someone who had "some less ultra democratic" credentials. John McLean wrote that while he might consent to the presidential nomination of the party he could not accept the second place, "knowing Mr. Van Buren, I could never expect to identify myself with his political principles." In the Western Reserve, one correspondent of Adams wrote, "With almost any other man in the Union, who was sound on Free Soil," the party could carry his county. In Maine a group of 200 voters informed Adams that "We are free *Soil men* but not *free trade* men." Besides Van Buren's Locofocism, he had as president committed himself to a number of positions that outraged antislavery people: he sought the return of the *Amistad* mutineers to slavery, he decided that Congress had not the right to abolish slavery in Washington, D.C., and he generally deferred to southerners on all matters concerning slavery. As Thomas Mumford of Seneca Falls told Adams, he would vote for Van Buren regardless, but many Whigs in his area said that while they could support a former Democrat, they could never back Van Buren, who had always been "a northern man with southern principles."[73]

Why Van Buren took the nomination is something of a puzzle. He should have known better. His various letters to the conventions leading up to the Buffalo Free-Soil finale certainly demonstrated his hostility to the expansion of slavery and his dismissal of southern constitutional objections, but very little else. The fires of antislavery that moved others—humanitarian, free labor, and dread of the slave power—were with him only embers or barely warm ashes. Cass supporters had no problem understanding Van Buren; they said he acted out of revenge for being denied the Democratic nomination in 1844.[74] It perhaps might be an unfair evaluation, but the charge of revenge may be the most accurate interpretation of Van Buren's motivations.

While Van Buren's name at the head of the Free-Soil ticket certainly attracted attention and gave notoriety to the infant party, it proved a major liability in attracting people to the organization. Van Buren's name also reignited the bonfires of past political combat. He was so identified with the battles of the Jacksonian period that Whigs and Democrats could hardly be expected to put aside their memories—and their partisan passions—of those quite recent days. Early in the campaign, one correspondent of Chase wondered in light of the Van Buren nomination "how then these discordant elements can be brought together." Chase recognized the importance of former party conciliation by arguing against a Van Buren–John Hale ticket because then the party "will take a more exclusively democratic character than it would otherwise assume." In short, the party needed to fuse antislavery elements from the Democratic Party, the Whig Party, and the Liberty Party—and the Van Buren nomination drove two of those elements away. No one cemented a relationship between the disparate antislavery forces. Thus, after the election Joshua Giddings admitted that "some of our members from the whig party will feel a lingering wish to hold on to their old prejudices and associations; so too of those who come from the democratic party."[75]

In this case, comparison with the Republican Party in 1856, and even in

1860, is instructive. The newly formed Republican Party chose as its first standard-bearer John C. Frémont, a person known to have had Democratic Party affiliations and one who possessed renown but had no real history of party battles. His record did not dredge up the partisan passions of the past. In 1860 Abraham Lincoln was sufficiently unknown in national politics not to raise offensive memories that could have generated ill-will among the party's coalition (whereas William H. Seward's past obviously did). Moreover, in Lincoln's case, his willingness to withdraw from the balloting for the Illinois senatorship in 1855 to enable a Republican to win—the ex-Democrat Lyman Trumbull—soothed any fears among ex-Democrat Republicans that Lincoln's Whig ancestry would lead to prejudice against them due to their Democratic antecedents.

That Van Buren's nomination was a mistake in the long run did not make it any less shocking in June and July 1848, when the Democrat bolters began publicizing his name as the leader of their cause. John W. Forney, the Pennsylvania editor and supporter of James Buchanan, called Van Buren's defection "dreadful[;] it has alarmed me & others considerably." The *Ohio State Journal* said the regular Democracy had gone into "spasms" over Van Buren's acceptance of the Free-Soil position. Southerners, who had their doubts about Van Buren's sincerity anyway, found him to be an interesting animal—"Is Martin really so old and imbecile as to be tickled with a straw?" One Mississippi paper lashed out at him as "*the American Machiavel—the 'Little Magician.'*" Southerners, nonetheless, seemed more concerned about the Free-Soil movement than Van Buren himself, for the rise of a political party based on antislavery sentiment represented a considerable threat to the peculiar institution.[76] Rather quickly party managers began to assess the appeal Van Buren might have and what damage he could do in the North. Initially, they felt a major revolt might occur, certainly in New York but also possibly in Ohio, New England, and the northern parts of Indiana and Illinois.[77]

In the heat of the campaign, many reassessed the impact of the Free-Soilers. An Ohio Whig correspondent of John J. Crittenden wrote that at first he feared the new party, but now realized "that with Van Buren they can have no principles in common [with Whigs] except that of free soil." President Polk wrote Cass that Van Buren's nomination "will produce not the slightest effect upon the Democracy of this State [Pennsylvania]." In Indiana, Whig campaigner Godlove Orth believed "Van Burenism is decidedly on the wane," while Abraham Lincoln predicted that any Whig loss to the Free-Soilers would be offset by Democratic defections from that party.[78] And because of Van Buren's prominent past, the Whigs had an easy method of arousing past angers at the head of the Free-Soil ticket. As Thomas Corwin explained to John G. Whittier, "While I agree with the Buffalo Convention in many of its sound doctrines, I cannot forget the reign of Andrew Jackson Van Buren."[79]

What the Free-Soilers did accomplish, however, was the murder of the economic issues of the Whig-Democrat party system. In the fall of 1846, the parties had girded their Second Party System armor to go forth and joust over the tariff; by the fall of 1848, the tariff as an issue had nearly disappeared, as had the national bank, internal improvements, and the Independent Treasury. National concern over slavery's expansion into the territories did not solely displace the economic issues of the past—the Free-Soilers targeted them for ridicule and derision. They did so by comparing how minuscule the issues of tariffs and banks were to the moral significance of human freedom. Charles Sumner and the Conscience Whigs of Massachusetts particularly chose to denigrate the tariff; the only reason the tariff continued to exist, said Sumner, was to enable old politicians to mount their old "battle-horse[s]"; but now the issue was "slavery versus freedom."[80] One editor described a speaker at a Cass meeting who talked wholly on the Bank of the United States; the oration was "much like stabbing a dead Percy to be in excellent taste." Even some northern Democrats found the old issues hollow. George M. Dallas, the vice-president, mentioned that banks and the tariff "have exhausted their power upon the legislation and congressional questions." As a writer in the *Massachusetts Quarterly Review* summarized, the old party system worked without "a great Moral Idea." That time was over, and a true moral issue had now entered politics.[81]

While charting the movement of ideological precepts and dispositions is always inexact, the Free-Soilers may have also affected the relationship between free labor exhortations and the parties. Prior to 1845 all northern parties used the free labor ideology in one form or another. But the Free-Soilers celebrated the idea unendingly in their praise of northern society and their denunciation of the slaveholding states. They may have then removed the free labor ideology from the Democratic Party and left it to float around until it could settle in a new home, the Republican Party of the 1850s. The administration Democrats—the Hunkers, popular sovereignty supporters, and generally committed partisans of the party—simply could not use the free labor ideology without threatening their party's alliance with the South. Except for a racist variant, the Free-Soilers in essence robbed the regular Democracy of its free labor appeal.[82]

The election determined the occupant of the White House but did not foreshadow a solution to the problem of slavery's status in the territories acquired from Mexico. In the Senate, an overwrought John C. Calhoun, sensing that if the territories were reserved for free states entirely, then the slaveholding states would forever be a minority in the nation, sought to destroy party lines. Using a conference of concerned southern congressmen in Washington, D.C., as his stepping-stone, Calhoun wrote an "Address to the People of the Southern States" in January 1849, calling for concerted southern action against northern "aggressions" by jettisoning party affiliations. Many southern congressmen complained that the document was too radical and demanded it be toned down. In its final version, only forty-eight southerners signed the address while seventy-three did not.

Zachary Taylor then really upset southern hopes, especially among the Whigs. Taylor, though a southern planter, had a national vision. He, too, thought climatic conditions in the Mexican cession militated against slavery's expansion and that those lands would become free states in the future. The trick was to let them in before Congress exploded over the Wilmot Proviso again. He tried to circumvent the territorial stage by having California and New Mexico write state constitutions, including a provision against slavery, and then hand them as a fait accompli to Congress. California complicated matters by writing a state constitution that prohibited slavery before any authorization to do so came from Washington. Southern Whigs were appalled, sensing that Taylor agreed with the North and that his actions would doom the party throughout the South.

By the meeting of the first session of the Thirty-first Congress in December 1849, the fuses leading to a sectional explosion over the territorial issue were burning short. A Mississippi convention had called for a meeting of southern delegates at Nashville in the spring of 1850 to concoct demands for northerners to accede to if the Union were to remain intact. On top of this, due to the Supreme Court ruling in the case of *Prigg v. Pennsylvania*, southerners became hypersensitive about the return of fugitive slaves, because the High Court had declared that only federal officials, not state officials, could be commanded to do this type of policing.[83]

The parties remained in confusion. Among the Democrats, remarked New York senator and Hunker William L. Marcy, "the general position of the free states [*sic*] is that our territories are now free; and the essential difference between the democrats and the free-soilers is this: that the democrats think nothing need be done by congress to keep them so, on the other hand the free soilers say though we agree with you that they are free the south do not agree with us and the Wilmot Proviso or something equivalent is necessary to guard them from the intrusion of slavery." Southern Democrats generally believed that the Missouri Compromise line was the best remedy, and James Buchanan agreed with them, but most others did not. Stephen A. Douglas, now in the Senate, found justification for his belief in popular sovereignty in the vote of Californians to be a free state: "[I] predicted [last session] that the people would decide against slavery if left to settle the question for themselves." Southern feelings did not need to be bruised or the North's morality assuaged by the passage of the Wilmot Proviso; popular sovereignty injured no one, but it effectively allowed the territories in the West to become free states. "The result has shown," he wrote, "that we were right & they wrong."[84]

Meanwhile, the Whigs suffered a severe sectional division. Northern Whigs continued their antislavery position, although Daniel Webster's speech of concession—the Wilmot Proviso need not be applied because climate had already decided the fate of the western territories—signaled a willingness of some conservatives to retreat from their insistence on congressional prohibition. Probably more typical of the northern Whig position was New York William H. Seward's declaration that there was a "higher law" than the constitution—the moral law of the divinity—that decreed that legislators needed to halt slavery's expansion and prepare the means for its ultimate demise. Meanwhile, southern Whigs were aghast at the actions of President Taylor and demanded that he act so as to safeguard southern rights. They also were not happy with their northern colleagues. "You would be mad to see the conduct of Toombs, Cabell, [and] Stephens," wrote one northern Whig; "They do not vote with us and I suppose do not intend to do it—mad and ugly as ever you saw hungry pigs." On top of slavery-related problems was a patronage fight between various Whigs and the Taylor administration. Taylor seemed bent on creating a new party, and many northern and southern Whigs were appalled at his appointments.[85]

In the debates in Congress, southerners continued to press their claims that slavery had to be considered as a species of property protected by the Constitution. At one point Jefferson Davis complained about the obtuseness of northerners. "What is there in the character of that property which excludes it from the general benefit of the principles applied to all other property?" The question must have been strictly rhetorical, because Davis knew the answer—northerners balked at lumping human beings in the category of property. In the extreme southern camp, however, the insistence on protection of property rights began to assume alarming proportions. About one year earlier, Georgia Whig senator John M. Berrien wrote an "Address to the People of the United States" declaring that slavery was a domestic institution wholly guarded by state government. Southerners would allow no attempt of the federal government to interfere with it or "to diminish its value" by "direct or indirect means."[86] That pronouncement implied a total southern control of the federal government because with only a little imagination one could always link various policies to various consequences to show that any federal law affected slavery in some fashion or another.

Northerners read southern intentions both cynically and perceptively. Southern constitutional arguments evoked only the cold analysis that southerners cloaked all their wants in constantly recreated constitutional doctrine. One correspondent of Democrat Hannibal Hamlin wondered how southerners could possibly object to the admission of California: "[B]ut they are given to hair splitting, and will doubtless find some pretext for a strenuous opposition."[87] Some northerners had no problem in discerning the economic problem southerners faced and its bearing on the slavery extension issue. In a long letter, Massachusetts Whig Julius Rockwell explained his interpretation of southern demands: "[Southerners say that they have a constitutional right to go into the territories and] that if the North is allowed to carry this point, it will be followed by the carrying [of] every other; and that the destruction of nine hundred millions of these property will assuredly follow. To the feelings of every slaveholder the matter is thus brought directly home, & he is taught to believe that he is to lose his property. This is enough for him, and it has always been the case in the slaveholding States, that the opinion of the Slaveholders is the opinion of the whole community."[88]

Henry Clay came to this Congress in one more attempt to arrange, as he had done in 1819–21 and 1832–33, a compromise. He offered a set of proposals in one bill, called the Omnibus, to take care of all existing sectional problems, at least those most dominating existing political life. His proposals consisted of the admission of California to the Union, the creation of a New Mexico territory with a broad and unclear provision that the question of slavery only involved the inhabitants there, a new fugitive slave law, the federal assumption of Texas state debts, the abolition of the slave trade in Washington, D.C., and the redrawing of the Texas–New Mexico boundary. Clay's Omnibus failed to attract a coalition and President Taylor threatened a veto should it pass. The measure failed in mid-July, and Clay was disgusted at the intransigence of his colleagues. But on July 9, Taylor died and Millard Fillmore became president. Fillmore affirmed his desire to resolve the crisis by compromise and was willing to sign such measures as Congress would pass. Stephen A. Douglas saw an opportunity to save the compromise by splitting the Omnibus into separate measures that shifting coalitions could accept. He and Speaker of the House Howell Cobb of Georgia then adroitly managed to pass through the Senate and the House in late August and early September the separate bills that became known as the Compromise of 1850. The key to victory was the willingness of some northern members, primarily Democrats, to forgo the Wilmot Proviso; the northern Democrats were the group that made passage of the several measures possible.[89]

Few people doubted that a true crisis had been averted. Letters from Washington were filled with reports of secessionist movements in the South.[90] However, a bitterness remained that only the electoral process could remove. Northerners looking at the compromise were convinced that southerners had won: the Wilmot Proviso, despite all the bluster about it being sacrosanct, had been defeated and rejected; the Fugitive Slave Law was an assault upon the integrity of northern states and their sovereignty; and slavery still had a chance to move into the New Mexico area.[91] Southern reaction to the compromise remained to be seen, but it was clear that the admission of California as a free state, giving the free states for the first time a numerical majority in the Union, upset people in the Gulf states.

Millard Fillmore had barely enough time to sign the Compromise measures of 1850 into law before numerous northern states had congressional elections in 1850—the compromise bills had been approved in August and

September, while congressional elections came in October and November. The elections did not seem to light much of a fire in the electorate. In New York and Boston, merchants held mass meetings to rouse sympathy for the compromise and to remind voters of the disastrous consequences of a severed Union. In Massachusetts, Free-Soilers and Democrats assisted each other in an informal coalition to topple the Whig establishment.

But northern voting showed an odd pattern. In the Great Lakes and New England regions, nothing really changed. The results of 1850 were almost identical to 1848 (see Table 6.1). Such was not the case in the Middle Atlantic states of Pennsylvania, New York, and New Jersey. There the Whigs were swamped. Some of this reversal originated in the election of 1848 when the Free-Soil revolt dramatically injured the New York Democratic Party, resulting in a swollen number of Whig victories; 1850 merely pulled the relative strength of the Whigs and Democrats back into a more usual pattern. Nonetheless the Democrats gained twenty-five members of Congress in these three states, while the Whigs lost twenty-one. To the extent that the election of 1850 showed acceptance of the Compromise of 1850—a dubious proposition—those returns indicated an acceptance of the compromise in three states only; New England and the Great Lakes are not easily interpretable on this score. (See Table 6.1.)[92]

Matters within the South were a different story. After the passage of the 1850 compromise, certain South Carolina politicians determined to secede, but not by themselves; they wanted other southern states to join the movement. South Carolina governor Whitemarsh Seabrook thus communicated with others to gauge their temperament. Governor George Towns of Georgia seemed ready. He called for elections to a state convention to determine the status of Georgia in the Union. From Washington, D.C., came Howell Cobb, Alexander H. Stephens, and Robert Toombs to stump for the Union. The result was a shocking Unionist victory (about 46,000 to 24,000). When the Convention met in December, instead of adopting a secession ordinance, they resolved to stand by a "Georgia Platform" that called the Compromise of 1850 acceptable but warned that Georgia would consider secession a legal remedy if ever northerners sought to exclude slavery from the territories, failed to capture and return runaway slaves, intruded on slavery's existence where established, or tried to abolish slavery in the nation's capitol. Moreover, the Nashville Convention in its two sessions—June and November of 1850—had failed to become the vehicle of radicals and had adopted the Missouri Compromise line as its major sectional demand—a mild demand indeed. The second session was poorly attended and had little influence. By December 1850 secessionists had virtually admitted that whatever would be the battle cry of the South, it would not be immediate secession.[93]

Most of the southern states held congressional elections in 1851, and the battle for the Union was fought over again. However, the question of secession

TABLE 6.1. *Party Victories in Congressional Races, 1848–1851*

Region/State	1848 *Democrat*	1848 *Whig*	1848 *Free-Soil*	1850 *Democrat*	1850 *Whig*	1850 *Free-Soil*
Great Lakes						
Illinois	6	1	0	6	2	0
Wisconsin	1	1	1	1	0	2
Michigan	2	1	0	1	2	0
Ohio	11	8	2	10	10	1
Total	20	11	3	18	12	3
Middle Atlantic						
New Jersey	1	4	0	4	1	0
New York	2	31	1	17	17	0
Pennsylvania	8	13	3[a]	15	9	0
Total	11	48	4[a]	36	27	0
New England						
Maine	5	2	0	5	2	0
Vermont	1	3	0	1	3	0
Massachusetts	0	8	2	1	6	3
Total	6	13	2	7	11	3

Region/State	1849 *Democrat*	1849 *Whig*	1849 *Free-Soil*	1851 *Democrat*	1851 *Whig*	1851 *Free-Soil*
New England						
New Hampshire	2	0	2	2	2	0
Connecticut	2	2	0	3	1	0
Rhode Island	1	1	0	1	1	0
Total	5	3	2	6	4	0
Great Lakes						
Indiana	8	1	1	8	2	0
Border South						
Kentucky	4	6	0	5	5	0
Maryland	3	3	0	2	4	0
North Carolina	3	6	0	4	5	0
Tennessee	7	4	0	6	5	0
Virginia	15	0	0	13	2	0
Total	32	19	0	30	21	0

Region/State	1849 *Democrat*	1849 *Whig*	1849 *Free-Soil*	1851 *States' Rights*	1851 *Union*	1851 *Free-Soil*
Deep South						
Alabama	4	3	0	2	5	0
Louisiana	3	1	0	2	2	0
Mississippi	4	0	0	1	3	0
Georgia (1848)	4	4	0	2	6	0
Total	15	8	0	7	16	0

Source: Moore, *Congressional Quarterly's Guide to U.S. Elections*, 587–94.

a. Includes 1 Nativist Party member.

was relegated to the Deep South states of South Carolina, Georgia, Mississippi, and Alabama. The Border South states accepted the compromise with a sigh of relief and little debate, and there was no great upheaval in vote tallies and partisan affiliations.[94] But the Gulf states reacted differently. Party lines broke down altogether in the Deep South, and instead of Whig versus Democrat the election became States' Rights (believers in secession) versus Constitutional Unionist (believers in the Union when directed by the Constitution). By throwing away all party lines and by discussing an issue beyond the boundaries of the Second Party System, the Deep South states inaugurated the realignment of the 1850s. It makes sense that the Deep South should start a reshuffling of party lines because they were the ones who felt the pressure on their property rights.

By the beginning of 1851, almost everyone knew that the public had no intention of permitting secession over the Compromise of 1850. States' Rights candidates, however, insisted that secession was a right that the South could exercise, that it was sanctioned by the Constitution. Unionists openly ran on the preservation of the Union and denied that secession was anything other than revolution. On this issue, the Unionists had all the advantages, for secession was not a live issue. While the States' Rights Party generally drew in Democrats and the Unionists gathered strength from Whigs, some amount of fusion had to occur or else the Unionists attracted a large number of previous nonvoters. The Unionist victory was hefty in 1851 and overthrew by a considerable amount the congressional majority that the Democrats had obtained in 1849 (see Table 6.1).[95]

Exactly what analysis, sentiment, or trepidation powered States' Rights fears in 1850–51 remains mysterious, for the seceders mentioned many. Generally, they were convinced that due to the Compromise of 1850, in the words of the *Georgia Weekly Constitutionalist*, "the rights of the South are prostrate at the feet of Anti-Slavery."[96] A basic cause of the unrest seems to have been the admission of California as a free state. Many felt that California should have been divided at the 36 degree 30 minute line and two states admitted into the Union, one free and one slave; they objected to Californians taking matters into their own hands and framing a state constitution before congressional authority to do so.[97]

Deep South secessionists saw in the California issue a portent of the future, and as they tried to divine the future they came up with several scenarios, all of them frightening. First, they believed that once the North obtained a majority in both the U.S. Senate—which it did with the admission of California—they could then pass Wilmot Proviso laws on the rest of the territories because the North already had secured the majority in the House of Representatives and before long could elect a northern president. A prohibition of slavery in the territories meant only free states would be admitted in the future. Here, the ability of southerners to peer into the future failed and became a fractured vision. By adding more free states some southerners feared that the North would destroy slavery by a constitutional amendment. Others felt that the cordon of free states around slave states allowed for such massive resistance to slavery by encouraging runaways that slavery could not survive. Some insisted that the South needed new lands to keep plantation slavery alive, that slavery had to march westward and southward in order to be profitable. A number used a Malthusian analysis: without expansion, only whites could leave the slave states but black slaves would remain behind; over time this process would produce such a horrific imbalance in the ratio between whites and blacks that race war would erupt. Many simply feared a majoritarian North. Even if the North did not directly attack slavery, its representatives could so shape laws to plunder and ruin Southern economic activity.[98]

Within this debate over secession and the future of the South without expansion, southerners offered numerous other reasons to resist the Compromise of 1850. Southern honor would be impugned for one, and no southerner should allow himself to be a member of an organization that singled him out for different treatment—another way of saying that the compromise violated the equality of the states. Running throughout the exhortations was a fear of race war and the need for the white race to keep Africans subservient. Some advocated separation because slavery had made North and South different civilizations.[99]

Secessionists never did a good job of explaining those "rights" except for one—the right to private property. The Compromise of 1850 had devalued the right of property in slaves by indicating that somehow slavery was different from other sorts of property. Thus, southerners, claimed a Joint Committee on the State of the Republic, would not "*even for the preservation of the Union*, permit their rights to be assailed; they will not permit their property to be rendered worthless; they will not permit their wives and children to be driven as wanderers into strange lands." John A. Quitman, erstwhile governor of Mississippi, called slavery the "great interest" of the South that absolutely needed governmental protection and encouragement. Christopher Memminger warned that without government approval, slavery would become "a property without protection of a law, which is only another name for that which is no property at all." South Carolinian Armistead Burt explained:

> The leading object to be attained by secession, will be admitted to be the preservation of the institution of African slavery, unimpaired and unmolested. It comprehends the quiet and undisturbed enjoyment of this species of property, as well as the means of making it profitable and desirable. These conditions are necessary to save fifteen hundred millions of property, the most profitable in the world, and the source of countless blessings to mankind—from becoming a nuisance and a curse.
>
> . . . The great function of government, in modern times, is the protection of property. Property in slaves, of all other property, can least endure aggression, and most needs the arm of government.[100]

This fear of property rights also explained southern dread of democratic government and the States' Righters' continuous assault on democratic principles during the 1850–51 electoral contests. In the address of the Nashville Convention in its first meeting, the proclamation read that democratic government only works when the interests of all parties are "entirely identical. Then the dominant cannot oppress the subject people without oppressing themselves." Slavery was confined to the South. An increasing northern majority created a disaster in political economy, for the majority had no reason to respect the property rights of the minority. This line of reasoning allowed John A. Quitman to argue that "whenever a government is hostile to any particular interest, it may cripple and destroy it, without ever infringing the constitution." By simply using the majority's constitutional right to pass laws, the majority may then neutralize the laws upholding the property rights of the minority. Thus the passage of power from a balance of slave and free states in the Senate to a free state majority represented a universe of future evil.[101]

The congressional and gubernatorial contests in southern states held in September and October 1851 produced an astonishing Unionist triumph, frequently registering some 60 percent of the vote.[102] This campaign across the Deep South had produced a sense of profound political change. "Developments every where around us, clearly indicate," said the editor of the *Milledgeville Federal Union* in late 1850, "that old party lines are broken down, and that Whig and Democrat as distinctive national parties, will soon cease to exist." Another editor cried, "Who cares now for the question of Bank or no Bank, distribution of the public lands, sub-treasury, veto power, and the other subordinate measures of policy?" Editors and politicians often exaggerated the results of elections, partly for their own benefit and partly because they had no experience with real party upheaval. But in this case they were right. The debate over property rights in slaves and whether the Compromise of 1850 endangered them reduced the old issues of tariff, currency, and internal improvements to baby babble. The old party names did not die, but the relative strengths became significantly different. After 1851 the Democrats grew in power and might as they became increasingly the party of state control of property rights in slaves; the Whigs simply weakened and opposition to the Democrats in general became enfeebled.[103]

The importance of the southern elections in 1850 and 1851 escaped northerners. Most northern politicians received no letters on the subject. Only Millard Fillmore closely watched developments in the South and seemed aware of their portent, but even then he seemed mostly concerned with Whig fortunes in New York and Pennsylvania.[104] The northern urban newspapers provided some coverage of the struggle of secessionists to take the Gulf states out of the Union but seemed rather smug that the seceders had been routed. Few ventured any analysis; that of the *New York Tribune* was unique. "Georgia, like Virginia, and less thoroughly Maryland, North Carolina and Alabama, is a

State containing two antagonist Social systems—the Slave system in the South-East and the Free Labor system in the North-West." Those "North-West" areas were the homes of small, thrifty, yeoman farmers, who naturally were for union and opposed to separation.[105] Numerous papers noted that the fight in the South was between Unionists and Secessionists, but the lesson they derived was that the southern cry of secession was bluster. Almost no one in the North noted a seismic shift in party allegiance.[106]

The impact of the southern elections of 1850 and 1851 is given in Figure 6.1. This illustration depicts the electoral results of congressional districts for five regions: New England (Massachusetts, Connecticut, Vermont, Maine, and New Hampshire), the Middle Atlantic (New York, Pennsylvania, and New Jersey), the Great Lakes (Ohio, Indiana, Illinois, Wisconsin, and Michigan), the Border South (North Carolina, Virginia, Tennessee, and Kentucky), and the Deep South (Georgia, Alabama, Mississippi, and Louisiana). Elections used in the chart were determined by presidential contests; if not presidential elections, then congressional elections; if neither presidential nor congressional contests, then state races. (A full explanation of the procedures in constructing the figures and a more complete analysis is given in Appendix B.) The lines of the chart represent the average percentage of the vote cast earned by the Democrats minus the percentage of the vote cast earned by the next major opposition party (which means third-party effects are not captured by this technique). When the parties were evenly matched, the lines would be flat around zero; if the Democrats earned more votes, the lines would reach into positive territory; when the Democrats lost votes, the lines would plunge into negative territory.

Figure 6.1 demonstrates how competitive the Second Party System of Whigs versus Democrats was. The curves seldom extended beyond the plus or minus 5 lines, and all regions showed a competitive situation. But the party system gyrated in 1851, when people in the Deep South reacted to the debate over slavery in the western territories. That debate touched the core of the institution of slavery—the legitimacy of property rights in people. That issue crushed out interest in tariffs, banks, and internal improvements. Thus, for the Border South and emphatically for the Deep South the figure shows a real breakage in the pattern of the Second Party System. As well, it should be noted that the North did not react in such a fashion—in the North the patterns of the Second Party System continued in 1851 and afterward. Northerners had yet to react fully to the implications of the slavery-extension debate, whereas Deep South southerners obviously had far more at stake. In short, Figure 6.1 reveals that the Deep South's reaction to the debate over the Wilmot Proviso commenced the destruction of the Second Party System.

Politics after 1851 fell into a lifeless dance between hollow parties emptied of their spirit. In 1852 came a presidential election. The Democrats found a useful general, Franklin Pierce of New Hampshire, who had volunteered to serve in

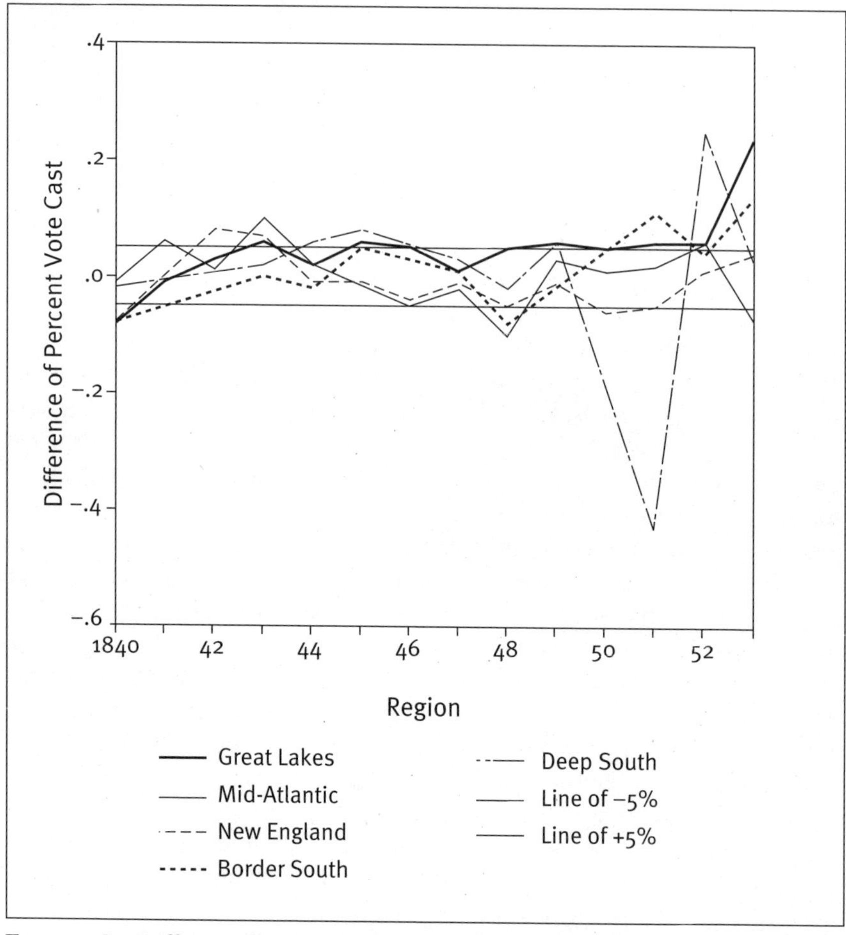

FIGURE 6.1. *Difference between Major Party Voting, 1840–1853: Democratic Party Percent Vote Cast Minus Second Strongest Party*

the Mexican War, and nominated him, ignoring the claims of James Buchanan, Stephen A. Douglas, and some southerners. Their platform boldly called for all the usual Jacksonian standards and the implementation of congressional nonintervention in the territories, a way of upholding the Compromise of 1850 and Lewis Cass's notion of popular sovereignty. Unlike the Democrats, the Whigs had no lovefeast. While they found a willing general, Winfield Scott, they could not soothe over party wounds from the fight over the Wilmot Proviso. Southern Whigs demanded an outright embrace of the Compromise of 1850 and the selection of Millard Fillmore as the standard-bearer; northern Whigs were outraged by the Fugitive Slave Law, wanted its repeal, and leaned toward the Wilmot Proviso standard. Although the Whigs managed a national campaign, the bitterness between northern antislavery Whigs and southern anti-proviso Whigs badly weakened the party. When the returns were added in November 1852, Pierce had demolished Scott, earning 1,600,000 votes to Scott's 1,385,000, and 254 electoral votes to 42. Twenty-seven of the thirty-one states voted Democratic, and the Democrats would have majorities in both houses of Congress during the next session.[107]

The election results were so bad that Whigs talked about the end of the party. "We are slayed—the party is dead—dead—dead!" wrote Lewis Campbell of Ohio. One Whig told William Seward that "I never believed such a result possible." Even Democrats wondered about the survival of their rivals. August Belmont of New York penned the sentiment that the election was the "complete annihilation of the Whig party," and it was a blessing because it destroyed that party's antislavery wing.[108] Blame for the election results included the role of illegal immigrants, the mighty power of the Democracy to attract the unwashed, and the fight between proslavery and antislavery wings of the party.[109] Few really sat down, evidently, and studied the results. While it was clear that Whig voting was less than it should have been, few tried to find out where Whig voting faltered. Indeed, analysis of this election was so slim that many did not even mention the lowered turnout in 1852.

The next year returned in greater measure the apathy that had settled over political affairs. Elections for congressional seats in the South, a few in the North, and various state offices throughout the country were held. Democrats maintained their edge over the Whigs, if anyone noticed. These state and congressional elections did not elicit much interest from newspapers or appear in political correspondence. It was probably the most uninspired election year of the antebellum era.[110] No one quite realized what was happening to politics or what had happened. Although the more spectacular upheaval was to come in the North between 1854 and 1856, the nation had just gone through the first phase of the realignment of the 1850s.

7

The Northern Realignment, 1854–1860

After 1852 southern politics was on a new trajectory that lifted the Democratic Party into a nearly unassailable position of dominance. Shortly thereafter, in 1854, northern politics burst asunder and underwent realignment. The old party system of Whigs and Democrats vanished, and a new system in the North took form. Unlike the southern one, the northern realignment was messy, and for two years considerable confusion about the Democrats' new foe existed. By the end of 1856, the uncertainty ended as the Republican Party emerged out of the chaos with an impressive command of northern voters. The end result of the northern and southern realignments was the sectionalization of American politics.

Although gales of cultural conflict buffeted northern communities, the northern realignment was basically due to the slavery issue in national politics. Animosity over the Fugitive Slave Law and lingering attempts at Manifest Destiny in the Caribbean provided a background of northern suspicion about southern designs. Those suspicions exploded in outrage over the passage of the Kansas-Nebraska Act in 1854. Then came the conflict in Kansas and the presidential election of 1856. Throughout these years northerners sounded the alarm over the slave power and expressed anxiety about the safety and perpetuity of their free labor village communities.

Southerners continued to insist that northerners recognize property rights in slaves. That continuing search for the ultimate sanctuary for the peculiar institution drove many southerners further away from compromise and led them to extreme positions. The question of property rights in slaves became amplified in the *Dred Scott* decision of the Supreme Court and the Lecompton Constitution battle in Congress, both of which created an alienation that cut many northern Democrats from their southern brethren. Indeed, by the beginning of 1860, as the party conventions drew near, the visible line between North and South was not simply the preservation of slavery; it was to what extent would the nation be governed by property rights in slaves. Republicans, of course, wanted the legal question of slaves entirely confined to southern states. Southern Democrats were forcing northern Democrats into the same position, because in the battles in Congress it became clear that the general southern demand was that democratic procedures had no business interfering with property rights, a position that entirely gutted Douglas's principle of popular sovereignty. Southerners saw the election of 1860 as the North's last chance to prove its fidelity to property rights in slaves. When northerners turned to the Republican Abraham Lincoln in massive numbers, southerners judged that northerners had failed in their commitments for the last time and secession was the only remedy for preserving their wealth.

In the heat of sectional anger in 1850, southerners demanded a new fugitive slave law because northerners had failed to perform their duties faithfully and because the Supreme Court in the case of *Prigg v. Pennsylvania* (1842) had relieved states of enforcement responsibilities and had placed them squarely on the shoulders of the federal government. In the clash of sections over the territorial expansion of slavery, the southern demand for national recognition of property rights in slaves spilled over to the fugitive slave issue. Here at least was a duty specifically described in the Constitution to which northerners had agreed, and here was a test of northern fidelity to past promises about slavery—that they would view runaways as property to be returned, like horses that had slipped out of a corral.

James Murray Mason of Virginia shaped the bill and pushed it through the Senate. He made no attempt to disguise its meaning. "The property held by that part of the United States, valued at hundreds of millions of dollars, is the subject of wanton depredation" by northerners who did not return escaped slaves back to their masters even though the obligation was clearly outlined in the Constitution. In his anger at northerners' refusal to see slaves as property, Mason leveled a blast that any northerner with an ounce of imagination could see as slave-master-inspired imperialism: "The Constitution, however, as the supreme law, recognizes this right of property, and carries its obligations and its incidents, for all purposes of reclamation, into every State in the Union, and makes the law of the domicile, *quo ad hoc*, the law of every State in the Union." Mason gave northerners ample reason to fear that slavery would eventually become a national institution and all the states would become slave states.[1]

Southerners never saw the Fugitive Slave Law of 1850 as an attack on northern communities but only as the fulfillment of constitutional obligations. That northerners complained about the lack of trial by jury and the abolition of the right of habeas corpus did not, so it seems from the research done on the subject, trouble them. They purposely made the law stringent and designed it as a "test" of northern fidelity. Behind the stringency may have been an explicit attitude: slaves were property like the animals of the fields; and animals had no right to trial by jury and habeas corpus. Some nonetheless understood that the provisions of the Fugitive Slave Act—giving federal marshals more in fees if arrested blacks were sent back to the South than if freed, relying solely upon evidence submitted by slaveholders, permitting U.S. marshals to force northerners to serve as slave catchers, and denying arrested blacks any means of appeal—would upset northerners; yet moderates demanded obedience to the law. The Virginia Whig luminary, William C. Rives, who was then minister to France, wrote to Connecticut readers of the *New Haven Register* to support the compromise measures and thereby save the Union. He understood "that painful and disagreeable circumstances may sometimes attend the enforcement of this law," but it was a duty that southerners demanded to be performed. The Union was based on trust, said Rives, and if northerners thwarted the Fugitive Slave Law of 1850, the Union "would not survive the blow."[2]

Northern conservatives rallied support for the Compromise of 1850 and the Fugitive Slave Act, suppressing their distaste for the provisions of the latter. Conservatives enunciated a consistent theme: the Fugitive Slave Law of 1850 was constitutional and the law had to be upheld because to follow one's conscience instead of the law was to invite anarchy. Indeed, in the aftermath of the Fugitive Slave Act conservatives stressed obedience to law rather than morality. This set up one of the great debates during the decade about which commandments individuals should follow—those of their religion and conscience, or those of the public authorities. John A. Bingham of Ohio, a future congressman, remarked in a letter that the answer to a bad law was to amend or repeal it, but no "foolish violations of law. The latter conduct is bad [in] every way and contravenes the first principles of Republican Government and also the first duty of Republican Citizens[,] to wit[:] *obedience to the* laws." Abolitionists and antislavery zealots noted a class division on this issue: the wealthy were the ones arguing for acceptance of the Fugitive Slave Law whereas the artisans and farmers demanded action governed by moral laws. One consequence of the Fugitive Slave Law, quite unintended by its authors, was its impact upon the northern clergy. The Fugitive Slave Law became the first slavery-related issue that drew the clergy into the political arena in a significant way.[3]

Ultimately northerners complied with the Fugitive Slave Law. Democrats demanded strict observance of the law, and Whigs generally fell into line as well. Certainly there were spectacular instances of community support for some runaways: the Christiana Riot in southeastern Pennsylvania, the "Jerry" case in Syracuse, the William Booth episode in Wisconsin, the Thomas Sims and Shadrach captures in Boston, and probably most famously the Anthony Burns trial, also in Boston. The law inspired Harriet Beecher Stowe to write *Uncle Tom's Cabin*, a melodrama that became the first national best-seller and soon an international sensation. Yet only an approximate total of 100 fugitive slave cases occurred between 1850 and 1860. Certainly only a relatively few northern communities ever experienced the operation of the law, and even fewer northerners were ever dragooned into a posse to hunt down runaways. Given the minor role it actually played in the North, the law hardly seemed to deserve the appellations given it by John Rankin, "a standing monument of the most high handed wickedness ever a nation had" or Charles Stuart's description of it as "that masterpiece of cowardly & ferocious iniquity." Yet the Fugitive Slave Law had important effects.[4]

The Fugitive Slave Law damaged the southern case in the North in three vital ways. First, it invoked the passion of northern clergymen and prepared them for more interventions in the political realm. Second, and quite unexpected given its origins, the bill humanized blacks in the North. Northern blacks had been the object of mob violence, of discriminatory laws, of an imposed poverty. In many ways, white northerners could look upon blacks as insignificant beings complicating their universe. But the Fugitive Slave Law made victims out of northern blacks and gave them a human visage because the law was imposed from outside the local community, thereby giving them a different stature, that of individuals oppressed by outside powers. Many northerners now found that they could conceive of blacks as human beings with normal desires for freedom. A correspondent of William Seward recorded this process at a meeting he went to in New Bedford, Massachusetts: "Last night in Liberty hall a very large room full and running over—gallery and all—and some very eloquent speakers among them, one darkie perfectly Illiterate, but in his native eloquence as good as the best of them, and to see such a giant mind of a man converted into a chattle, by his fellow man, and to be deprived of himself, and the power, and opertunity of knowing himself, by the development of those native tallents, and that too by cretures as much inferiour to him, perhaps as a monkey to a common man, is to my mind the most abominable and Demning sin that a nation could be guilty of." Instead of forcing northerners to treat blacks as property, southerners managed through the Fugitive Slave Law to erode some of the bitter racism rampant in the North.[5]

Third, the Fugitive Slave Law demonstrated southern aggression against the rights of the North. For the first time in the sectional conflict over slavery, one side imposed laws upon the other side that were not self-generated. Northerners found themselves forced to obey the laws of slavery. "By this late act of Congress," penned the Democratic editor of the *Cleveland Daily Plain Dealer*, "passed by Southern slave breeders and Northern compromisers, all the free States are made slavery ground, and all freemen, slave-catchers, if the law is to be enforced." In one pamphlet, a writer wailed, "It constitutes at the North, in our neighborhoods, and by our firesides, the most anomalous, over-shadowing, insulting, and despotic police that perverted mind can contrive, or guilty power sustain." In Wisconsin, the antislavery editor C. Latham Sholes hammered away at the southern violation of northern states' rights. South Carolina had the right to "her institutions" but "she has no right under the constitution, nor by any other authority, to demand that her institutions and laws, shall be recognized as of authority, outside her boundary. . . . The Fugitive Slave Law is in all practical effects an extension of slavery over the whole land."[6]

The small number of incidents involving slave catchers in the North may not adequately capture the sense of invasion. In some matters in this world, spectacular incidents have far more social power than they should. That some communities came under the command of slave catchers was communicated quickly to the rest of northern communities; in a sense, they shared the outrage of having their laws and customs set aside by the command of slaveholders.[7] That dictation rankled and let the northern public cast a dark and wary countenance on ultimate southern designs.

Coincident with the continuing anger over the Fugitive Slave Law was the remnant of Manifest Destiny in the 1850s. Various Americans still wanted to push the nation outward. However, those people all seemed to want lands that could embrace slavery—Cuba and Central America. In 1850 and 1851 "filibusters" invaded Cuba (the Lopez expeditions) and much of the financing and manpower for these attempts to foment insurrection came from southerners. Later in 1854 the fire-breathing John A. Quitman, former governor of Mississippi who had called for secession in 1850, became involved in a plot to seize Cuba. A few years afterward, the desire for expansion into Central America became personified in William Walker who for a while took over the nation of Nicaragua.[8]

These attempts to push the boundaries of the United States outward probably were not vital to southern society nor were they an important element of American civil life. Most southerners, particularly politicians, had had their fill of adding territories and wanted a little quiet. The only factor favoring expansion, however, was that if someone managed to seize new land adequate for plantation slavery, southerners would not object. They were essentially passively favorable to such projects, not wishing to initiate such action themselves but willing to receive any gifts that fell into their laps. Northerners by this time were probably actively opposed to extension, especially of territory that could sustain slavery. Thus the filibusterers were tangential to the main directions of American politics and economics. But the presence of the filibusterers gave northerners pause. Filibustering activity raised the question of ultimate designs of southerners and how they would use the power of the federal government. Like the Fugitive Slave Law, what mattered was not the frequency of incidents but the appearance of any incidents at all.

Thus the Fugitive Slave Law and filibustering were background conditions in the North. They nourished suspicions that slaveholders had an agenda for the nation that boded ill for northern freedoms and international tranquility. They created a northern environment hostile to alterations in sectional accords consummated in the past. Northern apprehensions about southern behavior that resulted from the Fugitive Slave Law and filibustering attempts help to explain the maniacal reaction of northerners to Stephen A. Douglas's attempt to organize the territories of Kansas and Nebraska by repealing the Missouri Compromise and instituting the policy of popular sovereignty.

Plans to connect California to the rest of the country by a transcontinental railroad were afoot by 1852, and the proposed routes used initial starting points either in New Orleans or St. Louis, bypassing altogether a Great Lakes connection (Chicago). Stephen A. Douglas did not want this to happen, and to insure consideration for a northern route he needed to organize the territories west of Iowa in the Louisiana Purchase area; without a political entity to protect operations, there could be no construction. However, Douglas had other concerns as well. He believed deeply in Manifest Destiny and wanted to bring in those western lands as states; his concern for the tribes there was minimal. His presidential ambitions for 1856 influenced him as well; helping to expand the nation could only enhance his fame. Beyond this was a desire to return the nation to the economic issues that had served the Democratic Party so well, the issues of tariffs, banking, internal improvements, and available western lands. Slavery had terrorized the old two-party system, and Douglas was eager to remove it forever from the halls of Congress. The means of doing so was to employ Lewis Cass's idea of popular sovereignty. Instead of having politicians wrangle about the subject in Congress, let settlers in the West debate the matter while Washington leaders kept their mouths shut. Without the issue of slavery undercutting the northern Democrat appeal and deranging southern loyalties, the party system could return to tariffs and banks, topics that had always produced Democrat electoral triumphs.[9]

As chairman of the Senate Committee on Territories, Douglas tried to write legislation enabling the area known as Nebraska to begin an organization process that would ultimately result in statehood—the appointment of a territorial governor, the sale of public lands to settlers, the creation of a legislative body once population reached 5,000. His attempt failed in the last session of the Thirty-second Congress (December 1852 to March 1853). Senator David Atchison of Missouri led southerners against the bill because, as a result of the Missouri Compromise, slaveholders could not migrate to the Nebraska area with their slaves.

Douglas reintroduced the plan of organizing territories in the land west of Iowa in January 1854 in the first session of the Thirty-third Congress. Southerners pressured him to remove the Missouri restriction. Douglas yielded to their demands probably due to his own desire for rapid organization, his belief that slavery would not go westward, and a general sympathy for the southern position that the Missouri restriction stigmatized the slaveholding states as being lesser members of the Union. His bill would create two territories, Kansas and Nebraska, set them both on the path of territorial organization leading to statehood, and permit settlers there to determine the question of slavery themselves. But the southern opposition to the Democrats, the remnant of the Whigs, did not want the Democrats to claim such a victory. Archibald Dixon, a Whig senator from Kentucky, moved an amendment that made the Missouri Compromise inapplicable to the territory under consideration. Douglas a week later moved a new bill in which popular sovereignty on the slavery question was made explicit and which stipulated that the Compromise of 1850 had replaced the Compromise of 1820, declaring the antislavery provision of the earlier compromise now "inoperative." Ultimately Douglas justified his position by stating that the Compromise of 1850 had superseded the Compromise of 1820. But the cat had escaped from its hiding place and was now in the open. The new measure, the Kansas-Nebraska Act, sought repeal of the Missouri Compromise.[10]

An immediate response to the proposal came from the antislavery group in Congress. In an "Appeal of the Independent Democrats in Congress to the People of the United States: Shall Slavery Be Permitted in Nebraska?" Salmon P. Chase, Charles Sumner, Joshua Giddings, Edward Wade, Gerrit Smith, and Alexander deWitte lambasted the proposal as a conspiracy by the slave power to expand its influence in the nation and seize the reins of the government. They made the compromise line of 36 degrees 30 minutes a sacrosanct agreement between northerners and southerners that prohibited slavery in the Louisiana Purchase area above that line. Slaveholders, they charged, wanted to nullify the compromise because they had carved slave states out of the Louisiana land given them (Louisiana, Arkansas, Missouri, Texas, and potentially Indian Territory). Now, slaveholders wanted more; they coveted the land they had once given to the free states. The consequences were monstrous. The western lands would become slave states because "Freemen, unless pressed by a hard and cruel necessity, will not, and should not, work besides slaves. Labor cannot be respected where any class of laborers is held in abject bondage." Moreover, the slave states would then surround the free states and subject them to political domination and finally throttle their freedoms.[11]

It should be remarked that from the first these individuals hit exactly the argument from which arose northern support for the Wilmot Proviso after 1846 and from which sprang the Free-Soil movement in 1848. For thirty years, land in the Louisiana Purchase area north of 36 degrees 30 minutes had been "pledged to freedom"; to take land pledged for freedom and to make it slave would be a "monstrous wrong."[12] This idea that land once free was always free had been in every statement made by Wilmot Proviso supporters from 1846 to 1848. Such a conviction had convulsed the nation in those years and produced a near secession of the Gulf states. Douglas badly miscalculated when he affirmed that popular sovereignty had replaced it. Indeed, the northern reaction to the Kansas-Nebraska Act was merely the northern reaction to slavery expansion in 1846–48—but this time written in much greater script because, while California and New Mexico had been recently acquired territories, the Kansas-Nebraska area had been reserved for freedom for thirty-four years.

The northern political upheaval in 1854 is not surprising at all when it is compared with the northern arguments surrounding the Wilmot Proviso.

The battle over the passage of the Kansas-Nebraska Act grew to gigantic proportions. Congressmen certainly felt it was the principal measure of the session, and the topic consumed all other matters.[13] The arguments for and against the measure, however, largely reiterated the ones between 1846 and 1850.

Democrats upheld the Kansas-Nebraska legislation with a variety of rationales. They insisted that the Compromise of 1850 had superseded the Compromise of 1820. Most Democrats, northern as well as southern, said both territories were destined to be free and that the slavery issue was inconsequential. The only reason that the legislation mentioned the peculiar institution was to remove the stigma placed upon the slaveholding states, not out of any design to obtain more slave states. More interesting was their handling of the Missouri Compromise line. Douglas insisted that the line was defunct anyway because of the vote in July 1848 in which northerners had refused to extend the line to the Pacific Ocean. That constituted a repeal of the Compromise of 1820, and for that reason the Compromise of 1850 replaced the older one. Moreover, as many southerners said, the Missouri Compromise line was not a constitutional amendment; it was merely ordinary legislation that could be repealed or amended at any time. Southerners offered this latter argument to defuse the constant antislavery cry about the sacrosanct quality of the 1820 agreement.[14]

Northern antislavery spokesmen angrily denounced the Kansas-Nebraska Act. In this session of Congress, some true abolitionists were present who particularly bemoaned the fate of Africans in slavery, but their speeches were notable because they were so rare.[15] One question asked was what prompted the repeal of the Missouri Compromise, for there were no movements or congressional emergencies demanding it; rather, the nation was at sectional peace and the question of slavery should have been left undisturbed. Only one or two antislavery congressmen actually brought up the question of why two territories were proposed instead of the original one of Nebraska. The implication was that a bargain had been made to bring one slave state and one free state into the Union. Surprisingly few others developed that charge. Several antislavery speakers reiterated the mantra of the 1840s: territory once free was always free, and slavery should never be allowed to expand where it was once banned or nonexistent. Many expressed concern over the fate of the Indians should the bill pass and believed that opening up the Kansas-Nebraska area was a betrayal of the promise President Jackson gave when Indian Removal was implemented in the 1830s.[16]

Of course, antislavery speakers in Congress emphasized the perfidy of rescinding the Missouri Compromise prohibition against the expansion of slavery in the Louisiana Purchase area above the 36 degree 30 minute line. This proved a conspiracy among slaveholders to obtain new land for new slave states. Slaveholders had exhausted their options in the Louisiana Purchase area and regretted their promise to give land to the North, so now they were willing to repeal their agreement to get more slave states. Northerners pounded away at this theme because it struck a chord with the public. Southerners had insisted that northerners live up to their agreements about slavery in the Constitution, a theme constantly reiterated between 1846 and 1850. But now southerners sought to annul their agreements with the North when they saw that they were not to be benefited. The idea that southerners only abided with agreements when it served their self-interest came out strongly among northerners, and they intimated that further compromise with slaveholders was now futile. Richard Yates in a later speech declared that "the day of compromize is gone forever. When Compromizes are trampled in the dust as the Mo. C. was, who in the North, retaining one particle of manhood, will ask for another compromize to be broken again when ever the South in her sovereign pleasure may see proper to break it." At a Bangor meeting against the Kansas-Nebraska Act, one of the resolutions read that the free states were "absolved from all obligations to maintain the Slavery compromises; that it is now only a question of power between slavery and freedom." One of William Seward's correspondents expressed the public anger in the North about "the proposed repeal of a compact which, for more than thirty-years has been regarded as a holy thing, above the reach of political legislation is universal & intense." Even John Bell recognized the impolicy of goading northerners with repeal, regardless if the compromise were or were not merely common legislation.[17]

Certainly the successful repeal of the Missouri Compromise line consumed much congressional and public attention, but other themes came out of the debates over the Kansas-Nebraska Act. Property rights in slavery constituted the main prop of the southern defense of their territorial position, and southerners began expressing themselves in unconditional terms. Northerners explained their hostility to repeal in terms of the slave power conspiracy and the free labor ideology. For the northern Democrats, however, popular sovereignty became a point of some contention but as well a new and vital principle.

In December 1847 Lewis Cass had stumbled upon popular sovereignty as a way to avoid the constitutional clash over Congress's power concerning slavery in the territories. By 1854 Douglas had refurbished it into the great principle of the Democratic Party, full of hallowed memories of the Revolution and as the gift that the founders had given the nation. Douglas declared emphatically that his principle of nonintervention by Congress and popular sovereignty in the territories was right. He had help. Bernhard Henn of Iowa emphasized that popular sovereignty was "*the fundamental principle of self-government*," while Henry Wright of Pennsylvania, who agreed with southerners that the Missouri Compromise was unfair, connected Douglas's doctrine with the Revolution: "The first gun of the Revolution sounded the note of popular sovereignty; the last one, at the gates of Mexico, reechoed the principle."[18] Democrats made popular sovereignty into a principle of the Revolution, not of the Constitution; they never really claimed that Congress had not the power to rule the territories and prohibit slavery, only that the exercise of such power would be prejudicial and unfair to one section of the country. Popular sovereignty was a practical compromise based on the ideals of the Revolution, not a Constitutional mandate.

In truth popular sovereignty gave the opposition fits—and would do so for several more years. The basic problem was that popular sovereignty *was* the gift of the revolutionary struggle and refuting its applicability in the case of the western territories required more thinking than most antislavery people were willing to give it. Mostly antislavery congressmen said that the Constitution granted Congress the power to prohibit slavery's expansion, that the territories did not possess sovereignty but were in a state of "tutelage." Most believed popular sovereignty was a doctrinal mask that hid the real motivation—to let slavery expand. Spoke Ohio's Andrew Stuart, "The right of self-government recognized in this bill is the power to establish the despotism of slavery. It gives one portion of the inhabitants the power to buy and sell another portion." Only Edward Wade and Israel Washburne pointed to the missing piece that might damage popular sovereignty. Popular sovereignty could not be allowed to overrule the right to "self-ownership." For them, the doctrine was misapplied, because it denied people of a different race citizenship.[19]

Many northern Democrats rallied behind the doctrines of nonintervention and popular sovereignty, for those claims had a legitimate public appeal.[20] Nonetheless, southerners had problems with popular sovereignty, calling Douglas's policy "squatter sovereignty." The reason was a confusion over when the people were allowed to vote on slavery. Southerners admitted that the people of a state could vote on slavery-related questions whenever they pleased because a state had sovereignty. But territories did not have sovereignty and only obtained it when they wrote a state constitution and were admitted into the Union. Without some definition, popular sovereignty could mean that the first handful of settlers in a territory could outlaw slavery and make their determination last throughout the territorial period. The Calhounite position, and the general southern position, was that the Constitution oversaw the territorial stage and guaranteed all settlers equal rights, and among those equal rights was the right to migrate to the territory with property from the state of origin and have that property protected, not outlawed. Many southern Democrats for practical reasons were willing to go along with popular sovereignty in the hopes that it provided a means out of the constitutional impasse; they hoped the cases in which it were invoked would be so obvious in one direction or another in regard to slavery that no one would quarrel with the outcome.[21]

When Lawrence Keitt of South Carolina discussed popular sovereignty, he declared that he thought the idea subversive of the Constitution: "As a southern man, sir, I demand that this Government shall protect, constitutionally, our slave property." Stephen A. Douglas never responded to the tension between property rights and majority voting. Perhaps he was afraid of the conflict, or more likely he hoped that the collision might simply be avoided by climatic conditions. In any event, Douglas did not provide any analysis of popular sovereignty in terms of property rights. Yet the danger was there. Cyrus L. Dunham of Indiana, a popular-sovereignty Democrat, did respond to the question—and what he said offered little comfort to southerners. Slavery existed by "municipal regulations only." The Constitution did not carry slave property into the territories because the Constitution did not define slavery, and without positive local law it could not exist. For southerners, the problem was that they possessed "a peculiar kind of property, which is, not only, not recognized or enjoyed by the people of the free States, but which is repugnant to their tastes and principles." Property in the states was one thing; in the territories, however, it was something else. The saving grace for the South was that if ever the nation acquired territory that allowed slavery to be profitable, then American greed would ensure that slavery would go there regardless of any law, Missouri Compromise or not, because the true rule of nature was that the strong ruled the weak. So, Dunham said, popular sovereignty could safely be imposed on the territories because it made no real difference: where slavery was profitable, no power on earth could stop white Americans from establishing it.[22]

Within the Democratic Party, the Achilles' heel of popular sovereignty was property rights. The tendency of southern demands was distinctly to repudiate majoritarian control over property rights, to elevate the rights of property above legislative tinkering. In this matter southerners were conservative in a very old sense, for the traditional fear of conservatives was that the mob sought to relieve the wealthy of their riches. Yet the doctrine of popular sovereignty for Douglas and his supporters was not a hollow argument used solely for avoiding sectional confrontations. Douglas and his followers did not repudiate the Jacksonian past, and in the heat of the battles between Whigs and Democrats in the 1830s and 1840s, it was the Democrats who cried "human rights above property rights." When push came to shove, Douglas and the northern Democrats would insist upon the primacy of popular sovereignty and that would create the breach between them and the radicals in the Gulf states. Up in New Hampshire, the low-tariff Democratic publicist Edmund Burke wrote a broadside for the Democrat Central Committee of New Hampshire supporting the Kansas-Nebraska Act. On its cover was an exhortation for the rights to life, liberty, and property, and government policies that favored no classes and established no monopolies, for "The DEMOCRATIC CREED WAS THE CREED OF JEFFERSON," "*Absolute acquiescence in the decisions of the majority, the vital principle of republics, from which there is no appeal but to force, the vital principle and immediate parent of despotism.*" Gulf state politicians increasingly wanted restrictions on this majoritarian sentiment in regard to property rights. Thus the eventual split between northern and southern Democrats was already visible, and the fault line would be when a majority attempted to rule on property rights.[23]

Besides their abhorrence of the repeal of the Missouri Compromise line and their rejection of popular sovereignty as a fruitful policy, antislavery opponents of the Kansas-Nebraska Act explained their hostility to slavery's expansion by reliance on two main themes. The first was dread of the slave power. Southern slaveholders and their northern lackeys—"doughfaces"—sought to give the slaveholding states more political power so as to convert the United States into a bastion of slavery, even to the point of changing free states into slave states. "They mean to Africanise America," stated an Illinois editor, while a writer in the *New York Times* mused, "certainly the Slave-power had been encroaching; month by month, year by year, for quite a cycle of years. The Slave-power is one." Indeed, one Henry Bennett of New York during the House debates over the bill gave the session's most startling slave power analysis of the situation. The South wanted political power, he said, not land, because the South already was twice as big geographically as the North but had only one-half the population. With more slave states, the South could control federal legislation and insure it benefited the peculiar institution. Slaveholders represented a dangerous power because they formed an aristocracy hostile to freedom. Why was this aristocracy so powerful? "This is a great property interest—more than three millions of slaves, covering fifteen States, and worth over $2,000,000,000." Because owners of similar property acted together so easily, the slave power exercised the most influence in Congress. Bennett then demanded that this interest not be allowed to grow further.[24]

Just as prominent, if not more so, was the theme of free labor. "Shall the United States Government, hereafter," asked New Jersey's Charles Skelton, "compel the free laborer of the North to enter into competition with the slavery of the South?" Many antislavery representatives raised that question, and others provided a comparison between some southern state, almost always Virginia, and a northern state, usually Ohio or New York. One of the strongest speeches came from Richard Yates of Illinois, who claimed that the "free laborer does not wish the labor of slaves to come into competition with his labor."[25] Many of these speakers were northern Democrats.

Indeed, the opposition use of free labor claims so clogged the chambers of Congress that it drew two memorable responses. Mississippi senator Albert Gallatin Brown blundered into a discussion that lent credence to the frequent northern cry that slaveholders were aristocrats. Early in the session, he gave a speech attacking the idea of popular sovereignty but then switched to a justification of slavery because of the institution's social benefits. Due to slavery, southerners only had one standard for judging others, and that was integrity: "Poverty is no crime, and labor is honorable." But then he stumbled into a damaging statement: "The line that separates menial from honorable labor with you [in the North] is not marked by a caste or distinct color as it is with us." Blacks, said Brown, did the menial labor of agriculture. The next day the Iowa Democrat senator Augustus C. Dodge attacked—not the Kansas Nebraska Act, not the enslavement of blacks, not the backwardness of Virginia or Maryland—but the notion of labor that Brown voiced. "Sir, I tell the Senator from Mississippi . . . that I have performed and do perform when at home all of those menial services to which the Senator referred in terms so grating to my feelings. As a general thing, I saw my own wood; do all my own marketing. I never had a servant of any color to wait upon me a day in my life. I have driven teams, horses, mules, and oxen, and considered myself as respectable then as I now do, or any Senator upon this floor is." Brown saw his damaging admission about labor—one that nearly justified antislavery pronouncements—and tried to find some way to define the labor of blacks so that northerners would not take offense; he failed. And Dodge's reaction, this free labor reaction, was from a Democratic supporter of the Kansas-Nebraska Act.[26]

The other episode came toward the end of the debate on the legislation. Mike Walsh of New York City had a distinct class viewpoint on the economics of American life, particularly on the sufferings of the Irish in New York City. He found no reason to celebrate the northern laborer in comparison with the lot of a slave. "I have to say," said this supporter of popular sovereignty, "that the only difference between the negro slave of the South, and the white wage slave of the North, is, that the one has a master without asking for him, and the other has to beg for the privilege of becoming a slave. [Great Laughter.]" He added, "the one is the slave of an individual; the other is the slave of an inexorable class." Walsh's statements were quite unique in the Kansas-Nebraska debate, but they obtained considerable reprinting in the northern press.[27]

But most prominent in the debates over Kansas-Nebraska was the issue of property rights in slaves because it was so intimately involved in the constitutional issue of slavery's expansion. Southerners raised the topic of property rights in nearly every speech they gave. James F. Dowdell of Alabama said that the South was willing to "rest her case—the security of her property—upon a strict construction of that sacred instrument [the constitution]." If the South allowed the federal government to legislate slavery out of the territories, "what barrier can be set up against its unlimited sway?" South Carolinian Lawrence Keitt put the subject entirely in property rights terms: "You deny that there is property in the slave. Your denial shakes the very foundation of property." The stress that southerners placed upon property rights led John W. Edmands of Massachusetts to remark, "So far as I have observed, our southern friends seem more sensitive on the subject of rights of property than on any other connection." And indeed, the reason for that concern was easily expressed. Alfred H. Colquitt of Georgia, upset at the intervention of the northern clergy in congressional proceedings, reminded his colleagues that slaves were worth

$1.5 billion and numbered 3 million individuals. Even an appropriation of $60 million for 100 years could not recompense slaveholders for the emancipation of their slaves, and that did not cover any cost of transportation of ex-slaves to new lands; thus, "emancipation is impossible."[28]

The constitutional argument given by southerners in 1854 was generally similar to the one they propounded in the debates of 1847–50. The states retained sovereignty, which included the right to define property; the federal government was the agent of the states and therefore could not discriminate against any of the states; the Constitution guaranteed the rights of property in the bill of rights and the Constitution recognized slaves as property; and southerners had as much right to take their forms of property into the territories as northerners had.[29] Sometimes they went beyond this defense and made arguments that could only raise northern eyebrows. Robert Toombs of Georgia did so by claiming that not only was the Constitution proslavery but that the Constitution, "far from its being true that [it] localized slavery, it nationalized it." At a time when northerners acted apprehensively about the slave power and its intentions, Toombs's pronouncements only added more fuel to the fires in the antislavery imagination.[30]

More than this, several southerners claimed that slavery was a product of natural law, not positive law. Virginia's William Smith rightly pointed out that slavery existed in Virginia in 1619 but no law established it until 1660. The whole history of the colonies testified to the existence of slavery without statute. Keitt claimed that the common law protected slavery as well. Thus the antislavery position that only municipal law could establish slavery was wrong. Indeed, the reverse was true: to end slavery a community had to pass positive law, but not to establish slavery. Thus slavery, not freedom, existed in all territories as soon as they were acquired by the United States.[31] This contention flabbergasted northern opponents of the Kansas-Nebraska Act. As Edmands of Massachusetts stated, after noting the obsession southerners had about property rights, "One would suppose that the slaveholders imagined that they had a *natural* right to their slaves as property." He then castigated these propositions and insisted on the necessity of municipal law in order for slavery to exist. In this he had much company, for almost all the northern antislavery speakers insisted that slavery required positive municipal law.[32]

The Senate, by its Democratic dominance, had no trouble in approving the Kansas-Nebraska Act, but the House took longer. After a considerable struggle, with many Democratic defections, the House affirmed the measure on May 22 by a vote of 113-100. It then received President Franklin Pierce's signature shortly thereafter. Northerners were upset, as was apparent in newspaper articles, public meetings, and the oratory of politicians. When Congress ended, Douglas said his passage back to Chicago was lit by the flames of his burning effigies along the railroad tracks. But southerners hardly seemed distraught. Alexander H. Stephens believed that the removal of the Missouri restriction was a good victory for the morale of the South and for the southern Whig Party, for he hoped that the southern Whigs could take credit for the removal of the antislavery 36 degree 30 minute line.[33] Southern editors in no sense played up the Kansas-Nebraska Act as they had the Wilmot Proviso, and they reported few meetings rallying around nonintervention in the territories. Most southern editors agreed that the Missouri Compromise was an unfair discrimination against them and that congressional noninterference in the territories was the appropriate policy. Many believed the territorial issue would wither and die, although a few did see the difference between the southern position and Douglas's popular sovereignty. Precious few of them figured in the manner of the proprietor of the *Raleigh (North Carolina) Weekly Register*. Why, asked the editor, reignite the issue when no demand for a reconsideration was in sight? He then warned prophetically that the South had claimed that all parties should abide by solemn compacts, and that for many in the North the Missouri Compromise was a solemn compact that the South decided to repeal—"and it will be difficult to repel the charge."[34]

As the session of Congress moved to adjournment, northern members understood that their section's politics was in tumult. For one thing, the Kansas-Nebraska Act had seemingly activated the northern clergy, which sent several protests to Congress about the legislation; the numbers of clerics signing the petition were startling—nearly 80 percent of all New England ministers. For Democrats, this boded ill.[35] Yet judging the impact of the Kansas-Nebraska Act on the public mind was difficult. Whig politicians were utterly irate and sought fusions with old Free-Soilers and others who would not stand for the repeal of the Missouri Compromise. In Jackson, Michigan, and Ripon, Wisconsin, those fusions were called Republican Parties after a while, and the name did migrate East to Maine by September.[36] While many politicians detested the Kansas-Nebraska Act and planned, in the words of James W. Grimes of Iowa, to "make it the sole issue," other politicians were not so sure.[37] Millard Fillmore obtained contradictory advice from his correspondents: Solomon G. Haven feared the effect of the legislation but John P. Kennedy believed the bill's impact was overrated. Indiana congressman John G. Davis received information at times saying that there was "little if any opposition" among Democrats to Douglas's bill, while others told him the legislation had made a mess of the party by dividing it into pro and anti camps. The same was true for Pennsylvanians James Buchanan and Simon Cameron.[38]

Despite intensive coverage of the Kansas-Nebraska battle in Congress and its aftermath in the states, people were quite aware of other influences buffeting politics. Temperance was an important subject to the parties. The activities of the ministry caused discomfort among Democrats. And then the secret organization, the Know-Nothings, had become visible. By the middle of 1854, calculating politicians realized the existence of the nativists and recognized that they had acquired a considerable foothold in the free states. "Have you heard of the new political combination called the Know Nothings?" asked a correspondent of James Buchanan. "These 'know nothings' act in perfect concert, it would seem; but where they meet, or how they are organized, no one can tell."[39]

Indeed, astute northern politicians in 1854 understood that a strange force was shaping the public life of their states. The Know-Nothings began organizing in 1851 under the direction of James Barker of New York City, a dry-goods merchant. Adopting many of the rituals of fraternal organizations, the Know-Nothings drew followers because of the upheavals that attended the massive immigration wave that hit the United States between 1840 and 1854. Composed largely of Irish, Germans, and English, this wave brought to the overwhelmingly Protestant United States a massive increase in Catholic adherents. This circumstance immediately touched off a cultural conflict; for decades native-born Americans believed Protestantism was supportive of self-government, whereas Catholicism inculcated notions of hierarchy and authoritarian government. Moreover, the clash between Catholicism and Protestantism was of long-standing, and anti-Catholicism had produced violent episodes and riots throughout the early part of the century. In addition there was an economic component. Native-born Americans blamed immigrants for lowering the wage rate, increasing taxes to take care of immigrant poor in almshouses, and ousting long-standing Americans from positions in both political parties. The nativists wanted a curtailment of immigrant participation in politics by increasing the number of years required for naturalization, and they probably —though usually not publicly—desired to stop the immigrant influx.[40]

The election year of 1854 was going to start a strange cycle. It happened that by 1850, most northern congressional elections occurred in even years. Thus, 1854 was a congressional election year for all but a few northern states (the exceptions were Rhode Island, Connecticut, and New Hampshire). Most southern states held their congressional contests in odd-numbered years (the exceptions being Arkansas, Delaware, Florida, Missouri, and South Carolina). Except for a few gubernatorial elections in the South, 1854 was almost exclusively an election year for the North. Southerners were reduced to being observers. This oddity in the timing of congressional elections between the slave and free states set up almost a call-response pattern in sectional affairs: southerners registered northern elections and then reacted to them the next year—and then northerners reacted to the southern reaction. This odd timing of congressional elections may have elevated sectional animosities above the level they might have attained if elections had been contemporaneous throughout the nation.

People acknowledged that party organization in the North was a shambles. True, the usual Whig and Democratic conventions met and put forth their platforms and nominees; yet many sensed that the Know-Nothing element would change allegiances. Conservative Whigs hoped that Fillmore could capture the movement because the Whig Party was dying. In Maine, a malaise seemed to overtake Democrats: "Indeed, I do not know of many working Democrats who *care* now to attempt to do much. They will not only try the virtue of 'masterly silence,' but of 'masterly inactivity!'" Others declared the old parties of Whig, Democrat, and Free-Soil "obsolete ideas." Parties were fusing strange elements together while out there unknown was lurking the secret order of Know-Nothings and their command over an uncertain number of voters. Wrote Lewis D. Campbell of Ohio, "The Whigs & free Soilers are *all* for one to *a man*; but we will lose what few foreign votes we have heretofore got. How the K.N's may strike no one knows.... They are said to be numerous throughout the Dist; but *I don't* know."[41] And to top it off, New York decided to add a little more confusion to the situation. The Democrats in 1853 had split into two major factions, Hardshell versus Softshell Democrats. Much of the split mirrored political infighting between Dan Dickinson (Hard) and William Marcy (Soft), some of it represented different patronage claimants, and some of it arose from antislavery sentiments, the Hards wanting retribution against Barnburners, the Softs urging reconciliation. In any event, the New York Democrats went into the congressional and state elections of 1854 a divided party.[42]

During the campaign in the North, anti–Kansas-Nebraska orators relied upon the incompatibility of free and slave labor, the designs of the slave power, the hostile purpose behind the repeal of the Missouri Compromise, and the need to make freedom, not slavery, the national standard. Several interesting additions to this expected commentary also appeared. In Detroit, Lewis Cass at the end of the campaign gave a speech in which he rebuked the South for its property rights doctrines. In particular, he insisted that property existed only by local law. If the views of the South became standard, then ultimately the southern property rights doctrine concerning slavery would nationalize the institution and override states' rights.[43] An opposition to the idea that slavery depended on local law came from an unlikely source: Abraham Lincoln. Lincoln commenced his journey on explaining why Douglas's doctrine of popular sovereignty was false. In doing so, he aimed his rhetorical cannons at the faith that slavery could not exist in Kansas. The climate there, he said at Peoria, was no different than the climate of Delaware, Maryland, Virginia, Kentucky, or Maryland. Unlike his fellow antislavery campaigners, Lincoln warned that if law did not prohibit slavery, then slave owners might try to sneak the institution into a territory and establish it.[44] Lincoln's analysis actually agreed with southerners in the last session of Congress. However, he used the main point of their arguments to demand an explicit congressional prohibition of slavery in the territories.

The usual way for Democrats to escape the dilemma of favoring slave labor over free labor, as the anti-Nebraskaites charged, was to declare that climate determined the matter and that slaves could not operate in Kansas and Nebraska. Seldom did Democrats, North or South, actually deal with the question of labor competition. Daniel S. Dickinson of New York did. He tried to calm fears about the competition by asserting that free labor would drive slave labor from the field, not the reverse. The reason was that slave labor is "slow . . . , expensive and unwieldy," whereas free labor "marches" boldly ahead. This was true even in the border states where free labor was displacing slave labor. The western territories would prove even more emphatically how superior free labor was.[45]

Antislavery individuals could not accept the claim. Horace Greeley looked at southern slavery from an economic vantage. Why should the North be afraid, and why should not everyone expect the slave system to collapse? Greeley's answer: the system was monopolistic and able to sustain itself. "Slavery impoverishes Virginia, but it enriches the Johnny Tylers, Johnny Masons, and Billy Smiths, that govern Virginia." Thus the elite had a reason to keep the institution going no matter if it impoverished everyone else—it enriched them and that was all the justification a self-interested slaveholder needed. Moreover, slavery truly resembled a monopoly. "Monopolies in trade and manufacturing, impoverish communities, but enrich proprietors; so does Slavery. The slaveholders understand this, and this is their answer to political economists." The real question for the North was whether continued union with these particular monopolists would result in beggary for the North. From Greeley's angle of vision, he saw the North slowly being drawn into the economy of the South.[46]

Election dates varied in the northern states. Maine's citizens went to the polls in August; the voters in the Great Lakes states, Pennsylvania, and New Jersey usually determined congressional and gubernatorial decisions on the second Tuesday of October; and Massachusetts and New York held their elections in early November. By the middle of October it was unmistakable that the Pierce administration had just received one of the greatest thumpings in all American political history. Who administered that thumping was a difficult question. There were two sets of elections, congressional and state, and they gave slightly different answers.

Victories in the congressional elections between 1852 and 1855 are given in Table 7.1. They tell a particular story of how badly mangled the Democrats were in this election. The northern states that voted in the even years gave Democrats a total of seventy-nine seats in 1852; in 1854 that number was reduced to twenty-four. Almost all of the Democrats who voted for the Kansas-Nebraska Act lost reelection (seven of forty-four reelected), and only one-third of the Democrats who opposed the measure found success at the polls.[47] The regional and state totals show a basic division within the North. The Republican Party in the Great Lakes region, undoubtedly aided to some extent by Know-Nothings, arose instantly to deliver the Democrats a massive rebuke. Indiana and Ohio in particular switched almost unanimously from the Democracy to the Republican Party; those two states, which had given twenty-two Democrats in 1852, produced only two congressional victories in 1854. At

TABLE 7.1. *Congressional Victors by Party, 1852–1855*

Region/State	*Congressional Elections*						
	1852			*1854*			
	Democrat	*Whig*	*Other*	*Democrat*	*Whig*	*Republican*	*Other*
Great Lakes							
Illinois	5	4	0	4	0	5	0
Indiana	10	1	0	2	0	9	0
Iowa	1	1	0	1	0	1	0
Michigan	3	1	0	1	0	3	0
Ohio	12	7	2	0	0	21	0
Wisconsin	3	0	0	1	0	2	0
Total	34	14	2	9	0	41	0
New England							
Maine	3	3	0	1	0	5	0
Massachusetts	1	9	1	0	0	0	11
Vermont	0	3	0	0	3	0	0
Total	4	15	1	1	3	5	11
Middle Atlantic							
New Jersey	4	1	0	1	4	0	0
New York	21	11	1	6	27	0	[15]
Pennsylvania	16	9	0	7	17	0	1
Total	41	21	1	14	48	0	1 [15]
Border South							
Arkansas	2	0	0	2	0	0	0
Delaware	1	0	0	0	0	0	1
Missouri	3	4	0	1	6	0	0
Total	6	4	0	3	6	0	1
Deep South							
Florida	1	0	0	1	0	0	0
South Carolina	6	0	0	6	0	0	0
Total	7	0	0	7	0	0	0

Region/State	*Congressional Elections*						
	1853			*1855*			
	Democrat	*Whig*	*Other*	*Democrat*	*Whig*	*Republican*	*Other*
New England							
Connecticut	4	0	0	0	0	0	4
New Hampshire	3	0	0	0	0	0	3
Rhode Island	2	0	0	0	0	0	2
Total	9	0	0	0	0	0	9
Border South							
Virginia	13	0	0	12	0	0	1
Tennessee	5	5	0	5	0	0	5
Kentucky	5	4	1	4	0	0	6
Maryland	3	2	1	2	0	0	4
North Carolina	5	3	0	5	0	0	3
Total	31	14	2	28	0	0	19
Deep South							
Alabama	5	2	0	5	0	0	2

TABLE 7.1. *Continued*

Region/State	*Congressional Elections*						
	1853			*1855*			
	Democrat	*Whig*	*Other*	*Democrat*	*Whig*	*Republican*	*Other*
Georgia	6	2	0	6	0	0	2
Louisiana	3	1	0	3	0	0	1
Mississippi	5	0	0	4	1	0	0
Texas	2	0	0	1	0	0	1
Total	20	5	0	19	1	0	6

Region	*Congressional Elections*						
	1852			*1854*			
	Democrat	*Whig*	*Other*	*Democrat*	*Whig*	*Republican*	*Other*
1852–54							
Great Lakes	34	14	2	9	0	41	0
New England	4	15	1	1	3	5	11
Middle Atlantic	41	21	1	14	48	0	1 [15]
Border South	6	4	0	3	6	0	1
Deep South	7	0	0	7	0	0	0
1853–55	*1853*			*1855*			
New England	9	0	0	0	0	0	9
Border South	31	14	2	28	0	0	19
Deep South	20	5	0	18	1	0	6

Source: Party identifications taken from Moore, *Congressional Quarterly's Guide to U.S. Elections*, 595–600.

Note: Other in 1852 and 1853 columns is Free-Soil or Abolitionist. Other in 1854 and 1855 columns is almost always American Party (Know-Nothings). The bracketed number for New York stands for hyphenated parties claiming Know-Nothing support in that state. The 1 in Maryland 1854 represents an independent candidate. South Carolina switched from odd year voting to even year voting in 1854, so I made its 1853 congressional vote an 1852 vote in the table.

least in this section, it would seem that antislavery emerged on top; the Know-Nothing organization simply could not muster the strength to run a separate organization. The fusion of groups in the Great Lakes was probably on antislavery, Barnburning principles rather than nativism.[48]

But in the New England and Middle Atlantic states, the results were not clear. The Republican Party, except for Maine—which seemingly had interesting ties with Wisconsin and almost could be grouped as a Great Lakes state—had virtually no formal existence. The American Party tended to dominate New England, especially Massachusetts. In the Middle Atlantic region, the much-maligned Whig Party held ground; however, it was frequently compromised by having to fuse with Know-Nothings. In New York, fifteen of the state's congressional victors were hyphenated Americans—that is, the Know-Nothings supported certain Whigs and certain Democrats for office, masking their true strength. In Pennsylvania the impact of the Know-Nothings was more muted, but its existence could not be questioned. (See Table 7.1.)[49]

In the state races, Republicans continued to dominate in the Great Lakes area, although the power of the Know-Nothings was clearer. Know-Nothings backed the Whig James Pollock for the Pennsylvania governorship and probably constituted one-third of the vote; a fusion had to be constructed in New York for Myron H. Clark to defeat the Know-Nothing Daniel Ullman. Know-Nothing Henry J. Gardner took the Massachusetts governorship with about two-thirds of the vote. Fusion parties prevailed in Vermont, Connecticut, Rhode Island, and New Hampshire; sometimes by 1855 they openly declared themselves American Party supporters.[50]

Contemporary reaction to the northern elections in 1854 showed both confusion and some sophistication. The common theme was how the northern voters "annihilated" the Pierce administration—"The crushers are crushed." In the northern comments, however, was a strong awareness that the crushing occurred in the congressional races. The Washington antislavery paper, the *National Era*, noted that eighteen of the twenty-five congressmen-elect in Pennsylvania were anti-Nebraska but did admit that in the governor's race the Know-Nothing vote was perhaps the strongest element of the opposition coalition. A confidant of James Buchanan remarked that all the disparate elements out in the political realm—Know-Nothings, anti-Nebraska feelings, Temperance, and Cass followers—hurt the Democrats, yet "We have been pretty effectually used up throughout the State in the matter of Congressmen. This is mainly owing to the Nebraska business." And he noted that anti-Nebraska sentiment worked even more against the Democrats the further west one went—Indiana and Ohio. Indeed, in the West the term "Republican" was used to describe the victory.[51]

"It is hard to make a plausible divination of the future on these strange dispositions in the North," wrote the Maryland novelist John P. Kennedy to Millard Fillmore, and he was not alone. Many saw the demise of the Whig Party. The governor-elect of Pennsylvania, James Pollock, wrote to Senator John Clayton that "The old parties, as National parties, are broken up, & their power gone." A correspondent of Supreme Court Justice John McLean surmised that "The old Northern Whig party has ceased to exist."[52]

Some Whigs saw the 1854 results as a glorious chance to rebuild the party. People writing to Millard Fillmore were thinking of him as the next presidential nominee of the party, and they expressed hopes that the Whig organization could capture the Know-Nothings. Fillmore wrote Edward Everett and asked him about the nature of the state's party, adding that he believed that the Americans could be the foundation for a new national party. At the moment, Old Whigs with new hopes found the prospects of purging sectionalism out of the Whig Party—that is, expulsion of conscience Whigs and the Seward faction—exhilarating. The possibility existed because the antislavery portion of the party was now replaceable with American Party followers. And as Solomon Haven wrote Fillmore, "The growth in numbers of these men is unparalleled."[53]

Northern Democrats found the 1854 electoral results humiliating. Just as they had been during the canvass, however, they were perplexed as to the forces operating against them. Some fingered the effects of the Kansas-Nebraska Act, but just as often they felt overwhelmed by all the disparate forces that united to inflict such a terrible defeat. As the *Cleveland Daily Plain Dealer* publicly whined in a column about "The Results," "Free soilism, Federalism, Know Nothingism, Whigism, ism, ism, ism combined" to destroy the Democrats. But the Know-Nothings in particular mightily impressed the Democrats. "No one can tell where this underground movement is going to hit," despaired a correspondent of James Buchanan. However, Democrats believed that their opposition in 1854 had been a strange fusion of discordant elements; that fusion could not last, and then the Democracy could reclaim its hold on victory at the polls.[54]

Of major importance was how difficult it was for the South to read the northern results. The confused southerners saw the congressional results and noted that anti-Nebraska candidates crushed out the Democrats; in that sense they read the results as a general northern opposition to the southern stand on equality in the territories.[55] But southern editors and politicians simply did not know what had happened. A strange brew of different factions arose, but no one party seemed to dominate. Old Whig papers immediately fastened onto the power of the American Party and trumpeted the new, and supposedly nonsectional, organization as the savior of the nation. No mention of a "Republican party" was made, however. Southern editors also did not betray a sense of desperation. The voter explosion in the North was not read, at least in 1854, as being hostile to southern interests; indeed, for some it was a welcome relief from the old party system.[56]

But this election was the death knell for the Whigs, and the cause of death was the slavery issue. Two circumstances foretold of its passing. Edward Everett, the Massachusetts Whig politician-intellectual, succinctly explained one problem to Millard Fillmore. While Everett favored a return of the national Whigs, he was skeptical of its occurrence. "[I]n order to make Such Success of any avail in a national point of view, our Southern whig friends must show some signs of returning reason. The leading men among them last winter turned to me not only indifferent to the continued existence [?] of a National Whig party, but really to exult in its being broken up." Southern Whigs never forgave the Conscience Whigs and the Sewardites of the party. In order to combat the southern Democrats, the southern opposition had to prove fidelity to slavery, and to do that meant they had to stand for repeal of the Missouri Compromise line, that whatever the imperfections of the Kansas-Nebraska Act—basically, no definition of popular sovereignty—the principle that the territories were free for slaveholder settlement was nonnegotiable. Two-thirds of Southern Whigs had voted for the Kansas-Nebraska Act.[57] Yet northern Whigs had joined fusions and been part of the northern outrage over repeal of the Missouri Compromise line. How, then, could the Whig Party be sewn back together?

This problem of slavery's expansion would become the outstanding one in the career of the American Party. The northern Know-Nothings had strong convictions on the Missouri Compromise, although they considered themselves "national" in their outlook and free of sectional prejudices. As the Know-Nothings matured and attempted a national organization, they ran right into the problem that had sunk the Whigs. Northern Know-Nothings moved to the restoration of the Missouri Compromise line as the solution to sectional questions; southern Know-Nothings demanded acquiescence in the Kansas-Nebraska Act. That impasse generated in 1855 and 1856 divisions that spoiled the possibility of Know-Nothings capturing the northern electorate. Moreover, it would be wrong to dismiss the antislavery element in the northern Know-Nothing ranks. As the chief organ of the Pennsylvania Know-Nothings declared, the party intended to let slavery alone where it existed, "but at the same time [the party] sets [its] face like flint against the *extension* of slavery to territory now belonging to or hereafter to come into this Union." The general distaste for the political culture of slavery was caught in its editorial on Democratic success in the congressional polls in South Carolina in 1854: "Hurrah! Bring out the old 'rooster!' Ring the bells, and fire the cannon! Rejoice, for the Democrats have carried South Carolina! Yes, South Carolina stands firm! . . . South Carolina, where there are six slaves to every voter! South Carolina, where no man can cast a ballot until he pays three shillings sterling in taxes, and where no man can sit in the Legislature unless he owns ten negroes, or the value thereof! South Carolina, where four-sevenths of the population can neither read nor write, and it is a crime by law to teach them!"[58]

The second obstacle to a revitalization of the Whigs was the pace of the realignment. The first part of the realignment occurred in the South in 1851. The struggle over the Wilmot Proviso and the Compromise of 1850 annihilated the Whigs in the Deep South and crippled them in the Border South. The second phase of the realignment in 1854, the northern phase, saw the Kansas-Nebraska legislation annihilating the Whigs in the Great Lakes states. Basically, the Whigs had lost their stand in nearly two-thirds of the Union. Only in the Middle Atlantic and New England regions did Whigs still have a viable organization. This fact was communicated to William H. Seward. One of his correspondents wrote, "Allow me to suggest that no time should be lost in organizing the Republican party! There is no longer a Whig party in the West. The South is availing itself of K. N.-ism to preserve and perpetuate its power." The assessment may have been unfair to southerners but was on the mark in terms of making obvious alliances. To whom would southerners rationally go?

To the Whigs whose organization had faltered in most of the country, or to the Know-Nothings who were a young—and presumably moldable—party that had possibilities in the West as well as in the East? Ultimately the Whig Party was ground to pieces by the sectionalism aroused by the Wilmot Proviso in the South and by the Kansas-Nebraska Act in the North.[59]

Though many hoped that the Kansas-Nebraska Act would remove the vexatious question of slavery extension from national discourse, such was not to be the case. Land-hungry people from the Great Lakes region started moving into the area, while Massachusetts Representative Eli Thayer created an Emigrant Aid Society to assist free-soil Yankees to migrate to Kansas and preserve that land for freedom. The number of New Englanders who so arrived to Kansas Territory was small but the publicity was great. Thus, some southerners reacted to a sense that the North was not going to play fair in letting normal flows of population move into Kansas and Nebraska. In Missouri, Senator David Atchison threatened guerrilla war; the movement of Missourians over the border to intimidate northern migrants and to vote illegally in territorial elections had begun. "Border Ruffianism" had commenced and soon would consume northern newspaper columns; a "Bleeding Kansas" was on the horizon.

Politics in 1855 changed only a little. In northern state races, Republicans remained the opposition party to the Democrats in the Great Lakes region, while the Know-Nothings seemed dominant in the Middle Atlantic states and in New England, although in the latter two regions the Republican Party had acquired more followers and was more visible. Democrats in the North, however, started to rebound from their disastrous showing in 1854. Southerners had congressional elections in 1855, and largely the Democrats emerged victorious (see Table 7.1). The major difference was that the Know-Nothings replaced the Whigs entirely, although it would appear that the old Whig supporters simply shrugged off their Whig buttons and simply put on Know-Nothing regalia. In 1853 Border South and Deep South states had elected fifty-one Democrats, nineteen Whigs, and two independents; in 1855, they elected forty-nine Democrats and twenty-four Americans (the extra congressional seat came from Mississippi finally creating its fifth congressional district). Voting was light during the contests, and voting for opposition candidates fell well beneath the levels the Whigs had obtained in the 1840s.[60]

Within the South, the Know-Nothings and Democrats fought over nativism. Slavery-related issues were distinctly muted. Indeed, most southern editors continued to overlook the Republican Party in the North, and instead considered that section's politics a struggle between Democrats and the Know-Nothings, with the Know-Nothings continuing to win.[61] However, a few did record the existence of the Republicans in the fall, and the term "Black Republicans" came into existence.[62] There was no panic in southern voices or letters yet.

The major development of 1855 was the political failure of the Know-Nothings on both the state and national levels, despite their continued electoral success. Essentially the Know-Nothings could not take the disparate anti-Democratic fragments in American society and forge them into an organization to battle the Democrats. On the state level, they proved incapable of producing the kind of legislation required to cement loyalty to the organization, and in Pennsylvania the Know-Nothings proved their ineptitude by failing to elect a U.S. senator from their ranks, even though they had the majority (supposedly) of members of the state legislature.[63] Their national failure, however, doomed the party. In the second week of June 1855, nativists came to Philadelphia to establish a national party and a national platform. There was talk of a readoption of the Missouri platform, but those rumors disappeared when southerners insisted on a twelfth section that affirmed all "existing laws upon the subject of Slavery to be a final and conclusive settlement of the Slavery question." This statement meant the Know-Nothing Party accepted the Kansas-Nebraska Act. Northerners dissented and although the convention adopted the platform with the twelfth section intact, many northerners bolted the meeting. About the same time, a "Know-Something" meeting was held in Cleveland. After the national meeting adjourned, northern local councils repudiated the twelfth section.[64] Northern Know-Nothings were not proslavery, and most wanted slavery confined to the states where it already existed, and they resented the imperious attitude of southerners on the question. In Congress in December 1855, New York representative Solomon G. Haven griped about how the southern Know-Nothings "insist on Phila. platform 12 section" and force northern congressional members into acquiescence. "To tell you the truth the Southern boys are too exacting & I will not yield to them."[65] Slavery was eroding the Know-Nothing organizational edifice.

The Know-Nothings might have lasted longer and had more of a chance for survival if affairs in Kansas had not refocused national attention to the slavery-expansion question. The battle between free state settlers and proslavery Missourians escalated. The settlers had elected members to a territorial legislature who were proslavery because of the invasion of Missourians at the ballot box; those legislators then passed laws legalizing slavery and protecting slaveholders, made it a felony to question slaveholding, and expelled antislavery territorial delegates. That circumstance then led the free state supporters to create a rival state government in Topeka (the existing and legal territorial government was in Shawnee Mission, near the Missouri border). A harsh winter obstructed any additional problems, but in the spring of 1856 hostilities between the free state and slave state factions boiled over. An army of Missourians attacked the free state town of Lawrence, thereafter known as the Sack of Lawrence, by burning a few buildings—but failed to capture free state leaders. On the day after the Sack of Lawrence, May 22, South Carolina representative Preston Brooks beat Massachusetts senator Charles Sumner into unconsciousness for giving a speech that insulted Brooks's uncle, Senator Andrew Butler. Then immediately after Sumner's beating, abolitionist John Brown, a settler in Kansas and enraged by the proslavery attack on Lawrence, took seven of his followers to Pottawatomie Creek and slew five unarmed men, presuming them to be proslavery southerners. After this, Kansas virtually erupted into civil war.[66]

Sectional disasters in Kansas occurred in a presidential election year just as the parties began their national conventions. The Democrats met in June in Cincinnati and adopted an extensive platform filled with traditional Democratic economic appeals and a statement demanding congressional nonintervention in the territories. For a presidential nominee, the convention chose James Buchanan of Pennsylvania, a northerner with considerable southern connections and one who was not connected with the Kansas-Nebraska Act because he had been U.S. ambassador to Great Britain at the time.

The Know-Nothings simply could not overcome the sectional division about restoring the Missouri Compromise line. In February 1856 they held a nominating convention, maintained a plank favoring the Kansas-Nebraska Act, and split the party into southern Know-Nothings and northern Know-Nothings, the latter agreeing to convene again in June. Millard Fillmore became the nominee at the February convention. Then the Republicans outfoxed the northern Know-Nothings in June. The Know-Nothings had called their convention just a few days before the Republicans so that the two sides could arrange a fusion. For the Know-Nothings, the fusion meant a prominent place on a joint ticket for the presidency, both sides retaining their organizations but nominating the same persons for president and vice-president. Nathaniel P. Banks was the choice of the Know-Nothings, but he had already made an agreement with the Republicans to join their party. When the Know-Nothings nominated him, Banks embarrassed the organization by turning down the nomination and publicly switching to the Republicans. The Republicans then rebuffed the Know-Nothings rather brutally by nominating John C. Frémont, a military man, a former Democrat with marital ties to Missouri's famous politician Thomas Hart Benton, and a person with ties to Catholicism. The northern Americans wanted some say in the nominees by having the Republicans nominate the Pennsylvanian William P. Johnston for vice-president, but the Republicans ignored the request and instead nominated William L. Dayton of New Jersey. Northern Know-Nothings then ran a separate ticket of Frémont and Johnston, but then later Johnston refused the nomination. So northern Know-Nothings were left with the choice of Frémont or Fillmore. Though their absorption into the Republican ranks took longer than expected, the political failures of 1856 sealed their doom.

Republicans sought to capture northern anger at the caning of Charles Sumner and proslavery nastiness in Kansas. They succeeded. When the votes were tallied in November, James Buchanan won the prize—but barely. The Republicans captured all the free states but five—California, New Jersey, Pennsylvania, Indiana, and Illinois. Frémont's bid for the presidency would have been successful if he had only carried Pennsylvania and New Jersey, and the main obstacle in those states was a continuing clump of Know-Nothing voters. Republicans referred to these states hereafter as the "uncertain states," and as early as 1857 they set their sights on capturing the essential state of Pennsylvania.[67]

In terms of the presidential contest, the Democrats appeared to be barely holding on to their edge in national politics. On the congressional level, the picture was different. In 1856 Democrats rebounded well and recaptured many of their former partisans; they erased some of the most embarrassing features of the congressional election of 1854. In the Great Lakes and Middle Atlantic regions, the numbers of Democrat congressmen elected rose from twenty-three in 1854 to forty-six in 1856, thereby giving the Democrats control of Congress. Ohio and Indiana recovered from their disastrous 1854 performances, Pennsylvanians rallied about Buchanan's nomination sufficiently so that the Democrats had a decided advantage in that state's delegation (fifteen Democrats, ten Republicans and Union Party members), and New York's obstreperous, unruly, and fratricidal Democrats stopped bickering long enough to elect twelve Democrats (up from six in 1854).[68]

But something dramatic had happened. Southerners took note now of the Republican Party, and stared in awe as the Republicans swept all but five northern states. The turning point came with the October results in Pennsylvania, Indiana, and Ohio where the Republicans clearly emerged as the principal opposition to the Democracy, and the Know-Nothings shrank into a potent but distant northern third party. "A party has arisen, bold, unscrupulous and powerful, in its opposition to us and our institutions," wrote the editor of the *Southern Banner*. Henry A. Wise, governor of Virginia, wrote by August 1856 that "The [the southern states] *will not* submit to a *sectional* election of a *Free-soiler* or *Black Republican*." Another editor in Georgia fretted that "The alarming result of the late conflict—the overwhelming defeat of both the American and Democratic parties at the North and West, is well calculated to fill all thoughtful and considerate minds with the most gloomy forebodings."[69] Southern fears had finally taken a political form; in the rise of an avowedly antislavery organization, the sanctity of property rights in slaves was jeopardized.

President James Buchanan had opportunities to smooth over sectional fears and had some hopes of doing so, but his presidency would only intensify the animosities that had been growing for a decade. The lasting illusion of the years of 1845–60 was that if only one last sectional hurdle could be successfully jumped, then sectional bickering would disappear. In Buchanan's case, that hurdle's name was Kansas. But the engine that drove sectional controversy always obtained fuel from the clash over the sanctity of property rights in slaves.

The expansion issue evoked the property rights question, but in truth almost any issue would have raised it. Southerners sought an ironclad guarantee that under all circumstances the sanctity of property rights in slaves would be observed. For northerners to have given that guarantee would have damaged badly—maybe fatally—their free labor, small-village society. Under Buchanan, the property rights nature of the controversy reached its peak moments: the *Dred Scott* decision, the battle over the Lecompton controversy, and the southern demand for a territorial slave code.

A few days after Buchanan was sworn into office, the Supreme Court handed down a decision in the case of *Dred Scott v. Sanford*, a legal battle concocted by antislavery lawyers to argue that once a slave was taken into free territory, as the slave Dred Scott had been taken, the slave was free. Their argument was that slavery only existed in the boundaries of the sovereignty that declared slavery legal.[70] The Court decided 6–3 that Dred Scott, being a slave, had no right to petition the court like a citizen—slaves, obviously, were not citizens and had no citizenship rights—and therefore he had no standing before the Court and the question was remanded back to the state of Missouri from which the litigation began.

Taney then pushed much further than that, perhaps at the urging of President Buchanan, who did try to influence the court and particularly the northern justice, Pennsylvanian Robert Grier, to side with the five southern justices on the bench. Taney gave three other distinct rulings. The first was that the Constitution recognized slaves as property, and, via the Fifth Amendment, no person could be deprived of property without due process of law. In this instance, Taney then moved to the idea of substantial due process instead of procedural due process by stating that a prohibition of slavery in the territories, as was the case with the Missouri Compromise, damaged the property rights of the slaveholder in slaves and thereby deprived the person of enjoyment of the property. Thus, the Missouri Compromise was unconstitutional. Second, by implication, the federal authority had to insure the sanctity of property rights in the territories and could not discriminate against one form of property from another. Third, African Americans had never been citizens, would never become citizens, and, given the historical record, they "had no rights which the white man was bound to respect." Ohio's John McLean dissented, as one would expect, because he believed that slavery was entirely a municipal institution that extended no further than the political power of that municipality—a position he had held since 1847. Benjamin Curtis also produced a long dissent, arguing for the power of Congress to rule the territories and claiming that the Constitution did not recognize property rights in man.[71] The opinion of Taney was a logical, historical, and legal disaster, a near farce that brought disrepute on the Supreme Court and its objectivity. The basic problem, besides the unwillingness of southern judges to accept the truth that the federal government had sovereign power over a territory until the moment of statehood (which Justice Campbell had admitted in 1848), was that the locus of defining property was neglected. States could only define property within their boundaries; they had no right, under any circumstance, to define property beyond their boundaries, whether it be a state, a territory, or a foreign nation. It was this attempt to claim for slavery a property right beyond a state's boundary that led historian Arthur Bestor years ago to claim that southerners sought for slavery a rule of "extraterritoriality."[72]

Certainly some northerners were upset at the callous reduction of African Americans to an inhuman status, but that was not the part of the decision that elicited outrage and genuine fear. Rather, the Court's willingness to bestow upon slaves a constitutional definition of property frightened all types of northerners. Wisconsin senator James R. Doolittle after March 1857 made the *Dred Scott* ruling a focus of his political efforts, in speechmaking, publications, and political organizations. "The truth is, that if the supremacy of the U.S. Court be conceded the Rep. Party may disband for they have *by a decree* settled the whole question in the controversy in favor of the slave power, the right to hold slaves in all the territories and next in the States. If their word is supreme —if as they say the U.S. Constitution says *slaves are property* is *supreme in the States* as well as territories." Any number of northern newspapers made the same leap of imagination—that by affirming that the Constitution recognized slaves as property, and because the Constitution was the supreme law of the land, the Supreme Court had paved the way to overthrowing state laws forbidding slavery.[73] At the least the Supreme Court ruling meant that the purpose of the federal government was the protection and advancement of human slavery, not human freedom, because the sanctity of property overruled all else. Screamed Columbus's *Ohio State Journal*, "THEY HAVE MADE SLAVERY NATIONAL, FREEDOM SECTIONAL."[74]

Southerners at times used words similar to Republican editorialists. In one editorial in a Georgia paper, the small headline on the editorial page read, "The Dred Scott Case—The Nationality of Slavery." Within the column, the writer declared that southern opinion on slavery "is now the supreme law of the land," and all northern views on slavery in the territories were repudiated because slavery "is recognised as a national institution, protected in the States and territories by the Constitution of the United States." Probably the intention of southern writers was different from that of northerners regarding the meaning of the phrase "nationality of slavery," but nonetheless there was a recognition that the Supreme Court had just given slavery a status in the Constitution that it had never before enjoyed. However, southerners were quick to doubt whether northerners would obey the ruling and whether it would change stances on slavery-related issues.[75]

Northern Democrats reacted quite differently to the *Dred Scott* decision. They counseled acceptance of the decision and saw no judicial barrier to their brand of popular sovereignty. What they focused upon, however, was race.

They lauded the decision of the Court that said Africans were not and could not be federal citizens, an affirmation of the Democrat creed (at least by 1857) that the United States was a white man's country. In the Ohio legislature, a speech was given by Mr. Payne that touched upon the *Dred Scott* decision; it was approvingly reprinted by the *Cleveland Daily Plain Dealer*. Said Payne, "That decision finds that the black race is inferior to the white race, and this is proven from history, and the Divine Law, and also from the history of all the States of the Union." What was missing in the northern Democrat analysis was property rights.[76] The northern Democracy simply avoided the topic. But that ability to bypass the property rights question in slavery was becoming impossible. Events between 1858 and 1860 would force the northern Democrats to face the matter squarely and to decide what would be their true principle: popular sovereignty or property rights.

The furor over the *Dred Scott* decision actually faded to some extent fairly quickly. Republicans later denounced the decision often enough in their state and local party conventions, but many recognized that Taney's real decision was that slaves could not sue in federal courts; his decisions that slaves were property by the Constitution, that the Missouri Compromise was unconstitutional, and that slaves had to be admitted and protected in the territories were opinions, not readings of the law—they were ober dicta. Thus the *Dred Scott* decision did not produce any immediate political pressure. Yet it may have unsettled northern lawyers and political leaders, if not the general northern public. Where was the law going over the course of time? In 1845 northerners convinced themselves that the law favored freedom over slavery, and that slavery was wholly a municipal institution. By 1857 the nation was on the verge of finding that slavery was a national institution protected by the Constitution. When Abraham Lincoln commenced the election campaign in Illinois in 1858, he used the startling metaphor of a "House Divided" to describe the condition of the United States. He also made the statement, "If we could first know where we are, and whither we are tending, we could better judge what to do, and how to do it."[77] If one looked at the evolution of the law of property rights in slaves—and Lincoln would do so repeatedly in the Lincoln-Douglas debates—then the tendency of the nation was obvious: slavery was becoming a sacrosanct national institution.

James Buchanan then faced the challenge of Bleeding Kansas. He replaced Kansas Territorial governor Wilson Shannon with Robert J. Walker, Pennsylvanian turned Mississippian, a career Democrat, and author of the tariff of 1846. Walker believed that Kansas could become a Democratic state but not a slave state. He courted the free state residents in Kansas and begged them to participate in elections. However, in a June election for a state constitutional meeting, the proslavery element won the majority of delegates because the free staters boycotted. In an October election for the legislature, the proslavery element won a majority again because of massive fraud in Johnson and McGee counties. Walker overturned those returns and, by such decision, enabled the free state element for the first time to control the legislature. Proslavers determined then upon a desperate bid to make Kansas a slave state; the Constitutional Convention at Lecompton, Kansas—hence the name Lecompton Constitution—drew up a document for the state that recognized slavery, forbade the passage of any laws thereafter (or at least up to eight years) freeing slaves already in the territory, and declared private property above the acts of any legislature. The convention at first was not going to allow the citizens to vote on the newly framed Kansas Constitution, but the leader of the proslavery forces, oddly named John Calhoun, prevailed upon the convention to at least let the citizenry vote on whether to take the constitution as formed or one that would forbid the further importation of slaves into Kansas. Thus Kansas citizens were not voting on slavery or nonslavery, but on whether future imports of slaves would be allowed or not. An irate Walker denounced the voting procedure and left the territory. In his place, the acting-governor, Tennessean Frederick Stanton, asked the state legislature to pass a law enabling the citizens to vote on the entire Lecompton Constitution, either for or against, and let the vote stand as an indication of citizen sentiment but not as a final determination of the legality of the document. On December 21, the vote commanded by the Lecompton Constitution was held; free staters abstained, and the result was 6,226 for the framework with slavery and 569 for it without slavery. The vote mandated by the legislature occurred on January 4 recorded 10,226 against the proposed constitution while 138 voted for the document with slavery and 24 for it without slavery. The combined results strongly argued that two-thirds of the settlers in Kansas did not want slavery.

President Buchanan, however, determined to accept the validity of the Lecompton Constitution and recommended that Congress approve it, thereby adding Kansas to the Union as a slave state. Behind him were powerful southern politicians demanding Kansas be permitted entrance as a slave state to demonstrate that northerners would not stymie future southern expansionist schemes. Moreover, southerners wanted proof of the North's willingness to accept the peculiar institution as a valid institution. Kansas became the test of the South's hope for expansion in the Union—but a poorly chosen test, unfortunately for them, as many acknowledged the illegalities performed by that territory's proslavery clique tinged the document with fraud.[78]

Stephen A. Douglas revolted from Buchanan's policy by announcing his intention to work against acceptance of the Kansas document because it was a perversion of popular sovereignty, his announcement leading to his censure by the party in caucus and his removal from the chairmanship of the Senate Committee on Territories. Douglas's motivation may be questioned to some degree. Douglas never believed slavery would go into the West, and the upheaval of 1854 taught him not to transgress the obvious sentiments of the Great Lakes states that the western territory was free territory.[79] But there are other reasons to suspect that Douglas was sincere in his desire to elevate popular sovereignty as the appropriate doctrine for the Democratic Party. For the next two years, Douglas fought for the soul of the Democracy, and the danger to the party's soul came from the incessant demand of southerners that democratic politics take second place to property rights in slaves.

The congressional fight over Lecompton rested primarily on whether fraud had been so widespread that the constitution was illegitimate. Anti-Lecompton speakers stressed fraud, violence, and the failure to submit the whole constitution to the entire population. Administration supporters responded by insisting that many states had entered the Union without a vote on the entire constitution, and that popular sovereignty was specifically designed to handle the slavery question, so whether the entire constitution went before the entire voting public or not was irrelevant. Southerners said Kansas was a test case for future slave states, and the motivation behind northern hostility to Lecompton was not voter fraud but a determination to see that no more slave states entered the Union. Several southerners said that the North desired more free states so they could use the federal government to plunder the South at will.[80]

Those basic questions did not squeeze out other topics or concerns. On March 3, William H. Seward rose to give a free labor address to the Senate, explaining how the North had already won the war and free labor was the ultimate destiny of the nation. He also said, to the consternation of western Republicans, that climate excluded slavery from the West and the Republican Party could adopt the policy of popular sovereignty because it worked in favor of free labor.[81] Seward was obviously trying to tempt Douglas and his followers into the Republican coalition. After all, the slavery extension issue had cracked the Democratic Party twice before, in 1846–48 and in 1854, and one more time would seal an antislavery victory. Douglas and the popular sovereignty Democrats were unmoved by Seward's entreaties, and all Seward accomplished was to anger the strong antislavery members of his own party.

A second development was a movement made by border state conservatives. John J. Crittenden of Kentucky and John Bell of Tennessee spoke in the Senate on March 17 and 18 against the Lecompton Constitution because of fraud. Both contended that all the ills of the nation came from one foolish move—the Kansas-Nebraska Act of 1854. They intimated that the Missouri Compromise line needed to be restored. Crittenden received many letters from northerners praising his speech and promising support for a new conservative party that was neither antislavery nor proslavery.[82] That party would become the Constitutional Union Party in the election of 1860.

William Seward's announcement that the free states had already won the battle for supremacy of the Union triggered a memorable response from South Carolina senator James Henry Hammond. Defending the record of the South and its policies, Hammond then launched into an advanced proslavery critique of northern free labor. He announced that all societies needed a lower class to do the manual labor of civilization so that an upper class could be freed to advance the arts and sciences. The northern free laborers were "mud-sills"; they were in truth slaves because the free states "had abolished the name, but not the thing" that comprised slavery—"in short your hireling class of manual laborers and operatives, as you call them, are slaves." Hammond then uttered the standard fear of the advanced proslavery thinkers: the unpropertied would revolt against the wealthy and plunge civilization into barbaric anarchy by destroying property rights. The northerners' special vulnerability to this circumstance was that they allowed their slaves to vote, and thus gave them the power to elect representatives pledged to violate property rights. Such was not the case with the South, where slavery removed the danger of the unpropertied masses from tinkering with the property of the wealthy.[83]

The dread of agrarianism in proslavery thought erupted in this session of Congress, sparked by the effects of an economic recession that had produced mob scenes and fiery laborite speeches in several northern cities. At least five southern congressmen, including Hammond, referred to the dangers of democracy and of allowing menial or common laborers the vote. And they made the point explicit: property rights were more vital to civilization than voting rights.[84] This outburst against political democracy from southern Democrats came at a moment when Stephen A. Douglas fought tooth and nail for the doctrine of popular sovereignty as the guiding light of the national Democratic Party. Property and Democracy were colliding in the intersectional coalition of the Democrats.

Republicans took Hammond's remarks as an insult to northern workingmen, and a number of them immediately obtained the floor to denounce Hammond's depiction of free workers as slaves. They, of course, glorified free labor. In this session of Congress, the free labor argument was indeed prominent. To explain why slavery should not spread into the territories and why they so earnestly fought the Lecompton Constitution, Republicans endlessly paraded their free labor beliefs. Moreover, they made it manifest that they were seeking to avoid placing slave labor and free labor in proximity to one another where they would compete against each other.[85] There was a humorous poignancy to the proceedings. In the House of Representatives, administration supporter William Bishop of Connecticut recognized that southerners during the debates kept uttering phrases that the Republicans would use to hammer the northern Democrats during elections. Now, he said, perhaps southerners believed that northern workers were not as well off as African slaves: "[T]hey have the right to think so; but it would be much more satisfactory to me, and much more gratifying to them, if they would only think so, and not incorporate their thoughts into their speeches. [Laughter]"[86]

Within the Lecompton controversy in Congress was as well a massive debate over property rights. Much of this discussion was repetitive. The South insisted that slaves were classified as property by the Constitution and that, via the compact theory of the Constitution, Congress could not deny southerners the right to take their property into the territories. Senator Judah Benjamin of Louisiana gave a learned talk about how the common law supported slavery and was fully met by Senator Clark, who found exacting references to show English law had declared slavery illegal throughout the realm by 1700 (see Chapter 5). Republicans insisted that slavery was only a municipal regulation and had no validity beyond its municipal confines. They read the property rights doctrines of the southern Democracy as nationalizing slavery and sectionalizing freedom; *Dred Scott* was thoroughly discussed. One of the gems of the session was James Harlan's dissection of the slavery issue by pitting property rights against human rights.[87]

It was during these debates that Stephen A. Douglas and the popular-sovereignty Democracy were forced to grapple with the property rights defense of the South. In their desperation to put slavery in Kansas above legislative tinkering, the proslavery forces put this language into the Lecompton Constitution, section 1, article 7: "The right of property is before and higher than any constitutional sanction; and the right of the owner of a slave to such and to its increase is the same, and as inviolable, as the right of the owner of any property whatever." This section was singled out by Republicans for condemnation because it placed property rights above human rights.[88] Some Democrats already had stated that such sentiments did not belong to the party of Democracy and the principle of popular sovereignty.[89]

On March 22, Senator James A. Bayard of Maryland gave a long speech on the inviolability of property, calling it the end for which civilization was brought into existence. Douglas entered the debate and sparred with Hammond of South Carolina over minority rights versus majority rights. Then Stuart of Michigan interjected a statement from the administration newspaper, the *Washington Daily Union* (dated November 17, 1857), that "The protection of property being, next to that of person, the most important object of all good government," the right of property in slaves had to be recognized, and thus the northern state emancipation achieved decades ago was "*an outrage on the rights of property*." Douglas returned to the center of debate. He denied that northern emancipation was illegal or that because of property rights in slaves southerners could move into the North with their slaves. Then he summed up a view that he had never before revealed: "I recognize the right of the slaveholding States to regulate their local institutions . . . but I do not admit, and I do not think they are safe in asserting, that their right of property in slaves is higher than and above constitutional obligations, is independent of constitutional obligations." He rejected the contentions of the *Washington Union* and then turned to the Lecompton Constitution. He had been read out of the party "for disputing this higher law, which is embodied in the Lecompton Constitution, that slavery, the right to slave property, does not depend upon human law nor constitutional sanction, but is above and beyond and before all constitutional sanctions and obligations! [He must] repudiate and rebuke this doctrine [as a Democrat and a free state citizen]."[90]

Douglas had avoided discussion of property rights throughout the sectional strife over the extension of slavery since 1846. Increasingly he found avoidance of the issue difficult. The truth of the matter was that the South's property rights doctrines were eating away at his principle of popular sovereignty, and that principle could not be sacrificed. Douglas came from the Jacksonian tradition, and that tradition included during the 1830s and 1840s the slogan, "Human Rights before Property Rights."[91] If Douglas were to let go the principle of majority rule, then for what did the Democratic Party stand? Had the Democrats replaced the Whigs as the party of property rights? The answer was no. Douglas had twisted and squirmed to keep the Democratic bisectional coalition together, but there was a limit to the twistings. Without the doctrine of popular sovereignty and the principle of majority rule behind it, the Democracy would become the most conservative party the country had yet seen—indeed, one step away from the embrace of aristocratic principles. It was too much to ask.

The House of Representatives did not accept the Lecompton Constitution and sent it back to Kansas for a new vote of the citizenry. It was massively defeated. However, 1858 was a congressional election year and politicians tried to figure out how the *Dred Scott* decision and the Lecompton struggle would play in the North. Added to the slavery-related issues was a new factor. In August 1857 the nation experienced a financial tumult, the Panic of 1857, which left parts of the North in a depressed economic state. Among certain states arose a cry for federal aid to alleviate the dark conditions, primarily the old Whig program of higher tariffs, internal improvements, and free western land for actual settlers.[92]

In the northern canvass, the Republicans relied on their standing appeals to elevate the free laborer by restricting slavery and to curb the power of slaveholders in national affairs. Douglas Democrats trumpeted popular sovereignty, while all Democrats emphasized Caucasian racial superiority. A central event of the election was the series of debates between Lincoln and Douglas, whose term in the Senate was about to expire; to recapture it he had to campaign vigorously in the state so that Democratic legislators would control the state legislature and send him back to the Senate. During these debates, Lincoln hammered away at the immorality of slavery, the tendency of the country to embrace slavery instead of freedom, and the impact of the *Dred Scott* decision. Lincoln asked Douglas in the face of this ruling by the Supreme Court, how could popular sovereignty work. Douglas replied in his famous "Freeport Doctrine" that any community that wished not to have slavery merely had to refuse to pass the local police laws that made slavery possible. Lincoln thought the answer an evasion; he later asked again, "how is it possible for any power to exclude slavery from the Territory unless in violation of that decision?"[93]

The Lincoln-Douglas debates were probably something of a draw, as the Republicans captured more votes than the Democrats, but due to the way the districts had been constructed the Democrats earned a majority of legislative seats and thus returned Douglas to the Senate. The Lincoln-Douglas debates were also something of an anomaly. Nowhere else did politicians rely so heavily on the questions of popular sovereignty and the morality of slavery. The rest of the country talked about the slave power, the need to elevate free laborers, corruption of the Buchanan administration, the true interests of the workingman, and race. States along the east coast in particular talked about economic issues, a subject on which neither Douglas nor Lincoln touched. The Panic of 1857 had reintroduced economic issues into political deliberations that had been absent for nearly ten years. And the place where the discussion was greatest was where the Democrats had the most strength—the Middle Atlantic states.[94]

The elections of 1858 were another shock to the Democratic Party, for the administration fared poorly. However, there was a pattern to the performance. Despite all kinds of fears about *Dred Scott* and the Lecompton controversy, voting in the Great Lakes and New England states followed the patterns that had emerged in the election of 1856. The difference came in the Middle Atlantic states in two forms. One, Pennsylvania proved susceptible to the tariff appeal, and in that state the Democrats got swamped: the fifteen Democrats elected in 1856 were reduced to four in 1858, and one of them (John Hickman) soon switched parties. In Pennsylvania a fusion party—but basically a Republican Party—brought the Americans fully into the Republican camp. New York Democrats, on the other hand, fell from twelve Democratic congressmen elected in 1856 to four in 1858. Most of the New York Democracy's problems, however, were internal. The bickering New York City Democrats divided and enabled Republican fusionists to make significant gains. But everyone knew that in the election of 1858 the opposition in Pennsylvania had successfully combined and entered the Republican camp. The key uncertain state was becoming more certain.[95]

Nothing went right for the Buchanan administration and the Democratic Party thereafter. Buchanan understood he had to answer some of the demands for altered economic policies, but his southern base of support absolutely refused to budge on the tariff and internal improvements. During the summer of 1859, Douglas tried to reclaim some stature for his doctrine of popular sovereignty by writing an essay for *Harper's Magazine*. For individuals knowledgeable about politics, the article contained no new arguments but merely carefully went over the old ones. Once again, however, Douglas carefully skirted the property rights issue.[96]

The damage inflicted upon the administration climaxed in the fall elections of 1859. Democrats swept the southern congressional elections of 1857 and piled up an unusual number of uncontested seats. Given the explosion over the Lecompton Constitution in Congress and the continued growth of the Republicans in the elections of 1858, it seemed most likely that the Democrats would again destroy any opposition that dared to stand before them. Such did not happen in the border states of Kentucky, Tennessee, and North Carolina. In 1857 these states (plus Maryland and Virginia) elected thirty-eight Democrats to nine American Party members. But in 1859, the Opposition (the new name chosen by southerners repudiating the Democratic Party) won twenty seats and the Democrats only twenty-seven. If Virginia is excluded, the Opposition actually won the border: eighteen Opposition to sixteen Democrats. The extremism had finally produced a reaction. Led by Crittenden and Bell, an organization was forming to contest both the Republicans and the Democrats, and it aimed distinctly at the Border South and the border parts of the the Great Lakes and Middle Atlantic states. The conservatives were going to preempt the tariff issue by recharging the old Whig allegiances, exhibit sufficient Americanism to appeal to the Know-Nothings, and attract conservative Democrats via constitutionalism. Although as yet unstipulated, they had a platform: the restoration of the Missouri Compromise line.[97]

Serendipitous fate intervened, however, and changed the conservatives' possibilities of winning the Border North and South by a unionist appeal. The elections in the southern states came in August in Kentucky and Tennessee, in April in Virginia, and in early October in North Carolina. While the Opposition leaders and presses crowed about their victory, John Brown on October 16 led a small band into Harpers Ferry in an effort to incite a slave rebellion. Within forty-eight hours he was captured, in two weeks brought to trial and found guilty of treason, and one month later hanged. John Brown's invasion changed the political mood of the South from sullenness to raw anger. This attack on the institution of slavery occurred in a state where the institution was born and fully established; it evoked the primal fear of slave revolts and all the horrors that attended uprisings of slaves—of the Haiti Revolution. After October 1859 various parts of the South underwent traumatic fears of slave revolts and being "John Browned." The raid, whatever its relation to property rights, powerfully evoked apprehensions for white supremacy throughout the South and made the Republicans appear even more demonic. The intense emotional fear of marauding abolitionists worked distinctly against the Opposition and its program of compromise and unionism.[98] It would have an uphill battle in 1860.

The year 1860 opened unpropitiously for the Union. In Congress, Republicans tried to use their swollen numbers to take over the House of Representatives by electing a speaker, but the numbers were so close that a stalemate of nearly two months ensued. (William Pennington of New Jersey, an American-Republican, was finally elected.) In the Senate, southerners coalesced around a set of seven resolutions authored by Jefferson Davis concerning slavery in the territories. These resolutions became known as the slave code for the territories resolutions, and they were the political demand of the South—at least of the Gulf states—in the presidential election year of 1860. They insisted that slaves be recognized as property, that southerners could take their property into the territories, that territorial government had no sovereignty to disapprove of slavery, that the federal government must intervene in a territory's affairs if slavery could not be protected by local authorities (the fifth resolution), that slavery's existence could only be decided when the territory applied for statehood, and that northern legislatures had to repeal their personal liberty laws that tried to nullify the Fugitive Slave Law. No one doubted that property rights were the heart of this debate. Behind those rights were income and wealth. Albert Gallatin Brown explained exactly why: if slavery were not protected, then southerners would lose "investments of more than forty hundred million dollars. Destroy our $2,000,000,000 worth of slaves and you destroy the value of the soil on which they work; you destroy the value of all our machinery; our stock becomes worthless . . . ; and yet, sir, this great interest—the greatest individual interest under the Government—gets no protection from the Federal head."[99]

Northern Democrats grew impatient with the continual demand of southerners that they adopt southern positions. Douglas gave a speech May 15 and 16 which he entitled "Property in the Territories" and then managed not to talk about property at all. He focused on how the Davis resolutions destroyed the fundamental principles of nonintervention of Congress and a weak central government; he also defended his record. He asked the central question that was building up within the northern Democratic Party: "Can you preserve the party by allowing a minority to overule and dictate to the majority?" In later comments he brought up the record of the Democratic Party in the North and showed how southern demands had reduced the party to near nonexistence. At one time the Democrats claimed Maine, New Hampshire, Rhode Island, Connecticut, New York, Pennsylvania, and Ohio. Only Illinois had been consistently faithful, but now the southerners pressed their demands further and demanded obedience to federal intervention in the territories. "I should like to know how many States will be 'certain,' if you repudiate the Cincinnati platform, strike away the flag-staff, pull down the old Democratic banner [of nonintervention], and run up this new one."[100]

Democrats assembled in Charleston on April 23 for their national nominating convention. Deep South delegates had come pledged to obtain a slave code for the territories or to secede from the convention; northerners generally demanded that the platform uphold the doctrine of popular sovereignty and federal nonintervention in the territories. These differing views clashed in the platform committee for days. Finally, five days later, the committee issued a report giving two platforms; the majority of the committee favored a slave code, while a minority demanded nonintervention. So the platforms were given to the delegates to vote on, and, because there were more northern than southern delegates, the minority or popular sovereignty platform won. The Gulf state delegates then seceded from the convention. The remaining delegates tried to effect a nomination but failed. The Democrats then reconvened in Baltimore in early June. The Gulf state seceders were denied entrance, and so they gathered elsewhere to hold their own convention. This time, the Border South states joined them. They nominated Vice-President John C. Breckinridge (of Kentucky) for the presidency upon a platform calling for a congressional slave code for the territories. The regular Democratic Party nominated Stephen A. Douglas upon a platform of popular sovereignty. Throughout the nation everyone realized the effect: a split Democratic Party surely augured the victory of some other party in the November election.

One week after the Charleston Democratic convention, the efforts of border state conservatives bore fruit in the creation of a new party, the Constitutional Union Party. Meeting at Baltimore, they fashioned a platform consisting of the Constitution and calling for all citizens to suppress their sectionalism and elevate their patriotic unionism. For candidates they chose John Bell of Tennessee and Edward Everett of Massachusetts. At this stage, the party leaders hoped they could overcome the animus produced by the John Brown raid and capture the key border states; in the Great Lakes and Middle Atlantic northern states, they expected to draw conservatives to their party by elevating the economic issues of the tariff and internal improvements. Part of their strategy was predicated upon a Republican nomination of a party radical—William H. Seward—who would dismay conservative Republicans and send them fleeing into the arms of the safe Constitutional Unionists.[101]

But they failed to do the one thing probably necessary for victory: they did not adopt a resolution calling for the reestablishment of the Missouri Compromise line. Probably they did not do so because the sentiment of the South had become so supercharged that if the Constitutional Union Party had given in to the northern stand, then their appeal would have been greatly diminished in the southern border states. On the other hand, without such a plank they forfeited their strongest appeal to northern conservatives. After all, the northern Know-Nothings and conservative Whigs had all demanded restoration of the compromise line between 1854 and 1856; most of them were willing to let their great god of Climate determine slavery's expansion, and many of them would not have declared that they would forever bar new slave states from the Union. Thus the restoration of the Missouri Compromise was their greatest asset in the election, one that had the potential of seriously undercutting the Republicans. But the Constitutional Union Party failed at this critical moment. When they did resurrect the idea—in the winter of secession in January–February 1861—it was too late.

On May 16 the Republicans convened their national nominating convention in Chicago. In their platform they took advantage of all the economic issues that the Panic of 1857 had given them, calling for a higher tariff, a transcontinental railroad, and internal improvements. They also demanded congressional prohibition of slavery in the territories. For their nominee, they completely outfoxed the Constitutional Union Party managers by avoiding well-known Republicans who had amassed enemies as well as friends, and instead came up with Abraham Lincoln, an individual known enough not to be considered totally incompetent for national office but sufficiently unknown so as not to have angered the various constituencies of the Republican Party. Moreover, Lincoln's alleged conservatism, his Whig antecedents, satisfied many northerners that the Republicans were not offering an irresponsible, quick-tempered, insulting radical. And their strategy worked in the two ways it was meant to. Constitutional Union Party leaders immediately felt their chances slip away, and the uncertain states of Pennsylvania and New Jersey were pleased. Thus the son of Senator James Doolittle of Wisconsin wrote, "The nominations of the convention was a surprise to many. . . . I think the great Union Savers under the lead of Bell, Everett & Co. were about as badly surprised as any, and think that a deal of wind has been taken out of their canvass."[102]

Two separate campaigns were run in the election of 1860. In the South, the Breckinridge Democrats battled the Bell conservatives, with the Douglas Democrats as a sort of minor third party. Largely they argued over which party best protected the institution of slavery. In the North, Republicans fought Douglas Democrats as the Constitutional Unionists fell behind the other contestants rather early. Republicans used their stock appeals of celebrations of free labor, fears of the competition of free labor with slave labor, admonitions about the slave power and its ultimate designs, and the absolute uselessness of popular sovereignty to settle sectional issues. Douglas argued for Union and for popular sovereignty; he also insisted that the territories now belonged to the free population of the country and so the moment of crisis had actually passed. Douglas broke the tradition of allowing others to campaign for him and took to the stump on a speaking tour of the nation starting in July.[103]

Northerners talked mainly about defeating the slave power and limiting the influence of slave labor on free labor, but they mentioned property rights often enough. President Buchanan, while speaking in favor of the Breckinridge nomination, virtually repudiated the Democratic Party past when he said about slavery in the territories and popular sovereignty, "When was property ever submitted to the will of the majority?" Republicans talked about the immorality of reducing human beings to the level of oxen, and they often explained southern behavior in terms of the planters' determination to hold onto their property. James Russell Lowell put the reform impulse behind antislavery before the public just before the election. The revolutionary ideas of the founders were "promoted, not by any unthinking hostility to the *rights* of property, but by a well-founded jealousy of its usurpations."[104]

In the South, of course, the rhetoric about property rights escalated considerably, and the right of property was explicitly linked to electoral outcomes. The reason why the South demanded that the federal government be composed of people pledged to slavery was because southerners needed sympathetic legislators to wield the police power required to sustain the institution. Reuben Davis of Mississippi complained in Congress of the potential results of a Republican presidential victory: "When the government gets into the hands of the Republican party, the arm of the General Government, we are told, will not be raised for the protection of our slave property." This fear led southerners to imagine the ways that a Lincoln administration could devalue slave property and impoverish the South. All the North needed to do to preserve the Union, said Howell Cobb, was to agree that "slaves are property under and by the Constitution" and that slave property would be allowed and protected in the territories.[105] Southerners did stress states' rights and limited federal power during the election of 1860, but for a distinct purpose. They wanted an ironclad guarantee from the government that all officials would adhere to basic principles as defined by their interpretation of the Constitution. By so agreeing, then, no action against property rights in slaves could be taken. That also meant the South would not agree to abide by any legislation supported by a majority that they saw as ruinous to their wealth. In the election of 1856, Robert Toombs had made this explicit in a letter to Lewis Cass: "We did not submit our rights to numbers but to the constitution & numbers can not take them away."[106]

In the second week of October, the large states of Indiana, Ohio, and Illinois voted for governors and congressmen; the Republicans swept the field. Every astute politician knew that the uncertainty of the uncertain states was gone and that Abraham Lincoln would be elected president. From that point on, political speeches in the South were over immediate secession upon Lincoln's victory or a secession contingent upon an overt act of northern aggression. On November 6 Lincoln carried all the northern states save New Jersey, where a fusion arrangement split the electoral vote. Lincoln polled some 1,860,000 votes to 980,000 for Douglas, 670,000 for Breckinridge, 580,000 for Bell, and some 600,000 for fusion tickets in New York, New Jersey, and Pennsylvania (the last-named basically Douglas votes). With but 40 percent of the popular vote, Lincoln became president because he won all the northern states by a majority and earned 180 electoral votes, 151 being needed for election.[107]

Figure 7.1 maps out the explosion of the Second Party System into a sectional configuration. The lines are constructed the same way as Figure 6.1. Figure 7.1 shows how crucial was the year 1854 and the virulent reaction in the

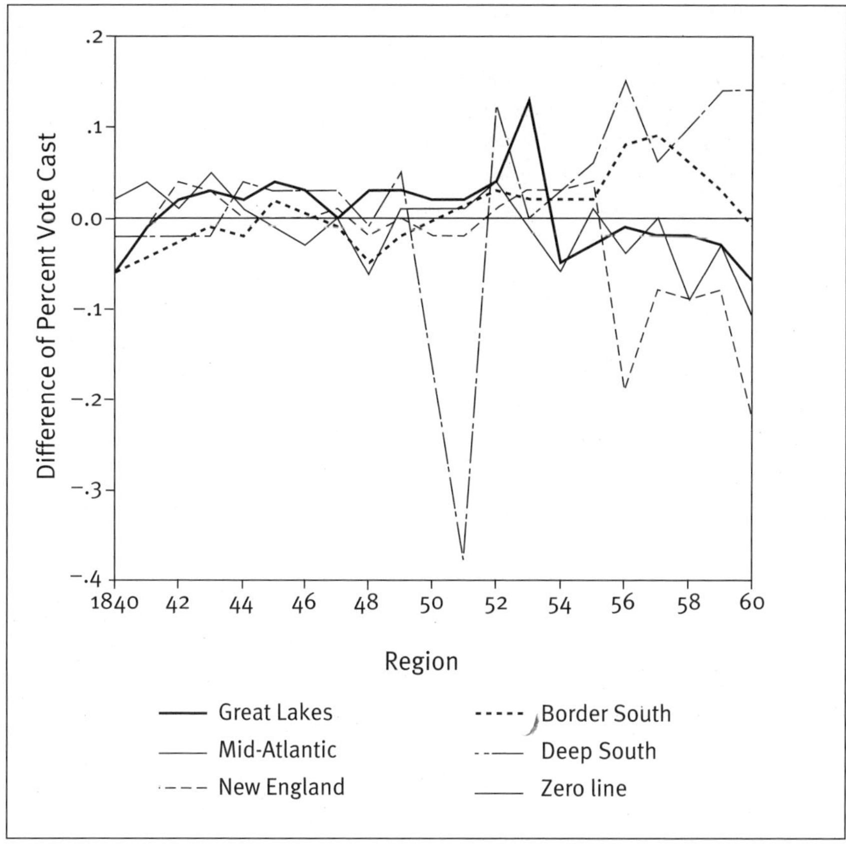

FIGURE 7.1. *Difference between Democratic Voting and Major Opposition Party by Votes Cast, All Regions, 1840–1860*

Great Lakes region and, to some extent, in the Middle Atlantic area. New England appears less potent because of the presence of other strong parties. Because in the congressional districts, the issue of slavery extension was paramount and because in the Great Lakes area the anti–Democratic Party fusion was distinctly called Republican, it may be inferred that the Kansas-Nebraska issue dominated the election results. In the other parts of the North, however, confusion reigned because of the strong showing of the Know-Nothings, especially in 1855. By 1856, however, the anti-Democratic elements had made their decision and fused into the national Republican Party. Meanwhile, the Democratic majorities in the South in congressional races were becoming absolutely awesome. Given the attention foisted on northern state realignment between 1854 and 1860, it is interesting that this figure indicates that stronger reaction to national affairs occurred in the Deep South and Border South. While New England indeed became a sectionalized region favoring the Republicans, both the Middle Atlantic and Great Lakes regions were still politically competitive, the Republicans holding only a slender lead over the Democrats. By 1860 the sectionalization of American politics is visible: the hegemony of the Democratic Party in the Border South and Deep South, and the supremacy of the Republicans in the North, with the Deep South and New England being the furthermost boundaries of sectionalism.[108]

South Carolina moved quickly to call a convention to terminate its connection with the Union. On December 20, South Carolina seceded, followed in January by Mississippi, Alabama, Louisiana, and Georgia; in February Texas departed. There was little doubt as to why they felt impelled to sever their ties to the northern states. James Mason of Virginia had written in November that the northern states had by overwhelming majorities put into power a party "whose open and avowed mission is to break up and destroy interests in property and in society in all the slaveholding States, which, when effected, must reduce their lands to deserts." The South Carolina Declaration of Causes insisted that the Union had been a compact in which the northern side failed to live up to its part of the bargain. In particular, northerners denied "the right of property in slaves" that had been part of the constitutional settlement; the nonslaveholding states had "assumed the right of deciding upon the propriety of our domestic institutions [that is, slavery]," denied the rights of property in fifteen states, and denounced "as sinful the institution of slavery." During the Georgia debate over secession, the proponents of a separate political existence constantly warned of the danger to their slave property by staying in the Union. And in New York City, the transplanted South Carolinian Richard Lathers told a meeting why secession had occurred and what the basic issue was. "The next question will be whether there can be such a thing as a claim for property in slaves. The Supreme Court has already decided that, as one portion of the country insists, but it is denied by another portion. The South will never come back until that principle is settled."[109]

Between December 1860 and March 1861, southerners demonstrated the limits of democracy. It was one thing to allow majorities to determine laws and regulations over the commonplaces of daily life; it was one thing to allow them to tax; and it was one thing to allow assemblies operating under majority rule to propose rule changes for activities in which few engaged. But on the giant propertied interests, a calculation unlike any other came into play; southerners called it rights, constitutional duties, and the like, but what they were really referring to was the presumption of a majority to change rules—or even to discuss the possibility of changing rules—that for decades had been the means to fortunes, social achievement, and political preferment. Then indeed it was time to calculate the value of the Union, or perhaps the future value of the Union. When Gulf state southerners finished the arithmetic, they concluded that the Union was a heavy drag upon southern prosperity because of the possibility that property rights in slaves would not be enforced.

Afterword

A central purpose of realignment theory was to connect political changes in the party system to policy changes. Indeed, for Walter Dean Burnham, one of the fathers of critical election theory and realignment, the reason to study upheavals in politics occurring periodically was to show how they revealed actual working democracy, when the "people" seized control of the agenda, changed it, and forced politicians to consider issues vital to them. In normal times—between realignments—politicians interacted with special interest groups to fashion policy, and voters counted only for elections but not policies.[1]

The realignment of the 1850s did set the agenda for the next several decades and did alter policy, but that altered agenda was not the one so many authors have insisted upon.[2] True, the wartime Republicans managed to pass legislation resulting in higher tariffs, easier western land acquisition (the homestead act), a new banking system, agricultural colleges, and the construction of transcontinental railroads. None of this represented a new agenda, for it was the old Whig program. Rather, it was far less than the old Whig program because it was an amalgam reflecting the coalitional nature of the Republican Party. The Old Whigs of the 1830s and 1840s wanted a national bank to control credit; the national banking system of 1862 and 1864 set up requirements for banking and outlined good banking practices but did not erect a central bank. In many ways, the national banking system reflected Democratic thinking, not Whig. The tariffs tended to be Whig protectionism reborn. Whether those tariffs were as protectionist as 1824 and 1828 is dubious. The Transcontinental Railroad was bipartisan in Whig-Democrat terms. After all, Stephen A. Douglas wanted the road badly enough to overturn the Missouri Compromise, and southern Democrats—not exactly bashful orators for states' rights—heartily wanted expenditures for a southern Pacific railroad. The homestead act probably had more Democrat antecedents than Whig, while the agricultural colleges legislation more demonstrated the Whig belief in beneficial education than the Democrat insistence on the virtues of the common man, but even that observation may have to be amended.

The truth is the Republican economic program during and after the Civil War reflected the old economic issues of the Democrat-Whig party system. The agenda was not replaced, it was merely recycled. Nothing in Republican economic policies foreshadows anything new—not only in terms of policy advocacy but in terms of argument, of economic knowledge, of general social problems. If one wanted to point to key departures that truly indicated a different agenda, one has two to look at. First, the Freedman's Bureau established in 1865 and operative to 1868 marked a different direction from Democrat-Whig battles. That institution was a bureaucracy that could have functioned as the buffer between white supremacists and black poverty; the bureau might have over time cooled racial passions and supported more economic progress for blacks than political reconstruction provided. But Republicans were obviously aware that they were building a bureaucracy, and instead of embracing the change they ran away from it. They offered southern blacks the vote as a mechanism to quell southern violence and economic inequality, a mechanism that failed miserably. The other possibility to consider as a bench mark for a change in agenda was the Interstate Commerce Commission of 1886. Here was a budding movement to consider the regulation of something new in American life—big business. For the Interstate Commerce Commission intended to oversee—by reports only in 1887—the activity of the nation's railroads, and, in the words of Alfred D. Chandler, the railroads were the nation's first big business. Four years later came the passage of the Sherman Anti-Trust Act. But 1887 and 1890 were nearly three decades after the realignment of the 1850s, and realignment theory posits that the time difference between moments of realignment runs about thirty-five years. In short, the Interstate Commerce Act and the Sherman Antitrust Act belong to another era, not the antislavery one.[3]

The realignment of the 1850s was about slavery, the slave power, and protection of a free labor village society—not about the economic issues of corporate capitalism or even about the tariffs and banks. Republicans changed the agenda of the country by altering the law of property rights in people. The Thirteenth Amendment, somewhat foisted upon the party and the public by the exigencies of the Civil War, was the massive agenda change of that realignment. By Lincoln's penstroke on the preliminary emancipation proclamation, and then by the states' ratification of the Thirteenth Amendment, the Republicans solved the problem of free labor versus slave labor. The amendment declared that property rights in human beings were no longer permissible anywhere in the United States. By doing that, the Thirteenth Amendment legitimated the destruction of $3 billion worth of property and reduced the slave power from national prominence to a landlord political entity that only had a regional influence.[4]

And the Thirteenth Amendment did the major task of preserving the free labor village community of the North. The danger to those communities was the property right slaveholders held in their slaves, a property right that enabled the slaveholders to use laborers economically in ways that ruined the wages of northern workers or monopolized the land to the detriment of small farmers. While the threat was a future one, northerners understood the basic, and new, commercial nature of their civilization. Better means of commerce stitched the country together and allowed localities to ship goods nationwide. Competition entered American life with a forcefulness it had never before known. It took no great imagination to conjecture that eventually slaveholders could use their slaves in ways so that the products of slaves competed with the products of free workers and free farmers. Indeed, northerners were well prepared for such an argument because it had been the heart of tariff arguments since the 1820s: Americans lived in a blessed state of freedom that enabled each person to reap the fruits of his labors, and to maintain that condition foreign goods by pauper labor had to be stopped because the pauper labor would destroy the high wages of American workers, and high wages were the economic birthright of a free society. Slave labor competition was fundamentally no different than foreign pauper labor competition.[5]

What enabled the slaveholder to act so ruinously, and thus unfairly, on free labor was the control of labor and its remuneration. Property rights in slaves gave southern slaveholders the power to push wages down should ever slaves be used in occupations in which free labor dominated. Northern workers' fear of slave labor wage competition had a long history in the United States, and the transportation revolution heightened the fear and made it more realistic. By passing the Thirteenth Amendment, the Republicans ended that particular threat. They destroyed the source of power—the right to hold property in people.

The centrality of the Thirteenth Amendment for the realignment of the 1850s because of its impact on property rights also aids in explaining why the Fourteenth and Fifteenth Amendments were ultimately so weak. The problem festering in the country was the collision of two sets of property rights; one in the South that permitted slavery, one in the North that did not. Solving the problem meant one of the two regimes of property rights had to triumph; the northern version did. That solved the northern fears about slave power domination and the destruction of a free labor village society. The Fourteenth and Fifteenth Amendments had little relationship to the central issue of power derived from property rights. They stand, perhaps, as a testament to the idealism of Republicans in their desire to carve out a place for ex-slaves in American life and were milestones in the centuries-old battle to erode European ethnocentrism. They show the humanitarian, antislavery quality of the Republican Party in its willingness to grant civil and political rights to those who had once been slaves. Nonetheless, Republicans had hardly been converted to racial egalitarianism.

Yet the commitment of the Republicans was to save their society and to eliminate the economic and political threat of the slave power. The Fourteenth and Fifteenth Amendments did little in that regard, except perhaps to attempt to stop the southern white elite from bolstering their representation in Congress by the elimination of the three-fifths compromise. Northerners were not all that committed to the civil and political equality promised in those amendments, and were obviously not committed to the use of government power to enforce them. Ultimately, Republicans proved to be very respectful of states' rights. So when white southerners challenged the Fourteenth and Fifteenth Amendments in order to control African Americans, the northern response was tepid. Northerners finally let the Fourteenth and Fifteenth Amendments lapse into impotence in terms of human rights and let states' rights override them.[6] If the Republicans could have obtained racial civil and political equality without any real cost to northerners, they probably would have been overjoyed. But as southerners raised the cost of providing that equality to southern blacks, northerners gave up the fight. They were committed to destroy property rights in slaves; the Thirteenth Amendment was a sine non qua, and it would be rigorously enforced. But the Fourteenth and Fifteenth Amendments were not central to the fears of northerners in the 1850s, and so they were allowed to slip into enforcement obscurity.

The property concentration of slavery represented a particularly momentous and violent problem in American history. The next concentration of property that would require a realignment would be the rise of big business, the consolidation of American enterprise in a few huge firms. That produced a realignment and its share of violence as well, but the outcome of the concentration of wealth in business enterprises had real differences from the concentration of wealth in slaves. One had much more of a moral impulse than the other; one was more regionally defined than the other; one was infinitely more violent than the other. A comparison between the two concentrations would be an interesting analysis indeed. But that is someone else's book.

Appendix A

A Theory of Political Realignment

> It is quite plain that your government will never be able to restrain a distressed and discontented majority. For with you the majority is the government, and has the rich, who are always a minority, absolutely at its mercy. The day will come when, in the State of New York, a multitude of people, none of whom has had more than half a breakfast, or expects to have more than half a dinner, will choose a Legislature. Is it possible to doubt what sort of Legislature will be chosen? On one side is a statesman preaching patience, respect for vested rights, strict observance of public faith. On the other is a demagogue ranting about the tyranny of capitalists and usurers, and asking why anybody should be permitted to drink champagne and to ride in a carriage, while thousands of honest folks are in want of necessaries. Which of the two candidates is likely to be preferred by a working man who hears his children cry for more bread?
>
> —Thomas B. Macaulay to Henry S. Randall, May 23, 1857, in *Littell's Living Age* 65 (May 19, 1860): 430–31

This appendix propounds a theory that suggests that political realignments in the United States are linked to periodic reformulations of property rights. Major economic transformations, meaning the creation of new technologies or methods of production, are responsible for the existence of political realignments, for transformations alter work rewards and investment paths; they generate new means of acquisition of property for which no rules exist. In order for society to return to a somewhat "contractual" basis—that is, consent to the rules of society without undue amounts of citizen violence that necessitate state coercion—the rules of property have to be reformulated. To iron out the social upheavals from basic economic transformations, politics will undergo two political realignments per every major economic transformation, economic upheavals occurring roughly every eighty years, realignments every thirty-five to forty years. The realignment period itself lasts approximately one decade, probably governed by prospective voting, the last two decades of the particular realignment era usually characterized by retrospective voting. The policy output of each realignment decade is a new formulation of property rights that alters the paths of investment and the rewards of economic activity. In the decades after the realignment decade, politics center on a debate as to how far deviations from the new rules will be allowed. Thus this presentation finds the origin of realignments primarily in the economic realm, not in cultural clashes; cultural clashes will not explain periodicity, but economic cycles may because of their potential regularity.[1] The following discussion details the foregoing thesis and is wholly theoretical.

The Theory of Political Realignment

Political Realignment theory arose in the 1940s from the need to understand the cycle of stability and disruption that seemingly characterized the path of American political history. Commencing with the ideas of V. O. Key about the role of critical elections and culminating in the writings of political scientist Walter Dean Burnham in the 1970s, realignment theory proposed to explain the rise and fall of political parties and the formulation of public policy. Between 1970 and 1990, this paradigm has guided research in American political history. It has produced a number of statistical techniques, a terminology for categorizing elections, and explanatory hypotheses for the causation of political change; it has been extended to account for party formation and partisan affiliation, congressional policy shifts, and decisions of the Supreme Court.[2]

The basic components of realignment theory are as follows. First, realignment produces vital shifts in public policy. Second, the realigning period takes from four to eight years and is usually signaled by a "critical election." During the period of realignment, third parties proliferate as the major parties ignore some vital issue that has upset a significant portion of the public. Third, a realignment of voting blocs occurs that produces either a new major party or reshuffles the allegiances of groups in the existing parties. In either case of continuing parties or the birth of new parties, large numbers of people change their political preferences. This alteration in preferences can be detected by switches in group voting, groups being defined in terms of economic, social, political, or ideological characteristics (e.g., class, religious denomination, ethnicity, race, or geography). A key component in the the shifting of groups is the action of young voters with weak partisan connections and nonvoting citizens who had not been politically active in the old party system. Frequently realignments are powered by the young and by nonvoters who attach themselves to some new issue in the political environment, disrupting the loyalty given to the older parties. Fourth, after the realignment individuals develop a partisan identity that strengthens over time so that people continuously vote a party ticket. This produces a party system that continuously delivers consistent voting for the major parties. On occasion, given the intrusion of some event or circumstance, one party accustomed to losing might win, but such "deviating" elections are rare. Normally most elections "sustain" a consistent pattern of either one party dominating or a close competition between the two parties. Fifth, party-system stability runs approximately thirty-four or so years; then a new issue enters politics that the old parties cannot handle, new parties or novel voting coalitions form, and a new process of realignment commences.

During the 1980s, realignment theory came under attack. The theory worked well enough between 1828 and 1945, but its predictive power faded in the post–World War II environment. Moreover, a number of scholars carped about the fuzziness of many of the theory's propositions. When was a critical election critical? How were elections characterized? Why did so many have trouble deciding upon realignment moments and critical elections? Other theories were developed to take place of realignment theory's deficiencies. Chief among these competitors was the theory of retrospective voting—that voters weighed how well the party in power governed, and then rewarded or punished parties on that basis. Rather than periods of stability, the theory of retrospective voting found voting change highly correlated with how well a party governed. And there are also theories of prospective voting, that voters act on how well a party may protect or advance the interests of the individual voter.[3]

It may be conceded that realignment theory is beset by unsettling problems of defining the moment of realignment, the duration of the realignment period, and categorization of elections. It may also be admitted that frequently retrospective or prospective voting theories are superior in predictive capacity and short-run understanding of voter behavior. Yet realignment theory has one capacity that the other voting theories do not: realignment theory has the possibility of explaining fundamental shifts in policy, as opposed to those shifts in policy which are primarily small deviations around stable, long-run governmental activities. Public policy in American history has aspects of unusual stability. Public policy gets set in its larger framework and then persists over time, although refinements may be added. Yet the party system operates consistently within that larger framework. Realignment theory allows an understanding of how such a framework is constructed, a framework that sets a policy agenda and then confines political discourse to that agenda for decades.

The Economic Formulation

Property Rights

Economists and economic historians have for several decades now been investigating the economic consequences of property rights and have produced a rich (if strange) literature on transactions costs, information costs, the prisoner's dilemma, the problem of the commons, and the formation of hierarchies. From the vantage point of economists, the interest in property rights is connected to maximizing economic growth rates, as individuals will make best use of resources when income flows from assets are secure—and that security comes from the guarantee of property rights.[4] Whatever the debates over the economic merits of property rights, the importance of the body of literature for realignment theory is clear: only government—in whatever form it takes—can establish property rights and enforce them. Government through its rules about property establishes the fundamental "rules of the game" for society, indicating what economic actions are acceptable and how rewards of activity are to be obtained—hence, a determination of sorts of the shape of income distribution.[5]

For many economists, the state then becomes the Jekyll-Hyde monster. For economic growth, the state must define (and in some cases assign) property rights. But the power to do so is also the power to change those rules. As an illustration, Terry Anderson and Peter Hill lament that, "clearly, any state that defines and enforces property rights can also redefine and reallocate rights." And the fear of these individuals is that governments will destroy economic efficiency by engaging in rent seeking, redistributionist policies, and government maximization of its own resources and power.[6]

Technology and Economic Transformation

Douglass C. North has posited that property rights assignments and definitions must change over time, regardless of the wisdom of the governing authorities and their potential failure to maximize economic growth. The reason is technology. Technological development creates new forms of property that require definition and devalues the property held in old technologies. In North's depiction, technology disrupts relative prices, thereby altering the opportunity set for actors and setting the stage for political actors to enact legislation to restore the returns obtained in the old price regime. Such political activity engenders social conflict because altering the definitions of property rights inherently alters income and property distributions, usually a most unsettling proposition for the propertied and property-aspiring classes. More generally among economists, the "market" for political power determines the equilibrium on the sanctity of property rights and the extent of rent-seeking and redistribution that will occur. This book, however, favors the technological interpretation.[7]

Technological change arises from the nature of the capitalist or free market economy. It was once believed that technological improvements were "manna from heaven" that were exogenous to the operations of the market. Now some economists believe that the investment process by itself produces a search for better means of production via technology, and so technological change is endogenous to a market society. That is the approach taken here.[8]

I posit (without any proof) that major technological transformations occur roughly every eighty years—and the timing probably comes from a sense of economic history as much as any other source. This scenario has perhaps a closer resemblance to the "leading industry" hypothesis of Walt W. Rostow than is wise, but it is broadened beyond the rise of a single industry to the ripple effects of a dominant technology through the various sectors of the economy and the amount of time it takes to accomplish that feat.[9] Usually investment extends existing productive units to their long-range equilibrium points, and thus one obtains a repetition of existing job routines, knowledge, and entrepreneurial activities. In periods of great technological change, however, usually twenty years in duration, new knowledge and new job routines are created. After the twenty-year introductory phase, the economy then adapts to pushing firms to long-run equilibrium.

The only material that comes close to substantiating such a view of the economy is long-run cycle theory, the investigators of the Kondratiev wave. This is evidently not an area beloved by most economists. Most of the work on the Kondratiev cycle is interested in whether the wave demonstrates economic growth or decline. However, the realignment theory I advance does not at all depend on the concepts behind Kondratiev cycles.[10]

Political Change

Technological Transformation and Social Disruption

Technological transformation induces a political effect by altering rewards of productive behavior. In economic language, technological change alters factor prices, enabling some enterprises to obtain positive economic profits while others fail to cover short-run costs. Over the long run, resources have to shift from older industries to new ones where factor prices indicate positive rewards. In more common parlance, technological change alters the incomes of economic actors. With the introduction of a new technology that has a broad application, people who create that technology and have knowledge of it earn a premium; their incomes advance. But individuals who live by the old technology find their skills devalued; their incomes suffer.

These differences in income for economic agents generate the basic dichotomy that powers realignment. Technology creates new ways of earning a living and usually introduces innovations in the way of doing business, new knowledge and skills, and new forms of property. The new mechanisms of economic life, being more productive and hence earning greater returns on investment, inevitably war on older business activities in the economy, either in the form of producing a competing product or in taking away resources from the older activities by bidding up input prices. Realignments invariably pit the forces for technological change against the forces against technological change.

Class

By viewing realignments as the political artifacts of technological change, it is possible to derive an explanation for the weakness of class influences upon partisanship. For several years now, a literature has grown up that insists that class has had little influence in politics. Yet other scholars, using different definitions and statistical procedures, continue to press for the importance of class in political preferences.[11] But the overall assessment is that class influences in American politics are at best surprisingly weak, while cultural influences appear much stronger. Realignment can offer an explanation for this phenomenon.

Although much of the literature on social disruption via technological change focuses on the working class, major technological transformations cut across income cohorts. This is because technological transformations affect whole segments of the economy or entire sectors. In any given sector of the economy, an entire spectrum of income classes will exist (in orthodox Marxist terminology, capitalists and proletarians; in broader terms, wage-earners, skilled workers, perhaps some managers, owners, stockholders, etc.). Moreover, groups of individuals will be associated with support activities to that sector of the economy—resource and transportation suppliers, retailers, and perhaps financial servicers. When transformation occurs, all those locked into the old technology are damaged. Individuals who made either significant or large amounts of money under the old technology may be resistant to the change and indeed grow angry over "younger" people making sudden new fortunes because of their knowledge of the new technology. Other citizens whose subsistence relied upon the old technology may be in a more desperate position. Some may successfully make the transition to another remunerative endeavor; many others will not. In other words, the dread of substantial change cuts across income lines, and the resentment will not be class-based but economic-sector based. Thus attempts to find class influences during realignment periods will not find strong correlations because the transformation has generated anger across class lines in the sector under attack. At the same time, the workers, artisans, managers, and owners in the technologically favored sector of the economy are, relatively speaking, doing well and do not exhibit resentment. Hence class analysis in moments of technological transformation is likely to come up empty-handed. Excepting those sectors that are largely unaffected, realignments really pit the technological ins versus the technological outs.

It is technology and its effects that upset class analysis and give rise to the common formulation that American politics reacts to economic change but not in the form of class politics. If technology did not change and these transformations did not occur, then Marxian class politics would probably arise because nothing would hinder the political division between propertied and unpropertied. An economy without technological change would eventually hit its final resting point of diminishing marginal returns in all fields (John Stuart Mill's "steady-state") and lock society into frozen class positions. Under that condition, politics would undoubtedly divide between haves and have-nots. Technological change, however, affects both propertied and unpropertied classes, thereby producing class coalitions either to mitigate or to protect the effects of technological change.[12]

Ideology and Realignment

A specific form of protest comes out of realigning periods associated with major technological transformations. It is based on rational expectations of future income streams. At this juncture, we part with economists' use of the term, especially associating rationality with economic efficiency; we instead use a broader understanding of rational expectations. The governing dictum in this discussion is A. K. Sen's comment about the assumptions of the economists' ideal economic actor: "The *purely* economic man is indeed close to being a social moron, . . . a rational fool."[13]

In periods of predictable technological change, that is, small improvements in production processes in which companies are moving to their long-run equilibrium points, individuals—wage earners, skilled workers, entrepreneurs, salespeople, capitalists—become accustomed to income streams from certain types of behavior. Doing certain things at the right time earns rewards. Knowledge of the rules of the game and of the correct behaviors to obtain a competence or a sufficient standard of living is widespread; the reward for this knowledge and these behaviors is an income stream. This becomes the "just fruits of labor," the "honest" way of earning a living.

When technological transformation arrives and unsettles whole sectors of the economy, the income stream to the older sectors—the ones that are in competition with the new one either in terms of product or acquisition of resources—lessens. The rewards to labor, to investment, to mental activity—that is, to wage labor, skilled labor, mental labor—decrease, either in the form of unemployment or in actually reduced wages. The response is anger. Individuals in the older sectors rationally expect the behaviors that earned them competences in days gone by should continue to do so in the future. When those competences become endangered, they feel cheated out of the "just fruits of labor," that dishonesty has crept into the system, that somewhere people are manipulating the economic system in a conspiracy to deprive "honest" people of their "just" rewards. And the people they point to are those who have innovated some new form of property or economic process.[14]

People riding the crest of technological change, however, are certain of the justice of their activity. They protect themselves with ideas claiming that their improvements advance humankind and ultimately create a more prosperous society. They also are aware that their innovations require the sanctity of law.

In one form or another, they have created new financial arrangements, working arrangements, enterprise forms, or intellectual property that the society is not accustomed to. They therefore seek legitimization of their pursuits in the law, an attempt that sets up the contest over property rights. The process shows why realignments are fundamental contests over the rules of the game and are so socially disruptive.

For these reasons, periods of realignment, especially connected with the onslaught of technological change, evoke such stirring calls for justice, morality, and conspiracy. One side is losing a way of life while the other is trying to obtain legal sanction for innovations. Realignments seldom evoke cries to end property rights, and it may be taken as a cultural fact that Americans are wedded to the notion of individual property rights.[15] But the area being contested is what constitutes property, what legitimately deserves to be considered rewards for honest endeavors. Not all forms of labor deserve rewards, and not all forms of ownership deserve the sanction of the law.[16] Realignments exist to resolve these problems.

Politics

In the normal functioning of the American two-party system, partisan alignments are created first by cultural reasons or an initial response to technological change. Partisan affiliations thereafter should be roughly stable because the process of change follows the path of investment over time, and expectations are generally met as to what behaviors and knowledge bring rewards. Major technological transformation raises the issue that disrupts the political parties by making life less predictable for a sizable segment of the population (10 to 20 percent). The issue raised has property rights implications. This produces third parties, new parties, and rearranges coalitions in the two-party system. Normally, the realignment phase occurs approximately one decade after the technological transformation has been at work. The reason is that economic phenomena will be judged by the criteria in the older party system—what policies will do what, how readjustments can be achieved using the old methods of governmental action. The lag is necessary to show that the old policies will not work, that the economic change is not transient but mighty and permanent, and that a sufficient number of people are motivated to tear political coalitions apart. The policy output will be accomplished by one of the realigned parties: a rewriting of the rules of property acquisition, a new set of property rights definitions.

Because redefining property rights affects so many interests and because property is so fundamental an aspect of life, there are limits to how far property rights can be changed in any single realignment. A drastic redefinition calls either for revolution or civil war. The purpose of realignment is to incorporate changes in property definitions so as to hold the society together, establish some consensus on justifiable means of property acquisition under the new technological regime, and to avoid social disaster over the question. For this reason, it takes two realignments to adjust society to a major technological transformation: one to set the ground rules, a space of two or three decades to enable citizens to accept the altered rules, and a second realignment to complete the transition.[17]

The scenario offered here does not invalidate cultural or contextual influences in any given realignment period. Depressions, immigration waves, clashes of cultural values, and remnant but persisting problems of earlier periods can all be factors in any given realignment. From a historian's perspective, there *must* be contextual peculiarities to each realignment because that is the nature of the human experience. The argument here, however, is that these influences serve to depress or heighten the crisis atmosphere. The main engine producing the crisis atmosphere derives from technological transformation that alters the expected income stream for a sizable segment of the population.

Testable Propositions

From the foregoing discussion, testable propositions can be derived to ascertain whether the ideas contained in this theory carry any weight.

For realignment theory and for technological change, certain assumptions are made. First, the economy is semicapitalist or market-oriented so that private decisions concerning disposition of property exist. The regulated, welfare state is no hindrance to the assumption. Second, the political environment requires the single-winner by plurality in electoral districts and an elective executive officer (the presidency).[18] Realignment theory may or may not work for parliamentary systems, although in many ways it should.

1. On a literary basis, realignment periods should be characterized by a heightened discussion of property rights. In other periods, discourse over property rights is limited to normal levels of background static among intellectuals, lawyers, and perhaps fringe elements. During realignments, however, the public becomes involved in the argument, and usually the argument is freighted with moralistic pronouncements about fairness, justice, and morality.

2. Technological transformation should be measurable by a variety of phenomena, and it can be posited that at least one of the following conditions should appear:

a. It should be detectable by shifts in investment flows. In nontransforming periods, the sectors of the economy—as, say, defined by the census reporters—should grow at a normal pace and new categories not be observable or of appreciable size. Transforming eras should be detectable by the emergence of new categories of endeavors that over a period of twenty years account for at least 5 percent of gross domestic product. Here, the growth of sectors is acting as the proxy for investment flows as altered by technological change.

b. Reorganization of the work environment is indicative of the impact of technology, for it alters the behaviors and skills necessary to acquire a competence. A proxy for reorganization of the work environment would be the average size of the workplace. If workplaces enlarge or contract, or if overall employment in the sector changes dramatically, then work is being either eliminated or reorganized.

c. Dramatic increases or decreases in lifetime expected earnings would also be indicators of realignment periods. In particular, given the impact of technology, expected incomes *within certain sectors* should decline for males aged thirty to fifty, and increase *within certain sectors* for young males, twenty to thirty. (As of 1970, women may be added to this criterion.)[19] This effect should exist because technology will devalue skills and knowledge in older technologies but enhance the income potential of younger people who are at the forefront of the new technology.

3. Policy outputs of realignment should be observable by one of two possible conditions.

a. Legislation or Supreme Court rulings redefine property rights. The consequence should be shifting investment flows away from areas deemed improper for property rights or to areas that acquire legal sanction, or simply modified because of a limit to property right protection.

b. Dramatic changes occur in government spending, federal or state or local—in particular, dramatic changes in taxes or creation of new categories of expenditure in the budget. If we assume a linear function to characterize taxes or budget outlays over time, realignment policy shifts would dramatically change the slopes of those functions over a new time period.

An Outline of Realignment Eras, Technological Change, and Property Rights Alterations

Given the foregoing explanation, U.S. political history could be organized in the following manner.[20]

Born out of the Revolution in 1776, the United States acquired the institutions of a rapidly modernizing nation (individualism, private property, small government, unobtrusive bureaucracy) but lacked the transportation facilities to make the jump from a subsistence economy to a market economy (that is, this is republicanism waiting for capitalism). The politics that emerged (Federalists versus Democratic-Republicans) was a variant on European politics in which the aristocracy split and vied for control of the state and in which the rest of society deferred to the wisdom of the social superiors. Because the Revolution had knocked the wind out of aristocratic sails, however, the American situation inherently possessed democratic potential.[21]

In the early nineteenth century, the economic transformation occurred that engendered the two major realignments of that era. The transportation revolution appeared in the form of canals, steamboats, and railroads, creating between 1825 and 1890 a national market (net addition to the railroad network peaked in the late 1880s). The technological change was the application of the steam engine to economic life. The ultimate change for society was the movement from local, semisubsistence agriculture to a national market and commercial agriculture. In this economic change, the basic characteristic was entrepreneurship: the small farm, the small bank, the small store, and the small factory.[22] Because of its entrepreneurial focus and its emphasis on individualism and smallness, the political response to the new economic environment was to tear down the remaining structures of hierarchy that survived the Revolution. Thus came the first realignment of 1838–54, the Democrat-Whig party system. The dominant party, the Democrats, attacked centralized banking, monopoly power, and special privileges. The policy outcomes were visible in free banking laws, the New York Constitution of 1846, and generally reduced governmental involvement in the economy. A particular signal of the change in property rights inspired by the realignment was the decision of Roger B. Taney in the *Charles River Bridge* case (1837), in which vested interests that obstructed entrepreneurial interests were voided in interest of the community at large. In short, the structures of eighteenth-century stability would not be allowed to thwart the dynamism of nineteenth-century enterprise.[23] Associated with the Second Party System was a fight over property rights—the extension of suffrage to all white males and the *rhetorical* claim of Democrats that human rights were more sacrosanct than property rights, or as Orestes Brownson charged, "So in the last analysis the dominant idea of the whigs is not MAN, but PROPERTY."[24]

The Jacksonian realignment of parties did not remove one vestige of the hierarchical past: slavery. Slavery presented enormous problems which the process of realignment could not resolve peacefully. The conflict was not social, political, or ideological: it was fundamentally economic in every aspect. As this particular realignment and its consequences were treated in the narrative of this book, suffice it to say that the realignment of the 1850s sought to establish a consistent standard of property rights throughout the nation, and that slavery was simply too antagonistic to be allowed in a national market system.

The second era of technological transformation can be dated 1890 to 1973. It was dominated by the large-scale corporation (that is, big business)—or, in Robert Sobel's phrase, *The Age of Giant Corporations*. The technology that dominated this phase was mass production, or the use of expensive, heavy, single-purpose machinery for the production of interchangeable parts for mass consumption. Historians of the nineteenth century have generally overrated the significance of the power of the transportation revolution because broadly speaking it involved no great upheaval of work routines or the mental requirements for work, although some alterations were obvious in early urban industrialization; and certainly the Civil War as a product of the transportation revolution was a mighty effect. But the grand transformation of American history occurred between 1880 and 1920, when the nation passed from rural agrarian to urban industrial; when mental labor began to surge in reward over manual labor, when machines replaced skilled craftsmen, and when the personal qualities of small business life groveled before the might of impersonal bureaucratic corporate giants. This was the birth of the core-periphery economy.[25]

The first realignment that arose from the new technological order was the crisis of 1896 and the progressive movement that followed it. In terms of policy, if not exactly in group reshuffling, the response was regulation: the Mann-Elkins Act, the Pure Food and Drug Act, the Federal Reserve Act, and the Fair Trade Commission, among others. The rise of big business had collectivized American economic life. Whereas the nineteenth century had sought the trinity of small business, small government, and small labor, the beginning of the twentieth century witnessed the power imbalance of big business, small government, and small labor. The work of the two realignments of the twentieth century was to balance the power mix to large entities: big business, big government, and big labor (or Theodore Lowi's beast of pluralism). The progressive period laid the groundwork for the first part of the required change, the institutional basis for big government, by carving out a bureaucracy. And in doing so it redefined property rights in two particular ways: one, by constitutional amendment, the Sixteenth Amendment (income tax), and by the Northern Securities Trust case, which made the Sherman Anti-Trust Act powerful in influencing business decisions. The rise of the antitrust *capability* of government influenced investing decisions and the acceptable size of enterprise.[26]

The second realignment associated with the era of mass-production technology, or the age of big business, was the New Deal realignment, 1932–73. The New Dealers completed the upgrading of the other areas of American society to match that of the original appearance of the corporate core economy: they fleshed out the bureaucratic apparatus, recognized labor unions, and created the welfare state, the two key policies being the Wagner Act and the Social Security Act (with, of course, a host of regulatory acts). After World War II, a few historians called the New Deal arrangement the "Corporate Commonwealth" and indicated it was a new social contract. Moreover, the New Deal era (roughly 1933–40) was a struggle with the Supreme Court over control of property rights. That struggle ended, according to legal scholars, in *U.S. v. Carolene Products Co.* (1938), in which the sanctity of absolute property rights was overthrown; it ended substantive due process and unimpaired freedom of contract.[27]

Political scientists could not locate a realignment in the 1970s when one should have appeared given the timing mechanism of the theory (it was thirty-plus years after the New Deal realignment), and thus the paradigm of realignment became criticized and in some circles discarded.[28] However, no one should dispute the shift in the policy framework that has occurred between 1970 and 1990, and explaining changes in the dimensions of the policy universe was the reason that realignment theory was born. In 1970 the United States was still in the throes of a general reform movement, and expectations were general that over time the nation would implement socialist measures or at least general-welfare ones. By 1990, the parties debated how much to reduce the federal government, how to reinvigorate the doctrine of states' rights, how far to deregulate economic enterprise, how much to lower taxes, and whether to abolish entirely inheritance taxes. By 1990, politics had experienced a triumph of individualism over community, just the reverse of the 1960s reformers' confident expectations. Anyone who lived through these years with any political awareness certainly understood that the foundations of public debate had dramatically shifted.

A policy realignment had occurred and it was matched by an economic transformation as well as a feeble voter realignment. The voter realignment has not been as marked as other realignments, basically involving the shift of conservative Democrats to a Republican affiliation and the capture of the Republican Party by proslavery, secessionist southerners (the modern Republican Party has no ideological linkage to the party of Lincoln at all). The cultural factor in the long realignment of 1976–95 has been the Caucasian reaction to the civil rights movement of the 1960s. More generally throughout the United States in the 1990s, Republicans won governorships and control of state legislatures in large numbers. The timing of the realignment may not have matched realignment theory, but that politics have realigned should no longer be a question.

Behind the policy shift and the political realignment was a transformation of the economy. Three distinct forces reshaped the economy. First, the mass-production model of American enterprise had reached its limits. In the 1970s the bureaucratic nature of large-scale American manufacturing became an object of derision, and unflattering comparisons were made between the bureaucracies of the Soviet Union and General Motors. Second, the rise of a new technology appeared in the form of computers, satellite communications, and electronic processing of information. But the new means of electronic communication changed, evidently, the cost structure of doing business. In particular, it destroyed some of the economies of size that large corporations had obtained, enabling small and middle-sized companies to compete with the Fortune 500. Hence, in the 1980s and 1990s one witnessed the "downsizing" of American firms, as they shed workers in order to become more nimble and efficient—and the group being downsized comprised middle managers. According to a report in the *Wall Street Journal*, Fortune 500 firms in 1979 employed 16,193,44 people (18.0 percent of the nonfarm work force); by 1991, Fortune 500 firms were down to 11,973,000 people (11.0 percent of the nonfarm work force). In short, the core firms of the corporate commonwealth (the era 1890 to 1973) were reducing in size while new firms arose that were smaller and more nimble. This economic development stressed entrepreneurial qualities, not administrative ones, and sought the nineteenth century's freedom to act or, as James Williard Hurst had phrased it, a "release of energy." Thus the economic change promoted a belief in the inefficiency of government regulation and an elevation of the beneficence of marketplace activity. In short, the technological transformation stimulated a desire to return to laissez-faire policy in government.[29]

At the same time, government policy pushed "globalization," which amounted to the transference of mass-production jobs to low-wage nations. Employment in steel, automobiles, tires, textiles, and shoes shockingly fell. This circumstance set up the tensions over economic change induced by technological change: one sector advanced wildly and with grand expectations, while another sector shrank, with individuals experiencing the horror of watching their future economic expectations explode.[30]

The third factor, more of a long-term force in promoting the realignment, has been the ecology movement. Until the 1970s—perhaps symbolized by the oil shocks—the marginal returns from wasteful use of the environment evidently far outweighed the marginal costs. During the 1960s and after, the marginal costs must have shot up as populations began pressing to the limits of resource acquisition and use by the older technologies. The costs took the form of water, air, and land pollution. The externalities coming out of plundering natural resources gave birth to the ecology movement, and that movement succeeded in passing all types of laws that restricted entrepreneurial activity, especially involving logging, land development, and pollution control. Environmental protection suddenly involved large costs; from nothing in 1960, they rose to hundreds of billions of dollars by the 1990s.[31]

Property rights had been a largely quiescent topic in the 1950s and 1960s, except for a few extreme conservatives, but then suddenly discussion of property rights issues exploded in the 1980s and 1990s. The computer and digital processing had elevated the question of "intellectual property rights" to a new level. One group of entrepreneurs tried to continue to open the United States to world trade (and enforce property rights), while another feared world trade and wanted either a new regulation of conditions (hours and remuneration of labor in Third World countries) or an elimination of foreign competition. Most of all, the ecology movement pushed property rights to the forefront, because the side effect of wanting to conserve nature from industrial pollution was to deny individuals unconditional property rights. Conservation has cut across class lines in a typical realignment fashion, for corporate owners, workers, and service providers alike find their livelihood threatened by government intrusion on their capacity to act.[32]

If the theory propounded in this chapter holds weight, then another realignment should occur between 2010 and 2020. However, the discussion has now ranged far beyond the usual borders of the historian and such conjectures will be confined to associates.[33] But one parallel between the present and the past will be offered. The violence of the Civil War era came about because the property right being questioned—slavery in the South—was so geographically concentrated. In the current situation, ecological concerns are nationwide, but the areas most upset with them are western states, and the result of this geographical concentration has also had small moments of violence (the "sagebrush rebellion") and realignment (from Democratic Party allegiance to the Republican Party). Of course, the scale of violence is immensely dissimilar but parallels between the two situations exist.

Appendix B

Graphing U.S. Politics, 1840–1860

For three decades, historians and political scientists have used various theories to explain the political explosion that ended the Second Party System (Whigs versus Democrats, 1828–54) and gave birth to the Third Party System (Republicans versus Democrats, 1854–96). The point of contention is what process was at the core of this seismic change. For many scholars, slavery stood foremost as the agent of political transformation. Since the 1960s, however, others have posited the importance of cultural factors in the North—the impact of immigration, ethnic hostilities, and religious animosities (the ethnocultural interpretation). Michael F. Holt has imaginatively argued that the economy after 1846 proved so strong and beneficent that the former Second Party System issues of the tariff, internal improvements, national banking, and western lands lost their salience. In the vacuum created by the demise of these standard economic issues, both the public and the politicians searched for new issues that could make political groupings look different; the Whigs and the Democrats no longer seemed distinct entities because their main area of disagreement had evaporated. Two possibilities appeared. The first, and to some the most powerful, was immigration restriction. This subject particularly concerned the North where massive immigration waves had produced urban turmoil, anger over the rise of Catholicism, distress at a bloated labor market that lowered wage rates, and increased taxes for pauper relief. At the same time, concern over slavery's expansion rose again but did not become vital in popular politics until 1856 when northern politicians manipulated the press and events to manufacture a northern indignation at southern behavior in Congress and in the Kansas Territory. Only then did the slavery issue become important.[1]

The interpretation offered here is that property rights problems connected with slavery after 1846 consumed national politics and was particularly insolvable in the only place it could have been solved, in the halls of Congress. In the preceding chapters, the narrative of events and arguments between 1846 and 1860 was presented in a way that emphasized the omnipresence of property rights arguments—that both northerners and southerners reasoned about slavery in terms of wealth and rights to property. The narrative and arguments by themselves, however, are insufficient to understand the politics of the 1850s. Some attention to elections and voting patterns is vital. By the start of the third millennium, however, it should be clear to most students of antebellum politics that statistical procedures by themselves will not absolutely confirm some interpretations over others. Statistical procedures have certainly revealed religious, ethnic, and class preferences in voting, and they have as well indicated how previous groups in one election have voted in succeeding ones. But the reasons for shifts in partisan voting remain in the realm of inference. That Presbyterians voted for Republicans in and after 1856 fails to establish the primary motive for the political preference of this group to be either anti-immigrant, Protestant cultural mentality, hypersensitivity to the question of the morality of slavery, antisouthernism, or the fear of the slave power.

The analysis offered here is both slightly different from other authors and somewhat simpler. It proceeds by graphing out the percentage of partisan affiliation in congressional districts for elections between 1840 and 1860. Most studies have used townships, counties, and precincts; they have typically been city, state, or, at times, regional studies. The one used herein is national. Congressional districts have been employed because they seem the natural unit for understanding national issues. This study also does not employ ecological regression, logit regression, multiple regression, analysis of variance, and other techniques. These procedures yield extremely fruitful information for short-term analyses but, in all honesty, the wealth of numbers that such techniques have produced have largely bored or overwhelmed historians; moreover, long-term processes became lost. In particular, the timing of change and the places of change may be overlooked because attention is too riveted to short-term variations. Graphical analysis has the potential of showing turning points and, just as important, communicating those results to a wider audience.[2]

The graphical depiction given in this chapter will yield certain basic interpretations. First, it will be suggested that the best theory for antebellum politics is realignment theory. Partisan voting in the Second Party System had a competitiveness and a constancy that may never again be repeated. Second, the first cracking in the Second Party System was in the Deep South and less emphatically but still noticeably in the Border South and the Great Lakes regions. Third, the failure of the Whigs to maintain party strength was the defection of southern Whigs. In the election of 1852, the Whigs actually held their constituency fairly well in the North, but in the Deep South they suffered a disaster. Fourth, the southern realignment makes sense in terms of the issues at stake: the weighty subjects of secession and property rights in slaves replaced the less vital ones of tariffs, banks, internal improvements, and western lands. Given the emphasis of this book, it would make sense that the party system should break down first in the South and then in the North, for the struggle over slavery in the territories most obviously affected southern property rather than northern property.

The slavery issue was primarily responsible for the realignment of politics in the North during the 1850s. While the importance of the Know-Nothings and ethnic hostilities need not be dismissed or downplayed, the immigration problems were secondary to the difficulties over the national question of slavery. The graphical analysis of this chapter intends to give some quantitative evidence based on congressional district voting that favors the primary significance of the slavery issue in tearing the Second Party System apart.

Methodology

Any statistical methodology has procedures, assumptions, and failures that require careful explication. In other words, pages of nonexhilarating reading are required. It was partly this aspect of voter analysis by historians that sent droves of graduate students into the embrace of the return of the narrative, meaning, deconstruction, and literary analysis. Boring though it may be, the presentation is necessary because faulty procedures lead to improper conclusions, and a critical evaluation of any numerical analysis requires an understanding of problems in data collection and tabulation.

The basic procedure was to use congressional districts for the unit of analysis between 1840 and 1860 for state, congressional, and presidential elections. By selecting the pertinent elections, one can then derive a series of partisan voting percentages over time that may reveal constancy, constant fluctuations, or sudden breaks. Moreover, I used regions to group election districts. Those regions are the Great Lakes (Ohio, Indiana, Illinois, Wisconsin, and Michigan), Middle Atlantic (New York, Pennsylvania, and New Jersey), New England (Massachusetts, Connecticut, Vermont, New Hampshire, and Maine), Border South (North Carolina, Virginia, Kentucky, and Tennessee), and the Deep South (Georgia, Alabama, Mississippi, and Louisiana). Not all the states are represented obviously, but enough so that generalizations for the nation may be hazarded with some expectation of success (out of 236 congressional districts in 1860, this study uses 174). To ensure a continuity over the same geographical units over time, the disturbance of reapportionment had to be dealt with. Between 1850 and 1853, the states redrew their congressional boundaries in accordance with census returns. That redrawing of congressional district boundaries can make a large difference in the computation of how a district voted over time (after all, the politicos who redraw the boundaries do so for obvious political advantages), so I adopted the procedure of using the configuration of congressional districts in 1860 as the standard. The election results of the 1840s were then recomputed by taking the counties (as they existed) between 1840 and 1853 and reassembling them into the congressional districts of the 1850s. Moreover, I figured all state and presidential elections in terms of congressional district results because usually sources reported state and presidential elections by counties; the electoral returns for presidential and state offices in the 1840s were thus placed in the congressional district configurations of the 1850s.[3]

Once the vote tallies for the congressional districts were obtained, they were then put into percentage form in two ways. One was a calculation based on percentage of eligible voters. To determine the eligible voter pool, I used the censuses of 1840, 1850, and 1860, aggregated the counties into congressional districts of the 1850s, and then computed an estimate of white males over the age of twenty-one years (in effect, that meant adding all the categories of white males over age thirty plus nine-tenths of the white males between age twenty and twenty-nine). This figure was not adjusted for immigrants, and so the extent of nonvoting may be exaggerated in the North, but it should nonetheless serve the purpose of showing in a relative sense how nonvoting rose and fell over the two decades. The second calculation was based on the percentage of the vote that a party obtained in an election. The summing was done by region—that is, the average vote obtained was formed by using congressional districts as the unit of analysis in the Great Lakes, the Middle Atlantic, New England, Border South, and Deep South regions. These percentage points were then plotted over time to form a graph of partisan voting. To choose elections for these points, I adhered to the following rule: presidential elections took precedence first, then congressional elections, then state elections.

To pursue elections over time, the counties had to remain intact from one reapportionment to another. When redistricters split counties and moved the fragments of counties from one congressional district to another, I could not arrange the vote tallies of the 1840s into the 1850s congressional district alignment because the vote returns were almost always in terms of counties. Moreover, estimating the eligible electorate would be extremely difficult because the published census reports were for either townships or counties. Thus I had to eliminate congressional districts in which a part of a county was included in the congressional district. This procedure had several distinct effects. First, all urban areas were eliminated because following precinct returns was too difficult, and I had no assurance that precinct boundaries were not changing. This had the greatest impact in the states of New York and Pennsylvania. The cities of Philadelphia, Pittsburgh, and New York City are not included in this study. The same holds true for New Orleans, Cincinnati, and Boston. In some instances, congressional districts were eliminated simply because for some reasons legislators chose to fragment counties in the formation of congressional districts. The reduction has worked this way: Ohio had twenty-one districts, nineteen of which are included in this study; New York had thirty-three, of which I used twenty-three; Pennsylvania had twenty-five, of which sixteen are incorporated; Louisiana had four, and I counted only two. Basically the results given in the figures speak to the voting patterns of nonurban American citizens.

And then there is the special problem of the New England states. They were a disaster in terms of the research agenda of this study. Some of the New England states had congressional districts based on counties, but largely they were determined by townships. That meant not only a potentially monstrous job of aggregation (and aggravation), but even worse many of the congressional districts were composed of fragments of townships. No wonder the South wanted to secede! Among the reasons for using congressional districts for the units of analysis is that the congressional districts are close in terms of population; they possessed fairly standard populations over a long stretch of time. This condition eliminated the need for weighting and other intrusive operations (which, given existing techniques, inflates the number of cases by such a large amount that the typical probability statistics are meaningless). Because New England proved to be research-design recalcitrant, I used county voting for the presidency and gubernatorial races (which occurred nearly every year between 1840 and 1860), then weighted the counties by the square root of the eligible electorate in the county. This weighting had to be done because of the population variation in the counties; for example, Essex County in Vermont had at most only 1,700 voters, while Middlesex County in Massachusetts had nearly 60,000. Because I had eliminated urban areas in the rest of the districts I employed, I did the same for Massachusetts and removed Essex County (Boston).

But the situation in New England was even worse than this. I could not use congressional voting at all. Some states in New England voted for congressional members in odd years (Connecticut, New Hampshire, and Rhode Island) while the others did so in even years (Maine, Massachusetts, and Vermont). Despite the mountain of studies on New England, it was the smallest regional bloc in Congress (only possessing twenty-nine congressmen), and splitting its delegation into two normally produced a number of cases too small to make the average reliable. Thus, very unfortunately, congressional voting had to factored out for New England.

Problems

Beyond counties split into parts for congressional districts and the statistically inhospitable nature of the New England states, a host of other problems arose. For one, states did not always have annual elections. New York and Pennsylvania, it turns out, almost always had some state officer up for election. Not so the other states. Governors were elected, but other state offices, such as treasurer, secretary of state, controller, and Supreme Court judges were either not elected officials or the voting went unrecorded. Votes for the assembly frequently only yielded party victors, not individual vote tallies. The consequence is that in the figures some years have no elections at all; for presentation's sake, the graph does not break at the missing election year but connects with the next closest point. This situation was made worse when state offices and congressional elections occurred simultaneously. This was especially the case in the South where gubernatorial and congressional elections came in odd years. In this vein, it should also be mentioned that state office elections (and in the

1840s congressional voting) came at different times within the regions. Thus Illinois, Indiana, and Michigan might vote for governor in one year, but not Ohio and Wisconsin. Generally I tried to insure that at least one-half of the states were voting in a given year, but when the number of cases became too small—frequently the case for the southern states—then I simply had to skip that election year. The appendix contains the list of the state races for the states used in this analysis, and another table indicates the number of cases for the elections.

A lack of election returns often afflicted this study, particularly in the 1840s. To some extent these problems could be overborne by checking newspapers and other sources, but a fundamental difficulty often arose. Sometimes the returns provided not a county breakdown but just the congressional district results. Because all results had to be set in the 1850s congressional district configuration by counties, it was impossible to use such information.

A perplexing problem was the existence of degraded election returns and uncontested elections. For some reason, the sources never obtained the complete results, one or two counties failing to report anything but which candidate obtained a majority. More problematic was the existence of uncontested elections. A few occurred in the North—Illinois had at least two (William A. Bissell and William A. Richardson in 1848), and Pennsylvania one (John Dick in 1854)—but the majority occurred in the South. Of the southern states, the worst by far was Virginia. When enough returns existed, I trusted Dame Fortuna and recorded the vote, imperfect though it was. When the election was uncontested, I recorded the winner as 100 and the loser as 0. Sometimes the vote for the winner was recorded but usually was not. In any event, how to interpret these results statistically is a real difficulty because the motivation of the nonvoters is unintelligible. Does the opposition refuse to vote because it supports the other candidate, or has the party given up the chance of victory? The extent of uncontested elections makes the amount of nonvoting in the southern elections enormously suspect.[4]

Although election data for the 1840s proved more inaccessible than one might expect, I have plodded onward with the material I have. My belief is that enough returns prior to 1847 exist so that the essential pattern of party voting per region appears and can be used to fashion interpretations. It must be noted that the level of aggregation in this study is the congressional district (except for Live Free or Die New Englanders), and that a different level of aggregation might produce different patterns.[5]

The Graphical Analysis of United States Voting by Region, 1840–1853

There are now three large theories of American voting, each of which has a number of subtheories for parts of the election process. They are realignment theory, the theory of retrospective voting, and the theory of prospective voting.

Retrospective theory argues that voters determine their party preferences based on how well the party in power performed over the immediate electoral period. Thus one may obtain significant swings in party preference as voters change their minds about how the incumbent party has functioned. Prospective voting theory is similar except that voters cast their ballots for parties that promise to enact policies that the voter favors.[6]

Realignment theory is perhaps the oldest theory of voting, and until recently historians have favored it. However, since 1990 some political scientists have looked upon it with disfavor because, among other reasons, it has nearly completely failed to explain voting after 1970. Realignment theory posits that groups form opinions or attitudes toward parties during "defining moments" in a society's history when some great problem or upheaval presents itself. Over a period of two to three decades, that set of issues persists; and the groups that initially took positions on those issues persist in their partisan affections as well. Families then socialize youth into partisan attachments, explaining why one party is unfair and one is not, and thereby perpetuate the group's identification with a party. However, periodically—meaning every twenty-five to thirty-two years—the social firmament changes. Population change, economic change, foreign affairs, or some circumstance new to the society intrudes in a powerful way. The old parties try to run on the issues that gave them strength and fail to respond adequately to the new issue. The public becomes upset with the inability of the old parties to deal with the novel situation; in particular, young voters not completely socialized into partisan feelings and previous nonvoters start moving into new associations. Third parties proliferate until either two new parties are formed or one of the old parties disappears. At first, scholars referred to "critical elections" as signals of the rise of new parties, but in practice they tend to use realignment years. In any event, the groups that once had firm partisan attachments undergo change; they reshuffle their loyalties in the new party system. And this is known as the theory of realignment —the voting blocs of the old party system realign themselves to form a new party system. Even if the names of the parties do not change, the supporters of those parties do. The theory of realignment arose not only to explain the periodicity of American party developments but also to show how democratic politics actually altered policies. During the stable phase of realignment, the issue base of politics is repetitive and resistant to change. Actual policy is perhaps due to pressure groups as to any other factor. But realignment alters the issue landscape and changes the agenda as to what policies Congress may or may not consider.[7]

In a small way this study can test certain propositions of realignment theory. The obvious inference is that party voting over time should be quite stable given the fluctuations of turnout for different types of election races (i.e., the amount of interest in the election). Third-party voting and power should be easy to chart and interpret in terms of cracking the major party system. Also, if realignment holds weight, the points at which the parties collapse should be obvious and sharp.

The Southern Realignment, 1840–1853

Before we begin the investigation of election results, some aspects of the congressional division by regions of the United States deserve comment. Table B.1 offers the number of actual congressional districts by state and region in the United States in 1850 and 1860. Certain conclusions leap out from this table. Although the number of free and slave states has usually drawn the most interest (basically indicating the balance in the Senate), the congressional districts tell a much different story. First, the two allegedly "radical" portions of the Union on the slavery issue were the smallest. New England only had twenty-nine congressmen and the Deep South only thirty-three. Even when combined the New England and the Deep South states barely have more members than the Great Lakes states or the Border South states, and less than the Middle Atlantic region. One has to ask how these two sections managed to embroil the country in Civil War when they were numerically so insignificant. Indeed, one has to ask why there are so many studies of the New England states and why Massachusetts and South Carolina in particular are so deserving of scholarly attention. Massachusetts in 1860 had no more congressmen than Indiana, and barely more than Illinois, Tennessee, and Kentucky. Virginia in 1860 still was a populous and powerful state, yet the studies on the Mother of States in the antebellum years is a short list indeed.[8] Looking at these numbers reinforces how badly the economy, culture, and society of the United States have been interpreted in the past few decades. The population of the country is in the middle, not the extremes. Yet because Boston and its environs became industrial, scholars have insisted that all the country was in the grips of rampant industrialism. Because South Carolina and Mississippi, with their less than overwhelming total of eleven congressmen, were violently proslavery and patriarchal, we assume all the South was. This is balderdash.

Two other facets from Table B.1 demand attention. Three states were the pivot of American politics—New York, Pennsylvania, and Ohio; they had seventy-nine of the nation's congressmen, fully one-third of the total. So why has there not been a proliferation of studies of these states? They hold more of the key to antebellum politics than anyone else, with one exception. If any region has been lost in antebellum studies—political, cultural, economic, or on any standard—it is the Border South. In 1860 it housed fifty-six congressmen and was markedly more important than the Great Lakes region. Yet studies on this section are far and few between. In a broader sense, the Border South is the key region. Together with their descendants in Illinois, Indiana, Ohio, and Pennsylvania, they probably had influence in seventy-five or so congressional districts. The Border South by itself should have stopped the process leading to

TABLE B.1. *Congressional Seat Distribution, by State and Region*

Region/State	*Congressional Delegation Total 1850*	*Regional Total 1850*	*Congressional Delegation Total 1860*	*Regional Total 1860*
New England				
Connecticut	4		4	
Maine	7		6	
Massachusetts	10	31	11	29
Rhode Island	2		2	
New Hampshire	4		3	
Vermont	4		3	
Middle Atlantic				
New York	34		33	
Pennsylvania	24	63	25	63
New Jersey	5		5	
Great Lakes				
Ohio	21		21	
Indiana	10		11	
Illinois	7	46	9	51
Michigan	3		4	
Wisconsin	3		3	
Iowa	2		2	
Minnesota	0		1	
Border South				
Maryland	6		6	
Virginia	15		13	
Tennessee	11		10	
Kentucky	10	58	10	56
North Carolina	9		8	
Missouri	5		7	
Arkansas	1		1	
Delaware	1		1	
Deep South				
South Carolina	7		6	
Alabama	7		7	
Georgia	8	33	8	33
Mississippi	4		5	
Louisiana	4		4	
Texas	2		2	
Florida	1		1	
Far West				
California	2	2	2	3
Oregon			1	
Total	233		236	

Source: Tabulated from Moore, *Congressional Quarterly's Guide to U.S. Elections.*

Civil War in 1860; it had none of the Deep South's commitment to slavery in the long run, it had an outlook favorable to economic development, it housed an active Whig element—and, if it had united politically, it had the power to stalemate the country and force a compromise on the New England and Deep South sections (if any, the 36 degree 30 minute line with an agreement to end landed expansion altogether). I would argue that the failure of compromise over slavery in the antebellum decade was the failure of the Border South to assert itself. And I would conjecture that the reason for the failure was that settling the issue of property rights was simply too great a hurdle for compromisers to make. The nature of the argument pulled the Border South to the Deep South's side—the need to maintain property rights in slaves—instead of separating them and enabling the Border South to dictate terms to the Deep South and threaten armed retaliation if necessary.[9]

Figures B.1–5 present the extent of nonvoting in the regions of the United States. Probably the most obvious fact is that presidential contests drew out the electorate more than any others, except at certain times in the South. Generally, people voted in state and congressional elections with about equal fervor. But there were distinct differences. Nonvoting overall was, surprisingly, highest in the New England states. This may be an artifact of not adjusting the total eligible electorate by eliminating immigrant noncitizens, but then none of the districts elsewhere were so adjusted and yet they show nonvoting rates similar to other studies.[10] New Englanders, it would seem, were not as politically motivated as were other people in the nation. Southerners were avid voters; they flocked to the polls as well, if not better, than anyone else. However, southerners in both the Border and Deep South states found state contests, especially governor's races, distinctly more exciting than did northerners. It is also clear from Figures B.4 and 5 that after 1851 southerners were abstaining from congressional races in great numbers. In fact, in all the figures it is obvious that voters made distinctions between state, congressional, and presidential races. Many of these elections were simultaneously held, especially state and congressional elections, and it is apparent that voters were making distinct choices about supporting candidates based on different issues. This argues that a significant number of voters had some concept about different issues operating on the state and national levels.

Nonvoting had some interesting patterns in all the regions. In the Great Lakes region, a spike occurred in the state and congressional elections of 1848. That was evidently due to the Liberty Party and Free-Soil Party insurgency and the willingness of Whigs, especially, to back Democrats opposed to slavery's territorial extension. Quite interestingly, the Great Lakes region does not show an aberration in the state races of 1853, but the Middle Atlantic region does. Elsewhere, the state elections of 1853 show no major deviation from earlier nonvoting patterns. The interpretation that the Second Party System collapsed in 1853 should really be refined to a collapse in New York, Pennsylvania, and

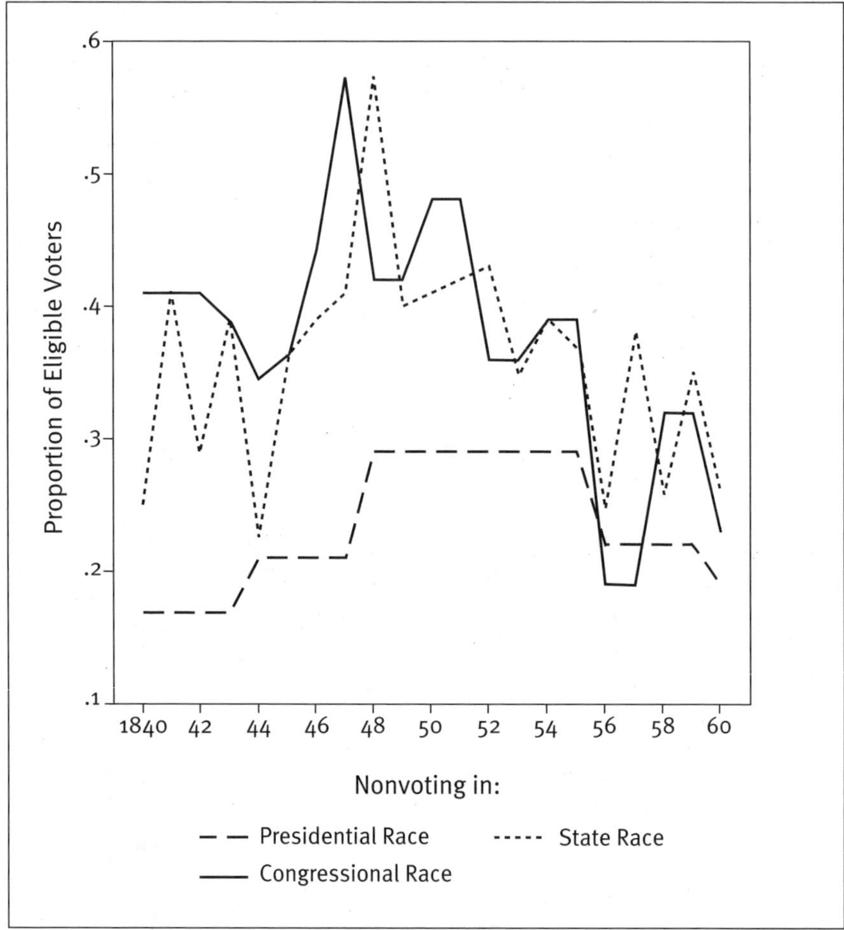

FIGURE B.1. *Great Lakes Nonvoting, 1840–1860*

New Jersey.[11] However, it should be pointed out that in the Middle Atlantic region nonvoting after a presidential election normally spiked anyway. The likely explanation is that those elections were nongubernatorial and noncongressional, thereby sparking little interest. Another set of spikes in the graphs of nonvoting occur at the congressional election of 1851 in the Border South and the presidential election of 1852 in the Deep South. The questions of secession and acceptance of the Compromise of 1850 dominated the congressional elections of 1851, and it may have been that a confused electorate in the Border South chose not to vote. Compared with the robust turnout in the Border South state elections of 1851, the small vote for congressional candidates in that region is remarkable. In the Deep South, one obtains a spike in nonvoting in 1852 that has no duplicate in any other region except for a small

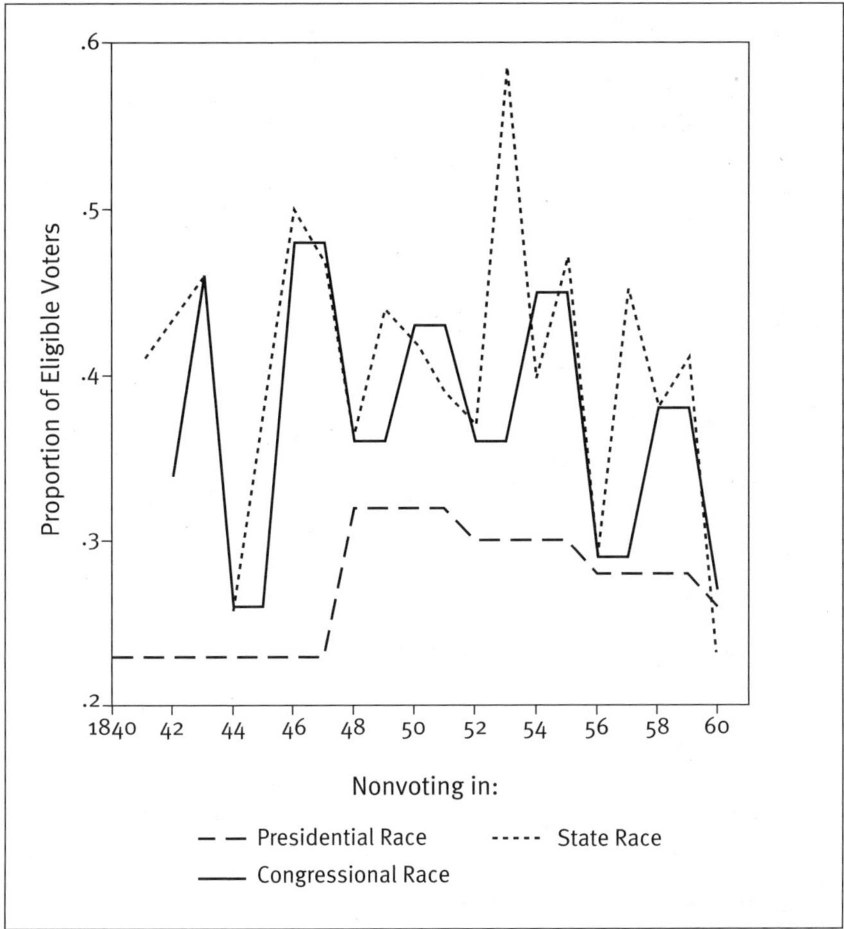

FIGURE B.2. *Middle Atlantic Nonvoting, 1840–1860: Presidential, Congressional, and State Races*

increase in New England. This circumstance made the election of 1852 remarkable. As will appear in the graphs of partisan voting, the Whigs retained their normal support throughout the nation—except for the Deep South where it nearly totally collapsed.[12] Oddly enough, contemporaries did not remark on this circumstance. Although politicians and editors frequently talked and wrote about nonvoters and analyzed elections with some thoroughness, no one explicitly wrote down that the Whig failure in 1852 was in the Deep South.[13]

One other observation merits consideration. All the figures (save the Border South and Deep South in congressional nonvoting) show a common trait. Nonvoting in the early part of the 1840s had a distinct pattern of numbering between 20 and 40 percent for most elections. Starting in 1846 (but more

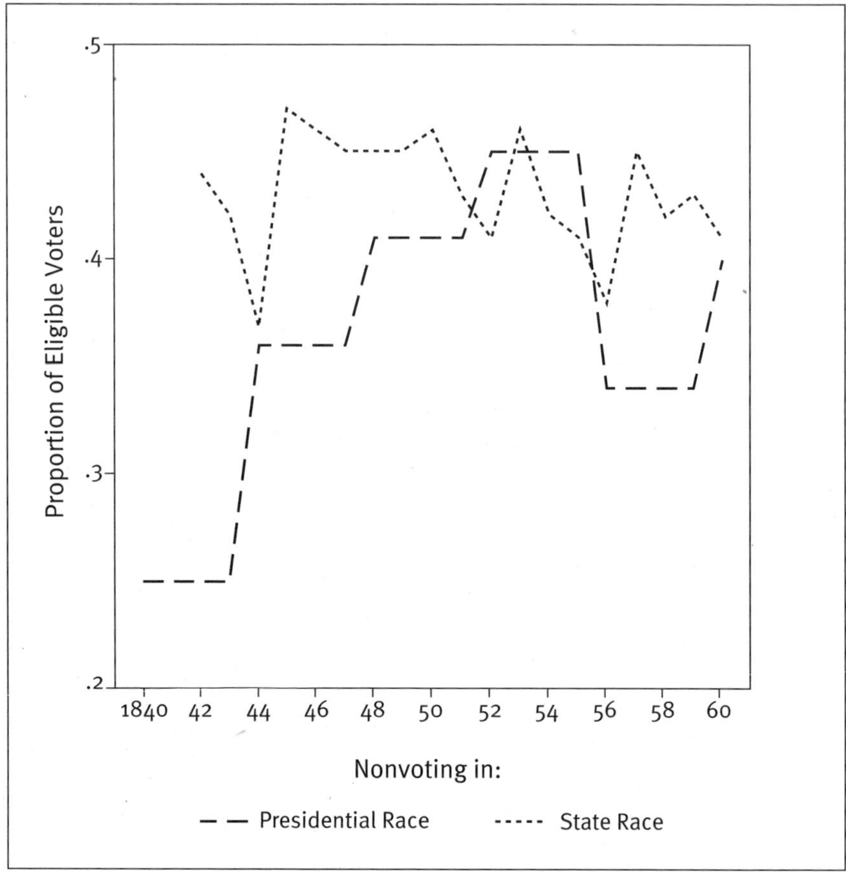

FIGURE B.3. *New England Nonvoting, 1840–1860: Presidential and State Races*

distinctly in 1848) and then lasting until 1856, nonvoting rises for all types of elections and in all regions. I have no evidence to support this explanation, which reduces it to speculation, but it would seem that the introduction of the slavery issue so jolted the entire country that a large segment of the voting population became confused. After eight years of debate, voters made decisions about how they would stand on the question of slavery's expansion into the territories. After 1856, nonvoting, except for congressional races in the South, began to trend downward.

Voting by partisan affiliation between 1840 and 1860 in the five regions is given in Figures B.6–10. The elections are a combination of presidential, congressional, and state races. The presidential elections were used in 1840, 1844, 1848, and 1852. Depending on when the region held congressional elections, those were used for nonpresidential voting years (for example, in the Middle Atlantic region, 1846, 1850), and state races in those years having neither

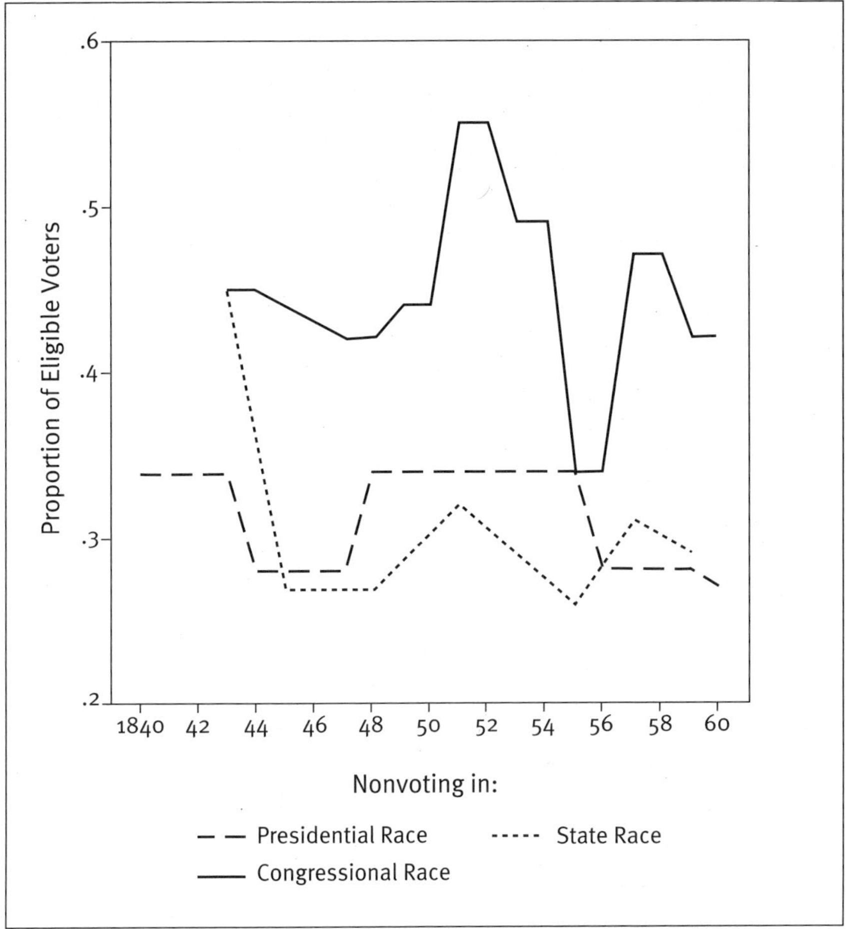

FIGURE B.4. *Border South Nonvoting, 1840–1860: Presidential, Congressional, and State Races*

presidential nor congressional contests. The points plotted are for each party's percentage of votes cast—that is, of the total vote at that election, rather than the percentage of eligible voters. Modern voting studies emphasize incorporation of nonvoters in the analysis because nonvoting is actually a viable choice of the electorate, and so current practice favors using percentages based on the eligible voter pool. In most forms of analysis, that procedure is indisputably correct, but in this instance of looking at patterns over time the calculation of party performance relying on percentage of votes cast yields superior information.[14] Because of the different drawing power of the various types of races—gubernatorial, congressional, and presidential—the results graphically fluctuate considerably. When the figures use percentages of votes cast, these devia-

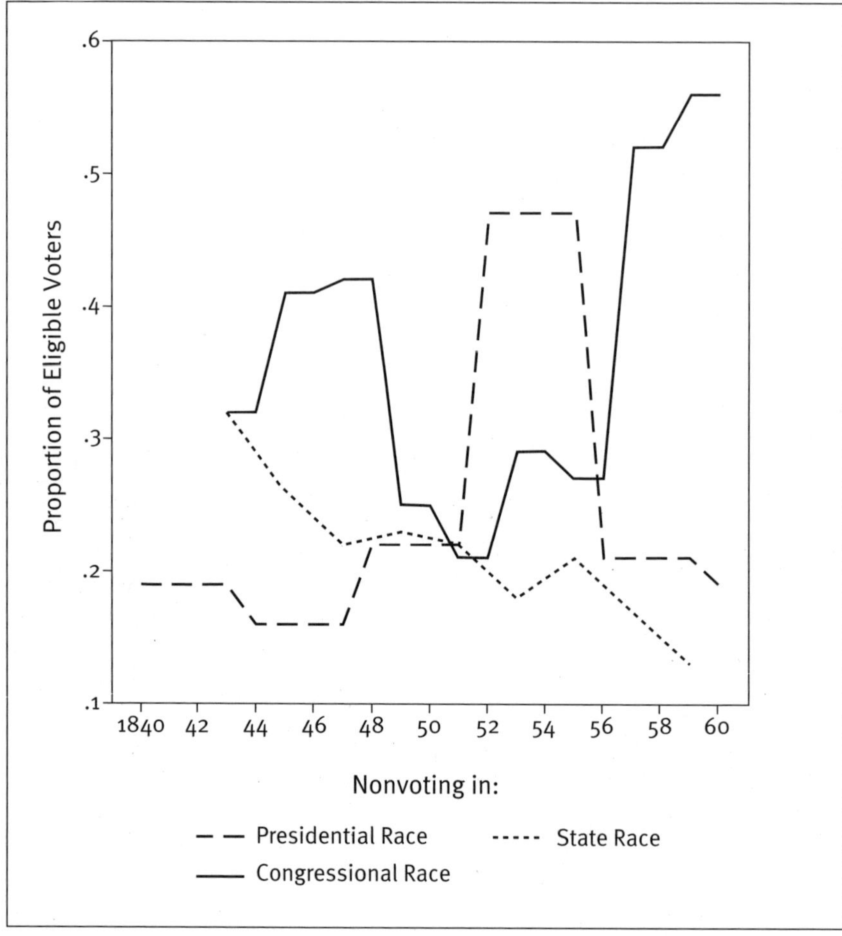

FIGURE B.5. *Deep South Nonvoting, 1840–1860: Presidential, Congressional, and State Races*

tions lessen considerably, and for the years 1840–53 the representations of party voting flatten out. Over time, the parties obtained a fairly stable percentage of the vote cast, with some fluctuations, but seldom deviating more than a few percentage points. Each election seemingly generated a level of excitement; that excitement apparently drove out Whigs, Democrats, and third-party voters in proportions about equal to the numbers they normally obtained. When the excitement abated, the drop-off in voting also fell proportionately. It may very well be that there is a constant confusion from one election to the next with voters switching parties, joining and then leaving the ranks of nonvoters, and surges in party support from new voters. Yet one would expect to see more variation in the the proportion of votes parties obtained per election.

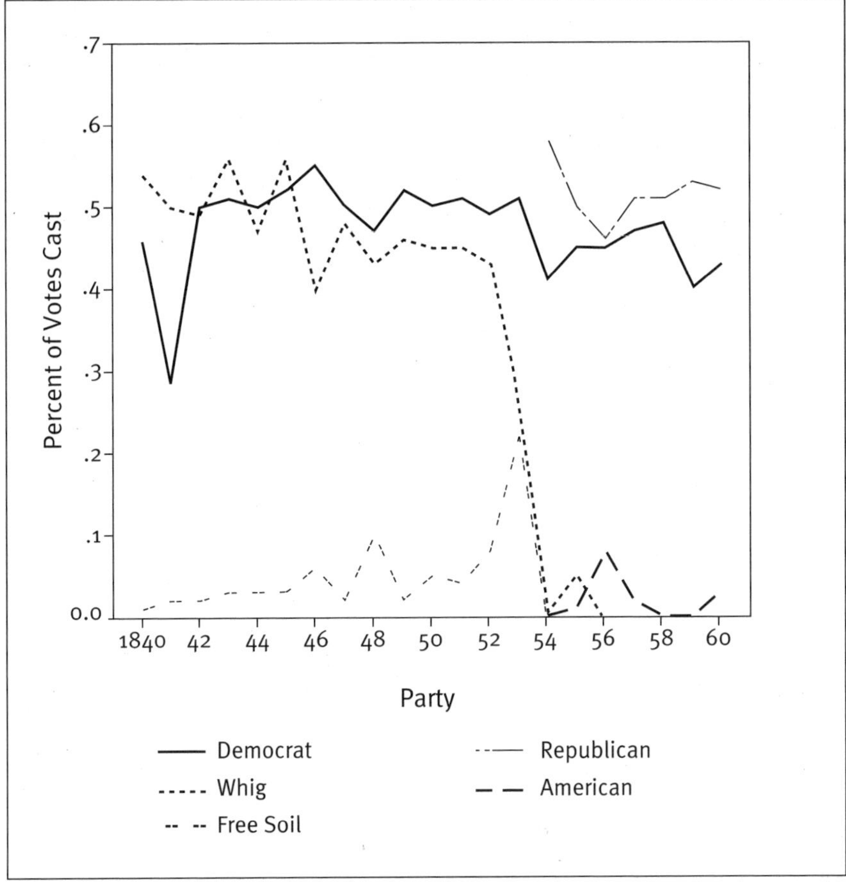

FIGURE B.6. *Great Lakes Party Voting (of Votes Cast), 1840–1860: Combination of Presidential, Congressional, and State Races*

What one sees, however, is constancy.[15] From Figures B.6–10, one sees confirmation of the interpretation that so many political historians have made about the Second Party System: it was national and competitive.[16]

These figures reveal important features of the Second Party System as it moved into the 1850s. First, the Whigs and Democrats were usually competitive in all regions of the country—that is, the curves of Whig and Democrat voting are fairly close to one another. Second, there were fluctuations of party triumph. Sometimes the Whigs held the ascendancy, other times the Democrats. It would seem that by the middle 1840s the Democrats had clearly outdistanced the Whigs in the Great Lakes region (Figure B.6). Some might be surprised by the near equivalence of Whigs and Democrats in New England (Figure B.8), usually considered safe Whig territory. The reason for this misinterpretation has been the focus on Massachusetts. True enough, the Bay State

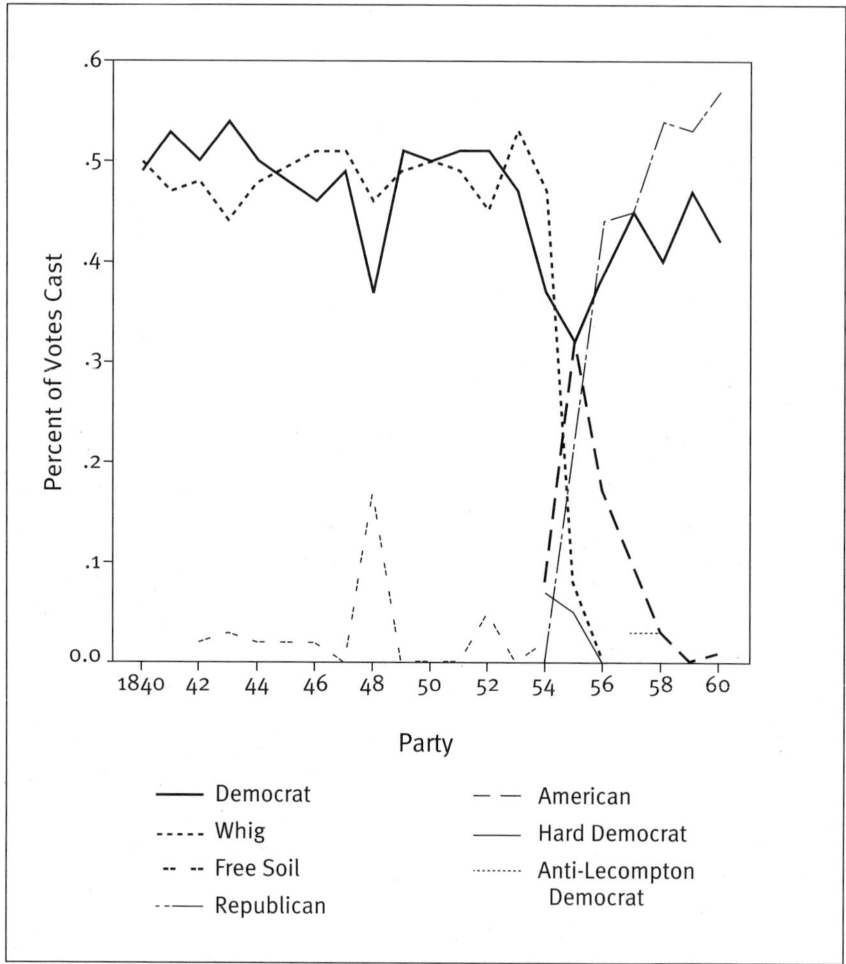

FIGURE B.7. *Middle Atlantic Party Voting (of Votes Cast), 1840–1860: Combination of Presidential, Congressional, and State Races*

was almost solid Whig; of its ten congressional delegates elected in 1848, eight were Whigs, two were Free-Soilers, and none were Democrats. But the rest of New England between 1848 and 1851 was more Democrat than Whig. The state of Maine was considered one of the jewels of the Democratic Party, Connecticut tipped toward the Democrats, and Rhode Island was fairly evenly divided. Of the forty-two congressmen elected between 1848 and 1851 in New England excluding Massachusetts, twenty-nine were Democrats. Only Massachusetts disrupted the tendency to the Democratic Party in New England. Whig strength actually centered in the Middle Atlantic and Border South regions—and if one excluded Virginia from the Border South, the Whig nature of the Border South would be overwhelming (Figures B.7 and 9).

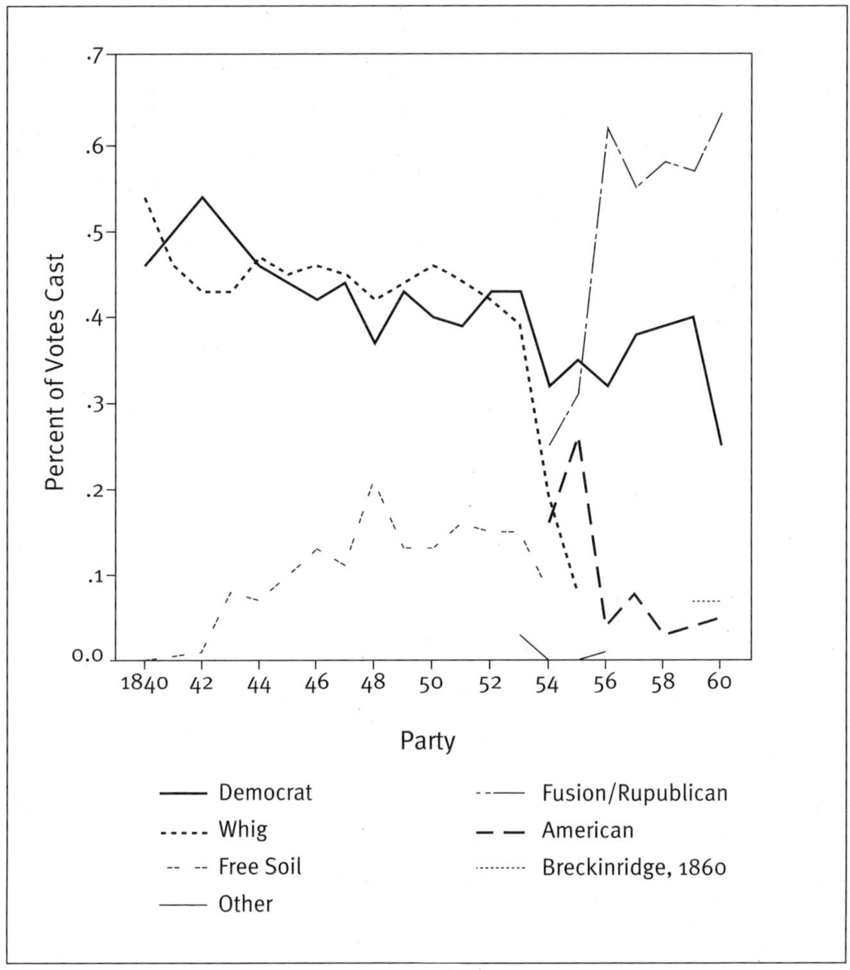

FIGURE B.8. *New England Party Voting (of Votes Cast), 1840–1860: Combination of Presidential and State Races*

Third parties have a marginal existence in these figures. The Great Lakes (Figure B.6) showed a blip in 1848, and in the 1853 state races a segment of Whigs evidently flowed over to the Free-Soilers. Between 1842 and 1848, the Liberty Party (or a local abolitionist organization in some districts) hardly counted. Even more marginal were antislavery parties in the Middle Atlantic Region (Figure B.7). Both Pennsylvania and New Jersey were stolid states that barely harbored a free thinker; even David Wilmot admitted that in the Keystone State only his district had antislavery convictions.[17] New York's experience with the Liberty Party was inconsequential, and while the Free-Soiler's caused some problems for the Democratic Party in 1848, it appeared to be only

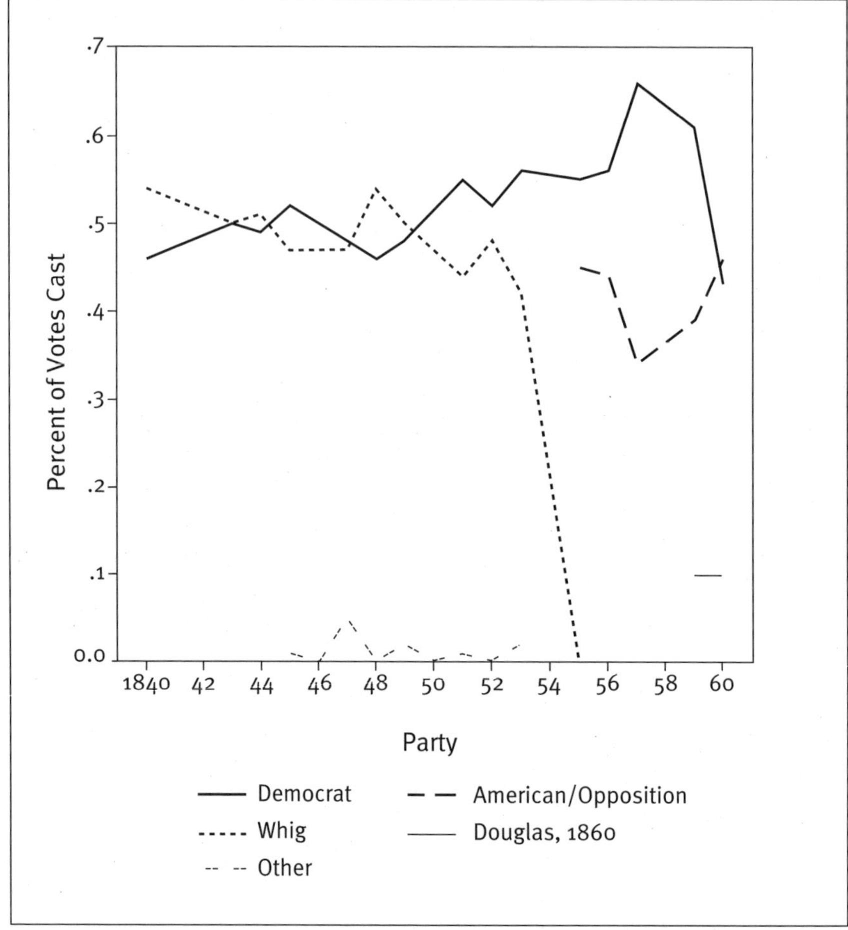

FIGURE B.9. *Border South Party Voting (of Votes Cast), 1840–1860: Combination of Presidential, Congressional, and State Races*

a momentary phenomenon, lending some credence to the view that in New York revenge against southern domination of the party mostly motivated the Free-Soilers. However, the Liberty Party and then the Free-Soilers had a more visible and persistent presence in the New England states—all of them, not just Massachusetts (Figure B.8). While these antislavery parties never captured more than 10 percent of the vote, they nonetheless carried political weight. In elections where the parties were so evenly matched, this large regiment of antislavery voters could only be viewed as vital to both parties. Thus in New England both the Whigs and Democrats wooed the antislavery vote—inducing increasing revulsion among party stalwarts in the South who translated such behavior into an interpretation that all northern parties were antislavery.

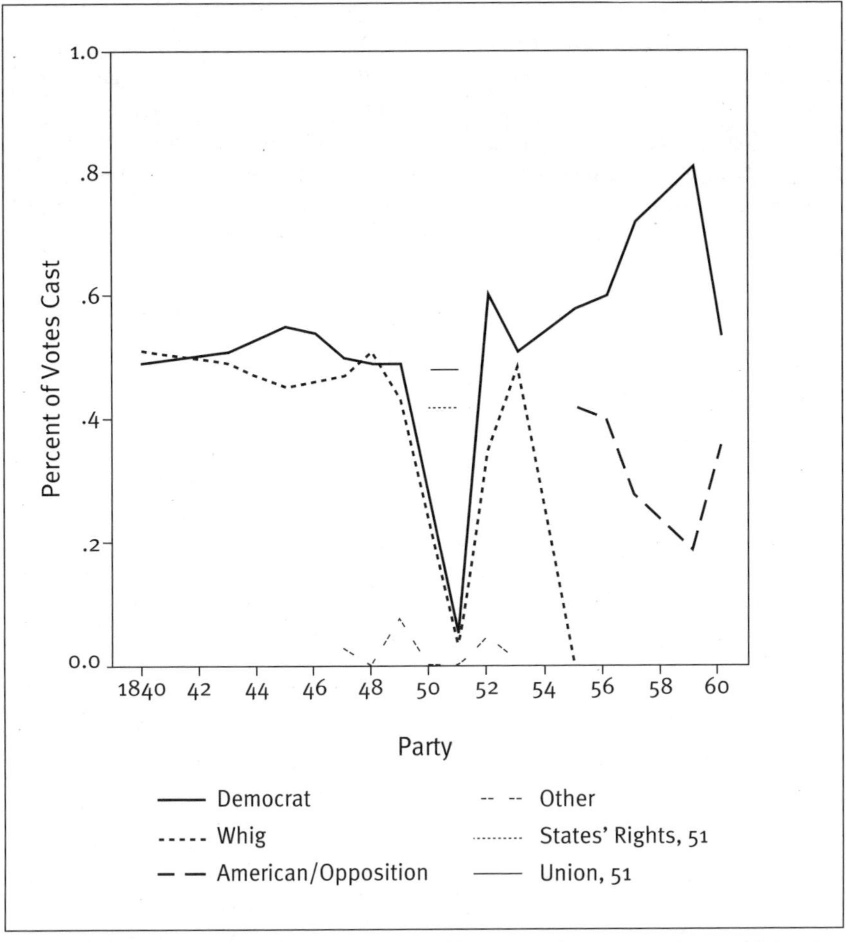

FIGURE B.10. *Deep South Party Voting (of Votes Cast), 1840–1860: Combination of Presidential, Congressional, and State Races*

In the South, a different story unfolds. Third parties did not exist; the dotted lines in Figures B.9 and 10 show intraparty personality feuds that erupted every once in a while in the congressional districts and did not represent the breakdown of political organizations. The major change to note in the Border South was the surge in Democratic power during the congressional elections of 1851. The figure for Deep South voting (Figure B.10), however, is the dramatic regional chart. Here the pattern of fairly constant voting and party competition breaks manifestly at the congressional elections of 1851. The rather consistent pattern of Whig and Democratic Party strength disappears in the congressional elections of 1851, and in the presidential election of 1852 Democrats climbed to a new height of supremacy while the Whigs performed much lower than they had ever done in the Second Party System. The Democrats and Whigs received a reprieve, it would seem, in the congressional elections (and state elections) of 1853, returning to somewhat accustomed positions of relative strength. Nonetheless, it was in the Deep South that the Second Party System first crashed; it commenced the realignment of the 1850s.

The congressional elections of 1851 require additional explanation because it begins to obtain the attributes of a "critical election," at least in regional terms. The emphasis upon this election as a critical one is manifold. First, party leaders assumed that they had to jettison old party names. In 1851 in Georgia, Alabama, and Mississippi, the names Whig and Democrat were dropped in favor of Constitutional Union Party and States' Rights Party. Although there was name confusion in this election ("States' Rights Whig"; "Constitutional Union Democrat"), the fact that the old parties no longer seemed appropriate reference points for determining issues signaled a failure of the old party system to function correctly. For voters socialized into partisan preferences, one would expect recalcitrance to giving up party identification except under immense pressure. Second, the new parties were not just stalking horses for the old parties. The Constitutional Union Party swept state races (in Georgia, Howell Cobb won the governorship, and in Mississippi, Henry S. Foote did so as well) by substantial margins. Whigs certainly supported the Constitutional Union Party, but they had to have attracted considerable numbers of Democrats. Moreover, voter turnout for this congressional election in the Deep South was unusually high, as good as in presidential races (see Figure B.5).[18] Additionally, the pattern of voting after 1851 in the Deep South changed. The Constitutional Union and States' Rights parties did not continue after 1851, although party name confusion seemed to persist for a while in Alabama. But Democrat hegemony in the Deep South soared, while the Whigs, with the exception of 1853, began their withering decline into nonexistence.[19]

The older historiography was correct. The first sectional battle over the issue of slavery in the territories transformed the political landscape. The realignment of American politics had begun, and its origin was the southern reaction to the northern demand that slavery be prohibited from expanding into the newly acquired territories. It only makes sense that this should be so. As William L. Yancey said at the 1848 Baltimore Democratic convention, "Far different is it [the influence of this issue] with the South. They own the property which the success of this principle will prevent them from carrying with them to the Territories."[20] Property rights in slavery—the wealth and income the institution represented—were issues that far outweighed any issues the Second Party System fought over. No one should have any trouble understanding why the realignment of American politics started in the South and was powered by fears of property rights.

The Northern Realignment, 1854–1860

The northern reaction to the slavery issue was in many respects a top-to-bottom phenomenon, although this is not meant at all to belittle grass-roots antislavery sentiment. The problem that continually pressed on the entire electoral system was the inability of Congress to overcome the slavery expansion issue. Probably leaders were more ideologically driven than their constituents, and they found themselves incapable of resolving this issue, behind which stood the ultimate fate of slavery (at least in many imaginations—most important, southern ones). Leaders communicated their constant turmoil in Congress to constituents through the party system and probably gave voice to a number of highly unflattering descriptions of southerners and southern demands.

The American electoral system was (and is) a federal one, and the parties have to operate well on all levels for a continued existence. Somehow parties have to produce a unified platform for both state and national issues; running on one level but not the other would lead to eventual disappearance to a competitor that could operate on both levels. In this sense, one can conceive of the means by which slavery-related issues came to dominate northern politics. Due to the congressional battle over slavery, that subject gravitated downward into congressional elections and there citizens became more aware of the controversy. Given the continuity of the fight over the extension of slavery and its failure to achieve resolution, the pressure to declare public positions on the issue was unrelenting. On the other hand, one might consider nativism more of a grass-roots movement—stronger in certain localities than in others—in which political pressure was exerted in state elections. The two pressures met each other in 1854, slavery-related issues descending from above in the congressional districts, nativism rising from below in the state elections. Nativism had difficulty penetrating the congressional districts, and it was vulnerable to any changes in immigration flows or economic conditions. Moreover, the Know-Nothings as a party depended for existence on its spread to other regions of the country; those other regions might have different responses given the set of potential issues. Nativism was actually centered along the east coast. Once one traveled over the Appalachian Mountains, its appeal vis-à-vis the slavery issue diminished quickly. In addition, nativism had for northerners the problem of being attached to the South and its proslavery demands. Finally, antislavery had the advantage of having widespread favorable sentiment throughout the North and thereby could draw in nativists on the basis of antislavery, whereas the reverse was not quite so true-antislavery northerners were not necessarily attracted to nativism.[21]

So what happened was the leadership crisis at the top of the political heap—congressional leaders—pushed their issue downward to, in truth, a willing public. The push upward from nativism in the localities was confined to certain geographical areas and weakened over time due to the southern connection, to a continuous uproar over the territories, and to the lessening immigrant influx after 1854. Because the congressional issue of slavery was relentless and growing, it simply overrode the pressure of nativism and finally swamped the states with the slavery issue. This is not to say that the grass roots were manipulated into antislavery, for the sentiment was already there and powerful; but it is to say the basic source of sectional friction was the political leadership.[22]

Table B.2 provides the victors in congressional races in the regions of the country (all states included except the Far West) between 1844 and 1860. Examination of the chart gives an indication of how the realignment of the 1850s moved. Although this material could be presented graphically, the numbers by themselves are quite obvious. In the New England states, the Democrats consistently elected about ten Democrats to Congress from 1844 to 1854. Then, in the years of 1854 and 1855, the Democratic representatives of New England disappeared. The Whigs died out as well. Replacing them were the hyphenated groups of Americans, Republicans, fusionists, and temperance advocates. By 1856–57 the Republicans had emerged as the hegemonic force in congressional elections, winning everything except for one Constitutional Union victory in Boston in 1860. Nearly as dramatic was the experience of the Great Lakes states. There the emergence of the Republicans in 1854 was almost instantaneous and overwhelming; the Democrats lost nearly one-half of their congressional numbers. Confusion reigned in the Middle Atlantic states. Whigs and Democrats there almost exchanged victory positions every two years. However, it appears that the Democrats suffered a permanent loss after 1854. Who won was not immediately clear for Whigs, Know-Nothings, Fusion-Unionists ("People's" parties), and Republicans vied for party dominance until the Republicans sealed their supremacy in 1860.

Table B.2 foreshadows Republican victory on antislavery grounds in three ways, however. First, the year in which the northern party system changed was obviously 1854. Second, the Republicans early and quickly seized the Great Lakes region. Know-Nothings existed there, but on the congressional level nativists were unable to mount much of a challenge. Both New England and the Middle Atlantic regions had enough of a Republican base to enable them to expand and contest the Know-Nothings and other coalitions. Third, the issue in the congressional districts in 1854 was the Kansas-Nebraska Act and the repeal of the Missouri Compromise line. Nativism may have made some kind of public noise in 1854 in the congressional districts, but it was ridiculously muted compared to antislavery. Everywhere in the North in 1854, congressional candidates ran on the question of Nebraska.[23]

Table B.2 also brings the southern part of the equation into view. It seems relatively clear that in the Deep South, Democratic Party supremacy increased after 1851 and opposition victories shrank. The Border South was less em-

TABLE B.2. *Summary of Congressional Seats Won by Regional District, 1844–1860*

Region/Party	*1844–45*	*1846–47*	*1848–49*	*1850–51*	*1852–53*	*1854–55*	*1856–57*	*1858–59*	*1860*
New England									
Democrat	10	9	12	14	13	1	2	0	0
Whig	20	21	15	13	15	3	0	0	0
Republican	0	0	0	0	0	5	25	29	19
Other1	0	0	0	0	1	18	0	1	0
Other2	0	0	0	0	0	0	0	0	1
Great Lakes									
Democrat	30	25	30	28	35	9	19	17	17
Whig	10	16	11	15	13	0	0	0	0
Republican	0	0	0	0	0	41	31	34	35
Other1	1	0	5	3	2	0	0	1	0
Other2	0	0	0	0	0	0	0	0	0
Middle Atlantic									
Democrat	34	19	11	36	41	14	27	7	16
Whig	23	43	48	26	21	48	0	0	0
Republican	0	0	0	0	0	0	25	22	45
Other1	6	1	5	0	1	1 [15]	8	33 [union]	0
Other2	0	0	0	0	0	0	0	0	3
Border South									
Democrat	38	30	38	33	37	31	43	36	NA
Whig	20	28	20	25	18	6	0	0	NA
Republican	0	0	0	0	0	0	0	0	NA
Other1	0	0	0	0	2	20	14	21	NA
Other2	0	0	0	0	0	0	0	0	NA
Deep South									
Democrat	24	24	24	11	29	26	29	30	NA
Whig	7	9	9	4	4	0	0	0	NA
Republican	0	0	0	0	0	0	0	0	NA
Other1	0	0	0	4	0	7	4	3	NA
Other2	0	0	0	14	0	0	0	0	NA

Notes: Other1 in New England, Middle Atlantic, and Great Lakes regions is American Party unless otherwise indicated; the 15 in brackets for Middle Atlantic is because 15 candidates were hyphenated Know-Nothing Whigs or Democrats.

Other1 in Deep South states are the States' Rights Party; Other2 is the Union Party.

NA for Deep South and Border South regions is for nonapplicability because either congressional elections were not held in 1860 or the states that would have held the elections seceded.

The Other2 in New England for 1860 is a Constitutional Unionist; the 3 in 1860 for Middle Atlantic region are fusionist candidates.

Source: Computed from Moore, *Congressional Quarterly's Guide to U.S. Elections.*

phatic, but after 1851 the Democrats showed more of an edge in winning congressional seats while the Opposition slipped a little in its capacity to elect its candidates. This is another way of stating that the realignment of the 1850s began with the South, and their realignment was over the protection of slavery's value. That movement almost logically required a countermovement in the North. In short, because southerners reacted to the slavery issue by altering their political party preferences, they elevated the slavery issue in the North and made it more salient. It was not likely that national elections could continue in which one part of the country campaigned only on one issue while the other part of the country campaigned entirely on another. The reason for the unlikelihood is that the victors would actually meet in Congress, and there have to decide which issue was supreme and which one was secondary. Southern strength on the slavery issue dictated that slavery-driven issues would triumph over nativism on the congressional battlefield. Ultimately, northerners would take that fact back to their congressional districts and thus enhance the primacy of the slavery issue in the North.

Figure B.6 shows voting by parties in the congressional districts of the Great Lakes region in the 1850s. The two-party system from 1848 to 1852 (and probably to 1853) was stable, the break coming in 1854.[24] That break has special features. First, the Whigs disappear; second, the Republicans—and they are so named in the returns in the *Whig Almanac* and elsewhere—come from nowhere to dominate absolutely the congressional elections. Third, in the congressional districts, other parties—the Whigs and Americans—are hardly a blip on the screen. Fourth, the decline in Democrat voting is remarkable.

In comparison with the Great Lakes region, the Middle Atlantic trio of states, New York, Pennsylvania, and New Jersey, in the 1850s are like a hidden code (Figure B.7). In 1854 the Republicans did not exist in the congressional races, the winner being the Whig Party. However, the Whigs were in that election a fusion of anti-Democrat elements. The Democrats collapsed in the face of the opposition, although the situation was made more difficult because of the Hard-Soft rift in the Democratic Party. In this region, the influence of the Americans was apparent. In the state elections of 1855, the Know-Nothings matched the Democrats (Softs), while the Republicans were a distant third party. The coalition nature of the Whigs in the congressional elections of 1854 became apparent in 1855 when that party virtually disappeared in all three states on the local level. Only in 1856 did the Republican Party achieve a nearly dominant position, and even then the Democrats were close competitors. In the Middle Atlantic region the importance of the congressional elections of 1858 becomes plain: those elections gave the Republicans supremacy.

To some extent, these figures may assist in determining why the Republicans emerged victorious. First, the coalition that won the congressional elections of 1854 clearly predicted the coalition that would become the Republican Party. In the congressional districts, that was an antislavery coalition. In the elections of 1855, the coalition of anti-Democrat forces fragmented and enabled the Democrats overall in the region to return to victory, or some semblance of it. That circumstance dictated the obvious: antislavery produced coalitions that enabled the opposition forces to triumph over the Democracy; other issues did not.

In the North, the odd region was New England; fortunately for the Republican Party, the New England region was not a tail that wagged the political dog because of its limited population and small number of representatives. Figure B.8 shows New England party voting by counties between 1848 and 1860 in percentage of eligible voters and percent of votes cast for presidential and state races. Over the entire period, the Democratic Party captured a highly consistent number of voters and actually edged out the Whigs between 1851 and 1853. The elections of 1852 and 1853, in fact, do not reveal abnormal changes from earlier patterns. But then, in 1854, the opposition to the Democracy fractured in the state races. The Republican Party did not actually exist in 1854 in New England states. The point representing the Republican Party in 1854 is really a fusion party of Free-Soilers and temperance people, who, for the purposes of this exposition, were the embryo of the Republican Party.

Part of the difficulty in dealing with New England as a region is that the states went very separate ways between 1854 and 1856. Republicans organized fast and triumphed quickly in Maine in the congressional race of 1854, but Vermont, which turned Republican by 1855, held true to the Whig Party in 1854. In state races, Maine and Vermont began with fusion parties that then quickly evolved into the Republicans. The American Party overwhelmed Massachusetts, Connecticut, and New Hampshire in 1854 and 1855. On the state level, the chief party characteristic was fragmentation; in the congressional districts, the opposition destroyed the Democrats, but the name of the opposition was anything but standard. Another difficulty in characterizing New England was the difference in voting for congressional representatives; Connecticut and New Hampshire (American Party states) voted in odd years, while Massachusetts (American), Maine (Republican), and Vermont (Whig-Republican) voted in even years. The only thing obvious was the power of the opposition to the Democracy in congressional races in 1854 and 1855. Together Massachusetts, Maine, and Vermont yielded in the 1854 congressional races, in terms of percentage of votes cast, 25 percent for the Whigs, 36 percent for the Americans, 14 percent for the Republicans, 1 percent for other (temperance), and 23 percent for the Democrats, the Democrats' lowest percentage share of the vote for the two decades under consideration. In the 1855 congressional vote, New Hampshire and Connecticut gave 58 percent for the American Party and 42 percent for the Democracy.[25]

Outside of the obvious turmoil in New England in 1854, ultimate Republican victory is not obvious from Figure B.8. By 1856, however, the triumph of the Republicans is overwhelming. Why Republicans won the battle for the disparate anti-Democrat factions has been told elsewhere and will not be repeated here. Suffice it to say that the larger and more potent regions of the Middle Atlantic and Great Lakes had already indicated in the congressional elections of 1854 that a coalition based on antislavery was to be the eventual winner; it took New England two more years to come to the same conclusion.[26]

Voting patterns in the Border South and Deep South in the 1850s have a common theme: the growing, even awesome, hegemony of the Democratic Party. Figures B.9 and 10 exhibit voting for both regions between 1853 and 1860. What the figures show is how the Democratic Party after 1851 commenced a near total control of southern politics, except in the Border South where the Opposition in 1859 began a resurgence. In the Deep South, Democratic hegemony was almost grotesque; by 1859 the Deep South Democrats obtained nearly 80 percent of the votes cast. Part of the difficulty with these figures, and particularly with Figure B.9, is the extent of uncontested elections. This was especially true for Virginia, a state that had had thirteen congressional districts, and in 1859 five of them were uncontested, and one other was virtually uncontested as the Democrat racked up nearly 65 percent of the vote.[27] The surge in Democratic strength had a reservation, however. In state races, the opposition was far more powerful than in congressional contests, indicating that voters were making obvious distinctions about the issues they considered worthy of partisan dispute.[28]

For an overall assessment of what happened to the Second Party System, Figure B.11 was constructed by taking the Democratic percentage of votes cast in presidential, congressional, and state elections per region and subtracting from them the next major opposition party vote, be it American, Republican, or fusion. The continuity of politics, its amazing competitiveness, between 1840 and 1850 is obvious, confined as it is to a small region of plus or minus five percentage points. Within that narrow range of fluctuation, one can also discern a rising Democratic cycle between 1842 and 1846, and then a cycle of Whig strength from 1847 to 1850. Beginning in 1851, the pattern of the Second Party System starts gyrating, with the Border South and the Great Lakes becoming more Democratic while the Deep South Democracy, in the mess of the congressional elections of 1851, suffered a large setback only to rebound to large victories over their Whig opponents in 1852 and afterward. The northern pattern, however, continues the Jacksonian party system until 1854. Then the Great Lakes Democrats suffered an amazing reversal as did the Middle Atlantic region. But the New Englanders, living free rather than dying, held out until 1856 before completely embarrassing the Democrats. By 1858 and 1860, the sectionalization of politics, as shown in Figure B.11, was nearly complete. Interestingly but not unexpectedly, the Deep South and New England regions were the new boundaries, the New England states being highly anti-Democratic while the Deep South being nearly wholly Democratic. The Border South

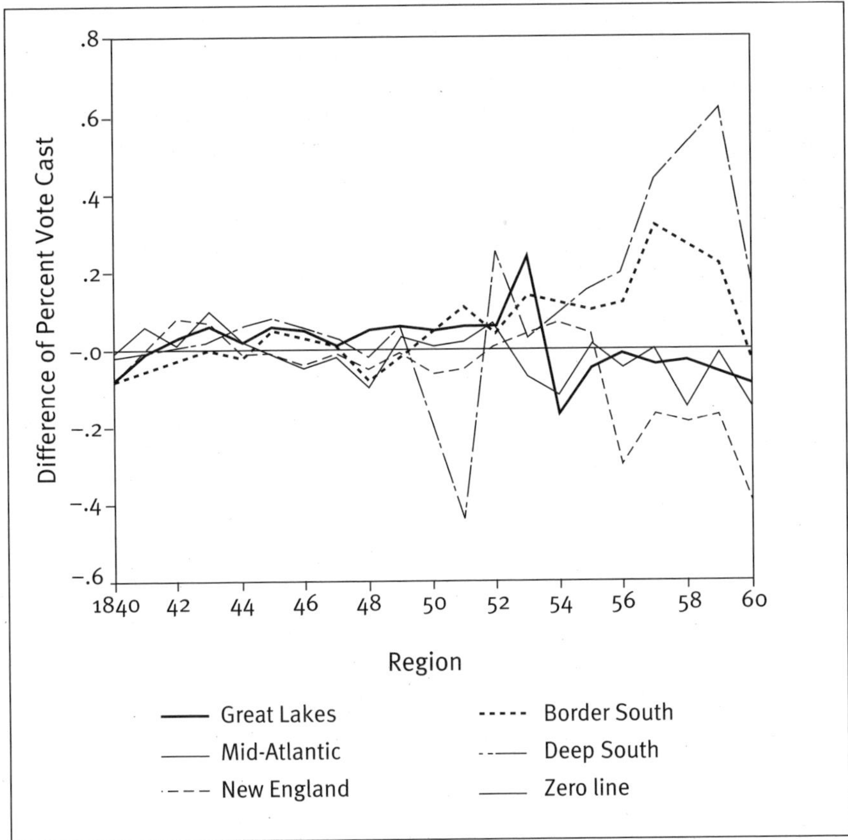

FIGURE B.11. *Difference between Democratic Voting and Major Opposition Party by Votes Cast, All Regions, 1840–1860*

had become markedly pro–Democratic Party as well, but of significance, given the historiography that has so much focused on northern state realignment, the Great Lakes and Middle Atlantic regions were only mildly anti-Democratic.[29] The Great Lakes and Middle Atlantic regions demonstrated a change of heart: the Great Lakes states went from being a strong Democratic region to a distinctly Republican region, while the Middle Atlantic states seemed to have followed a sort of pattern of political party indecision (or perhaps cycling). (Figure B.12 is given for the purists who would like to see a graphing based on percentage of eligible voters; the same information is provided, but the extent of regional divergence is less pronounced.)

These figures demonstrate the central characteristics of the realignment of the 1850s. The realignment started in the South in 1851 and transformed the politics of the area from a competitive party system to one of near absolute Democratic dominance. It is only logical that this should be the case. Con-

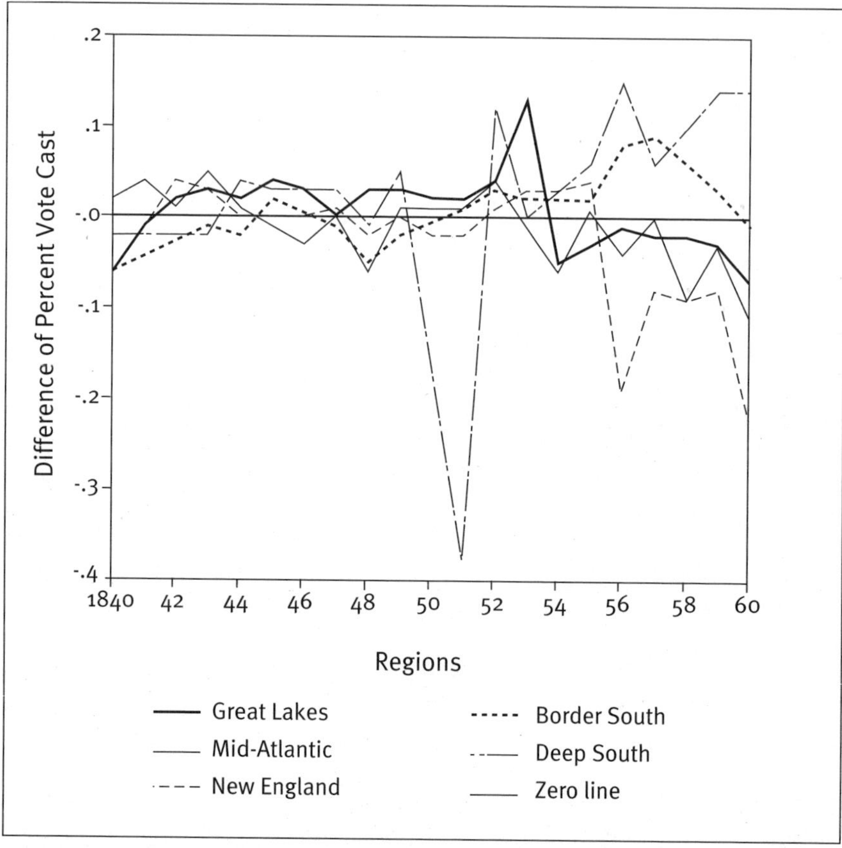

FIGURE B.12. *Difference between Democratic Voting and Major Opposition Party by Percentage of Eligible Voters, All Regions, 1840–1860*

gressional fighting over slavery and property rights in slaves would lead to the obvious inference that southerners would have reacted massively to this debate and have swung to the one party that offered the sanctuary of state dominance over slavery. For southerners, slavery was, as William Lowndes Yancey said, a matter of dollars and cents, not a metaphysical question to contemplate with a glass of claret in an easy chair before a comfortable fireplace. The change in southern politics probably begged an alteration in northern politics because the Whigs could not function as a national party when it was being shut out of two regions of the country. Moreover, the figures also reveal that though northerners weathered the 1846–53 crisis stage fairly well, with the pattern of party competition holding to its previous performance, the North reacted strongly in 1854 and then reshuffled its party system. The anti-Nebraska winning coalition in the congressional elections of 1854 clearly foreshadowed the coalition that became the national Republican Party. In the Great Lakes, the

Republicans had already won the organizational contest and thereby influenced both the Middle Atlantic and New England regions. In the Middle Atlantic, the 1854 congressional coalition was crucial, revealing the winning combination of elements that could overthrow Democratic power; the state races showed fragmentation and the inability of the Americans to reorganize politics so that they could effectively counter the Democrats. The northern political sluggard was New England, and the worst state in the mix was Massachusetts. There the American Party in both congressional and state elections had the punch to organize politics and overcome the Republicans. On a national level, though, the Americans of New England could not impose their organizational form on the Great Lakes and Middle Atlantic states, which were already jettisoning the American cause and embracing the Republican Party. In 1856 all the cards fell into place and the Republicans swept to dominance in every region of the North. And by 1860, although a reaction against extremism along the border had set in, the result was plain: the realignment of the 1850s had caused a nearly complete sectionalization of American politics. And what caused the realignment of the 1850s was the issue of property rights in slavery.

Appendix C

State and Congressional Elections Used in Figures 6.1, 7.1, and B.1–10

PART I. *Great Lakes Region*

Year	*Ohio*	*Indiana*	*Illinois*	*Wisconsin*	*Michigan*
1840					
1841	Legislature	Congress	Congress		Governor
1842			Governor		
1843	Congress	Governor	Congress	Delegates	Governor
1844			Congress	Governor	
1845	Governor	Congress		Delegates	Governor
1846	Governor	Governor	Governor		Congress
1847				Delegates	Governor
1848		Governor	Governor	Governor	
1849		Governor		Governor	Secretary of State
1850	Governor				Secretary of State
1851	Governor			Governor	Governor
1852	Supreme Court		Governor		
1853	Governor			Governor	Maine Law
1854	Public Works	Secretary of State	Treasurer		Governor
1855	Governor		Treasurer	Governor	
1856		Governor	Governor		Governor
1857	Governor			Governor	Chief Justice
1858	Supreme Court	Governor	Treasurer		Governor
1859	Governor		Superintendent of Instruction	Governor	Chief Justice
1860		Governor	Governor		

Note: Congressional election used as proxy for state election.

PART II. *State Elections in the Middle Atlantic Region*

Year	*New York*	*Pennsylvania*	*New Jersey*
1841	Senator	Governor	
1842			
1843	Senator	Canal Commissioner	
1844	Governor	Governor	Governor
1845		Canal Commissioner	
1846	Governor	Canal Commissioner	
1847	Lt. Governor	Governor	Governor
1848	Governor	Governor	
1849	Controller	Canal Commissioner	
1850	Governor	Canal Commissioner	Governor
1851	Treasurer	Governor	Governor
1852	Governor	Canal Commissioner	
1853	Secretary of State	Canal Commissioner	Governor
1854	Governor	Supreme Court	
1855	Secretary of State	Canal Commissioner	
1856	Governor	Canal Commissioner	Governor
1857	Secretary of State	Governor	
1858	Governor	Supreme Court	
1859	Secretary of State	Surveyor General	Governor
1860	Governor	Governor	

PART III. *State Elections in the New England Region*

Year	*Maine*	*New Hampshire*	*Massachusetts*	*Vermont*	*Connecticut*
1841					
1842	Governor			Governor	Governor
1843		Governor	Governor		Governor
1844	Governor				
1845	Governor	Governor	Governor	Governor	Governor
1846	Governor	Governor		Governor	Governor
1847	Governor	Governor	Governor	Governor	Governor
1848			Governor		Governor
1849	Governor	Governor	Governor	Governor	Governor
1850					Governor
1851		Governor	Governor	Governor	Governor
1852	Governor	Governor	Governor		
1853	Governor	Governor	Governor	Governor	
1854	Governor	Governor	Governor	Governor	Governor
1855	Governor	Governor	Governor	Governor	Governor
1856	Governor	Governor	Governor	Governor	Governor
1857	Governor	Governor	Governor	Governor	Governor
1858	Governor	Governor	Governor	Governor	Governor
1859	Governor	Governor	Governor	Governor	
1860	Governor	Governor	Governor	Governor	Governor

PART IV. *State Elections in the Border South Region*

Date	*Tennessee*	*Virginia*	*North Carolina*	*Kentucky*
1841	Governor			
1842			Governor	
1843	Governor			
1844			Governor	Governor
1845	Governor			
1846			Governor	
1847	Governor			
1848			Governor	Governor
1849	Governor			
1850			Governor	
1851	Governor	Governor		Governor
1852			Governor	
1853	Governor			
1854			Governor	
1855	Governor	Governor		Governor
1856			Governor	
1857	Governor			Treasurer
1858			Governor	
1859	Governor	Governor		Governor
1860				

PART V. *State Elections in the Deep South Region*

Year	*Louisiana*	*Georgia*	*Alabama*	*Mississippi*
1841		Governor		
1842	Governor			
1843				Governor
1844				
1845		Governor	Governor	
1846	Governor			
1847		Governor	Governor	
1848		Governor		
1849	Governor	Governor		Governor
1850				
1851	Auditor	Governor		Governor
1852				
1853	Treasurer	Governor		Governor
1854				
1855	Governor	Governor	Governor	Governor
1856				
1857	Auditor	Governor		
1858				
1859	Governor	Governor		
1860				

Appendix D

Number of Cases for Regions in Average Vote in Elections Used for Figures 6.1, 7.1, and B.1–10

PART I. *Number of Cases in State Elections in the Regions*

Year	*Great Lakes*	*Middle Atlantic*	*New England*	*Border South*	*Deep South*
1841	43	0	0	0	0
1842	28	33	35	0	0
1843	46	43	31	33	0
1844	22	44	33	0	0
1845	15	0	58	28	15
1846	39	39	58	0	0
1847	39	44	58	0	15
1848	12	39	0	18	0
1849	17	39	58	0	15
1850	21	44	48	0	0
1851	37	39	45	23	15
1852	39	39	58	0	0
1853	22	44	58	0	14
1854	43	39	60	0	0
1855	31	39	60	33	22
1856	24	44	60	0	0
1857	26	39	59	20	0
1858	43	39	60	0	0
1859	26	43	60	33	10
1860	39	39	47	0	0

PART II. *Number of Cases in Congressional Elections in the Regions*

Year	*Great Lakes*	*Middle Atlantic*	*New England*	*Border South*	*Deep South*
1841	0	0	NA	0	0
1842	0	23	NA	0	0
1843	0	44	NA	0	0
1844	9	28	NA	0	0
1845	0	0	NA	0	0
1846	13	44	NA	0	10
1847	0	0	NA	41	14
1848	34	44	NA	0	0
1849	0	0	NA	41	22
1850	35	44	NA	0	0
1851	0	0	NA	41	22
1852	46	44	NA	0	0
1853	0	0	NA	41	21
1854	46	44	NA	0	0
1855	0	0	NA	41	22
1856	46	44	NA	0	0
1857	0	0	NA	41	22
1858	46	44	NA	0	0
1859	0	0	NA	0	0
1860	46	44	NA	0	0

Note: New England counties were used in the figures instead of congressional election districts.

PART III. *Number of Cases in Presidential Elections in the Regions*

Year	*Great Lakes*	*Middle Atlantic*	*New England*	*Border South*	*Deep South*
1840	43	44	56	41	22
1844	43	44	58	41	22
1848	46	44	58	41	22
1852	46	44	58	41	22
1856	46	44	60	41	22
1860	46	44	60	41	22

Note: Number of cases for number of congressional districts used in Figures 6.1, 7.1, and B.1–10 except for New England, which instead represents counties.

Notes

Chapter 1

1. This brief narrative draws most heavily on Thomas Morris, *Southern Slavery and the Law*, chap. 2. It is supplemented by Handlin and Handlin, "Origins of the Southern Labor System"; Galenson, *White Servitude in Colonial America*; Morgan, *American Slavery, American Freedom*, chap. 15; Betty Wood, *Origins of American Slavery*, 7, 15–16, 27–28, 79–90.

2. Figures from U.S. Bureau of the Census, Department of Commerce, *Historical Statistics of the United States*, table Z 1–19, p. 1168; see fig. 4 in Fogel, *Without Consent or Contract*, 33.

3. Wood, *Origins of American Slavery*, 7–8, 12, 20–25, 27, 63, 89.

4. For a libertarian evaluating slavery, see Hummel, *Emancipating Slaves, Enslaving Free Men*, chap. 2.

5. See Domar, *Capitalism, Socialism, and Serfdom.*

6. In the preceding sentence, the descriptions of slavery are historical, but, of course, the question of removal is conjectural. In the author's opinion a peaceful end to slavery might have been possible, although it is difficult to think of the appropriate conditions under which such a demise might have occurred.

7. Hofstadter, *America at 1750*, chap. 5; Nash, *Red, White, and Black*, 199–219; also relevant, though emphasizing the emergence of elite dominance, is Henretta, *Evolution of American Society*, chap. 3.

8. Ely, *Guardian of Every Other Right*, 3–4, 28–32, 42, 50–57; Alexander, *Commodity and Propriety*, 2–9, 37–42, 68–69.

9. Richard Bland, *An Inquiry into Rights of the British Colonies*, 1766, in Hyneman and Lutz, *American Political Writing during the Founding Era*, 1:82; James Otis, *The Rights of the British Colonies Asserted and Proved*, [1764], in Bailyn, *Pamphlets of the American Revolution*, 447; Continental Congress, "Address to the People of Great Britain," October 21, 1774, in Ford et al., *Journals of Continental Congress*, 1:82; Continental Congress, "Address by the Twelve United Colonies, by Their Delegates in Congress, to the Inhabitants of Great Britain," July 8, 1775, in ibid., 2:168–69; Continental Congress, "Address to the Inhabitants of the Province of Quebec," October 26, 1774, in ibid., 1:107.

10. John Adams, *A Defence of the Constitutions of Government of the United States of America*, 1778, in Charles Adams, *Works of John Adams*, 6:8–9; James Madison, *Federalist* 10, in Hutchinson and Rachal, *Papers of Madison*, 10:265. See McIlwaine, *American Revolution*, 156–57; Greene, "Society, Ideology, and Politics," 46–47.

11. See Chipman, *Sketches of the Principles of Government* (1793), 64–69. This evidently came from the school of "common sense" philosophy of Lord Kames.

12. A famous example of this sentiment is Charles Thomson to Benjamin Franklin, September 24, 1765, in Labaree and Willcox, *Papers of Franklin*, 12:278–79.

13. Schlatter, *Private Property*, 143–44; Appleby, *Capitalism and a New Social Order*, 9, 17; Reck, "Moral Philosophy and the Framing of the Constitution," 29–31; Pocock, "The Mobility of Property and the Rise of Eighteenth-Century Sociology," 141–66.

14. Schlatter, *Private Property*, 151–55; Appleby, *Capitalism and a New Social Order*, 19–21; Bailyn, *Ideological Origins of the American Revolution*, 36; Scott, *In Pursuit of Happiness*, 37–38.

15. On fear of the propertied toward the willingness of the majority to violate property rights, see Noah Webster, *An Examination into the Leading Principles of the Federal Constitution*, 40–45; remarks of Edmund Randolph at the Constitutional Convention, in Farrand, *Records of the Federal Convention of 1787*, 1:58; Fisher Ames, "Equality," in Seth Ames, *Works of Fisher Ames*, 2:210–11, 217–18; "Account of the Insurrection in New Hampshire, in September, 1786," *American Museum* 5 (March 1789): 263–64; James Madison, "Madison's Observations on Jefferson's Draft of a Constitution for Virginia," [c. 1783], in Boyd et al., *Papers of Jefferson*, 6:308–31. For secondary treatments, see, for example, Jensen, *New Nation*, 4–23, 42–51; Fischer, *Revolution of American Conservatism*, 3–8; Countryman, *People in Revolution*, 46–49, 211–13, 242–44, 254–66.

16. Dickinson, *Liberty and Property*, 198–230; Schlatter, *Private Property*, 159–60; Huston, *Securing the Fruits of Labor*, chaps. 1–2.

17. On Locke, see remarks of Laslett in Locke, *Two Treatises of Government*, 101–6; Locke on the labor theory of property, ibid., 287–88. For differing views, see Macpherson, *Political Theory of Possessive Individualism*, chap. 5; Buckle, *Natural Law and the Theory of Property*, vii–ix, 124–53, 169.

18. James Wilson, "On the History of Property," in McCloskey, *Works of Wilson*, 2:719; Logan [A Farmer], *Letters Addressed to the Yeomanry of the United States . . .* (1791), 27; Warren, *An Oration: Delivered March Sixth, 1775, at the Request of the Inhabitants of Boston; to Commemorate the Bloody Tragedy of the Fifth of March, 1770* (1775), 6. A full elaboration of the revolutionaries' ideas about the labor theory of property or value is contained in Huston, *Securing the Fruits of Labor*, chap. 1.

19. Morgan, *Challenge of the American Revolution*, 91; Huston, *Securing the Fruits of Labor*, chap. 2.

20. James Wilson, "Lectures on Law," in McCloskey, *Works of Wilson*, 1:233, 241. See Address of Continental Congress to the Inhabitants of the Province of Quebec, October 26, 1774, in Ford et al., *Journals of Continental Congress*, 1:108. The idea that property rights could be used to fend off feudalistic excesses has been suggested by Hunt, "Marx's Theory of Property and Alienation," 300; Dickinson, *Liberty and Property*, 217, 227–28, 249–58; Schlatter, *Private Property*, 159–60.

21. Edward Everett, "Accumulation, Property, Capital, Credit: Address before the Mercantile Library Association of Boston," September 13, 1838, in Everett, *Orations and Speeches on Various Occasions*, 2:293–94; Nathan Appleton, "Labor—Its Relations in the United States and Europe, Compared," *Hunt's Merchants' Magazine* 11 (September 1844): 217–19.

22. William Leggett, in Blau, *Social Theories of Jacksonian Democracy*, 75; Samuel J. Tilden, "Currency, Princes, and Wages," October 1840, in Bigelow, *Writings and Speeches of Tilden*, 1:151–53. See Huston, *Securing the Fruits of Labor*, chaps. 4, 5, and 6. Of course, the mid-nineteenth century saw those who questioned property rights, such as Thomas Skidmore, various labor leaders, and particularly the utopians; see Huston, chap. 8.

23. John Adams to Thomas Jefferson, July 16, 1814, in Lipscomb, *Writings of Jefferson*, 14:158. James Otis, *Rights of British Colonies Asserted*, [1764], in Bailyn, *Pamphlets of the American Revolution*, 423–27; Noah Webster, *Sketches of American Policy*, in Noah Webster, *On Being American*, 39. On the difficulties the revolutionaries had with the meaning of property rights, see Kammen, "'The Rights of Property, and the Property in Rights.'"

24. Samuel Adams [Candidus], 1771, in Cushing, *Writings of Samuel Adams*, 2:299; James Wilson, "On the History of Property," in McCloskey, *Works of Wilson*, 2:711; Thomas Jeffer-

son to Isaac McPherson, August 13, 1818, in Lipscomb, *Writings of Jefferson*, 13:333; Benjamin Franklin to Robert Morris, December 25, 1783, in Bigelow, *Life of Benjamin Franklin*, 3:242–43; Thomas Paine, *Agrarian Justice*, [1795–96], in Foner, *Complete Writings of Paine*, 1:620. See Wills, *Inventing America*, 229–30; Yarbrough, "Jefferson and Property Rights," 65–83; Matthews, *Radical Politics of Thomas Jefferson*, 20–29.

25. This is the "property rights paradigm." For examples, see North, *Structure and Change in Economic History*; North, *Institutions, Institutional Change and Economic Performance*; Demsetz, "Toward a Theory of Property Rights," 347–59; Alchian and Demsetz, "Property Rights Paradigm," 16–27; Getzler, "Theories of Property and Economic Development"; Firmin-Sellers, "The Politics of Property Rights"; Umbeck, "Might Makes Rights"; Novack, *People's Welfare*, chap. 1.

26. Stephen Hopkins, *The Rights of the Colonies Examined*, in Bailyn, *Pamphlets of the American Revolution*, 516. See Bailyn, *Ideological Origins of the American Revolution*, 232–33; John Reid, *The Concept of Liberty in the Age of the American Revolution*, 7, 69–73. Slaveholders knew the Revolution made their cries for freedom hypocritical because of their slaveholding; see remarks of Tucker, *A Dissertation on Slavery with a Proposal for the Gradual Abolition of It, in the State of Virginia* (1796), 48.

27. Rice [Philanthropos], *Slavery Inconsistent with Justice and Good Policy* (1792), 40; Benjamin Rush, "On Slave-Keeping," [1773], in Runes, *Selected Writings of Rush*, 12; Tom Paine in *Pennsylvania Journal and the Weekly Advertiser*, March 8, 1775, in Foner, *Complete Writings of Paine*, 19. Note the comment of Englishman William Cobbett about slavery and the fruits of labor in Mandel, *Labor Free and Slave*, 79.

28. Woolman, *Consideration on Keeping Negroes . . . Part Second* (1762), 16–17, quotation from 34; Othello, "Negro Slavery," in Woodson, *Negro Orators and Their Orations*, 18; Franklin, "Observations Concerning the Increase of Mankind," [1751], in Labaree and Willcox, *Papers of Franklin*, 4:231; Rushton, *Expostulatory Letter to George Washington, of Mount Vernon, on His Consenting to Be a Holder of Slaves* (1797), 4.

29. For two examples of how the aristocratic policies of England would deprive the colonies of a prosperous future, see John Dickinson, "Letters of a Pennsylvania Farmer," in Ford, *Political Writings of Dickinson*, 400–401; Alexander Hamilton, *A Full Vindication*, 1774, in Syrett and Cooke, *Papers of Hamilton*, 1:53. On the poverty and alleged backwardness of southern life, see John Adams to Joseph Hawley, November 25, 1775, in Charles Adams, *Works of John Adams*, 9:367; Ramsey, *History of the American Revolution*, 1:24–25; Timothy Pickering to Rufus King, March 8, 1785, in Charles King, *Life and Correspondence of Rufus King*, 1:45; Rush, "On Slave-Keeping," in Runes, *Selected Writings of Rush*, 5–6; Buchanan, *An Oration upon the Moral and Political Evil of Slavery* (1793), 16.

30. See Scott, *In Pursuit of Happiness*, 94; Zilversmit, *First Emancipation*, 57–60, 93–99, 227–28.

31. The incipient defense of slavery because it treated the laborer better than free laborers in England can be found in Boucher, *Reminiscences of an American Loyalist*, 97–98, who also defended slavery because he disliked equality. Also, Benjamin Franklin expressed proslavery ideas when in London defending the action of the colonists by comparing slaves in America to workers in England; "A Conversation on Slavery," in *Public Advertiser*, January 30, 1770, in Labaree and Willcox, *Papers of Franklin*, 17:38–44. See Robinson, *Slavery in the Structure of American Politics*, 148, 178, 180–87, 203; David Davis, *Problem of Slavery in the Age of Revolution*, 84, 164–71, 264–68. Larry Tise has found more proslavery sentiment in the North during the early period of the Republic, while Paul Finkelman has decided that the Constitution was purposely written to protect slavery; Tise, *Proslavery*; Finkelman, *Slavery and the Founders*.

32. July 30, 1776, in Ford et al., *Journals of Continental Congress*, 6:1079–80. This incident is also stressed in Robinson, *Slavery in the Structure of American Politics*, 148.

33. For example, *Constitution of the Pennsylvania Society for Promoting the Abolition of Slavery* (1787), 5, 9–10; *Constitution of the Maryland Society, for Promoting the Abolition of Slavery* (1789), 3; [Cooper], *A Mite Cast into the Treasury* (1772), 7, 13; John Wesley, "Thoughts upon Slavery," in [Benezet], *Collection of Religious Tracts* (1773), 4, 18–26; Othello, "Negro Slavery," in Woodson, *Negro Orators and Their Orations*, 15–17; A Free Negro, "Slavery," in ibid., 27–28; Rice, *Slavery Inconsistent with Justice and Good Policy*, 19, 35.

34. [Cooper], *A Mite Cast into the Treasury* (1772), 5–7; de Warville, *New Travels in the United States of America, 1788*, 229; Rice, *Slavery Inconsistent with Justice and Good Policy*, 20–21.

35. [Benezet], *Collection of Religious Tracts*, 36; Rice, *Slavery Inconsistent with Justice and Good Policy*, 20–22; [Cooper], *A Mite Cast into the Treasury*, quotation of Locke from 23, discussion of property rights, 11, 14–16, 22–23; Adam Smith, *An Inquiry into the Nature and Causes of the Wealth of Nations*, 121. See Buckle, *Natural Law and the Theory of Property*, 49, 52, 124–33.

36. Paine, *The Rights of Man*, in Foner, *Complete Writings of Paine*, 1:251.

37. Madison, *Notes of Debates*, quotation from 244; others from 245, 194, 247.

38. Ibid., remarks of Gerry, 39.

39. Madison speeches, June 6, ibid., 75–77, and June 26, ibid., 193–95, quotation from 194. See also Hamilton, 135. For support for majority rule, see comments of James Wilson, 287; Oliver Ellsworth, 222; and George Mason, 167.

40. Ibid., remarks of Gerry, 103; G. Morris, 271; Sherman, 507; Madison, 532. See comments of Patterson, 259.

41. Speech of Alexander Hamilton, June 21, 1788, in Lodge, *Works of Hamilton*, 2:14; Ferdinando Fairfax, "Plan for Liberating the Negroes within the United States," *American Museum* 8 (September 1790): 285.

42. Madison, *Notes of Debates*, Pinckney, 278–79; Mason, 269; Randolph, 279; Butler, 286.

43. Ibid., Randolph, 508; Rutledge, 502; Ellsworth, 503; Pinckney, 505. The question of race already was in the air as well; see fears of Pennsylvania's James Wilson, 275.

44. Discussion in ibid., 412, 502, 503.

45. Ibid., 411, 504.

46. Morris quotation in ibid., 412. Southerners in convention did not apologize for economic backwardness or lassitude among laborers; see speeches of Pinckney, 281, Butler, 268, and even Mason, 269, in ibid. Rufus King of Massachusetts indeed accepted the superior wealth position of the South: "[He] had always expected that as the Southern States are the richest, they would not league themselves with the Northn. unless some respect were paid to their superior wealth." Ibid., 260.

47. John Adams, "Notes of Debates," in Ford et al., *Journals of Continental Congress*, 6:1099.

48. Thomas Jefferson, "Notes of Proceedings in the Continental Congress," in Boyd et al., *Papers of Jefferson*, 1:322.

49. John Adams, "Notes of Debates," in Ford et al., *Journals of Continental Congress*, 6:1082, 1100. On the three-fifths compromise, see Madison, *Notes of Debates*, 268; Fehrenbacher, *Slaveholding Republic*, 24–25.

50. Madison, *Notes of Debates*, 224–25, 283, 285.

51. Speeches of Morris in ibid., 286, 411–12; James Madison, "Notes for the National Gazette Essays," [ca. December 19, 1791–March 3, 1792], in Hutchinson and Rachal, *Papers of*

Madison, 14:163. A good description of the battles over slavery in the convention is given in Richards, *Slave Power*, 32–40.

52. James Winthrop, "Letters of Agrippa," [1787–88], in Storing, *Complete Anti-Federalist*, 4:80, 94; George Bryan, "Letters of Centinel," in Kenyon, *Antifederalists*, 23.

53. Remarks of Patrick Henry, July 12, 1788, in Elliot, *Elliot's Debates*, 3:314, 327, 328.

54. Remarks of Charles C. Pinckney, January 17, 1788, in ibid., 4:283, 285, 286.

55. Remarks of George Mason, June 11, 1788, in ibid., 3:269–70, emphasis added. There was extensive discussion in the South over the proposed powers of the new national government and how it could injure slavery either through direct legislation such as taxes or indirect legislation such as control of commerce or by tinkering with the definition of property rights. That discussion will not be presented fully here; however, see *Elliot's Debates*, 3:135–52, 215–30, 242–53, 264–70, 5:474; Lee, *The Letters of Richard Henry Lee*, 2:282, 369, 383.

56. Speech of Smith, March 17, 1790, House of Representatives, *Annals of Congress*, 1st Cong., 2d sess., 1501–14, quote from 1508. The early debates over slavery have been fully laid out in Robinson, *Slavery in the Structure of American Politics*, 49–50, 59–63; David Davis, *Problem of Slavery in the Age of Revolution*, 148–52; and John Miller, *Federalist Era*, 104.

57. John Taylor, *An Argument Respecting the Constitutionality of the Carriage Tax* (1795), 20.

58. Remark of Rutledge, January 2, 1800, *Annals of Congress*, 6th Cong., 1st sess., 232. See comment of Dodd, *Expansion and Conflict*, 164–65.

59. On the constitution, see Wiecek, "The Witch at the Christening"; and Finkelman, *Slavery and the Founders*, chap. 1. Fehrenbacher did not find slavery so prominent at the convention, nor did he believe it had shaped greatly the final product; Fehrenbacher, *Slaveholding Republic*, 3–5 and chap. 2.

Chapter 2

1. Yancey speech, October 23, 1860, in *Louisville Daily Courier*, October 24, 1860.

2. Excerpts taken from Thomas Roderick Dew, "Abolition of Negro Slavery," in Faust, *Ideology of Slavery*, 29.

3. Remarks of John C. Calhoun in U.S. Senate, January 6, 1838, in Meriwether et al., *Papers of Calhoun*, 14:66; J. D. B. DeBow, "The Cause of the South," in Paskoff and Wilson, *Cause of the South*, 185; Message of Governor Pettus in *Vicksburg (Miss.) Weekly Whig*, November 23, 1859; Jabez Curry, *Civil History of the Government of the Confederate States*, 16. These comments were considerably more pervasive than historians have allowed, for these values have not been dominant in the historiography.

4. The importance of amount of land for the Civil War resides in the military fact that it is far easier to defend an extensive area than it is for an opponent to conquer an extensive area. According to population theory, the lack of population in the South was a plus because it meant the Malthusian moment of plunging the masses into misery was to be postponed; this was not the case for the North, for as innumerable proslavery writers would say, the North was shortly to face a population crisis that would destroy its liberty.

5. Historians have been slow to seize what the economists have provided, for economists have been quite aware of the property dimensions of slavery; in particular, see Gavin Wright, *Political Economy of the Cotton South*, chap. 5, esp. pp. 139–50; see also Ransom and Sutch, *One Kind of Freedom*, 51–53; Lee and Passell, *New Economic View of American History*, chap. 10, esp. pp. 214–18; Gunderson, "The Origin of the American Civil War"; Goldin and Lewis, "The Economic Cost of the American Civil War"; Coclanis, *Shadow of a Dream*, 85–91, 126–27. Oddly, Fogel and Engerman, *Time on the Cross*, and Fogel, *Without Consent or Contract*, do

not deal with the question of wealth holding. Most of these works also deal with the matter of property rights in slaves but not necessarily with illuminating results.

6. Computed from Kennedy, *Preliminary Report on the Eighth Census, 1860*, 131.

7. See Ransom and Sutch, *One Kind of Freedom*, 52–53; Goldin and Lewis, "The Economic Cost of the American Civil War"; Lee and Passell, *New Economic View of American History*, 215; Gunderson, "The Origin of the American Civil War," 917. Gunderson, Goldin and Lewis, and Lee and Passell accept a figure of about $2.7 billion. Ransom and Sutch argue for $1.5 billion for the 2 million slaves in five cotton states. Roger Ransom offers a figure of $3.058 billion in Ransom, *Conflict and Compromise*, 70 n. 52; Hummel, *Emancipating Slaves, Enslaving Free Men*, 52. Clement Eaton suggested a possible value of slaves in 1860 of $4 billion; Eaton, *Freedom-of-Thought Struggle in the Old South*, 36.

8. Families listed in U.S. Department of the Interior, *Eighth Census*, vol. 4: *Statistics*, 351; slaveholding numbers in ibid., vol. 2: *Agriculture*, 247. McPherson, *Ordeal by Fire*, 34, gives the common statistic that planters owned more than one-half of all slaves. On wealth of southern planters, see Soltow, *Men and Wealth in the United States*, 66–67, 100–101, 133–41; Gavin Wright, "Economic Democracy and the Concentration of Agricultural Wealth in the Cotton South"; Fogel, *Without Consent or Contract*, 82–88.

9. Gavin Wright, *Old South, New South*, 17–50.

10. De Bow, *Statistical View of the United States*, 190–91.

11. U.S. Department of the Interior, *Eighth Census*, vol. 4: *Statistics*, 294–95.

12. Charles Sumner, "The Antislavery Enterprise," May 9, 1855, in Sumner, *Works of Sumner*, 4:27.

13. Fogel and Engerman, *Time on the Cross*, 1: table 4, p. 248; numbers in text from Fogel, *Without Consent or Contract*, table 1, p. 85; tables 2 and 3, pp. 88–89; see also Ransom, *Conflict and Compromise*, fig. 3.2, p. 49.

14. Ransom, *Conflict and Compromise*, 63–68; Fogel, *Without Consent or Contract*, 81–84; Gavin Wright, *Political Economy of the Cotton South*, 24–37. On the nonslaveholder, see Eaton, *History of the Old South*, 226–29, 400–409; Winters, "'Plain Folk' of the Old South Reexamined"; Ford, *Origins of Southern Radicalism*, 44–95; Cecil-Fronsman, *Common Whites*; and Inscoe, *Mountain Masters, Slavery, and the Sectional Crisis in Western North Carolina*.

15. Fogel, *Without Consent or Contract*, 87, 90–92; Fogel and Engerman, *Time on the Cross*, 1:254–57; see also Bateman and Weiss, *Deplorable Scarcity*, 10–21, 158–63; Stampp, *Peculiar Institution*, 397; Starobin, *Industrial Slavery in the Old South*.

16. On the question of development, see Vatter, *Drive to Industrial Maturity*, 6–11; Conrad et al., "Slavery an Obstacle to Economic Growth in the United States."

17. In Keynesian economics, this is called the multiplier effect. An addition to a nation's income from one source will circulate through the economy several times in the course of a year and thus stimulate additional economic activity. One can surmise a multiplier effect between 2 and 3 from a permanent addition to the national income. The point, of course, is that the income earned from slavery was not confined to slaveholders; rather, the income then began a circulation that created an economic climate that allowed others to enjoy prosperity as well, whether or not they had any direct connection to slaveholding. The multiplier effect is well known and can be found in any elementary macroeconomics textbook.

18. Kettell, *Southern Wealth and Northern Profits* (1860); David Christy, *Cotton Is King*, in E. N. Elliott, *Cotton Is King*, 19–267; speech of Alfred H. Colquitt, May 10, 1854, *Cong. Globe*, 33d Cong., 1st sess., *Appendix*, 751; message of John A. Quitman to legislature, November 18, 1850, in *Jackson Mississippian*, November [22], 1850; "South-West, No. 2" in *August (Ga.)*

Daily Constitutionalist, January 17, 1860. See Rainwater, *Mississippi Storm Center of Secession*, 218–20.

19. Compare Guion Johnson, *Ante-Bellum North Carolina*, 57.

20. On southern manufacturing, see Bateman and Weiss, *Deplorable Scarcity*; a useful summation can be found in Eaton, *History of the Old South*, 372–83.

21. See the dispute over economies of scale in cotton production between Fogel, *Without Consent or Contract*, 74–76; and Ransom and Sutch, *One Kind of Freedom*, 73–78; Gavin Wright, *Political Economy of the Cotton South*, 87–91.

22. Statistics from U.S. Department of the Interior, *Eighth Census*, vol. 2: *Agriculture*, 247. The antebellum South had 383,637 slaveholders and 3,930,513 slaves. There were 211,614 holders of 1–5 slaves; 65,278 holders of 6–9 slaves; 61,710 holders of 10–19 slaves; and 46,274 holders of more than 20 slaves. Concentrated holdings of slaves, that is, states in which more than 100 slaveholders held more than 100 slaves, were in the Deep South: Alabama (312), Georgia (181), Louisiana (460), Mississippi (279), North Carolina (118), South Carolina (363), and Virginia (105). Number of families from U.S. Department of the Interior, *Eighth Census*, vol. 4: *Statistics*, 351. The classic treatment of southern planters as aristocrats is Genovese, *Political Economy of Slavery*, 16–18, 23, 33–34, 180–201; see also Dodd, *Cotton Kingdom*, 22–24; Simms, *Decade of Sectional Controversy*, 3–4; Eaton, *History of the Old South*, 366–71; Barney, *Secessionist Impulse*, 91.

23. On limitations of the planters as an aristocracy, see Gavin Wright, *Political Economy of Cotton South*, 37–39; Gavin Wright, "Economic Democracy and the Concentration of Agricultural Wealth in the Cotton South," 84–85; Bowman, *Masters and Lords*, 95, 109, 112–33, 158, 204–5; Takaki, *Pro-Slavery Crusade*, viii–x; Ford, *Origins of Southern Radicalism*, 102.

24. On the nonslaveholding yeoman farmer and his world, see McCurry, *Masters of Small Worlds*; Ford, *Origins of Southern Radicalism*, 47–74; Hahn, *Roots of Southern Populism*; Bond, *Political Culture in the Nineteenth-Century South*, 47–79; Campbell, "Planters and Plain Folks"; Winters, "'Plain Folk' of the Old South Reexamined"; McWhiney, *Cracker Culture*; Eaton, *History of the Old South*, 207, 226, 401–7. The classic statement about the yeomen of the antebellum South is Owsley, *Plain Folk of the Old South*; see rebuttal by Linden, "Economic Democracy in the Slave South." The "dual economy" of the South is in Rothstein, "Antebellum South as a Dual Economy"; while the family first farming was initially argued by Gavin Wright, *Political Economy of the Cotton South*, 62–74; and then extended by Ford, *Origins of Southern Radicalism*, 72–88 and chap. 2 generally. On the folkways interpretation, see Collins, *White Society in the Antebellum South*, 145–59; and Potter, *The South and the Sectional Conflict*, 16.

25. Arthur Cole, *Irrepressible Conflict*, 37–41; Barney, *Secessionist Impulse*, 11–12, 31–32, 271, 274; Clarence Norton, *Democratic Party in Ante-Bellum North Carolina*, 200–206; Carey, *Parties, Slavery, and the Union in Antebellum Georgia*, 11–12.

26. This is a well-known interpretation, of course. See Genovese, *World the Slaveholders Made*; Genovese, *Slaveholders' Dilemma*, chap. 1; Jenkins, *Pro-Slavery Thought in the Old South*; Faust, *Sacred Circle*; on the proslavery argument, see Faust, *Ideology of Slavery*, 1–20.

27. For example, Crenshaw, *Slave States in the Presidential Election of 1860*, 180–81; speech of William L. Yancey, in *Knoxville Whig*, September 22, 1860; William Harper, "Memoir on Slavery," in Faust, *Ideology of Slavery*, 109–10; speech of John Johnson, in *Charleston Courier*, July 28, 1858. For an example of a modern historian relating the idea that slavery debased labor, see McPherson, *Ordeal by Fire*, 39–41.

28. Bonner, "Profile of a Late Ante-Bellum Community," 680; May, *John A. Quitman*, 31, 71; Wiltse, *John C. Calhoun: Nullifier*, 324–25; Eaton, *Mind of the Old South*, 87. On the acquisitive nature of southern society, see Oakes, *Slavery and Freedom*, 92–116; Oakes, *Ruling*

Race, 39–59, 127. The free-labor ideology is fully developed in Eric Foner, *Free Soil, Free Labor, Free Men*, chap. 1.

29. Speech of Philip P. Barbour, April 27, 1820, *Annals of Congress*, 16th Cong., 1st sess., 2075; speech of Barry, April 27, 1854, *Cong. Globe*, 33d Cong., 1st sess., *Appendix*, 616. For other such contemporary expressions, *Brownlow's Knoxville Whig*, October 13, 1860; "Rising in the World," from *Vermont Patriot*, in *Tuscaloosa (Ala.) Independent Monitor*, August 10, 1847; "True Wealth," in *Natchez Mississippi Free Trader*, November 22, 29, 1848; "The Way to Get Rich," from *Hunt's Merchants' Magazine*, quoted in *Macon Georgia Journal and Messenger*, November 8, 1848; "The Dignity of Labor," from *Philadelphia Inquirer*, quoted in ibid., August 8, 1849; address of Kenneth Rayner at North Carolina State Agricultural Fair, in *North Carolina Weekly Raleigh Register*, October 25, 1854; "Feudalism in the Nineteenth Century," *Southern Literary Messenger* 15 (August 1849): 466, 471; Andrew Johnson to William W. Pepper, July 17, 1854, in Graf and Haskins, *Papers of Johnson*, 2:238; Young, *Domesticating Slavery*, 4–7.

30. Wolfe, *Helper's Impending Crisis Dissected*, 57–58; *Southern Planter* 20 (January 1860): 58–60; "Philadelphia Lawyer's View of the Constitution," *Russell's Magazine* 1 (April 1857): 75–76; Coulter, *William G. Brownlow*, 92–93.

31. *Charleston Mercury*, February 25, 1859. For other examples, speech of Jefferson Davis, September 2, 1845, in Monroe and McIntosh, *Papers of Davis*, 2:324–25; Address of the Republican Members of Congress [John C. Calhoun], July 6, 1838, in Meriwether et al., *Papers of Calhoun*, 14:369–73; Niven, *John C. Calhoun and the Price of Union*, 162–64; Cassandra, *Charleston Mercury*, September 8, 1857; *Natchez Mississippi Free Trader*, May 30, 1859; Huston, *Panic of 1857*, 85–97; Shore, *Southern Capitalists*, 11–12, 19, 35–41.

32. Quotation from Wolfe, *Helper's Impending Crisis Dissected*, 60. See also speech of Jefferson Davis, May 26, 1851, in Rowland, *Jefferson Davis: Constitutionalist*, 2:73–74; Ford, *Origins of Southern Radicalism*, chaps. 2, 6, 7, 9; Oakes, *Ruling Race*, 42–43, 69–95; speech of Rust, December 28, 1859, *Cong. Globe*, 36th Cong., 1st sess., 269. Probably the work most associated with an extreme vision of a capitalist South—to include the slaves as well—is Fogel and Engerman, *Time on the Cross*, 1:4–6; Fogel, *Without Consent or Contract*, 64–72, 154–98.

33. *Jackson Mississippian*, January 18, 1859; S. W. C., "The Voluntary Principle," *United States Review* 36 (November 1855): quotations from 387, 392, 386–95; prospectus of the *Natchez Mississippi Free Trader*, February 8, 1858. On the competitive nature of the southern states and their politics, see Shade, *Democratizing the Old Dominion*, 160–77; Thomas Brown, *Politics and Statesmanship*, 170–87; Atkins, *Parties, Politics, and Sectional Conflict in Tennessee*, 68–78; Carey, *Parties, Slavery, and the Union in Antebellum Georgia*, 106–10; Bergeron, *Antebellum Politics in Tennessee*, chap. 2; Ford, *Origins of Southern Radicalism*, 102. On state constitutional development, see Eaton, *History of the Old South*, 293–98; Green, *Constitutional Development in the South Atlantic States*, 153–64, 254–91; Sydnor, *The Development of Southern Sectionalism*, 275–93; Williamson, *American Suffrage*, 223–41, 265–99; Kruman, *Parties and Politics in North Carolina*, 45–47. For views doubting the democratic quality of southern politics, see Christopher Morris, *Becoming Southern*, chap. 5; McCurry, *Masters of Small Worlds*, chap. 7; Edmunds, *Francis W. Pickens and the Politics of Destruction*, xi, 104–5.

34. Huston, *Panic of 1857*, 81–97.

35. The classic treatment of the proslavery argument as exemplifying a labor argument opposed to the free market is Genovese, *World the Slaveholders Made*, 118–94. For examples of proslavery writers and race, see Albert T. Bledsoe, "Liberty and Slavery," in E. N. Elliot, *Cotton Is King*, 411–26; S. A. Cartwright, "Slavery in Light of Ethnology," in ibid., 691–728; quotation from Chancellor Harper, "Slavery in Light of Social Science," in ibid., 575–86, 93; see Olmsted, *The Cotton Kingdom* (1861), 512–13; Horsman, *Josiah Nott of Mobile*, 81–98.

36. Alfred Iverson at a public dinner, 1859, in *Milledgeville (Ga.) Federal Union*, July 26, 1859; inaugural of John J. Pettus, in *Vicksburg (Miss.) Weekly Whig*, November 23, 1859; James Hammond, quoted in Merritt, *James Henry Hammond*, 112; Barney, *Secessionist Impulse*, 38–43; Shore, *Southern Capitalists*, 35–38, 43–50; Thornton, *Politics and Power in a Slave Society*, 204–27; Fredrickson, *Black Image in the White Mind*, 43–70.

37. Lathers, *Reminiscences*, 4–5.

38. Gavin Wright, *Old South, New South*, chap. 2.

39. On the diversity of the South, see Degler, *The Other South*; Freehling, *The Road to Disunion: Secessionists at Bay*; and, generally, Eaton, *Mind of the Old South*.

40. *Natchez Mississippi Free Trader*, September 25, 1850.

41. Numerous scholars have focused attention on slaveholders only seeing slaves as property: Oakes, *Slavery and Freedom*, 72–75; Oakes, *Ruling Race*, 26, 109; McCurry, *Masters of Small Worlds*, 7, 13, 114–17; Durden, *Self-Inflicted Wound*, x; Phillips, *Life and Labor in the Old South*, 161–62; Brian Reid, *Origins of the American Civil War*, 41.

42. Thomas B. Macaulay to Henry S. Randall, May 23, 1857, in *Littell's Living Age* 65 (May 19, 1860): 430–31. On the relation between English economics and democratic ideas in the nineteenth century, see Stromberg, *Democracy*, chap. 3.

43. Speech of February 13 and 14, 1850, in Rowland, *Jefferson Davis: Constitutionalist*, 1:283; see also speech of Alexander H. Stephens in *Macon Georgia Journal and Messenger*, September 11, 1850.

44. "Slavery as a Moral Relation," *Southern Literary Messenger* 17 (July 1851): 402–3; Sawyer, *Southern Institutes* (1859), 248–49.

45. *Charleston Mercury*, March 13, 1848; also Cassandra, "The Political Position of the South, No. 1," in ibid., September 8, 1857; speech of Horace Maynard, March 20, 1858, *Cong. Globe*, 35th Cong., 1st sess., 1208; see Fields, *Slavery and Freedom on the Middle Ground*, 62–65.

46. Ben Franklin during the Constitutional Convention reminded the members that slavery brought with it the fear of slave revolts, and that slave property was different from all other kinds of property, for whoever heard of an insurrection of sheep? Reidy, *From Slavery to Agrarian Capitalism*, 6; see Morris, *Southern Slavery and the Law*, 1–2; Franklin, *Militant South*, viii, 63–87.

47. Livermore, *Story of My Life*, 183, 187; see also narrative of Frederick Douglass and his encounter with the professional "slave-breaker"; Douglass, *Narrative of the Life of Frederick Douglass, an American Slave*, 71–86. For discussion of cruelty in slavery, which I think woven inextricably into the system, see Blassingame, *Slave Community*, chap. 7; Stampp, *Peculiar Institution*, chap. 4. On property rights in slaves generally, Thomas Morris, *Southern Slavery and the Law*; Genovese, *Roll, Jordan, Roll*, 4–17; Turner, *From Chattel Slaves to Wage Slaves*, 2, 9; Sydnor, *Slavery in Mississippi*, chap. 5, esp. p. 90; Parish, *Slavery: History and Historians*, 34; Wahl, *Bondsman's Burden*, 15–17, 24–25, 49–50. For modern economists' treatment of coercion, see Friedman, *Capitalism and Freedom*, 13–15, 109; Sowell, *Economics and Politics of Race*, 84–100; Hummel, *Emancipating Slaves, Enslaving Free Men*, 40–41, 69–70. In contradistinction, somewhat interestingly, see Engerman, "Some Considerations Relating to Property Rights in Man."

48. Joshua F. Speed to Salmon P. Chase, September 2, 1861, in Niven, McClure, and Johnsen, *Chase Papers*, 3:93; *Macon Georgia Journal and Messenger*, October 24, 1849; Julius Rockwell to Artemas Hale, December 28, 1850, Hale Papers; Armistead Burt to Thomas B. Byrd et al., in *Columbus (Ga.) Enquirer*, June 3, 1851; see Reidy, *From Slavery to Agrarian Capitalism*, 6; Hummel, *Emancipating Slaves, Enslaving Free Men*, 52–55, 69; Wahl, *Bondsman's Burden*, chaps. 5, 6.

49. Memminger speech in *Charleston Mercury*, October 10, 1850.

50. For treatments of the subject of law and slavery from different ideological perspectives, see Stampp, *Peculiar Institution*, chap. 5; Tushnet, *American Law of Slavery*; Phillips, *Life and Labor in the Old South*, 161–70; Randolph Campbell, *An Empire for Slavery*, 97–98, 151. See analysis of Wahl, *Bondsman's Burden*.

51. William Cooper acknowledges the property aspect in the southerners' demand for liberty but believes their idea of liberty had a much broader perspective; William Cooper, *Liberty and Slavery*, 175–81.

52. Eaton, *History of the Old South*, 299.

53. Law[rence] T. Dade to Daniel F. Slaughter, March 13, 1832, in Slaughter Papers. Ambler, *Sectionalism in Virginia*, 50–86, 193; Williamson, *American Suffrage*, 231–34; Sydnor, *The Development of Southern Sectionalism*, 288–90; Green, *Constitutional Development in the South Atlantic States*, 288–91, 277–78; Eaton, *History of the Old South*, 293–98; Conway, *Testimonies concerning Slavery* (1864), 33–34; William C. Harris, *Leroy Pope Walker*, 9.

54. On rule within the South, see Kruman, *Parties and Politics in North Carolina*, 45–54; Wooster, *People in Power*, 9–25, 33–40, 105–13; see also Michael Johnson, *Toward a Patriarchal Republic*, 32–34, 54–58, 83–101.

55. This point has also been raised by Frayssé, *Lincoln, Land, and Labor*, 162, 166.

56. D. H. London, "Enfranchisement of Southern Commerce," *De Bow's Review* 28 (March 1860): 315; William J. Grayson, "The Dual Form of Labour," *Russell's Magazine* 6 (October 1859): 14; speech of Robert B. Rhett, December 22, 1841, in *Cong. Globe*, 27th Cong, 2d sess., *Appendix*, 43. An analysis of how the federal government could damage southern slavery was given in a speech by Robert Barnwell Rhett, *Charleston Mercury*, September 25, 1850. See also Eaton, *History of the Old South*, 383–84; Dodd, *Cotton Kingdom*, 29; Wiltse, *John C. Calhoun: Nationalist*, 197, 390–93.

57. Claiborne, *Life and Correspondence of Quitman*, 2:189; John C. Calhoun to Virgil Maxcy, September 11, 1830, in Meriwether et al., *Papers of Calhoun*, 11:229. See Freehling, *Prelude to Civil War*, ix–x, 192–96, 255–59.

58. William H. Trescot to James H. Hammond, December 5, 1858, Hammond Papers, Library of Congress; see roughly the same comments of Henry Clay to Joshua R. Giddings, October 6, 1847, in Hay, *Papers of Clay*, 10:356; *Milledgeville (Ga.) Federal Union*, October 31, 1854.

59. Speech of Yancey in *Athens (Ga.) Southern Banner*, June 8, 1848.

60. How the federal government was used in a proslavery manner is the thesis of Fehrenbacher, *Slaveholding Republic*.

61. The sentiment was widespread. However, see Thomas R. Dew, "The Abolition of Slavery," in Faust, *Ideology of Slavery*, 39–40; William A. Graham speech, in Hamilton, *Papers of Graham*, 4:555. A particularly good explanation of the connection between property rights, voting, and taxation is William O. Goode to Robert M. T. Hunter, May 11, 1850, in Ambler, *Correspondence of Hunter*, 112. Brian Reid, *Origins of the American Civil War*, 42–43.

62. Message of Seabrook in Capers, *Life of Memminger*, 197; Beverly Tucker to James H. Hammond, December 29, 1846, in Hammond Papers, Library of Congress; John Forsyth, "The North and the South," *De Bow's Review* 17 (October 1854): 367. On the other hand, see the defense of majority rule by Judge Garnett Andrews of Georgia in *Macon Georgia Journal and Messenger*, October 2, 1850. See also speech of Alfred H. Colquitt of Georgia, May 10, 1854, *Cong. Globe*, 33d Cong., 1st sess., *Appendix*, 752; Dabney, *Defence of Virginia* (1867), 298–300; speech of Jefferson Davis in *Yazoo (Miss.) Democrat*, May 7, 1851; Sinha, *Counterrevolution of Slavery*, 2–5, 89–91; Freehling, "Divided South," 146–49, 172–74.

63. Carsel, "The Slaveholders' Indictment of Northern Wage Slavery"; Faust, *Ideology of Slavery*, 2–18; Mitchell, *Edmund Ruffin*, 83, 104–17; Genovese, *World the Slaveholders Made*,

165–94; Jenkins, *Pro-Slavery Thought in the Old South*, 295–300. A peculiar addition to the literature, finding proslavery thought among northerners first, is Tise, *Proslavery*. Those emphasizing property rights and population theory would include Kaufman, *Capitalism, Slavery, and Republican Values*, 99, 101, 107–8, 112; Jenkins, *Pro-Slavery Thought in the Old South*, 294, 300; Wish, *George Fitzhugh*, 191–92, 224.

64. Shore, *Southern Capitalists*, 20, 26; Hietala, *Manifest Design*, 110–18; McCoy, *Elusive Republic*, 190–95. For examples of southern use of population theory, see James Madison to Richard Rush, April 21, 1821, in Hunt, *The Writings of Madison*, 9:45–53; Dabney, *Defence of Virginia*, 297–307; James K. Paulding to John C. Calhoun, April 5, 1848, in Meriwether et al., *Papers of Calhoun*, 25:296; *Huntsville (Ala.) Southern Advocate*, March 4, 1848; Cobb, *An Inquiry into the Law of Negro Slavery in the United States of America* (1858), xlvii; Robert Toombs quotation from Stephens, *Constitutional View of the Late War between the States* (1870), 1:644–45; Fitzhugh, *Cannibals All!*, 237–38.

65. Claiborne, *Life and Correspondence of Quitman*, 2:263; E. N. Elliot, *Cotton Is King*, 898; George Fitzhugh, "The Conservative Principle," *De Bow's Review* 22 (April 1857): 422. The explicit link between the danger to property and democracy can as well be seen in Murphy, *L. Q. C. Lamar*, 48; Python, "Relative Political Positions of the North and the South," *De Bow's Review* 22 (February 1857): 114–15; James Henry Hammond, "Letter to an English Abolitionist," January 28, 1845, in Faust, *Ideology of Slavery*, 176–77.

66. For this subject, see Benjamin Wright, *American Interpretations of Natural Law*, 212–37, 307–11; Genovese, *World the Slaveholders Made*, 158, 211–13.

67. Quotations from Jackson, Mississippi, meeting in *Vicksburg (Miss.) Whig*, October 9, 1849; Sawyer, *Southern Institutes*, 14; Kentucky law quoted from Howard, *Evangelical War against Slavery and Caste*, 46. Discussions of natural law and slavery can be found in Cobb, *Historical Sketch of Slavery*, ccxxx–cclxiv, esp. ccxxxvi; remarks of James Mason, March 2, 1858, *Cong. Globe*, 35th Cong., 1st sess., 925; speech of W. T. Hamilton of Maryland, May 19, 1854, ibid., 33d Cong., 1st sess., *Appendix*, 824; speech of Muscoe R. H. Garnett, March 22, 1858, ibid., 35th Cong., 1st sess., 1244; remarks of Jefferson Davis, February 25, 1850, ibid., 31st Cong., 1st sess., 420; Pearce, *Benjamin H. Hill*, 37–38.

68. There is a willingness to accord states' rights a power independent of the slavery issue, a position which I find wholly inadequate. This has been frequently suggested in connection with the ideals of republicanism. For examples, consult Ford, "Republican Ideology in a Slave Society: The Political Economy of John C. Calhoun"; Harris, "Last of the Classical Republicans"; Michael Morrison, *Slavery and the American West*, 6–10, 258–78. For older views, Hesseltine, *Lincoln's Plan of Reconstruction*, 19, 33–37; Osborne, "The Last Hope of the South—To Establish a Principle." For the anti-Democratic nature of states' rights views, see Freehling, "Nullification, Minority Blackmail, and the Crisis of Majority Rule"; Shade, *Democratizing the Old Dominion*, 228–64. For a work connecting slavery to states' rights, Carpenter, *South as a Conscious Minority*, 128, 142. A book that treats northern states' rights as well as southern is Richard E. Ellis, *Union at Risk*, 2–65. See the skeptical comments about states' rights by a libertarian: Hummel, *Emancipating Slaves, Enslaving Free Men*, 14–26. The best statements of states' rights as the cause of the Civil War are by Jefferson Davis and Alexander H. Stephens: Davis, *The Rise and Fall of the Confederate Government*, 1:1–15, 52, 78–79; Stephens, *Constitutional View of the Late War between the States*, 1:539, 2:28–29.

69. On states' rights doctrines, see McDonald, *States' Rights and the Union*; Dumond, *Secession Movement*, 2–5; Sellers, *Southerner as American*, 42; Eaton, *Freedom-of-Thought Struggle in the Old South*, 144–45. An excellent treatment is Freehling, *Prelude to Civil War*, 134–76. For contemporary examples, see Virginia resolutions offered by Arthur Bagby, December 12, 1848, *Cong. Globe*, 30th Cong., 2d sess., 28; "The Nebraska Bill and Speech of

Senator Chase," *Southern Literary Messenger* 20 (March 1854): 185–87; "Centralization," *United States Magazine and Democratic Review* 26 (April 1850): 289–300.

70. Quotations from remarks on Senate Resolutions, January 6, 1838, in Meriwether et al., *Papers of Calhoun,* 14:6; and John C. Calhoun to Virgil Maxcy, September 11, 1830, in ibid., 11:229; see also draft of address to People of South Carolina, December 1, 1830, in ibid., 11:268–70; John C. Calhoun to Frederick W. Symmes, in ibid., 11:427–34.

71. Calhoun, *A Disquisition on Government and Selections from the Discourse,* 13–22, quotation on p. 13. See comments of message of Governor Seabrook of South Carolina to the General Assembly, November 25, 1850, in Capers, *Life of Memminger,* 197; James Madison had a similar idea about the importance of differing interests to explain the Revolution; comments of Madison, June 6, 1787, in Madison, *Notes of Debates,* 76–77. For interpretations of Calhoun, see Niven, *John C. Calhoun and the Price of Union,* 328–35; Ford, *Origins of Southern Radicalism,* chap. 8. For others seeing Calhoun's position as a defense of property, Dodd, *Expansion and Conflict,* 164–65; Eaton, *History of the Old South,* 312–15; Sinha, *Counterrevolution of Slavery,* 20–35.

72. Correspondence in John C. Calhoun to Robert L. Dorr, March 21, 1847, Meriwether et al., *Papers of Calhoun,* 24:274–75; Robert L. Dorr to Calhoun, March 1, 1847, ibid., 24:229. Such attitudes disturbed northern Democrats; see Benjamin Tappan to Lewis Tappan, March 6, 1847, Benjamin Tappan Papers. In contrast to Calhoun, see the speech of Robert Toombs, March 18, 1858, *Cong. Globe,* 35th Cong., 1st sess., *Appendix,* 125–26.

73. Speech of Laurence M. Keitt, March 30, 1854, *Cong. Globe,* 33d Cong., 1st sess., *Appendix,* 465; William O. Goode, May 19, 1854, ibid., 33d Cong., 1st sess., *Appendix,* 907–8; speech of Clement C. Clay, March 19, 1858, ibid., 35th Cong., 1st sess., *Appendix,* 147; D. J. Bailey, February 28, 1855, ibid., 33d Cong., 2d sess., *Appendix,* 328; Albert G. Brown, December 29, 1848, ibid., 30th Cong., 2d sess., 126.

74. Quotation from *New York Express,* quoted by *Greensborough (N.C.) Patriot,* July 15, 1848; *Natchez Mississippi Free Trader,* March 14, 1849; Report of Southern State Convention, in *Vicksburg (Miss.) Weekly Whig,* October 9, 1849; speech of Shelton F. Leake, January 15, 1847, *Cong. Globe,* 29th Cong., 2d sess., *Appendix,* 127; Hampden in *Mobile Register and Journal,* September 14, 1847; speech of Curry, December 10, 1859, *Cong. Globe,* 36th Cong., 1st sess., 96; William Davis, *The Cause Lost,* 180–82.

75. Call for a southern congress in *Natchez Mississippi Free Trader,* April 9, 1851; editorial in ibid., October 9, 1850. See also *Charleston Mercury,* January 4, 10, 1851.

76. Jefferson Davis to S. Cobun et al., November 7, 1850, in Rowland, *Jefferson Davis: Constitutionalist,* 1:595; William P. Miles, March 31, 1858, *Cong. Globe,* 35th Cong., 1st sess., *Appendix,* 287; Bayard, March 22, 1858, ibid., *Appendix,* 191.

77. James L. Seward, May 10, 1854, *Cong. Globe,* 33d Cong, 1st sess., *Appendix,* 619; *Toledo Blade,* January 27, 1847; *New Orleans Picayune,* March 9, 1850; speech of Lewis Cass, March 14, 1850, *Cong. Globe,* 31st Cong., 1st sess., 529. See Carpenter, *South as a Conscious Minority*; Williams, *Romance and Realism in Southern Politics,* 12.

78. Quotation from Sydnor, *The Development of Southern Sectionalism,* 189; see also Peterson, *The Great Triumvirate,* 173; Malone, *Public Life of Thomas Cooper,* chap. 10, esp. pp. 310–14. The reference here of course is to the revisionist historians who stressed the emotionalism of abolitionists and fire-eaters; Milton, *The Eve of Conflict*; Randall, "The Blundering Generation."

79. Owsley, "The Fundamental Cause of the Civil War"; Osborne, "The Last Hope of the South—To Establish a Principle"; Hesseltine, *Sections and Politics,* 98–112; Hesseltine, *Lincoln's Plan of Reconstruction,* 33. Of course, Confederate memoirs are filled with states' rights explanations for southern secession, but see analysis of Dew, *Apostles of Disunion,* 74–77.

80. Degler, *The Other South*, 119; Craven, *Growth of Southern Nationalism*, 118.

81. Examples of the revisionist school include Randall, "The Blundering Generation"; Craven, *Growth of Southern Nationalism*, 19, 119–22, 286–88; Craven, *An Historian and the Civil War*, 46–62; Craven, *Civil War in the Making*, viii–ix, 66–69; Simms, *Decade of Sectional Controversy*, viii; Milton, *The Eve of Conflict*, 1–2, 237–38; Ramsdell, "The Natural Limits of Slavery Expansion." A sophisticated treatment that relies on the breakdown of the Second Party System to release sectional agitators who sought to shore up their positions by appeal to sectional animosities is Holt, *The Political Crisis of the 1850s*, 3–9. See the trenchant criticisms offered by Robert E. May, "Psychobiography and Secession"; Stampp, *Imperiled Union*, chap. 7.

82. Ford, *Origins of Southern Radicalism*, 121–25, 138, 351–54, 372; Greenberg, *Masters and Statesmen*, ix–x, 3–14, 125–35. Watson, *Liberty and Power*, though dealing nationally with republicanism in the Jacksonian age, makes the agrarian versus commerce or industry quality of this interpretation quite clear. See also Oakes, "From Republicanism to Liberalism"; for a general description of how the interpretation of republicanism has developed, see Rodgers, "Republicanism."

83. For example, Dumond, *Secession Movement*, 5–21; Freehling, *Prelude to Civil War*, 307–9. On preserving the South from internal enemies, see Michael Johnson, *Toward a Patriarchal Republic*, xx–xxi.

84. Siegel, *Roots of Southern Distinctiveness*; Koeniger, "Climate and Southern Distinctiveness"; McWhiney, *Cracker Culture*. See Allan Nevins, "Contrast of Cultures," in Nevins, *Ordeal of the Union*, 2:515–54, for the classic statement of differences between North and South.

85. Cole, *Irrepressible Conflict*, xiii, 46–52; Anne Norton, *Alternative Americas*, chap. 4; McPherson, "Antebellum Southern Exceptionalism"; Craven, *Growth of Southern Nationalism*, 9–12; Phillips, *Course of the South to Secession*, 152.

86. Oakes, *Slavery and Freedom*, 55–56, 62; Collins, *Origins of America's Civil War*, 4–13, 28–30; Pessen, "How Different from Each Other Were the Antebellum North and South?"; Govan, "Was the Old South Different?"; William Taylor, *Cavalier and Yankee*, 15–22, 334–40; Boney, *Southerners All*; Brian Reid, *Origins of the American Civil War*, 97–101.

87. The "prebourgeois" society theory is of course most prominently tied to Genovese, *Political Economy of Slavery*, 7–10, 15–34. The best introduction to modernization as relates to the Civil War is Richard Brown, *Modernization*, chap. 7; Raimondo Lurgahi, "The Civil War and the Modernization of American Society." Modernization was presaged by a number of historians; Craven, *An Historian and the Civil War*, 102–12.

88. Wyatt-Brown, *Yankee Saints and Southern Sinners*, chap. 7; and Wyatt-Brown, *Southern Honor*. Wyatt-Brown has recently restated his belief that while slavery in general was responsible for southern secession, it was the honor aspect of southern culture that determined the decision; Wyatt-Brown, *Shaping of Southern Culture*, 179.

89. Speech of Gartrell, January 25, 1858, *Cong. Globe*, 35th Cong., 1st sess., 391; *Yazoo (Miss.) Democrat*, February 2, 1851; *Natchez Mississippi Free Trader*, October 9, 1857; Merritt, *James Henry Hammond*, 102; Thomas Cooper, "Slavery," *Southern Literary Journal* 1 (1835): 188–91; *Brownlow's Knoxville Whig*, May 8, 1858. See Huston, *Panic of 1857*, 93–94; for racism in proslavery, merely consult any collection of proslavery writing, such as E. N. Elliot, *Cotton Is King*, and Faust, *Ideology of Slavery*. On northern Democrat effusions, see, for example, *Easton (Pa.) Argus*, August 19, 1858; *Cleveland Daily Plain Dealer*, October 20, 1860; Baker, *Affairs of Party*, 177, 185–92, 212–58; Dykstra, *Bright Radical Star*, 157, 189. Mitigating the charge of racism against the Democrats is Feller, "A Brother in Arms."

90. For an example of this line of thinking, see speech of James H. Hammond, March 3,

1858, *Cong. Globe,* 35th Cong., 1st sess., 961–62; William Harper, "Memoir on Slavery," in Faust, *Ideology of Slavery,* 78–135; letter of Joseph E. Brown, December 7, 1860, in Freehling and Simpson, *Secession Debated,* 149–55.

91. The two basic books for this interpretation are Steven Channing, *Crisis of Fear,* 258–69, 289–93; and Thornton, *Politics and Power in a Slave Society,* 204–27. Two recent additions stressed the racial appeal of prosecessionist agitators to nonslaveholders and border state Unionists: Dew, *Apostles of Disunion,* 74–81; Fehrenbacher, *Slaveholding Republic,* 306–7, 342–43. On the rise of the racist argument, see Betty Wood, *Origins of American Slavery,* 53–55, 89–92; Morgan, *American Slavery, American Freedom,* 376–81.

92. Beringer et al., *Elements of Confederate Defeat,* 179–86; Rable, *But There Was No Peace,* 187–91; Tunnell, *Crucible of Reconstruction,* 173–218.

93. On the fallacy of using "race" as a category at all, see Fields, "Ideology and Race in American History"; Ignatiev, *How the Irish Became White,* 1.

94. Speech of Wilmot, February 8, 1847, *Cong. Globe,* 29th Cong., 2d sess., *Appendix,* 357; for others, see speech of Fessenden, March 3, 1854, ibid., 33d Cong., 1st sess., *Appendix,* 318–19; speech of Tompkins, February 18, 1858, ibid., 774; speech of Bishop Perkins, May 10, 1854, ibid., 33d Cong., 1st sess., *Appendix,* 646; E. W. Farley, May 10, 1854, ibid., 33d Cong., 1st sess., *Appendix,* 680. Inequality of blacks pervaded the Lincoln-Douglas debates; see David Potter, *Impending Crisis,* 339–54; on how slavery would eventually end, see remark of Johannsen, *Lincoln, the South, and Slavery,* 59–60, 77.

95. Thomas Roderick Dew, "Abolition of Negro Slavery," in Faust, *Ideology of Slavery,* 23–77, quotation from 27, bulk of material 23–30. See also remarks of Governor Joseph E. Brown of Georgia in Freehling and Simpson, *Secession Debated,* 149–50.

96. Hacker, *Triumph of American Capitalism,* 323–35; Beard and Beard, *Rise of American Civilization,* 1:632–39, 2:1–54. In one fashion or another, this viewpoint informs Billings, *Planters and the Making of a "New South,"* chap. 3; Genovese, *Political Economy of Slavery,* 248–70; Wiltse, *John C. Calhoun: Nationalist,* 197; Sydnor, *The Development of Southern Sectionalism,* 132.

97. Genovese, *Political Economy of Slavery,* 34, 35; Bensel, *Yankee Leviathan,* 11, 416.

98. Speech of Reuben Davis, January 27, 1858, *Cong. Globe,* 35th Cong., 1st sess., 440–41. Same sentiment shared by Jefferson Davis and Alexander H. Stephens; Jefferson Davis, *The Rise and Fall of the Confederate Government,* 1:6, 32, 83; Johnston and Browne, *Life of Alexander H. Stephens,* 109–22.

99. Actually, the Beards did refer to the census numbers, but they misinterpreted them and did not pay attention to the results for personal and real wealth. The Beards claimed that northerners finally outdistanced slave wealth when *all* northern wealth was combined—which was a highly unusual way for showing that slave property was becoming insignificant. Beard and Beard, *Rise of American Civilization,* 1:635.

100. Frayssé, *Lincoln, Land, and Labor,* 162–68. In the twentieth century, most historians of the antebellum United States have deemphasized the wealth that slaves represented. This trend has been reversed in the last four decades by economic historians. They rediscovered the immensity of the value of slavery, yet they have been generally reticent in linking that investment to the origins of the Civil War except in the most obvious manner—wealth holders do not enjoy being deprived of their wealth. They seemed to have been most intrigued by capital gains, the territorial issue, or the sectional impact of federal policy. More important, political historians have not incorporated the economists' findings in current interpretations of sectional conflict. Gunderson, "The Origin of the American Civil War"; Gavin Wright, *Political Economy of the Cotton South,* chap. 5; Ransom and Sutch, "Capitalists

without Capital"; Ransom and Sutch, *One Kind of Freedom*, 52; Ransom, *Conflict and Compromise*, 68–72.

101. See the statistical results of Formisano, *The Birth of Mass Political Parties*, 290–96; Gienapp, *Origins of the Republican Party*, 437–38; Gienapp, "Who Voted for Lincoln?," 50–97; Holt, *Forging a Majority*, 184–88, 303; Renda, *Running on the Record*, 39, 68–69; Cook, *Baptism of Fire*, 8–11, 31–32; Hansen, *Making of the Third Party System*, 40–44, 51, 92–93; Baum, *Civil War Party System*, 75–89; Philip Foner, *Business and Slavery*, esp. 2–5; Mandel, *Labor Free and Slave*, 154–55; O'Connor, *Lords of the Loom*, 81–124, 161–64; Gregory, *Nathan Appleton*, 302–4. Kenneth Stampp underscored how many occupations slave laborers filled in the Old South: Stampp, *Peculiar Institution*, 60–66.

102. Spahr, *An Essay on the Present Distribution of Wealth in the United States*, 31, 34.

103. Gunderson, "The Origin of the American Civil War"; Gavin Wright, *Political Economy of the Cotton South*, chap. 5; Ransom and Sutch, "Capitalists without Capital"; Ransom and Sutch, *One Kind of Freedom*, 52; Ransom, *Conflict and Compromise*, 68–72.

104. Speech of Preston S. Brooks, May 15, 1854, *Cong. Globe*, 33d Cong., 1st sess., *Appendix*, 372. See also Jefferson Davis, July 12, 1848, in Monroe and McIntosh, *Papers of Davis*, 3:356; *Greensborough (N.C.) Patriot*, October 2, 1847; John Miller, *Wolf by the Ears*, 96; Takaki, *Pro-Slavery Crusade*, 35, 113; Saunders, *John Archibald Campbell*, 62–63.

Chapter 3

1. Yates, *Speech of Hon. Richard Yates . . . Delivered at Springfield, Ill., 7 June 1860*, 7; speech of Oglesby in *Chicago Press and Tribune*, August 1, 1860.

2. For examples of the emphasis on the moral question of slavery, see Potter, *Impending Crisis*, 328–55; the religious component of those moral convictions can be found in Carwardine, *Evangelicals and Politics in Antebellum America*, 323; Brian Reid, *Origins of the American Civil War*, 142. The northern elite interpretation is the progressive interpretation: Beard and Beard, *Rise of American Civilization*, 2:3–10, 28–31, 50–51, 99–115; and Bensel, *Yankee Leviathan*, 10–15, 57–67. A recent restatement of the blundering generation approach is Aldrich, *Why Parties?*, chap. 5; the original view was propagated by Randall, "The Blundering Generation." The view that northern discontent was a result of a disheveled society coping with modernization, or that class formation created a new arrogant class, is implied in Richard Brown, *Modernization*, 3–22, 150–76; McPherson, *Ordeal by Fire*, 5–25; Levine, *Half Slave and Half Free*, chaps. 2, 3, 5. Two particular applications based on the change from a barter economy to a wage-labor economy are Ashworth, *Slavery, Capitalism, and Politics in the Antebellum Republic*, ix–x, 149, 157–66; and Dawley, *Class and Community*, 100–102. The northern side of culture is given in Wyatt-Brown, *Yankee Saints and Southern Sinners*, chaps. 2, 3, 7. An inference can be made that the rise of the middle class helped spark northern antisouthernism: Blumin, *Emergence of the Middle Class*. On cultural conflict, shaped by the difference between rural life and industrial life, see Anne Norton, *Alternative Americas*.

3. On the slave power, see Richards, *Slave Power*; Holt, *The Political Crisis of the 1850s*, 51, 148–52; and Gienapp, *Origins of the Republican Party*, 357–64. For the free labor ideology, Eric Foner, *Free Soil, Free Labor, Free Men*, chap. 1.

4. Paludan, *A People's Contest*, 3–31.

5. The basic interpretation I am offering is in Huston, *Securing the Fruits of Labor*, chap. 4. See also Atack and Bateman, *To Their Own Soil*; Kulikoff, *Agrarian Origins of American Capitalism*; and any number of good economic histories, such as Hughes, *American Economic History*; Brownlee, *Dynamics of Ascent*; Lebergott, *The Americans*.

6. Huston, *Securing the Fruits of Labor*, chap. 4. A somewhat pessimistic view of labor and wages is given in Margo, *Wages and Labor Markets*, 4, 5, 43–44, 80–85, 91–92, 108, 153–56. For a different division by occupations, see Ferrie, *Yankeys Now*, 36; on wages and immigration, see ibid., 161–83.

7. The census of 1850 also gave an occupational listing based on the census of 1840, which would have been enlightening because it was before the immigration wave and at the initial stages of the transportation revolution. Unfortunately, those results, already tabulated by census officials, were for all people, including gender and race. Thus, they are not standardized somehow by household. Moreover, the breakdown of labor is inadequate for the questions I am pursuing. U.S. Department of the Census, *Seventh Census*, vol. 1: *Population*, lxxx, table LII.

8. *Buffalo Courier and Pilot*, October 7, 1846; *Detroit Democratic Free Press*, August 8, 1846; description of the northern economy here accords with the earlier assessment of Collins, *Origins of America's Civil War*, 30–35.

9. Ashworth, *Slavery, Capitalism, and Politics in the Antebellum Republic*, ix–x, 10–12, 115–17, 149; Steinfeld, *Invention of Free Labor*, 129–37, 143–63; Eric Foner, "The Idea of Free Labor in Nineteenth-Century America," introductory essay to 1995 edition of Eric Foner, *Free Soil, Free Labor, Free Men*, xvi–xxii; Stanley, *From Bondage to Contract*, 4–11.

10. Fogel, *Without Consent or Contract*, 354–62.

11. U.S. Census Office, *Twelfth Census*, vol. 7: *Manufactures*, Part 1, p. cxxviii. When women and children were added, the number for 1870 was 2,054,000, and in 1900 was 5,315,000. For the entire work force the increase was 80 percent between 1880 and 1900.

12. See discussion in U.S. Census Office, *Twelfth Census*, vol. 12: *Special Reports: Employees and Wages*, xiii, xxi–xxiii.

13. Note discussion in Gavin Wright, *Political Economy of the Cotton South*, 22–29.

14. Speech of Perkins, May 10, 1854, *Cong. Globe*, 33d Cong., 1st sess., *Appendix*, 647; untitled speech of McClernand in Untitled Speech Fragments, box 2, folder "Speeches," second fragment with D 70 on corner, in McClernand Papers. See *Milwaukee Weekly Wisconsin*, October 1, 1856; speech of David D. Field, in *New York Tribune*, September 25, 1860.

15. Eric Foner, *Free Soil, Free Labor, Free Men*, chap. 2; Grant, *North over South*, 41–58, 81–110.

16. Boritt, *Lincoln and the Economics of the American Dream*, 115, 172–73, 176–80; Huston, *Securing the Fruits of Labor*, chaps. 1–3.

17. Abraham Lincoln speech at New Haven, Conn., March 6, 1860, in Basler, Pratt, and Dunlap, *Collected Works of Lincoln*, 4:24; speech of Daniel Webster, March 7, 1850, *Cong. Globe*, 31st Cong., 1st sess., 482; letter of Theodore Parker in *New York National Anti-Slavery Standard*, January 27, 1848, p. 137; Martin, *Mind of Frederick Douglass*, 254–60.

18. *Baltimore Niles Weekly Register*, November 13, 1819, p. 162; A[lonzo] Potter, *Political Economy* (1841), 62.

19. Colwell, *Claims of Labor* (1861), 5. On the dimensions of the European problem, see *Philadelphia Public Ledger*, April 14, 1848; "Civilization: American and European," in *American [Whig] Review* 3 (June 1846): 622. On the angry movements of urban labor, see Laurie, *Artisans into Workers*; Pessen, *Most Uncommon Jacksonians*; Wilentz, *Chants Democratic*.

20. Brownlow and Pryne, *Ought Slavery to Be Perpetuated?* (1858), 52; Lincoln speech at Kalamazoo, August 27, 1856, in Basler, Pratt, and Dunlap, *Collected Works of Lincoln*, 2:365; speech of Henry Bennett, May 17, 1854, *Cong. Globe*, 33d Cong., 1st sess., *Appendix*, 694; see Wendell Phillips in *Philadelphia Pennsylvania Freeman*, May 18, 1848; *Buffalo Daily Courier*, December 29, 1846.

21. Tappan, *Modern Democracy the Ally of Slavery* ([1856]), 4–6.

22. Speech of James Wilson, February 16, 1849, *Cong. Globe*, 30th Cong., 2d sess., *Appendix*, 196; Calhoun remark in Charles Adams, *Memoirs of John Quincy Adams*, 5:10; Judge Ruffin quotation in Goodell, *American Slave Code in Theory and Practice* (1853), 33; speech of Wendell Phillips in *Philadelphia Pennsylvania Freeman*, May 23, 1850. See Olmsted, *The Cotton Kingdom*, 19; Frederick Douglass, "Freedom in the West Indies," August 2, 1858, in Blassingame, *Frederick Douglass Papers*, ser. 1, 3:219; letter of Commodore Stewart, May 4, 1861, published in Drake, *Union and Antislavery Speeches* (1864), 110.

23. Fessenden, *Life and Public Services of William Pitt Fessenden*, 1:54; speech of Davis of Massachusetts, May 4, 1830, *Cong. Debates*, 21st Cong., 1st sess., 882–83; James G. Birney to Myron Holley et al., May 11, 1840, in Dumond, *Letters of Birney*, 1:566–67; John G. Whittier to the *Newburyport Herald*, October 1842, in Pickard, *Letters of Whittier*, 1:578; Sam L. DeFord to Caleb Cushing, April 5, 1842, Cushing Papers. On the role of the three-fifths compromise, see esp. Richards, *Slave Power*, 41–50.

24. W. B. Thrall to Ben Wade, August 5, 1856, Wade Papers; C. H. Ray to Elihu B. Washburne, December 24, 1854, Washburne Papers; Gideon Wells to Martin Van Buren, July 28, 1846, Van Buren Papers; Moses M. Davis to John F. Potter, October 25, 1857, Potter Papers.

25. *New York National Anti-Slavery Standard*, November 9, 1848, pp. 93–94.

26. Speech of Banks in *New York Times*, September 10, 1857. Some of the more pointed "Slave Power" documents would include Charles Adams, *What Makes Slavery a Question of National Concern?* (1855); Webb, *Slavery and Its Tendencies* (1856); William H. Seward, "The Advent of the Republican Party," speech at Albany, October 12, 1855, in Baker, *Works of Seward* (1887), 4:226–36; Seward, "The Slaveholding Class Dominant in the Republic," speech at Detroit, October 2, 1856, in ibid., 4:254–55; Charles Sumner, "Union among Men of All Parties against the Slave Power and the Extension of Slavery," June 28, 1848, in Sumner, *Works of Sumner*, 2:77–85; Julian, *Speeches on Political Questions*, 24–28; Henry Wilson, *History of the Rise and Fall of the Slave Power in America* (1872). Examples of northerners complaining about being governed by a minority of slaveholders would include letter of OLD DEMOCRAT in *Indianapolis Daily Journal*, October 4, 1860; Lyman Trumbull speech in *Chicago Press and Tribune*, September 29, 1859; *Chicago Daily Democrat*, September 22, 1860. For discussion of the slave power theory, see Gara, "Slavery and the Slave Power: A Crucial Distinction"; Gienapp, "The Republican Party and the Slave Power"; Richards, *Slave Power*.

27. See Eric Foner, *Free Soil, Free Labor, Free Men*, chap. 2.

28. Upham, March 1, 1847, *Cong. Globe*, 29th Cong., 2d sess., 548. Hogeboom reply to George Fitzhugh in Fitzhugh and Hogeboom, *Controversy on Slavery* (1857), 36; see Gerteis, *Morality and Utility in American Antislavery Reform*, 36–37.

29. Burleigh, *Slavery and the North* (1855), 3; speech of Kellogg, March 23, 1858, *Cong. Globe*, 35th Cong., 1st sess., 1269; speech of Seward at New York City, October 20, 1853, in Seward, *Seward at Washington*, 208; Conway, *Testimonies concerning Slavery*, 33; Barnburner resolutions from Utica Convention, in *Chicago Gem of the Prairie*, July 8, 1848; speech of Benjamin Wade, March 13, 1858, *Cong. Globe*, 35th Cong., 1st sess., 1113.

30. Adam Smith, *An Inquiry into the Nature and Causes of the Wealth of Nations*, 81, 365; *The Injurious Effects of Slave Labour* (1824), 7–10; Palfrey, *Papers on the Slave Power*, 66; see also speech of Cassius M. Clay at New York, 1846, in Greeley, *Writings of Cassius Marcellus Clay* (1848), 189; Alvan Stewart, "An Address by the 'National Committee of Correspondence,'" April 1840, in Marsh, *Writings and Speeches of Stewart* (1860), 238–39.

31. "The Financial Crisis," *North American Review* 86 (January 1858): 181–82.

32. Preston King, January 5, 1847, *Cong. Globe*, 29th Cong., 2d sess., 114; see report of New York Democratic Convention in *Washington (D.C.) National Era*, July 13, 1848; John

Abbott, *History of the Civil War in America* (1863–66), 1:20; speech of John Van Buren in *Rochester (N.Y.) Advertiser*, June 27, 1848; Convention call of Free-Soilers in *Toledo Blade*, May 10, 1848; Goodell, *Slavery and Anti-Slavery* (1852), 319–20. Compare Glickstein, *American Exceptionalism, American Anxiety*, chap. 3.

33. *Appeal of the Independent Democrats in Congress to the People of the United States* ([1854?]), 5. For examples, speech of Benjamin F. Wade, March 13, 1858, *Cong. Globe*, 35th Cong., 1st sess., 1113; *Chicago Press and Tribune*, August 24, 1859; *Providence Journal*, March 30, 1860; speech of Cortlandt Parker, *Newark Daily Advertiser*, September 1, 1860; consult Glickstein, *American Exceptionalism, American Anxiety*, 76–80.

34. George Patterson to George Washington Julian, [December 4, 1852?], Julian Papers. The idea of the value and respect of labor being lost due to the presence of slaves can be found in the famous tracts of the time: Helper, *Impending Crisis of the South* (1857), 41–44; *Poor Whites of the South* ([1860?]), 2–3, 5. This type of comment surfaced repeatedly, and it was hardly a novel observation; it was prevalent during the revolutionary era. For an earlier example, see Benjamin Franklin, *Observation on the Increase of Mankind*, 1751, in Labaree, *Writings of Franklin*, 4:231.

35. Speech of Dean, March 25, 1858, *Cong. Globe*, 35th Cong, 1st sess., 1357; speech of Charles W. Gardner, May 9, 1837, in Ripley, *Black Abolitionist Papers*, 3:206; William Lloyd Garrison to *Boston Evening Transcript*, November 6, 1830, in Merrill and Ruchames, *Letters of Garrison*, 1:112; *Prairieview (Wisc.) American Freeman*, August 18, 1846; Sumner, "Example of Massachusetts against Slavery," September 18, 1860, in Sumner, *Works of Sumner*, 5:277; Weston, *Southern Slavery Reduces Northern Wages* (1856), 5. *Chicago Press and Tribune*, October 19, 1858; [Lemuel Shaw], "Slavery and the Missouri Question," *North American Review* 10 (January 1820): 142; speech of Elizabeth Cady Stanton in Stanton, Anthony, and Gage, *History of Women Suffrage* (1887), 1:599; speech of Samuel T. Glover, in *New York Tribune*, August 1, 1860; *New York Tribune*, May 27, 1854. It should be noted that Weston later retreated, believing that as free labor was more intelligent it should be able to compete with slavery; Weston, *Progress of Slavery in the United States* (1858), 7–11.

36. Olmsted, *The Cotton Kingdom*, 90. On free labor versus slave labor in the South, see Gavin Wright, "Prosperity, Progress, and American Slavery," 332; Siegel, "Artisans and Immigrants in the Politics of Late Antebellum Georgia"; Shugg, *Origins of Class Struggle in Louisiana*, 88–94; Sydnor, *The Development of Southern Sectionalism*, 25; Green, *Constitutional Development in the South Atlantic States*, 159–61; Eaton, *History of the Old South*, 412; Berlin and Gutman, "Natives and Immigrants, Free Men and Slaves"; Jackson, *Free Negro Labor and Property Holding in Virginia*, 59–69; Takaki, *Pro-Slavery Crusade*, 44–49; Mandel, *Labor Free and Slave*, 24, 28–31; Gillespie, *Free Labor in an Unfree World*, 18–22, 150–57. These ideas that slave labor lowered ("degraded") free labor wages had a long pedigree: see *Baltimore Niles Weekly Register*, January 29, 1820, p. 368; Taylor of New York in Missouri Compromise debate of 1820, *Annals of Congress*, 15th Cong., 2d sess., 1176; Edgar McManus, *History of Negro Slavery in New York*, 183; Zilversmit, *First Emancipation*, 46–47; Goldin, *Urban Slavery in the American South*, 28–31.

37. Douglass, *Life and Times of Frederick Douglass* (1892), 180; Greeley, *Writings of Clay*, 205; Smiley, *Lion of White Hall*, 48; Eaton, *Mind of the Old South*, 114–16.

38. *Lebanon (Pa.) Courier*, April 7, 1854. For other examples of antislavery advocates promoting a dread of competition between slave and free labor, see William Smith, *Francis Preston Blair Family in Politics*, 1:219; *Cincinnati Daily Gazette*, October 1, 1858; *Evansville (Ind.) Daily Journal*, August 24, 1860; *Washington (Pa.) Reporter*, August 8, 1856; Hamlin, *The Life and Times of Hannibal Hamlin*, 299; Salter, *The Life of James W. Grimes*, 45; Kraut, "The Forgotten Reformers: A Profile of Third Party Abolitionists in Antebellum New York," 143–

44; Nordhoff, *America for Free Working Men* (1865), 5; [Bigelow?], *Life, Explorations and Public Services of John Charles Fremont* (1856), 458.

39. *Springfield Daily Illinois State Journal*, September 29, 1857; see also *Philadelphia Sun*, quoted in *Milwaukee Daily Free Democrat*, August 28, 1857. A clash between labor systems was a fundamental problem in the United States regardless of territorial expansion, which is why the expansion of the 1840s was not the sole reason for the sectional quarrel of the 1850s; its appearance evoked the underlying conflict between the labor systems. For those stressing the expansionist issue, see David Potter, *Impending Crisis*, 6–7, 47–50, 52–54; Parish, *American Civil War*, 24–25; Brian Reid, *Origins of the American Civil War*, 25–42, 52–56, 63–65, 102, 108–15.

40. *Chicago Weekly Democrat*, March 12, 1848; see the same sentiments in *Milwaukee Daily Free Democrat*, November 14, 1857. The reduction of free wages by competition with slave labor can also be found in Richard Yates, February 28, 1855, *Cong. Globe*, 33d Cong., 2d sess., *Appendix*, 251; Seward, *Immigrant White Free Labor, or Imported Black African Slave Labor* (1857), 4–5; copy of address of Democratic members of the New York legislature, 13–15, extra, April 1848, *Albany Atlas*, copy in the Van Buren Papers; *Washington (D.C.) National Era*, July 20, 1848; Blake, *History of Slavery and the Slave Trade, Ancient and Modern* (1858), 59; *Philadelphia North American*, October 14, 1856; speech of Lincoln at Cincinnati, September 17, 1859, in Basler, Pratt, Dunlap, *Collected Works of Lincoln*, 3:446; [Nordhoff?], *What Democratic Leaders Think of Slavery* ([1865?]), 3, 5, 9, 12, 13, 21; *Poor Whites of the South*, 4–6; Bourke and DeBats, *Washington County*, 67.

41. *New York National Anti-Slavery Standard*, November 15, 1849, p. 98; *Rochester Advertiser*, October 27, 1848; see *Philadelphia Pennsylvania Freeman*, July 10, 1851; *Lebanon (Pa.) Courier*, August 23, 1860. On Herschel V. Johnson, *Chicago Press and Tribune*, October 6, 1860; *Pottsville Miner's Journal*, June 23, 30, 1860; *Richmond (Ind.) Palladium*, September 6, 1860; *Springfield Daily Illinois State Journal*, August 29, 1860. On Hammond's speech, *Chicago Daily Tribune*, March 16, 1858; *New York Tribune*, March 11, 1858, p. 6; *Bedford (Pa.) Inquirer*, April 30, 1858.

42. Etcheson, *Emerging Midwest*, 5, 67–70, 99; other studies note the fear of competition between slaves and free workers; Richardson, *Greatest Nation of the Earth*, 23, 210; Bourke and DeBats, *Washington County*, 67; Cook, *Baptism of Fire*, 31–42; Ratcliffe, *Party Spirit in a Frontier Republic*, 47, 232; Buenger, *Secession and the Union in Texas*, 18–19.

43. John C. Calhoun to John McLean, August 4, 1828, in Meriwether et al., *Papers of Calhoun*, 10:407; Calhoun's draft of the "Exposition and Protest," in ibid., 10:460.

44. See Huston, *Securing the Fruits of Labor*, chap. 5; this idea also detected by Glickstein, *American Exceptionalism, American Anxiety*, chap. 7.

45. Martindale, February 17, 1824, *Annals of Congress*, 18th Cong., 1st sess., 1653–54; see Huston, *Securing the Fruits of Labor*, 174–82, 247–51.

46. Gavin Wright, *Old South, New South*, 27–28.

47. For example, Martineau, *Society in America* (1837), 2:131–32; Eaton, *Henry Clay and the Art of American Politics*, 136; Phillips, *Life of Robert Toombs*, 163–64; R. M. T. Hunter to James R. Mocou, Thomas Croxton, et al., December 12, 1860, in Ambler, *Correspondence of Hunter*, 346; Cobb, *Historical Sketch of Slavery*, xlvii; Jefferson Davis speech July 12, 1848, in Monroe and McIntosh, *Papers of Davis*, 3:356. For the role of Malthusian population theory in southern thinking, merely look at Fitzhugh, *Cannibals All!* In the voluminous literature on the economics of slavery, one should consult as well the pointed and libertarian comments of Hummel, *Emancipating Slaves, Enslaving Free Men*, 38–70.

48. The people who would have felt a broad and not local labor market effects of early American slaveholding would have been cotton, tobacco, rice, and sugar producers and

workers in other lands. Most of that competition was slave-based also, so that the broad labor market effect would have been unnoticed.

49. The transportation revolution is now a well-documented change in United States history, most of the literature dealing with the effects of the switch from a semicommercial society to a fully commercial society. For the economics, the best book remains George Taylor, *The Transportation Revolution*; see also a decent textbook, like Hughes, *American Economic History*; or even an older work, such as Russel, *A History of the American Economic System*. For an example of how some historians have used the transportation revolution to explain social and political developments, see Sellers, *The Market Revolution*.

50. In newspapers and increasingly in personal correspondence, the railroad became a centerpiece of discussion and speculation starting about 1848. On the limitations of the railroad in creating a seamless transportation system, see Chandler, *The Visible Hand*; and George Taylor and Neu, *American Railroad Network*.

51. L. C. B., "The Country in 1950, or the Conservatism of Slavery," *Southern Literary Messenger* 22 (June 1856): 426. See comments of Peter Parish on the effects of improved transportation facilities, Parish, *American Civil War*, 32.

52. See Huston, "The Experiential Basis of the Northern Antislavery Impulse"; Seward, "Irrepressible Conflict," 1858, in Baker, *Works of Seward*, 4:292. See also Huston, *Securing the Fruits of Labor*, chap. 4, on the results of the transportation revolution economically and socially.

53. This interpretation is the opposite of the one usually advanced. Genovese and Bensel —and the progressive school generally—argue that capitalism is inherently imperialistic and northern capitalists had designs on the wealth and prosperity of the South. Let it be noted that the only way that this interpretation can be upheld is by assuming the federal government had the power by legislation to impoverish the South and transfer its wealth to the North. Much writing on the coming of the Civil War has been in this vein. It is wrong. First, the federal government was not that strong, and the proposed legislation—tariffs, internal improvements, banking requirements, and homestead acts—are hardly the measures capable of carrying out such a grandiose scheme. This school has seen the transportation revolution largely in the light of creating new and highly avaricious capitalists loaded with the money to control the legislation of Congress. The effort to make the North the aggressor in the Civil War scenario has been so intense that it has overlooked the obvious impact of the transportation system—that the effects of slave labor could no longer be localized.

54. Seward speech at Rochester, 1858, in Baker, *Works of Seward*, 4:292; speech in U.S. Senate, July 2, 1850, in ibid., 1:108. See Edward Channing, *A History of the United States*, 6:3; Schurz, *Reminiscences of Carl Schurz*, 2:89; speech of John Hickman, in supplement to *Chicago Daily Press and Tribune*, May 7, 1859.

55. Weston, *Southern Slavery Reduces Northern Wages*, 5; for an opposing view, see "The Financial Crisis," *North American Review* 85 (January 1858): 181; *Boston Emancipator*, July 29, 1846, p. 54. On Weston, see analysis of Glickstein, *American Exceptionalism, American Anxiety*, chap. 5.

56. Speech of Jenkins, February 13, 1847, *Cong. Globe*, 29th Cong., 2d sess., 420; *Columbus Ohio State Journal*, May 25, 1854.

57. James M. Morrison to William H. English, February 16, 1858, English Papers. See *Gettysburg Compiler*, October 29, 1860; *Chicago Times and Herald*, September 5, 1860; speech of Charles Skelton of New Jersey, February 14, 1854, *Cong. Globe*, 33d Cong., 1st sess., *Appendix*, 190–91. On the southern climatic justification of slavery, Huston, *Panic of 1857*, 93–94.

58. Alfred H. Colquitt, May 10, 1854, *Cong. Globe*, 33d Cong., 1st sess., *Appendix*, 750–51;

speech of Calhoun, March 9, 1847, in *Charleston Mercury*, March 23, 1847. On the racist interpretation of slavery, see Steven Channing, *Crisis of Fear*. On the idea that slave and free labor inhabited different spheres, *Richmond Enquirer*, May 28, 1858; *Charleston Courier*, July 2, 1858; Sawyer, *Southern Institutes*, 356–57; *Natchez Mississippi Free Trader*, October 24, 1859; Russel, "The Effects of Slavery upon Nonslaveholders in the Ante Bellum South"; Kettell, *Southern Wealth and Northern Profits*, 62; Colton, *Rights of Labor* (1847), 5–7.

59. For studies of southern manufacturing, see Stampp, *Peculiar Institution*, 60–73; Fogel, *Without Consent or Contract*, 102–13; Starobin, *Industrial Slavery in the Old South*; Preyer, "The Historian, the Slave, and the Ante-Bellum Textile Industry"; Ronald Lewis, *Coal, Iron, and Slaves*; Aufhauser, "Slavery and Technological Change"; Wahl, *Bondsman's Burden*, 49–52.

60. Gavin Wright, "Slavery and the Cotton Boom," 437; also in Gavin Wright, *Political Economy of the Cotton South*, 90–97. Wright additionally believed that the southern economic response would have been to put slaves into factories and then that would have generated a social apocalypse; Wright, "Prosperity, Progress, and American Slavery," 303–32.

61. For the particulars of this debate, see Fields, *Slavery and Freedom on the Middle Ground*, 54–56, 84; Genovese, *Political Economy of Slavery*, 23, 24, 28–29, 43–44, 46, 55, 112, 117, 158–59, 165–73; Randall Miller, *Cotton Mill Movement in Antebellum Alabama*, 1–2, 208–13; Ashworth, *Slavery, Capitalism, and Politics in the Antebellum Republic*, 92–99; Cohen, *Karl Marx's Theory of History*, 65, 70, 72, 82–83, 189, 191–93; Wyatt-Brown, "Slavery's Cross Resurrected—and Recast"; Phillips, *American Negro Slavery*, 389, 396, 401; Eaton, *History of the Old South*, 274–75; Craven, *Coming of the Civil War*, 81–82; Russel, *Economic Aspects of Southern Sectionalism*, 54–57, 230; Fischbaum and Rubin, "Slavery and the Economic Development of the American South"; Schmitz and Schaefer, "Slavery, Freedom, and the Elasticity of Substitution"; Wade, *Slavery in the Cities*, 246–48; Christopher Morris, *Becoming Southern*, 166; Stampp, *Peculiar Institution*, 400–404; Gray, "Economic Efficiency and Competitive Advantages of Slavery under the Plantation System"; Shugg, *Origins of Class Struggle in Louisiana*, 88–94; Robert Smith, "Was Slavery Profitable in the Ante-Bellum South?"; Kenneth Johnson, "Slavery and Racism in Florence, Alabama, 1841–1862"; Sutch, "Profitability of Ante-Bellum Slavery"; Majewski, *House Dividing*, 42–44, 113, 178, 142–63.

62. On the alteration of work processes in the American economy during and after the 1880s, consult Livesay, *Andrew Carnegie and the Rise of Big Business*, 83–90; Chandler, *The Visible Hand*, chaps. 8, 9, 11; Porter, *Rise of Big Business*, 1–84; Hounshell, *From the American System to Mass Production*, 1–13, 217–61. On factory towns, see Irving Bernstein, *Lean Years*, 148–57; Brody, *Labor in Crisis*, 89–95, 148–55. For police forces in factories, Fine, *Sit-Down*, 37–42; Halberstam, *The Reckoning*, 87–97; Sward, *Legend of Henry Ford*, 291–342.

63. For the argument against slavery in industry, see Fields, *Slavery and Freedom on the Middle Ground*, 54–56, 84; Genovese, *Political Economy of Slavery*, chap. 9; Randall Miller, *Cotton Mill Movement in Antebellum Alabama*, 1–2, 208–13; Ashworth, *Slavery, Capitalism, and Politics in the Antebellum Republic*, 92–99.

64. Nye, *Fettered Freedom*, 254–57; Lofton, "Abolition and Labor"; Rayback, "American Workingman and the Antislavery Crusade"; Schlüter, *Lincoln, Labor, and Slavery*, 44–65.

65. Fogel, *Without Consent or Contract*, 355–60; Carsel, "The Slaveholders' Indictment of Northern Wage Slavery"; Nye, *Fettered Freedom*, 254–57; Dumond, *Antislavery*, 353–55; Mandel, *Labor Free and Slave*, 81–92, 103–4; Ignatiev, *How the Irish Became White*, 96–113.

66. For the antislavery animus of workers, see Mandel, *Labor Free and Slave*, esp. 113–41; Jentz, "The Anti-Slavery Constituency in Jacksonian New York City"; Rayback, "American Workingman and the Antislavery Crusade."

67. On the troubles with definition, see, for example, Gilje, "The Rise of Capitalism in

the Early Republic"; Gordon S. Wood, "The Enemy Is Us: Democratic Capitalism in the Early Republic"; Appleby, "The Vexed Story of Capitalism Told by American Historians." On the tendency to elevate "wage labor" as the key structure of capitalism, consult Macpherson, *Political Theory of Possessive Individualism*, 53–55; Cohen, *Karl Marx's Theory of History*, 64–66; Ashworth, *Slavery, Capitalism, and Politics in the Antebellum Republic*, ix–x, 82–84; Stanley, *From Bondage to Contract*, 8–17.

68. Ashworth, *Slavery, Capitalism, and Politics in the Antebellum Republic*, 131–49; Steinfeld, *Invention of Free Labor*, 143–57, 175–84. Eric Foner, "The Idea of Free Labor in Nineteenth-Century America," xiii–xxxix. Foner thinks that, although the abolitionists were moralists, they did justify the wage contract (xxii) while the Republicans were more sympathetic to labor (xxv). On the legal problems of defining freedom and coercion, see Steinfeld and Engerman, "Labor—Free or Coerced?"

69. Certain Marxian theorists insist that the Marxian analysis of exploitation does not require subsistence wages, e.g., Elster, *Introduction to Karl Marx*, 74–75; Wolff and Resnick, *Economics: Marxian versus Neoclassical*, 168–71. On the other hand, the analytical Marxist theoretician, John E. Roemer, finds subsistence wages an irreplaceable part of the theory if exploitation and class conflict are to be explained: Roemer, *A General Theory of Exploitation and Class*, 150.

70. See Huston, "A Political Response to Industrialism: The Republican Embrace of Protectionist Labor Doctrines"; Huston, *Securing the Fruits of Labor*, chaps. 5, 6, 7; and Huston, "Abolitionists, Political Economists, and Capitalism." Virtually all political parties up to 1860 wanted the foundation of the nation to be yeoman farmers; Democrats may have wanted to avoid the factory system, but they certainly were not low-wage advocates, whereas the abolitionists, Free-Soilers, and Republicans were clearly high-wage proponents.

71. Huston, *Securing the Fruits of Labor*, chaps. 2, 6; Alexander, *Commodity and Propriety*, 50–61.

72. Clark, March 15, 1858, *Cong. Globe*, 35th Cong., 1st sess., *Appendix*, 92; speech of Tompkins, February 18, 1858, ibid., 774; speech of E. W. Farley, May 10, 1854, ibid., 33d Cong., 1st sess., *Appendix*, 678; *Chicago Daily Democrat*, April 26, 1848.

73. Bishop Perkins, May 10, 1854, *Cong. Globe*, 33d Cong., 1st sess., *Appendix*, 647; *Rochester Democrat*, February 11, 1847; *Milwaukee Daily Free Democrat*, October 10, 1850; *Philadelphia Pennsylvania Freeman*, July 20, 1848; Henry Wilson, *Speech of Hon. Henry Wilson, at the Republican Mass Metting at Bangor, Me., August 27, 1868* (1868), 9. Other expressions equating free labor with yeoman farmers may be found in *Ottawa (Ill.) Free Trader*, March 3, 1848; *Rochester Advertiser*, October 19, 1848; speech of Benjamin F. Wade, March 7, 1860, *Cong. Globe*, 36th Cong., 1st sess., *Appendix*, 154; speech of Samuel Mayall, May 16, 1854, ibid., 33d Cong., 1st sess., *Appendix*, 714; Going, *David Wilmot, Free-Soiler*, 168, 174; speech of Oliver P. Morton, quoted in Foulke, *Life of Oliver P. Morton*, 2:72; Schurz, *Speech Delivered at Verandah Hall, St. Louis, August 1, 1860* ([1860]), 3. Note the discussion of the northern farm labor economy in Majewski, *House Dividing*, 39–42.

74. Sedgwick, *Public and Private Economy*, 1:254; Garfield, "Joshua R. Giddings," July 25, 1870, in Hinsdale, *Works of Garfield*, 1:596; note emphasis of Jonathan Glickstein on metropolitan centers in his studies of free labor ideology; Glickstein, *American Exceptionalism, American Anxiety*, 13–15.

Chapter 4

1. Huston, *Securing the Fruits of Labor*, chaps. 1–2.
2. Madison, *Notes of Debates*, 194.

3. For the classics, see James Wilson, "Of Man, as a Member of Society" and "On the History of Property," in McCloskey, *Works of Wilson*, 1:233–41, 2:711–19; Lieber, *Essays on Property and Labour as Connected with Natural Law and the Constitution of Society* (1841). For examples of property rights as vested rights, see the descriptions of Justice William Storey and Chancellor Kent given in Kutler, *Privilege and Creative Destruction*.

4. Noah Webster to Daniel Webster, 1837, in Warfel, *Letters of Noah Webster*, 489–94, quotation from 501–2.

5. J. Loud to Artemas Hale, April 24, 1848, Hale Papers; Weed, *Autobiography of Thurlow Weed*, 2:560–61.

6. A Northern Conservative, "A Word to Southern Democrats," *American [Whig] Review* 10 (August 1849): 194. For some reason, much of the literature on Jacksonian politics between 1828 and 1846 fails to capture the division between the parties over the sanctity of property rights, yet it used to be a standard in the historiography; Howe, *Political Culture of the American Whigs*, 108–22; Schlesinger, *Age of Jackson*, 311–12. See discussion of the advent of democracy and the safety of property rights in Keyssar, *Right to Vote*, 39–52. Keyssar perhaps undervalued the continuing belief that majority rule inherently warred on property rights.

7. Thomas Babington Macaulay to Henry S. Randall, May 23, 1857, published in *Littell's Living Age* 65 (May 19, 1860): 430–31; see response of *New York Tribune*, April 7, 1860, p. 4.

8. For example, Pennsylvania Society for Promoting the Abolition of Slavery, *Memorials* (December 1792), 7, 23, 29; Brackenridge, *Brackenridge Reader*, 104; Woolman, *Some Considerations on the Keeping of Negroes* (1754), 2–3; Rush [A Pennsylvanian], *An Address . . . upon Slave-Keeping* (1773), 7; Benezet, *A Short Account of That Part of Africa Inhabited by the Negroes* (1762), 5–7; Benezet, *Observations on Inslaving, Importing and Purchasing of Negroes* (1759), 2–9; Swift, *Oration on Domestic Slavery* (1791), 5–6; Noah Webster, *Effects of Slavery* (1793), 7–8; *Constitution of the Maryland Society, for Promoting the Abolition of Slavery* (1789), 3; Amynto [unknown], *Reflections on the Inconsistency of Man* (1796), 5–7. See Huston, *Securing the Fruits of Labor*, 60–66.

9. Rush, *An Address . . . upon Slave-Keeping*, 19–20.

10. Woolman, *Some Considerations on the Keeping of Negroes*, 16, 19–20; Noah Webster, *Effects of Slavery*, 18–21; Benezet, *Observations on Inslaving, Importing and Purchasing of Negroes*, 12; Edwards, *Injustice and Impolicy of the Slave Trade*, 11–12.

11. Wiecek, *Sources of Antislavery Constitutionalism*, 25–35, 42.

12. Dwight, *An Oration Before, The Connecticut Society, for the Promotion of Freedom and the Relief of Persons Unlawfully Holden in Bondage* (1794), 8–9; Appleton, *Considerations on Slavery in a Letter to a Friend* (1767), 4; [Cooper], *A Mite Cast into the Treasury*, 10–11, quotation from 23; Wiecek, *Sources of Antislavery Constitutionalism*, 42; Gerteis, *Morality and Utility in American Antislavery Reform*, 13.

13. [Hopkins], *A Dialogue concerning the Slavery of the Africans* (1776), 37–39; Elihu Smith, *A Discourse . . . before the New-York Society for Promoting the Manumission of Slaves* (1798), 26; Rice, *Slavery Inconsistent with Justice and Good Policy*, 4–5, 20–21.

14. Woolman, *Consideration on Keeping Negroes* (1762), 16–17; Elihu Smith, *A Discourse . . . before the New-York Society for Promoting the Manumission of Slaves* (1798), 24.

15. Tom Paine, *The Rights of Man*, in Foner, *Complete Writings of Paine*, 1:251; Rice, *Slavery Inconsistent with Justice and Good Policy*, 3, 20–21; Cover, *Justice Accused*, 34, 44.

16. On the abolitionist movement, see Stewart, *Holy Warriors*; Goodman, *Of One Blood*; Huston, "The Experiential Basis of the Northern Antislavery Impulse."

17. Speech of Stewart, 1838, in Marsh, *Writings and Speeches of Stewart*, 53; Nathaniel Paul, "The Abolition of Slavery," 1827, in Woodson, *Negro Orators and Their Orations*, 66;

Fee, *Anti-Slavery Manual* (1848), 140–41; Frederick Douglass, "Lecture on Slavery, No. 1," Rochester, N.Y., 1850, in Foner, *Life and Writings of Douglass*, 2:135. See also William Lloyd Garrison to editor *Boston Evening Transcript*, November 6, 1830, in Merrill and Ruchames, *Letters of Garrison*, 1:112.

18. Ruffin quoted, emphasis in original, in Goodell, *American Slave Code in Theory and Practice*, 33; the same sentiment is quoted in Cobb, *An Inquiry into the Law of Negro Slavery in the United States of America*, 235.

19. It will be quickly noted that the escape from this dilemma for proslavery writers and politicians was by reference to race. In their view, Africans would not work except by coercion; thus, without force, blacks would not work at all and thereby create no fruits. Hence, proslavery advocates could argue that they indeed deserved the fruits of the slave's labor because without the guidance of slave masters no fruits would exist at all. Needless to say, northern antislavery folk were entirely unmoved by this racial justification; Huston, *Panic of 1857*, 93–94.

20. Bassett, *Slavery Examined by the Light of Nature* ([1858?]), 4; [Weld?], *The Bible against Slavery* (1838), 17; James M. Dickinson, "An Anti-Slavery Sermon, Delivered at Norwich, July 4, 1834," 4; Charles Sumner speech in the Senate, February 24, 1854, *Cong. Globe*, 33d Cong, 1st sess., *Appendix*, 263; *Hallowell (Me.) Liberty Standard*, March 26, 1846. For example, in William E. Channing's short book on slavery the first chapter was on the slave as property; Channing, *Slavery* (1836), chap. 1.

21. For the moral attack on slavery, see Huston, "Abolitionists, Political Economists, and Capitalism."

22. Henry Stanton, *Remarks on Slavery* (1837), 21.

23. Among the religious abolitionists, the reduction of people to property was sinful because it denied the enslaved individual moral development and thwarted personal responsibility. In the Protestant tradition, each individual had to be responsible for his or her salvation. Slavery interfered with the development of Christian moral attributes. Martha V. Ball to James G. Birney, May 10, 1848, Birney Papers; *Augusta (Me.) Kennebec Journal*, November 3, 1854; resolutions of New England Conference Methodist Episcopal Church, in *Philadelphia Pennsylvania Freeman*, July 16, 1846.

24. Henry Stanton, *Remarks on Slavery*, 21, see 19–26; Brownlow and Pryne, *Ought Slavery to Be Perpetuated?*, 63; Joshua Giddings, February 13, 1847, *Cong. Globe*, 29th Cong., 2d sess., *Appendix*, 457.

25. Phillips in *New York Tribune*, March 21, 1860, p. 8; John Abbott, *History of the Civil War in America*, 1:iii, iv.

26. *Washington (D.C.) National Era*, April 13, 1848; *New York Independent*, February 21, 1850, p. 30; James Russell Lowell to G. B. Loring, November 15, 1838, in Norton, *Letters of James Russell Lowell*, 1:33–34; Clarke, *Anti-Slavery Days*, 122. However, it must be mentioned that the morality of the abolitionists probably held them back from a full endorsement of democracy, as morality is not, at least for moralists, determined by majority voting.

27. Charles F. Adams to the Subscribers of the Whig, June 1, 1846, Adams [Family] Papers; "Aristocracy" in *Hallowell (Me.) Liberty Standard*, June 18, 1846; Clarke, *Anti-Slavery Days*, 114; speech of Wendell Phillips, 1853, in Phillips, *Speeches, Lectures, and Letters*, 143; Maria Weston Chapman, "The Beginning and the Ending," *Liberty Bell*, October 6, 1857, 14.

28. Hildreth, *Despotism in America*, 86–88, 97–99; Lowell, "The Election in November," in Lowell, *Political Essays*, 24–27; Henry Stanton, *Remarks on Slavery*, 19–20, 25–27; Charles Elliott, *Sinfulness of Slavery*, 1:104–17.

29. Henry Stanton, *Remarks on Slavery*, 20; Hildreth, *Despotism in America*, 55.

30. Frothingham, *Theodore Parker*, 135–36; Rogers, *A Collection from the Miscellaneous*

Writings of Nathaniel Peabody Rogers (1849), 285–87; [Elder], *Third Parties* (1851), 12, 13, 16–17; Charles Adams, *An Oration, Delivered before the Municipal Authorities of the City of Fall River, July 4, 1860* (1860), 7–8.

31. Whittier to the *National Era*, February 5, 1847, in Pickard, *Letters of Whittier*, 2:69; Lowell, "Election in November," in Lowell, *Political Essays*, 29.

32. Nathan Appleton letter in *Boston Liberator*, September 8, 1848, p. 143. For example, Henry Wilson wrote a classic book about the era, and one of his chapters (37) was titled "Demand for the Recognition of Property in Slaves"; Wilson, *History of the Rise and Fall of the Slave Power in America*, 1:528–44. For earlier debates on slavery, see William Miller, *Arguing about Slavery*, 9–10, 54–55, 256–57.

33. *Milwaukee Daily Sentinel and Gazette*, February 17, 1851, in Commons et al., *Documentary History of American Industrial Society*, 8:57. On the connection between property and labor among the Republicans, see Huston, *Securing the Fruits of Labor*, 324–28.

34. Cyrus L. Dunham, May 19, 1854, *Cong. Globe*, 33d Cong., 1st sess., *Appendix*, 1132.

35. Foulke, *Life of Oliver P. Morton*, 1:78; speech of Andrews, February 23, 1858, *Cong. Globe*, 35th Cong., 1st sess., 826; speech of Hale, January 20, 1858, ibid., 341.

36. Edward Wade, May 17, 1854, *Cong. Globe*, 33d Cong., 1st sess., *Appendix*, 665; Samuel Gordon, February 11, 1847, ibid., 29th Cong., 2d sess., 387; Francis Gillette, July 6, 1854, ibid., 33d Cong., 1st sess., 1617.

37. See remarks of William Pennington and John Sherman in *Newark Daily Advertiser*, September 14, 1860; V. Wright Kingsley to James Doolittle, January 26, 1860, Doolittle Papers.

38. *New York Tribune*, February 22, 1847. Clay made his remark in response to abolitionist petitions claiming there could be no property rights in man; Clay's remark was simply that property rights in slaves were valid because only the law determined property rights. At the time, abolitionists were outraged because Clay did not side with them. However, Clay's position also was a weakness of slavery, because it then made majority rule the arbiter of the fate of property rights in slaves, a position slaveholders could never accept. Clay speech in the Senate, on abolitionist petitions, February 7, 1839, quoted from Swain, *Life and Speeches of Henry Clay*, 2:398, 410. See the fuller citation from Clay given at the beginning of Part I of this work.

39. Salter, *The Life of James W. Grimes*, 57; speech of Henry Waldron, March 20, 1858, *Cong. Globe*, 35th Cong., 1st sess., 1212.

40. William H. Seward, "The Destiny of America," 1853, in Baker, *Works of Seward*, 4:122–38; speech in the Senate, February 29, 1860, *Cong. Globe*, 36th Cong., 1st sess., 910.

41. William H. Seward, "The Dominant Class in the Republic," 1856, in Baker, *Works of Seward*, 4:254–55.

42. Speech at Kalamazoo, August 27, 1856, in Basler, Pratt, and Dunlap, *Collected Works of Lincoln*, 2:365; quotation from speech at Columbus, Ohio, September 16, 1859, in ibid., 3:418.

43. Speech at Hartford, Conn., March 5, 1860, in ibid., 4:3–4; see also speech at New Haven, Conn., March 6, 1860, in ibid., 4:15–16; speech at Leavenworth, Kans., December 3, 1859, in ibid., 3:499; speech at Janesville, Wisc., October 1, 1859, in ibid., 3:485. These statements deserve more attention than they have received. Gabor Boritt's treatment of Lincoln's economic ideas, while admirable in most other respects, does not seem to pick up Lincoln's varied stand on property, and Olivier Frayssé's attempt to paint Lincoln as an obsessed democratic bourgeois overlooks Lincoln's reasoning on the limits of property; Boritt, *Lincoln and the Economics of the American Dream*, 163–64, 169–72; Frayssé, *Lincoln, Land, and Labor*, 25–26, 45, 123–28, 162–71.

44. Abraham Lincoln to Henry L. Pierce and others, April 6, 1859, in Basler, Pratt, and Dunlap, *Collected Works of Lincoln,* 3:375. See also speech of Charles Durkee, *Cong. Globe,* 35th Cong., 1st sess., *Appendix,* 152–53; H. D. Shanks to William H. Seward, November 13, 1851, Seward Papers; William H. Seward, "The Dominant Class in the Republic," 1856, in Baker, *Works of Seward,* 4:255.

45. Harlan speech, January 25, 1858, *Cong. Globe,* 35th Cong., 1st sess., 385–86. On the Democratic Party struggle with property rights, see Chapter 7.

46. *Charleston Mercury,* quoted in *Washington (D.C.) National Intelligencer,* June 26, 1858.

47. On legal developments generally, consult Wiecek, *Constitutional Development in a Modernizing Society,* 7, 55–59; Lawrence Friedman, *History of American Law,* 301–2; Horwitz, *Transformation of American Law,* 102–8, 160–82, 211–12. The linkage between abolitionism, the market, and legal decrees can, in one fashion or another, be found in David Davis, *Problem of Slavery in the Age of Revolution,* 254, 264–69, 304, 350; Stanley, *From Bondage to Contract*; Forbath, "Ambiguities of Free Labor," 768–77, 785–88. This emphasis on self-ownership has quite an interesting pedigree. See Macpherson, *Political Theory of Possessive Individualism,* 200–202; Nozick, *Anarchy, State, and Utopia,* 151–82; Richard J. Ellis, *American Political Cultures,* 28–33; Christman, "Self-Ownership, Equality, and the Structure of Property Rights"; Richard Curry and Goodheart, "Individualism in Trans-National Context," 16–18; Curry and Valois, "The Emergence of an Individualistic Ethos in American Society," 21–29; Genovese, *Slaveholders' Dilemma,* 56; Walters, *Antislavery Appeal,* 129; Goodheart, *Abolitionist, Actuary, Atheist,* 130.

Chapter 5

1. This interpretation is the reverse of Michael Morrison who argues that for southerners property rights were a lesser concern than their dread of a federal government with expansive power that could trample the rights of a white minority; Michael Morrison, *Slavery and the American West,* 60–61. The work by Forrest McDonald is unfortunately not greatly informative on states' rights and slavery expansion; McDonald, *States' Rights and the Union,* chaps. 7, 8.

2. Richard W. Thompson to Vigo County Whigs Constitutional Convention, June 8, 1847, Thompson Papers; Daniel Webster speech taken from *Yazoo (Miss.) Democrat,* June 18, 1851.

3. I have not located the McLean letter in the *Washington (D.C.) National Intelligencer*; but see S. W. H. to John McLean, February 4, 1847, McLean Papers; John Teasdale to McLean, January 11, 1847, ibid.; *Cleveland Daily Plain Dealer,* June 22, 1848; *Chicago Daily Democrat,* December 9, 1847.

4. Samuel Lahm, February 17, 1849, *Cong. Globe,* 30th Cong., 2d sess., *Appendix,* 108; *Washington (D.C.) National Era,* November 4, 1852; Charles Sumner to J. R. Giddings, December 21, 1846, Giddings Papers; *Lewistown (Pa.) Gazette,* October 23, 1856; exchange between Lawrence Keitt and Thomas Corwin, January 25, 1860, *Cong. Globe,* 36th Cong., 1st sess., 581–82; *Rochester Democrat,* January 14, 1847; *Pittsburgh Morning Post,* February 20, 1847; *Springfield Daily Illinois State Register,* December 8, 1849.

5. *Columbus Ohio State Journal,* September 5, 1846; resolution in *Albany Argus,* February 8, 1847; Thompson Campbell to Charles Lanphier, December 4, 1848, Lanphier Papers. For further examples, see *Pottsville (Pa.) Miner's Journal,* September 14, 1850; *Albany Argus,* October 14, 18, 24, 25, 1848; Daniel Mace, February 14, 1854, *Cong. Globe,* 33d Cong., 1st sess., *Appendix,* 166; Hannibal Hamlin, January 16, 1847, ibid., 29th Cong., 2d sess., 196; *Ottawa (Ill.) Free Trader,* September 15, 1848; speech of Lincoln at Bloomington, Ill., September 12,

1854, in Basler, Pratt, and Dunlap, *Collected Works of Lincoln*, 2:230–31; *Green Bay (Wisc.) Advocate*, October 19, 1848; *Hartford (Conn.) Times*, July 6, 1848; "Dangers and Safeguards of the Union," *American [Whig] Review* 9 (February 1849): 117; Richard W. Yates, fragment of a speech [1856], in Speeches, 1856 folder, Yates Papers; Broadside, "To the Independent Democratic Whigs, of the County of Oneida," July 4, 1848, Utica, N.Y., by Jno. S. Peckham et al., copy in Adams [Family] Papers.

6. Quotation from Robert Dale Owen, manuscript, "The Annexation of Texas," April 16, 1848, p. 45, Owen Papers; "Address of the Free Soil Convention of Massachusetts," in *New York National Anti-Slavery Standard*, September 21, 1848, pp. 65–66; *Albany Argus*, February 3, 1847; *Hartford (Conn.) Times*, March 30, 1848.

7. Letter of John Van Buren to John P. Epply et al., July 19, 1848, Van Buren Papers; *Washington (D.C.) National Era*, February 25, 1847; John A. Dix to Charles F. Adams, July 12, 1848, Adams [Family] Papers; Charles F. Adams to John Palfrey, July 16, 1848, ibid. References to the Northwest Ordinance of 1787 and to the Missouri Compromise are in nearly all antislavery constitutional arguments.

8. Morrison, May 19, 1854, *Cong. Globe*, 33d Cong., 1st sess., *Appendix*, 849, 852; Chandler, April 5, 1854, ibid., *Appendix*, 469–71; *Hallowell (Me.) Free Soil Republican*, October 26, 1848; V. Wright Kingsley to James Doolittle, January 8, 1860, Doolittle Papers.

9. Wentworth, May 18, 1854, *Cong. Globe*, 33d Cong., 1st sess., *Appendix*, 737; Samuel Waterbury et al. to Martin Van Buren, June 16, 1848, Van Buren Papers. See also Clay's letter to Wickliffe, September 2, 1844, in Hay, *Papers of Clay*, 10:108.

10. Dix speech June 26, 1848, in Dix, *Memoirs*, 1:224.

11. *Cincinnati Daily Enquirer*, March 9, 1847; Richard W. Thompson to delegates from Vigo to Whig County Meeting, June 8, 1847, Thompson Papers; Hamlin, March 9, 1858, *Cong. Globe*, 35th Cong., 1st sess., 1004.

12. Letter of Martin Van Buren to the Committee of the Buffalo Convention, August 22, 1848, in *Orleans Republican*, September 6, 1848, in Van Buren Papers; Martin Van Buren to Convention of New York City, June 20, in ibid.; copy of "Address of the Democratic Members of the Legislature of the State of New York," *Albany Atlas*, extra, April 1848, in ibid.; message of Maine governor Dana, in *Milwaukee Weekly Wisconsin*, June 16, 1847; Edward Bates to Schuyler Colfax, June 16, 1859, Bates Papers. See extended defense of slavery restriction by John Farnsworth, March 20, 1858, *Cong. Globe*, 35th Cong., 1st sess., 1204–5, who quotes southern judicial decisions stipulating that slavery was only a municipal institution; *Washington (D.C.) National Era*, January 27, 1848; John McLean to John Teesdale, November 2, 1855, McLean Papers.

13. For example, Palfrey, *Papers on the Slave Power*; Charles Sumner, "Necessity of Political Action against the Slave Power and the Extension of Slavery," September 29, 1847, in Sumner, *Works of Sumner*, 1:56–61; *Rochester Democrat*, January 25, 1847; *Columbus Ohio State Journal*, March 13, 1847.

14. Speech of John Van Buren, June 6, 1848, *New York Tribune*, quoted in *Utica (N.Y.) Oneida Morning Herald*, June 9, 1848; William Upham, March 1, 1847, *Cong. Globe*, 29th Cong., 2d sess., 548; speech of Wilmot, November 26, 1847, in Going, *David Wilmot, Free-Soiler*, 291; Address of the Democratic Members of the Legislature of the State of New York, April 1848, copy in Van Buren Papers.

15. Martin Van Buren to Convention of New York City, June 20, 1848, Van Buren Papers.

16. *Hartford Times*, March 8, 1847; *Cleveland Daily Plain Dealer*, January 30, 1847, March 4, 1848; Simon Cameron to Edmund Burke, June 15, 1849, Burke Papers.

17. *Macon Georgia Journal and Messenger*, September 19, 1848; "A Countryman," in *Charleston Mercury*, March 11, 1847; James H. Hammond to S. Fouché and others, September

26, 1850, Hammond Papers, Library of Congress; Address of Christopher Memminger, September 1851, in Capers, *Life of Memminger*, 212; *Columbus (Ga.) Enquirer*, January 19, 1847.

18. Hilliard, January 5, 1847, *Cong. Globe*, 29th Cong., 2d sess., 120; Dargan, January 7, 1847, ibid., 135–36; Seddon, January 7, 1847, ibid., *Appendix*, 86–87; Leake, January 15, 1847, ibid., *Appendix*, 127; Dobbin, February 11, 1847, ibid., 384; see Howell Cobb, February 9, 1847, ibid., 361–62; *Augusta (Ga.) Constitutionalist*, quoted in *Charleston Mercury*, January 18, 1847. On states' rights theories, see Dumond, *Secession Movement*, 2–5; Richard E. Ellis, *Union at Risk*, 3–11; Russel, "Constitutional Doctrines with Regard to Slavery in the Territories."

19. Calhoun, February 19, 1847, *Cong. Globe*, 29th Cong., 2d sess., 454–55; February 20 comments in Crallé, *Works of Calhoun*, 4:358–61.

20. Calhoun, speech on Oregon bill, June 27, 1848, in Crallé, *Works of Calhoun*, 4:482–85, quotation from p. 484.

21. Ibid., 486–96.

22. Ibid., 496–98.

23. Ibid., 505–11. On Calhoun's theories generally, see Niven, *John C. Calhoun and the Price of Union*, 156–60, 316–17, 324–28; Freehling, *Prelude to Civil War*, 159–73; Clyde N. Wilson and Shirley Bright Cook, Introduction to Meriwether et al., *Papers of Calhoun*, 25:xiii–xvii; Fehrenbacher, *Sectional Crisis and Southern Constitutionalism*, 36–38.

24. Speech of July 12, 1848, in Monroe and McIntosh, *Papers of Davis*, 3:332–35, 339–40, 343–47, 355–68, quotation from 265.

25. Ibid., 335–38, quotation from 335.

26. Ibid., 343; this speech is also summarized by Cooper, *Jefferson Davis*, 169–74.

27. See William O. Goode to Robert M. T. Hunter, May 11, 1850, in Ambler, *Correspondence of Hunter*, 112; James A. Bayard, March 22, 1858, *Cong. Globe*, 35th Cong., 1st sess., *Appendix*, 191.

28. *Natchez Mississippi Free Trader*, March 14, 1849; on the Constitution being primarily a form of government designed to protect property in slaves, see *Greensborough (N.C.) Patriot*, July 15, 1848; *Charleston Mercury*, March 13, 14, April 24, 1848; states' rights meeting in *Yazoo (Miss.) Democrat*, October 10, 1850.

29. Goode, May 19, 1854, *Cong. Globe*, 33d Cong., 1st sess., *Appendix*, 907–8. See Judge Daniel to Martin Van Buren, November 1, 1847, Van Buren Papers.

30. For examples of the equality of states, common property, and protection of slave property, see "The Nebraska Bill and Speech of Senator Chase," *Southern Literary Messenger* 20 (March 1854): 177–87; "The Wilmot Proviso," *United States Magazine and Democratic Review* 23 (September 1848): 219–22; message of Governor Reuben Chapman, in *Mobile Register and Journal*, November 16, 1849; H. Garnett, "The South and the Union," *De Bow's Review* 18 (February 1855): 145–47; Stanton, March 11, 1850, *Cong. Globe*, 31st Cong., 1st sess., 498–99; speech of James Seward, May 10, 1854, ibid., 33d Cong., 1st sess., *Appendix*, 621; Preston Pond Jr. to Millard Fillmore, November 1, 1856, Fillmore Papers, State University of New York at Oswego; Resolutions of Virginia Legislature on Wilmot Proviso published in *Boston Liberator*, February 16, 1849, 25; Hinds County resolutions in *Yazoo (Miss.) Democrat*, October 3, 1850; Resolves of Florida Democracy in *Charleston Mercury*, April 10, 1848; Southern Rights Meeting at Claibornville in *Natchez Mississippi Free Trader*, April 16, 1851; Report of State Convention, in *Vicksburg Whig*, October 9, 1849; Judge Daniel to Martin Van Buren, November 1, 1847, Van Buren Papers; *Raleigh North Carolina Standard*, June 20, 1849.

31. For examples of those arguing that property rights were above the touch of territorial legislatures, see R. H. Chamberlayne to Millard Fillmore, June 24, 1848, Fillmore Papers, State University of New York at Oswego; Yulee remarks in *Charleston Mercury*, April 7, 1848;

Raleigh Star and North Carolina Gazette, August 14, 1850; *Athens (Ga.) Southern Banner*, October 14, 1852; William Cullom, April 11, 1854, *Cong. Globe*, 33d Cong., 1st sess., *Appendix*, 541.

32. *Raleigh (N.C.) Weekly Register*, June 14, 1848.

33. *Augusta Georgia Weekly Constitutionalist*, August 2, 1848; *Columbus (Ga.) Enquirer*, March 2, 1847; remarks of Calhoun at Charleston, March 9, 1847, in *Charleston Mercury*, March 23, 1847.

34. Toombs speech quoted in Phillips, *Life of Robert Toombs*, 81–82.

35. Arthur Bestor called the southern quest for the expansion of slave law into the territories a demand for "extrajurisdicational" authority; Bestor, "The American Civil War as a Constitutional Crisis"; see also Bestor, "State Sovereignty and Slavery."

36. "Address of the Southern Delegates," February 1 or 2, 1847, in Crallé, *Works of Calhoun*, 6:297; Burt speech, January 14, 1847, *Cong. Globe*, 29th Cong., 2d sess., *Appendix*, 132; speech of Rhett in *Charleston Mercury*, September 25, 1850.

37. Israel Washburne, April 7, 1854, *Cong. Globe*, 33d Cong., 1st sess., *Appendix*, 496; this point was also brought up early in the Oregon admission debate: Henry C. Murphy of New York, February 24, 1849, ibid., 30th Cong., 2d sess., *Appendix*, 169.

38. It was by use of the Fifth Amendment that Chief Justice Taney argued that Congress could not prohibit slavery in the territories because then it would amount to a violation of the due process of law clause for the slaveholder. The point skirted by Taney was the determination of property definition in a territory in the first place, because without a state authority operation, there was no agency to do the definition. See Russel, "Constitutional Doctrines with Regard to Slavery in the Territories," 475–78, 480–81; Fehrenbacher, *Dred Scott Case*, 383–84.

39. *New York Globe*, quoted in *Cleveland Daily Plain Dealer*, April 22, 1848; *Toledo Blade*, January 25, 1847; speech of Cass reported in *New York Herald*, November 9, 1854; speech of Culver at Buffalo in *Philadelphia Pennsylvania Freeman*, August 31, 1848; *Pittsburgh Morning Post*, February 23, 1847.

40. John A. Dix to Hannibal Hamlin, March 6, 1850, Hamlin Papers. From what I can tell between 1846 and 1850 Calhoun was constantly derided in the northern press and much of the southern.

41. Fayette in *Rochester Advertiser*, June 21, 1848; *Washington (D.C.) National Era*, January 27, 1848.

42. *Rochester Advertiser*, April 24, 1848; Arnold Buffum to Joshua Giddings, April 16, 1850, Giddings Papers, Ohio Historical Society; E. P. Walton, March 31, 1858, *Cong. Globe*, 35th Cong., 1st sess., *Appendix*, 333; Abraham Lincoln, Cooper Institute Address, February 27, 1860, in Basler, Pratt, and Dunlap, *Collected Works of Lincoln*, 3:543.

43. William R. King to James Buchanan, March 11, 1850, Buchanan Papers; James H. Hammond to William G. Simms, June 20, 1848, Hammond Papers, Library of Congress; Henry Clay quoted by Isaac N. Morris, December 28, 29, 1859, *Cong. Globe*, 36th Cong., 1st sess., *Appendix*, 62.

44. *Athens (Ga.) Southern Banner*, August 24, 31, September 7, 1848; speech of Stephens in *Macon Georgia Journal and Messenger*, September 11, 1850; speech of Toombs, ibid., October 16, 1850. On the internal politics of Georgia and the fight between Stephens and Toombs with John M. Berrien, see Holt, *Rise and Fall of the American Whig Party*, 468–70.

45. James A. Seddon to Robert M. T. Hunter, June 16, 1848, in Ambler, *Correspondence of Hunter*, 91; James H. Hammond to William G. Simms, June 20, 1848, Hammond Papers, Library of Congress; letter of M. J. Wellborn in *Columbus (Ga.) Enquirer*, July 8, 1851.

46. William H. Hodgson to James H. Hammond, March 20, 1850, Hammond Papers, Library of Congress; *Macon Georgia Messenger*, February 11, 1847; speech of Henry Wise, *Columbus Ohio State Journal*, September 20, 1854.

47. Speech on Wilmot Proviso, December 22, 1847, in Clingman, *Selections from the Speeches and Writings of Hon. Thomas L. Clingman*, 200, 202; John A. Campbell to John C. Calhoun, March 1, 1848, in Meriwether et al., *Papers of Calhoun*, 25:213; see also John Stafford to William A. Graham, October 19, 1848, in Hamilton, *Papers of Graham*, 3:250–51. The letter of Cambell to Calhoun is well known; see commentary in Saunders, *John Archibald Campbell*, 76–81, 87–94.

48. INDEPENDENT DEMOCRAT in *Charleston Mercury*, June 24, 1848.

49. *Raleigh (N.C.) Weekly Register*, July 11, 30, 1849.

50. Letter of Judge Andrews, in *Macon Georgia Journal and Messenger*, October 2, 1850; *Athens (Ga.) Southern Banner*, August 14, 1851.

51. "The Slavery Question," May 14, 1850, in Julian, *Speeches on Political Questions*, 5, quotation from 6, analysis 6–9; Wade, March 13, 1858, *Cong. Globe*, 35th Cong., 1st sess., 1111–12.

52. Northerners had a number of specific comments about the constitution and the territorial problem. They recognized that slave property was not the only property in question in the territories, but that all state laws concerning property presented conflict that some agency had to sort out. They said that all rights of citizens in the territories were equal under prohibition of slave property, and that giving southerners the right to take slaves in fact gave them a privilege others did not have—to which Robert Toombs remarked everyone had an equal right to become slaveholders when they went to the territories. On these points, see *Rochester Democrat*, July 17, 1848; Israel Washburn, May 19, 1860, *Cong. Globe*, 36th Cong., 1st sess., *Appendix*, 351; Henry C. Murphy, February 24, 1849, ibid., 30th Cong., 2d sess., *Appendix*, 169; James Cooper, February 27, 1854, ibid., *Appendix*, 507; Martin Grover, January 7, 1847, ibid., 29th Cong., 2d sess., 138; Edward Ball, May 9, 1854, ibid., 33d Cong., 1st sess., *Appendix*, 579; Farnsworth, March 20, 1858, ibid., 35th Cong., 1st sess., 1204; *Washington (D.C.) National Era*, Feb. 25, 1847; message of Maine governor John W. Dana in *Milwaukee Weekly Wisconsin*, June 16, 1847; speech of Benjamin F. Hallett in *Madison Wisconsin Democrat*, October 7, 1848. Remark of Toombs, January 8, 1847, *Cong. Globe*, 29th Cong., 2d sess., 142.

53. Robert C. Schenck, August 1, 1848, *Cong. Globe*, 30th Cong., 1st sess., 1023; Israel Washburn, May 19, 1860, ibid., *Appendix*, 350; Hammond, *Freedom National—Slavery Sectional* (1860), 3–5, 8. The claim that the Constitution was naturally antislavery had Liberty Party and abolitionist antecedents; Wiecek, *Sources of Antislavery Constitutionalism*, 216–19, 282–84.

54. Gordon, February 11, 1847, *Cong. Globe*, 29th Cong., 2d sess., 387; Caleb Smith, July 31, 1848, ibid., 30th Cong., 1st sess., 1015; Hallett speech in *Madison Wisconsin Democrat*, October 7, 1848. See Bliss, *Complaints of the Extensionists—Their Falsity* (1856), 13–15.

55. On Pacheco case, see Wilson, December 29, 1848, *Cong. Globe*, 30th Cong., 2d sess., 124–25; reply of Brown, ibid., 125–26; Cabell, 126; Burt, 126–28; Giddings, 172–75; Turner, 239; Jones, 240; Palfrey, 240. Martin Grover, January 7, 1847, ibid., 29th Cong., 2d sess., 138; Abbott, March 22, 1858, ibid., 35th Cong., 1st sess., 1255; *Washington (D.C.) National Intelligencer*, December 22, 1847; Julian, May 14, 1850, in Julian, *Speeches on Political Questions*, 18.

56. Chase, February 3, 1854, *Cong. Globe*, 33d Cong., 1st sess., *Appendix*, 138; Dunham, May 19, 1854, ibid., *Appendix*, 1132; Wade, March 3, 1854, ibid., *Appendix*, 311; *Cincinnati Herald*, quoted by *Boston Emancipator*, May 17, 1848; *Washington (D.C.) National Era*, January 14, 1847.

57. On common law, see James F. Simmons, March 19, 1858, *Cong. Globe*, 35th Cong., 1st sess., *Appendix*, 159–60; John P. Hale, January 20, 1858, ibid., 35th Cong., 1st sess., 343; Chandler, March 12, 1858, ibid., 35th Cong., 1st sess., 1089; Lyman Trumbull, March 17, 1858, ibid., 35th Cong., 1st sess., 1161; Galusha Grow, May 10, 1854, ibid., 33d Cong., 1st sess., *Appendix*, 974; Charles Sumner, ibid., 33d Cong., 1st sess., *Appendix*, 268; FAYETTE in *Rochester Advertiser*, June 21, 1848; *Washington (D.C.) National Era*, January 14, 1847.

58. Woodward, May 17, 1848, *Cong. Globe*, 30th Cong., 1st sess., 776; William Smith, April 27, 1854, ibid., 33d Cong., 1st sess., *Appendix*, 553; Garnett, March 22, 1858, ibid., 35th Cong., 1st sess., 1244; Keitt, March 30, 1854, ibid., 33d Cong., 1st sess., *Appendix*, 466; see also Mason, March 15, 1858, ibid., 35th Cong., 1st sess., *Appendix*, 79–81. The importance of the Somerset case, to some, was that it defined slavery as a local institution solely; see invitation from a Committee, signed Daniel E. Huger et al., to William A. Graham, in Hamilton, *Papers of Graham*, 3:204.

59. On evolution of slavery, see Morgan, *American Slavery, American Freedom*, chaps. 9, 15–18; Thomas Morris, *Southern Slavery and the Law*, chaps. 2, 3. On maximizing all individuals' utilities by allowing free choice without government intervention, see Zajac, *Political Economy of Fairness*, 21, 69–77. Compare with Hummel, *Emancipating Slaves, Enslaving Free Men*, 44–46. The issue raised here will be made explicit. Current microeconomic theory asserts (the Libertarian variety) that the market erodes racism. The debate in the 1850s showed that the market created racism.

60. Lincoln speech at Peoria, October 16, 1854, in Basler, Pratt, and Dunlap, *Collected Works of Lincoln*, 2: quote 262, 263; also 2:262–70; see also his fear of the political power of slaveholders in a territory due to their social position, in speech at Janesville, Wisc., October 1, 1859, ibid., 3:485; and in his speech at Leavenworth, Kans., December 3, 1859, ibid., 3:499. Lincoln's view on the ability of an elite to influence commoners because of the elite's social position is almost the modern theory of hegemony used by Marxists.

61. Benjamin, March 11, 1858, *Cong. Globe*, 35th Cong., 1st sess., 1066–69.

62. Quotations taken from Clark, March 15, 1858, *Cong. Globe*, 35th Cong., 1st sess., *Appendix*, 88; the same case was mentioned earlier by Hale, January 20, 1858, ibid., 35th Cong., 1st sess., 343. See discussion in Bush, "The British Constitution and the Creation of American Slavery," 387–88.

63. *Woodville (Miss.) Republican*, October 3, 1848.

64. Speech of Jefferson Davis, February 13 and 14, 1850, in Rowland, *Jefferson Davis: Constitutionalist*, 1:283. See Report of Southern State Convention, Jackson, Miss., in *Vicksburg Whig*, October 9, 1849.

65. James S. Green, March 23, 1858, *Cong. Globe*, 35th Cong., 1st sess., *Appendix*, 211; R. M. T. Hunter, March 12, 1858, ibid., 35th Cong., 1st sess., 1096; Syndeham Moore, March 25, 1858, ibid., 1344; speech of James H. Hammond, *New York Times*, November 6, 1858; *Augusta Georgia Weekly Constitutionalist*, September 18, 1850; Saunders, *John Archibald Campbell*, 70, 93–94.

66. On fears of majority rule, William Porcher Miles to Christopher Memminger, January 10, 1860, Memminger Papers; John Slidell, March 15, 1858, *Cong. Globe*, 35th Cong., 1st sess., *Appendix*, 117; Jefferson Davis, December 9, 1859, ibid., 36th Cong., 1st sess., 68–69. On demand for guarantees, message of Governor John A. Quitman in *Jackson Mississippian*, November 22, 1850; quotation from Fisher [Cecil], *Kanzas and the Constitution* (1856), 11; Carpenter, *South as a Conscious Minority*, 27–28, 42, 154.

67. Berrien's Address to the People of the United States in *Huntsville (Ala.) Southern Advocate*, February 16, 1849; Toombs, February 23, 1854, *Cong. Globe*, 33d Cong., 1st sess., *Appendix*, 350.

68. Dowdell, May 10, 1854, *Cong. Globe*, 33d Cong., 1st sess., *Appendix*, 706; see Augustus E. Maxwell, May 16, 1854, ibid., 33d Cong., 1st sess., *Appendix*, 675; *New York Journal of Commerce*, quoted in *Boston Liberator*, October 27, 1848; Jefferson Davis to S. Cobun et al., November 7, 1850, in Rowland, *Jefferson Davis: Constitutionalist*, 1:595.

69. Godlove S. Orth to Oliver P. Morton, February 1, 1861, Morton Papers; see also P. S. Haekliman to Oliver P. Morton, February 1, 1861, ibid.

70. Charles E. Stuart, March 22, 1858, *Cong. Globe*, 35th Cong., 1st sess., *Appendix*, 199; Douglas speech, March 22, 1858, ibid., *Appendix*, 200. See Benjamin Tappan to E. T. Tappan, March 28, 1847, Tappan Papers. On Democrats and free labor, see the views of Glickstein, *American Exceptionalism, American Anxiety*, 159–60, 190–91.

71. For example, S. P. Chase, February 3, 1854, *Cong. Globe*, 33d Cong., 1st sess., *Appendix*, 134; John Farnsworth, March 20, 1858, ibid., 35th Cong., 1st sess., 1205; Israel Washburn, May 19, 1860, ibid., 36th Cong., 1st sess., *Appendix*, 349.

72. See, for example, Address of the Democratic Members of the Legislature, in *Rochester Advertiser*, April 24, 1848; E. P. Walton, March 31, 1858, *Cong. Globe*, 35th Cong., 1st sess., *Appendix*, 333; Letter of Martin Van Buren to the Committee of the Buffalo Convention, August 22, 1848, in *Orleans Republican*, September 6, 1848, in Van Buren Papers; "The Slave Compromises of the Constitution," *New Englander* 7 (August 1849): 345–46.

73. William Goodell to John F. Potter, [1858], Potter Papers; Aaron Harlan, May 19, 1854, *Cong. Globe*, 33d Cong., 1st sess., *Appendix*, 1004.

74. John C. Calhoun to Percy Walker, October 23, 1847, in Meriwether et al., *Papers of Calhoun*, 24:617. This sentiment came out in more diluted form in his famous and last public address on the compromise proposals of Henry Clay in the Senate, March 4, 1850.

75. That restriction might be unfair yet constitutional was the position of Justice Benjamin Curtis in the *Dred Scott* case; Russel, "Constitutional Doctrines with Regard to Slavery in the Territories," 478.

76. See comment of *Hartford (Conn.) Times*, August 2, 1848.

77. Wyatt-Brown, *Yankee Saints and Southern Sinners*, 184–88, 198–99; for reasons other than honor, see Barney, *Secessionist Impulse*, 3–21.

Chapter 6

1. David Potter, *Impending Crisis*, 21.

2. Basic chronology taken from *New York Herald*, July 24, 27, 28, 30, 1846, August 1, 2, 4, 5, 1846.

3. *Alton Telegraph and Democrat*, August 7, 14, 21, 1846.

4. *Cong. Globe*, 29th Cong., 1st sess., 1214–16, Senate handling of the matter on 1220–21. Elaboration of the dissident northerners in *New York Tribune*, August 18, 1846.

5. *New York Tribune*, August 18, 1846; *Boston Liberator*, September 11, 1846, p. 145; A. R. W. Twain to J. R. Giddings, August 9, 1849, in Giddings Papers, Ohio Historical Society; Salmon P. Chase to Gerrit Smith, September 1, 1846, Chase Papers, ed. Niven.

6. John C. Calhoun to Lewis S. Coryell, November 7, 1846, in Meriwether et al., *Papers of Calhoun*, 23:530; Nous Verrons in *Charleston Mercury*, August 14, 1846. See *Richmond Enquirer*, quoted in *Athens (Ga.) Southern Banner*, August 18, October 27, 1846; *Mobile Register and Journal*, August 17, 19 ("JOHN TAYLOR of Caroline"), 21, 28, 1846; *Richmond Whig*, August 14, 1846; *Huntsville Southern Advocate*, August 28, 1846.

7. Compare with Chaplain Morrison, *Democratic Politics and Sectionalism*, 21–26.

8. *Philadelphia North American*, August 17, 19, 1846; *Columbus Ohio State Journal*, September 5, 1846; *Alton (Ill.) Telegraph and Democrat*, August 21, 1846; *Pottsville (Pa.) Miners'*

Journal, August 15, 1846; the proviso is also discussed in *Washington (D.C.) Daily National Intelligencer*, August 15, 1846.

9. *Cleveland Daily Plain Dealer*, August 12, 1846; see report of Democratic meeting of Hamilton County in ibid., August 28, 1846; *Detroit Democratic Free Press*, August 25, 1846; *Cincinnati Daily Enquirer*, August 25, 31, 1846.

10. *Cleveland Daily Plain Dealer*, August 8, 1846; *Detroit Democratic Free Press*, August 11, 1846; *Buffalo Courier and Pilot*, August 6, 1846; *New York Herald*, August 10, 1846; *Toledo Blade*, August 7, 1846; *Columbus Ohio State Journal*, August 8, 1846; *Indianapolis Indiana State Journal, Weekly*, August 12, 19, 1846.

11. *Columbus Ohio State Journal*, July 28, 1846, quote of August 1, 1846; *Indianapolis Indiana State Journal, Weekly*, August 5, 1846; *Toledo Blade*, July 29, August 3, 1846; *Pottsville (Pa.) Miners' Journal*, June, July, and August 1846. On southern Whig reaction to the Walker tariff, see *Richmond Whig*, August 7, 1846; *Columbus (Ga.) Enquirer*, August 19, September 23, 1846; *Macon Georgia Messenger*, August 13, 1846; *Hillsborough (N.C.) Record*, August 20, 27, September 24, 1846; *Greensborough (N.C.) Patriot*, July 25, 1847; see letter of North Carolina senator William H. Haywood Jr., in ibid., August 29, 1846; J. N. Reynolds to John J. Crittenden, August 4, 1846, Crittenden Papers.

12. Charles H. Allen to Armistead Burt, July 25, 1846, Burt Papers; William B. Williamson to James K. Polk, August 16, 1846, Polk Papers; James H. Hammond to W. B. Hodgson, August 23, 1846, Hammond Papers, University of South Carolina; James Hamilton Jr. to John C. Calhoun, August 2, 1846, in Meriwether et al., *Papers of Calhoun*, 23:384; *Charleston Mercury*, July 29, August 1, 3, 1846; *Raleigh North Carolina Standard*, August 12, 1846; *Memphis Weekly Appeal*, September 4, 1846; *Pittsburgh Morning Post*, July 23, 24, 28, 1846; *Detroit Democratic Free Press*, August 5, 6, 7, 31, 1846; *Portland (Me.) Daily Argus*, July 31, August 4, 7, 14, 1846; *Hartford (Conn.) Times*, July 24, August 4, 5, 6, 1846.

13. *Indianapolis Indiana State Journal, Weekly*, November 17, 1846.

14. Thomas Ritchie to Edmund Burke, October 21, 1846, Burke Papers.

15. Hudson speech, December 16, 1846, *Cong. Globe*, 29th Cong., 2d sess., 51; see also (all dates are 1846) remarks of Giddings, December 15, ibid., 34–36; Gentry, December 16, ibid., 47–48; Washington Hunt, December 23, ibid., 72; Frederick P. Stanton, December 23, ibid., 82–83; and Samuel Gordon, December 24, ibid., 83–84.

16. Ibid., January 5, 1847, 114.

17. Seddon speech, ibid., *Appendix*, 86–87; speech of Grover, ibid., 137, 138. Other expressions of slaves as property include Shelton Leake of Virginia, January 15, 1847, ibid., *Appendix*, 127; Allan G. Thurman of Ohio, January 15, 1847, ibid., 190–91; George Rathbun of New York, February 9, 1847, ibid., 364–65; James C. Dobbin of North Carolina, February 10, 1847, ibid., 384; Samuel Gordon of New York, February 11, 1847, ibid., 387; Joshua R. Giddings, February 13, 1847, ibid., *Appendix*, 457.

18. William C. Rives to John J. Crittenden, February 8, 1847, Rives Papers; for southern Whigs, see also *Columbus (Ga.) Enquirer*, January 19, 1847; *Hillsborough (N.C.) Record*, February 25, April 1, 1847; *Richmond Whig*, February 19, July 20, 1847.

19. Quote from "A Countryman" in *Charleston Mercury*, March 11, 1847. *Memphis Weekly Appeal*, April 9, 1847; *Macon Georgia Journal and Messenger*, February 11, 1847; HALIFAX correspondence in *Raleigh North Carolina Standard*, January 13, 1847; *New Orleans Picayune*, February 28, 1847; report from D. C. in *Charleston Mercury*, January 16, 1847; *Milledgeville (Ga.) Southern Recorder*, February 16, 1847; ibid., February 2, 9, 10, March 13, 17, 1847; W. F. DeSaussure to James H. Hammond, March 13, 1847, Hammond Papers, Library of Congress.

20. Percy Walker to John C. Calhoun, October 10, 1847, in Meriwether et al., *Papers of Calhoun*, 24:609; *Richmond Whig*, February 19, 1487; *Charleston Mercury*, February 17, 1847.

21. Calhoun's resolutions, February 19, 1847, *Cong. Globe*, 29th Cong., 2d sess., 454–55; *Columbus (Ga.) Enquirer*, March 2, 1847; *Macon Georgia Journal and Messenger*, March 18, 1847. See also *Natchez Mississippi Free Trader*, March 3, 1847; *Jackson Mississippian*, March 12, 1847; *Memphis Weekly Appeal*, March 9, 1847; *New Orleans Picayune*, February 28, 1847.

22. James Graham to W. A. Graham, January 10, 1847, in Hamilton, *Papers of Graham*, 3:171; Calhoun to Governor David Johnson, January 13, 1847, in Meriwether et al., *Papers of Calhoun*, 24:67. See also *Greensborough (N.C.) Patriot*, January 2, 1847; *Jackson Mississippian*, November 5, 1847; report on Congress, *Charleston Mercury*, January 7, 1847; *Milledgeville (Ga.) Federal Union*, January 19, 1847; *Richmond Whig*, January 12, February 2, 1847; *Charleston Mercury*, March 13, 1847.

23. Joshua R. Giddings to Charles Francis Adams, January 13, 1847, Adams [Family] Papers; on fear of the Democrats, see Charles F. Adams to Joshua R. Giddings, January 16, 1847, Giddings Papers, Ohio Historical Society; and Henry Wilson to Giddings, February 6, 1847, ibid. The Whig reaction was generally summed up in *New York Tribune*, February 22, 1847.

24. Chaplain Morrison believed the reaction to the Wilmot Proviso was due to infighting among the Van Buren and Calhoun wings of the party and that it was irrational. William R. Brock has concluded that Democrat fear of slavery expansion was real, that slavery injured free society, and that the principle of freedom mattered. John Schroeder maintained that the northern Democrats had to assert their independence from southerners in order to remain viable in northern politics. Eric Foner found the roots of the proviso in the annexation of Texas when southern demands trumped northern desires on every issue, and northern Democrats, especially in New York, felt the public swinging to an antislavery stand. Michael Morrison seems to agree with Foner's interpretation and finds that Wilmot acted because of the northern political situation and that Free-Soilers tended to use the free labor argument. Chaplain Morrison, *Democratic Politics and Sectionalism*, 11–12, 53–58; Brock, *Parties and Political Conscience*, 165–66, 180–83; Schroeder, *Mr. Polk's War*, 20–22, 46; Eric Foner, "The Wilmot Proviso Revisited"; Michael Morrison, *Slavery and the American West*, 42–44, 56; see also Donald Cole, *Martin Van Buren and the American Political System*, 393–94, 409.

25. *Cincinnati Daily Enquirer*, August 12, 1846; see Eric Foner, "The Wilmot Proviso Revisited," 262–79; and Chaplain Morrison, *Democratic Politics and Sectionalism*, 11–63.

26. Gideon Wells to Martin Van Buren, July 28, 1846, Van Buren Papers; *Buffalo Courier and Pilot* quoted by *Detroit Democratic Free Press*, August 10, 1846; *Cleveland Daily Plain Dealer*, August 8, 1846; *Fort Wayne (Ind.) Sentinel*, July 11, 1846; *Toledo Blade*, August 17, 19, 1846.

27. On Barnburners, see Dix, *Memoirs*, 1:187–88, 231; Donald Cole, *Martin Van Buren and the American Political System*, 409–10. The meeting of the Democrats initiating the proviso in David Wilmot, Sketch of Life, Wilmot Papers; Jacob Brinkerhoff to Mr. Glessner, September 16, 1846, in *Cleveland Daily Plain Dealer*, October 6, 1846. On Wilmot's reputation, see *Detroit Democratic Free Press*, October 27, 1846; *Mobile Register and Journal*, July 29, 1846. On the New York State Constitutional Convention, see Gunn, *The Decline of Authority*, 170–97.

28. John Law to Martin Van Buren, August 2, 1847, Van Buren Papers; David Smith to William Allen, January 15, 1847, Allen Papers; Brinkerhoff letter in *Cleveland Daily Plain Dealer*, October 6, 1846; *Madison (Wisc.) Express*, August 18, 1846.

29. *Columbus Ohio State Journal*, March 13, 1847; Whig meeting in *Augusta (Me.) Kennebec Journal*, August 28, 1846; see *Cincinnati Daily Times*, January 19, 1847; *New York Tribune*, August 6, 1846; James H. Cravins to R. W. Thompson, December 23, 1846, Thompson Papers; William Slade to Joshua Giddings, July 30, 1846, Giddings Papers; Thomas P. Beal to Artemas Hale, December 28, 1846, Hale Papers; John McLean to John Teasdale, April 6, 29,

1847, McLean Papers, Ohio Historical Society; *New York Tribune*, quoted in *Indianapolis Indiana State Journal, Weekly*, September 2, 1846.

30. John M. Whiton to Artemas Hale, May 19, 1848, Hale Papers; Millard Fillmore to Edward Everett, October 21, 1850, Everett Papers, Massachusetts Historical Society; R. W. Thompson to Delegates of Whig Party from Vigo County, June 8, 1847, Thompson Papers; John C. Calhoun to Mrs. Sarah Maury, February 18, 1847, in Meriwether et al., *Papers of Calhoun*, 24:165; Henry Clay speech in Lexington, Ky., November 13, 1847, in Hay, *Papers of Clay*, 10:367; see Holt, *Rise and Fall of the American Whig Party*, 258–79.

31. Edmund Burke to Franklin Pierce, June 21, 1847, Pierce Papers; Joshua R. Giddings to Son, January 15, 1847, Giddings Papers; Charles W. Marsh to Caleb Cushing, January 17, 1847, Cushing Papers; John Hogan to J. C. Calhoun, September 21, 1846, in Meriwether et al., *Papers of Calhoun*, 23:453; Lewis Cass to Andrew T. McReynolds, December 26, 1846, Cass Papers; Morris Longstreth to James Buchanan, February 21, 1847, Buchanan Papers.

32. On observing southern rights, letter of Senex to *Albany Argus*, March 3, 1847; on Federalist desires to harm the Democracy, *Portland (Me.) Daily Argus*, September 9, 1846; James Buchanan to Charles Kessler et al., August 25, 1847, in Moore, *Works of Buchanan*, 7:386–87. For comments calling for winning the war first, see *Pennsylvanian* and *Niagara Democrat*, quoted in *Albany Argus*, January 23, 1847; *Springfield Daily Illinois State Register*, February 5, March 19, October 8, 1847; *Fort Wayne (Ind.) Sentinel*, February 20, March 27, 1847; *Detroit Democratic Free Press*, January 26, April 3, 9, 1847.

33. *Buffalo Daily Courier*, December 29, 1846; *Springfield Daily Illinois State Register*, December 17, 1847; see Michael Morrison, *Slavery and the American West*, 99; Johannsen, *Douglas*, 185–205.

34. Quotes from *Boston Post* in *Detroit Democratic Free Press*, January 30, 1847; *Hartford Times*, March 8, 1847; *Peoria (Ill.) Democratic Press*, February 10, 1847; *Pittsburgh Morning Post*, February 20, 1847; *Catskill Democrat*, quoted in *Albany Argus*, February 3, 1847.

35. *Portland (Me.) Daily Argus*, February 5, 1847; see also *Albany Argus*, February 3, 1847; resolution of Buffalo Democratic meeting in ibid., February 11, 1847; *Hartford Times*, April 13, June 21, 1848; the fear of disunion can be seen in ibid., March 3, 8, 1847.

36. See Chapter 5; *Pittsburgh Morning Post*, February 20, 1847; *Chicago Daily Democrat*, December 9, 1847, March 2, 1848; *Madison Wisconsin Democrat*, October 14, 1848; message of Maine governor John W. Dana in *Milwaukee Weekly Wisconsin*, June 16, 1847; *Portland (Me.) Daily Argus*, February 25, 1847; *Cincinnati Daily Enquirer*, March 9, 1847; *Rochester Advertiser*, June 1, 1848. The Whig response can be found in *New York Tribune*, February 22, 1847. For the abolitionist position—essentially the same as the Democrats and Whigs—see Charles Sumner to J. R. Giddings, December 21, 1846, Giddings Papers; and the extensive analysis in *Washington (D.C.) National Era*, January 14, February 25, 1847, January 27, 1848.

37. Brinkerhoff speech, February 10, 1847, *Cong. Globe*, 29th Cong., 2d sess., 378–79; speech of Clark in *Albany Argus*, February 8, 1847.

38. John Van Buren speech at Utica, in *Utica (N.Y.) Oneida Morning Herald*, June 9, 1848; John Pettit speech, January 14, 1847, *Cong. Globe*, 29th Cong., 2d sess., 181; David Wilmot speech, February 8, 1847, ibid., *Appendix*, 357–58. For southern racial comments, see James C. Dobbin, February 11, 1847, ibid., 385–86.

39. *New York Evening Post*, quoted by *Fort Wayne (Ind.) Sentinel*, January 30, 1847; Governor Dana, quoted in *Milwaukee Weekly Wisconsin*, June 16, 1847; *New York Globe*, quoted by *Albany Argus*, January 30, 1847; David Wilmot, quoted in Going, *David Wilmot, Free-Soiler*, 298; remark on repeal of corn laws in *Detroit Democratic Free Press*, July 27, 1846; Martin Van Buren to Convention of New York City, June 20, 1848, Van Buren Papers.

40. Resolution in *Rochester Democrat*, February 11, 1847; speech of John A. Dix, March 1,

1847, *Cong. Globe*, 29th Cong., 2d sess., 543; Sedgwick, *Public and Private Economy*, 1:241, 247–54. For other Democratic references against letting free and slave labor compete, see speech of David Wilmot, February 8, 1847, *Cong. Globe*, 29th Cong., 2d sess., *Appendix*, 357; speech of Preston King, January 5, 1847, ibid., 114; speech of Timothy Jenkins, February 13, 1847, ibid., 420; letter of Brinkerhoff in *Cleveland Daily Plain Dealer*, October 6, 1846; message of Maine governor John W. Dana, in *Milwaukee Weekly Wisconsin*, June 16, 1847; Hamlin, *The Life and Times of Hannibal Hamlin*, 109, 188–89.

41. See *Cleveland Plain Dealer*, August 8, 1846; *Detroit Democratic Free Press*, March 22, 1847; Hannibal Hamlin, quoted in Hamlin, *The Life and Times of Hannibal Hamlin*, 107; John Martin to Martin Van Buren, June 27, 1848, Van Buren Papers; Gideon Welles to Martin Van Buren, July 28, 1846, ibid.; George Rathburn, February 9, 1847, *Cong. Globe*, 29th Cong., 2d sess., *Appendix*, 199. See Huston, "The American Revolutionaries, the Political Economy of Aristocracy, and the American Concept of the Distribution of Wealth, 1765–1900," 1100 and n. 43.

42. Thomas Dowling to John Dowling, August 21, 1847, Dowling Papers; Edwin M. Stanton to Jacob Brinkerhoff, January 19, 1848, Stanton Papers.

43. Letter of Brinkerhoff, *Cleveland Daily Plain Dealer*, October 6, 1846; Wilmot speech in Going, *David Wilmot, Free-Soiler*, 289; Rathbun speech, February 9, 1847, *Cong. Globe*, 29th Cong., 2d sess., 364; Jno. S. Peckham et al., *To the Independent Democratic Whigs, of the County of Oneida*, July 4, 1848 [Utica], broadside in Adams [Family] Papers; meeting of Independent Democrats in *Augusta (Me.) Kennebec Journal*, September 11, 1846; *Green Bay (Wisc.) Advocate*, October 19, 1848.

44. John Reed to Artemas Hale, February 11, 1847, Hale Papers; Chase and Cleveland, *Anti-Slavery Addresses of 1844–45* (1867), 29; Palfrey, *Papers on the Slave Power*; Charles Sumner, "Union among Men of All Parties against the Slave Power and the Extension of Slavery," June 28, 1848, in Sumner, *Works of Sumner*, 2:77–78; Sumner, "Necessity of Political Action against the Slave Power and the Extension of Slavery," September 29, 1847, ibid., 1:59; "Antislavery Duties of the Whig Party," September 23, 1846, ibid., 1:307; *New York National Anti-Slavery Standard*, November 9, 1848.

45. David Potter, *Impending Crisis*, 64–67.

46. Listing of wayward northerners in *Indianapolis Indiana State Journal, Weekly*, March 9, 1847; *Detroit Advertiser*, quoted in *Madison (Wisc.) Express*, March 23, 1847; votes in *Cong. Globe*, 29th Cong., 2d sess., 425 and 573. Washington Hunt to Salmon P. Chase, February 15, 1847, Chase Papers, ed. Niven; Edwin M. Stanton to Chase, March 11, 1847, ibid.; Joshua R. Giddings to Charles F. Adams, March 3, 1847, Adams [Family] Papers. Account of last moments of Congress found in David Potter, *Impending Crisis*, 66.

47. David Potter, *Impending Crisis*, 74–76. For example, see *Jackson Mississippian*, January 22, 1847; *Covington (Ky.) Licking Valley Register*, January 30, 1847; John W. Tibbatts, January 8, 1847, *Cong. Globe*, 29th Cong., 2d sess., 147; Edward Dargan, January 7, 1847, ibid., 136.

48. Broadside for "Taylor Meeting," [January 1847?], in Adams [Family] Papers; James Buchanan to Charles Kesler et al., August 25, 1847, in Moore, *Works of Buchanan*, 7:386–87; James Buchanan to William R. King, May 13, 1850, in ibid., 8:383–84.

49. James Buchanan to William R. King, May 13, 1850, in Moore, *Works of Buchanan*, 8:383.

50. *Augusta (Me.) Kennebec Journal*, July 7, 1848; *New York Tribune*, quoted in *Indianapolis Indiana State Journal, Weekly*, September 28, 1847; *Columbus Ohio State Journal*, January 28, 1847; Benjamin F. Butler (of New York) to R. H. Gillet, May 8, 1848 [but in 1847 series], in Van Buren Papers; *Toledo Blade*, January 27, 1847; Thompson Campbell to Charles Lanphier, December 4, 1848, Lanphier Papers; Charles Hudson to Artemas Hale, July 13, 1848, Hale Papers.

51. For details, see David Potter, *Impending Crisis*, 73–75; L. A. Ward to John Clayton, July 21, 1848, Clayton Papers. On Stephens's actions, *Macon Georgia Journal and Messenger*, September 11, 1850; *Athens (Ga.) Southern Banner*, August 24, September 7, 1848.

52. Speech of Armistead Burt, January 14, 1847, *Cong. Globe*, 29th Cong., 2d sess., *Appendix*, 132–33.

53. Yulee quoted by congressional correspondent in *Charleston Mercury*, April 7, 1848; see Virginia legislative resolutions in *Macon Georgia Messenger*, March 18, 1847; *Mobile Register and Journal*, September 14, 1847; "The Wilmot Proviso," *United States Democratic Review* 23 (September 1848): 224. See Calhoun's speech on the Oregon bill, June 27, 1848, in Crallé, *Works of Calhoun*, 4:481–511; Davis's speech on Oregon Bill, July 12, 1848, in Monroe and McIntosh, *Papers of Davis*, 3:332–68.

54. *Charleston Mercury*, March 17, 1848; *Natchez Mississippi Free Trader*, March 14, 1849; Jefferson Davis to S. Cobun et al., November 7, 1850, in Rowland, *Jefferson Davis: Constitutionalist*, 1:595; *Woodville (Miss.) Republican*, October 3, 1848.

55. Giddings, January 6, 1849, *Cong. Globe*, 30th Cong., 2d sess., 172, 174–75. The same analysis was offered by Massachusetts's Palfrey, January 12, 1849, ibid., 240.

56. Holt, *Rise and Fall of the American Whig Party*, 330.

57. Text taken from General Cass to Mr. Nicholson, December 24, 1847, in *Albany Argus*, October 23, 1848. On Cass and the slavery issue, see Klunder, *Lewis Cass and the Politics of Moderation*, 162–69.

58. Ellwood Fisher to John C. Calhoun, August 22, 1847, in Meriwether et al., *Papers of Calhoun*, 24:502; A. R. Johnson to Sidney Breese, June 29, 1848, Breese Papers; "The Wilmot Proviso," *Springfield Daily Illinois State Register*, October 8, 1847. Cass immediately noted how people absorbed the idea: Lewis Cass to Henry Clay, January 6, 1848, Cass Papers.

59. There was a difference, of course. The antislavery cry of individual freedom had no need for reservations or qualifications. The Democrats' cry of popular sovereignty did: the people were defined explicitly as European descendants. It was precisely this difference that Lincoln attacked in 1858.

60. Quoted from *Charleston Mercury*, March 2, 1848; see Frank Blair to Martin Van Buren, January 23, 1847 [1848], Van Buren Papers; *Chicago Daily Democrat*, December 22, 1847, March 2, 1848; Letter of "W." in *Huntsville (Ala.) Southern Advocate*, March 4, 1848.

61. The term arose from a skeptical point of view on the basis of a fight for the spoils of office. The Albany Regency supposedly had control of appointments, and younger men of the party plus older malcontents grew angry and jealous at being overlooked. Rather than reform the system, they would rather "burn down the barn" with all the rats in it—hence, Barnburners. Hunkers were so named because of their hunkering for office. However, the division came to mean those favoring the Wilmot Proviso versus the Democrats favorable to a sectional compromise. See column on Barnburners in *Indianapolis Indiana State Journal, Weekly*, May 29, 1848.

62. For the genesis of the Free-Soil Party, see the description in Dix, *Memoirs*, 1:232–47; Mayfield, *Rehearsal for Republicanism*, 9–30; Blue, *The Free Soilers*, 31–80.

63. On Van Buren, see Van Buren letter to Buffalo Committee, in *Orleans (N.Y.) Republican*, September 6, 1848, in Van Buren Papers; Van Buren to Convention in New York City, June 20, 1848, in ibid.; quotation from Address of the Democratic Members of the Legislature, in *Rochester Advertiser*, April 25, 1848; see speech of John Van Buren in ibid., June 27, 1848; Address to the Electors of Monroe County, in ibid., October 19, 1848; Broadsheet, "People's Convention—To the People of Ohio," March 1848, Chase Papers; resolutions of Utica meeting quoted in *Chicago Gem of the Prairie*, July 8, 1848.

64. *Oneida (N.Y.) Morning Herald*, June 28, 1848.

65. Speech and resolution taken from *Athens (Ga.) Southern Banner*, June 8, 1848; also found in *Huntsville (Ala.) Southern Advocate*, June 10, 1848; *Rochester Democrat*, June 1, 1848; *Cincinnati Daily Enquirer*, May 31, 1848; *Raleigh (N.C.) Weekly Register*, June 14, 1848.

66. Quotation of McDowell taken from speech of Benjamin F. Halleck printed in *Madison Wisconsin Democrat*, October 7, 1848; incident involving Freeman reported in *Raleigh (N.C.) Weekly Register*, June 14, 1848; vote on Yancey resolution in *Cincinnati Daily Enquirer*, May 31, 1848.

67. For example, *Milwaukee Weekly Wisconsin*, March 15, 1848; *Hartford (Conn.) Times*, July 6, August 2, 1848; *Albany Argus*, October 4, 7, 1848; *Ottawa (Ill.) Free Trader*, August 4, 1848; *Cincinnati Enquirer*, quoted by *Madison Wisconsin Democrat*, September 7, 1848; *Pittsburgh Morning Post*, October 20, 1848; *Fort Wayne (Ind.) Sentinel*, September 16, 1848.

68. See, for example, R. H. Chamberlayne to Millard Fillmore, June 24, 1848, Fillmore Papers, State University of New York at Oswego.

69. See Johannsen, *Douglas*, 238–40. Of course, the Calhounites immediately picked up on the issue of the precise moment when popular majorities might rule, but most southern Whigs and Democrats ignored them in 1848.

70. For discussion of the Whig convention, see Holt, *Rise and Fall of the American Whig Party*, 320–30.

71. On the election of 1848 see David Potter, *Impending Crisis*, 79–82; Holt, *Rise and Fall of the American Whig Party*, 348–82. The election is treated in Appendix B.

72. Benjamin Tappan, fragment, "Who Will Be President in 1848?," box 1, folder 20, Tappan Papers; Benjamin Tappan to Lewis Tappan, September 8, 1848, ibid.; D. Radebaugh Jr. and William Weed to Martin Van Buren, December 1847, Van Buren Papers; Charles Francis Adams to John Palfrey, July 6, 1848, Adams [Family] Papers; E. A. Stansbury to Charles Francis Adams, July 5, 1848, ibid.; H. B. Stanton to C. F. Adams, June 26, 1848, ibid.; C. F. Adams to John Palfrey, July 9, 1848, ibid.; J. R. Giddings to Son, June 23, 1848, Giddings Papers, Ohio Historical Society.

73. William Sprague to Charles F. Adams, July 8, 1848, Adams [Family] Papers; H. B. Stanton to C. F. Adams, June 26, 1848, ibid.; John McLean to Mr. Denny, July 31, 1848, McLean Papers; Seth M. Gates to C. F. Adams, July 24, 1848, Adams [Family] Papers; Two Hundred Voters to C. F. Adams, July 24, 1848, ibid.; Thomas J. Mumford to C. F. Adams, July 17, 1848, ibid.

74. *Portland (Me.) Daily Argus*, June 29, 1848; *Buffalo Daily Courier*, June 24, 1848; *Madison Wisconsin Democrat*, July 8, August 26, 1848; *Cleveland Daily Plain Dealer*, June 22, 27, 1848; *Albany Argus*, July 1, 5, 8, 11, 1848; William R. King to James Buchanan, June 28, 1848, Buchanan Papers; Daniel S. Dickinson to Lewis Cass, July 10, 1848, Cass Papers.

75. H. C. Stewart to S. P. Chase, July 24, 1848, Chase Papers; Salmon P. Chase to John McLean, August 3, 1848, McLean Papers; Joshua R. Giddings to Thomas Bolton, November 14, 1848, Giddings Papers, Ohio Historical Society.

76. John W. Forney to Buchanan, June 25, 1848, Buchanan Papers; *Columbus Ohio State Journal*, June 27, 1848; Benjamin F. Whitnor to James H. Hammond, July 1, 1848, Hammond Papers, Library of Congress; *Jackson Mississippian*, September 22, 1848.

77. B. B. Thurston to Dutee J. Pearce, July 6, 1848, Cass Papers; John Y. Mason to Lewis Cass, September 25, 1848, ibid.; William L. Marcy to General P. M. Wetmore, June 10, July 9, 1848, Marcy Papers; Sandy Harris to James Buchanan, July 16, 1848, Buchanan Papers; Thaddeus Sanford to James Buchanan, August 12, 1848, ibid.; Schuyler Colfax to D. D. Pratt, July 15, 1848, Pratt Papers.

78. O. Hoffman to J. J. Crittenden, September 20, 1848, Crittenden Papers; James K. Polk to Lewis Cass, August 24, 1848, Cass Papers; Godlove Orth to Schuyler Colfax, [Octo-

ber 1848], Orth Papers; Abraham Lincoln to Walter Davis, June 26, 1848, in Basler, Pratt, and Dunlap, *Collected Works of Lincoln*, 1:493.

79. Thomas Corwin to John G. Whittier, August 21, 1848, Corwin Papers.

80. Sumner, "The Free-Soil Party Explained and Vindicated," September 12, 1849, in Sumner, *Works of Sumner*, 2:288; "Union among Men of All Parties against the Slave Power and the Extension of Slavery," June 28, 1848, in ibid., 2:84–85; "The Party of Freedom," August 22, 1848, in ibid., 2:143. For the attack on the tariff, see Edward S. Hamlin to S. P. Chase, May 14, 1848, Chase Papers, ed. Niven; Charles Sumner to Thomas Corwin, September 7, 1847, in Palmer, *Selected Letters of Sumner*, 1:195; Sumner to Samuel Lawrence, November 29, 1848, in ibid., 1:256–58; Sumner, *Memoir and Letters of Sumner*, 3:129–32; O. W. Allen to Charles F. Adams, June 21, 1848, Adams [Family] Papers; Julian, *Political Recollections*, 37–38; Dana, *Richard Henry Dana*, 147–48.

81. *Oneida Morning Herald*, June 28, 1848; George M. Dallas to Lewis Cass, October 21, 1848, Cass Papers; "The Free Soil Party and the Late Election," *Massachusetts Quarterly Review* 2 (December 1848): 106–8, quotation from 115–16.

82. This observation was hinted at by Stephen Maizlish, *Triumph of Sectionalism*, 3–4, 6–7, 11–12.

83. This is a typical treatment; see David Potter, *Impending Crisis*, 84–89; Holt, *Rise and Fall of the American Whig Party*, chaps. 12, 13; Elbert Smith, *Presidencies of Taylor and Fillmore*, 60–66; Bauer, *Zachary Taylor*, 226–27, 249–58, 290–310.

84. William L. Marcy to James Buchanan, March 10, 1850, Buchanan Papers; Stephen A. Douglas to Charles H. Lanphier and George Walker, January 7, 1850, in Johannsen, *Letters of Douglas*, 182; Joshua R. Giddings to Son, January 9, 1850, Giddings Papers, Ohio Historical Society. On southern support for the Missouri Compromise line, see Thomas L. Harris to Charles Lanphier, June 26, 1850, Lanphier Papers; Resolution of Jefferson Davis et al., [December 1849–February 1850?], in Ambler, *Correspondence of Hunter*, 104; Isaac Toucey to James Buchanan, July 5, 1850, Buchanan Papers; Samuel J. Ray to Buchanan, August 1, 1850, ibid.; Henry S. Foote to Buchanan, May 13, 1850, ibid.; Jonathan M. Foltz to Buchanan, May 20, 1850, ibid.; James Buchanan to Jefferson Davis, March 16, 1850, ibid.

85. David Potter, *Impending Crisis*, 100–104; Holt, *Rise and Fall of the American Whig Party*, chap. 13; Schott, *Alexander H. Stephens of Georgia*, 118–20; Stegmaier, *Texas, New Mexico, and the Compromise of 1850*, 85–100; Daniel P. King to Artemas Hale, February 8, 1850, Hale Papers.

86. Jefferson Davis, February 13, 1850, in Rowland, *Jefferson Davis: Constitutionalist*, 1:283; Berrien's Address in *Huntsville (Ala.) Southern Advocate*, February 16, 1849.

87. James S. Wiley to Hannibal Hamlin, December 26, 1849, Hamlin Papers; Arnold Buffum to Joshua R. Giddings, April 16, 1850, Giddings Papers, Ohio Historical Society.

88. Julius Rockwell to Artemas Hale, January 19, 1850, Hale Papers.

89. This is a standard account taken from David Potter, *Impending Crisis*, 107–13; Hamilton, *Prologue to Conflict*; Stegmaier, *Texas, New Mexico, and the Compromise of 1850*; and Holt, *Rise and Fall of the American Whig Party*, chaps. 14, 15, 16.

90. William H. Bissell to William Martin, February 5, 1850, Bissell Papers; William H. Bissell to Joseph Gillespie, February 12, 1850, Gillespie Papers; Thomas L. Harris to Charles Lanphier, January 12, 1850, Lanphier Papers; Hannibal Hamlin to William R. Haines [?], February 23, 1850, Hamlin Papers; Edmund Burke to Stephen A. Douglas, February 13, 1850, Douglas Papers; Hugh O'Neal to Henry S. Lane, March 7, 1850, Lane Papers; Thomas Corwin to J. A. Briggs, March 20, 1850, Corwin Papers; Herman Lincoln to John McLean, February 16, 1850, McLean Papers.

91. See J. Hoffman to William H. Seward, September 26, 1850, Seward Papers; Daniel

Henshaw to Seward, October 7, 1850, ibid.; Silas A. Andrews to Seward, September 26, 1850, ibid.; Charles Coburn to Seward, September 26, 1850, ibid.; *Fort Wayne (Ind.) Sentinel*, September 14, 1850; A. Nourse to Hannibal Hamlin, March 16, 1850, Hamlin Papers.

92. On the elections of 1850, for Massachusetts, see Donald, *Charles Sumner and the Coming of the Civil War*, 182–86, 199; for New York merchants, Philip Foner, *Business and Slavery*, 35–54; and O'Connor, *Lords of the Loom*, 81–97. For Whigs generally, Holt, *Rise and Fall of the American Whig Party*, chap. 16. The figures in Table 6.1 were simplified for the cases of Democrat Free-Soil and Whig Free-Soil. Usually, I placed the individual in the Whig or Democratic camp if the party name came first; only for obvious Free-Soilers (such as Joshua Giddings) did I place such a person in the Free-Soil category.

93. David Potter, *Impending Crisis*, 104–5, 122–30.

94. Based on my impression of newspapers in the border states.

95. Huston, "Southerners against Secession," 287–88.

96. *Augusta Georgia Weekly Constitutionalist*, September 18, 1850.

97. See Hinds County Resolutions in *Yazoo (Miss.) Democrat*, October 3, 1850; message of Reuben Chapman of Alabama in *Mobile Register and Journal*, November 16, 1849; protest against admission of California as a state in Mason, *Public Life and Diplomatic Correspondence of James M. Mason*, 78–81; Letter of James A. Hamilton in *Charleston Mercury*, November 28, 1850; Southern Rights Meeting at Raymond in *Jackson Mississippian*, September 13, 1850.

98. Proceedings of the States Rights Convention: Its Address, in *Charleston Mercury*, May 7, 1851; letter of Charles J. McDonald in *Athens (Ga.) Southern Banner*, August 7, 1851; speech of R. B. Rhett, in *Charleston Mercury*, September 25, 1850; speech of John A. Quitman, in *Natchez Mississippi Free Trader*, May 28, 1851; Matthew F. Maury to William A. Graham, October 8, 1850, in Hamilton, *Papers of Graham*, 3:434–36; Address of the Southern Rights Association of Natchez in *Natchez Mississippi Free Trader*, April 16, 1851; Littleton Waller Tazewell to Robert M. T. Hunter, August 18, 1850, in Ambler, *Correspondence of Hunter*, 117; speech of Christopher Memminger, in *Charleston Mercury*, October 10, 1850; Address of the Committee in *Yazoo (Miss.) Democrat*, January 1, 1851; St. Mary's Southern Rights Organization, in *Charleston Mercury*, September 3, 1850; *Jackson Mississippian*, September 20, 1850. See Barney, *Secessionist Impulse*, 3–19.

99. For example, James H. Hammond to S. Fouché and others, September 26, 1850, Hammond Papers, Library of Congress; James H. Hammond to Lewis Tappan, September 6, 1850, ibid.; *Mobile (Ala.) Daily Register*, November 30, 1850; report of speech of John Townshend, South Carolina, in *New York Herald*, October 26, 1850; *Yazoo (Miss.) Democrat*, February 26, 1851; *St. Louis Intelligencer*, quoted by *Raleigh North Carolina Standard*, July 2, 1851; Felix Huston in *Natchez Mississippi Free Trader*, September 25, 1850. See Thornton, *Politics and Power in a Slave Society*, chap. 4, esp. pp. 204–27.

100. Report of a Joint Committee on the State of the Republic, in *Raleigh North Carolina Standard*, January 9, 1850; Message of Quitman, in *Jackson Mississippian*, November 22, 1850; speech of Memminger in *Charleston Mercury*, October 10, 1850; letter of Burt, quoted in *Columbus (Ga.) Enquirer*, June 3, 1851.

101. *Huntsville (Ala.) Southern Advocate*, June 26, 1850; Quitman, quoted in *Yazoo (Miss.) Democrat*, June 4, 1851.

102. Huston, "Southerners against Secession," table 1, pp. 287–88.

103. *Milledgeville (Ga.) Federal Union*, November 26, 1850, and October 14, 1851; *Macon Georgia Journal and Messenger*, February 19, 1851; Albert G. Fahnstock to Millard Millmore, November 4, 1850, Fillmore Papers, Buffalo and Erie County Historical Society. Writers on southern politics currently tend to favor the idea of a southern realignment in 1851; Christo-

pher Morris, *Becoming Southern*, 154; Bond, *Political Culture in the Nineteenth-Century South*, 104–5; Carey, *Parties, Slavery, and the Union in Antebellum Georgia*, 160–72; Cooper, *The South and the Politics of Slavery*, 304–19. For a version of a nonpartisan South, in which personal relations rather than party affiliation prevailed, see Olsen, *Political Culture and Secession in Mississippi*, 39–52, 74–111.

104. F. M. Robertson to Millard Fillmore, December 6, 1850, Fillmore Papers, Buffalo and Erie County Historical Society; J. J. Flournoy to Fillmore, October [31?], 1850, ibid.; A. Hamilton to Fillmore, August 22, 1851, ibid.; William F. Herring to Fillmore, September 18, 1851, ibid.; Benjamin F. Perry to Fillmore, October 10, 1851, ibid.; James E. Harvey to Fillmore, October 19, 1851, ibid.; D. Lewis to Fillmore, October 19, 1851, ibid.; W. F. Boone to Fillmore, October 20, 1851, ibid.

105. *New York Tribune*, October 14, 1851. See reports of *Washington (D.C.) National Intelligencer*, November 5, 8, 18, 1851; *Philadelphia Evening Bulletin*, August 19, October 10, 1851; *New York Times*, September 22, 26, 27, October 17, 1851; *New York Herald*, August 15, October 20, 24, November 4, 1851; *Boston Daily Advertiser*, August 16, 1851. The quotation from the *New York Tribune* in this instance is unusually important because it is a great indicator of what northerners intended when they said "free labor."

106. Most northern newspapers ran columns of current events that included election news. Southern elections accounted usually for one or two lines in them, typically rejoicing that secession had been so completely rejected or snidely commenting on how feeble secessionists really were. Even the standard abolitionist journals—*National Era, National Anti-Slavery Standard, Independent, Pennsylvania Freeman*, and *Liberator*—had few comments on southern elections.

107. David Potter, *Impending Crisis*, 231–38; Cooper, *The South and the Politics of Slavery*, 323–41. Michael F. Holt, while detailing all the problems slavery presented southern and northern Whigs, nonetheless concludes that personality fights and cultural tensions had more to do with the Whig failure in 1852; see Holt, *Rise and Fall of the American Whig Party*, chaps. 19–20, and his generalization on pp. 674, 727.

108. Lewis D. Campbell to Isaac Strohm, November 4, 1852, Strohm Letters; W. G. Snethen [?] to William H. Seward, November 4, 1852, Seward Papers; August Belmont to James Buchanan, November 5, 1852, Buchanan Papers.

109. J. Teesdale to John McLean, November 19, 1852, McLean Papers; *Pottsville (Pa.) Miners' Journal*, November 6, 1852; *Raleigh (N.C.) Weekly Register*, December 1, 1852; John M. McCrae [?] to J. A. Trimble, November 9, 1852, Trimble Papers; F. J. Stratton to W. H. Seward, November 22, 1852, Seward Papers; C. B. Wheeler to Seward, November 29, 1852, ibid.; Robert Toombs to John J. Crittenden, December 5, 1852, Crittenden Papers; *Jackson Mississippian*, November 26, 1852; *Macon Georgia Journal and Messenger*, November 10, 1852.

110. Holt, *The Political Crisis of the 1850s*, 136–38; Gienapp, *Origins of the Republican Party*, 65–67.

CHAPTER 7

1. Speech of Mason, January 28, 1850, *Cong. Globe*, 31st Cong., 1st sess., quotations from 233, 235.

2. News clipping of *New Haven Register*, December 16, 1850, Rives Papers. On the Fugitive Slave Law, see Thomas Morris, *Free Men All*, esp. 130–48; Pease and Pease, *Fugitive Slave Law and Anthony Burns*, 3–8.

3. John A. Bingham to Samuel Galloway, December 2, 1850, Galloway Papers. See *New York Herald*, October 8, 1850; Spencer, *Religious Duty of Obedience to Law*, 5–24; *Portland*

(Me.) Daily Argus, December 19, 1850; John McLean to Elihu B. Washburne, June 14, 1856, Washburne Papers; Thomas Morris, *Free Men All*, 149–50. On the Abolitionist charge of class, and the general religious argument that developed, see Howe, *Reminiscences*, 218; Arvine, *Our Duty to the Fugitive Slave* (1850), 5–15; "A Word for the Clergy," *United States Magazine and Democratic Review* 34 (September 1854): 241–53; "Puritanism and Abolitionism," ibid., 36 (July 1855): 79–85; John F. Morse to Salmon P. Chase, October 21, 1850, Chase Papers; speech of Abby Kelly Foster in *Rochester Democrat*, October 7, 1850; Address to the People of Massachusetts by the Board of Managers of the Massachusetts Anti-Slavery Society, in *Boston Liberator*, September 27, 1850, p. 154; "Shall We Compromise?," *New York Independent*, February 21, 1850, p. 30; ibid., October 3, 1850, p. 162; *New York National Anti-Slavery Standard*, October 28, 1852, p. 90; Colver, *Fugitive Slave Bill*, 11–15; *Philadelphia Public Ledger*, October 16, 1850; *Rochester Democrat*, November 9, 1850; and *Pittsburgh Morning Post*, September 30, 1850.

4. John Rankin, copy of *Life of Rev. John Rankin Written by Himself in His Eightieth Year*, 1873, p. 49, copy in Clements Library, University of Michigan; Charles Stuart to Theodore Weld, October 15, 1852, Weld-Grimké Papers. Number of cases somewhat estimated from Samuel May, *The Fugitive Slave Law and Its Victims* (1861). See Stanley Campbell, *Slave-Catchers*, chaps. 3–4, 6; David Potter, *Impending Crisis*, 130–40; James McPherson, *Ordeal by Fire*, 79–84.

5. Isaac Sisson to William H. Seward, October 8, 1850, Seward Papers. On northern race relations, Litwack, *North of Slavery*; Field, *Politics of Race in New York*, 100–106; Baker, *Affairs of Party*, chaps. 5, 6; Horton and Horton, *In Hope of Liberty*, 72, 101–2, 239, 243–44. For the humanization angle, note treatment toward blacks in certain Democratic newspapers, such as *Pittsburgh Morning Post*, September 26, 1850; meeting in ibid., September 30, 1850; *Monmouth (Ill.) Atlas*, November 29, 1851; *Cleveland Daily Plain Dealer*, September 28, 1850.

6. *Cleveland Daily Plain Dealer*, quoted in *Milwaukee Daily Free Democrat*, October 5, 1850; *The Fugitive Slave Bill* (1850), 20; speech of Sholes in *Milwaukee Daily Free Democrat*, November 5, 1851. See Gara, "Antislavery Congressmen, 1848–1856," 204; Michael McManus, " 'Freedom and Liberty First and the Union Afterwards.' "

7. This is something of a personal observation without evidentiary support. In recent times, accidents or mishaps—such as a plane crash or tampered medicine—cause reactions that make no statistical sense. The probability of ingesting tampered medicine or being involved in an airplane crash is infinitesimally small; yet because of the public reaction to such events, companies and the government go to extreme lengths to assure the public that the problems involved have been reacted to and mitigated in all other circumstances. Examples of southern slave catchers in antebellum northern communities may have been of this character. It was not that a few incidents occurred that mattered; it was that any incidents occurred at all.

8. Robert May, *Southern Dream of a Caribbean Empire*; James McPherson, *Ordeal by Fire*, 75–79.

9. Consult Johannsen, *Douglas*, 386–400; Holt, *The Political Crisis of the 1850s*, 144–45; David Potter, *Impending Crisis*, 145–54.

10. On the January stages of the Kansas-Nebraska Act, see printing of bill, January 4, 1854, *Cong. Globe*, 33d Cong., 1st sess., 115; speech of Dixon, January 16, 1854, ibid., 175; speech of Douglas, January 23, ibid., 221–22; speech of Dixon, January 24, 1854, ibid., 240; Douglas, January 30, 1854, ibid., 275–77: Johannsen, *Douglas*, 401–18; Gara, *Presidency of Pierce*, 89–92.

11. *Appeal of the Independent Democrats in Congress to the People of the United States* (1854), 1–7, quotation from 6, found in Giddings Papers, Indiana State Library.

12. Ibid., 3.

13. Sion H. Rogers to W. A. Graham, May 11, 1854, in Hamilton, *Papers of Graham*, 4:514; Joshua R. Giddings to Son, January 12, 1854, Giddings Papers, Ohio Historical Society; John W. Forney to James Buchanan, May 25, 1854, Buchanan Papers; Charles Sumner to Mrs. Frances A. Seward, March 30, 1854, Seward Papers; Solomon G. Haven to James M. Smith, February 7, May 7, 1854, Haven Papers; Hannibal Hamlin to William P. Haines [?], January 25, 1854, Hamlin Papers, supplement II.

14. On the 1850 legislative acts replacing 1820, see speeches of (all dates 1854) A. H. Stephens, February 17, *Cong. Globe*, 33d Cong., 1st sess., *Appendix*, 193–95; J. R. Thomson, February 28, ibid., *Appendix*, 255–56; Samuel A. Smith, April 5, ibid., 856. On the prediction that the two territories would be free due to climate and economic reasons, Butler, March 2, ibid., *Appendix*, 292; John Bell, March 3, ibid., *Appendix*, 414; J. S. Millson, March 23, ibid., 426; J. R. Franklin, March 28, ibid., *Appendix*, 421; William Cullom, April 11, ibid., *Appendix*, 538; A. B. Greenwood, May 19, ibid., *Appendix*, 844; M. Macdonald, April 10, ibid., *Appendix*, 515. On the idea that the Missouri Compromise was not above amendment or repeal, Douglas, January 30, ibid., 276–77; John Bell, March 3, ibid., *Appendix*, 412; P. Phillips, April 24, ibid., *Appendix*, 530–33.

15. See speeches of Gerrit Smith, April 6, 1854, ibid., *Appendix*, 519; Charles Sumner, February 24, 1854, ibid., *Appendix*, 263; Edward Ball, May 9, 1854, ibid., *Appendix*, 579; Joshua Giddings, May 16, 1854, ibid., *Appendix*, 986–87.

16. On why resurrect the agitation, R. W. Peckham, May 18, 1854, ibid., *Appendix*, 870; G. W. Morrison, May 19, 1854, ibid., *Appendix*, 849; John Bell, May 24–25, 1854, ibid., *Appendix*, 938; A. Harlan, May 19, 1854, ibid., *Appendix*, 1002. On free territory always free territory, Edward Everett, February 8, 1854, ibid., *Appendix*, 162; D. Mace, February 14, 1854, ibid., *Appendix*, 166; J. O. Norton, March 29, 1854, ibid., *Appendix*, 453. On why two territories, Bernhart Henn, May 20, 1854, ibid., *Appendix*, 886. On the question of the title of Indians to the land and the promise made justifying removal under Jackson, Houston, February 14–15, 1854, ibid., *Appendix*, 201–2; Seward, February 17, 1854, ibid., 153.

17. Richard Yates, manuscript of a speech, 1856, Yates Papers; *Augusta (Me.) Kennebec Journal*, June 9, 1854; Ogden Hoffman to William H. Seward, March 5, 1854, Seward Papers. See also John Holcomb to Benjamin F. Wade, January 24, 1854, Wade Papers; Martin Van Buren to Moses Tilden, September 1, 1856, in Bigelow, *Letters and Memorials of Tilden*, 1:119–20; resolutions of a Harrison and Vicinity meeting, March 28, 1854, Fessenden Papers; John Bell, March 3, 1854, *Cong. Globe*, 33d Cong., 1st sess., *Appendix*, 408–12, 414; Crittenden to Archibald Dixon, March 7, 1854, Crittenden Papers. For some congressional speeches on the repeal of the Missouri Compromise, see (all dates 1854) Salmon P. Chase, February 3, *Cong. Globe*, 33d Cong., 1st sess., *Appendix*, 134; M. H. Nichols, April 5, ibid., *Appendix*, 475–77; E. W. Farley, May 10, ibid., *Appendix*, 677–79; Nathaniel P. Banks, May 18, ibid., *Appendix*, 878–80; C. W. Upham, May 10, ibid., *Appendix*, 712–13; A. Harlan, May 19, ibid., *Appendix*, 1004–6.

18. Douglas speech (all dates 1854), January 30, *Cong. Globe*, 33d Cong., 1st sess., 280; Henn, May 20, ibid., *Appendix*, 887; Wright, April 4, ibid., *Appendix*, 460; Johannsen, *Douglas*, 430–32.

19. Quotations from (all dates 1854) Stuart, May 20, *Cong. Globe*, 33d Cong., 1st sess., *Appendix*, 843; Wade, May 17, ibid., *Appendix*, 665; Washburne, April 7, ibid., *Appendix*, 493, 496. For other criticisms based on antislavery and the power of Congress, see speech of Edward Ball, May 9, ibid., *Appendix*, 578; D. Carpenter, May 10, ibid., *Appendix*, 599–600; G. W. Morrison, May 19, ibid., *Appendix*, 852; Henry Bennett, May 17, ibid., *Appendix*, 692; Charles Hughes, April 27, ibid., *Appendix*, 536.

20. *Springfield Illinois State Register*, January 27, 1854; Jonathan Garrgies [?] to John G. Davis, April 10, 1854, Davis Papers, Indiana Historical Society; *Fort Wayne (Ind.) Sentinel*, February 18, 1854; *Cincinnati Enquirer*, January 11, May 24, 1854; *Cleveland Daily Plain Dealer*, May 19, 23, 1854; C. S. H., "The Missouri Prohibition," *United States Magazine and Democratic Review* 34 (August 1854): 134–38; *Washington (D.C.) Daily Union*, January 20, May 23, 27, 1854.

21. For attacks on popular sovereignty, see William Cullom, April 11, 1854, *Cong. Globe*, 33d Cong., 1st sess., *Appendix*, 541; Archibald Dixon, January 24, 1854, ibid., 240; John S. Caskie, May 19, 1854, ibid., *Appendix*, 1143; Lawrence M. Keitt, March 30, 1854, ibid., *Appendix*, 466; James L. Seward, May 10, 1854, ibid., *Appendix*, 620. These differences were picked up; see *Washington (D.C.) National Intelligencer*, May 18, 1854; Johannsen, *Douglas*, 426–28.

22. Keitt, March 30, 1854, *Cong. Globe*, 33d Cong., 1st sess., *Appendix*, 467; speech of Dunham, May 19, 1854, ibid., *Appendix*, 1132–33.

23. Address of the Democratic Republican Central Committee to the Freemen of New-Hampshire, Broadside, Burke Papers. I assume that Burke wrote the pamphlet, although it is not signed. The issue of property rights in slaves was the reason compromise was not viable in the 1850s despite the pleas of several historians who insist that the sectional problems over slavery were compromisable; those who have argued for the possibility of compromise include Craven, *An Historian and the Civil War*, 82–93; Milton, *The Eve of Conflict*, 1–2, 237–38; and a recent restatement, Grant, *North over South*, 36.

24. *Springfield Daily Illinois State Journal*, May 26, 1854; *New York Times*, May 23, 1854; H. Bennett, May 17, 1854, *Cong. Globe*, 33d Cong., 1st sess., *Appendix*, 693–95, quotation from 694.

25. Skelton, February 14, 1854, *Cong. Globe*, 33d Cong., 1st sess., *Appendix*, 191; Yates, March 28, 1854, ibid., *Appendix*, 447. Other individuals making speeches or portions of their speeches devoted to the topic are James Cooper, February 27, 1854, ibid., *Appendix*, 507; Harlan, May 19, 1854, ibid., *Appendix*, 1007; Giddings, May 16, 1854, ibid., *Appendix*, 988; E. W. Farley, May 10, 1854, ibid., *Appendix*, 678–80; Thomas Davis, May 9, 1854, ibid., *Appendix*, 639–42; Bishop Perkins, May 10, 1854, ibid., *Appendix*, 646–47; G. A. Simmons, May 10, 1854, *Appendix*, 591–92; Edward Ball, May 9, 1854, ibid., *Appendix*, 579–80.

26. Brown, February 24, 1854, ibid., *Appendix*, 230; Dodge, February 25, 1854, ibid., *Appendix*, 376–78 (quotation and Brown's response from 376).

27. Walsh, May 19, 1854, ibid., 1232.

28. Keitt, March 30, 1854, ibid., *Appendix*, 466; Dowdell, May 10, 1854, ibid., *Appendix*, 704, 706; Boyce, May 20, 1854, ibid., *Appendix*, 725; Edmands, May 20, 1854, ibid., *Appendix*, 753; Colquitt, May 10, 1854, ibid., *Appendix*, 751. New England ministers and Chicago ministers petitioned Congress to reject the Kansas-Nebraska Act and inspired quite a discussion over clerical interference in political activity; Huston, "Democracy by Scripture vs. Democracy by Process."

29. For example, Keitt, March 30, 1854, *Cong. Globe*, 33d Cong., 1st sess., *Appendix*, 464–67; Robert Toombs, February 23, 1854, ibid., *Appendix*, 347–49; P. Phillips, April 24, 1854, ibid., *Appendix*, 532–34; Dowdell, May 10, 1854, ibid., 705–6.

30. Toombs, February 23, 1854, ibid., *Appendix*, 350. The same claim was made by North Carolina's Thomas Clingman, April 4, 1854, ibid., *Appendix*, 491.

31. William Smith, April 27, 1854, ibid., *Appendix*, 553; Keitt, March 30, 1854, ibid., *Appendix*, 465; William Barry, April 27, 1854, ibid., *Appendix*, 618; C. J. Faulkner, April 10, 1854, ibid., *Appendix*, 487.

32. Edmands, May 20, 1854, ibid., *Appendix*, 753. See Charles Sumner, February 24, 1854, ibid., *Appendix*, 268; Dunham, May 19, 1854, ibid., *Appendix*, 1132–33; Benjamin F. Wade,

March 3, 1854, ibid., *Appendix*, 313; Yates, March 28, 1854, ibid., *Appendix*, 447; George S. Hillard in *Boston Semi-Weekly Advertiser*, February 25, 1854.

33. On passage, see David Potter, *Impending Crisis*, 165–67; Johannsen, *Douglas*, 428–47; Alexander H. Stephens to Col. T. W. Thomas, May 23, 1854, Stephens Papers; A. H. Stephens to M. Barnwell, June 26, 1854, ibid.; A. H. Stephens to M. Burwell, June 27, 1854, ibid.

34. Quote from *Raleigh Weekly Register*, February 1, 1854. Generalizations based on *Greensborough (N.C.) Patriot*, May 6, 1854; *Covington (Ky.) Journal*, February 11, May 27, 1854; *Athens (Ga.) Southern Banner*, February 2, May 18, 1854; *Macon Georgia Journal and Messenger*, February 1, May 17, 31, 1854; *Richmond Whig*, May 23, 25, 1854; *Natchez Mississippi Free Trader*, March 14, 21, 1854; *Milledgeville (Ga.) Federal Union*, May 30, 1854; *Raleigh North Carolina Standard*, February 8, May 31, 1854; *Hillsborough (N.C.) Recorder*, March 22, April 26, 1854; *Milledgeville (Ga.) Southern Recorder*, May 30, 1854; *Raleigh Star and North Carolina Gazette*, May 21, June 7, 1854; *Yazoo (Miss.) Democrat*, February 1, 8, 15, 22, 1854; *Jackson Mississippian*, February 10, May 19, June 9, 1854.

35. Huston, "Democracy by Scripture vs. Democracy by Process"; *New York Times*, February 13, 1854; *Chicago Journal*, March 18, 28, April 13, 1854; Stephen Douglas, *Letter of Senator Douglas, Vindicating His Character and His Position on the Nebraska Bill* (1854), 3–10.

36. Crandall, *Early History of the Republican Party*, 20–23; Gienapp, *Origins of the Republican Party*, 89–91, 104–6; *Augusta (Me.) Kennebec Journal*, September 22, 1854; R. S. Wilson to Elihu Washburne, September 19, 1854, Washburne Papers; Schuyler Colfax to Friend Shryock, August 24, 1854, Colfax Papers.

37. James W. Grimes to Elihu B. Washburne, July 13, 1854, Washburne Papers.

38. Solomon G. Haven to Millard Fillmore, February 18, May 15, 1854, Fillmore Papers, State University of New York at Oswego; John P. Kennedy to Fillmore, May 28, 1854, ibid.; quotation in John Law to John G. Davis, April 3, 1854, Davis Papers, Indiana Historical Society; Samuel A. Fisher to John G. Davis, April 4, 1854, ibid.; Eli Davis to John G. Davis, April 2, July 16, 1854, Davis Papers, State Historical Society of Wisconsin; J. Bohonann to William English, February 8, 1854, English Papers; J. B. Archer to English, February 23, 1854, ibid.; Jonathan L. Robsage [?] to English, May 19, 1854, ibid.; G. G. Graham to English, May 30, 1854, ibid.; J. Glancy Jones to James Buchanan, May 18, 1854, Buchanan Papers; Wilson McCandless to Buchanan, June 12, 1854, ibid.; Lewis P. Clover to Buchanan, June 15, 1854, ibid.; John M. Butler to Simon Cameron, June 10, 1854, Cameron Papers, Library of Congress; F. J. Grund to Simon Cameron, April 23, 1854, Cameron Correspondence and Papers, Historical Society of Dauphin County; William H. Davis to Cameron, May 27, 1854, ibid.

39. A. L. Hayes to James Buchanan, May 8, 1854, Buchanan Papers; Daniel T. Jenks to Buchanan, June 9, 1854, ibid.; George Sanderson to Buchanan, June 22, 1854, ibid. On temperance and the ministry, see B. P. Douglass to William H. English, April 4, 1854, English Papers; W. Z. Stuart to English, March 13, 1854, ibid.; W. W. Wick to English, June 5, 1854, ibid.; William Bigler to Simon Cameron, July 10, 1854, Cameron Papers, Library of Congress; Westcott, *New Men, New Issues*, 90–131.

40. On the Know-Nothings, see the standard works of Billington, *Protestant Crusade*; Anbinder, *Nativism and Slavery*; Mulkern, *Know-Nothing Party in Massachusetts*; Baker, *Ambivalent Americans*; Gienapp, *Origins of the Republican Party*, 92–100; and Holt, "The Politics of Impatience."

41. George W. Mitchell to H. H. Stuart, June 20, 1854, Stuart Papers; Solomon G. Haven to Millard Fillmore, June 29, 1854, Fillmore Papers, George Peabody Branch of the Enoch Pratt Free Library; quotation from William P. Haines to Hannibal Hamlin, July 28, 1854, Hamlin Papers; quotation from J. B. Turner to Richard Yates, April 8, 1854, Yates Papers; quotation from Lewis D. Campbell to Isaac Strohm, September 9, 1854, Strohm Papers.

42. Nevins, *Ordeal of the Union,* 2:70–72; Gienapp, *Origins of the Republican Party,* 39–40; see also Berger, *Revolution in the New York Party Systems,* 2, 26–36; Booraem, *Formation of the Republican Party in New York,* 22–24.

43. Cass speech at Detroit in *New York Herald,* November 9, 1854.

44. Lincoln speech at Peoria, October 16, 1854, in Basler, Pratt, and Dunlap, *Collected Works of Lincoln,* 2:262, 263.

45. Dickinson speech in *New York Herald,* October 4, 1854.

46. "Slavery and the Future," *New York Tribune,* May 27, 1854. The assumption is that Greeley wrote this editorial.

47. David Potter, *Impending Crisis,* 175 n. 47. Potter evidently included the New England states holding elections in 1855 for his computation for ninety-one Democrats. My total is seventy-nine Democrats elected from the free states in 1852, excluding the nine from Connecticut, Rhode Island, and New Hampshire; I also did not include the three Far Western Democrats (I presume), two from California and one from Oregon.

48. Gienapp focuses more on the forces of the Know-Nothings, finding little party cohesion in the Great Lakes. However, he pays most attention to state races. Gienapp, *Origins of the Republican Party,* 104–27. The division between the Great Lakes states and the northern seaboard states was pointed out by Aldrich, *Why Parties?,* 146–49, 155.

49. Compare with Gienapp, *Origins of the Republican Party,* 129–66; see Aldrich, *Why Parties?,* 146–49; Westcott, *New Men, New Issues,* 114–19.

50. Some results taken from *Whig Almanac and Politician's Register* for 1855; see also David Potter, *Impending Crisis,* 250; Gienapp, *Origins of the Republican Party,* chaps. 4, 5.

51. *Toledo Blade,* October 11, 1854; *Washington (D.C.) National Era,* October 19, 1854; George Sanderson to James Buchanan, October 24, 1854, Buchanan Papers; *Milwaukee Daily Free Democrat,* October 14, 16, 1854; *Fort Wayne (Ind.) Sentinel,* October 13, 1854; Godlove Orth to Schuyler Colfax, October 14, 1854, Orth Papers; G. W. Southwick to Elihu B. Washburne, December 28, 1854, Washburne Papers. The term Republican Party or Republican fusion for the western states found in the *Milwaukee Daily Free Democrat,* November 15, 1854; *Washington (D.C.) National Era,* November 16, 1854.

52. John P. Kennedy to Millard Fillmore, October 26, 1854, Fillmore Papers, State University of New York at Oswego; James Pollock to John M. Clayton, October 30, 1854, Clayton Papers; Robert I. Arundel to John McLean, October 14, 1854, McLean Papers; remarks of *Cleveland Daily Plain Dealer,* October 18, 1854.

53. Millard Fillmore to Edward Everett, December 13, 1854, Fillmore Papers, Massachusetts Historical Society; Solomon G. Haven to Fillmore, December 9, 1854, Fillmore Papers, State University of New York at Oswego; William A. Graham to Fillmore, December 3, 1854, ibid.; Francis Granger to Fillmore, October 24, 1854, ibid.; Alexander H. Stuart to Fillmore, November 11, 1854, ibid.; John T. Bush to Fillmore, November 15, 1854, ibid.; Winfield Scott to John J. Crittenden, November 9, 1854, Crittenden Papers. The Seward people also saw the election largely in terms of the Know-Nothing insurgency, although they predicted that eventually the party of freedom, not nativism, would dominate: Charles Sumner to Mrs. Francis A. M. Seward, October 26, 1854, Seward Papers; George E. Baker to Seward, November 10, 15, 1854, ibid.; Laban Hoskins to Seward, November 15, 1854, ibid.

54. *Cleveland Daily Plain Dealer,* October 12, 1854; Daniel T. Jenks to James Buchanan, October 3, 1854, Buchanan Papers. See H. B. Pickett to John G. Davis, October 25, 1854, Davis Papers, Indiana Historical Society; H. W. Daniels to John G. Davis, October 12, 1854, ibid.; *Fort Wayne (Ind.) Sentinel,* October 13, 1854; *Madison Wisconsin Democrat,* November 11, 1854; Daniel T. Jenks to Buchanan, October 17, 1854, Buchanan Papers; Joseph A. Wright to James Buchanan, November 14, 1854, ibid.; John Saco to William H. English, November 6,

1854, English Papers; R. M. DeFrance to Simon Cameron, October 12, 1854, Cameron Correspondence and Papers, Historical Society of Dauphin County; Isaac Huger to Cameron, October 17, 1854, ibid.; *New York Herald*, October 12, 13, 25, November 8, 1854. See analysis of Gara, *Presidency of Pierce*, 96–100.

55. *Huntsville (Ala.) Southern Advocate*, October 25, 1854; *Natchez Mississippi Free Trader*, November 1, 1854; *Raleigh North Carolina Standard*, October 18, November 1, 1854; *Vicksburg (Miss.) Weekly Whig*, November 22, 1854; *Louisville Daily Courier*, October 13, 1854; *Macon Georgia Journal and Messenger*, October 18, 1854. Howell Cobb believed that sectional parties would form out of the upheaval in the North; Cobb to James Buchanan, December 5, 1854, Buchanan Papers.

56. *Raleigh (N.C.) Star and Gazette*, October 12, 1854; *Hillsborough (N.C.) Recorder*, October 18, 1854; *Raleigh North Carolina Standard*, October 11, 1854; *Richmond Whig*, October 17, November 10, 1854; *Athens (Ga.) Southern Banner*, October 12, 26, 1854; *Covington (Ky.) Journal*, October 14, 1854; *Greensborough (N.C.) Patriot*, October 14, 1854; *Columbus (Ga.) Enquirer*, October 17, 1854; *Natchez Mississippi Free Trader*, November 8, 15, December 13, 1854; *Macon Georgia Journal and Messenger*, October 25, November 1, 8, 1854; C. R. Harris [of Virginia] to John A. Trimble, November 21, 1854, John A. Trimble Family Papers.

57. Edward Everett to Millard Fillmore, November 10, 1854, Fillmore Papers, State University of New York at Oswego; the breakdown on voting for the Kansas-Nebraska Act is given in *Jackson Mississippian*, June 9, 1854. See Cooper, *The South and the Politics of Slavery*, 349–60; Cooper, *Liberty and Slavery*, 242–46.

58. Quotations from *Harrisburg (Pa.) Herald*, December 13, 1854, and second quotation October 25, 1854. See Huston, "The Demise of the Pennsylvania American Party"; Anbinder, *Nativism and Slavery*, chaps. 5, 7, 8. One southern paper did call for restoration of the Missouri Compromise: the *Louisville Journal*, as reported in the *Milwaukee Daily Sentinel*, October 24, 1854. This is exactly what the whole of the Border South should have done to stave off the rise of the Republicans, at least for a few years. It is what the Border South offered in the Crittenden Resolutions of 1861, when it was too late and secession already acted upon.

59. William Lansing to William H. Seward, November 13, 1854, Seward Papers. The interpretation of Holt over the past twenty years has been that slavery did not lead to the demise of the Second Party System, that other influences—ethnocultural and economic, for example—played at the least as important a role. See Holt, *Rise and Fall of the American Whig Party*, chaps. 21–23; his interpretation may be found more succinctly in Holt, *Political Crisis of the 1850s*, vii–viii, 4–6, 9–16, 148–56, 172–81.

60. On the elections of 1855, see Gienapp, *Origins of the Republican Party*, chap. 7; Cooper, *The South and the Politics of Slavery*, 349–60; Atkins, *Parties, Politics, and Sectional Conflict in Tennessee*, 195–205; Carey, *Parties, Slavery, and the Union in Antebellum Georgia*, 185–95. On Kansas events, David Potter, *Impending Crisis*, chap. 9.

61. For example, *Raleigh (N.C.) Star and Gazette*, October 12, 24, November 14, 1855; *Vicksburg (Miss.) Weekly Whig*, November 2, 8, 1855; *Macon Georgia Journal and Messenger*, October–November 1855; *Hillsborough (N.C.) Recorder*, November 14, 1855; *Natchez Mississippi Free Trader*, November 1855; *Covington (Ky.) Journal*, October–November 1855.

62. *Natchez Mississippi Free Trader*, October 10, 1855; *Richmond Whig*, September 28, 1855.

63. Huston, "The Demise of the Pennsylvania American Party"; Anbinder, *Nativism and Slavery*, 145–61; Holt, *The Political Crisis of the 1850s*, 172–74.

64. Reports on the Know-Nothing convention from *New York Times*, June 13, 14, 15, 1855; Know-Something convention discussed ibid., June 15, 1855. See reports of *Pittsburgh Dis-*

patch, June 8, 19, 1855; *Harrisburg Pennsylvania Telegraph*, July 11, 1855; *Harrisburg (Pa.) Herald*, July 7, 10, 1855; Huston, "The Demise of the Pennsylvania American Party"; Anbinder, *Nativism and Slavery*, 162–74; Gienapp, *Origins of the Republican Party*, 179–87.

65. Solomon G. Haven to James M. Smith, December 20, 1855, Haven Papers; see Anbinder, *Nativism and Slavery*, 162–74.

66. The description here is a summary of Nevins, *Ordeal of the Union*, 2:380–93, 408–11, 416–19, 428–50, 471–86; David Potter, *Impending Crisis*, 199–224; Gienapp, *Origins of the Republican Party*, 295–303; Gara, *Presidency of Pierce*, 112–26.

67. On election of 1856, see Gienapp, *Origins of the Republican Party*, chaps. 10–13; David Potter, *Impending Crisis*, 253–65. For the uncertain states, see Huston, *Panic of 1857*, 231, 241.

68. Computed from Moore, *Congressional Quarterly's Guide to U.S. Elections*, 598–602. See Table B.2.

69. *Athens (Ga.) Southern Banner*, October 16, 1856; Henry A. Wise to Robert Tyler, August 15, 1856, in Tyler, *Letters and Times of the Tylers*, 2:531; *Macon Georgia Journal and Messenger*, November 12, 1856. See *Covington (Ky.) Journal*, October 18, 1856; *Memphis Weekly Appeal*, June 18, October 15, 1856; *Greensborough (N.C.) Patriot*, September 19, October 17, 1856; *Columbus (Ga.) Enquirer*, September 16, November 18, 1856; *Richmond Whig*, November 11, 1856; *Vicksburg (Miss.) Weekly Whig*, October 22, 24, 1856.

70. The somewhat convoluted background of the *Dred Scott* case may be found in Hopkins, *Dred Scott's Case*; Ehrlich, *They Have No Rights*; and Fehrenbacher, *Dred Scott Case*.

71. David Potter, *Impending Crisis*, 271–80; Hopkins, *Dred Scott's Case*, 79, 87; Fehrenbacher, *Dred Scott Case*, 323–25, 367–84.

72. See opinions of Fehrenbacher, *Dred Scott Case*, 383–84, 395, 557–61; David Potter, *Impending Crisis*, 279–85, 291–94; Wiecek, "Slavery and Abolition before the United States Supreme Court"; Bestor, "State Sovereignty and Slavery."

73. James R. Doolittle to Moses M. Davis, March 9, 1860, Moses M. Davis Papers; Timothy O. Howe to [Horace] Rubles, April 5, 1857, Howe Papers; *New York Tribune*, March 11, 1857; *New York Herald*, March 12, 14, 15, 1857; *Pottsville (Pa.) Miner's Journal*, March 21, 1857; *New York Evening Post*, quoted in *Boston Liberator*, March 20, 1857; *Cincinnati Daily Gazette*, March 9, 11, 12, 16, 1857; *Milwaukee Weekly Wisconsin*, March 18, 1857; *Toledo Blade*, March 13, 1857; *Boston Semi-Weekly Advertiser*, March 14, 27, June 10, 1857; Benton, *Historical and Legal Examination of That Part of the Decision of the Supreme Court of the United States in the Dred Scott Case* (1857), 17–22. The abolitionist William Goodell took the occasion of the Dred Scott decision to send letters to congressmen warning of the impact of the judgment on local law and that southerners sought to buttress slavery by claims to its origin in natural law and common law. William Goodell to John F. Potter, 1858, Potter Papers; William Goodell to E. B. Washburne, March 20, 1858, Washburne Papers.

74. *Columbus Ohio State Journal*, March 11, 1857; *Chicago Daily Tribune*, March 12, 1857; *Milwaukee Weekly Wisconsin*, March 18, 1857.

75. *Augusta Georgia Weekly Constitutionalist*, March 18, 1857; *Athens (Ga.) Southern Banner*, March 26, 1857; *New Orleans Daily Picayune*, March 20, 1857; *Macon Georgia Journal and Messenger*, March 18, 1857; *Greensborough (N.C.) Patriot*, April 3, 10, 1857; *Hillsborough (N.C.) Recorder*, April 1, 1857; "Dred Scott in the Supreme Court," *De Bow's Review* 22 (April 1857): 403–9; *Baltimore Patriot*, quoted in *Covington (Ky.) Journal*, March 28, 1857; *Milledgeville (Ga.) Southern Recorder*, March 17, 1857.

76. *Cleveland Daily Plain Dealer*, September 2, 1857; see ibid., March 19, 24, 1857; *Springfield Illinois State Register*, March 12, 19, 31, 1857; *Washington (D.C.) Daily Union*, March 11, 1857; Rawley, *Race and Politics*, 195; Fehrenbacher, *Dred Scott Case*, 415–595.

77. Johannsen, *Lincoln-Douglas Debates*, 14. Idea of ober dicta in *Milwaukee Daily Sen-*

tinel, March 19, 1857; *Pottsville (Pa.) Miner's Journal*, March 21, 1857; *Toledo Blade*, March 16, 1857.

78. For events surrounding Kansas, see David Potter, *Impending Crisis*, 297–327.

79. Johannsen, *Douglas*, 576–87, 590–93.

80. See David Potter, *Impending Crisis*, 310–27; Johannsen, *Douglas*, 592–613; Klein, *President James Buchanan*, 303–11. On southern explanations of northern behavior, see Thomas L. Anderson, January 26, 1858, *Cong. Globe*, 35th Cong., 1st sess., 419; L. Q. C. Lamar, January 13, 1858, ibid., *Appendix*, 49–51; John Bell, March 18, 1858, ibid., *Appendix*, 132; James S. Green, March 23, 1858, ibid., *Appendix*, 211; Reuben Davis, January 27, 1858, ibid., 440–41; Stephen R. Mallory, March 16, 1858, ibid., 1137; Samuel O. Peyton, March 28, 1858, ibid., 1332.

81. Seward, March 3, 1858, *Cong. Globe*, 35th Cong., 1st sess., 941–43. Republican attitudes toward Douglas can be found in Henry D. Cooke to John Sherman, March 2, 1858, Sherman Papers; Edward Potter to John F. Potter, April 13, 1858, Potter Papers; Schuyler Colfax to Powell, February 17, 1858, Colfax Papers; Charles Sumner to Chase, January 18, 1858, Chase Papers, Library of Congress; Richard Mott to Chase, January 15, 1858, ibid.

82. Bell, March 18, 1858, *Cong. Globe*, 35th Cong., 1st sess., 1231–39; Crittenden, March 17, 1858, ibid., 1153; Washington Hunt to John J. Crittenden, March 18, 1858, Crittenden Papers; Jonathan Edwards to Crittenden, March 18, 1858, ibid.; R. A. Sommerville to Crittenden, March 31, 1858, ibid.; Thomas E. Bramletter to Crittenden, April 2, 1858, ibid.; J. Scott Harrison to Crittenden, March 22, 1858, ibid.; J. Harlan to Crittenden, March 22, 1858, ibid.; William H. Vanderbilt to Crittenden, March 22, 1858, ibid.; and many others.

83. Hammond, March 4, 1858, *Cong. Globe*, 35th Cong., 1st sess., 959–62; see Huston, *Panic of 1857*, 124–27.

84. Speeches of the following individuals, without the dates, from *Cong. Globe*, 35th Cong., 1st sess.: J. L. M. Curry, 320, 819; John D. C. Atkins, 750; Muscoe R. H. Garnett, 1245; Miles Taylor, *Appendix*, 231–32.

85. Probably most free labor speeches contained warnings of the slave power as well, but my sense is that the free labor argument overwhelmed most other Republican rationalizations about the dangers of slavery. Free labor speeches, without the dates, are from *Cong. Globe*, 35th Cong., 1st sess.: Cydnor B. Tompkins, 774; Silas M. Burroughs, 815–16; Calvin C. Chaffee, 854; William H. Seward, 942, 944; James R. Doolittle, 982; Hannibal Hamlin, 1005–6; Lafayette S. Foster, 1043; Benjamin Franklin Wade, 1113; John Farnsworth, 1205; Emory B. Pottle, 1249; William Kellogg, 1269; Francis P. Blair Jr., 1283–84; William A. Howard, 1277; John F. Potter, 1290; Sidney Dean, 1357; John Covode, 1365. From the *Appendix*: Daniel Clark, 91–92; David C. Broderick, 192–93; Henry Wilson, 168–72; Edward Wade, 220–21; John R. Thomson, 298; Freeman H. Morse, 312; Charles B. Hoard, 275.

86. Bishop, March 22, 1858, ibid., 1246. This is one of the most humorous congressional speeches given during the decade.

87. The following individuals made comments about the *Dred Scott* case, dates not given. *Cong. Globe*, 35th Cong., 1st sess.: Elihu B. Washburne, 233, 1349; Lyman Trumbull, 523–24; James Doolittle, 665; Cydnor B. Tompkins, 774; Charles Case, 1082; Zachariah Chandler, 1089; Nehemiah Abbott, 1255; John Covode, 1362; Eli Thayer, 1341. Ibid., *Appendix*: James F. Simmons, 159, Abram B. Olin, 235–36; James Wilson, 245; Mason W. Tappan, 329; E. P. Walton, 331–32. Property rights discussed in the following speeches, dates not given. *Cong. Globe*, 35th Cong., 1st sess.: Elihu B. Washburne, 235; John P. Hale, 341; Aaron Harlan, 384–85; John B. Cochrane, 426; Silas M. Burroughs, 816; Samuel G. Andrews, 826; Calvin C. Chaffee, 854; William Pitt Fessenden, 620; Jefferson Davis, 856; Jacob Collamer, 924; William H. Seward, 941; Judah P. Benjamin, 1066–72; Zachariah Chandler, 1089; Benjamin F.

Wade, 1116; Lyman Trumbull, 1160–61; John F. Farnsworth, 1204–5; Horace Maynard, 1207; Muscoe R. H. Garnett, 1244; Nehemiah Abbott, 1255; Francis P. Blair Jr., 1284. Ibid., *Appendix*: James M. Mason, 79–80; Clement C. Clay, 146; James A. Bayard, 191; Henry Wilson, 246; William S. Groesbeck, 306; Mason W. Tappan, 328; Eliakim P. Walton, 331–32; Daniel W. Gooch, 229.

88. Quotation from Henry Waldron, March 20, 1858, *Cong. Globe*, 35th Cong., 1st sess., 1212; Elihu Washburne, March 25, 1858, ibid., 1349, generally, 1346–68.

89. Charles E. Stuart, March 22, 1858, ibid., *Appendix*, 180; James Hughes, March 31, 1858, ibid., *Appendix*, 324; William Groesbeck, March 31, 1858, ibid., 306.

90. Bayard, March 22, 1858, *Cong. Globe*, 35th Cong., 1st sess., *Appendix*, 191; Douglas and Stuart remarks and quotes, ibid., *Appendix*, 199–200. Toombs responded that no southerner had assaulted the principles and constitutions of the free states; ibid., *Appendix*, 201.

91. On Douglas and popular sovereignty, see Douglas to John A. McClernand, November 23, 1857, in Johannsen, *Letters of Douglas*, 403; Douglas to John W. Forney, February 6, 1858, ibid., 408; Douglas to ——, February 11, 1858, ibid., 411.

92. Huston, *Panic of 1857*, 261–67.

93. Johannsen, *Lincoln-Douglas Debates*, 79, 88, quotation from 145. See comments of Jaffa, *Crisis of the House Divided*, 288–89, 304; David Potter, *Impending Crisis*, 328–55; Johannsen, *Douglas*, 661–79. For a philosopher's probing of popular sovereignty and the Lincoln-Douglas debates, see Jaffa, *New Birth of Freedom*, 112–16, 179–80, 309–36, 473–87.

94. Huston, *Panic of 1857*, 139–72.

95. Ibid., 152–66.

96. Ibid., 173–209; Stephen A. Douglas, "The Dividing Line between Federal and Local Authority: Popular Sovereignty in the Territories," *Harper's Monthly* 19 (September 1859): 519–37; Johannsen, *Douglas*, 707–12; Jaffa, *New Birth of Freedom*, 473–87.

97. Huston, *Panic of 1857*, n. 59, pp. 208–9; Table 7.1; Holt, *The Political Crisis of the 1850s*, 207–9, 213–14.

98. David Potter, *Impending Crisis*, 369–78; Steven Channing, *Crisis of Fear*, 252–56, 287–90.

99. Davis resolutions debated and passed May 25, 1860, *Cong. Globe*, 36th Cong., 1st sess., 2344–52; speech of Albert G. Brown, March 6, 1860, ibid., 1003; Davis defense of resolutions, May 16, 18, 1860, ibid., 2121, 2151. William J. Cooper argues that Davis's resolutions were more ambiguous and had a "Freeport doctrine" quality to them, allowing settlers to deny the establishment of slavery by passing hostile police laws; the radical version of federal intervention, says Cooper, was authored by Albert G. Brown; Cooper, *Jefferson Davis*, 304–7.

100. Douglas speech, May 15, 16, 1860, *Cong. Globe*, 36th Cong., 1st sess., *Appendix*, 301–16, quotation from 316; Douglas remarks, May 17, 1860, ibid., 2153. Also see bitter remarks of New York's Charles H. Van Wyck, March 7, 1860, ibid., 1027–35.

101. On the two conventions, see David Potter, *Impending Crisis*, 407–18; for the Constitutional Unionists, see Huston, *Panic of 1857*, 236–37. Organizational work for the party can be found in the Alexander H. H. Stuart Papers.

102. Henry Doolittle to James R. Doolittle, May 24, 1860, Doolittle Papers; see Huston, *Panic of 1857*, 237–45.

103. The election of 1860 is covered in many places. For easy reference, consult David Potter, *Impending Crisis*, 405–47; Johannsen, *Douglas*, 774–807; Crenshaw, *Slave States in the Presidential Election of 1860*; Luthin, *The First Lincoln Campaign*.

104. Buchanan speech, July 9, 1860, in Moore, *Works of Buchanan*, 10:460; [James Russell Lowell], "Election in November," *Atlantic Monthly* 6 (October 1860): 496; *Philadelphia Eve-*

ning Bulletin, August 21, 1860; Dix, *Memoirs*, 1:344; *Indianapolis Daily Journal*, August 3, 1860; speech of John Sherman, *Newark Daily Advertiser*, September 14, 1860; speech of William Evarts, 1860, in Evarts, *Arguments and Speeches of William Maxwell Evarts*, 2:516–22.

105. Reuben Davis, December 9, 1859, *Cong. Globe*, 36th Cong., 1st sess., 69; Cobb comment in Thomas E. Massie to William Allen, June 16, 1860, Allen Papers; *Richmond Enquirer*, July 10, 1860, in Dumond, *Southern Editorials on Secession*, 141; *Charleston Mercury*, October 11, 1860, ibid., 179–80; Benjamin H. Hill in *Milledgeville (Ga.) Southern Recorder*, July 17, 1860.

106. Robert A. Toombs to Lewis Cass, September 29, 1856, Cass Papers. The states' rights theme can be found in *Richmond Semi-Weekly Examiner*, October 26, 1860, in Dumond, *Southern Editorials on Secession*, 191, 193; speech of William L. Yancey at Washington, D.C., in *Richmond Enquirer*, September 25, 1860.

107. Numbers taken from David Potter, *Impending Crisis*, 443.

108. The plunging of the graphs in the election of 1860 for the Border South and the Deep South is due to the presence of a strong third party—that is, the Douglas Democracy.

109. James M. Mason to Nathaniel Tyler, editor of *Richmond Enquirer*, November 23, 1860, printed in Mason, *Public Life and Diplomatic Correspondence of James M. Mason*, 156; South Carolina Declaration of Causes in Frank Moore, *Rebellion Record* (1861–65), 1:3–4; Freehling and Simpson, *Secession Debated*, 13, 39–41, 84, 147–52; Pamphlet on Pine Street Meeting, December 15, 1860, Lathers Papers.

Afterword

1. Burnham, *Current Crisis in American Politics*, 10, 51–52, 100–113.

2. The economic ramifications of Republican victory in 1860 are the themes of Beard and Beard, *Rise of American Civilization*; Hacker, *Triumph of American Capitalism*; Bensel, *Yankee Leviathan*; Richardson, *Greatest Nation of the Earth*; Leonard Curry, *Blueprint for Modern America*.

3. On Reconstruction policy and Republican laissez-faire, see Gillette, *Retreat from Reconstruction*, 198, 363–66. On the Freedmen's Bureau, Cimbala, *Under the Guardianship of the Nation*; and McFeely, *Yankee Stepfather*.

4. See Soltow, *Men and Wealth in the United States*, 101, 140–43, 181–83; Gavin Wright, *Old South, New South*, 31–34.

5. See Huston, *Securing the Fruits of Labor*, 170–83, 243–51. The Republicans' fight with their labor ideals, African American yearnings, actual labor conditions, and working-class unrest is the subject of Richardson, *Death of Reconstruction*, ix–xv, chaps. 4–6.

6. The story is contained in any decent history of Reconstruction: Stampp, *Era of Reconstruction*, chap. 7; Gillette, *Retreat from Reconstruction*; Franklin, *Reconstruction after the Civil War*, chap. 11; Eric Foner, *Reconstruction*; Rable, *But There Was No Peace*; Beringer et al., *Elements of Confederate Defeat*, 179–86. On the continued vitality of states' rights, see McDonald, *States' Rights and the Union*, 223–29.

Appendix A

1. For nineteenth-century historians, of course, the major determinant powering realignments has been ethnocultural tensions. My book posits an economic determinant. For the ethnocultural argument, see, as an example of the interpretation, Kleppner, *Third Electoral System*, 3–12, 144, 359–73.

2. Basic works on realignment would include Key, "A Theory of Critical Elections";

Burnham, *Critical Elections and the Mainsprings of American Politics*; Clubb, Flanigan, and Zingale, *Partisan Realignment*; Sundquist, *Dynamics of the Party System*; Brady, *Critical Elections and Congressional Policy Making*; Gates, "The American Supreme Court and Electoral Realignment: A Critical Review"; Lasser, "The Supreme Court in Periods of Critical Realignment"; Adamany, "The Supreme Court's Role in Critical Elections"; Nardulli, "The Concept of a Critical Realignment, Electoral Behavior, and Political Change."

3. For the attack on realignment theory and the theories of retrospective, and now a renewed interest in prospective voting, see Fiorina, *Retrospective Voting in American National Elections*; Lichtman, "The End of Realignment Theory?"; articles by Silbey and Shafer, in Shafer, *End of Realignment?*

4. Anderson and Hill, "The Race for Property Rights"; Alchian and Demsetz, "Property Rights Paradigm"; Barzel, *Economic Analysis of Property Rights*, chap. 1; Leblan, "Property Rights, Democracy, and Economic Growth," 5–7; Gary Miller, *Managerial Dilemmas*, 1–18.

5. This is largely the work of Douglass C. North. North and Weingast, "Constitutions and Commitment," 803–8; North, *Institutions, Institutional Change and Economic Performance*, 3–9, 47–48; Gary Miller, *Managerial Dilemmas*, 9; Olson, "Dictatorship, Democracy, and Development," 567.

6. Anderson and Hill, *Birth of a Transfer Society*, 9–11, quotation from 7; Lance Davis and North, *Institutional Change and American Economic Growth*, 30–31; McChesney, "Government as Definer of Property Rights," 109–10; Riker and Sened, "A Political Theory of Property Rights," 954; Epstein, *Takings*, 24–25.

7. North, *Structure and Change in Economic History*, 17, 29, 61, 67; see Demsetz, "Toward a Theory of Property Rights," 350; Libecap, *Contracting for Property Rights*, 1–6, 16–18, 116; remarks of Epstein, *Takings*, 25. In this literature, the idea of policy by interest group reaches its fullest expression, and the godfathers of the analysis seem to be George J. Stigler, James Buchanan, and Benjamin Tulloch. See also Becker, "A Theory of Competition among Pressure Groups for Political Preference." North evidently sees property rights formulations as being a constant pressure rather than points of heated debate; Lance Davis and North, *Institutional Change and American Economic Growth*, chaps. 1, 2.

8. See, for example, Romer, "Endogenous Technological Change"; Romer, "Increasing Returns and Long-Run Economy"; Lichtenberg and Diegel, "The Impact of R&D Investment on Productivity—New Evidence Using Linked R&D-LRD Data"; Mowery and Rosenberg, *Technology and the Pursuit of Economic Growth*, chaps. 1, 2, 4; Rosenberg, *Perspectives on Technology*, chaps. 4, 6.

9. Rostow, *Stages of Economic Growth*, 39, 53–55.

10. Generally, see Berry, *Long-Wave Rhythms*, 2–10, 38, 40–52, 144–55; Duijn, *Long Wave in Economic Life*, 32–33, 93–106, 173–83; Tylecote, *Long Wave in the World Economy*, xiii, 7–11, 36–37. Berry also tries to unite economic cycle theory with political realignment; Berry, *Long-Wave Rhythms*, 144–55.

11. For historical literature, see Kleppner, *Third Electoral System*. More recently, see Katznelson, "Working-Class Formation and the State"; Hout, Brooks, and Manza, "The Democratic Class Struggle in the United States, 1948–1992"; Leigley and Nagler, "Socioeconomic Class Bias in Turnout, 1964–1988."

12. This is not to say that class effects cannot be found in realignments; there are specific contexts that can evoke class responses. The most common are those which endanger the "glue" of any economic society, income flows. During depressions, when the income flow is halted, one can rationally expect a class response.

13. Sen, "Rational Fools," 336.

14. To wit: the radical agrarians of the Jacksonian period, the antislavery cry against slaveholders, the Populist and progressives' cry against the trusts, labor's anger at the mass production industrial corporation, and everybody's disgust at "yuppies" and "nerds."

15. See discussion in Burnham, *Critical Elections and the Mainsprings of American Politics*, chap. 7.

16. Just to clarify the obvious: narcotics are obviously things, but the law does not assign property rights to them. Another area is fetuses; women do not have property rights in their fetuses so that they may be sold to laboratories. A pertinent historical example is primogeniture and entail, both of which are forms of property rights that are deleterious to long-run economic growth and which the revolutionaries decided were "unjust" forms of property rights. The list of activities and material objects that do not have the sanction of property rights is long, and even then, as Douglass North contends, property rights are seldom absolute. North, *Institutions, Institutional Change and Economic Performance*, 33.

17. The process of realignment among voters, emergence and disappearance of parties, and the rise of defining issues is discussed in any number of good works. See Burnham, *Critical Elections and the Mainsprings of American Politics*; Sundquist, *Dynamics of the Party System*; Clubb, Flanigan, and Zingale, *Partisan Realignment*; and Trilling and Campbell, "Toward a Theory of Realignment." My emphasis on property rights and technological transformation is not in these works.

18. See Richard P. McCormick, *The Presidential Game*. No form of government can handle redefinitions of property rights easily. For this reason, democracies fare no better than other power arrangements, and it was precisely this aspect that led to Civil War. Several historians have noted the failure of democratic processes in the 1850s to resolve the question of slavery's expansion, and the answer is simply that property rights so concentrated geographically were too powerful for any government to redefine or restrict. On this question, see Craven, *An Historian and the Civil War*, 64, 82; Eric Foner, *Free Soil, Free Labor, Free Men*, 8–9; Gienapp, "Crisis of American Democracy," 81; Freehling, "Divided South," 128–29.

19. This test derives from human capital theory, or life-cycle earnings. See Wykstra, *Human Capital Formation and Manpower Development*, xiii–xxvi.

20. Kondratiev wave theorists have offered alternative political or economic cycles that can be compared with the ones I offer here. Brian Berry suggests 1830–70 by canal, iron rails, and steamboat; 1870–1920, steel rail and oceanic liner; 1920–present, automobile and airplane. Chris Freeman, a scholar mentioned by Berry, suggested 1770s–1840s, cotton, pig iron; 1840s–1890s, steam and railroad; 1890s–1940s, electricity and heavy engineering; 1940s–1990s, Fordism. Berry, *Long-Wave Rhythms*, 43–48. On politics, see the attempt by Benjamin Ginsberg to flesh out realignments by policy initiatives: Ginsberg, "Elections and Public Policy," and Ginsberg, "Critical Elections and Substance of Party Conflict."

21. Goodman, "The First American Party System"; Formisano, "Deferential-Participant Politics: The Early Republic's Political Culture, 1789–1840"; Wiebe, *Opening of American Society*, 11–18; Sharp, *American Politics in the Early Republic*, 10, 285–86.

22. The economic historian Peter Temin has written, accurately in my opinion, "To the extent that workers were being transferred from agriculture to commerce and related activities rather than to manufacturing, it would be more correct to speak of a *commercial revolution* than an industrial revolution for this period." Temin, *Causal Factors in American Economic Growth in the Nineteenth Century*, 16. On the impact of railroads, see Fishlow, *American Railroads and the Transformation of the Ante-Bellum Economy*; George Taylor, *The Transportation Revolution*; Haites, Mak, and Walton, *Western River Transportation*; Danhof, *Change in Agriculture*. For examples of how this change produced conflict, see Durill, "Pro-

ducing Poverty"; Shirley, "Yeoman Culture and Millworker Protest in Antebellum Salem, North Carolina"; and Barron, "Listening to the Silent Majority: Change and Continuity in the Nineteenth-Century Rural North."

23. On the entrepreneurial use of the law and especially the *Charles River Bridge* case, see Kutler, *Privilege and Creative Destruction*, 4–5, 43–61, 86–101; Hurst, *Legitimacy of the Business Corporation in the Law of the United States*, 1, 13, 20–34; Horwitz, *Transformation of American Law*, xv, 20–24, 31–33, 109–37; Ely, *Guardian of Every Other Right*, 8, chap. 4; Pisani, "Promotion and Regulation"; Hovencamp, *Enterprise and American Law*, 112–13. For an emphasis on the Revolution creating capitalist interpretations of property rights, see Nelson, *Americanization of Common Law*. General treatments of the impact of the market revolution upon politics can be gleaned from Watson, *Liberty and Power*; and Sellers, *The Market Revolution.*

24. [Orestes Brownson?], "Democracy and Reform," *Boston Quarterly Review* 2 (October 1839): 508. Ashworth, *"Agrarians" and "Aristocrats,"* 22–31; Remini, *Legacy of Andrew Jackson*, 14–16; Schlesinger, *Age of Jackson*, 510–18; Welter, *The Mind of America*, 79–90, 138–46.

25. Sobel, *Age of Giant Corporations*; McCraw, "Rethinking the Trust Question"; Hounshell, *From the American System to Mass Production*, chaps. 6–8; Chandler, "The Emergence of Managerial Capitalism"; Chandler, *The Visible Hand*, chaps. 6–11. On the impact on labor and the middle class, Wiebe, *Search for Order*, 2, 12, 20, 44–45; Cochran, *Challenges to American Values*, 65–72; Keller, *Regulating a New Economy*, chap. 1.

26. On the contested realignment of the 1890s, see Burnham, *Current Crisis in American Politics*, 32–50; Baum, *Civil War Party System*, 16–22; Richard L. McCormick, *Party Period and Public Policy*, 18–25, and chap. 7; McGerr, *Decline of Popular Politics*, chap. 8; Reynolds and McCormick, "Outlawing 'Treachery.'" On regulation and the popular outcry against the trusts, see Hurst, *Law and Social Order in the United States*, 248–52; Painter, *Standing at Armageddon*, x–xii; Sklar, *Corporate Reconstruction of American Capitalism*, esp. 14–19; Wiebe, *Search for Order*, 52–53; Keller, *Regulating a New Economy*, chap. 2; Hays, *Response to Industrialism*, chaps. 6, 7. The question of property rights dominated much discussion of the period, and a number of economists using the property rights paradigm see the Sherman Anti-Trust Act as the crucial point of transition from free contract to a transfer society; North, *Institutions, Institutional Change and Economic Performance*, 8; Anderson and Hill, *Birth of a Transfer Society*, 56–69; Kleitt, "Common Law, Statute Law, and the Theory of Legislative Choice"; McWilliams, Turk, and Zardkoohi, "Antitrust Policy and Mergers." On other treatments of the Sherman Act, see Lamoreaux, *Great Merger Movement in American Business*, chaps. 5–6; Hurst, *Law and Social Order in the United States*, 251–52; Hurst, *Legitimacy of the Business Corporation in the Law of the United States*, 13–14; Keller, "The Pluralist State"; Ely, *Guardian of Every Other Right*, chap. 6; Pisani, "Promotion and Regulation," 758–59; Keller, *Affairs of State*, 367; Chandler, *The Visible Hand*, 375–76.

27. Galambos and Pratt, *Rise of the Corporate Commonwealth*; Ely, *Guardian of Every Other Right*, chap. 7; Pisani, "Promotion and Regulation," 763–67; Skocpol, *Protecting Soldiers and Mothers*, 525–29; Weir and Skocpol, "State Structures and the Possibilities for 'Keynesian' Responses to the Great Depression in Sweden, Britain, and the United States"; Lewis-Beck and Squire, "Transformation of the American State"; Biles, *New Deal for the American People*, chaps. 5, 8, and pp. 225–33; Brinkley, "The New Deal and the Idea of the State"; Milkis, "New Deal Party Politics, Administrative Reform, and the Transformation of the American Constitution"; Shenfield, "The New Deal and the Supreme Court"; Frisch, "An Appraisal of Roosevelt's Legacy"; Wettergreen, "The Regulatory Policy of the New Deal."

28. For example, see Shafer, "The Notion of an Electoral Order."

29. "For New Jobs, Help Small Business," *Wall Street Journal*, August 10, 1992, p. A10; some other contemporary literature focusing on the bureaucratic nature of big business is "Lexmark: The Typing on the Wall," *Economist*, October 3, 1992, pp. 74–75; "Can GM Fix Itself?," *Newsweek*, November 9, 1992, pp. 54–60; "The Fall of the Dinosaurs," ibid., February 8, 1993, pp. 42–44; Review of *Control Your Destiny or Someone Else Will* by Noel Tichy and Stratform Sherman, *Economist*, February 6, 1993, pp. 96–97; review of *Liberation Management* by Tom Peters, ibid., December 5, 1992, p. 96. The year 1973 has been chosen as the point of change by several economists; see, for example, Duijn, *Long Wave in Economic Life*, 198–200; Ely, *Guardian of Every Other Right*, 136–42; Michael Bernstein, "Understanding American Economic Decline."

30. See Michael Bernstein, "Understanding American Economic Decline"; U.S. Bureau of the Census, *Statistical Abstract of the United States 1994*, 756, 757, 770.

31. Vogel, "The 'New' Social Regulation in Historical and Comparative Perspective." The key enactments were the 1955 Air Pollution Control Act, the 1956 Water Pollution Control Act, the 1965 Water Quality Act, the 1963 Clean Air Act, the 1965 Motor Vehicle Air Pollution Control Act, and the 1973 Endangered Species Act.

32. Yandle, *The Political Limits of Environmental Regulation*; Yandle, *Land Rights*; "Saving Endangered Species: Wildlife and Property Rights," *Congressional Digest* 11 (March 1996): 68–85.

33. I made such statements in a paper I delivered, "Property Rights and Nineteenth-Century Politics and Beyond: A Theory," presented at a meeting of the Social Science History Association, New Orleans, October 11, 1996.

Appendix B

1. The older interpretation of emphasizing slavery in one fashion or another can be found in Nevins, *Ordeal of the Union*; Nevins, *The Emergence of Lincoln*; Nichols, *Disruption of American Democracy*; David Potter, *Impending Crisis*. Interpretations based on realignment theory and ethnocultural interpretations are given by Holt, *The Political Crisis of the 1850s*; Kleppner, *Third Electoral System*, 24–57; Silbey, *The Partisan Imperative*, chap. 9; and Gienapp, *Origins of the Republican Party*. Gienapp affirms that the breakdown of the Second Party System due to ethnocultural pressures permitted the slavery issue to erupt and thereby cause the Civil War; Gienapp, "Crisis of American Democracy." The small narrative is largely taken from Gienapp and Holt.

2. It is no secret that quantitative analysis of politics has fallen on less than glorious times in the 1990s. Part of the reason is that only a few could continually upgrade their statistical skills to keep pace with the ever increasing sophistication of statistical analysis. As a result, quantitative analysis has suffered in the historical profession (but not in most other social sciences). It may be that historians will have to rethink their tools in order to find the procedures that best communicate with other members of the profession.

3. The sources for this study are as follows. The counties composing the congressional districts of the United States in the 1850s can be found in Martis, *Historical Atlas of United States Congressional Districts*. For voter results, I relied heavily upon the *The Whig Almanac and Politician's Register* or the *Tribune Almanac and Political Register* between 1840 and 1861 (the title varies). Supplemental sources include John L. Moore, *Congressional Quarterly's Guide to U.S. Elections*; Allen and Lacey, *Illinois Elections*; Riker and Thornbrough, *Indiana Election Returns*; Donoghue, *How Wisconsin Voted*; Pease, "Illinois Election Returns, 1818–1848"; Baum, "Electoral and Demographic Data, 1848–1876"; State of Michigan, Depart-

ment of State, Records of Elections and Archives Division, Record Group RG 56-26, RG 65-38; *Lancaster (Wisc.) Grant County Herald*, November 18, 1843; *Albany Argus*, November 21, 1848, November 18, 1852; *Harrisburgh (Pa.) Telegraph*, November 7, 1848, November 6, 1850, October 27, 1852; *Philadelphia Evening Bulletin*, October 23, 1860; *Springfield Daily Illinois State Register*, November 11, 1858; *Philadelphia North American*, November 3, 1846; and personal aid from Lex Renda and Dale Baum.

4. The following is a list of degraded and uncontested elections for Congress unless indicated otherwise.

Degraded. Virginia, district 1 (1843, 1847), district 2 (1843, 1847), district 3 (1843, 1847), district 13 (1851 governor); Tennessee, district 10 (1849, 1851); North Carolina (1843 missing), district 4 (1847, 1849, 1851, division among Democrats), district 6 (1847, division among Whigs); Illinois, district 4-9 (1848), district 9 (1846).

Uncontested. Virginia, district 1 (1851, 1853, 1855, 1859), district 2 (1857, 1859), district 4 (1853), district 5 (1857, 1859), district 6 (1857), district 7 (1855), district 9 (1851, 1853, 1855, 1857), district 10 (1843, 1847, 1853, 1859), district 12 (1853, 1857, 1859), district 13 (1851, 1853); Tennessee, district 6 (1857, 1859), district 9 (1853); North Carolina, district 3 (1851), district 6 (1851); Kentucky, district 1 (1845, 1849), district 3 (1853), district 4 (1851); Illinois, district 8 (1850), district 9 (1850); Indiana, district 2 (1846 governor), district 10 (1846 governor); Pennsylvania, district 25 (1854).

5. I used in three places in the 1840s manuscript returns for Michigan congressional and gubernatorial voting. Some of the returns were faded beyond recognition and others were nearly illegible. My counts for Michigan are best guesses only. However, those guesses do not seem to have disturbed the basic patterns of the region.

6. Historians who have used retrospective voting theory include Renda, *Running on the Record*; Holt, *Political Parties and American Political Development*, chap. 4. For the basic theory, see Fiorina, *Retrospective Voting in American National Elections*. The problem for historians using the theory is that it requires data collection that is distinctly post-1960: voter surveys. For the nineteenth century, there is no statistical test per se about retrospective voting; the behavior is rather postulated and inferred. On prospective voting, see Lanoue, "Retrospective and Prospective Voting in Presidential-Year Elections."

7. On the theory of realignment, see Sundquist, *Dynamics of the Party System*; Burnham, *Current Crisis in American Politics*; Clubb, Flanigan, and Zingale, *Partisan Realignment*. Historical studies that have used the realignment viewpoint include Baum, *Civil War Party System*; Kleppner, *Third Electoral System*; Gienapp, *Origins of the Republican Party*. It probably needs to be mentioned that realignment theory evidently operates for the United States because it is a two-party system dominated by the presidential office and plurality-winner takes all in the electoral districts. A current interpretation among some historians argues that partisanship was much thinner than realignment theory posits; Altschuler and Blumin, *Rude Republic*, 3–10; Olsen, *Political Culture and Secession in Mississippi*, 8–14.

8. For Virginia, Ambler, *Sectionalism in Virginia*; Crofts, *Reluctant Confederates*; Crofts, *Old Southampton*; and Shade, *Democratizing the Old Dominion*. Of course, South Carolina has gained attention (Steven Channing, *Crisis of Fear*; McCurry, *Masters of Small Worlds*; Ford, *Origins of Southern Radicalism*) because it had the most percentage of slaves and the most patriarchal and anachronistic society; Massachusetts draws its scholars from those interested in industrialism and elite power (Baum, *Civil War Party System*; Abbott, *Cotton and Capital*; Dalzell, *Daniel Webster and the Trial of American Nationalism*; Brooke, *Heart of the Commonwealth*; Brauer, *Cotton versus Conscience*).

9. Among the studies of the Border South are Shade, *Democratizing the Old Dominion*; Crofts, *Reluctant Confederates*; Atkins, *Parties, Politics, and the Sectional Conflict in Tennessee*;

Kruman, *Parties and Politics in North Carolina*; Baker, *Ambivalent Americans*; Evitts, *A Matter of Allegiances*; Bergeron, *Antebellum Politics in Tennessee*; Woods, *Rebellion and Realignment.*

10. In particular, see Silbey, *American Political Nation*, 145–47.

11. The importance of the state elections in 1853 has been noted by Gienapp, *Origins of the Republican Party*, chap. 2, esp. pp. 65–67; and Holt, *The Political Crisis of the 1850s*, 137–38.

12. The presidential election of 1852 has sometimes been used to show the Whig descent into oblivion, but many historians have noted that the Whig failure was primarily in the South: David Potter, *Impending Crisis*, 142–43, 234–36, 245–46; Cooper, *The South and the Politics of Slavery*, 338–41.

13. This conclusion, of course, is based on the materials I have researched. As not every manuscript collection and newspaper has fallen within my purview, it is possible that various people did remark on the collapse of the Whigs in the Deep South—but it is strikingly odd that among the numerous sources I have consulted no one ever mentioned the surge in Whig nonvoting in 1852.

14. Figures based on party preference by eligible voters have been made, but given space considerations, they have been omitted from this work. People interested in figures showing party preference by eligible voters may contact the author.

15. Ecological regression is the technique used by those arguing for a more volatile electorate. However, most of those studies show that partisans usually drop to nonvoting status during some elections and then return to voting for their party in the next election. See Gienapp, *Origins of the Republican Party*; Renda, *Running on the Record*; Baum, *Civil War Party System.*

16. For the Second Party System, see Silbey, *American Political Nation.*

17. David Wilmot to Salmon P. Chase, May 29, 1848, Chase Papers, ed. Niven; Simon Cameron to Edmund Burke, June 15, 1849, Burke Papers; Richard Brodhead to John A. McClernand, May 7, 1850, McClernand Papers.

18. See table 1 in Huston, "Southerners against Secession," 287–88.

19. On the failure of the Constitutional Union Party to maintain itself, see Schott, *Alexander H. Stephens of Georgia*, 129–40; Carey, *Parties, Slavery, and the Union in Antebellum Georgia*, 168–73; Simpson, *Howell Cobb*, 86–87; Cooper, *The South and the Politics of Slavery*, 311–19.

20. *Athens (Ga.) Southern Banner*, June 8, 1848.

21. For example, David Potter, *Impending Crisis*, 250–53; Anbinder, *Nativism and Slavery*, 103–26; Gienapp, *Origins of the Republican Party*, 95–99.

22. It is sometimes forgotten that the "North" was not a homogeneous lump but was composed of hundreds of thousands of southerners, as well as Yankees and Puritans and others, who inhabited the southern border region of the Great Lakes and Middle Atlantic states. These individuals had carried with them an animus to slavery that was perhaps different from other groups but one that carried a political punch. Etcheson, *Emerging Midwest*, 66–70; Ratcliffe, *Party Spirit in a Frontier Republic*, 47, 232.

23. I assume that somewhere in the northern United States, some congressional nominee ran on the issue of restricting immigration or changing the naturalization laws. I have never encountered such a speech. Various platforms, however, may have included nativist planks, at the congressional district level. But all the literary evidence holds for the primary importance of the Kansas-Nebraska Act in the congressional elections of 1854.

24. One oddity of the Great Lakes region, left here unexplained, is the falling allure of the Whig Party in 1853 due to defections, evidently, to Free-Soilers in state elections (however, the only states that had state elections in the Great Lakes in 1853 were Ohio and Wisconsin).

25. Computed from John L. Moore, *Congressional Quarterly's Guide to U.S. Elections*,

and from the *Whig Almanac* for 1855 and the *Tribune Almanac* for 1856. The political division seems as well to reflect the economic division in New England; see Rosenbloom, "The Challenge of Economic Maturity: New England, 1880–1940," 158–60.

26. Compare with Gienapp who emphasizes local issues, not congressional ones; Gienapp, *Origins of the Republican Party*, 129–39, 205–8, 214–23. Basically, the continued problems with Bleeding Kansas, the caning of Charles Sumner, and then the collapse of the American program and the ineptitude of some of its novice representatives gave the Republicans the chance to shepherd the anti-Democrat forces under their banner; see ibid., 295–303. Even still, it is worth mentioning that Massachusetts seems, compared with the other states, to have been politically highly unusual, abnormally conservative, and bizarrely hostile to immigrants. Know-Nothingism persisted there with strength until at least 1859, whereas in all the other states it was quickly becoming an ungainly rump of a party. In many ways, the size of Massachusetts—it contained one-third of the congressional representation of the region—has tended to overshadow developments in the other states, which, upon comparison, are strikingly similar to those in the rest of the country. To make a long story short: Massachusetts is no test case politically for any other part of the country; it was one of the three grand outliers of American political and social tendencies in the nineteenth century—the other bizarre cases being, of course, South Carolina and Virginia.

27. John L. Moore, *Congressional Quarterly's Guide to U.S. Elections*, 606. The district mentioned in the narrative is district 4, William O. Goode; the uncontested districts were 1, 2, 5, 10, 12.

28. This fact is evident in the nonvoting levels of state and congressional races in Figures B.4 and 5. Figures demonstrating the difference in party strength for state and congressional contests could be constructed but are not given here. One of the reasons that the curvatures of the lines of party preference in Figures B.9 and 10 are so pronounced is that southern states most often had their gubernatorial and congressional races in the same year, and by the methodology I adopted the congressional race was given priority over the state election.

29. The plunge of both the Border South and the Deep South lines in the election of 1860 in Figures B.9 and 10 requires an extra explanation. The procedure of subtracting the major opposition party percentage from the Democratic Party percentage works well for two parties but obviously fails to capture the contortions in a three-party race. In the South, the presence of the small but substantial Douglas ticket was sufficient to turn the curves radically downward.

Sources

PRIMARY SOURCES

Manuscripts

Ann Arbor, Michigan
- William L. Clements Library, University of Michigan
  - James G. Birney Papers
  - Lewis Cass Papers
  - Artemas Hale Papers
  - Solomon G. Haven Papers
  - John Rankin autobiography
  - Weld-Grimké Papers

Baltimore, Maryland
- George Peabody Branch of the Enoch Pratt Free Library
  - Millard Fillmore Papers

Boston, Massachusetts
- Massachusetts Historical Society
  - Adams [Family] Papers [microfilm]
  - Edward Everett Papers
  - Millard Fillmore Papers

Buffalo, New York
- Buffalo and Erie County Historical Society
  - Millard Fillmore Papers

Chapel Hill, North Carolina
- University of North Carolina
  - Christopher Memminger Papers

Columbia, South Carolina
- University of South Carolina
  - James Henry Hammond Papers

Columbus, Ohio
- Ohio Historical Society
  - Samuel Galloway Papers
  - Joshua R. Giddings Papers
  - Isaac Strohm Letters
  - Benjamin Tappan Papers
  - John A. Trimble Family Papers

Durham, North Carolina
- Special Collections Division, Duke University
  - Armistead Burt Papers
  - Daniel French Slaughter Papers

Frederick, Maryland
- University Publications of America
  - Salmon P. Chase Papers. Edited by John Niven. 1987. Microfilm edition.

Harrisburg, Pennsylvania
- Historical Society of Dauphin County
  - Simon Cameron Correspondence and Papers

Indianapolis, Indiana
- Indiana Historical Society
  - John Givan Davis Papers
  - John Dowling Papers
  - William H. English Papers
- Indiana State Library
  - Schuyler Colfax Papers
  - Joshua R. Giddings Papers
  - George Washington Julian Papers
  - Henry S. Lane Papers
  - Oliver P. Morton Papers
  - Godlove Orth Papers
  - Robert Dale Owen Papers
  - Daniel D. Pratt Papers
  - Richard W. Thompson Papers

Madison, Wisconsin
- State Historical Society of Wisconsin
  - John G. Davis Papers
  - Moses M. Davis Papers
  - James R. Doolittle Papers
  - Timothy O. Howe Papers
  - John F. Potter Papers
  - Nathaniel P. Tallmadge Papers

New York, New York
- Columbia University
  - Hannibal Hamlin Papers

Oswego, New York
- Penfield Library, SUNY at Oswego
  - Millard Fillmore Papers

Philadelphia, Pennsylvania
- Historical Society of Pennsylvania
  - William Bigler Papers
  - James Buchanan Papers

Rochester, New York
- Rush Rees Library, University of Rochester
  - William H. Seward Papers

Springfield, Illinois
- Illinois State Historical Library
  - Edward Bates Papers
  - William H. Bissell Papers
  - Sidney Breese Papers
  - Stephen A. Douglas Papers
  - Joseph Gillespie Papers

Charles H. Lanphier Papers
John A. McClernand Papers
Richard Yates Papers

Washington, D.C.

Library of Congress, Manuscripts Division

William Allen Papers
Edmund Burke Papers
Simon Cameron Papers
Salmon P. Chase Papers
John M. Clayton Papers
Thomas Corwin Papers
John Jordan Crittenden Papers
Caleb Cushing Papers
William Pitt Fessenden Papers
James H. Hammond Papers
Richard Lathers Papers
John McLean Papers
William L. Marcy Papers
Franklin Pierce Papers
James K. Polk Papers
William C. Rives Papers
John Sherman Papers
Edwin M. Stanton Papers
Alexander H. Stephens Papers
Alexander H. H. Stuart Papers
Lyman Trumbull Papers
Martin Van Buren Papers
Benjamin Franklin Wade Papers
Elihu B. Washburne Papers
David Wilmot Papers

Government Documents

Annals of Congress, 15th Cong., 2d sess.; 16th Cong., 1st sess.; 18th Cong., 1st sess.

Congressional Debates, 20th Cong., 2d sess.; 21st Cong., 1st sess.

Congressional Globe, 22d Cong., 1st sess.; 27th Cong., 2d sess.; 29th Cong., 2d sess.; 30th Cong., 2d sess.; 31st Cong., 1st sess.; 33d Cong., 1st sess.; 33d Cong., 2d sess.; 35th Cong., 1st sess.; 36th Cong., 1st sess.

Congressional Record, 20th Cong., 1st sess.

Register of Debates, 22d Cong., 1st sess.

De Bow, J. D. B. *Statistical View of the United States.* Washington, D.C.: A. O. P. Nicholson, 1854.

Ford, Worthington Chauncey, et al., eds. *Journals of the Continental Congress, 1774–1789*. 34 vols. Washington, D.C.: Government Printing Office, 1904–37.

Kennedy, Joseph C. G. *Preliminary Report on the Eighth Census, 1860*. Washington, D.C.: Government Printing Office, 1862.

U.S. Bureau of the Census. *Statistical Abstract of the United States 1994*. Washington, D.C.: Government Printing Office, 1994.

U.S. Bureau of the Census. Department of Commerce. *Historical Statistics of the United States: Colonial Times to 1970*. Washington, D.C.: Government Printing Office, 1975.

U.S. Census Office. *Twelfth Census of the United States Taken in the Year 1900*. Vol. 2: *Population*, Part 2. Washington, D.C.: U.S. Census Office, 1902.

———. *Twelfth Census of the United States Taken in the Year 1900*. Vol. 7: *Manufactures*, Part 1. Washington, D.C.: U.S. Census Office, 1902.

———. *Twelfth Census of the United States Taken in the Year 1900*. Vol. 12: *Special Reports: Employees and Wages*. Washington, D.C.: U.S. Census Office, 1903.

———. *Twelfth Census of the United States Taken in the Year 1900*. Vol. 13: *Special Reports: Occupations at the Twelfth Census*. Washington, D.C.: Government Printing Office, 1904.

U.S. Department of the Census. *The Seventh Census of the United States*. Vol. 1: *Population in 1850*. Washington, D.C.: Robert Armstrong, 1853.

U.S. Department of the Interior. *Eighth Census*. Vol. 1: *Population of the United States in 1860*. Washington, D.C.: Government Printing Office, 1864.

———. *Eighth Census*. Vol. 2: *Agriculture of the United States in 1860*. Washington, D.C.: Government Printing Office, 1864.

———. *Eighth Census*. Vol. 3: *Manufactures of the United States in 1860*. Washington, D.C.: Government Printing Office, 1865.

———. *Eighth Census*. Vol. 4: *Statistics of the United States (Including Mortality, Property, &c.) in 1860*. Washington, D.C.: Government Printing Office, 1866.

Newspapers

Albany Argus
Albany Atlas
Alton (Ill.) Telegraph and Democrat
Athens (Ga.) Southern Banner
Augusta (Ga.) Daily Constitutionalist (*Augusta Georgia Weekly Constitutionalist*)
Augusta (Me.) Kennebec Journal
Baltimore Niles Weekly Register
Bedford (Pa.) Inquirer
Bellefonte (Pa.) Democratic Watchman
Boston Semi-Weekly Advertiser
Boston Emancipator
Boston Herald
Boston Liberator
Boston Post
Buffalo Daily Courier (*Buffalo Courier and Pilot*)
Charleston Courier
Charleston Mercury
Chicago Daily Democrat (*Chicago Weekly Democrat*)
Chicago Gem of the Prairie
Chicago Journal
Chicago Press and Tribune (*Chicago Daily Tribune*)
Chicago Times and Herald
Cincinnati Daily Enquirer
Cincinnati Daily Gazette
Cincinnati Daily Times
Cleveland Daily Plain Dealer
Columbus (Ga.) Enquirer
Columbus Ohio State Journal

Concord New Hampshire Patriot and State Gazette
Covington (Ky.) Journal
Covington (Ky.) Licking Valley Register
Detroit Democratic Free Press (*Detroit Free Press*)
Easton (Pa.) Argus
Erie (Pa.) Weekly Observer
Evansville (Ind.) Daily Journal
Fort Wayne (Ind.) Sentinel
Gettysburg Compiler
Green Bay (Wisc.) Advocate
Greensborough (N.C.) Patriot
Hallowell (Me.) Free Soil Republican
Hallowell (Me.) Liberty Standard
Harrisburg (Pa.) Herald
Harrisburg (Pa.) Telegraph (*Harrisburg Pennsylvania Telegraph*)
Hartford (Conn.) Times
Hillsborough (N.C.) Recorder
Huntsville (Ala.) Southern Advocate
Indianapolis Daily Journal (*Indiana State Journal, Weekly*)
Jackson Mississippian
Knoxville Whig (*Brownlow's Knoxville Whig*)
Lancaster (Wisc.) Grant County Herald
Lebanon (Pa.) Courier
Lewistown (Pa.) Gazette
Louisville Daily Courier
Macon Georgia Journal and Messenger
Madison (Wisc.) Express
Madison Wisconsin Democrat
Memphis Weekly Appeal
Milledgeville (Ga.) Federal Union
Milledgeville (Ga.) Southern Recorder
Milwaukee Daily Free Democrat
Milwaukee Daily Sentinel
Milwaukee Weekly Wisconsin
Mobile (Ala.) Daily Register (*Mobile Register and Journal*)
Monmouth (Ill.) Atlas
Natchez Mississippi Free Trader
New Orleans Picayune
New York Herald
New York National Anti-Slavery Standard
New York Times
New York Tribune
Newark Daily Advertiser
Ottawa (Ill.) Free Trader
Peoria (Ill.) Democratic Press
Philadelphia Evening Bulletin
Philadelphia North American
Philadelphia Pennsylvania Freeman
Philadelphia Public Ledger

Pittsburg[h] Dispatch
Pittsburgh Gazette
Pittsburgh Morning Post
Portland (Me.) Daily Argus
Pottsville (Pa.) Miner's Journal
Prairieview (Wisc.) American Freeman
Providence Evening Press
Providence Journal
Raleigh North Carolina Standard
Raleigh Star and North Carolina Gazette
Raleigh (N.C.) Weekly Register
Richmond Enquirer
Richmond (Ind.) Palladium
Richmond Whig
Rochester (N.Y.) Advertiser
Rochester Democrat
Springfield Daily Illinois State Journal (Sangamo Journal)
Springfield Daily Illinois State Register
Toledo Blade
Trenton (N.J.) True American
Tuscaloosa (Ala.) Independent Monitor
Utica (N.Y.) Oneida Morning Herald
Vicksburg (Miss.) Weekly Whig (Vicksburg Whig)
Washington (D.C.) Daily Union
Washington (D.C.) National Era
Washington (D.C.) National Intelligencer
Washington (Pa.) Reporter
Woodville (Miss.) Republican
Yazoo (Miss.) Democrat

Periodicals

American Museum
American Quarterly Observer
American [Whig] Review
Atlantic Monthly
Boston Quarterly Review
Brownson's Review
De Bow's Review
Harper's Monthly Magazine
Hunt's Merchants' Magazine
Liberty Bell
Littell's Living Age
Massachusetts Quarterly Review
New Englander
New York Independent
North American Review
Russell's Magazine
Southern Literary Messenger

Southern Planter
Southern Review
United States Magazine and Democratic Review (*United States Review*)

Election Data

Allen, Howard W., and Vincent A. Lacey. *Illinois Elections, 1818–1990: Candidates and County Returns for President, Governor, Senate, and House of Representatives.* Carbondale: Southern Illinois University Press, 1992.

Baum, Dale. "Electoral and Demographic Data, 1848–1876: Massachusetts." *Inter-University Consortium for Political and Social Research,* 8242. Ann Arbor, 1984.

Donoghue, James R. *How Wisconsin Voted, 1848–1960.* Madison: University of Wisconsin Press, 1962.

Martis, Kenneth C. *The Historical Atlas of United States Congressional Districts, 1789–1983.* New York: Free Press, 1982.

Moore, John L., ed. *Congressional Quarterly's Guide to U.S. Elections.* 2d ed. Washington, D.C.: Congressional Quarterly, 1985.

Pease, Theodore Calvin, ed. "Illinois Election Returns, 1818–1848." *Collections of the Illinois State Historical Library.* Vol. 18. Springfield: Trustees of the Illinois State Historical Library, 1923.

Riker, Dorothy, and Gayle Thornbrough, comps. *Indiana Election Returns, 1816–1851.* Indianapolis: Indiana Historical Bureau, 1960.

State of Michigan, Department of State, Records of Elections and Archives Division, Record Group RG 56-26, RG 65-38.

The Whig Almanac and Politician's Register (*Tribune Almanac and Political Register*). 1838–61.

Published Works

Abbott, John S. C. *The History of the Civil War in America.* 2 vols. Springfield, Mass.: Gurdon Bill, 1863–66.

Adams, Charles Francis. *An Oration, Delivered before the Municipal Authorities of the City of Fall River, July 4, 1860.* Fall River, Mass.: Almy and Milne, 1860.

——. *What Makes Slavery a Question of National Concern? A Lecture, Delivered, by Invitation, at New York, January 1830, and at Syracuse, February 1, 1855.* Boston: Little, Brown, 1855.

Address of the Southern Delegation in Congress. N.p., [1848?].

Amynto [unknown]. *Reflections on the Inconsistency of Man, Particularly Exemplified in the Practice of Slavery in the United States.* New York: John Buel, 1796.

Appeal of the Independent Democrats in Congress to the People of the United States: Shall Slavery Be Permitted in Nebraska? Washington, D.C., [1854?].

Appleton, Nathaniel. *Considerations on Slavery in a Letter to a Friend.* Boston: Edes and Gill, 1767.

Arvine, Rev. K. *Our Duty to the Fugitive Slave: A Discourse Delivered on Sunday, Oct. 6, in West Boylston, Ms., and in Worcester, Dec. 15.* Boston: John P. Jewett, 1850.

Bassett, Rev. George M. *Slavery Examined by the Light of Nature.* N.p., [1858?].

Benezet, Anthony. *Observations on Inslaving, Importing and Purchasing of Negroes. . . .* Germantown, Pa.: Christopher Sower, 1759.

——. *A Short Account of That Part of Africa Inhabited by the Negroes. . . .* Philadelphia: N.p., 1762.

[——, ed.]. *A Collection of Religious Tracts.* Philadelphia: Joseph Crukshank, 1773.

Benton, Thomas Hart. *Historical and Legal Examination of That Part of the Decision of the Supreme Court of the United States in the Dred Scott Case, Which Declares the Unconstitutionality of the Missouri Compromise Act. . . .* New York: D. Appleton, 1857.

[Bigelow, John?]. *Life, Explorations and Public Services of John Charles Fremont.* Boston: Ticknor and Fields, 1856.

Blake, W. O., comp. *The History of Slavery and the Slave Trade, Ancient and Modern. . . .* Columbus, Ohio: J. & H. Miller, 1858.

Bliss, Philemon. *Complaints of the Extensionists—Their Falsity. Speech of Hon. Philemon Bliss, of Ohio, in House of Representatives, May 21, 1856.* Washington, D.C.: Buell and Blanchard, 1856.

Boucher, Jonathan. *Reminiscences of an American Loyalist, 1738–1789.* Edited by Jonathan Bouchier. 1925. Reprint, Port Washington, N.Y.: Kennikat Press, 1967.

Bowen, Francis. *American Political Economy. . . .* New York: Charles Scribner, 1870.

Brownlow, Rev. William G., and Rev. A[braham?] Pryne. *Ought Slavery to Be Perpetuated? A Debate between Rev. W. G. Brownlow and Rev. A. Pryne; Held at Philadelphia, September, 1858.* Philadelphia: J. B. Lippincott, 1858.

Buchanan, George. *An Oration upon the Moral and Political Evil of Slavery.* Baltimore: Philip Edwards, 1793.

Burleigh, Charles C. *Slavery and the North.* New York: American Anti-Slavery Society, 1855.

Calhoun, John C. *A Disquisition on Government and Selections from the Discourse.* Edited by C. Gordon Post. New York: Liberal Arts Press, 1953.

Channing, William E. *Slavery.* 4th ed. Boston: James Munroe, 1836.

Chase, Salmon Portland, and Charles Dexter Cleveland. *Anti-Slavery Addresses of 1844–45.* Philadelphia: J. A. Bancroft, 1867.

Chicago Press and Tribune. Life of Abraham Lincoln. Chicago: Press and Tribune, 1860.

Chipman, Nathaniel. *Sketches of the Principles of Government.* Rutland, Vt.: J. Lyon, 1793.

Claiborne, J. F. H. *Life and Correspondence of John A. Quitman.* 2 vols. New York: Harper and Bros., 1860.

Clarke, James Freeman. *Anti-Slavery Days.* New York: R. Worthington, 1884.

Cobb, Thomas R. R. *An Inquiry into the Law of Negro Slavery in the United States of America. To Which Is Prefixed an Historical Sketch of Slavery.* 1858. Reprint, New York: Negro Universities Press, 1968.

Colton, Calvin. *The Rights of Labor.* 3d ed. New York: A. S. Barnes, 1847.

Colver, Rev. Nathaniel. *The Fugitive Slave Bill; or, God's Laws Paramount to the Laws of Men.* Boston: J. M. Hewes, 1850.

Colwell, Stephen. *The Claims of Labor, and Their Precedence to the Claims of Free Trade.* Philadelphia: C. Sherman and Son, 1861.

Constitution of the Maryland Society, for Promoting the Abolition of Slavery, and the Relief of Free Negroes, and Others, Unlawfully Held in Bondage. Baltimore: William Goddard and James Angell, 1789.

Constitution of the Pennsylvania Society for Promoting the Abolition of Slavery, and the Relief of Free Negroes Unlawfully Held in Bondage; Enlarged at Philadelphia, April 23, 1787. Philadelphia: Joseph James, 1787.

Conway, Moncure. *Testimonies concerning Slavery.* London: Chapman and Hall, 1864.

[Cooper, David]. *A Mite Cast into the Treasury; or, Observations on Slave-Keeping.* Philadelphia: Joseph Crukshank, 1772.

Curry, Jabez Lamar Monroe. *Civil History of the Government of the Confederate States.* Richmond: B. F. Johnson Publishing, 1901.

Dabney, Robert. *A Defence of Virginia, [and through Her, of the South,] in Recent and Pending Contests against the Sectional Party*. New York: E. J. Hale and Son, 1867.

Davis, Jefferson. *The Rise and Fall of the Confederate Government*. 2 vols. 1881. Reprint, New York: Thomas Yoseloff, 1958.

Dickinson, James M. "An Anti-Slavery Sermon, Delivered at Norwich, July 4, 1834." In *Legal and Moral Aspects of Slavery: Selected Essays*, by James M. Dickinson, 4–18. New York: Negro Universities Press, 1969.

Dix, John Adams. *Memoirs of John Adams Dix*. Compiled by Morgan Dix. 2 vols. New York: Harper and Bros., 1883.

Douglas, Stephen A. *Letter of Senator Douglas, Vindicating His Character and His Position on the Nebraska Bill against the Assaults Contained in the Proceedings of a Public Meeting Composed of Twenty-Five Clergymen of Chicago*. Washington, D.C.: Sentinel Office, 1854.

Douglass, Frederick. *Life and Times of Frederick Douglass*. 1892. Rev. ed. Reprint, New York: Crowell, 1962.

——. *Narrative of the Life of Frederick Douglass, an American Slave*. New York: Signet, 1968.

Dwight, Timothy. *An Oration Spoken Before, "The Connecticut Society, for the Promotion of Freedom and the Relief of Persons Unlawfully Holden in Bondage."* Hartford: Hudson and Goodwin, 1794.

Edwards, Jonathan. *The Injustice and Impolicy of the Slave Trade; and of the Slavery of the Africans . . . A Sermon*. New Haven: Thomas and Samuel Green, 1791.

[Elder, William]. *Third Parties: The Duty of Anti-Slavery Voters*. Philadelphia: N.p., 1851.

Elliott, Charles. *Sinfulness of Slavery; Proven from Its Evil Sources*. Edited by B. F. Tefft. 2 vols. Cincinnati: L. Suormstedt and J. H. Power, 1851.

Elliott, E. N., ed. *Cotton Is King, and Pro-Slavery Arguments: Comprising the Writings of Hammond, Harper, Christy, Stringfellow, Hodge, Bledsoe, and Cartwright, on This Important Subject*. Augusta, Ga.: Abbott and Loomis, 1860.

Fee, John Gregg. *An Anti-Slavery Manual*. 1848. Reprint, New York: Arno Press, 1969.

Fisher, Sidney George. [Cecil]. *Kanzas and the Constitution*. Boston: Damrell and Moore, 1856.

Fitzhugh, George. *Cannibals All! or Slaves without Masters*. Edited by C. Vann Woodward. Cambridge, Mass.: Harvard University Press, 1960.

Fitzhugh, George, and A. Hogeboom. *A Controversy on Slavery, between George Fitzhugh, Esq., of Virginia, Author of "Sociology for the South," etc., and A. Hogeboom, Esq., of New York*. Oneida, N.Y.: Oneida Sachem Office, 1857.

The Fugitive Slave Bill: Its History and Unconstitutionality. . . . New York: William Harned, 1850.

Goodell, William . *The American Slave Code in Theory and Practice: Its Distinctive Features Shown by Its Statutes, Judicial Decisions, and Illustrative Facts*. 1853. Reprint, New York: Johnson Reprint Corp., 1968.

——. *Slavery and Anti-Slavery; A History of the Great Struggle in Both Hemispheres; with a View of the Slavery Question in the United States*. 1852. Reprint, New York: Negro Universities Press, 1968.

Hammond, Samuel H. *Freedom National—Slavery Sectional: Speech of the Hon. S. H. Hammond, of the 27th Senate District, on the Governor's Message, in Senate, February, 1860*. Albany, N.Y.: Weed, Parsons, 1860.

Helper, Hinton Rowan. *The Impending Crisis of the South: How to Meet It*. New York: Burdick Brothers, 1857.

Hildreth, Richard. [Author of "Archy Moore"]. *Despotism in America; or, An Inquiry into the Nature and Results of the Slave-holding System in the United States.* Boston: Whipple and Damrell, 1840.

[Hopkins, Samuel]. *A Dialogue concerning the Slavery of the Africans. . . .* Norwich, Conn.: Judah P. Spooner, 1776.

Howe, Julia Ward. *Reminiscences, 1819–1899.* Boston: Houghton, Mifflin, 1899.

The Injurious Effects of Slave Labour: An Impartial Appeal to the Reason, Justice, and Patriotism of the People of Illinois on the Injurious Effects of Slave Labour. Philadelphia and London: n.p., 1824.

Julian, George W. *Political Recollections, 1840 to 1872.* Chicago: Jansen, McClug, 1884.

——. *Speeches on Political Questions.* New York: Hurd and Houghton, 1872.

Kettell, Thomas Prentice. *Southern Wealth and Northern Profits.* New York: George W. and John A. Wood, 1860.

Lathers, Richard. *Reminiscences of Richard Lathers.* Edited by Alvan F. Sanborn. New York: Grafton Press, 1907.

Lieber, Francis. *Essays on Property and Labour as Connected with Natural Law and the Constitution of Society.* New York: Harper and Bros., 1841.

Livermore, Mary A. *The Story of My Life or the Sunshine and Shadow of Seventy Years.* Hartford, Conn.: D. Worthington, 1899.

Locke, John. *Two Treatises of Government.* [1690]. Edited by Peter Laslett. Student edition. Cambridge: Cambridge University Press, 1988.

Logan, George. [A Farmer]. *Letters Addressed to the Yeomanry of the United States. . . .* Philadelphia: Eleazer Oswald, 1791.

Lunt, George. *The Origin of the Late War.* New York: D. Appleton, 1866.

McNeil, George E., ed. *The Labor Movement: The Problem of To-Day.* Boston: A. M. Bridgman, 1887.

Madison, James. *Notes of Debates in the Federal Convention of 1787 Reported by James Madison.* Edited by Gaillard Hunt and James Brown Scott. 1920. Reprint, New York: W. W. Norton, 1987.

Martineau, Harriet. *Society in America.* 3 vols. 1837. Reprint, New York: Ams Press, 1966.

May, Samuel. *The Fugitive Slave Law and Its Victims.* Rev. ed. 1861. Reprint, Freeport, N.Y.: Books for Libraries Press, 1970.

Nordhoff, Charles. *America for Free Working Men.* New York: Harper and Brothers, 1865.

[Nordhoff, Charles?]. *What Democratic Leaders Think of Slavery.* N.p., [1865?].

Olmsted, Frederick Law. *The Cotton Kingdom: A Traveller's Observations on Cotton and Slavery in the American Slave States.* Edited by Arthur M. Schlesinger. 1861. Reprint, New York: Alfred A. Knopf, 1953.

Palfrey, John G. *Papers on the Slave Power, First Published in the "Boston Whig."* Boston: Merrill, Cobb, [1846].

Pennsylvania Society for Promoting the Abolition of Slavery. *Memorials.* Philadelphia: Francis Bailey, 1792.

The Poor Whites of the South: The Injury Done Them by Slavery. Republican Executive Congressional Committee, Washington, D.C., [1860?].

Potter, A[lonzo]. *Political Economy: Its Objects, Uses, and Principles: Considered with Reference to the Condition of the American People.* New York: Harper and Bros., 1841.

Potter, John F. *Speech of Hon. John F. Potter of Wisconsin: In the House of Representatives, March 23, 1858.* Washington, D.C.: By the Author, 1858.

Ramsey, David. *The History of the American Revolution.* 2 vols. Philadelphia: R. Aitken and Son, 1789.

Rice, David. [Philanthropos]. *Slavery Inconsistent with Justice and Good Policy*. Lexington: J. Bradford, 1792.

Rush, Benjamin. [A Pennsylvanian]. *An Address to the Inhabitants of the British Settlements in America upon Slave-Keeping*. Philadelphia: John Dunlap, 1773.

Rushton, Edward. *Expostulatory Letter to George Washington, of Mount Vernon, on His Consenting to Be a Holder of Slaves*. Lexington, Ky.: John Bradford, 1797.

Sawyer, George S. *Southern Institutes; or, An Inquiry into the Origins and Early Prevalence of Slavery and the Slave Trade*. Philadelphia: J. B. Lippincott, 1859.

Schurz, Carl. *The Reminiscences of Carl Schurz*. 3 vols. Garden City, N.Y.: Doubleday, Page, 1908.

——. *Speech Delivered at Verandah Hall, St. Louis, August 1, 1860*. N.p., [1860].

Sedgwick, Theodore. *Public and Private Economy*. 3 vols. New York: Harper and Brothers, 1836.

Seward, William H. *Immigrant White Free Labor, or Imported Black African Slave Labor: Speech of William H. Seward at Oswego, New York, November 3, 1856*. Washington, D.C.: Buell and Blanchard, 1857.

Smith, Adam. *An Inquiry into the Nature and Causes of the Wealth of Nations*. Edited by Edwin Cannan. New York: Modern Library, 1937.

Smith, Elihu Hubbard. *A Discourse, Delivered April 11, 1798, at the Request of and before the New-York Society for Promoting the Manumission of Slaves, and Protecting Such of Them As Have Been or May Be Liberated*. New York: T. and J. Swords, 1798.

Spencer, Ichabod S. *The Religious Duty of Obedience to Law: A Sermon. . . .* New York: M. W. Dodd, 1850.

Stanton, Henry B. *Remarks of Henry B. Stanton, in the Representatives' Hall, on the 23d and 24th of February, 1837, . . . on the Subject of Slavery*. 5th ed. Boston: Isaac Knapp, 1837.

Stephens, Alexander H. *A Constitutional View of the Late War between the States. . . .* 2 vols. Philadelphia: National Publishing, 1870.

Swift, Zephaniah. *An Oration on Domestic Slavery*. Hartford, Conn.: Hudson and Goodwin, 1791.

Taney, Roger B. *The Dred Scott Decision: Opinion of Chief Justice Taney. . . .* Edited by J. H. Van Evrie. New York: Horton, 1860.

Tappan, M. W. *Modern Democracy the Ally of Slavery, Speech of Hon. M. W. Tappan, of New Hampshire, in the House of Representatives, July 29, 1856*. [New York: Greeley and McElrath, 1856].

Taylor, John. *An Argument Respecting the Constitutionality of the Carriage Tax*. Richmond: Augustine Davis, 1795.

Tucker, St. George. *A Dissertation on Slavery with a Proposal for the Gradual Abolition of It, in the State of Virginia*. Philadelphia: Mathew Carey, 1796.

Warren, Dr. Joseph. *An Oration: Delivered March Sixth, 1775, at the Request of the Inhabitants of Boston; to Commemorate the Bloody Tragedy of the Fifth of March, 1770*. Boston: Edes and Gill, 1775.

Webb, J. Watson. *Slavery and Its Tendencies: A Letter from General J. Watson Webb of the New York Courier and Enquirer*. Washington, D.C.: Buell and Blanchard, 1856.

Webster, Noah, Jr. *Effects of Slavery on Morals and Industry*. Hartford: Hudson and Goodwin, 1793.

——. *An Examination into the Leading Principles of the Federal Constitution, Proposed by the Late Convention Held at Philadelphia*. Philadelphia: Prichard and Hall, 1787.

[Weld, Theodore?]. *The Bible against Slavery. . . .* 1838. Reprint, Detroit: Negro History Press, 1970.

Weston, George M. *The Progress of Slavery in the United States.* Washington, D.C.: George M. Weston, 1858.

——. *Southern Slavery Reduces Northern Wages.* Washington, D.C.: Republican Association, 1856.

Wilson, Henry. *History of the Rise and Fall of the Slave Power in America.* 3 vols. Boston: Houghton Mifflin, 1872.

——. *Speech of Hon. Henry Wilson, at the Republican Mass Metting at Bangor, Me., August 27, 1868.* New York: N.p., 1868.

Wilson, William A. M. *The Great American Question: Democracy vs. Doulocracy: or, Free Soil, Free Labor, Free Men and Free Speech against the Extension and Domination of the Slaveholding Interest. A Letter. . . .* Cincinnati: E. Shepard, 1848.

Wolfe, Samuel M. *Helper's Impending Crisis Dissected.* Philadelphia: J. T. Lloyd, 1860.

Woolman, John. *Consideration on Keeping Negroes; Recommended to the Professors of Christianity, of Every Denomination. Part Second.* Philadelphia: B. Franklin and D. Hall, 1762.

——. *Some Considerations on the Keeping of Negroes. Recommended to the Professors of Christianity of Every Denomination.* Philadelphia: James Chattin, 1754.

Yates, Richard. *Speech of Hon. Richard Yates . . . Delivered at Springfield, Ill., 7 June 1860.* N.p., [1860].

Edited Collections

Adams, John. *The Works of John Adams, Second President of the United States. . . .* Edited by Charles Francis Adams. 10 vols. Boston: Little, Brown, 1856.

Adams, John Quincy. *Memoirs of John Quincy Adams.* Edited by Charles Francis Adams. 12 vols. Philadelphia: J. B. Lippincott, 1874–77.

Adams, Samuel. *The Writings of Samuel Adams.* Edited by Harry Alonzo Cushing. 4 vols. 1904. Reprint, New York: Octagon Books, 1968.

Ames, Seth, ed. *The Works of Fisher Ames. With a Selection from His Speeches and Correspondence.* 2 vols. Boston: Little, Brown, 1854.

Bailyn, Bernard, ed. *Pamphlets of the American Revolution, 1750–1776.* Cambridge, Mass.: Harvard University Press, 1965.

Barnes, Gilbert H., and Dwight L. Dumond, eds. *Letters of Theodore Dwight Weld, Angelina Grimké Weld, and Sarah Grimké.* 2 vols. 1934. Reprint, Gloucester, Mass.: Peter Smith, 1965.

Beale, Howard K., ed. *The Diary of Edward Bates, 1859–1860.* Washington, D.C.: Government Printing Office, 1933.

Bigelow, John, ed. *Writings and Speeches of Samuel J. Tilden.* 2 vols. New York: Harper and Brothers, 1885.

——. *The Life of Benjamin Franklin, Written by Himself.* 3d ed. 3 vols. Philadelphia: J. B. Lippincott, 1893.

Birney, James G. *Letters of James Gillespie Birney, 1837–1857.* Edited by Dwight L. Dumond. 2 vols. 1938. Reprint, Gloucester, Mass.: Peter Smith, 1966.

Blau, Joseph L., ed. *Social Theories of Jacksonian Democracy: Representative Writings of the Period, 1825–1850.* New York: Hafner Publishing, 1947.

Brackenridge, Hugh Henry. *A Hugh Henry Brackenridge Reader, 1770–1815.* Edited by Daniel Marder. Pittsburgh: University of Pittsburgh Press, 1970.

Brownson, Orestes A. *The Works of Orestes A. Brownson.* Edited by Henry F. Brownson. 20 vols. Reprint, New York: Ams Press, 1966.

Buchanan, James. *The Works of James Buchanan: Comprising His Speeches, State Papers, and Private Correspondence.* Edited by John Bassett Moore. 12 vols. 1908–11. Reprint, New York: Antiquarian Press, 1950.

Calhoun, John C. *The Papers of John C. Calhoun.* Edited by Robert L. Meriwether et al. 25 vols. to date. Columbia: University of South Carolina Press, 1959–.

——. *Works of John C. Calhoun.* Edited by Richard K. Crallé. 6 vols. New York: D. Appleton, 1856.

Chase, Salmon P. *The Salmon P. Chase Papers.* Vol. 3: *Correspondence, 1858–March 1863.* Edited by John Niven, James P. McClure, and Leigh Johnsen. Kent, Ohio: Kent State University Press, 1996.

Clay, Cassius Marcellus. *The Writings of Cassius Marcellus Clay, Including Speeches and Addresses.* Edited by Horace Greeley. 1848. Reprint, New York: Negro Universities Press, 1969.

Clay, Henry. *The Life and Speeches of Henry Clay.* Edited by James B. Swain. 2 vols. New York: James B. Swain, 1842–43.

——. *The Papers of Henry Clay.* Edited by Melba Porter Hay. 10 vols. Lexington: University of Kentucky Press, 1959–91.

Clingman, Thomas L. *Selections from the Speeches and Writings of Hon. Thomas L. Clingman, of North Carolina, with Additions and Explanatory Notes.* 2d ed. Raleigh, N.C.: John Nichols, 1878.

Commager, Henry Steele, and Richard B. Morris, eds. *The Spirit of 'Seventy-Six: The Story of the American Revolution as Told by Participants.* 2 vols. Indianapolis: Bobbs-Merrill, 1958.

Commons, John R., et al., eds. *A Documentary History of American Industrial Society.* 10 vols. Cleveland: Arthur H. Clark, 1910.

Dana, Richard H., III, ed. *Richard Henry Dana, Jr.: Speeches in Stirring Times and Letters to a Son.* Boston: Houghton Mifflin, 1910.

Davis, Jefferson. *Jefferson Davis: Constitutionalist; His Letters, Papers, and Speeches.* Edited by Dunbar Rowland. 10 vols. Jackson: Mississippi Department of Archives and History, 1923.

——. *The Papers of Jefferson Davis.* Edited by Haskell M. Monroe Jr. and James T. McIntosh. 6 vols. to date. Baton Rouge: Louisiana State University Press, 1971–.

de Warville, J. P. Brissot. *New Travels in the United States of America, 1788.* Translated by Mara Soceanu Vamos and Durand Echeverria. Edited by Durand Echeverria. Cambridge, Mass.: Harvard University Press, 1964.

Dickinson, John. *The Political Writings of John Dickinson, 1764–1774.* Edited by Paul Leicester Ford. 1895. Reprint, New York: Da Capo Press, 1970.

Douglas, Stephen A. *The Letters of Stephen A. Douglas.* Edited by Robert W. Johannsen. Urbana: University of Illinois Press, 1961.

Douglass, Frederick. *The Frederick Douglass Papers.* Edited by John W. Blassingame et al. 3 vols. to date. New Haven: Yale University Press, 1979–.

Drake, Charles D., ed. *Union and Antislavery Speeches, Delivered during the Rebellion.* 1864. Reprint, Miami, Fla.: Mnemosyne Publishing, 1969.

Dumond, Dwight L., ed. *Southern Editorials on Secession.* New York: Century Company, 1931.

Elliot, Jonathan. *Elliot's Debates [on the Ratification of the Constitution].* 5 vols. 1836. Reprint, Philadelphia: J. B. Lippincott, 1937.

Evarts, William M. *Arguments and Speeches of William Maxwell Evarts.* Edited by Sherman Evarts. 3 vols. New York: Macmillan, 1919.

Everett, Edward. *Orations and Speeches on Various Occasions.* 4 vols. 12th ed. Boston: Little, Brown, 1895.

Farrand, Max, ed. *The Records of the Federal Convention of 1787.* 3 vols. New Haven: Yale University Press, 1911.

Faust, Drew Gilpin, ed. *The Ideology of Slavery: Proslavery Thought in the Antebellum South, 1830–1860.* Baton Rouge: Louisiana State University Press, 1981.

Foner, Philip S., ed. *The Life and Writings of Frederick Douglass.* 4 vols. New York: International Publishers, 1950–55.

Franklin, Benjamin. *The Papers of Benjamin Franklin.* Edited by Leonard W. Labaree and William B. Willcox. 28 vols. New Haven: Yale University Press, 1959–90.

Freehling, William W., and Craig M. Simpson, eds. *Secession Debated: Georgia's Showdown in 1860.* New York: Oxford University Press, 1992.

Garfield, James A. *The Works of James Abram Garfield.* Edited by Burke A. Hinsdale. 2 vols. Boston: James R. Osgood, 1882–83.

Garrison, William Lloyd. *The Letters of William Lloyd Garrison.* Edited by Walter M. Merrill and Louis Ruchames. 6 vols. Cambridge, Mass.: Harvard University Press, 1971–81.

Graham, William A. *The Papers of William Alexander Graham.* Edited by J. G. DeRoulhac Hamilton. 5 vols. Raleigh, N.C.: State Department of Archives and History, 1957–73.

Hamilton, Alexander. *The Papers of Alexander Hamilton.* Edited by Harold C. Syrett and Jacob E. Cooke. 27 vols. New York: Columbia University Press, 1961–87.

——. *The Works of Alexander Hamilton.* Edited by Henry Cabot Lodge. 2d ed. 12 vols. New York: G. P. Putnam's Sons, 1904.

Hunter, Robert M. T. *Correspondence of Robert M. T. Hunter, 1826–1876.* Edited by Charles Henry Ambler. 1918. Reprint, New York: DaCapo Press, 1971.

Hyneman, Charles S., and Donald S. Lutz, eds. *American Political Writing during the Founding Era, 1760–1805.* 2 vols. Indianapolis: Liberty Press, 1983.

Jefferson, Thomas. *The Papers of Thomas Jefferson.* Edited by Julian P. Boyd et al. 29 vols. to date. Princeton: Princeton University Press, 1950–.

——. *The Writings of Thomas Jefferson.* Edited by Andrew A. Lipscomb. 20 vols. Washington, D.C.: Thomas Jefferson Memorial Association, 1904.

Johannsen, Robert W., ed. *The Lincoln-Douglas Debates of 1858.* New York: Oxford University Press, 1965.

Johnson, Andrew. *The Papers of Andrew Johnson.* Edited by Leroy P. Graf and Ralph W. Haskins. 8 vols. to date. Knoxville: University of Tennessee Press, 1967–.

Kenyon, Cecelia M., ed. *The Antifederalists.* Indianapolis: Bobbs-Merrill, 1966.

King, Rufus. *The Life and Correspondence of Rufus King.* Edited by Charles R. King. 6 vols. 1894–1900. Reprint, New York: DaCapo Press, 1971.

Lee, Richard Henry. *The Letters of Richard Henry Lee.* Edited by James C. Ballagh. 2 vols. 1911. Reprint, New York: Da Capo Press, 1970.

Leggett, William. *A Collection of the Political Writings of William Leggett.* Edited by Theodore Sedgwick. 2 vols. New York: Taylor and Dodd, 1840.

Lincoln, Abraham. *The Collected Works of Abraham Lincoln.* Edited by Roy P. Basler, Marion Dolores Pratt, and Lloyd A. Dunlap. 9 vols. New Brunswick, N.J.: Rutgers University Press, 1953–55.

Lowell, James Russell. *The Anti-Slavery Papers of James Russell Lowell.* 2 vols. Boston: Houghton, Mifflin, 1902.

——. *Letters of James Russell Lowell.* Edited by Charles Eliot Norton. 3 vols. Cambridge, Mass.: Riverside Press, 1904.

——. *Political Essays.* Cambridge, Mass.: Riverside Press, 1904.

McKitrick, Eric L., ed. *Slavery Defended: The Views of the Old South*. Englewood Cliffs, N.J.: Prentice-Hall, 1963.

Madison, James. *The Papers of James Madison*. Edited by William T. Hutchinson and William M. E. Rachal. 17 vols. Chicago: University of Chicago Press, 1962–91.

——. *The Writings of James Madison*. Edited by Gaillard Hunt. 9 vols. New York: G. P. Putnam's Sons, 1900–1910.

Mangum, Willie P. *The Papers of Willie Person Mangum*. Edited by Henry Thomas Shanks. 5 vols. Raleigh, N.C.: State Department of Archives and History, 1950–56.

Moore, Frank, ed. *The Rebellion Record: A Diary of American Events*. 11 vols. New York: G. P. Putnam, 1861–65.

Osofky, Gilbert, ed. *Puttin' on Ole Massa: The Slave Narratives of Henry Bibb, William Wells Brown, and Solomon Northrup*. New York: Harper and Row, 1969.

Paine, Thomas. *The Complete Writings of Thomas Paine*. Edited by Philip S. Foner. 2 vols. New York: Citadel Press, 1945.

Parker, Theodore. *The Collected Works of Theodore Parker*. Edited by Francis Power Cobbe. 14 vols. London: Trubner, 1864–71.

Paskoff, Paul F., and Daniel J. Wilson, eds. *The Cause of the South: Selections from De Bow's Review, 1846–1867*. Baton Rouge: Louisiana State University Press, 1982.

Phillips, Wendell. *Speeches, Lectures, and Letters*. 2 vols. Boston: Lee and Shepard, 1884–91.

Polk, James K. *Correspondence of James K. Polk*. Edited by Herbert Weaver et al. 7 vols. to date. Nashville: Vanderbilt University Press, 1969–.

Rawick, George P., ed. *The American Slave: A Composite Autobiography*. Westport, Conn.: Greenwood Press, 1972.

Ricardo, David. *The Works and Correspondence of David Ricardo*. Edited by Piero Sraffa. 9 vols. Cambridge: Cambridge University Press, 1951.

Ripley, Peter C., ed. *The Black Abolitionist Papers*. 5 vols. Chapel Hill: University of North Carolina Press, 1985–92.

Rogers, Nathaniel Peabody. *A Collection from the Miscellaneous Writings of Nathaniel Peabody Rogers*. Manchester, N.H.: William H. Fisk, 1849.

Rush, Benjamin. *The Selected Writings of Benjamin Rush*. Edited by Dagobert D. Runes. New York: Philosophical Library, 1947.

Seward, William H. *The Works of William H. Seward*. Edited by George E. Baker. 5 vols. 2d ed. Boston: Houghton, Mifflin, 1887.

Stanton, Elizabeth Cady, Susan B. Anthony, and Matilda Joslyn Gage. *History of Women Suffrage*. 4 vols. Rochester, N.Y.: Charles Mann, 1887.

Stewart, Alvan. *Writings and Speeches of Alvan Stewart, on Slavery*. Edited by Luther Rawson Marsh. New York: A. B. Burdick, 1860.

Storing, Herbert J., ed. *The Complete Anti-Federalist*. 7 vols. Chicago: University of Chicago Press, 1981.

Sumner, Charles. *Memoir and Letters of Charles Sumner*. Edited by Edward L. Pierce. 4 vols. Boston: Roberts Brothers, 1877.

——. *The Selected Letters of Charles Sumner*. Edited by Beverly Wilson Palmer. 2 vols. Boston: Northeastern University Press, 1990.

——. *The Works of Charles Sumner*. 11 vols. Boston: Lee and Shepard, 1870–75.

Tyler, Lyon, ed. *The Letters and Times of the Tylers*. 3 vols. 1884–98. Reprint, New York: Da Capo Press, 1970.

Webster, Daniel. *The Papers of Daniel Webster*. Edited by Charles M. Wiltse and Harold D. Moser. 14 vols. to date. Hanover, N.H.: University Press of New England, 1974.

Webster, Noah. *Letters of Noah Webster*. Edited by Harry R. Warfel. New York: Library Publishers, 1953.

——. *On Being American: Selected Writings, 1783–1828*. Edited by Homer D. Babbidge Jr. New York: Frederick A. Praeger, 1967.

Weed, Thurlow. *Life of Thurlow Weed, Including His Autobiography and a Memoir*. Edited by Harriet A. Weed. 2 vols. Boston: Houghton Mifflin, 1883–84.

Whittier, John G. *The Letters of John Greenleaf Whittier*. Edited by John B. Pickard. 3 vols. Cambridge, Mass.: Harvard University Press, 1975.

——. *The Works of John Greenleaf Whittier*. 7 vols. Boston: Houghton Mifflin, 1892.

Wilson, James. *The Works of James Wilson*. Edited by Robert Green McCloskey. 2 vols. Cambridge, Mass.: Harvard University Press, 1967.

Winthrop, Robert C. *Addresses and Speeches on Various Occasions*. 4 vols. Boston: Little, Brown, 1852–86.

Woodson, Carter G., ed. *Negro Orators and Their Orations*. 1925. Reprint, New York: Russell and Russell, 1969.

SECONDARY SOURCES

Abbott, Richard H. *Cotton and Capital: Boston Businessmen and Antislavery Reform, 1854–1868*. Amherst: University of Massachusetts Press, 1991.

Abzug, Robert H., and Stephen E. Maizlish, eds. *New Perspectives on Race and Slavery in America: Essays in Honor of Kenneth M. Stampp*. Lexington: University of Kentucky Press, 1986.

Adamany, David. "The Supreme Court's Role in Critical Elections." In *Realignment in American Politics: Toward a Theory*, edited by Bruce A. Campbell and Richard J. Trilling, 229–59. Austin: University of Texas Press, 1980.

Aitken, Hugh G. J., ed. *Did Slavery Pay? Readings in the Economics of Black Slavery in the United States*. Boston: Houghton Mifflin, 1971.

Alchian, Armen, and Harold Demsetz. "The Property Rights Paradigm." *Journal of Economic History* 33 (March 1973): 16–27.

Aldrich, John H. *Why Parties? The Origin and Transformation of Political Parties in America*. Chicago: University of Chicago Press, 1995.

Alexander, Gregory S. *Commodity and Propriety: Competing Visions of Property in American Legal Thought, 1776–1970*. Chicago: University of Chicago Press, 1997.

Altschuler, Glenn C., and Stuart M. Blumin. *Rude Republic: Americans and Their Politics in the Nineteenth Century*. Princeton: Princeton University Press, 2000.

Ambler, Charles Henry. *Sectionalism in Virginia, from 1776 to 1861*. 1910. Reprint, New York: Russell and Russell, 1964.

Anbinder, Tyler. *Nativism and Slavery: The Northern Know Nothings and the Politics of the 1850s*. New York: Oxford University Press, 1992.

Anderson, Terry L., ed. *Property Rights and Indian Economies*. Boston: Rowman and Littlefield, 1992.

Anderson, Terry L., and Peter J. Hill. *The Birth of a Transfer Society*. Lanham, Md.: University Press of America, 1989.

——. "The Race for Property Rights." *Journal of Law and Economics* 33 (April 1990): 177–97.

Appleby, Joyce. *Capitalism and a New Social Order: The Republican Vision of the 1790s*. New York: New York University Press, 1984.

——. "The Vexed Story of Capitalism Told by American Historians." *Journal of the Early Republic* 21 (Spring 2001): 1–18.

Ashworth, John. *"Agrarians" and "Aristocrats": Party Political Ideology in the United States, 1837–1846*. Cambridge: Cambridge University Press, 1983.

——. *Slavery, Capitalism, and Politics in the Antebellum Republic*. Vol. 1: *Commerce and Compromise, 1820–1850*. Cambridge: Cambridge University Press, 1995.

Atack, Jeremy, and Fred Bateman. *To Their Own Soil: Agriculture in the Antebellum North*. Ames: Iowa State University Press, 1987.

Atkins, Jonathan M. *Parties, Politics, and Sectional Conflict in Tennessee, 1832–1861*. Knoxville: University of Tennessee Press, 1977.

Aufhauser, R. Keith. "Slavery and Technological Change." *Journal of Economic History* 34 (March 1974): 36–50.

Bailyn, Bernard. *The Ideological Origins of the American Revolution*. Cambridge, Mass.: Harvard University Press, 1967.

Baker, Jean H. *Affairs of Party: The Political Culture of Northern Democrats in the Mid-Nineteenth Century*. Ithaca: Cornell University Press, 1983.

——. *Ambivalent Americans: The Know-Nothing Party in Maryland*. Baltimore: Johns Hopkins University Press, 1977.

Barney, William L. *The Secessionist Impulse: Alabama and Mississippi in 1860*. Princeton: Princeton University Press, 1974.

——. "Towards the Civil War: The Dynamics of Change in a Black Belt County." In *Class, Conflict and Consensus: Antebellum Southern Community Studies*, edited by Orville Vernon Burton and Robert C. McMath Jr., 146–72. Westport, Conn.: Greenwood Press, 1982.

Barron, Hal S. "Listening to the Silent Majority: Change and Continuity in the Nineteenth-Century Rural North." In *Agriculture and National Development: Views on the Nineteenth Century*, edited by Lou Ferleger, 3–23. Ames: Iowa State University Press, 1990.

Barzel, Yoram. *Economic Analysis of Property Rights*. Cambridge: Cambridge University Press, 1989.

Bateman, Fred, and Theodore Weiss. *A Deplorable Scarcity: The Failure of Industrialization in the Slave Economy*. Chapel Hill: University of North Carolina Press, 1981.

Bauer, K. Jack. *Zachary Taylor: Soldier, Planter, Statesman of the Old Southwest*. Baton Rouge: Louisiana State University Press, 1985.

Baum, Dale. *The Civil War Party System: The Case of Massachusetts, 1848–1876*. Chapel Hill: University of North Carolina Press, 1984.

Beard, Charles A., and Mary Beard. *The Rise of American Civilization*. 2 vols. New York: Macmillan, 1927.

Becker, Gary S. "A Theory of Competition among Pressure Groups for Political Preference." *Quarterly Journal of Economics* 97 (August 1983): 371–400.

Bensel, Richard Franklin. *Yankee Leviathan: The Origins of Central State Authority in America, 1859–1877*. New York: Cambridge University Press, 1990.

Berger, Mark. *The Revolution in the New York Party Systems, 1840–1860*. Port Washington, N.Y.: Kennikat Press, 1973.

Bergeron, Paul H. *Antebellum Politics in Tennessee*. Lexington: University Press of Kentucky, 1982.

Beringer, Richard E., Herman Hattaway, Archer Jones, and William N. Still Jr. *The Elements of Confederate Defeat: Nationalism, War Aims, and Religion*. Athens: University of Georgia Press, 1988.

Berlin, Ira, and Herbert G. Gutman. "Natives and Immigrants, Free Men and Slaves: Urban Workingmen in the Antebellum American South." *American Historical Review* 88 (December 1983): 1176–1200.

Bernstein, Irving. *The Lean Years: A History of the American Worker, 1920–1933*. Boston: Houghton Mifflin, 1972.

Bernstein, Michael A. "Understanding American Economic Decline: The Contours of the Late-Twentieth-Century Experience." In *Understanding American Economic Decline*, edited by Michael A. Bernstein and David E. Adler, 3–33. Cambridge: Cambridge University Press, 1994.

Bernstein, Michael A., and David E. Adler, eds. *Understanding American Economic Decline*. Cambridge: Cambridge University Press, 1994.

Berry, Brian L. *Long-Wave Rhythms in Economic Development and Political Behavior*. Baltimore: Johns Hopkins University Press, 1991.

Bestor, Arthur. "The American Civil War as a Constitutional Crisis." *American Historical Review* 69 (January 1964): 327–52.

——. "State Sovereignty and Slavery—A Reinterpretation of Proslavery Constitutional Doctrine, 1846–1860." *Journal of the Illinois State Historical Society* 54 (1961): 147–80.

Biles, Roger. *A New Deal for the American People*. DeKalb: Northern Illinois University Press, 1991.

Billings, Dwight B., Jr. *Planters and the Making of a "New South": Class, Politics, and Development in North Carolina, 1865–1900*. Chapel Hill: University of North Carolina Press, 1979.

Billington, Ray Allen. *The Protestant Crusade, 1800–1860: A Study of the Origins of American Nativism*. Rev. ed. New York: Rinehard, 1952.

Blassingame, John W. *The Slave Community: Plantation Life in the Antebellum South*. Rev. ed. New York: Oxford University Press, 1979.

Blight, David, and Brooks D. Simpson, eds. *Union and Emancipation: Essays on Politics and Race in the Civil War Era*. Kent, Ohio: Kent State University Press, 1997.

Blue, Frederick J. *The Free Soilers: Third Party Politics, 1848–54*. Urbana: University of Illinois Press, 1973.

Blumin, Stuart M. *The Emergence of the Middle Class: Social Experience in the American City, 1760–1900*. Cambridge: Cambridge University Press, 1989.

Boles, John B., and Evelyn Thomas Nolen, eds. *Interpreting Southern History: Historiographical Essays in Honor of Sanford W. Higginbothan*. Baton Rouge: Louisiana State University Press, 1987.

Bond, Bradley G. *Political Culture in the Nineteenth-Century South: Mississippi, 1830–1900*. Baton Rouge: Louisiana State University Press, 1995.

Boney, F. N. *Southerners All*. Macon, Ga.: Mercer University Press, 1984.

Bonner, James C. "Profile of a Late Ante-Bellum Community." *American Historical Review* 49 (July 1944): 663–80.

Booraem, Hendrik V. *The Formation of the Republican Party in New York: Politics and Conscience in the Antebellum North*. New York: New York University Press, 1983.

Boritt, Gabor S. *Lincoln and the Economics of the American Dream*. Memphis: Memphis State University Press, 1978.

——, ed. *Why the Civil War Came*. New York: Oxford University Press, 1996.

Bourke, Paul, and Donald DeBats. *Washington County: Politics and Community in Antebellum America*. Baltimore: Johns Hopkins University Press, 1995.

Bowman, Shearer Davis. *Masters and Lords: Mid-19th-Century U.S. Planters and Prussian Junkers*. New York: Oxford University Press, 1993.

Brady, David W. *Critical Elections and Congressional Policy Making*. Stanford: Stanford University Press, 1988.

Brauer, Kinley J. *Cotton versus Conscience: Massachusetts Whig Politics and Southwestern Expansion, 1843–1848*. Lexington: University of Kentucky Press, 1967.

Brinkley, Alan. "The New Deal and the Idea of the State." In *The Rise and Fall of the New Deal Order, 1930–1980*, edited by Steve Fraser and Gary Gerstle, 85–121. Princeton: Princeton University Press, 1989.

Brock, William R. *Parties and Political Conscience: American Dilemmas 1840–1850*. Millwood, N.Y.: KTO Press, 1979.

Brody, David. *Labor in Crisis: The Steel Strike of 1919*. Philadelphia: Lippincott, 1965.

——. *Steelworkers in America: The Nonunion Era*. Cambridge, Mass.: Harvard University Press, 1960.

Brooke, John L. *The Heart of the Commonwealth: Society and Political Culture in Worcester County, Massachusetts, 1713–1861*. Cambridge: Cambridge University Press, 1989.

Brown, Richard D. *Modernization: The Transformation of American Life, 1600–1865*. New York: Hill and Wang, 1976.

Brown, Thomas. *Politics and Statesmanship: Essays on the American Whig Party*. New York: Columbia University Press, 1985.

Brownlee, W. Elliott. *Dynamics of Ascent: A History of the American Economy*. 2d ed. New York: Alfred A. Knopf, 1988.

Bruchey, Stuart W., ed. *Small Business in American Life*. New York: Columbia University Press, 1980.

Buckle, Stephen. *Natural Law and the Theory of Property: Grotius to Hume*. Oxford: Oxford University Press, 1991.

Buenger, Walter L. *Secession and the Union in Texas*. Austin: University of Texas Press, 1984.

Burnham, Walter Dean. *Critical Elections and the Mainsprings of American Politics*. New York: W. W. Norton, 1970.

——. *The Current Crisis in American Politics*. Oxford: Oxford University Press, 1982.

Burton, Orville Vernon, and Robert C. McMath Jr., eds. *Class, Conflict and Consensus: Antebellum Southern Community Studies*. Westport, Conn.: Greenwood Press, 1982.

Bush, Jonathan A. "The British Constitution and the Creation of American Slavery." In *Slavery and the Law*, edited by Paul Finkelman, 379–418. Madison, Wisc.: Madison House, 1997.

Campbell, Bruce A., and Richard J. Trilling, eds. *Realignment in American Politics: Toward a Theory*. Austin: University of Texas Press, 1980.

Campbell, Randolph B. *An Empire for Slavery: The Peculiar Institution in Texas, 1821–1865*. Baton Rouge: Louisiana State University Press, 1989.

——. "Planters and Plain Folks: The Social Structure of the Antebellum South." In *Interpreting Southern History: Historiographical Essays in Honor of Sanford W. Higginbothan*, edited by John B. Boles and Evelyn Thomas Nolen, 48–77. Baton Rouge: Louisiana State University Press, 1987.

Campbell, Stanley W. *The Slave-Catchers: Enforcement of the Fugitive Slave Law, 1850–1860*. Chapel Hill: University of North Carolina Press, 1968.

Capers, Henry D. *The Life and Times of C. G. Memminger*. Richmond, Va.: Everett Waddy, 1893.

Carey, Anthony Gene. *Parties, Slavery, and the Union in Antebellum Georgia*. Athens: University of Georgia Press, 1997.

Carpenter, Jesse T. *The South as a Conscious Minority*. New York: New York University Press, 1930.

Carsel, Wilfred. "The Slaveholders' Indictment of Northern Wage Slavery." *Journal of Southern History* 6 (November 1940): 504–20.

Carwardine, Richard J. *Evangelicals and Politics in Antebellum America*. New Haven: Yale University Press, 1993.

Cecil-Fronsman, Bill. *Common Whites: Class and Culture in Antebellum North Carolina.* Lexington: University Press of Kentucky, 1992.

Chambers, William Nisbet, and Walter Dean Burnham, eds. *The American Party Systems: Stages of Political Development.* New York: Oxford University Press, 1967.

Chandler, Alfred D., Jr. "The Emergence of Managerial Capitalism." *Business History Review* 58 (Winter 1984): 473–503.

——. *The Visible Hand: The Managerial Revolution in American Business.* Cambridge, Mass.: Harvard University Press, 1977.

Channing, Edward. *A History of the United States.* 6 vols. New York: Macmillan, 1925.

Channing, Steven A. *Crisis of Fear: Secession in South Carolina.* New York: W. W. Norton, 1970.

Christman, John. "Self-Ownership, Equality, and the Structure of Property Rights." *Political Theory* 19 (February 1991): 29–39.

Cimbala, Paul A. *Under the Guardianship of the Nation: The Freedmen's Bureau and the Reconstruction of Georgia.* Athens: University of Georgia Press, 1997.

Clubb, Jerome E., William H. Flanigan, and Nancy H. Zingale. *Partisan Realignment: Voters, Parties, and Government in American History.* Beverly Hills, Calif.: Sage Publications, 1980.

Cochran, Thomas C. *Challenges to American Values: Society, Business and Religion.* New York: Oxford University Press, 1985.

Coclanis, Peter A. *The Shadow of a Dream: Economic Life and Death in the South Carolina Low Country, 1670–1920.* New York: Oxford University Press, 1989.

Cohen, G. A. *Karl Marx's Theory of History: A Defence.* Princeton: Princeton University Press, 1978.

Cole, Arthur Charles. *The Irrepressible Conflict, 1850–1865.* New York: Macmillan, 1934.

Cole, Donald B. *Martin Van Buren and the American Political System.* Princeton: Princeton University Press, 1984.

Collins, Bruce. *The Origins of America's Civil War.* New York: Holmes and Meier, 1981.

——. *White Society in the Antebellum South.* London: Longman, 1985.

Conrad, Alfred H., et al. "Slavery an Obstacle to Economic Growth in the United States: A Panel Discussion." *Journal of Economic History* 27 (December 1967): 518–60.

Cook, Robert J. *Baptism of Fire: The Republican Party in Iowa, 1838–1878.* Ames: Iowa State University Press, 1994.

Cooke, Jacob E., ed. *Alexander Hamilton: A Profile.* New York: Charles Scribner's Sons, 1967.

Cooper, William J., Jr. *Jefferson Davis, American.* New York: Alfred A. Knopf, 2000.

——. *Liberty and Slavery: Southern Politics to 1860.* New York: Alfred A. Knopf, 1983.

——. *The South and the Politics of Slavery, 1828–1856.* Baton Rouge: Louisiana State University Press, 1978.

Coulter, E. Merton. *William G. Brownlow: Fighting Parson of the Southern Highlands.* Chapel Hill: University of North Carolina Press, 1937.

Countryman, Edward. *A People in Revolution: The American Revolution and Political Society in New York, 1760–1790.* Baltimore: Johns Hopkins University Press, 1981.

Cover, Robert M. *Justice Accused: Antislavery and the Judicial Process.* New Haven: Yale University Press, 1975.

Crandall, Andrew W. *The Early History of the Republican Party, 1854–1856.* Boston: Goreham Press, 1930.

Craven, Avery O. *Civil War in the Making.* Baton Rouge: Louisiana State University Press, 1959.

——. *The Coming of the Civil War.* New York: Charles Scribner's Sons, 1942.

——. *The Growth of Southern Nationalism, 1848–1861*. Baton Rouge: Louisiana State University Press, 1953.

——. *An Historian and the Civil War*. Chicago: University of Chicago Press, 1964.

Crenshaw, Ollinger. *The Slave States in the Presidential Election of 1860*. Baltimore: Johns Hopkins University Press, 1945.

Crofts, Daniel W. *Old Southampton: Politics and Society in a Virginia County, 1834–1869*. Charlottesville: University Press of Virginia, 1992.

——. *Reluctant Confederates: Upper South Unionists in the Secession Crisis*. Chapel Hill: University of North Carolina Press, 1989.

Curry, Leonard P. *Blueprint for Modern America: Nonmilitary Legislation of the First Civil War Congress*. Nashville: Vanderbilt University Press, 1968.

Curry, Richard O., and Lawrence B. Goodheart. "Individualism in Trans-National Context." In *American Chameleon: Individualism in Trans-National Context*, edited by Richard O. Curry and Lawrence B. Goodheart, 1–19. Kent, Ohio: Kent State University Press, 1991.

Curry, Richard O., and Karl E. Valois. "The Emergence of an Individualistic Ethos in American Society." In *American Chameleon: Individualism in Trans-National Context*, edited by Richard O. Curry and Lawrence B. Goodheart, 20–43. Kent, Ohio: Kent State University Press, 1991.

Dalzell, Robert F., Jr. *Daniel Webster and the Trial of American Nationalism, 1843–1852*. Boston: Houghton Mifflin, 1973.

Danhof, Clarence H. *Change in Agriculture: The Northern United States, 1820–1870*. Cambridge, Mass.: Harvard University Press, 1969.

David, Paul, et al. *Reckoning with Slavery: A Critical Study in the Quantitative History of American Negro Slavery*. New York: Oxford University Press, 1976.

Davis, David Brion. *The Problem of Slavery in the Age of Revolution, 1770–1823*. Ithaca: Cornell University Press, 1975.

Davis, Lance E., and Douglass C. North. Assisted by Calla Smorodio. *Institutional Change and American Economic Growth*. Cambridge: Cambridge University Press, 1971.

Davis, William C. *The Cause Lost: Myths and Realities of the Confederacy*. Lawrence: University Press of Kansas, 1996.

Dawley, Alan. *Class and Community: The Industrial Revolution in Lynn*. Cambridge, Mass.: Harvard University Press, 1976.

Degler, Carl N. *The Other South: Southern Dissenters in the Nineteenth Century*. New York: Harper and Row, 1974.

Demsetz, Harold. "Toward a Theory of Property Rights." *American Economic Review* 57 (May 1967): 347–59.

Dew, Charles B. *Apostles of Disunion: Southern Secession Commissioners and the Causes of the Civil War*. Charlottesville: University Press of Virginia, 2001.

Dickinson, H. T. *Liberty and Property: Political Ideology in Eighteenth-Century Britain*. New York: Holmes and Meier, 1977.

Dodd, William E. *The Cotton Kingdom: A Chronicle of the Old South*. New Haven: Yale University Press, 1919.

——. *Expansion and Conflict*. Boston: Houghton Mifflin, 1915.

Domar, Evsey D. *Capitalism, Socialism, and Serfdom*. Cambridge: Cambridge University Press, 1989.

Donald, David. *Charles Sumner and the Coming of the Civil War*. New York: Alfred A. Knopf, 1960.

Duijn, J. J. Van. *The Long Wave in Economic Life*. London: George Allen and Unwin, 1983.

Dumond, Dwight L. *Antislavery: The Crusade for Freedom in America*. Ann Arbor: University of Michigan Press, 1961.

———. *The Secession Movement, 1860–1861*. New York: Macmillan, 1931.

Durden, Robert F. *The Self-Inflicted Wound: Southern Politics in the Nineteenth Century*. Lexington: University of Kentucky Press, 1985.

Durill, Wayne K. "Producing Poverty: Local Government and Economic Development in a New South County, 1874–1884." *Journal of American History* 71 (March 1985): 764–81.

Dykstra, Robert R. *Bright Radical Star: Black Freedom and White Supremacy on the Hawkeye Frontier*. Cambridge, Mass.: Harvard University Press, 1993.

Eaton, Clement. *The Freedom-of-Thought Struggle in the Old South*. Rev. ed. New York: Harper and Row, 1964.

———. *Henry Clay and the Art of American Politics*. Boston: Little, Brown, 1957.

———. *A History of the Old South*. 2d ed. New York: Macmillan, 1966.

———. *The Mind of the Old South*. Rev. ed. Baton Rouge: Louisiana State University Press, 1969.

Eden, Robert, ed. *The New Deal and Its Legacy: Critique and Reappraisal*. Westport, Conn.: Greenwood Press, 1989.

Edmunds, John B. *Francis W. Pickens and the Politics of Destruction*. Chapel Hill: University of North Carolina Press, 1986.

Ehrlich, Walter. *They Have No Rights: Dred Scott's Struggle for Freedom*. Westport, Conn.: Greenwood Press, 1979.

Ellis, Richard E. *The Union at Risk: Jacksonian Democracy, States' Rights, and the Crisis of the Union*. New York: Oxford University Press, 1987.

Ellis, Richard J. *American Political Cultures*. New York: Oxford University Press, 1993.

Elster, Jon. *An Introduction to Karl Marx*. Cambridge: Cambridge University Press, 1986.

Ely, James W., Jr. *The Guardian of Every Other Right: A Constitutional History of Property Rights*. 2d ed. New York: Oxford University Press, 1998.

Engerman, Stanley. "Slavery and Emancipation in Comparative Perspective: A Look at Some Recent Debates." *Journal of Economic History* 46 (June 1986): 323.

———. "Some Considerations Relating to Property Rights in Man." *Journal of Economic History* 33 (March 1973): 43–65.

Epstein, Richard A. *Takings: Private Property and the Power of Eminent Domain*. Cambridge, Mass.: Harvard University Press, 1985.

Escott, Paul D. "Jefferson Davis and Slavery in the Territories." *Journal of Mississippi History* 39 (May 1977): 97–116.

Etcheson, Nichole. *The Emerging Midwest: Upland Southerners and the Political Culture of the Old Northwest, 1787–1861*. Bloomington: Indiana University Press, 1996.

Evans, Peter, Dietrich Rueschemeyer, and Theda Skocpol, eds. *Bringing the State Back In*. Cambridge: Cambridge University Press, 1985.

Evitts, William J. *A Matter of Allegiances: Maryland from 1850 to 1861*. Baltimore: Johns Hopkins University Press, 1974.

Faust, Drew Gilpin. *A Sacred Circle: The Dilemma of the Intellectual in the Old South, 1840–1860*. Baltimore: Johns Hopkins University Press, 1977.

Fehrenbacher, Don E. *The Dred Scott Case: Its Significance in American Law and Politics*. New York: Oxford University Press, 1978.

———. "The New Political Historians and the Coming of the Civil War." *Pacific Historical Review* 54 (May 1985): 117–42.

———. *Sectional Crisis and Southern Constitutionalism*. Baton Rouge: Louisiana State University Press, 1995.

———. *The Slaveholding Republic: An Account of the United States Government's Relation to Slavery*. Completed and edited by Ward M. McAfee. New York: Oxford University Press, 2001.

Feller, Daniel. "A Brother in Arms: Benjamin Tappan and the Antislavery Democracy." *Journal of American History* 88 (June 2001): 48–74.

Ferleger, Lou, ed. *Agriculture and National Development: Views on the Nineteenth Century.* Ames: Iowa State University Press, 1990.

Ferrie, Joseph P. *Yankeys Now: Immigrants in the Antebellum United States, 1840–1860.* New York: Oxford University Press, 1999.

Fessenden, Francis. *Life and Public Services of William Pitt Fessenden.* 2 vols. Boston: Houghton, Mifflin, 1907.

Field, Phyllis F. *The Politics of Race in New York: The Struggle for Black Suffrage in the Civil War Era.* Ithaca: Cornell University Press, 1982.

Fields, Barbara Jean. "Ideology and Race in American History." In *Region, Race, and Reconstruction: Essays in Honor of C. Vann Woodward,* edited by J. Morgan Kousser and James M. McPherson, 143–77. New York: Oxford University Press, 1982.

——. *Slavery and Freedom on the Middle Ground: Maryland during the Nineteenth Century.* New Haven: Yale University Press, 1985.

Fine, Sidney. *Sit-Down: The General Motors Strike of 1936–1937.* Ann Arbor: University of Michigan Press, 1969.

Finkelman, Paul. *Slavery and the Founders: Race and Liberty in the Age of Jefferson.* Armonk, N.Y.: M. E. Sharpe, 1996.

——, ed. *Slavery and the Law.* Madison, Wisc.: Madison House, 1997.

Fiorina, Morris P. *Retrospective Voting in American National Elections.* New Haven: Yale University Press, 1981.

Firmin-Sellers, Kathryn. "The Politics of Property Rights." *American Political Science Review* 89 (December 1995): 867–81.

Fischbaum, Marvin, and Julius Rubin. "Slavery and the Economic Development of the American South." *Explorations in Economic History* 6 (Fall 1968): 119.

Fischer, David Hackett. *The Revolution of American Conservatism: The Federalist Party in the Era of Jeffersonian Democracy.* New York: Harper and Row, 1965.

Fishlow, Albert. *American Railroads and the Transformation of the Ante-Bellum Economy.* Cambridge, Mass.: Harvard University Press, 1965.

Fogel, Robert W. *Without Consent or Contract: The Rise and Fall of American Slavery.* New York: Norton, 1989.

Fogel, Robert W., and Stanley L. Engerman. *Time on the Cross: The Economics of American Negro Slavery.* 2 vols. Boston: Little, Brown, 1974.

Foner, Eric. *Free Soil, Free Labor, Free Men: The Ideology of the Republican Party before the Civil War.* 2d ed. New York: Oxford University Press, 1995.

——. "The Idea of Free Labor in Nineteenth-Century America." In *Free Soil, Free Labor, Free Men: The Ideology of the Republican Party before the Civil War,* by Eric Foner, ix–xxxix. 2d ed. New York: Oxford University Press, 1995.

——. *Reconstruction: America's Unfinished Revolution, 1863–1877.* New York: Harper and Row, 1988.

——. "The Wilmot Proviso Revisited." *Journal of American History* 56 (September 1969): 262–79.

Foner, Philip S. *Business and Slavery: The New York Merchants and the Irrepressible Conflict.* 1941. Reprint, New York: Russell and Russell, 1968.

Forbath, William E. "The Ambiguities of Free Labor: Labor and the Law in the Gilded Age." *Wisconsin Law Review* (1985): 767–817.

Ford, Lacy K. *The Origins of Southern Radicalism: The South Carolina Upcountry, 1800–1860.* New York: Oxford University Press, 1988.

——. "Republican Ideology in a Slave Society: The Political Economy of John C. Calhoun." *Journal of Southern History* 54 (August 1988): 405–24.

Formisano, Ronald P. *The Birth of Mass Political Parties: Michigan, 1827–1861.* Princeton: Princeton University Press, 1971.

——. "Deferential-Participant Politics: The Early Republic's Political Culture, 1789–1840." *American Political Science Review* 68 (June 1974): 473–87.

——. "Federalists and Republicans—Parties Yes, System No." In *The Evolution of American Electoral Systems,* by Paul Kleppner et al., 33–76. Westport, Conn.: Greenwood Press, 1981.

——. "The Invention of the Ethnocultural Interpretation." *American Historical Review* 99 (April 1994): 453–77.

Foulke, William Dudley. *Life of Oliver P. Morton.* 2 vols. Indianapolis: Bowen-Merrill, 1899.

Franklin, John Hope. *The Militant South, 1800–1861.* Cambridge, Mass.: Harvard University Press, 1956.

——. *Reconstruction after the Civil War.* Chicago: University of Chicago Press, 1961.

Franklin, John Hope, and Loren Schweninger. *Runaway Slaves: Rebels on the Plantation.* New York: Oxford University Press, 1999.

Fraser, Steve, and Gary Gerstle, eds. *The Rise and Fall of the New Deal Order, 1930–1980.* Princeton: Princeton University Press, 1989.

Frayssé, Olivier. *Lincoln, Land, and Labor, 1809–60.* Translated by Sylvia Neely. Urbana: University of Illinois Press, 1994.

Fredrickson, George M. *The Black Image in the White Mind: The Debate on Afro-American Character and Destiny, 1817–1914.* New York: Harper and Row, 1971.

——, ed. *A Nation Divided: Problems and Issues of the Civil War and Reconstruction.* Minneapolis: Burgess Publishing, 1975.

Freehling, William W. "The Divided South, Democracy's Limitations, and the Causes of the Peculiarly North American Civil War." In *Why the Civil War Came,* edited by Gabor S. Boritt, 125–75. New York: Oxford University Press, 1996.

——. "Nullification, Minority Blackmail, and the Crisis of Majority Rule." In *A Nation Divided: Problems and Issues of the Civil War and Reconstruction,* edited by George M. Fredrickson, 5–13. Minneapolis: Burgess Publishing, 1975.

——. *Prelude to Civil War: The Nullification Controversy in South Carolina, 1816–1836.* New York: Harper and Row, 1965.

——. *The Road to Disunion: Secessionists at Bay, 1776–1854.* New York: Oxford University Press, 1990.

Friedman, Lawrence M. *A History of American Law.* 2d ed. New York: Touchstone, 1985.

——. "Law and Small Business in the United States: One Hundred Years of Struggle and Accommodation." In *Small Business in American Life,* edited by Stuart M. Bruchey, 305–10. New York: Columbia University Press, 1980.

Friedman, Milton, with the assistance of Rose D. Friedman. *Capitalism and Freedom.* Chicago: University of Chicago Press, 1962.

Frisch, Morton J. "An Appraisal of Roosevelt's Legacy: How the Moderate Welfare State Transcended the Tension between Progressivism and Socialism." In *The New Deal and Its Legacy: Critique and Reappraisal,* edited by Robert Eden, 191–98. Westport, Conn.: Greenwood Press, 1989.

Frothingham, Paul Revere. *Theodore Parker: A Biography.* Boston: James R. Osgood, 1874.

Galambos, Louis, and Joseph Pratt. *The Rise of the Corporate Commonwealth: United States Business and Public Policy in the 20th Century.* New York: Basic Books, 1988.

Galenson, David. *White Servitude in Colonial America: An Economic Analysis.* Cambridge: Cambridge University Press, 1981.

Gara, Larry. "Antislavery Congressmen, 1848–1856: Their Contribution to the Debate between the Sections." *Civil War History* 32 (September 1986): 197–207.

——. *The Presidency of Franklin Pierce.* Lawrence: University Press of Kansas, 1991.

——. "Slavery and the Slave Power: A Crucial Distinction." *Civil War History* 15 (March 1969): 5–18.

Gates, John B. "The American Supreme Court and Electoral Realignment: A Critical Review." *Social Science History* 8 (Summer 1984): 267–90.

Genovese, Eugene D. *The Political Economy of Slavery: Studies in the Economy and Society of the Slave South.* New York: Pantheon Books, 1966.

——. *Roll, Jordan, Roll: The World the Slaves Made.* New York: Pantheon Books, 1974.

——. *The Slaveholders' Dilemma: Freedom and Progress in Southern Conservative Thought, 1820–1860.* Columbia: University of South Carolina Press, 1992.

——. *The World the Slaveholders Made: Two Essays in Interpretation.* 2d ed. Middleton, Conn.: Wesleyan University, 1988.

Gerteis, Louis. *Morality and Utility in American Antislavery Reform.* Chapel Hill: University of North Carolina Press, 1987.

Getzler, Joshua. "Theories of Property and Economic Development." *Journal of Interdisciplinary History* 26 (Spring 1996): 639–69.

Gienapp, William E. "The Crisis of American Democracy: The Political System and the Coming of the Civil War." In *Why the Civil War Came*, edited by Gabor S. Boritt, 79–124. New York: Oxford University Press, 1996.

——. *Origins of the Republican Party, 1852–56.* New York: Oxford University Press, 1987.

——. "The Republican Party and the Slave Power." In *New Perspectives on Race and Slavery in America: Essays in Honor of Kenneth M. Stampp*, edited by Robert H. Abzug and Stephen E. Maizlish, 51–78. Lexington: University of Kentucky Press, 1986.

——. "Who Voted for Lincoln?" In *Abraham Lincoln and the American Political Tradition*, edited by John L. Thomas, 50–97. Amherst: University of Massachusetts Press, 1986.

Gilje, Paul A. "The Rise of Capitalism in the Early Republic." In *Wages of Independence: Capitalism in the Early American Republic*, edited by Paul A. Gilje, 1–22. Madison, Wisc.: Madison House, 1997.

——, ed. *Wages of Independence: Capitalism in the Early American Republic.* Madison, Wisc.: Madison House, 1997.

Gillespie, Michele. *Free Labor in an Unfree World: White Artisans in Slaveholding Georgia, 1789–1860.* Athens: University of Georgia Press, 2000.

Gillette, William. *Retreat from Reconstruction, 1869–1879.* Baton Rouge: Louisiana State University Press, 1979.

Ginsberg, Benjamin. "Critical Elections and Substance of Party Conflict." *Midwest Journal of Political Science* 16 (November 1972): 603–25.

——. "Elections and Public Policy." *American Political Science Review* 70 (March 1976): 41–49.

Glickstein, Jonathan A. *American Exceptionalism, American Anxiety: Wages, Competition, and Degraded Labor in the Antebellum United States.* Charlottesville: University of Virginia Press, 2002.

Going, Charles Buxton. *David Wilmot, Free-Soiler: A Biography of the Great Advocate of the Wilmot Proviso.* New York: D. Appleton, 1924.

Goldin, Claudia Dale. *Urban Slavery in the American South, 1820–1860: A Quantitative History.* Chicago: University of Chicago Press, 1976.

Goldin, Claudia Dale, and Frank D. Lewis. "The Economic Cost of the American Civil War: Estimates and Implications." *Journal of Economic History* 35 (June 1975): 299–336.

Goodheart, Lawrence B. *Abolitionist, Actuary, Atheist: Elizur Wright and the Reform Impulse.* Kent, Ohio: Kent State University Press, 1990.

Goodman, Paul. "The First American Party System." In *The American Party Systems: Stages of Political Development,* edited by William Nisbet Chambers and Walter Dean Burnham, 56–89. New York: Oxford University Press, 1967.

——. *Of One Blood: Abolitionism and the Origins of Racial Equality.* Berkeley: University of California Press, 1998.

Govan, Thomas P. "Was the Old South Different?" *Journal of Southern History* 21 (November 1955): 447–55.

Grant, Susan-Mary. *North over South: Northern Nationalism and American Identity in the Antebellum Era.* Lawrence: University Press of Kansas, 2000.

Gray, Lewis Cecil. "Economic Efficiency and Competitive Advantages of Slavery under the Plantation System." *Agricultural History* 4 (April 1930): 31–47.

Green, Fletcher M. *Constitutional Development in the South Atlantic States, 1776–1860: A Study in the Evolution of Democracy.* Chapel Hill: University of North Carolina Press, 1930.

Greenberg, Kenneth S. *Masters and Statesmen: The Political Culture of American Slavery.* Baltimore: Johns Hopkins University Press, 1985.

Greene, Jack P. "Society, Ideology, and Politics: An Analysis of the Political Culture of Mid-Eighteenth-Century Virginia." In *Society, Freedom, and Conscience: The American Revolution in Virginia, Massachusetts, and New York,* edited by Richard M. Jellison, 14–76. New York: W. W. Norton, 1976.

Gregory, Francis W. *Nathan Appleton: Merchant and Entrepreneur, 1779–1861.* Charlottesville: University of Virginia Press, 1975.

Gunderson, Gerald. "The Origin of the American Civil War." *Journal of Economic History* 34 (December 1974): 915–50.

Gunn, L. Ray. *The Decline of Authority: Public Economic Policy and Political Development in New York, 1800–1860.* Ithaca: Cornell University Press, 1988.

Hacker, Louis M. *Triumph of American Capitalism: The Development of Forces in American History to the End of the Nineteenth Century.* New York: Columbia University Press, 1940.

Hahn, Stephen. *The Roots of Southern Populism: Yeoman Farmers and the Transformation of the Georgia Upcountry, 1850–1890.* New York: Oxford University Press, 1983.

Haites, Erik F., James Mak, and Gary M. Walton. *Western River Transportation: The Era of Early Internal Development, 1810–1860.* Baltimore: Johns Hopkins University Press, 1975.

Halberstam, David. *The Reckoning.* New York: Morrow, 1986.

Hamilton, Holman. *Prologue to Conflict: The Crisis and Compromise of 1850.* New York: W. W. Norton, 1964.

Hamlin, Charles Eugene. *The Life and Times of Hannibal Hamlin.* Cambridge, Mass.: Riverside Press, 1899.

Handlin, Oscar, and Mary Handlin. "Origins of the Southern Labor System." *William and Mary Quarterly* 7 (April 1950): 199–222.

Hansen, Stephen L. *The Making of the Third Party System: Voters and Parties in Illinois, 1850–1876.* Ann Arbor, Mich.: UMI Research Press, 1978.

Harris, J. William. "Last of the Classical Republicans: An Interpretation of John C. Calhoun." *Civil War History* 30 (September 1984): 255–67.

Harris, William C. *Leroy Pope Walker: Confederate Secretary of War.* Tuscaloosa: Confederate Publishing Company, 1962.

Hart, Albert Bushnell. *Salmon Portland Chase.* Boston: Houghton Mifflin, 1899.

Hays, Samuel P. *The Response to Industrialism, 1885–1914*. Chicago: University of Chicago Press, 1957.

Heller, H. Brandon, and Helmut Norpoth. "Let the Good Times Roll: The Economic Expectations of U.S. Voters." *American Journal of Political Science* 38 (August 1994): 625–50.

Henretta, James A. *The Evolution of American Society, 1700–1815: An Interdisciplinary Analysis*. Lexington, Mass.: D. C. Heath, 1973.

Hesseltine, William B. *Lincoln's Plan of Reconstruction*. Tuscaloosa, Ala.: Confederate Publishing, 1960.

——. *Sections and Politics: Selected Essays by William B. Hesseltine*. Edited by Richard N. Current. Madison: State Historical Society of Wisconsin, 1968.

Hietala, Thomas R. *Manifest Design: Anxious Aggrandizement in Late Jacksonian America*. Ithaca: Cornell University Press, 1985.

Hofstadter, Richard. *America at 1750: A Social Portrait*. New York: Vintage, 1971.

Holt, Michael F. *Forging a Majority: The Formation of the Republican Party in Pittsburgh, 1848–1860*. New Haven: Yale University Press, 1969.

——. *The Political Crisis of the 1850s*. New York: John Wiley and Sons, 1978.

——. *Political Parties and American Political Development from the Age of Jackson to the Age of Lincoln*. Baton Rouge: Louisiana State University Press, 1992.

——. "The Politics of Impatience: The Origins of Know Nothingism." *Journal of American History* 60 (September 1973): 309–31.

——. *The Rise and Fall of the American Whig Party: Jacksonian Politics and the Onset of the Civil War*. New York: Oxford University Press, 1999.

Hopkins, Vincent. *Dred Scott's Case*. 1951. Reprint, New York: Atheneum, 1967.

Horsman, Reginald. *Josiah Nott of Mobile: Southerner, Physician, and Racial Theorist*. Baton Rouge: Louisiana State University Press, 1987.

Horton, James Oliver, and Lois E. Horton. *In Hope of Liberty: Culture, Community, and Protest among Northern Free Blacks, 1700–1860*. New York: Oxford University Press, 1997.

Horwitz, Morton J. *The Transformation of American Law, 1780–1860*. Cambridge, Mass.: Harvard University Press, 1977.

Hounshell, David A. *From the American System to Mass Production, 1800–1932: The Development of Manufacturing Technology in the United States*. Baltimore: Johns Hopkins University Press, 1984.

Hout, Michael, Clem Brooks, and Jeff Manza. "The Democratic Class Struggle in the United States, 1948–1992." *American Sociological Review* 60 (December 1995): 805–28.

Hovencamp, Herbert. *Enterprise and American Law, 1836–1937*. Cambridge, Mass.: Harvard University Press, 1991.

Howard, Victor B. *The Evangelical War against Slavery and Caste: The Life and Times of John G. Fee*. Cranbury, N.J.: Associated University Presses, 1996.

Howe, Daniel Walker. *The Political Culture of the American Whigs*. Chicago: University of Chicago Press, 1979.

Hughes, J. R. T. *American Economic History*. 3d ed. Glenview, Ill.: Scott-Foresman, Little Brown, 1990.

Hummel, Jeffrey Rogers. *Emancipating Slaves, Enslaving Free Men: A History of the American Civil War*. Chicago: Open Court, 1996.

Hunt, E. K. "Marx's Theory of Property and Alienation." In *Theories of Property: Aristotle to the Present*, edited by Anthony Parel and Thomas Flanagan, 283–315. Waterloo, Canada: Wilfrid Laurier University Press, 1979.

Hurst, James Willard. *Law and Social Order in the United States*. Ithaca: Cornell University Press, 1977.

———. *The Legitimacy of the Business Corporation in the Law of the United States, 1780–1970.* Charlottesville: University Press of Virginia, 1970.

Huston, James L. "Abolitionists, Political Economists, and Capitalism." *Journal of the Early Republic* 20 (Fall 2000): 487–521.

———. "The American Revolutionaries, the Political Economy of Aristocracy, and the American Concept of the Distribution of Wealth, 1765–1900." *American Historical Review* 98 (October 1993): 1079–1105.

———. "The Demise of the Pennsylvania American Party, 1854–1858." *Pennsylvania Magazine of History and Biography* 109 (October 1985): 473–97.

———. "Democracy by Scripture vs. Democracy by Process: A Reflection on Stephen A. Douglas and Popular Sovereignty." *Civil War History* 43 (September 1997): 189–200.

———. "The Experiential Basis of the Northern Antislavery Impulse." *Journal of Southern History* 56 (November 1990): 609–40.

———. *The Panic of 1857 and the Coming of the Civil War*. Baton Rouge: Louisiana State University Press, 1987.

———. "A Political Response to Industrialism: The Republican Embrace of Protectionist Labor Doctrines." *Journal of American History* 70 (June 1983): 35–57.

———. *Securing the Fruits of Labor: The American Concept of Wealth Distribution, 1765–1900.* Baton Rouge: Louisiana State University Press, 1998.

———. "Southerners against Secession: The Arguments of the Constitutional Unionists in 1850–51." *Civil War History* 46 (December 2000): 281–99.

Ignatiev, Noel. *How the Irish Became White*. New York: Routledge, 1995.

Inscoe, John C. *Mountain Masters, Slavery, and the Sectional Crisis in Western North Carolina.* Knoxville: University of Tennessee Press, 1989.

Jackson, Luther P. *Free Negro Labor and Property Holding in Virginia, 1830–1860*. 1942. Reprint, New York: Atheneum, 1969.

Jaffa, Harry V. *Crisis of the House Divided: An Interpretation of the Issues in the Lincoln-Douglas Debate*. Garden City, N.Y.: Doubleday, 1959.

———. *A New Birth of Freedom: Abraham Lincoln and the Coming of the Civil War*. Lanham, Md.: Rowman and Littlefield, 2000.

Jellison, Richard M., ed. *Society, Freedom, and Conscience: The American Revolution in Virginia, Massachusetts, and New York*. New York: W. W. Norton, 1976.

Jenkins, William Sumner. *Pro-Slavery Thought in the Old South*. Chapel Hill: University of North Carolina Press, 1935.

Jensen, Merrill. *The New Nation: A History of the United States during the Confederation, 1781–1789*. New York: Alfred A. Knopf, 1967.

Jentz, John B. "The Anti-Slavery Constituency in Jacksonian New York City." *Civil War History* 27 (June 1981): 119–21.

Johannsen, Robert W. *Lincoln, the South, and Slavery: The Political Dimension*. Baton Rouge: Louisiana State University Press, 1991.

———. *Stephen A. Douglas*. New York: Oxford University Press, 1973.

———. "Stephen A. Douglas and the South." *Journal of Southern History* 23 (February 1967): 26–50.

Johnson, Guion Griffis. *Ante-Bellum North Carolina: A Social History*. Chapel Hill: University of North Carolina Press, 1937.

Johnson, Kenneth R. "Slavery and Racism in Florence, Alabama, 1841–1862." *Civil War History* 27 (June 1981): 155–71.

Johnson, Michael P. *Toward a Patriarchal Republic: The Secession of Georgia*. Baton Rouge: Louisiana State University Press, 1977.

Johnston, Richard Malcolm, and William Hand Browne. *Life of Alexander H. Stephens*. Philadelphia: J. B. Lippincott, 1878.

Kammen, Michael. "'The Rights of Property, and the Property in Rights': The Problematic Nature of 'Property' in the Political Thought of the Founders and the Early Republic." In *Liberty, Property, and the Foundations of the American Constitution*, edited by Ellen Frankel Paul and Howard Dickman, 1–22. Albany: State University of New York Press, 1989.

Katznelson, Ira. "Working-Class Formation and the State: Nineteenth-Century England in American Perspective." In *Bringing the State Back In*, edited by Peter Evans, D. Rueschemeyer, and Theda Skocpol, 257–84. Cambridge: Cambridge University Press, 1985.

Kaufman, Allen. *Capitalism, Slavery, and Republican Values: Antebellum Political Economists, 1819–1848*. Austin: University of Texas Press, 1982.

Keller, Morton. *Affairs of State: Public Life in Late Nineteenth Century America*. Cambridge, Mass.: Harvard University Press, 1977.

——. "The Pluralist State: American Economic Regulation in Comparative Perspective, 1900–1930." In *Regulation in Perspective: Historical Essays*, edited by Thomas K. McCraw, 56–94. Cambridge, Mass.: Harvard University Press, 1981.

——. *Regulating a New Economy: Public Policy and Economic Change in America, 1900–1933*. Cambridge, Mass.: Harvard University Press, 1990.

Key, V. O., Jr. "A Theory of Critical Elections." *Journal of Politics* 17 (February 1955): 3–18.

Keyssar, Alexander. *The Right to Vote: The Contested History of Democracy in the United States*. New York: Basic Books, 2000.

Klein, Philip Shriver. *President James Buchanan: A Biography*. University Park: Pennsylvania State University Press, 1962.

Kleitt, Andrew N. "Common Law, Statute Law, and the Theory of Legislative Choice: An Inquiry into the Goal of the Sherman Act." *Economic Inquiry* 31 (October 1993): 647–62.

Kleppner, Paul. *The Cross of Culture: A Social Analysis of Midwestern Politics, 1850–1900*. New York: Free Press, 1970.

——. *The Third Electoral System, 1853–1892: Parties, Voters, and Political Cultures*. Chapel Hill: University of North Carolina Press, 1979.

Kleppner, Paul, et al. *The Evolution of American Electoral Systems*. Westport, Conn.: Greenwood Press, 1981.

Klunder, Willard Carl. *Lewis Cass and the Politics of Moderation*. Kent, Ohio: Kent State University Press, 1996.

Knupfer, Peter B. *The Union As It Is: Constitutional Unionism and Sectional Compromise, 1787–1861*. Chapel Hill: University of North Carolina Press, 1991.

Koeniger, A. Cash. "Climate and Southern Distinctiveness." *Journal of Southern History* 54 (February 1988): 21–44.

Kousser, J. Morgan, and James M. McPherson, eds. *Region, Race, and Reconstruction: Essays in Honor of C. Vann Woodward*. New York: Oxford University Press, 1982.

Kraut, Alan M. "The Forgotten Reformers: A Profile of Third Party Abolitionists in Antebellum New York." In *Antislavery Reconsidered: New Perspectives on the Abolitionists*, edited by Lewis Perry and Michael Fellman, 119–45. Baton Rouge: Louisiana State University Press, 1979.

Kremm, Thomas W. "Cleveland and the First Lincoln Election: The Ethnic Response to Nativism." *Journal of Interdisciplinary History* 8 (Summer 1977): 69–86.

Kruman, Marc. *Parties and Politics in North Carolina, 1836–1865*. Baton Rouge: Louisiana State University Press, 1983.

Kulikoff, Allan. *The Agrarian Origins of American Capitalism*. Charlottesville: University Press of Virginia, 1992.

Kutler, Stanley I. *Privilege and Creative Destruction: The Charles River Bridge Case*. Philadelphia: J. B. Lippincott, 1971.

Lacy, Eric Russell. *Vanquished Volunteers: East Tennessee Sectionalism from Statehood to Secession*. Johnson City: East Tennessee State University Press, 1965.

Lamoreaux, Naomi. *The Great Merger Movement in American Business, 1895–1904*. Cambridge: Cambridge University Press, 1985.

Lander, Ernest M., Jr. "Manufacturing in South Carolina, 1815–60." *Business History Review* 28 (March 1954): 60–66.

Lanoue, David J. "Retrospective and Prospective Voting in Presidential-Year Elections." *Political Research Quarterly* 47 (March 1994): 193–205.

Lasser, William. "The Supreme Court in Periods of Critical Realignment." *Journal of Politics* 47 (November 1985): 1174–87.

Laurie, Bruce. *Artisans into Workers: Labor in Nineteenth Century America*. New York: Hill and Wang, 1988.

Lebergott, Stanley. *The Americans: An Economic Record*. New York: W. W. Norton, 1984.

Leblan, David A. "Property Rights, Democracy, and Economic Growth." *Political Research Quarterly* 49 (March 1996): 5–26.

Lee, Susan Previant, and Peter Passell. *A New Economic View of American History*. New York: W. W. Norton, 1979.

Leigley, Jan E., and Jonathan Nagler. "Socioeconomic Class Bias in Turnout, 1964–1988: The Voters Remain the Same." *American Political Science Review* 86 (September 1992): 725–36.

Levine, Bruce. *Half Slave and Half Free: The Roots of Civil War*. New York: Hill and Wang, 1992.

Levy, Leonard W., and Dennis J. Mahoney, eds. *The Framing and Ratification of the Constitution*. New York: Macmillan, 1987.

Lewis, Ronald L. *Coal, Iron, and Slaves: Industrial Slavery in Maryland and Virginia, 1715–1865*. Westport, Conn.: Greenwood Press, 1979.

Lewis, Walker. *Without Fear or Favor: A Biography of Chief Justice Roger Brooke Taney*. Boston: Houghton Mifflin, 1965.

Lewis-Beck, Michael, and Peverill Squire. "The Transformation of the American State: The New Era–New Deal Test." *Journal of Politics* 53 (February 1991): 106–21.

Libecap, Gary D. *Contracting for Property Rights*. Cambridge: Cambridge University Press, 1989.

Licht, Walter. *Industrializing America: The Nineteenth Century*. Baltimore: Johns Hopkins University Press, 1995.

Lichtenberg, Frank R., and Donald Diegel. "The Impact of R&D Investment on Productivity —New Evidence Using Linked R&D-LRD Data." *Economic Inquiry* 29 (April 1991): 203–25.

Lichtman, Allan J. "The End of Realignment Theory? Toward a New Research Program for American Political History." *Historical Methods* 15 (Fall 1982): 170–88.

Linden, Fabian. "Economic Democracy in the Slave South: An Appraisal of Some Recent Views." *Journal of Negro History* 21 (April 1946): 140–89.

Litwack, Leon F. *North of Slavery: The Negro in the Free States, 1790–1860*. Chicago: University of Chicago Press, 1961.

Livesay, Harold C. *Andrew Carnegie and the Rise of Big Business*. Boston: Little, Brown, 1975.

Lofton, Williston H. "Abolition and Labor." *Journal of Negro History* 33 (July 1948): 254–69.

Lurgahi, Raimondo. "The Civil War and the Modernization of American Society: Social Structure and Industrial Revolution in the Old South before and during the War." *Civil War History* 18 (September 1972): 230–50.

Luthin, Reinhard Henry. *The First Lincoln Campaign.* Cambridge, Mass.: Harvard University Press, 1944.

McChesney, Fred S. "Government as Definer of Property Rights: Indian Lands, Ethnic Externalities, and Bureaucratic Budgets." In *Property Rights and Indian Economies,* edited by Terry L. Anderson, 109–46. Boston: Rowman and Littlefield, 1992.

McCormick, Richard L. *The Party Period and Public Policy: American Politics from the Age of Jackson to the Progressive Era.* New York: Oxford University Press, 1986.

——. "The Realignment Synthesis in American History." *Journal of Interdisciplinary History* 13 (Summer 1982): 85–105.

McCormick, Richard P. *The Presidential Game: The Origins of American Presidential Politics.* New York: Oxford University Press, 1982.

McCoy, Drew. *The Elusive Republic: Political Economy in Jeffersonian America.* Chapel Hill: University of North Carolina Press, 1980.

McCraw, Thomas K. "Rethinking the Trust Question." In *Regulation in Perspective: Historical Essays,* edited by Thomas K. McCraw, 1–55. Cambridge, Mass.: Harvard University Press, 1981.

——, ed. *Regulation in Perspective: Historical Essays.* Cambridge, Mass.: Harvard University Press, 1981.

McCurry, Stephanie. *Masters of Small Worlds: Yeoman Households, Gender Relations, and the Political Culture of the Antebellum South Carolina Low Country.* New York: Oxford University Press, 1995.

McDonald, Forrest. *States' Rights and the Union: Imperium in Imperio, 1776–1876.* Lawrence: University Press of Kansas, 2000.

McDonald, Forrest, and Grady McWhiney. "The South from Self-Sufficiency to Peonage: An Interpretation." *American Historical Review* 85 (December 1980): 1095–118.

McFeely, William S. *Yankee Stepfather: General O. O. Howard and the Freedmen.* New Haven: Yale University Press, 1968.

McGerr, Michael E. *The Decline of Popular Politics: The American North, 1865–1928.* New York: Oxford University Press, 1986.

McIlwaine, Charles Howard. *The American Revolution: A Constitutional Interpretation.* New York: Macmillan, 1923.

McManus, Edgar J. *A History of Negro Slavery in New York.* Syracuse: Syracuse University Press, 1966.

McManus, Michael J. " 'Freedom and Liberty First and the Union Afterwards': State Rights and the Wisconsin Republican Party, 1854–1861." In *Union and Emancipation: Essays on Politics and Race in the Civil War Era,* edited by David Blight and Brooks D. Simpson, 29–56. Kent, Ohio: Kent State University Press, 1997.

Macmillan, Malcolm Cook. *Constitutional Development in Alabama, 1798–1901: A Study in Politics, the Negro, and Sectionalism.* Chapel Hill: University of North Carolina Press, 1955.

Macpherson, C. B. *The Political Theory of Possessive Individualism: Hobbes to Locke.* Oxford: Clarendon Press, 1962.

McPherson, James M. "Antebellum Southern Exceptionalism: A New Look at an Old Question." *Civil War History* 29 (September 1983): 230–44.

——. *Ordeal by Fire.* 2d ed. New York: Alfred A. Knopf, 1992.

McWhiney, Grady. *Cracker Culture: Celtic Ways in the Old South.* Tuscaloosa: University of Alabama Press, 1988.

McWilliams, Abagail, Thomas A. Turk, and Asghar Zardkoohi. "Antitrust Policy and Mergers: The Wealth Effect of Supreme Court Decisions." *Economic Inquiry* 31 (October 1993): 517–33.

Maizlish, Stephen E. *The Triumph of Sectionalism: The Transformation of Ohio Politics, 1844–1856*. Kent, Ohio: Kent State University Press, 1983.

Maizlish, Stephen E., and John J. Kushma, eds. *Essays on American Antebellum Politics, 1840–1860*. College Station: Texas A&M University Press, 1982.

Majewski, John. *A House Dividing: Economic Development in Pennsylvania and Virginia before the Civil War*. New York: Cambridge University Press, 2000.

Malone, Dumas. *The Public Life of Thomas Cooper, 1783–1839*. New Haven: Yale University Press, 1926.

Mandel, Bernard. *Labor Free and Slave: Workingmen and the Anti-Slavery Movement in the United States*. New York: Associated Authors, 1955.

Margo, Robert A. *Wages and Labor Markets in the United States, 1820–1860*. Chicago: University of Chicago Press, 2000.

Martin, Waldo E., Jr. *The Mind of Frederick Douglass*. Chapel Hill: University of North Carolina Press, 1984.

Mason, Virginia. *The Public Life and Diplomatic Correspondence of James M. Mason, with Some Personal History*. New York: Neale Publishing, 1906.

Matthews, Richard K. *The Radical Politics of Thomas Jefferson: A Revisionist View*. Lawrence: University Press of Kansas, 1984.

May, Robert E. *John A. Quitman: Old South Crusader*. Baton Rouge: Louisiana State University Press, 1985.

——. "Psychobiography and Secession: The Southern Radical as Maladjusted 'Outsider.'" *Civil War History* 34 (March 1988): 46–69.

——. *The Southern Dream of a Caribbean Empire, 1854–1861*. Baton Rouge: Louisiana State University Press, 1973.

Mayes, Edward. *Lucius Q. C. Lamar: His Life, Times, and Speeches, 1828–1893*. 2d ed. Nashville: Publishing House of the Methodist Episcopal Church, 1896.

Mayfield, John. *Rehearsal for Republicanism: Free Soil and the Politics of Antislavery*. Port Washington, N.Y.: Kennikat Press, 1980.

Merritt, Elizabeth. *James Henry Hammond, 1807–1864*. Baltimore: Johns Hopkins University Press, 1923.

Milkis, Sidney M. "New Deal Party Politics, Administrative Reform, and the Transformation of the American Constitution." In *The New Deal and Its Legacy: Critique and Reappraisal*, edited by Robert Eden, 123–54. Westport, Conn.: Greenwood Press, 1989.

Miller, Gary J. *Managerial Dilemmas: The Political Economy of Hierarchy*. Cambridge: Cambridge University Press, 1992.

Miller, John C. *The Federalist Era, 1789–1801*. New York: Harper and Brothers, 1960.

——. "Hamilton: Democracy and Monarchy." In *Alexander Hamilton: A Profile*, edited by Jacob E. Cooke, 150–65. New York: Hill and Wang, 1967.

——. *The Wolf by the Ears: Thomas Jefferson and Slavery*. New York: Free Press, 1977.

Miller, Randall Martin. *The Cotton Mill Movement in Antebellum Alabama*. New York: Arno Press, 1978.

Miller, William Lee. *Arguing about Slavery: The Great Battle in the United States Congress*. New York: Alfred A. Knopf, 1996.

Milton, George Fort. *The Eve of Conflict: Stephen A. Douglas and the Needless War*. Boston: Houghton Mifflin, 1934.

Mitchell, Betty L. *Edmund Ruffin: A Biography*. Bloomington: Indiana University Press, 1981.

Moore, Barrington, Jr. *Social Origins of Dictatorship and Democracy: Lord and Peasant in the Making of the Modern World*. Boston: Beacon Press, 1966.

Moore, John Hebron. "Economic Conditions of Mississippi on the Eve of the Civil War." *Journal of Mississippi History* 22 (July 1960): 167–91.

Morgan, Edmund S. *American Slavery, American Freedom: The Ordeal of Colonial Virginia.* New York: W. W. Norton, 1975.

——. *The Challenge of the American Revolution.* New York: W. W. Norton, 1976.

Morris, Christopher. *Becoming Southern: The Evolution of a Way of Life, Warren County and Vicksburg, Mississippi, 1770–1860.* New York: Oxford University Press, 1995.

Morris, Thomas D. *Free Men All: The Personal Liberty Laws of the North, 1780–1861.* Baltimore: Johns Hopkins University Press, 1974.

——. *Southern Slavery and the Law, 1619–1860.* Chapel Hill: University of North Carolina Press, 1996.

Morrison, Chaplain W. *Democratic Politics and Sectionalism: The Wilmot Proviso Controversy.* Chapel Hill: University of North Carolina Press, 1967.

Morrison, Michael A. *Slavery and the American West: The Eclipse of Manifest Destiny and the Coming of the Civil War.* Chapel Hill: University of North Carolina Press, 1997.

Mowery, David C., and Nathan Rosenberg. *Technology and the Pursuit of Economic Growth.* Cambridge: Cambridge University Press, 1989.

Mulkern, John R. *The Know-Nothing Party in Massachusetts: The Rise and Fall of a People's Movement.* Boston: Northeastern University Press, 1990.

Murphy, James B. *L. Q. C. Lamar: Pragmatic Patriot.* Baton Rouge: Louisiana State University Press, 1973.

Nardulli, Peter F. "The Concept of a Critical Realignment, Electoral Behavior, and Political Change." *American Political Science Review* 84 (March 1995): 10–22.

Nash, Gary B. *Red, White, and Black: The Peoples of Early America.* 2d ed. Englewood Cliffs, N.J.: Prentice-Hall, 1982.

Nelson, William E. *Americanization of Common Law: The Impact of Legal Change on Massachusetts Society, 1760–1830.* Cambridge, Mass.: Harvard University Press, 1975.

Nevins, Allan. *The Emergence of Lincoln.* 2 vols. New York: Charles Scribner's Sons, 1950.

——. *Ordeal of the Union.* 2 vols. New York: Charles Scribner's Sons, 1947.

Nichols, Roy Franklin. *The Disruption of American Democracy.* New York: Macmillan, 1948.

Niven, John. *John C. Calhoun and the Price of Union: A Biography.* Baton Rouge: Louisiana State University Press, 1988.

North, Douglass C. *Institutions, Institutional Change and Economic Performance.* Cambridge: Cambridge University Press, 1990.

——. *Structure and Change in Economic History.* New York: W. W. Norton, 1981.

North, Douglass C., and Barry R. Weingast. "Constitutions and Commitment: The Evolution of Institutions Governing Public Choice in Seventeenth-Century England." *Journal of Economic History* 49 (December 1989): 803–32.

Norton, Anne. *Alternative Americas: A Reading of Antebellum Political Culture.* Chicago: University of Chicago Press, 1986.

Norton, Clarence C. *Democratic Party in Ante-Bellum North Carolina, 1835–1861.* Chapel Hill: University of North Carolina Press, 1930.

Novack, William J. *The People's Welfare: Law and Regulation in Nineteenth-Century America.* Chapel Hill: University of North Carolina Press, 1996.

Nozick, Robert. *Anarchy, State, and Utopia.* New York: Basic Books, 1974.

Nye, Russel B. *Fettered Freedom: Civil Liberties and the Slavery Controversy.* 2d ed. Urbana: University of Illinois Press, 1972.

Oakes, James. "From Republicanism to Liberalism: Ideological Change and the Crisis of the Old South." *American Quarterly* 37 (Fall 1985): 551–71.

——. *The Ruling Race: A History of American Slaveholders.* New York: Alfred A. Knopf, 1982.

——. *Slavery and Freedom: An Interpretation of the Old South.* New York: Alfred A. Knopf, 1990.

O'Connor, Thomas. *Lords of the Loom: The Cotton Whigs and the Coming of the Civil War.* New York: Charles Scribner's Sons, 1968.

Olsen, Christopher J. *Political Culture and Secession in Mississippi: Masculinity, Honor, and the Antiparty Tradition, 1830–1860.* New York: Oxford University Press, 2000.

Olson, Mancur. "Dictatorship, Democracy, and Development." *American Political Science Review* 87 (September 1993): 567–76.

Osborne, D. F. "The Last Hope of the South—To Establish a Principle." *Georgia Historical Quarterly* 15 (September 1931): 225–51.

Owsley, Frank L. "The Fundamental Cause of the Civil War: Egocentric Sectionalism." *Journal of Southern History* 7 (February 1941): 3–18.

——. *Plain Folk of the Old South.* Baton Rouge: Louisiana State University Press, 1949.

Painter, Nell Irvin. *Standing at Armageddon: The United States, 1877–1919.* New York: W. W. Norton, 1987.

Paludan, Philip Shaw. *A People's Contest: The Union and Civil War, 1861–1865.* 2d ed. Lawrence: University Press of Kansas, 1996.

Parel, Anthony, and Thomas Flanagan, eds. *Theories of Property: Aristotle to the Present.* Waterloo, Canada: Wilfrid Laurier University Press, 1979.

Parish, Peter J. *The American Civil War.* New York: Holmes and Meier, 1975.

——. *Slavery: History and Historians.* New York: Harper and Row, 1989.

Parker, William N. *Commerce, Cotton, and Westward Expansion, 1820–1860.* Chicago: Scott, Foresman, 1964.

Paul, Ellen Frankel, and Howard Dickman, eds. *Liberty, Property, and the Foundations of the American Constitution.* Albany: State University of New York Press, 1989.

Pearce, Haywood J., Jr. *Benjamin H. Hill: Secession and Reconstruction.* Chicago: University of Chicago Press, 1928.

Pease, William, and Jane Pease. *The Fugitive Slave Law and Anthony Burns: A Problem in Law Enforcement.* Philadelphia: J. B. Lippincott, 1975.

Pessen, Edward. "How Different from Each Other Were the Antebellum North and South?" *American Historical Review* 85 (December 1980): 1119–49.

——. *Most Uncommon Jacksonians: The Radical Leaders of the Early Labor Movement.* Albany: State University of New York Press, 1967.

Peterson, Merrill D. *The Great Triumvirate: Webster, Clay, and Calhoun.* New York: Oxford University Press, 1987.

Phillips, Ulrich Bonnell. *American Negro Slavery: A Survey of the Supply, Employment and Control of Negro Labor as Determined by the Plantation Regime.* 1918. Reprint, New York: Peter Smith, 1952.

——. *The Course of the South to Secession.* Edited by E. Merton Coulter. New York: D. Appleton-Century, 1939.

——. *Life and Labor in the Old South.* Boston: Little, Brown, 1963.

——. *The Life of Robert Toombs.* New York: Macmillan, 1913.

——. *The Slave Economy of the Old South: Selected Essays in Economic and Social History.* Edited by Eugene D. Genovese. Baton Rouge: Louisiana State University Press, 1968.

Pisani, Donald J. "Promotion and Regulation: Constitutionalism and the American Economy." *Journal of American History* 74 (December 1987): 73–101.

Pocock, J. G. A. "The Mobility of Property and the Rise of Eighteenth-Century Sociology." In *Theories of Property: Aristotle to the Present*, edited by Anthony Parel and Thomas Flanagan, 144–66. Waterloo, Canada: Wilfrid Laurier University Press, 1979.

Porter, Glenn. *The Rise of Big Business, 1860–1910*. Arlington Heights, Ill.: Harlan Davidson, 1973.

Potter, David M. *The Impending Crisis, 1848–1861*. Edited by Don E. Fehrenbacher. New York: Harper and Row, 1976.

——. *The South and the Sectional Conflict*. Baton Rouge: Louisiana State University Press, 1968.

Preyer, Norris. "The Historian, the Slave, and the Ante-Bellum Textile Industry." *Journal of Negro History* 46 (April 1961): 67–82.

Rable, George C. *But There Was No Peace: The Role of Violence in the Politics of Reconstruction*. Athens: University Press of Georgia, 1984.

Rainwater, Percy L. *Mississippi Storm Center of Secession, 1856–1861*. Baton Rouge: Louisiana State University Press, 1938.

Ramsdell, Charles W. "The Natural Limits of Slavery Expansion." *Mississippi Valley Historical Review* 16 (September 1929): 151–71.

Randall, James G. "The Blundering Generation." *Mississippi Valley Historical Review* 27 (June 1940): 3–28.

Ransom, Roger L. *Conflict and Compromise: The Political Economy of Slavery, Emancipation, and the American Civil War*. Cambridge: Cambridge University Press, 1989.

Ransom, Roger L., and Richard Sutch. "Capitalists without Capital: The Burden of Slavery and the Impact of Emancipation." *Agricultural History* 62 (Summer 1988): 133–60.

——. *One Kind of Freedom: The Economic Consequences of Emancipation*. Cambridge: Cambridge University Press, 1977.

Ratcliffe, Donald J. *Party Spirit in a Frontier Republic: Democratic Politics in Ohio, 1793–1821*. Columbus: Ohio State University Press, 1998.

Rawley, James A. *Race and Politics: "Bleeding Kansas" and the Coming of the Civil War*. Philadelphia: J. B. Lippincott, 1969.

Rayback, Joseph G. "The American Workingman and the Antislavery Crusade." *Journal of Economic History* 3 (November 1943): 156–57.

Reck, Andrew J. "Moral Philosophy and the Framing of the Constitution." In *Liberty, Property, and the Foundations of the American Constitution*, edited by Ellen Frankel Paul and Howard Dickman, 23–42. Albany: State University of New York Press, 1989.

Reid, Brian Holden. *The Origins of the American Civil War*. London: Longman, 1996.

Reid, John Phillip. *The Concept of Liberty in the Age of the American Revolution*. Chicago: University of Chicago Press, 1988.

Reidy, Joseph P. *From Slavery to Agrarian Capitalism in the Cotton Plantation South: Central Georgia, 1800–1880*. Chapel Hill: University of North Carolina Press, 1992.

Remini, Robert V. *The Legacy of Andrew Jackson: Essays on Democracy, Indian Removal and Slavery*. Baton Rouge: Louisiana State University Press, 1988.

Renda, Lex. *Running on the Record: Civil War–Era Politics in New Hampshire*. Charlottesville: University of Virginia Press, 1997.

Reynolds, John F., and Richard L. McCormick. "Outlawing 'Treachery': Split Tickets and Ballot Laws in New York and New Jersey, 1880–1910." *Journal of American History* 7 (March 1986): 835–58.

Richards, Leonard L. *The Slave Power: The Free North and Southern Domination, 1780–1860*. Baton Rouge: Louisiana State University Press, 2000.

Richardson, Heather C. *The Death of Reconstruction: Race, Labor, and Politics in the Post–Civil War North, 1865–1901*. Cambridge, Mass.: Harvard University Press, 2001.

——. *The Greatest Nation of the Earth: Republican Economic Policies during the Civil War.* Cambridge, Mass.: Harvard University Press, 1997.

Riker, William H., and Itai Sened. "A Political Theory of Property Rights." *American Journal of Political Science* 35 (November 1991): 951–69.

Robinson, Donald L. *Slavery in the Structure of American Politics, 1765–1820.* New York: Harcourt Brace Jovanovich, 1971.

Rodgers, Daniel T. "Republicanism: The Career of a Concept." *Journal of American History* 79 (June 1992): 11–38.

Roemer, John E. *A General Theory of Exploitation and Class.* Cambridge, Mass.: Harvard University Press, 1982.

Romer, Paul M. "Endogenous Technological Change." *Journal of Political Economy* 100 (October 1990): S71–S102.

——. "Increasing Returns and Long-Run Economy." *Journal of Political Economy* 94 (October 1986): 1002–37.

Rosenberg, Nathan. *Perspectives on Technology.* Cambridge: Cambridge University Press, 1976.

Rosenbloom, Joshua L. "The Challenge of Economic Maturity: New England, 1880–1940." In *Engines of Enterprise: An Economic History of New England,* edited by Peter Temin, 153–99. Cambridge, Mass.: Harvard University Press, 2000.

Rostow, W. W. *The Stages of Economic Growth: A Non-Communist Manifesto.* Cambridge: Cambridge University Press, 1965.

Rothstein, Morton. "The Antebellum South as a Dual Economy: A Tentative Hypothesis." *Agricultural History* 41 (October 1967): 373–82.

Russel, Robert R. "Constitutional Doctrines with Regard to Slavery in the Territories." *Journal of Southern History* 32 (November 1966): 466–86.

——. *Economic Aspects of Southern Sectionalism, 1840–1861.* Urbana: University of Illinois Press, 1923.

——. "The Effects of Slavery upon Nonslaveholders in the Ante Bellum South." *Agricultural History* 15 (April 1941): 112–26.

——. *A History of the American Economic System.* New York: Appleton-Century-Crofts, 1964.

Salter, William. *The Life of James W. Grimes. . . .* New York: D. Appleton, 1876.

Saunders, Robert, Jr. *John Archibald Campbell, Southern Moderate, 1811–1899.* Tuscaloosa: University of Alabama Press, 1997.

"Saving Endangered Species: Wildlife and Property Rights." *Congressional Digest* 75 (March 1996): 68–85.

Schlatter, Richard. *Private Property: The History of an Idea.* New Brunswick, N.J.: Rutgers University Press, 1951.

Schlesinger, Arthur M., Jr. *The Age of Jackson.* Boston: Little, Brown, 1949.

Schlüter, Herman. *Lincoln, Labor, and Slavery: A Chapter from the Social History of America.* 1913. Reprint, New York: Russell and Russell, 1965.

Schmitz, Mark D., and Donald F. Schaefer. "Slavery, Freedom, and the Elasticity of Substitution." *Explorations in Economic History* 15 (July 1978): 332–34.

Schott, Thomas E. *Alexander H. Stephens of Georgia: A Biography.* Baton Rouge: Louisiana State University Press, 1988.

Schroeder, John H. *Mr. Polk's War: American Opposition and Dissent, 1846–1848.* Madison: University of Wisconsin Press, 1973.

Scott, William B. *In Pursuit of Happiness: American Conceptions of Property from the Seventeenth to the Twentieth Century.* Bloomington: Indiana University Press, 1977.

Sellers, Charles G. *The Market Revolution: Jacksonian America, 1815–1846*. New York: Oxford University Press, 1991.

——, ed. *The Southerner as American*. Chapel Hill: University of North Carolina Press, 1960.

Sen, Amartya K. "Rational Fools: A Critique of the Behavioral Foundations of Economic Theory." *Philosophy and Public Affairs* 6 (Summer 1977): 317–44.

Shade, William G. *Democratizing the Old Dominion: Virginia and the Second Party System, 1824–1861*. Charlottesville: University Press of Virginia, 1996.

——. "Society and Politics in Antebellum Virginia's Southside." *Journal of Southern History* 53 (May 1987): 188–92.

Shafer, Byron E. "The Notion of an Electoral Order: The Structure of Electoral Politics at the Accession of George Bush." In *The End of Realignment? Interpreting American Electoral Eras*, edited by Byron E. Shafer, 38–43. Madison: University of Wisconsin Press, 1991.

——, ed. *The End of Realignment? Interpreting American Electoral Eras*. Madison: University of Wisconsin Press, 1991.

Sharp, James Rogers. *American Politics in the Early Republic: The New Nation in Crisis*. New Haven: Yale University Press, 1993.

Shenfield, Arthur. "The New Deal and the Supreme Court." In *The New Deal and Its Legacy: Critique and Reappraisal*, edited by Robert Eden, 167–76. Westport, Conn.: Greenwood Press, 1989.

Shirley, Michael W. "Yeoman Culture and Millworker Protest in Antebellum Salem, North Carolina." *Journal of Southern History* 57 (August 1991): 427–57.

Shore, Lawrence. *Southern Capitalists: The Ideological Leadership of an Elite, 1832–1885*. Chapel Hill: University of North Carolina Press, 1986.

Shugg, Roger W. *Origins of Class Struggle in Louisiana: A Social History of White Farmers and Laborers during Slavery and After, 1840–1875*. 1939. Reprint, Baton Rouge: Louisiana State University Press, 1966.

Siegel, Frederick F. "Artisans and Immigrants in the Politics of Late Antebellum Georgia." *Civil War History* 27 (September 1981): 221–30.

——. *The Roots of Southern Distinctiveness: Tobacco and Society in Danville, Virginia, 1780–1865*. Chapel Hill: University of North Carolina Press, 1984.

Silbey, Joel. *The American Political Nation, 1838–1893*. Stanford: Stanford University Press, 1991.

——. "Beyond Realignment and Realignment Theory: American Political Eras, 1789–1989." In *The End of Realignment? Interpreting American Electoral Eras*, edited by Byron E. Shafer, 3–23. Madison: University of Wisconsin Press, 1991.

——. *The Partisan Imperative: The Dynamics of American Politics before the Civil War*. New York: Oxford University Press, 1985.

——. "The Surge of Republican Power: Partisan Antipathy, American Social Conflict, and the Coming of the Civil War." In *Essays on American Antebellum Politics, 1840–1860*, edited by Stephen E. Maizlish and John J. Kushma, 199–229. College Station: University of Texas A&M Press, 1982.

Silbey, Joel, Allan G. Bogue, and William H. Flanigan, eds. *The History of American Electoral Behavior*. Princeton: Princeton University Press, 1978.

Simms, Henry H. *A Decade of Sectional Controversy, 1851–1861*. Chapel Hill: University of North Carolina Press, 1942.

Simpson, John E. *Howell Cobb: The Politics of Ambition*. Chicago: Adams Press, 1973.

Sinha, Manisha. *The Counterrevolution of Slavery: Politics and Ideology in Antebellum South Carolina*. Chapel Hill: University of North Carolina Press, 2000.

Sklar, Martin J. *The Corporate Reconstruction of American Capitalism, 1890–1906: The Market, the Law, and Politics*. Cambridge: Cambridge University Press, 1988.

Skocpol, Theda. *Protecting Soldiers and Mothers: The Political Origin of Social Policy in the United States*. Cambridge, Mass.: Harvard University Press, 1992.

Smiley, David L. *Lion of White Hall: The Life of Cassius M. Clay*. Madison: University of Wisconsin Press, 1962.

Smith, Elbert B. *The Presidencies of Zachary Taylor and Millard Fillmore*. Lawrence: University Press of Kansas, 1988.

Smith, Robert Worthington. "Was Slavery Profitable in the Ante-Bellum South?" *Agricultural History* 20 (January 1946): 62–64.

Smith, William Ernest. *The Francis Preston Blair Family in Politics*. 2 vols. New York: Oxford University Press, 1933.

Sobel, Robert. *The Age of Giant Corporations: A Microeconomic History of American Business, 1914–1970*. Westport, Conn.: Greenwood Press, 1972.

Soltow, Lee. *Men and Wealth in the United States, 1850–1860*. New Haven: Yale University Press, 1975.

Sowell, Thomas. *The Economics and Politics of Race: An International Perspective*. New York: W. Morrow, 1983.

Spahr, Charles B. *An Essay on the Present Distribution of Wealth in the United States*. New York: Thomas Y. Crowell, 1896.

Stampp, Kenneth M. *The Era of Reconstruction, 1865–1877*. New York: Vintage, 1965.

——. *The Imperiled Union: Essays on the Background of the Civil War*. New York: Oxford University Press, 1980.

——. *The Peculiar Institution: Slavery in the Ante-Bellum South*. 1956. Reprint, New York: Alfred A. Knopf, 1972.

Stanley, Amy Dru. *From Bondage to Contract: Wage Labor, Marriage, and the Market in the Age of Slave Emancipation*. Cambridge: Cambridge University Press, 1998.

Starobin, Robert S. *Industrial Slavery in the Old South*. New York: Oxford University Press, 1970.

Stegmaier, Mark J. *Texas, New Mexico, and the Compromise of 1850: Boundary Dispute and Sectional Crisis*. Kent, Ohio: Kent State University Press, 1996.

Steinfeld, Robert J. *The Invention of Free Labor: The Employment Relation in English and American Law and Culture, 1350–1870*. Chapel Hill: University of North Carolina Press, 1991.

Steinfeld, Robert J., and Stanley L. Engerman. "Labor—Free or Coerced? A Historical Reassessment of Differences and Similarities." In *Free and Unfree Labor: The Debate Continues*, edited by Tom Brass and Marcel Van der Linden, 107–26. Bern: Peter Lang, 1997.

Stewart, James Brewer. *Holy Warriors: The Abolitionists and American Society*. 2d ed. New York: Hill and Wang, 1996.

Stromberg, Roland S. *Democracy: A Short, Analytical History*. Armonk, N.Y.: M. E. Sharpe, 1996.

Sundquist, James L. *Dynamics of the Party System: Alignment and Realignment of Political Parties in the United States*. Washington, D.C.: Brookings Institute, 1983.

Sutch, Edward. "Profitability of Ante-Bellum Slavery—Revisited." In *Did Slavery Pay? Readings in the Economics of Black Slavery in the United States*, edited by Hugh G. J. Aitken, 221–41. Boston: Houghton Mifflin, 1971.

Sward, Keith. *The Legend of Henry Ford*. New York: Atheneum, 1968.

Sydnor, Charles S. *The Development of Southern Sectionalism, 1819–1848*. Baton Rouge: Louisiana State University Press, 1948.

——. *Slavery in Mississippi*. New York: D. Appleton-Century, 1933.

Takaki, Ronald T. *A Pro-Slavery Crusade: The Agitation to Reopen the African Slave Trade.* New York: Free Press, 1971.

Taylor, George Rogers. *The Transportation Revolution.* New York: Rinehart, 1951.

Taylor, George Rogers, and Irene D. Neu. *The American Railroad Network, 1861–1890.* Cambridge, Mass.: Harvard University Press, 1956.

Taylor, Rosser H. *Ante-Bellum South Carolina: A Social and Cultural History.* 1942. Reprint, New York: Da Capo Press, 1970.

Taylor, William R. *Cavalier and Yankee: The Old South and American National Character.* 1957. Reprint, New York: Harper and Row, 1969.

Temin, Peter. *Causal Factors in American Economic Growth in the Nineteenth Century.* Houndmills: Macmillan, 1975.

Thornton, J. Mills, III. *Politics and Power in a Slave Society: Alabama, 1800–1860.* Baton Rouge: Louisiana State University Press, 1977.

Tise, Larry E. *Proslavery: A History of the Defense of Slavery in America, 1701–1840.* Athens: University of Georgia Press, 1987.

Trilling, Richard J., and Bruce A. Campbell. "Toward a Theory of Realignment: An Introduction." In *Realignment in American Politics: Toward a Theory,* edited by Bruce A. Campbell and Richard J. Trilling, 3–20. Austin: University of Texas Press, 1980.

Tunnell, Ted. *Crucible of Reconstruction: War, Radicalism and Race in Louisiana, 1862–1877.* Baton Rouge: Louisiana State University Press, 1984.

Turner, Mary, ed. *From Chattel Slaves to Wage Slaves: The Dynamics of Labour Bargaining in the Americas.* London: James Curry, 1995.

Tushnet, Mark V. *The American Law of Slavery, 1810–1860: Considerations of Humanity and Interest.* Princeton: Princeton University Press, 1981.

Tylecote, Andrew. *The Long Wave in the World Economy: The Current Crisis in Historical Perspective.* London: Routledge, 1991.

Umbeck, John. "Might Makes Rights: A Theory of the Formation and Initial Distribution of Property Rights." *Economic Inquiry* 19 (January 1981): 38–59.

Vatter, Harold. *The Drive to Industrial Maturity: The U.S. Economy, 1860–1914.* Westport, Conn.: Greenwood Press, 1975.

Vogel, David. "The 'New' Social Regulation in Historical and Comparative Perspective." In *Regulation in Perspective: Historical Essays,* edited by Thomas K. McCraw, 155–86. Cambridge, Mass.: Harvard University Press, 1981.

Wade, Richard C. *Slavery in the Cities: The South, 1820–1860.* New York: Oxford University Press, 1964.

Wahl, Jenny Bourne. *The Bondsman's Burden: An Economic Analysis of the Common Law of Southern Slavery.* Cambridge: Cambridge University Press, 1998.

Walters, Ronald G. *The Antislavery Appeal: American Abolitionism after 1830.* Baltimore: Johns Hopkins University Press, 1976.

Walther, Eric H. *The Fire-Eaters.* Baton Rouge: Louisiana State University Press, 1992.

Watson, Harry L. *Liberty and Power: The Politics of Jacksonian America.* New York: Noonday Press, 1990.

Weir, Margaret, and Theda Skocpol. "State Structures and the Possibilities for 'Keynesian' Responses to the Great Depression in Sweden, Britain, and the United States." In *Bringing the State Back In,* edited by Peter B. Evans, Dietrich Rueschemeyer, and Theda Skocpol, 107–63. Cambridge: Cambridge University Press, 1985.

Welter, Rush. *The Mind of America, 1820–1860.* New York: Columbia University Press, 1975.

Westcott, Richard R. *New Men, New Issues: The Formation of the Republican Party in Maine.* Portland: Maine Historical Society, 1986.

Wettergreen, John A. "The Regulatory Policy of the New Deal." In *The New Deal and Its Legacy: Critique and Reappraisal*, edited by Robert Eden, 199–213. Westport, Conn.: Greenwood Press, 1989.

Wiebe, Robert H. *The Opening of American Society: From the Adoption of the Constitution to the Eve of Disunion*. New York: Vintage Books, 1984.

——. *The Search for Order, 1877–1920*. New York: Hill and Wang, 1967.

Wiecek, William M. *Constitutional Development in a Modernizing Society: The United States, 1803 to 1917*. Washington, D.C.: American Historical Association, 1985.

——. "Slavery and Abolition before the United States Supreme Court, 1820–1860." *Journal of American History* 65 (June 1978): 34–59.

——. *The Sources of Antislavery Constitutionalism in America, 1760–1848*. Ithaca: Cornell University Press, 1977.

——. "The Witch at the Christening: Slavery and the Constitution's Origins." In *The Framing and Ratification of the Constitution*, edited by Leonard W. Levy and Dennis J. Mahoney, 167–84. New York: Macmillan, 1987.

Wilentz, Sean. *Chants Democratic: New York City and the Rise of the American Working Class, 1788–1850*. New York: Oxford University Press, 1984.

Williams, T. Harry. *Romance and Realism in Southern Politics*. Athens: University of Georgia Press, 1961.

Williamson, Chilton. *American Suffrage: From Property to Democracy, 1760–1860*. Princeton: Princeton University Press, 1960.

Wills, Garry. *Inventing America: Jefferson's Declaration of Independence*. Garden City, N.Y.: Doubleday, 1978.

Wiltse, Charles M. *John C. Calhoun: Nationalist, 1782–1828*. Indianapolis: Bobbs-Merrill, 1944.

——. *John C. Calhoun: Nullifier, 1829–1839*. Indianapolis: Bobbs-Merrill, 1949.

Winters, Donald L. "'Plain Folk' of the Old South Reexamined: Economic Democracy in Tennessee." *Journal of Southern History* 53 (November 1987): 565–86.

Wish, Harvey. *George Fitzhugh: Propagandist of the Old South*. Baton Rouge: Louisiana State University Press, 1943.

Wolff, Richard D., and Stephen A. Resnick. *Economics: Marxian versus Neoclassical*. Baltimore: Johns Hopkins University Press, 1987.

Wood, Betty. *The Origins of American Slavery: Freedom and Bondage in the English Colonies*. New York: Hill and Wang, 1997.

Wood, Gordon S. "The Enemy Is Us: Democratic Capitalism in the Early Republic." In *Wages of Independence: Capitalism in the Early American Republic*, edited by Paul A. Gilje, 137–53. Madison, Wisc.: Madison House, 1997.

Woods, James M. *Rebellion and Realignment: Arkansas's Road to Secession*. Fayetteville: University of Arkansas Press, 1987.

Wooster, Ralph A. *The People in Power: Courthouse and Statehouse in the Lower South, 1850–1860*. Knoxville: University of Tennessee Press, 1969.

Wright, Benjamin Franklin. *American Interpretations of Natural Law: A Study in the History of Political Thought*. 1931. Reprint, New York: Russell and Russell, 1962.

Wright, Gavin. "Economic Democracy and the Concentration of Agricultural Wealth in the Cotton South." *Agricultural History* 44 (January 1970): 72–85.

——. *Old South, New South: Revolutions in the Southern Economy since the Civil War*. New York: Basic Books, 1986.

——. *The Political Economy of the Cotton South: Households, Markets, and Wealth in the Nineteenth Century*. New York: W. W. Norton, 1978.

——. "Prosperity, Progress, and American Slavery." In *Reckoning with Slavery: A Critical Study in the Quantitative History of American Negro Slavery*, by Paul David et al., 302–38. New York: Oxford University Press, 1976.

——. "Slavery and the Cotton Boom." *Explorations in Economic History* 12 (October 1975): 439–51.

Wyatt-Brown, Bertram. *Shaping of Southern Culture: Honor, Grace, and War, 1760s–1880s.* Chapel Hill: University of North Carolina Press, 2001.

——. "Slavery's Cross Resurrected—and Recast." *Reviews in American History* 18 (June 1990): 190–96.

——. *Southern Honor: Ethics and Behavior in the Old South.* New York: Oxford University Press, 1982.

——. *Yankee Saints and Southern Sinners.* Baton Rouge: Louisiana State University Press, 1985.

Wykstra, Ronald A., ed. *Human Capital Formation and Manpower Development.* New York: Free Press, 1971.

Yandle, Bruce. *Land Rights: The 1990s' Property Rights Rebellion.* Lanham, Md.: Rowman and Littlefield, 1995.

——. *The Political Limits of Environmental Regulation: Tracking the Unicorn.* New York: Quorum Books, 1989.

Yarbrough, Jean. "Jefferson and Property Rights." In *Liberty, Property, and the Foundations of the American Constitution*, edited by Ellen Frankel Paul and Howard Dickman, 65–83. Albany: State University of New York Press, 1989.

Young, Jeffrey Robert. *Domesticating Slavery: The Master Class in Georgia and South Carolina, 1670–1837.* Chapel Hill: University of North Carolina Press, 1999.

Zajac, Edward E. *The Political Economy of Fairness.* Cambridge, Mass.: MIT Press, 1995.

Zilversmit, Arthur. *The First Emancipation: The Abolition of Slavery in the North.* Chicago: University of Chicago Press, 1967.

Index